WOMEN
OF EASTERN
AND SOUTHERN
AFRICA

Recent Titles in
African Special Bibliographic Series

American-Southern African Relations: Bibliographic Essays
Mohamed A. El-Khawas and Francis A. Kornegay, Jr.

A Short Guide to the Study of Ethiopia: A General Bibliography
Alula Hidaru and Dessalegn Rahmato

Afro-Americans and Africa: Black Nationalism at the Crossroads
William B. Helmreich

Somalia: A Bibliographical Survey
Mohamed Khalief Salad

Ethiopian Perspectives: A Bibliographical Guide to the History of Ethiopia
Clifton F. Brown

A Bibliography of African Ecology: A Geographically and Topically Classified
List of Books and Articles
Dilwyn J. Rogers, compiler

Demography, Urbanization, and Spatial Planning in Kenya: A Bibliographical Survey
Robert A. Obudho

Population, Urbanization, and Rural Settlement in Ghana: A Bibliographic Survey
Joseph A. Sarfoh, compiler

African Women: A General Bibliography, 1976-1985
Davis A. Bullwinkle, compiler

Women of Northern, Western, and Central Africa: A Bibliography, 1976-1985
Davis A. Bullwinkle, compiler

WOMEN OF EASTERN AND SOUTHERN AFRICA

A Bibliography, 1976–1985

Compiled by
Davis A. Bullwinkle

African Special Bibliographic Series, Number 11

Greenwood Press
New York • Westport, Connecticut • London

Library of Congress Cataloging-in-Publication Data

Bullwinkle, Davis.
    Women of eastern and southern Africa : a bibliography, 1976-1985 /
compiled by Davis A. Bullwinkle.
        p. cm.—(African special bibliographic series, ISSN
0749-2308 ; no. 11)
    Includes index.
    ISBN 0-313-26606-9 (lib. bdg. : alk. paper)
    1. Women—Africa, Sub-Saharan—Bibliography. 2. Women—Africa,
Eastern—Bibliography. 3. Women—Africa, Southern—Bibliography.
I. Title. II. Series.
Z7964.A337B84 1989
[HQ1787]
016.3054′09676—dc20   89-2154

British Library Cataloguing in Publication Data is available.

Library of Congress Catalog Card Number: 89-2154
ISBN: 0-313-26606-9
ISSN: 0749-2308

First published in 1989

Greenwood Press, Inc.
88 Post Road West, Westport, Connecticut 06881

Printed in the United States of America

The paper used in this book complies with the
Permanent Paper Standard issued by the National
Information Standards Organization (Z39.48-1984).

10 9 8 7 6 5 4 3 2 1

For Judy

Who in my middle years I have
found to share my life
And who brings joy and love,
support, kindness and meaning
to my life

And for Carol

Who showed me the true value of loving
another human being and whose
lifetime of love
I shall cherish for all my years

I dedicate this work

Contents

FOREWORD   xv

PREFACE   xvii

INTRODUCTION   xix

GENERAL SUBJECT BIBLIOGRAPHY--EASTERN AFRICA   1
  AGRICULTURE   1
  BIBLIOGRAPHIES   1
  CULTURAL ROLES   2
  DEVELOPMENT AND TECHNOLOGY   5
  ECONOMICS   6
  EDUCATION AND TRAINING   6
  EMPLOYMENT AND LABOR   7
  FAMILY LIFE   8
  FAMILY PLANNING AND CONTRACEPTION   8
  FERTILITY AND INFERTILITY   9
  HEALTH, NUTRITION AND MEDICINE   10
  HISTORY   12
  LAW AND LEGAL ISSUES   12
  LITERATURE   12
  MARITAL RELATIONS AND NUPTIALITY   12
  MASS MEDIA   13
  MIGRATION   13
  MISCELLANEOUS   13
  ORGANIZATIONS   14
  POLITICS AND GOVERNMENT   14
  RELIGION AND WITCHCRAFT   14
  RESEARCH   15
  SEX ROLES   15
  SEXUAL MUTILATION/CIRCUMCISION   15

CONTENTS

STATUS OF WOMEN   17
WOMEN AND THEIR CHILDREN   17
NATIONS OF EASTERN AFRICA   18

DJIBOUTI   19

ETHIOPIA   20
AGRICULTURE   20
BIBLIOGRAPHIES   21
CULTURAL ROLES   21
DEVELOPMENT AND TECHNOLOGY   24
ECONOMICS   25
EDUCATION AND TRAINING   26
EMPLOYMENT AND LABOR   27
FAMILY LIFE   27
FAMILY PLANNING AND CONTRACEPTION   28
FERTILITY AND INFERTILITY   28
HEALTH, NUTRITION AND MEDICINE   29
HISTORY   31
LAW AND LEGAL ISSUES   32
MARITAL RELATIONS AND NUPTIALITY   32
MIGRATION   32
MISCELLANEOUS   33
NATIONALISM   33
ORGANIZATIONS   33
POLITICS AND GOVERNMENT   34
RELIGION AND WITCHCRAFT   34
RESEARCH   34
SEX ROLES   34
SEXUAL MUTILATION/CIRCUMCISION   35
STATUS OF WOMEN   36
URBANIZATION   36
WOMEN AND THEIR CHILDREN   36

KENYA   37
ABORTION   37
AGRICULTURE   37
ARTS   41
BIBLIOGRAPHIES   42
CULTURAL ROLES   42
DEVELOPMENT AND TECHNOLOGY   58
ECONOMICS   63
EDUCATION AND TRAINING   69
EMPLOYMENT AND LABOR   72
EQUALITY AND LIBERATION   77
FAMILY LIFE   77
FAMILY PLANNING AND CONTRACEPTION   80
FERTILITY AND INFERTILITY   84
HEALTH, NUTRITION AND MEDICINE   89
HISTORY   94
LAW AND LEGAL ISSUES   96
LITERATURE   97

CONTENTS

MARITAL RELATIONS AND NUPTIALITY   98
MIGRATION   101
MISCELLANEOUS   102
NATIONALISM   103
ORGANIZATIONS   103
POLITICS AND GOVERNMENT   104
RELIGION AND WITCHCRAFT   105
RESEARCH   106
SEX ROLES   106
SEXUAL MUTILATION/CIRCUMCISION   111
SLAVERY   111
STATUS OF WOMEN   112
URBANIZATION   113
WOMEN AND THEIR CHILDREN   114

SEYCHELLES   115

SOMALIA   116

SUDAN   119
  ABORTION   119
  AGRICULTURE   119
  BIBLIOGRAPHIES   122
  CULTURAL ROLES   123
  DEVELOPMENT AND TECHNOLOGY   136
  ECONOMICS   139
  EDUCATION AND TRAINING   140
  EMPLOYMENT AND LABOR   142
  EQUALITY AND LIBERATION   145
  FAMILY LIFE   145
  FAMILY PLANNING AND CONTRACEPTION   146
  FERTILITY AND INFERTILITY   149
  HEALTH, NUTRITION AND MEDICINE   151
  HISTORY   158
  LAW AND LEGAL ISSUES   159
  LITERATURE   159
  MARITAL RELATIONS AND NUPTIALITY   159
  MIGRATION   161
  MISCELLANEOUS   161
  ORGANIZATIONS   161
  POLITICS AND GOVERNMENT   161
  RELIGION AND WITCHCRAFT   162
  RESEARCH   164
  SEX ROLES   164
  SEXUAL MUTILATION/CIRCUMCISION   168
  STATUS OF WOMEN   172
  URBANIZATION   174
  WOMEN AND THEIR CHILDREN   174

TANZANIA   176
  ABORTION   176
  AGRICULTURE   176

CONTENTS

ARTS   181
BIBLIOGRAPHIES   181
CULTURAL ROLES   181
DEVELOPMENT AND TECHNOLOGY   190
ECONOMICS   197
EDUCATION AND TRAINING   202
EMPLOYMENT AND LABOR   204
EQUALITY AND LIBERATION   210
FAMILY LIFE   210
FAMILY PLANNING AND CONTRACEPTION   212
FERTILITY AND INFERTILITY   214
HEALTH, NUTRITION AND MEDICINE   215
HISTORY   217
LAW AND LEGAL ISSUES   218
LITERATURE   219
MARITAL RELATIONS AND NUPTIALITY   219
MASS MEDIA   221
MISCELLANEOUS   222
NATIONALISM   222
ORGANIZATIONS   222
POLITICS AND GOVERNMENT   223
RELIGION AND WITCHCRAFT   224
RESEARCH   225
SEX ROLES   225
SEXUAL MUTILATION/CIRCUMCISION   231
SLAVERY   232
STATUS OF WOMEN   232
URBANIZATION   233
WOMEN AND THEIR CHILDREN   234

UGANDA   235

GENERAL SUBJECT BIBLIOGRAPHY--SOUTHERN AFRICA   238
AGRICULTURE   238
BIBLIOGRAPHIES   239
CULTURAL ROLES   239
DEVELOPMENT AND TECHNOLOGY   241
ECONOMICS   242
EDUCATION AND TRAINING   243
EMPLOYMENT AND LABOR   244
EQUALITY AND LIBERATION   245
FAMILY LIFE   245
FAMILY PLANNING AND CONTRACEPTION   246
FERTILITY AND INFERTILITY   246
HISTORY   246
LAW AND LEGAL ISSUES   246
LITERATURE   246
MARITAL RELATIONS AND NUPTIALITY   247
MASS MEDIA   247
MIGRATION   247
MISCELLANEOUS   248

CONTENTS

NATIONALISM   248
POLITICS AND GOVERNMENT   248
RELIGION AND WITCHCRAFT   249
RESEARCH   249
SEX ROLES   250
STATUS OF WOMEN   250
NATIONS OF SOUTHERN AFRICA   252

ANGOLA   253

BOTSWANA   254
  AGRICULTURE   254
  BIBLIOGRAPHIES   255
  CULTURAL ROLES   256
  DEVELOPMENT AND TECHNOLOGY   261
  DIVORCE   263
  ECONOMICS   263
  EDUCATION AND TRAINING   265
  EMPLOYMENT AND LABOR   266
  FAMILY LIFE   268
  FAMILY PLANNING AND CONTRACEPTION   270
  FERTILITY AND INFERTILITY   271
  HEALTH, NUTRITION AND MEDICINE   271
  HISTORY   272
  LAW AND LEGAL ISSUES   273
  MARITAL RELATIONS AND NUPTIALITY   273
  MIGRATION   274
  MISCELLANEOUS   275
  ORGANIZATIONS   276
  POLITICS AND GOVERNMENT   276
  RELIGION AND WITCHCRAFT   277
  RESEARCH   277
  SEX ROLES   277
  STATUS OF WOMEN   281
  URBANIZATION   281
  WOMEN AND THEIR CHILDREN   282

COMORO ISLANDS   283

LESOTHO   284
  AGRICULTURE   284
  BIBLIOGRAPHIES   285
  CULTURAL ROLES   285
  DEVELOPMENT AND TECHNOLOGY   288
  DIVORCE   290
  ECONOMICS   290
  EDUCATION AND TRAINING   292
  EMPLOYMENT AND LABOR   292
  FAMILY LIFE   294
  FAMILY PLANNING AND CONTRACEPTION   296
  FERTILITY AND INFERTILITY   296
  HEALTH, NUTRITION AND MEDICINE   297

xi

CONTENTS

HISTORY   298
LAW AND LEGAL ISSUES   298
MARITAL RELATIONS AND NUPTIALITY   298
MIGRATION   300
MISCELLANEOUS   301
POLITICS AND GOVERNMENT   302
RESEARCH   302
SEX ROLES   302

MADAGASCAR   305

MALAWI   306

MAURITIUS   310

MOZAMBIQUE   312

NAMIBIA   315

SOUTH AFRICA   318
  ABORTION   318
  AGRICULTURE   319
  APARTHEID AND RACE RELATIONS   320
  ARTS   327
  BIBLIOGRAPHIES   327
  CULTURAL ROLES   328
  DEVELOPMENT AND TECHNOLOGY   348
  DIVORCE   351
  ECONOMICS   352
  EDUCATION AND TRAINING   359
  EMPLOYMENT AND LABOR   360
  EQUALITY AND LIBERATION   373
  FAMILY LIFE   378
  FAMILY PLANNING AND CONTRACEPTION   382
  FERTILITY AND INFERTILITY   385
  HEALTH, NUTRITION AND MEDICINE   387
  HISTORY   397
  LAW AND LEGAL ISSUES   404
  LITERATURE   410
  MARITAL RELATIONS AND NUPTIALITY   412
  MASS MEDIA   418
  MIGRATION   419
  MISCELLANEOUS   420
  NATIONALISM   421
  ORGANIZATIONS   423
  POLITICS AND GOVERNMENT   427
  RELIGION AND WITCHCRAFT   435
  RESEARCH   437
  SEX ROLES   438
  SLAVERY   445
  STATUS OF WOMEN   445
  URBANIZATION   449

CONTENTS

WOMEN AND THEIR CHILDREN   450

SWAZILAND   451

ZAMBIA   454
    AGRICULTURE   454
    ARTS   456
    BIBLIOGRAPHIES   456
    CULTURAL ROLES   456
    DEVELOPMENT AND TECHNOLOGY   463
    ECONOMICS   467
    EDUCATION AND TRAINING   471
    EMPLOYMENT AND LABOR   471
    EQUALITY AND LIBERATION   475
    FAMILY LIFE   476
    FAMILY PLANNING AND CONTRACEPTION   477
    FERTILITY AND INFERTILITY   478
    HEALTH, NUTRITION AND MEDICINE   478
    HISTORY   479
    LAW AND LEGAL ISSUES   480
    LITERATURE   481
    MARITAL RELATIONS AND NUPTIALITY   481
    MIGRATION   484
    NATIONALISM   484
    ORGANIZATIONS   484
    POLITICS AND GOVERNMENT   485
    RELIGION AND WITCHCRAFT   486
    RESEARCH   486
    SEX ROLES   486
    STATUS OF WOMEN   490
    URBANIZATION   490
    WOMEN AND THEIR CHILDREN   491

ZIMBABWE   492
    AGRICULTURE   492
    BIBLIOGRAPHIES   493
    CULTURAL ROLES   493
    DEVELOPMENT AND TECHNOLOGY   498
    ECONOMICS   501
    EDUCATION AND TRAINING   503
    EMPLOYMENT AND LABOR   504
    EQUALITY AND LIBERATION   506
    FAMILY LIFE   507
    FAMILY PLANNING AND CONTRACEPTION   508
    FERTILITY AND INFERTILITY   508
    HEALTH, NUTRITION AND MEDICINE   508
    HISTORY   509
    LAW AND LEGAL ISSUES   510
    LITERATURE   510
    MARITAL RELATIONS AND NUPTIALITY   511
    MIGRATION   511
    NATIONALISM   511

CONTENTS

ORGANIZATIONS   512
POLITICS AND GOVERNMENT   513
RELIGION AND WITCHCRAFT   514
SEX ROLES   515
STATUS OF WOMEN   517
URBANIZATION   518
WOMEN AND THEIR CHILDREN   518

AUTHOR INDEX   519

Foreword

This work is the outgrowth of a paper I wrote a number of years ago that was published by the African Bibliographic Center in Washington, D.C. That paper, a bibliography on women in Africa during the 1970's stimulated my interest in creating a work that would bring together all the English language publications written about women in Africa during the United Nations Decade for Women from 1976-1985.

The work could never have been completed without the tremendous help of two people. During the research phase of this work, I discussed the computer needs of the work with a friend named Vicki Tynan. Over the next five months, Vicki wrote a complete computer program for this project. Due to the size and complexity of a project like this, the program was extremely time consuming to produce. Few works of this scope have ever been attempted and we were soon to learn we were on the fringe of computer technology as it applies to manipulating a large amount of data.

Vicki's son Dylan, already a computer whiz at sixteen, helped get me through my first major computer project and orientation with my computer and the integrated software.

Their help during every conceivable hour of the day made this project a much easier and manageable one. I am very grateful to them both for their time and patience.

Preface

'Women of Eastern and Southern Africa: A Bibliography, 1976-1985' is the third of a three volume Africana Special Bibliographic Series to be published by Greenwood Press. This third volume includes materials divided into general subjects by regions and subjects by nations of Eastern and Southern Africa.

Thirty-four subject headings will be utilized over the scope of the entire three volume set. Unique to the last two volumes is the heading of divorce, which was not used in the first volume. The subject heading of apartheid and race relations, while not unique to South Africa, will only be used in the South Africa bibliography.

Countries with fewer than thirty citations will not be divided by subjects. Instead, their data will be alphabetized by author.

The complete three-volume work indexes over 4,100 original English language research works on women in Africa and covers all aspects of their lives. The original citations are cross-referenced by as many subject headings as possible for best coverage. The scope of this work covers all subject areas where materials on or about women might appear. It differs from some previous bibliographic projects that covered very specialized materials.

A follow-up volume of this three-volume work is already being researched. Covering the years from 1986-1990, it will hopefully be published in 1993. I will continue to publish this research in as timely a manner as possible. Those of you completing research that might be relevant to upcoming works and would like to have information about your work disseminated may contact me at 213 Colonial Court, Little Rock, Arkansas, 72201 or by phone at either (501) 682-2867 or (501) 666-9048.

Introduction

In 1945, the nations of the world met in San Francisco to sign the charter of a new international organization to be known as the United Nations. Among its stated goals were the "attainment of world peace, the reaffirmation of faith in human rights, the dignity of worth of the human person as well as the equal rights of men and women of all nations."

Since then, the United Nations has encountered a greater degree of difficulty than anticipated in achieving the goals of its original charter. Nations are constantly warring with each other and the number of repressive governments has increased through the years. Hundreds of thousands of people have been oppressed by their own governments for their actions of speaking out against government policies to quash the goals of human dignity and freedom. Thousands of women, children and men have died of starvation and disease because governments have neither taken the steps needed to prevent the problems nor the steps needed to have the international community involved in the solutions.

Due to the conditions that created these problems, as well as the traditional, social and economic roles played by women in the developing world, the United Nations became alarmed that the goal of equality among the sexes was not being achieved by its members. Two years after the United Nations charter was signed, the organization created its Commission on the Status of Women.

In 1972, twenty-four years after the creation of the U.N., a group of nongovernmental organizations (NGOs) sent a request to the United Nations Commission on the Status of Women to look into the possibility of having the U.N. choose a one-year period to focus attention on the problems faced by women in the world. Egypt, Finland, France, Hungary Romania and the Philippines introduced a resolution to the

U.N. General Assembly which had been previously adopted by
the Commission. The year 1975 was declared International
Women's Year. The goals of this one year period were stated
as being, "to intensify action to promote equality between
women and men and to increase women's contribution to
national and international development." The U.N. delegates
agreed, while approving the Commission's declaration, to add
peace and equality to the already stated goals for the year.

Specific objectives for each of the individual goals
stated in the declaration were established. Among them
were... "to achieve full equality before the law in all
fields where it did not already exist; to meet the health
needs of girls and women equally with those of boys and men;
to promote equality of economic rights; to improve the
quality of rural life; and to eliminate illiteracy and
ensure equality of educational opportunities." Emphasis was
placed on "realizing the principle of the rights of people
to self-determination; combating racism and racial
discrimination wherever it manifests itself; and lending
support to the victims of racism, apartheid and colonialism
as well as supporting women and children in armed struggle."

In May of 1974, the United Nations Economic and Social
Council requested a United Nations conference to scrutinize
U.N. agencies as to how they had carried out the
recommendations for the elimination of discrimination
against women made by the Commission on the Status of Women.
In November of that year, the United Nations chose Mexico as
the site of what would be the first of three world
conferences on the plight of women throughout the world.

In June of 1975, the World Conference of the
International Women's Year convened in Mexico City. United
Nations members from one hundred and thirty-three nations
attended. The African continent was represented by
thirty-nine delegates. Other than United Nations delegates,
representatives from one hundred and fourteen
nongovernmental organizations also attended. Specific
African NGOs attending were the African National Congress
(ANC), the African National Council, and four national
liberation groups.

During the two weeks of meetings, the delegates labored
to create a World Plan of Action that could be used to
implement the stated objectives of the International Women's
Year. The plan was divided into actions that could be taken
by national governments and actions that could be undertaken
by NGOs and other international organizations. Those
actions included social, economic, legal, administrative and
educational proposals. To governments it was suggested that
a "national machinery" be established to manage and promote
efforts in each country to advance the status of women. To
international and regional organizations, particularly the
United Nations and its agencies, it was proposed that they
extend assistance to individual governments and

nongovernmental organizations to support their efforts in
achieving the recommendations.

The conference stressed the objective of achieving a
partial number of the goals from the Plan of Action by 1980.
Among the goals for that-five year period were a decrease in
the illiteracy rate; a concerted effort to create more
employment opportunities; the acknowledgment of the economic
value of women's work in the home, in food production and in
marketing; and the commitment to the development of modern
rural technology. Another important objective of this five
year period was that individual governments undertake the
responsibility to guarantee women equality in the execution
of their civil, social and political rights, especially
those associated with economic, marital and civil matters.

Once the Plan of Action was complete, thirty-five
resolutions attached to the plan were approved by the
conference. These resolutions dealt with such diverse
issues as the integration of women in development; the
establishment of research and training centers for women in
Africa; the status of women under apartheid; the condition
of women in rural areas, and the health needs of Third World
women.

From this two-week conference came the recommendation
that the United Nations proclaim the decade from 1976-1985
as the United Nations Decade for Women and Development. The
delegates believed that this proclamation would guarantee
that national and international activity on the equality of
women would maintain its momentum and continue, and that
agencies of the United Nations would take steps to enact the
Plan of Action and evaluate their previous achievements to
advance the status of women. Support from international and
regional intergovernmental organizations outside the United
Nations would result in the development of programs to carry
out the Plan of Action and achieve the objectives of the
United Nations International Women's Year as well as the
United Nations Decade for Women.

At the end of 1975, the U.N. General Assembly voted to
support the report of the World Plan of Action and its
resolutions. The assembly proclaimed the years 1976-1985 as
"The United Nations Decade for Women, Equality, Development
and Peace." They declared this ten year period to be one in
which a concerted effort would be made by national,
regional, and international organizations to implement the
Plan of Action and related resolutions. Nations were called
upon to act quickly and establish short, medium and long
term goals, including by 1980 the implementation of a
minimum number of the plan's objectives.

As a final action on this issue, the United Nations
announced that a second world conference would be held
in 1980 to evaluate and appraise the accomplishments made by
member nations in achieving the partial goals and

and objectives of the International Women's Year and Decade. Held in Copenhagen, Denmark in mid-July of 1980, the conference attracted delegates from one hundred forty-five nations. This almost ten percent increase in participation by member nations once again emphasized the growing importance of women's issues on the international scene. Among the African NGOs who attended were representatives from the African National Congress (ANC), the South West Africa People's Organization (SWAPO), and the Pan African Congress. Along with the reevaluation of the previous five years' work and the realization of the objectives drawn in Mexico City, the important issues of health, education and employment were added as additional themes of this conference.

The program of the conference included four important topics. Among these were the effects of apartheid on women in Southern Africa and special measures to assist them; a mid-decade review and evaluation of the successes and obstacles to achieving the objectives of the decade; the effects of the Israeli occupation on Palestinian women; and the study and creation of proposals for advancing the status of women and reinforcing established strategies to displace hurdles to full and equal participation in development.

A second Plan of Action for the concluding five years of the decade (1980-1985) was discussed and promulgated. This Plan of Action emphasized the achievement of equality, development and peace with special emphasis on health, education and employment. The forty-eight resolutions adopted by the conference were aimed at attaining the goals of the next five-year period and the decade overall.

On December 11, 1980, the United Nations General Assembly adopted a resolution supporting the conference's Plan of Action for the second half of the decade. Also set in motion was the planning for the end of the decade world conference to be held in Nairobi, Kenya, in mid-1985.

The last of the three world conferences convened in Nairobi, July 25, 1985. Representatives from one hundred forty nations attended. Eighteen thousand women, nearly three times as many as had attended the first world conference in Mexico City, arrived in Nairobi. The conference's theme was the review and appraisal of the achievements and the failures of the decade. Almost twelve hundred NGO workshops were conducted in overcrowded classrooms and outdoor spaces. Oriented around the main themes of development, equality and peace, the workshops also dealt with the issues of health, education, and employment.

The results of the three world conferences and the United Nations Decade for Women highlighted the wretched conditions faced by the women of Africa and the Third World. As a continent, Africa has the highest percent of illiterate women in the world. It is estimated that under

twenty percent of all African women can read and write and
that may be a liberal figure. Children are brought into
this world by the fewest number of trained maternity
personnel and suffer from the lowest birthrates in the
developing world. It is believed that African infant
mortality rates in excess of ninety-five per one thousand
live births, while being the highest in the world, are also
responsible for the low expectation of life in Africa.
Female children attend primary schools in smaller numbers
than males. Secondary education, while limited to both
sexes, is still undertaken by three times as many boys as
girls. African women marry at younger ages than their peers
throughout the world, usually between fifteen and seventeen
years of age. They also produce more children than any
group of women on earth, averaging six and a half children
for every childbearing woman in Africa. It is no wonder
that African women have the lowest life expectancy on earth.
That tragic age is just 48.6 years.

Historically, the women of Africa have been the
principal contributors for labor needed to produce Africa's
food crops. They have suffered from unequal access to
extension services and training and have been discriminated
against in their efforts to gain credit. It is estimated
that African women deliver eighty percent of the labor and
organization needed in the production of Africa's food.
Women often spend from nine to ten hours a day laboring in
the fields, then a sizeable number of hours performing other
tasks such as gathering firewood, preserving food, caring
for their children and elderly relatives, putting food in
storage, making meals and retrieving water. They may also
be involved in some form of work that produces saleable
commodities such as soap, vegetables and handicrafts that
can be traded for necessities such as food and household
items.

In the not too distant past, Africa as a continent
fulfilled her needs by producing all of the food her people
required. By 1980, Africa was forced to import almost
fifteen percent of her total food essentials. Africa's
inability to produce enough food to feed her people is due
to a number of factors, not the least of which were colonial
policies and the introduction of cash crop economies by
those governments. As a result of these governmental
policies, women have found themselves overburdened in their
roles as primary food producers. Over the last twenty-five
to thirty years, large numbers of African men have left
their native land holdings and migrated to Africa's cities
looking for work. While African men historically have never
had a great penchant for working the land, the loss of their
labor has seriously affected Africa's women. The amount of
work expected or required of women has increased
dramatically.

In Sub-Saharan Africa the rights to land have
traditionally belonged to women. Colonial governments,
ignoring historic cultural patterns, allocated land

ownership to men. These policies displaced subsistence agriculture with cash crop commodities such as coffee and cotton. Development projects instigated by new national governments also discriminated against women by recognizing men as the owners of projects. Men have been encouraged to grow cash crops for the economic rewards available to them while women have still been responsible for a large part of the labor required to grow these crops. The rewards of independence and supposedly egalitarian governments have not been kind to Africa's women. The benefits still elude them.

Another of the major problems faced by women throughout the Third World has been the failure of governments and development agencies to acknowledge women as a factor in development projects and in the decision making process. While women make up over fifty percent of the world's population, only a small percentage of them hold administrative careers in Third World governments. As a result of this, women are not involved in the decision-making processes and their opinions are often ignored. A crisis of self image has also hurt African and Third World women. They themselves do not value their own labor in food production by the same criteria as men's labor in agriculture. The same views are prevalent among agricultural economists and development planners who do not take into consideration the time women spend planting, weeding, harvesting and other daily chores previously mentioned. Acceptance of the facts concerning the role of women in food production is still slow in coming. Many research studies support the efforts of women to execute and oversee agricultural projects successfully. Still, agricultural development planning continues to ignore their position of importance and their capabilities. The role of women as food producers must be recognized before the problems of food shortages can be eliminated.

If conditions for women in Africa and the Third World are to be improved, governments must provide their female citizens the same opportunities they afford their male citizens. Equal opportunities in the areas of education and training, the elimination of illiteracy, and the equal access to credit sources would provide some solutions to the problems women face in Third World development. Women must have equal access to agricultural extension services to help provide them with the information and technological data they need to compete and increase crop yields. The employment of more female agricultural extension professionals might also be of great help. Between 1977 and 1984 less than one-fifth of all those sent overseas for professional training programs were women. The introduction of modern rural technology is a necessity women must have for them to gain advancements in mechanization, improved water systems, better methods of food production and preservation, and greater access to fuel resources.

INTRODUCTION

A special emphasis by African governments is also quickly needed in the field of women's health. Programs begun by the World Health Organization (WHO) in 1980 in a number of African nations have been very successful. Women's volunteer organizations are being trained at the WHO Regional Training Center in Mauritius. There they are instructed in maternal health care, family planning and child health. Promising results have been achieved in West Africa. The vaccination of children against childhood diseases such as tetanus, measles, poliomyelitis, tuberculosis and diphtheria have commenced. Governments throughout the Third World must move quickly and have relative success in dealing with the problems of their female citizens. The health of their nations sit in the balance. Development of any kind cannot succeed without a population free of the worries of catastrophic diseases that plague the African continent and other Third World nations. In Africa, 48.6 years of age certainly cannot be accepted as a fulfilled lifetime.

While the achievements of the United Nations Decade for Women, or the lack of them, will be discussed and debated for years, it is promising to know that the decade forced many governments to take a more objective look at the position women hold and the problems they face in their countries. The world conference and the media forced them to recognize the reality they refused to face. Two-thirds of all illiterates are women and most refugees are women and children. It is they who are facing major health problems that could dramatically alter the history of nations.

Technology, while helping to develop nations and making labor less difficult for men, and therefore more profitable, has actually failed to help women and in many cases has made their lives more demanding. Technology must be shared amongst all people in rural developing countries.

While achievements during the decade were exemplified by dramatic increases in women's and girls' participation in educational programs and small gains in employment opportunities, they have been minimal to say the least. Access to credit through new organizations such as the Women's Bank will be helpful if they continue to receive support from the international financial institutions.

This bibliographic research project was initiated in the anticipation of it becoming a major contribution in the Social Sciences and the field of African Studies. The citations that follow are arranged into five specific groups. They include articles appearing in journals and edited books, as well as Masters theses, Ph.D dissertations, conference papers and individual books on women in Africa and the Third World.

INTRODUCTION

Unlike the two previous world conferences in Mexico City and Copenhagen, a complete bibliography of papers presented at the conference has not and probably will not be published by the NGO committee. Research on this project was delayed for a period of time in the hope that such a list would be forthcoming. A final document for the Nairobi conference was published by the NGO. This document lists titles of some papers by the themes by which they were presented. Access to these papers may be possible through the Economic Commission for Africa's African Training and Research Center for Women in Addis Ababa, Ethiopia, the International Women's Tribunal Center in New York City, or the International Center for Research on Women in Washington, D.C. Addresses for these organizations can be found in Appendix A of this document.

It is unfortunate, to say the least, that a document as comprehensive as this one is not able to contain a list of the papers from the last world conference and the NGO workshops. Their inclusion would have made this a more complete work.

In publishing this comprehensive work on previously written research on African women, I hope that those using this document and contemplating further research on African and Third World women will use it to analyze where future research might best take place. This work is unique. No other book, periodical, or database has in the past brought together the amount of information on African women that this project has. This work is only the beginning of an ongoing project that will disseminate accumulated data on women in Africa. A five-year update of the research covering the post-decade period is forthcoming.

The gains of the decade have been disappointing. That a decade had to be chosen to underscore the injustices and widespread inequalities of women throughout the world is a tragedy in itself. I hope the decade and its poor results will demonstrate to all who care in this world that so much more needs to be done to guarantee that all peoples of this planet have the chance to live fulfilling lives. And, I hope it will inspire further research to help solve the problems of the oppressed and underprivileged.

WOMEN OF EASTERN AND SOUTHERN AFRICA

General Subject Bibliography— Eastern Africa

AGRICULTURE

Germain, Adrienne
"Research on Women in Agricultural Production in Eastern and Southern Africa." Paper Presented at a Workshop on Women in Agricultural Production in Eastern and Southern Africa. Nairobi, Kenya. April 9-11, 1980.

McDowell, James and Hazzard, Virginia
"Village Technology and Women's Work in Eastern Africa." Assignment Children. Volume 36 October-December, 1976. pp. 53-65.

Mies, M.
"Consequences of Capitalist Penetration for Women's Subsistence Reproduction." Paper Presented at the Seminar on Underdevelopment and Subsistence Production in South East Africa. April, 1978.

Wright, Marcia
"Technology and Women's Control Over Production: Three Case Studies From East-Central Africa and Their Implications for Esther Boserup's Thesis About the Displacement of Women." Paper Presented at the Rockefeller Foundation Workshop on Women, Household and Human Capital Development in Low Income Countries. New York: Rockefeller Foundation. July, 1982.

BIBLIOGRAPHIES

Wadsworth, Gail M.
Women in Development: A Bibliography of Materials Available in the Library and Documentation Centre, Eastern and Southern African Management Institute. Arusha, Tanzania: Eastern and Southern African Management Institute. Library and Documentation Centre. February, 1982. 106p.

CULTURAL ROLES

Abdalla, Raqiya
    Sisters in Affliction: Circumcision and Infibulation of
    Women in Africa. London: Zed Press. 1982. 122p.
Alpers, Edward
    "The Story of Swema: Female Vulnerability in
    Nineteenth-Century East Africa." (In) Robertson, Claire
    C. and Klein, Martin A. (eds.). Women and Slavery in
    Africa. Madison, Wisconsin: University of Wisconsin
    Press. 1983. pp. 185-219.
Berger, Iris
    "Rebels or Status Seekers? Women as Spirit Mediums in
    East Africa." (In) Hafkin, N.J. and Bay, Edna (eds.).
    Women in Africa: Studies in Social and Economic Change.
    Stanford, California: Stanford University Press. 1976.
    pp. 157-181.
Berger, Iris
    "Women, Religion and Social Change: East and Central
    African Perspectives." Paper Presented at the Conference
    on Women and Development. Wellesley, Massachusetts:
    Wellesley College. Wellesley College Center for Research
    on Women. June 2-6, 1976. 25p.
Caplan, Patricia
    "Cognatic Descent, Islamic Law, and Women's Property on
    the East African Coast." (In) Hirschon, Renbee (ed.).
    Women and Property--Women as Property. New York:
    St.Martin's Press. 1983.
Erasto, Muga
    Studies in Prostitution: East, West and South Africa,
    Zaire and Nevada. Nairobi: Kenya Literature Bureau.
    1980.
Gebre-Selassie, Alasebu
    The Situation of Women in Africa: A Review. Nairobi:
    UNICEF. Eastern Africa Regional Office. 1979. 65p.
Germain, Adrienne
    "Research on Women in Agricultural Production in Eastern
    and Southern Africa." Paper Presented at a Workshop on
    Women in Agricultural Production in Eastern and Southern
    Africa. Nairobi, Kenya. April 9-11, 1980.
Henin, Roushdi A.
    "Fertility, Infertility and Sub-Fertility in Eastern
    Africa." (In) International Union for the Scientic Study
    of Population (IUSSP). International Population
    Conference: Solicited Papers. Liege, Netherland: IUSSP.
    Volume Three. 1981. pp. 667-697.
Hosken, Fran P.
    "Female Circumcision and Fertility in Africa." Women and
    Health. Volume 1 #6 November-December, 1976. pp. 3-11.
Hosken, Fran P.
    "Female Circumcision in Africa." Victimology. Volume 2
    #3/4 1977. pp. 487-498.

Hosken, Fran P.
"Female Circumcision in the World of Today: A Global
Review." Paper Presented at the Seminar on Traditional
Practices Affecting the Health of Women and Children.
World Conference of the United Nations Decade for Women.
New York: United Nations. Copenhagen, Denmark. July
14-30, 1980.
Hosken, Fran P.
"Female Circumcision in the World of Today: A Global
View." Paper Presented at the Seminar on Traditional
Practices Affecting the Health of Women and Children:
Female Circumcision, Childhood Marriage, Nutritional
Taboos, etc. Alexandria, Egypt: World Health
Organization. Eastern Mediterranean Regional Office.
Khartoum, Sudan. February 10-15, 1979.
Hosken, Fran P.
"Female Genital Mutilation in the World Today: A Global
Review." International Journal of Health Services.
Volume 11 #3 1981. pp. 415-430.
Hosken, Fran P.
"Genital Mutilation of Women in Africa." Munger Africana
Library Notes. #36 October, 1976. 21p.
Hosken, Fran P.
"The Epidemiology of Female Genital Mutilation."
Tropical Doctor. July, 1978. pp. 150-156.
Hosken, Fran P.
"The Violence of Power: The Genital Mutilation of
Females." Heresies. Volume 6 #2 Summer, 1978. pp.
28-36.
Hosken, Fran P.
"Towards an Epidemiology of Genital Mutilation of Females
in Africa." Paper Presented at the Annual Meeting of the
African Studies Association. Paper #43. Baltimore,
Maryland. 1978. 20p.
Hosken, Fran P.
"Women and Health in East and West Africa: Family
Planning and Female Cicumcision." Paper Presented at the
Seminar on Traditional Practices Affecting the Health of
Women and Children. World Conference of the United
Nations Decade for Women. New York: United Nations.
Copenhagen, Denmark. July 14-30, 1980.
Hosken, Fran P.
"Women and Health in East and West Africa: Family
Planning and Female Circumcision." Paper Presented at
the Seminar on Traditional Practices Affecting the Health
of Women and Children: Female Circumcision, Childhood
Marriage, Nutritional Taboos, etc. Alexandria, Egypt:
World Health Organization. Eastern Mediterranean
Regional Office. Khartoum, Sudan. February 10-15, 1979.
Hosken, Fran P.
"Women and Health: Genital And Sexual Mutilation of
Females." International Journal of Women's Studies.
Volume 3 #3 May-June, 1980. pp. 300-316.

Hosken, Fran P.
   Female Sexual Mutilations: The Facts and Proposals for
   Action. Lexington, Massachusetts: Women's International
   Network News. 1980. 102p.
Hosken, Fran P.
   The Hosken Report: Genital and Sexual Mutilation of
   Females. Lexington, Massachusetts: Women's International
   Network News. 1982. 327p.
Huelsman, Ben R.
   "An Anthropological View of Clitoral and Other Female
   Genital Mutilations." (In) Lowery, T.P. and Lowery, T.S.
   (eds.). The Clitoris. St. Louis, Missouri: Warren H.
   Green. 1976. pp. 111-161.
Igbinovia, Patrick E.
   "Prostitution in Black Africa." International Journal of
   Women's Studies. Volume 7 #5 November-December, 1984.
   pp. 430-449.
Klein, H.
   "Crimes Against Thirty Million." New Statesman. Volume
   98 August 24, 1979. pp. 266-268.
MacGaffey, Wyatt
   "Lineage Structure, Marriage and the Family Amongst the
   Central Bantu." Journal of African History. Volume 24
   #2 1983. pp. 173-187.
McDowell, James and Hazzard, Virginia
   "Village Technology and Women's Work in Eastern Africa."
   Assignment Children. Volume 36 October-December, 1976.
   pp. 53-65.
Mgone, C.S.
   "Reproductive Behavior and Attitudes of African Mothers
   Following Birth of a Downs Syndrome Child." East African
   Medical Journal. Volume 59 #8 1982. pp. 555-559.
Mushanga, Tibamanya M.
   "Wife Victimization in East and Central Africa."
   Victimology. Volume 2 #3/4 1977. pp. 479-486.
Onyango, Philista P.M.
   "The Working Mother and the Housemaid as a Substitute:
   Its Complications on the Children." Journal of Eastern
   African Research and Development. Volume 13 1983. pp.
   24-31.
Oucho, John O.
   "Socio-Economic Perspectives of Fertility Regulation in
   Traditional and Modern African Societies." (In)
   University of Nairobi. Papers of the Seminar on Oral
   Traditions: Past Growth and Future Development in East
   Africa. Nairobi: University of Nairobi. UNESCO
   Institute of African Affairs. Kisumu, Kenya. April
   18-22, 1979. 18p.
Pieters, Guy and Lowenfels, A.
   "Infibulation in the Horn of Africa." New York State
   Journal of Medicine. Volume 77 April, 1977. pp.
   729-731.

Szklut, Jay
  "Bride Wealth, An Alternate View." Behavior Science
  Research. Volume 16 #3/4 1981. pp. 225-247.

DEVELOPMENT AND TECHNOLOGY

Elias, Misrak
  Training for Development Planning and Women, an African
  Perspective: Report on the Second Training Programme.
  Arusha, Tanzania: Eastern and Southern Africa Management
  Institute. April 5-May 14, 1982. 55p.
Elias, Misrak
  Training for Development Planning and Women: An African
  Perspective. Arusha, Tanzania: Eastern and Southern
  African Management Institute. Annual Report and Report
  of the First Training Programme. September 16,
  1980-September 15, 1981. 1981.
Gebre-Selassie, Alasebu
  The Situation of Women in Africa: A Review. Nairobi:
  UNICEF. Eastern Africa Regional Office. 1979. 65p.
Germain, Adrienne
  "Research on Women in Agricultural Production in Eastern
  and Southern Africa." Paper Presented at a Workshop on
  Women in Agricultural Production in Eastern and Southern
  Africa. Nairobi, Kenya. April 9-11, 1980.
Johnston, Bruce F. and Meyer, Anthony J.
  "Nutrition, Health and Population in Strategies for Rural
  Development." Economic Development and Cultural Change.
  Volume 26 #1 October, 1977. pp. 1-23.
Johnston, Bruce F. and Meyer, Anthony J.
  Nutrition, Health and Population in Strategies for Rural
  Development. Nairobi: University of Nairobi. Institute
  for Development Studies. Discussion Paper #238. 1976.
  45p.
Kayongo-Male, Diana
  "Helping Self-Help Groups Help Themselves: Training of
  Leaders of Women's Groups." Journal of Eastern African
  Research and Development. Volume 13 1983. pp. 88-103.
McDowell, James and Hazzard, Virginia
  "Village Technology and Women's Work in Eastern Africa."
  Assignment Children. Volume 36 October-November, 1976.
  pp. 53-65.
Wadsworth, Gail M.
  Women in Development: A Bibliography of Materials
  Available in the Library and Documentation Centre,
  Eastern and Southern African Management Institute.
  Arusha, Tanzania: Eastern and Southern African Management
  Institute. Library and Documentation Centre. February,
  1982. 106p.
Weisner, Thomas S. and Abbott, Susan
  "Women, Modernity and Stress: Three Contrasting Contexts

for Change in East Africa." Southwestern Journal of
Anthropology. Volume 33 #4 Winter, 1977. pp. 421-451.
Wright, Marcia
    "Technology and Women's Control Over Production: Three
    Case Studies From East-Central Africa and Their
    Implications for Esther Boserup's Thesis About the
    Displacement of Women." Paper Presented at the
    Rockefeller Foundation Workshop on Women, Household and
    Human Capital Development in Low Income Countries. New
    York: Rockefeller Foundation. July, 1982.

ECONOMICS

Caplan, Patricia
    "Cognatic Descent, Islamic Law, and Women's Property on
    the East African Coast." (In) Hirschon, Renbee (ed.).
    Women and Property--Women as Property. New York:
    St.Martin's Press. 1983.
Marks, Shula and Unterhalter, Elaine
    Women and the Migrant Labour System in Southern Africa.
    Lusaka, Zambia: United Nations Economic Commission for
    Africa. Multinational Programming and Operational Centre
    for Eastern and Central Africa. 1978. 15p.
Mies, M.
    "Consequences of Capitalist Penetration for Women's
    Subsistence Reproduction." Paper Presented at the
    Seminar on Underdevelopment and Subsistence Production in
    South East Africa. April, 1978.
Onyango, Philista P.M.
    "The Working Mother and the Housemaid as a Substitute:
    Its Complications on the Children." Journal of Eastern
    African Research and Development. Volume 13 1983. pp.
    24-31.
Wright, Marcia
    "Technology and Women's Control Over Production: Three
    Case Studies From East-Central Africa and Their
    Implications for Esther Boserup's Thesis About the
    Displacement of Women." Paper Presented at the
    Rockefeller Foundation Workshop on Women, Household and
    Human Capital Development in Low Income Countries. New
    York: Rockefeller Foundation. July, 1982.

EDUCATION AND TRAINING

Elias, Misrak
    Training for Development Planning and Women, an African
    Perspective: Report on the Second Training Programme.
    Arusha, Tanzania: Eastern and Southern Africa Management
    Institute. April 5-May 14, 1982. 55p.

Elias, Misrak
    Training for Development Planning and Women: An African
    Perspective. Arusha, Tanzania: Eastern and Southern
    African Management Institute. Annual Report and Report
    of the First Training Programme. September 16,
    1980-September 15, 1981. 1981.
Kayongo-Male, Diana
    "Helping Self-Help Groups Help Themselves: Training of
    Leaders of Women's Groups." Journal of Eastern African
    Research and Development. Volume 13 1983. pp. 88-103.
Mbilinyi, Marjorie J.
    "Research Priorities in Women's Studies in Eastern
    Africa." Women's Studies International Forum. Volume 7
    #4 1984. pp. 289-300.
Muriuki, Margaret N.
    "The Role of Women in African Librarianship: The Next 25
    Years." Paper Presented at the Standing Conference of
    Eastern, Central and Southern African Libraries. Lusaka,
    Zambia. October 4-9, 1976.
Wright, Marcia
    "Technology and Women's Control Over Production: Three
    Case Studies From East-Central Africa and Their
    Implications for Esther Boserup's Thesis About the
    Displacement of Women." Paper Presented at the
    Rockefeller Foundation Workshop on Women, Household and
    Human Capital Development in Low Income Countries. New
    York: Rockefeller Foundation. July, 1982.

EMPLOYMENT AND LABOR

Besha, R.M.
    The Mass Media and Entertainment. Dar-es-Salaam,
    Tanzania: University of Dar-es-Salaam. Bureau of
    Resource Assessment and Land Use Planning. Workshop on
    Women's Studies and Development. Paper #34. September
    24-29, 1979.
Igbinovia, Patrick E.
    "Prostitution in Black Africa." International Journal of
    Women's Studies. Volume 7 #5 November-December, 1984.
    pp. 430-449.
Kayongo-Male, Diana
    "Helping Self-Help Groups Help Themselves: Training of
    Leaders of Women's Groups." Journal of Eastern African
    Research and Development. Volume 13 1983. pp. 88-103.
Marks, Shula and Unterhalter, Elaine
    Women and the Migrant Labour System in Southern Africa.
    Lusaka, Zambia: United Nations Economic Commission for
    Africa. Multinational Programming and Operational Centre
    for Eastern and Central Africa. 1978. 15p.
McDowell, James and Hazzard, Virginia
    "Village Technology and Women's Work in Eastern Africa."

Assignment Children. Volume 36 October-December, 1976. pp. 53-65.

Mies, M.
"Consequences of Capitalist Penetration for Women's Subsistence Reproduction." Paper Presented at the Seminar on Underdevelopment and Subsistence Production in South East Africa. April, 1978.

Muriuki, Margaret N.
"The Role of Women in African Librarianship: The Next 25 Years." Paper Presented at the Standing Conference of Eastern, Central and Southern African Libraries. Lusaka, Zambia. October 4-9, 1976.

N'ska, Leci
"The Discrimination Against Women in the Civil Service." Viva. Volume 7 #2 1981. pp. 15-17, 45.

Onyango, Philista P.M.
"The Working Mother and the Housemaid as a Substitute: Its Complications on the Children." Journal of Eastern African Research and Development. Volume 13 1983. pp. 24-31.

FAMILY LIFE

MacGaffey, Wyatt
"Lineage Structure, Marriage and the Family Amongst the Central Bantu." Journal of African History. Volume 24 #2 1983. pp. 173-187.

Onyango, Philista P.M.
"The Working Mother and the Housemaid as a Substitute: Its Complications on the Children." Journal of Eastern African Research and Development. Volume 13 1983. pp. 24-31.

Oucho, John O.
"Socio-Economic Perspectives of Fertility Regulation in Traditional and Modern African Societies." (In) University of Nairobi. Papers of the Seminar on Oral Traditions: Past Growth and Future Development in East Africa. Nairobi: University of Nairobi. UNESCO Institute of African Affairs. Kisumu, Kenya. April 18-22, 1979. 18p.

FAMILY PLANNING AND CONTRACEPTION

Hosken, Fran P.
"Women and Health in East and West Africa: Family Planning and Female Cicumcision." Paper Presented at the Seminar on Traditional Practices Affecting the Health of Women and Children. World Conference of the United Nations Decade for Women. New York: United Nations. Copenhagen, Denmark. July 14-30, 1980.

Hosken, Fran P.
"Women and Health in East and West Africa: Family
Planning and Female Circumcision." Paper Presented at
the Seminar on Traditional Practices Affecting the Health
of Women and Children: Female Circumcision, Childhood
Marriage, Nutritional Taboos, etc. Alexandria, Egypt:
World Health Organization. Eastern Mediterranean
Regional Office. Khartoum, Sudan. February 10-15, 1979.
Johnston, Bruce F. and Meyer, Anthony J.
"Nutrition, Health and Population in Strategies for Rural
Development." Economic Development and Cultural Change.
Volume 26 #1 October, 1977. pp. 1-23.
Johnston, Bruce F. and Meyer, Anthony J.
Nutrition, Health and Population in Strategies for Rural
Development. Nairobi: University of Nairobi. Institute
for Development Studies. Discussion Paper #238. 1976.
45p.
Oucho, John O.
"Socio-Economic Perspectives of Fertility Regulation in
Traditional and Modern African Societies." (In)
University of Nairobi. Papers of the Seminar on Oral
Traditions: Past Growth and Future Development in East
Africa. Nairobi: University of Nairobi. UNESCO
Institute of African Affairs. Kisumu, Kenya. April
18-22, 1979. 18p.

FERTILITY AND INFERTILITY

Henin, Roushdi A.
"Fertility, Infertility and Sub-Fertility in Eastern
Africa." (In) International Union for the Scientic Study
of Population (IUSSP). International Population
Conference: Solicited Papers. Liege, Netherland: IUSSP.
Volume Three. 1981. pp. 667-697.
Hosken, Fran P.
"Female Circumcision and Fertility in Africa." Women and
Health. Volume 1 #6 November-December, 1976. pp. 3-11.
Ladipo, O.A.
"The Role of Artificial Insemimation in the Management of
Infertility." East African Medical Journal. Volume 56
#5 May, 1979. pp. 219-222.
Oucho, John O.
"Socio-Economic Perspectives of Fertility Regulation in
Traditional and Modern African Societies." (In)
University of Nairobi. Papers of the Seminar on Oral
Traditions: Past Growth and Future Development in East
Africa. Nairobi: University of Nairobi. UNESCO
Institute of African Affairs. Kisumu, Kenya. April
18-22, 1979. 18p.

HEALTH, NUTRITION AND MEDICINE

Abdalla, Raqiya
    Sisters in Affliction: Circumcision and Infibulation of
    Women in Africa. London: Zed Press. 1982. 122p.
Henin, Roushdi A.
    "Fertility, Infertility and Sub-Fertility in Eastern
    Africa." (In) International Union for the Scientic Study
    of Population (IUSSP). International Population
    Conference: Solicited Papers. Liege, Netherland: IUSSP.
    Volume Three. 1981. pp. 667-697.
Hosken, Fran P.
    "Female Circumcision and Fertility in Africa." Women and
    Health. Volume 1 #6 November-December, 1976. pp. 3-11.
Hosken, Fran P.
    "Female Circumcision in Africa." Victimology. Volume 2
    #3/4 1977. pp. 487-498.
Hosken, Fran P.
    "Female Circumcision in the World of Today: A Global
    Review." Paper Presented at the Seminar on Traditional
    Practices Affecting the Health of Women and Children.
    World Conference of the United Nations Decade for Women.
    New York: United Nations. Copenhagen, Denmark. July
    14-30, 1980.
Hosken, Fran P.
    "Female Circumcision in the World of Today: A Global
    View." Paper Presented at the Seminar on Traditional
    Practices Affecting the Health of Women and Children:
    Female Circumcision, Childhood Marriage, Nutritional
    Taboos, etc. Alexandria, Egypt: World Health
    Organization. Eastern Mediterranean Regional Office.
    Khartoum, Sudan. February 10-15, 1979.
Hosken, Fran P.
    "Female Genital Mutilation in the World Today: A Global
    Review." International Journal of Health Services.
    Volume 11 #3 1981. pp. 415-430.
Hosken, Fran P.
    "Genital Mutilation of Women in Africa." Munger Africana
    Library Notes. #36 October, 1976. 21p.
Hosken, Fran P.
    "The Epidemiology of Female Genital Mutilation."
    Tropical Doctor. July, 1978. pp. 150-156.
Hosken, Fran P.
    "The Violence of Power: The Genital Mutilation of
    Females." Heresies. Volume 6 #2 Summer, 1978. pp.
    28-36.
Hosken, Fran P.
    "Towards an Epidemiology of Genital Mutilation of Females
    in Africa." Paper Presented at the Annual Meeting of the
    African Studies Association. Paper #43. Baltimore,
    Maryland. 1978. 20p.
Hosken, Fran P.
    "Women and Health in East and West Africa: Family

Planning and Female Cicumcision." Paper Presented at the
Seminar on Traditional Practices Affecting the Health of
Women and Children. World Conference of the United
Nations Decade for Women. New York: United Nations.
Copenhagen, Denmark. July 14-30, 1980.

Hosken, Fran P.
"Women and Health in East and West Africa: Family
Planning and Female Circumcision." Paper Presented at
the Seminar on Traditional Practices Affecting the Health
of Women and Children: Female Circumcision, Childhood
Marriage, Nutritional Taboos, etc. Alexandria, Egypt:
World Health Organization. Eastern Mediterranean
Regional Office. Khartoum, Sudan. February 10-15, 1979.

Hosken, Fran P.
"Women and Health: Genital And Sexual Mutilation of
Females." International Journal of Women's Studies.
Volume 3 #3 May-June, 1980. pp. 300-316.

Hosken, Fran P.
Female Sexual Mutilations: The Facts and Proposals for
Action. Lexington, Massachusetts: Women's International
Network News. 1980. 102p.

Hosken, Fran P.
The Hosken Report: Genital and Sexual Mutilation of
Females. Lexington, Massachusetts: Women's International
Network News. 1982. 327p.

Huelsman, Ben R.
"An Anthropological View of Clitoral and Other Female
Genital Mutilations." (In) Lowery, T.P. and Lowery, T.S.
(eds.). The Clitoris. St. Louis, Missouri: Warren H.
Green. 1976. pp. 111-161.

Johnston, Bruce F. and Meyer, Anthony J.
"Nutrition, Health and Population in Strategies for Rural
Development." Economic Development and Cultural Change.
Volume 26 #1 October, 1977. pp. 1-23.

Johnston, Bruce F. and Meyer, Anthony J.
Nutrition, Health and Population in Strategies for Rural
Development. Nairobi: University of Nairobi. Institute
for Development Studies. Discussion Paper #238. 1976.
45p.

Ladipo, O.A.
"The Role of Artificial Insemination in the Management of
Infertility." East African Medical Journal. Volume 56
#5 May, 1979. pp. 219-222.

Mati, J.K.
"Focusing on Maternal Mortality and Morbidity." East
African Medical Journal. Volume 57 #2 February, 1980.
pp. 70-71.

Mgone, C.S.
"Reproductive Behavior and Attitudes of African Mothers
Following Birth of a Downs Syndrome Child." East African
Medical Journal. Volume 59 #8 1982. pp. 555-559.

Pieters, Guy and Lowenfels, A.
"Infibulation in the Horn of Africa." New York State

Journal of Medicine. Volume 77 April, 1977. pp. 729-731.

Weisner, Thomas S. and Abbott, Susan
"Women, Modernity and Stress: Three Contrasting Contexts for Change in East Africa." Southwestern Journal of Anthropology. Volume 33 #4 Winter, 1977. pp. 421-451.

HISTORY

Alpers, Edward
"The Story of Swema: Female Vulnerability in Nineteenth-Century East Africa." (In) Robertson, Claire C. and Klein, Martin A. (eds.). Women and Slavery in Africa. Madison, Wisconsin: University of Wisconsin Press. 1983. pp. 185-219.

Klein, H.
"Crimes Against Thirty Million." New Statesman. Volume 98 August 24, 1979. pp. 266-268.

MacGaffey, Wyatt
"Lineage Structure, Marriage and the Family Amongst the Central Bantu." Journal of African History. Volume 24 #2 1983. pp. 173-187.

LAW AND LEGAL ISSUES

Caplan, Patricia
"Cognatic Descent, Islamic Law, and Women's Property on the East African Coast." (In) Hirschon, Renbee (ed.). Women and Property--Women as Property. New York: St.Martin's Press. 1983.

LITERATURE

Mutiso, G.C.
"Women in African Literature." East Africa Journal. Volume 14 March, 1977. pp. 4-14.

MARITAL RELATIONS AND NUPTIALITY

Caplan, Patricia
"Cognatic Descent, Islamic Law, and Women's Property on the East African Coast." (In) Hirschon, Renbee (ed.). Women and Property--Women as Property. New York: St.Martin's Press. 1983.

MacGaffey, Wyatt
"Lineage Structure, Marriage and the Family Amongst the Central Bantu." Journal of African History. Volume 24 #2 1983. pp. 173-187.

Mushanga, Tibamanya M.
    "Wife Victimization in East and Central Africa."
    Victimology. Volume 2 #3/4 1977. pp. 479-486.
Oucho, John O.
    "Socio-Economic Perspectives of Fertility Regulation in
    Traditional and Modern African Societies." (In)
    University of Nairobi. Papers of the Seminar on Oral
    Traditions: Past Growth and Future Development in East
    Africa. Nairobi: University of Nairobi. UNESCO
    Institute of African Affairs. Kisumu, Kenya. April
    18-22, 1979. 18p.
Pieters, Guy and Lowenfels, A.
    "Infibulation in the Horn of Africa." New York State
    Journal of Medicine. Volume 77 April, 1977. pp.
    729-731.
Szklut, Jay
    "Bride Wealth, An Alternate View." Behavior Science
    Research. Volume 16 #3/4 1981. pp. 225-247.

MASS MEDIA

Anonymous
    "Women in East Africa Media Were 1% of Total: Now are 5%
    to 10%." Media Report to Women. Volume 8 January 1,
    1980. pp. 6.
Besha, R.M.
    The Mass Media and Entertainment. Dar-es-Salaam,
    Tanzania: University of Dar-es-Salaam. Bureau of
    Resource Assessment and Land Use Planning. Workshop on
    Women's Studies and Development. Paper #34. September
    24-29, 1979.

MIGRATION

Marks, Shula and Unterhalter, Elaine
    Women and the Migrant Labour System in Southern Africa.
    Lusaka, Zambia: United Nations Economic Commission for
    Africa. Multinational Programming and Operational Centre
    for Eastern and Central Africa. 1978. 15p.

MISCELLANEOUS

Erasto, Muga
    Studies in Prostitution: East, West and South Africa,
    Zaire and Nevada. Nairobi: Kenya Literature Bureau.
    1980.
Igbinovia, Patrick E.
    "Prostitution in Black Africa." International Journal of
    Women's Studies. Volume 7 #5 November-December, 1984.
    pp. 430-449.

Johnston, Bruce F. and Meyer, Anthony J.
    "Nutrition, Health and Population in Strategies for Rural
    Development." Economic Development and Cultural Change.
    Volume 26 #1 October, 1977. pp. 1-23.
Johnston, Bruce F. and Meyer, Anthony J.
    Nutrition, Health and Population in Strategies for Rural
    Development. Nairobi: University of Nairobi. Institute
    for Development Studies. Discussion Paper #238. 1976.
    45p.
Mati, J.K.
    "Focusing on Maternal Mortality and Morbidity." East
    African Medical Journal. Volume 57 #2 February, 1980.
    pp. 70-71.
Muriuki, Margaret N.
    "The Role of Women in African Librarianship: The Next 25
    Years." Paper Presented at the Standing Conference of
    Eastern, Central and Southern African Libraries. Lusaka,
    Zambia. October 4-9, 1976.
Mushanga, Tibamanya M.
    "Wife Victimization in East and Central Africa."
    Victimology. Volume 2 #3/4 1977. pp. 479-486.

ORGANIZATIONS

Kayongo-Male, Diana
    "Helping Self-Help Groups Help Themselves: Training of
    Leaders of Women's Groups." Journal of Eastern African
    Research and Development. Volume 13 1983. pp. 88-103.

POLITICS AND GOVERNMENT

N'ska, Leci
    "The Discrimination Against Women in the Civil Service."
    Viva. Volume 7 #2 1981. pp. 15-17, 45.

RELIGION AND WITCHCRAFT

Berger, Iris
    "Rebels or Status Seekers? Women as Spirit Mediums in
    East Africa." (In) Hafkin, N.J. and Bay, Edna (eds.).
    Women in Africa: Studies in Social and Economic Change.
    Stanford, California: Stanford University Press. 1976.
    pp. 157-181.
Berger, Iris
    "Women, Religion and Social Change: East and Central
    African Perspectives." Paper Presented at the Conference
    on Women and Development. Wellesley, Massachusetts:
    Wellesley College. Wellesley College Center for Research
    on Women. June 2-6, 1976. 25p.

Caplan, Patricia
    "Cognatic Descent, Islamic Law, and Women's Property on
    the East African Coast." (In) Hirschon, Renbee (ed.).
    Women and Property--Women as Property. New York:
    St.Martin's Press. 1983.

RESEARCH

Germain. Adrienne
    "Research on Women in Agricultural Production in Eastern
    and Southern Africa." Paper Presented at a Workshop on
    Women in Agricultural Production in Eastern and Southern
    Africa. Nairobi, Kenya. April 9-11, 1980.
Mbilinyi, Marjorie J.
    "Research Priorities in Women's Studies in Eastern
    Africa." Women's Studies International Forum. Volume 7
    #4 1984. pp. 289-300.
Wadsworth, Gail M.
    Women in Development: A Bibliography of Materials
    Available in the Library and Documentation Centre,
    Eastern and Southern African Management Institute.
    Arusha, Tanzania: Eastern and Southern African Management
    Institute. Library and Documentation Centre. February,
    1982. 106p.

SEX ROLES

Igbinovia, Patrick E.
    "Prostitution in Black Africa." International Journal of
    Women's Studies. Volume 7 #5 November-December, 1984.
    pp. 430-449.
MacGaffey, Wyatt
    "Lineage Structure, Marriage and the Family Amongst the
    Central Bantu." Journal of African History. Volume 24
    #2 1983. pp. 173-187.
McDowell, James and Hazzard, Virginia
    "Village Technology and Women's Work in Eastern Africa."
    Assignment Children. Volume 36 October-December, 1976.
    pp. 53-65.

SEXUAL MUTILATION/CIRCUMCISION

Abdalla, Raqiya
    Sisters in Affliction: Circumcision and Infibulation of
    Women in Africa. London: Zed Press. 1982. 122p.
Hosken, Fran P.
    "Female Circumcision and Fertility in Africa." Women and
    Health. Volume 1 #6 November-December, 1976. pp. 3-11.

Hosken, Fran P.
"Female Circumcision in Africa." Victimology. Volume 2
#3/4 1977. pp. 487-498.

Hosken, Fran P.
"Female Circumcision in the World of Today: A Global
Review." Paper Presented at the Seminar on Traditional
Practices Affecting the Health of Women and Children.
World Conference of the United Nations Decade for Women.
New York: United Nations. Copenhagen, Denmark. July
14-30, 1980.

Hosken, Fran P.
"Female Circumcision in the World of Today: A Global
View." Paper Presented at the Seminar on Traditional
Practices Affecting the Health of Women and Children:
Female Circumcision, Childhood Marriage, Nutritional
Taboos, etc. Alexandria, Egypt: World Health
Organization. Eastern Mediterranean Regional Office.
Khartoum, Sudan. February 10-15, 1979.

Hosken, Fran P.
"Female Genital Mutilation in the World Today: A Global
Review." International Journal of Health Services.
Volume 11 #3 1981. pp. 415-430.

Hosken, Fran P.
"Genital Mutilation of Women in Africa." Munger Africana
Library Notes. #36 October, 1976. 21p.

Hosken, Fran P.
"The Epidemiology of Female Genital Mutilation."
Tropical Doctor. July, 1978. pp. 150-156.

Hosken, Fran P.
"The Violence of Power: The Genital Mutilation of
Females." Heresies. Volume 6 #2 Summer, 1978. pp.
28-36.

Hosken, Fran P.
"Towards an Epidemiology of Genital Mutilation of Females
in Africa." Paper Presented at the Annual Meeting of the
African Studies Association. Paper #43. Baltimore,
Maryland. 1978. 20p.

Hosken, Fran P.
"Women and Health in East and West Africa: Family
Planning and Female Cicumcision." Paper Presented at the
Seminar on Traditional Practices Affecting the Health of
Women and Children. World Conference of the United
Nations Decade for Women. New York: United Nations.
Copenhagen, Denmark. July 14-30, 1980.

Hosken, Fran P.
"Women and Health in East and West Africa: Family
Planning and Female Circumcision." Paper Presented at
the Seminar on Traditional Practices Affecting the Health
of Women and Children: Female Circumcision, Childhood
Marriage, Nutritional Taboos, etc. Alexandria, Egypt:
World Health Organization. Eastern Mediterranean
Regional Office. Khartoum, Sudan. February 10-15, 1979.

Hosken, Fran P.
   "Women and Health: Genital And Sexual Mutilation of
   Females." International Journal of Women's Studies.
   Volume 3 #3 May-June, 1980. pp. 300-316.
Hosken, Fran P.
   Female Sexual Mutilations: The Facts and Proposals for
   Action. Lexington, Massachusetts: Women's International
   Network News. 1980. 102p.
Hosken, Fran P.
   The Hosken Report: Genital and Sexual Mutilation of
   Females. Lexington, Massachusetts: Women's International
   Network News. 1982. 327p.
Huelsman, Ben R.
   "An Anthropological View of Clitoral and Other Female
   Genital Mutilations." (In) Lowery, T.P. and Lowery, T.S.
   (eds.). The Clitoris. St. Louis, Missouri: Warren H.
   Green. 1976. pp. 111-161.
Klein, H.
   "Crimes Against Thirty Million." New Statesman. Volume
   98 August 24, 1979. pp. 266-268.
Pieters, Guy and Lowenfels, A.
   "Infibulation in the Horn of Africa." New York State
   Journal of Medicine. Volume 77 April, 1977. pp.
   729-731.

STATUS OF WOMEN

Caplan, Patricia
   "Cognatic Descent, Islamic Law, and Women's Property on
   the East African Coast." (In) Hirschon, Renbee (ed.).
   Women and Property--Women as Property. New York:
   St.Martin's Press. 1983.
Gebre-Selassie, Alasebu
   The Situation of Women in Africa: A Review. Nairobi:
   UNICEF. Eastern Africa Regional Office. 1979. 65p.

WOMEN AND THEIR CHILDREN

Mgone, C.S.
   "Reproductive Behavior and Attitudes of African Mothers
   Following Birth of a Downs Syndrome Child." East African
   Medical Journal. Volume 59 #8 1982. pp. 555-559.
Onyango, Philista P.M.
   "The Working Mother and the Housemaid as a Substitute:
   Its Complications on the Children." Journal of Eastern
   African Research and Development. Volume 13 1983. pp.
   24-31.

NATIONS OF
EASTERN AFRICA

Djibouti

Aitchison, Roberta
    "Reluctant Witnesses: Sexual Abuse of Refugee Women in
    Djibouti." Cultural Survival Quarterly. Volume 8 #2
    Summer, 1984. pp. 26-27.

Ethiopia

AGRICULTURE

Anonymous
"Socio-Economic Transformations in Liberated Ertitrea and
the Impact on Peasant Women." ISIS International
Bulletin. #11 Spring, 1979. pp. 22-24.
Bourgoyne, Clarissa
"Position of Women in Feudal Ethiopia." (In) Institute
of Ethiopian Studies and the Historical Society of
Ethiopia. Papers of the Conference on Ethiopian
Feudalism. Addis Ababa, Ethiopia: The Institute. March,
1976. 6p.
Chiffelle, Suzanne
Women's Occupations and Social Standing in Gofa Awradja.
Addis Ababa, Ethiopia: Service of Documentation and
Communication for Development. 1978. 58p.
Comhaire, Jean
Significance of Feudalism to the Position of Ethiopian
Women. Addis Ababa, Ethiopia: Institute of Ethiopian
Studies and the Historical Society of Ethiopia. Papers
of the Conference on Ethiopian Feudalism. March, 1976.
7p.
Crummey, Donald
"Women and Landed Property in Gondarine Ethiopia." Paper
Presented at the Annual Meeting of the African Studies
Association. Paper #17. Baltimore, Maryland. 1978.
12p.
Crummey, Donald
"Women, Property and Litigation Among the Bagemder
Amhara, 1750's to 1850's." (In) Hay, Margaret J. and
Wright, Marcia (eds.). African Women and the Law:
Historical Perspectives. Boston: Boston University.
African Studies Center. Boston University Papers on
Africa. Volume 7. 1982. pp. 19-32.
Crummey, Donald
"Women and Landed Property in Gondarine Ethiopia."

International Journal of African Historical Studies.
Volume 14 #3 1981. pp. 444-465.
Mackay, B.
"The Effects of Socialist Transformation on the Fertility
of the Rural Population of Ethiopia." Ethiopian Journal
of Development. Volume 3 #2 October, 1979. pp. 55-64.
Tadesse, Zenebeworke
"The Impact of Land Reform on Women: The Case of
Ethiopia." ISIS International Bulletin. #11 Spring,
1979. pp. 18-21.
Tadesse, Zenebeworke
"The Impact of Land Reform on Women: The Case of
Ethiopia." (In) Beneria, L. (ed.). Women and
Development: The Sexual Division of Labor in Rural
Societies. New York: Praeger Publishers. 1982. pp.
203-222.

BIBLIOGRAPHIES

Gebre-Selassie, Alasebu
Women and Development in Ethiopia: An Annotated
Bibliography. Addis Ababa, Ethiopia: United Nations
Economic Commission for Africa. African Training and
Research Centre for Women. 1981. 58p.
Hafkin, Nancy J. (ed.)
Women and Development in Ethiopia: An Annotated
Bibliography. Addis Ababa, Ethiopia: United Nations
Economic Commission for Africa. African Training and
Research Centre for Women. 1978. 117p.

CULTURAL ROLES

Almagor, Uri
Pastoral Partners: Affinity and Bond Partnership Among
the Dassanetch of South-West Ethiopia. Manchester,
England: Manchester University Press. 1978. 258p.
Anonymous
"Socio-Economic Transformations in Liberated Ertitrea and
the Impact on Peasant Women." ISIS International
Bulletin. #11 Spring, 1979. pp. 22-24.
Anonymous
"Women in Struggle." Third World Quarterly. Volume 5 #4
October, 1983. pp. 874-914.
Barnabas, G.
"Hagosa, the Traditional Midwife--A Tale From Ethiopia."
World Health Forum: An International Journal of Health
Development. Volume 3 #3 1982.
Bauer, Dan F.
Household and Society in Ethiopia: An Economic and Social
Analysis of Tigray Social Principles and Household
Organization. East Lansing, Michigan: Michigan State

University. African Studies Center. Committee on
Ethiopian Studies. Occasional Paper #6. 1977. 183p.
Beddada, Belletech
   "Female Circumcision in Ethiopia." Paper Presented at
   the Seminar on Traditional Practices Affecting the Health
   of Women and Children. World Conference of the United
   Nations Decade for Women. Copenhagen, Denmark. July
   14-30, 1980.
Beddada, Belletech
   "Female Circumcision in Ethiopia." Paper Presented at
   the Seminar on Traditional Practices Affecting the Health
   of Women and Children: Female Circumcision, Childhood
   Marriage, Nutritional Taboos, etc. Alexandria, Egypt:
   World Health Organization. Eastern Mediterranean
   Regional Office. Khartoum, Sudan. February 10-15, 1979.
Beddada, Belletech
   "Traditional Practices in Pregnancy and Childbirth in
   Ethiopia." Paper Presented at the Seminar on Traditional
   Practices Affecting the Health of Women and Children:
   Female Circumcision, Childhood Marriage, Nutritional
   Taboos, etc. Alexandria: Egypt: World Health
   Organization. Eastern Mediterranean Regional Office.
   Khartoum, Sudan. February 10-15, 1979.
Beddada, Belletech
   "Traditional Practices in Pregnancy and Childbirth in
   Ethiopia." Paper Presented to the Seminar on Traditional
   Practices Affecting the Health of Women and Children.
   World Conference of the United Nations Decade for Women.
   Copenhagen, Denmark. July 14-30, 1980.
Bjeren, Gunilla
   Migration to Shashemene: Ethnicity, Gender and Occupation
   in Urban Ethiopia. Uppsala, Sweden: Scandanavian
   Institute of African Studies. 1985. 271p.
Bliese, Loren F.
   "The Tragedies of Three Afar Girls." Ethiopanist Notes.
   Volume 2 #3 1978. pp. 45-59.
Bourgoyne, Clarissa
   "Position of Women in Feudal Ethiopia." (In) Institute
   of Ethiopian Studies and the Historical Society of
   Ethiopia. Papers of the Conference on Ethiopian
   Feudalism. Addis Ababa, Ethiopia: The Institute. March,
   1976. 6p.
Cassiers, Anne
   "Mercha: An Ethiopian Woman Speaks of Her Life."
   Northeast African Studies. Volume 5 #2 1983. pp. 57-81.
Chiffelle, Suzanne
   Women's Occupations and Social Standing in Gofa Awradja.
   Addis Ababa, Ethiopia: Service of Documentation and
   Communication for Development. 1978. 58p.
Comhaire, Jean
   Significance of Feudalism to the Position of Ethiopian
   Women. Addis Ababa, Ethiopia: Institute of Ethiopian
   Studies and the Historical Society of Ethiopia. Papers

of the Conference on Ethiopian Feudalism. March, 1976.
7p.

Crummey, Donald
"Women and Landed Property in Gondarine Ethiopia." Paper
Presented at the Annual Meeting of the African Studies
Association. Paper #17. Baltimore, Maryland. 1978.
12p.

Crummey, Donald
"Women, Property and Litigation Among the Bagemder
Amhara, 1750's to 1850's." (In) Hay, Margaret J. and
Wright, Marcia (eds.). African Women and the Law:
Historical Perspectives. Boston: Boston University.
African Studies Center. Boston University Papers on
Africa. Volume 7. 1982. pp. 19-32.

Crummey, Donald
"Women and Landed Property in Gondarine Ethiopia."
International Journal of African Historical Studies.
Volume 14 #3 1981. pp. 444-465.

Crummey, Donald
"The Settlement of Litigation Within the Ethiopian Ruling
Class, With Special Reference to the Position of Women:
The Bagemder Amhara from the 1750's to the 1850's."
Unpublished Manuscript. 1979.

Crummey, Donald
"Family and Property Amongst the Amhara Nobility."
Journal of African History. Volume 24 #2 1983. pp.
207-220.

Daka, Kebebew
"The Place of the Family in Ethiopian Society and Some
Observations on the Emerging Changes." Paper Presented
at the Seminar on the Changing Family in the African
Context, Maseru, Lesotho, 1983. Paris: United Nations
Educational, Scientific and Cultural Organization.
1984. 24p.

Dirasse, Laketch
"The Socio-Economic Position of Women in Addis Ababa: The
Case of Prostitution." Ph.D Dissertation: Boston
University. Boston, Massachusetts. 1978. 203p.

Foucher, Emile
"Ethiopia--The Unique Community of Muslim 'Nuns'."
Exchange. Volume 12 September, 1983. pp. 51.

Haile, Daniel
Law and the Status of Women in Ethiopia. Addis Ababa,
Ethiopia: United Nations Economic Commission for Africa.
African Training and Research Centre for Women. Research
Series. 1980. 49p.

Hecht, Elisabeth-Dorothea
The Voluntary Associations and the Social Status of
Harari Women in Harar, Eastern Ethiopia. Nairobi:
University of Nairobi. Institute of African Studies.
Paper #136. 1980. 17p.

Junge, B.J. and Tegegne, D.
"The Effects of Liberation From Illiteracy on the Lives

of 31 Women: A Case Study." Journal of Reading. Volume 28 April, 1985. pp. 606-613.

Pankhurst, Richard K.
The Ethiopian Women in Former Times: An Anthology Prepared for the International Women's Year Anniversary Exhibition at Revolutionary Square. Addis Ababa, Ethiopia. 1976. 25p.

Pankhurst, Richard K.
"Correspondent's Report: Women in Ethiopia Today." Africa Today. Volume 28 #4 4th Quarter, 1981. pp. 49-51.

Silkin, Trish
"Eritrea: Women in Struggle." Third World Quarterly. Volume 5 #4 1983. pp. 909-913.

Tadesse, Zenebeworke
Condition of Women in Ethiopia. Addis Ababa, Ethiopia: Swedish International Development Authority. Unpublished Paper. 1976.

Tsehai, Berhane S.
"'Man's World', 'Women's Position': The Case of the Darasa Widow." N.E.A. (Oxford). Volume 1 #1 Summer, 1981. pp. 51-61.

Turton, David
"The Economics of Mursi Bridewealth: A Comparative Perspective." (In) Comaroff, J.L. (ed.). The Meaning of Marriage Payments. New York: Academic Press. 1980. pp. 67-92.

Williams, Larry and Finch, Charles S.
"The Great Queens of Ethiopia." Journal of African Civilzations. Volume 6 #1 1984. pp. 12-35.

Wright, K.
"How War is Affecting Eritrean Women." Sudanow. Volume 3 #3 1978. pp. 44-46.

DEVELOPMENT AND TECHNOLOGY

Anonymous
"African Training and Research Centre for Women: It's Work and Program." Africa Report. Volume 26 #2 March-April, 1981. pp. 17-21.

Gebre-Selassie, Alasebu
Women and Development in Ethiopia: An Annotated Bibliography. Addis Ababa, Ethiopia: United Nations Economic Commission for Africa. African Training and Research Centre for Women. 1981. 58p.

Hafkin, Nancy J. (ed.)
Women and Development in Ethiopia: An Annotated Bibliography. Addis Ababa, Ethiopia: United Nations Economic Commission for Africa. African Training and Research Centre for Women. 1978. 117p.

Ketema, Teserach
"Modernization and Differential Fertility in Ethiopia--A

Multivariate Analysis." Ph.D Dissertation: University of
Illinois-Urbana-Champaign. Urbana, Illinois. 1985.
177p.
Mackay, B.
"The Effects of Socialist Transformation on the Fertility
of the Rural Population of Ethiopia." Ethiopian Journal
of Development. Volume 3 #2 October, 1979. pp. 55-64.
Palmer, Ingrid
"New Official Ideas on Women and Development." Institute
for Development Studies. Volume 10 #3 1979. pp. 42-53.
Tadesse, Zenebeworke
Condition of Women in Ethiopia. Addis Ababa, Ethiopia:
Swedish International Development Authority. Unpublished
Paper. 1976.
Tadesse, Zenebeworke
"The Impact of Land Reform on Women: The Case of
Ethiopia." ISIS International Bulletin. #11 Spring,
1979. pp. 18-21.
Tadesse, Zenebeworke
"The Impact of Land Reform on Women: The Case of
Ethiopia." (In) Beneria, L. (ed.). Women and
Development: The Sexual Division of Labor in Rural
Societies. New York: Praeger Publishers. 1982. pp.
203-222.

ECONOMICS

Anonymous
"Socio-Economic Transformations in Liberated Ertitrea and
the Impact on Peasant Women." ISIS International
Bulletin. #11 Spring, 1979. pp. 22-24.
Bourgoyne, Clarissa
"Position of Women in Feudal Ethiopia." (In) Institute
of Ethiopian Studies and the Historical Society of
Ethiopia. Papers of the Conference on Ethiopian
Feudalism. Addis Ababa, Ethiopia: The Institute. March,
1976. 6p.
Comhaire, Jean
Significance of Feudalism to the Position of Ethiopian
Women. Addis Ababa, Ethiopia: Institute of Ethiopian
Studies and the Historical Society of Ethiopia. Papers
of the Conference on Ethiopian Feudalism. March, 1976.
7p.
Dirasse, Laketch
"The Socio-Economic Position of Women in Addis Ababa: The
Case of Prostitution." Ph.D Dissertation: Boston
University. Boston, Massachusetts. 1978. 203p.
Kromstedt, Katherine
Women Textile Workers in Ethiopia. Addis Ababa,
Ethiopia: United Nations Economic Commission for Africa.
Handicrafts and Small-Scale Industries Unit. 1979. 25p.

Palmer, Ingrid
    "New Official Ideas on Women and Development." Institute
    for Development Studies. Volume 10 #3 1979. pp. 42-53.
Tadesse, Zenebeworke
    "The Impact of Land Reform on Women: The Case of
    Ethiopia." ISIS International Bulletin. #11 Spring,
    1979. pp. 18-21.
Tadesse, Zenebeworke
    An Oveview on the Role of Women's Organizations in
    Africa: Case Study of Ethiopia, Zambia, Mozambique and
    Tanzania. Lusaka, Zambia: P/O Box RW 514. 1978.
Tadesse, Zenebeworke
    "An Overview on Women's Organizations in Africa: The Case
    of Ethiopia, Mozambique and Tanzania." Paper Presented
    at the 9th World Conference of Sociology. Uppsala,
    Sweden. 1978.
Tadesse, Zenebeworke
    "The Impact of Land Reform on Women: The Case of
    Ethiopia." (In) Beneria, L. (ed.). Women and
    Development: The Sexual Division of Labor in Rural
    Societies. New York: Praeger Publishers. 1982. pp.
    203-222.
United Nations Economic Commission for Africa (UNECA)
    Women Textile Workers in Ethiopia. Addis Ababa,
    Ethiopia: UNECA. Handicraft and Small-Scale Industries
    Unit. African Training and Research Centre for Women.
    1979. 19p.

EDUCATION AND TRAINING

Anonymous
    "African Training and Research Centre for Women: It's
    Work and Program." Africa Report. Volume 26 #2
    March-April, 1981. pp. 17-21.
Junge, B.J. and Tegegne, D.
    "The Effects of Liberation From Illiteracy on the Lives
    of 31 Women: A Case Study." Journal of Reading. Volume
    28 April, 1985. pp. 606-613.
Pettit, John J.
    Integrated Family Life Education Project: A Project of
    the Ethiopian Women's Association. New York: World
    Education. 1977. 98p.
Tadesse, Zenebeworke
    An Oveview on the Role of Women's Organizations in
    Africa: Case Study of Ethiopia, Zambia, Mozambique and
    Tanzania. Lusaka, Zambia: P/O Box RW 514. 1978.
Tadesse, Zenebeworke
    "An Overview on Women's Organizations in Africa: The Case
    of Ethiopia, Mozambique and Tanzania." Paper Presented
    at the 9th World Conference of Sociology. Uppsala,
    Sweden. 1978.

United Nations Economic Commission for Africa (UNECA)
"Training and Employment Opportunities for Out-of-School
Girls in Ethiopia." Paper Presented at the Expert
Meeting for English Speaking Personnel Involved in
Programmes for Out-of-School Girls. Addis Ababa,
Ethiopia: UNECA. Lusaka, Zambia. August 17-30, 1981.

EMPLOYMENT AND LABOR

Chiffelle, Suzanne
Women's Occupations and Social Standing in Gofa Awradja.
Addis Ababa, Ethiopia: Service of Documentation and
Communication for Development. 1978. 58p.
Kromstedt, Katherine
Women Textile Workers in Ethiopia. Addis Ababa,
Ethiopia: United Nations Economic Commission for Africa.
Handicrafts and Small-Scale Industries Unit. 1979. 25p.
Palmer, Ingrid
"New Official Ideas on Women and Development." Institute
for Development Studies. Volume 10 #3 1979. pp. 42-53.
Tadesse, Zenebeworke
"The Impact of Land Reform on Women: The Case of
Ethiopia." (In) Beneria, L. (ed.). Women and
Development: The Sexual Division of Labor in Rural
Societies. New York: Praeger Publishers. 1982. pp.
203-222.
United Nations Economic Commission for Africa (UNECA)
Women Textile Workers in Ethiopia. Addis Ababa,
Ethiopia: UNECA. Handicraft and Small-Scale Industries
Unit. African Training and Research Centre for Women.
1979. 19p.
United Nations Economic Commission for Africa (UNECA)
A Profile of Women Textile Workers in Addis Ababa.
Background Document to the Regional Prepatory Meeting of
the United Nations Economic Commission for Africa 2nd
Regional Conference for the Integration of Women in
Development. Addis Ababa, Ethiopia: UNECA. December
3-7, 1979.
United Nations Economic Commission for Africa (UNECA)
"Training and Employment Opportunities for Out-of-School
Girls in Ethiopia." Paper Presented at the Expert
Meeting for English Speaking Personnel Involved in
Programmes for Out-of-School Girls, Lusaka, Zambia,
August 17-30, 1981. Addis Ababa, Ethiopia: UNECA.
1981.

FAMILY LIFE

Almagor, Uri
Pastoral Partners: Affinity and Bond Partnership Among
the Dassanetch of South-West Ethiopia. Manchester,
England: Manchester University Press. 1978. 258p.

Bauer, Dan F.
   Household and Society in Ethiopia: An Economic and Social
   Analysis of Tigray Social Principles and Household
   Organization. East Lansing, Michigan: Michigan State
   University. African Studies Center. Committee on
   Ethiopian Studies. Occasional Paper #6. 1977. 183p.
Bjeren, Gunilla
   Migration to Shashemene: Ethnicity, Gender and Occupation
   in Urban Ethiopia. Uppsala, Sweden: Scandanavian
   Institute of African Studies. 1985. 271p.
Cassiers, Anne
   "Mercha: An Ethiopian Woman Speaks of Her Life."
   Northeast African Studies. Volume 5 #2 1983. pp. 57-81.
Chiffelle, Suzanne
   Women's Occupations and Social Standing in Gofa Awradja.
   Addis Ababa, Ethiopia: Service of Documentation and
   Communication for Development. 1978. 58p.
Daka, Kebebew
   "The Place of the Family in Ethiopian Society and Some
   Observations on the Emerging Changes." Paper Presented
   at the Seminar on the Changing Family in the African
   Context, Maseru, Lesotho, 1983. Paris: United Nations
   Educational, Scientific and Cultural Organization.
   1984. 24p.
Pettit, John J.
   Integrated Family Life Education Project: A Project of
   the Ethiopian Women's Association. New York: World
   Education. 1977. 98p.

FAMILY PLANNING AND CONTRACEPTION

Ketema, Teserach
   "Modernization and Differential Fertility in Ethiopia--A
   Multivariate Analysis." Ph.D Dissertation: University of
   Illinois-Urbana-Champaign. Urbana, Illinois. 1985.
   177p.
Wenlock, R. June and Wenlock, R.W.
   "Maternal Nutrition, Prolonged Lactation and Birth
   Spacing in Ethiopia." Journal of Biosocial Science.
   Volume 13 #3 July, 1981. pp. 261-268.

FERTILITY AND INFERTILITY

Abegaz, Berhanu
   "Papers in Ethiopian Demography II: Levels and Patterns
   of Fertility and Mortality." Northeast African Studies.
   Volume 7 #2 1985. pp. 1-22.
Ketema, Teserach
   "Modernization and Differential Fertility in Ethiopia--A
   Multivariate Analysis." Ph.D Dissertation: University of
   Illinois-Urbana-Champaign. Urbana, Illinois. 1985.
   177p.

Mackay, B.
"The Effects of Socialist Transformation on the Fertility
of the Rural Population of Ethiopia." Ethiopian Journal
of Development. Volume 3 #2 October, 1979. pp. 55-64.
Shamebo, D.
"Fertility and Infant Mortality Rates in Dembia Plain,
Gondar." Ethiopian Medical Journal. Volume 16 #3 July,
1978. pp. 95-97.

HEALTH, NUTRITION AND MEDICINE

Abegaz, Berhanu
"Papers in Ethiopian Demography II: Levels and Patterns
of Fertility and Mortality." Northeast African Studies.
Volume 7 #2 1985. pp. 1-22.
Barnabas, G.
"Hagosa, the Traditional Midwife--A Tale From Ethiopia."
World Health Forum: An International Journal of Health
Development. Volume 3 #3 1982.
Beddada, Belletech
"Female Circumcision in Ethiopia." Paper Presented at
the Seminar on Traditional Practices Affecting the Health
of Women and Children. World Conference of the United
Nations Decade for Women. Copenhagen, Denmark. July
14-30, 1980.
Beddada, Belletech
"Female Circumcision in Ethiopia." Paper Presented at
the Seminar on Traditional Practices Affecting the Health
of Women and Children: Female Circumcision, Childhood
Marriage, Nutritional Taboos, etc. Alexandria, Egypt:
World Health Organization. Eastern Mediterranean
Regional Office. Khartoum, Sudan. February 10-15, 1979.
Beddada, Belletech
"Traditional Practices in Pregnancy and Childbirth in
Ethiopia." Paper Presented at the Seminar on Traditional
Practices Affecting the Health of Women and Children:
Female Circumcision, Childhood Marriage, Nutritional
Taboos, etc. Alexandria: Egypt: World Health
Organization. Eastern Mediterranean Regional Office.
Khartoum, Sudan. February 10-15, 1979.
Beddada, Belletech
"Traditional Practices in Pregnancy and Childbirth in
Ethiopia." Paper Presented to the Seminar on Traditional
Practices Affecting the Health of Women and Children.
World Conference of the United Nations Decade for Women.
Copenhagen, Denmark. July 14-30, 1980.
Duncan, M.E.
"The Message of 'Rheumatism': A Sympton of Leprosy in
Pregnancy and Lactation." Ethiopian Medical Journal.
Volume 23 #2 April, 1985. pp. 49-58.
Forsey, T.
"Chlamydial Gential Infection in Addis Ababa, Ethiopia.
A Seroepidemiological Survey." British Journal of

Venereal Diseases. Volume 58 #6 December, 1982. pp. 370-373.

Frost, O.
"Maternal and Perinatal Deaths in an Addis Ababa Hospital, 1980." Ethiopian Medical Journal. Volume 22 #3 July, 1984. pp. 143-146.

Gebre-Medhim, M.
"Subclinical Protein-Energy Malnutrition in Under-Privileged Ethiopian Mothers and Their Newborn Infants." ACTA Paediatrica Scandinavica. Volume 67 #2 March, 1978. pp. 213-217.

Haile, A.
"Menarcheal Age in Gondar, North Western Ethiopia." East African Medical Journal. Volume 61 #1 January, 1984. pp. 63-72.

Hernell, Olle and Gebre-Medhin, Mehari and Olivecrona, Thomas
"Breast-Milk Composition in Ethiopian and Swedish Mothers, IV: Milk Lipases." American Journal of Clinical Nutrition. Volume 30 #4 April, 1977. pp. 508-511.

Ketema, Teserach
"Modernization and Differential Fertility in Ethiopia--A Multivariate Analysis." Ph.D Dissertation: University of Illinois-Urbana-Champaign. Urbana, Illinois. 1985. 177p.

Kwast, B.E. and Kidane-Mariam, Widad and Saed, Ebrahim M. and Fowkes, F.G.
"Epidemiology of Maternal Mortality in Addis Ababa: A Community-Based Study." Ethiopian Medical Journal. Volume 23 #1 January, 1985. pp. 7-16.

Lonnerdal, Bo
"Breast Milk Composition in Ethiopian and Swedish Mothers. II--Lactose, Nitrogen and Protein Contents." American Journal of Clinical Nutrition. Volume 29 #10 October, 1976. pp. 1134-1141.

Shamebo, D.
"Fertility and Infant Mortality Rates in Dembia Plain, Gondar." Ethiopian Medical Journal. Volume 16 #3 July, 1978. pp. 95-97.

Svanberg, Ulf
"Breast Milk Composition in Ethiopian and Swedish Mothers. III--Amino Acids and Other Nitrogenous Substances." American Journal of Clinical Nutrition. Volume 30 #4 April, 1977. pp. 499-507.

Thein, M.
"Study on Milk Vitamin A, Serum Vitamin A and Serum Protein Levels of Lactating Mothers of Bochessa Village, Rural Ethiopia." East African Medical Journal. Volume 56 #11 November, 1979. pp. 542-547.

Wenlock, R. June and Wenlock, R.W.
"Maternal Nutrition, Prolonged Lactation and Birth Spacing in Ethiopia." Journal of Biosocial Science. Volume 13 #3 July, 1981. pp. 261-268.

HISTORY

Bourgoyne, Clarissa
"Position of Women in Feudal Ethiopia." (In) Institute of Ethiopian Studies and the Historical Society of Ethiopia. Papers of the Conference on Ethiopian Feudalism. Addis Ababa, Ethiopia: The Institute. March, 1976. 6p.

Comhaire, Jean
Significance of Feudalism to the Position of Ethiopian Women. Addis Ababa, Ethiopia: Institute of Ethiopian Studies and the Historical Society of Ethiopia. Papers of the Conference on Ethiopian Feudalism. March, 1976. 7p.

Crummey, Donald
"Women, Property and Litigation Among the Bagemder Amhara, 1750's to 1850's." (In) Hay, Margaret J. and Wright, Marcia (eds.). African Women and the Law: Historical Perspectives. Boston: Boston University. African Studies Center. Boston University Papers on Africa. Volume 7. 1982. pp. 19-32.

Crummey, Donald
The Settlement of Litigation Within the Ethiopian Ruling Class, With Special Reference to the Position of Women: The Bagemder Amhara from the 1750's to the 1850's. Unpublished Manuscript. 1979.

Crummey, Donald
"Family and Property Amongst the Amhara Nobility." Journal of African History. Volume 24 #2 1983. pp. 207-220.

Pankhurst, Richard K.
The Ethiopian Women in Former Times: An Anthology Prepared for the International Women's Year Anniversary Exhibition at Revolutionary Square. Addis Ababa, Ethiopia. 1976. 25p.

Rosenfeld, Chris P.
"Eight Ethiopian Women of the 'Zemene Mesafint' (c. 1769-1855)." Paper Presented at the Annual Meeting of the African Studies Association. Paper #68. Houston, Texas. 1977. 25p.

Rosenfeld, Chris P.
"Gossip, Proclamation and Women in Ethiopia (1500-1900): As Revealed in the Royal Chronicle." Paper Presented at the Annual Meeting of the African Studies Association. Paper #81. 1979. 18p.

Van Sertima, Ivan
Black Women in Antiquity. New Brunswick, New Jersey: Transaction Books. 1985. 160p.

Williams, Larry and Finch, Charles S.
"The Great Queens of Ethiopia." Journal of African Civilzations. Volume 6 #1 1984. pp. 12-35.

LAW AND LEGAL ISSUES

Crummey, Donald
   "Women, Property and Litigation Among the Bagemder
   Amhara, 1750's to 1850's." (In) Hay, Margaret J. and
   Wright, Marcia (eds.). African Women and the Law:
   Historical Perspectives. Boston: Boston University.
   African Studies Center. Boston University Papers on
   Africa. Volume 7. 1982. pp. 19-32.

Crummey, Donald
   The Settlement of Litigation Within the Ethiopian Ruling
   Class, With Special Reference to the Position of Women:
   The Bagemder Amhara from the 1750's to the 1850's.
   Unpublished Manuscript. 1979.

Haile, Daniel
   Law and the Status of Women in Ethiopia. Addis Ababa,
   Ethiopia: United Nations Economic Commission for Africa.
   African Training and Research Centre for Women. Research
   Series. 1980. 49p.

MARITAL RELATIONS AND NUPTIALITY

Daka, Kebebew
   "The Place of the Family in Ethiopian Society and Some
   Observations on the Emerging Changes." Paper Presented
   at the Seminar on the Changing Family in the African
   Context, Maseru, Lesotho, 1983. Paris: United Nations
   Educational, Scientific and Cultural Organization.
   1984. 24p.

Ketema, Teserach
   "Modernization and Differential Fertility in Ethiopia--A
   Multivariate Analysis." Ph.D Dissertation: University of
   Illinois-Urbana-Champaign. Urbana, Illinois. 1985.
   177p.

Turton, David
   "The Economics of Mursi Bridewealth: A Comparative
   Perspective." (In) Comaroff, J.L. (ed.). The Meaning of
   Marriage Payments. New York: Academic Press. 1980. pp.
   67-92.

MIGRATION

Bjeren, Gunilla
   Migration to Shashemene: Ethnicity, Gender and Occupation
   in Urban Ethiopia. Uppsala, Sweden: Scandanavian
   Institute of African Studies. 1985. 271p.

32

MISCELLANEOUS

Dirasse, Laketch
  "The Socio-Economic Position of Women in Addis Ababa: The
  Case of Prostitution." Ph.D Dissertation: Boston
  University. Boston, Massachusetts. 1978. 203p.

NATIONALISM

Anonymous
  "Socio-Economic Transformations in Liberated Ertitrea and
  the Impact on Peasant Women." ISIS International
  Bulletin. #11 Spring, 1979. pp. 22-24.
Anonymous
  "Women in Struggle." Third World Quarterly. Volume 5 #4
  October, 1983. pp. 874-914.
National Union of Eritrean Women
  Women and Revolution in Eritrea. Rome: National Union of
  Eritrean Women. 1980. 30p.
Silkin, Trish
  "Eritrea: Women in Struggle." Third World Quarterly.
  Volume 5 #4 1983. pp. 909-913.
Wright, K.
  "How War is Affecting Eritrean Women." Sudanow. Volume
  3 #3 1978. pp. 44-46.

ORGANIZATIONS

Anonymous
  "African Training and Research Centre for Women: It's
  Work and Program." Africa Report. Volume 26 #2
  March-April, 1981. pp. 17-21.
Hecht, Elisabeth-Dorothea
  The Voluntary Associations and the Social Status of
  Harari Women in Harar, Eastern Ethiopia. Nairobi:
  University of Nairobi. Institute of African Studies.
  Paper #136. 1980. 17p.
Pettit, John J.
  Integrated Family Life Education Project: A Project of
  the Ethiopian Women's Association. New York: World
  Education. 1977. 98p.
Tadesse, Zenebeworke
  An Overview on the Role of Women's Organizations in
  Africa: Case Study of Ethiopia, Zambia, Mozambique and
  Tanzania. Lusaka, Zambia: P/O Box RW 514. 1978.
Tadesse, Zenebeworke
  "An Overview on Women's Organizations in Africa: The Case
  of Ethiopia, Mozambique and Tanzania." Paper Presented
  at the 9th World Conference of Sociology. Uppsala,
  Sweden. 1978.

POLITICS AND GOVERNMENT

Mackay, B.
"The Effects of Socialist Transformation on the Fertility
of the Rural Population of Ethiopia." Ethiopian Journal
of Development. Volume 3 #2 October, 1979. pp. 55-64.
National Union of Eritrean Women
Women and Revolution in Eritrea. Rome: National Union of
Eritrean Women. 1980. 30p.
Palmer, Ingrid
"New Official Ideas on Women and Development." Institute
for Development Studies. Volume 10 #3 1979. pp. 42-53.
Silkin, Trish
"Eritrea: Women in Struggle." Third World Quarterly.
Volume 5 #4 1983. pp. 909-913.

RELIGION AND WITCHCRAFT

Foucher, Emile
"Ethiopia--The Unique Community of Muslim 'Nuns'."
Exchange. Volume 12 September, 1983. pp. 51.

RESEARCH

Gebre-Selassie, Alasebu
Women and Development in Ethiopia: An Annotated
Bibliography. Addis Ababa, Ethiopia: United Nations
Economic Commission for Africa. African Training and
Research Centre for Women. 1981. 58p.
Hafkin, Nancy J. (ed.)
Women and Development in Ethiopia: An Annotated
Bibliography. Addis Ababa, Ethiopia: United Nations
Economic Commission for Africa. African Training and
Research Centre for Women. 1978. 117p.

SEX ROLES

Almagor, Uri
Pastoral Partners: Affinity and Bond Partnership Among
the Dassanetch of South-West Ethiopia. Manchester,
England: Manchester University Press. 1978. 258p.
Bauer, Dan F.
Household and Society in Ethiopia: An Economic and Social
Analysis of Tigray Social Principles and Household
Organization. East Lansing, Michigan: Michigan State
University. African Studies Center. Committee on
Ethiopian Studies. Occasional Paper #6. 1977. 183p.
Bjeren, Gunilla
Migration to Shashemene: Ethnicity, Gender and Occupation
in Urban Ethiopia. Uppsala, Sweden: Scandanavian

Institute of African Studies. 1985. 271p.
Bourgoyne, Clarissa
"Position of Women in Feudal Ethiopia." (In) Institute
of Ethiopian Studies and the Historical Society of
Ethiopia. Papers of the Conference on Ethiopian
Feudalism. Addis Ababa, Ethiopia: The Institute. March,
1976. 6p.
Chiffelle, Suzanne
Women's Occupations and Social Standing in Gofa Awradja.
Addis Ababa, Ethiopia: Service of Documentation and
Communication for Development. 1978. 58p.
Daka, Kebebew
"The Place of the Family in Ethiopian Society and Some
Observations on the Emerging Changes." Paper Presented
at the Seminar on the Changing Family in the African
Context, Maseru, Lesotho, 1983. Paris: United Nations
Educational, Scientific and Cultural Organization.
1984. 24p.
Hecht, Elisabeth-Dorothea
The Voluntary Associations and the Social Status of
Harari Women in Harar, Eastern Ethiopia. Nairobi:
University of Nairobi. Institute of African Studies.
Paper #136. 1980. 17p.
Tsehai, Berhane S.
"'Man's World', 'Women's Position': The Case of the
Darasa Widow." N.E.A. (Oxford). Volume 1 #1 Summer,
1981. pp. 51-61.
Wright, K.
"How War is Affecting Eritrean Women." Sudanow. Volume
3 #3 1978. pp. 44-46.

SEXUAL MUTILATION/CIRCUMCISION

Beddada, Belletech
"Female Circumcision in Ethiopia." Paper Presented at
the Seminar on Traditional Practices Affecting the Health
of Women and Children. World Conference of the United
Nations Decade for Women. Copenhagen, Denmark. July
14-30, 1980.
Beddada, Belletech
"Female Circumcision in Ethiopia." Paper Presented at
the Seminar on Traditional Practices Affecting the Health
of Women and Children: Female Circumcision, Childhood
Marriage, Nutritional Taboos, etc. Alexandria, Egypt:
World Health Organization. Eastern Mediterranean
Regional Office. Khartoum, Sudan. February 10-15, 1979.
Bliese, Loren F.
"The Tragedies of Three Afar Girls." Ethiopanist Notes.
Volume 2 #3 1978. pp. 45-59.

STATUS OF WOMEN

Haile, Daniel
    Law and the Status of Women in Ethiopia. Addis Ababa,
    Ethiopia: United Nations Economic Commission for Africa.
    African Training and Research Centre for Women. Research
    Series. 1980. 49p.
Junge, B.J. and Tegegne, D.
    "The Effects of Liberation From Illiteracy on the Lives
    of 31 Women: A Case Study." Journal of Reading. Volume
    28 April, 1985. pp. 606-613.
National Union of Eritrean Women
    Women and Revolution in Eritrea. Rome: National Union of
    Eritrean Women. 1980. 30p.
Pankhurst, Richard K.
    "Correspondent's Report: Women in Ethiopia Today."
    Africa Today. Volume 28 #4 4th Quarter, 1981. pp.
    49-51.
Silkin, Trish
    "Eritrea: Women in Struggle." Third World Quarterly.
    Volume 5 #4 1983. pp. 909-913.
Tadesse, Zenebeworke
    Condition of Women in Ethiopia. Addis Ababa, Ethiopia:
    Swedish International Development Authority. Unpublished
    Paper. 1976.

URBANIZATION

Abegaz, Berhanu
    "Papers in Ethiopian Demography II: Levels and Patterns
    of Fertility and Mortality." Northeast African Studies.
    Volume 7 #2 1985. pp. 1-22.

WOMEN AND THEIR CHILDREN

Gebre-Medhim, M.
    "Subclinical Protein-Energy Malnutrition in
    Under-Privileged Ethiopian Mothers and Their Newborn
    Infants." ACTA Paediatrica Scandinavica. Volume 67 #2
    March, 1978. pp. 213-217.

Kenya

ABORTION

Aggarwal, V.P. and Mati, J.K.G.
"Epidemiology of Induced Abortion in Nairobi, Kenya."
Journal of Obstetrics and Gynaecology of Eastern and
Central Africa. Volume 1 #2 June, 1982. pp. 54-57.
Aggarwal, V.P. and Mati, J.K.G.
"Review of Abortions in Kenyatta National Hospital,
Nairobi." East African Medical Journal. Volume 57 #2
February, 1980. pp. 38-144.
Wanjala, S. and Murugu, N.M. and Mati, J.K.G.
"Mortality Due to Abortion at Kenyatta National Hospital,
1974-1983." CIBA Foundation Symposia. #115 1985. pp.
41-48.

AGRICULTURE

Ahlberg, B.M.
The Rural Water Supply (RWS) Programme in Kenya: Its
Impact on Women. Stockholm, Sweden: Swedish
International Development Agency (SIDA). October, 1983.
21p.
Anderson, Mary B.
"Kenya: Egerton College." (In) Overholt, Catherine and
Anderson, Mary B. and Cloud, Kathleen and Austin, James
(eds.). Gender Roles in Development Projects: A Case
Book. West Hartford, Connecticut: Kumarian Press. 1985.
pp. 185-213.
Anderson, Mary B.
"Kenya: Kitui District Arid and Semi-Arid Lands Project."
(In) Overholt, Catherine and Anderson, Mary B. and Cloud,
Kathleen and Austin, James E. (eds.). Gender Roles in
Development Projects: A Case Book. West Hartford,
Connecticut: Kumarian Press. 1985. pp. 309-326.

Anker, Richard and Knowles, James C.
   Population Growth, Employment and Economic Demographic
   Interactions in Kenya: Bachue-Kenya. New York: St.
   Martin's Press. 1983. 735p.
Anonymous
   "The Women Sing of Harambee." Agenda. Volume 1 #2
   February, 1978. pp. 15-18.
Barnes, Carolyn
   "Differentiation by Sex Among Small Scale Farming
   Households in Kenya." Rural Africana. #15-16 1983. pp.
   41-64.
Broche-Due, Vigdis
   Women at the Backstage of Development: A
   Socio-Anthropological Case Study From Katilu Irigation
   Scheme, Turkana, Kenya. Rome: United Nations Food and
   Agriculture Organization. 1983.
Clark, Carolyn M.
   "Land and Food, Women and Power, in 19th Century Kikuyu."
   Africa. Volume 50 #4 1980. pp. 357-370.
Clark, Noreen
   Education for Development and the Rural Women. New York:
   World Education Inc. Volume One--A Review of Theory and
   Principles With Emphasis on Kenya and the Philippines.
   1979. 66p.
Cooper, Frederick
   From Slaves to Squatters: Plantation Labor and
   Agriculture in Zanzibar and Coastal Kenya, 1890-1925.
   New Haven, Connecticut: Yale University Press. 1980.
   328p.
Davison, Jean
   "Voices From Mutira: Education in the Lives of Rural
   Gikuyu Women." Ph.D Dissertation: Stanford University.
   Stanford, California. 1985. 422p.
Ensminger, J.
   "Theoretical Perspectives on Pastoral Women: Feminist
   Critiques." Nomadic Peoples. #16 1984. pp. 59-71.
Feldman, Rayah
   "Women's Groups and Women's Subordination: An Analysis of
   Policies Towards Rural Women in Kenya." Review of
   African Political Economy. #27/28 1983. pp. 67-85.
Feldman, Rayah
   Employment Problems of Rural Women in Kenya. Addis
   Ababa, Ethiopia: International Labour Office. JASPA.
   1981.
Gachukia, Eddah W.
   "Mothers Role in Rural Kenya." Ekistics. Volume 45 #272
   September-October, 1978. pp. 356-357.
Gachukia, Eddah W.
   "Women's Self-Help Efforts for Water Supply in Kenya."
   Appropriate Technology. Volume 9 #3 1982. pp. 19-21.
Gachukia, Eddah W.
   "Women's Self-Help Efforts for Water Supply in Kenya: The

Important Role of NGO Support." Assignment Children.
Volume 45/46 Spring, 1979. pp. 167-174.
Getechah, W.
"The Role of Women in Rural Water Development in Kenya."
(In) International Development Research Centre (IDRC).
Rural Water Supply in Developing Countries. A Workshop
on Training, Zomba, Malawi, August 5-12, 1980. Ottawa,
Canada: IDRC. 1981. pp. 85-88.
Gold, Alice
"Women in Agricultural Change: The Nandi in the 19th
Century." Paper Presented at the Annual Meeting of the
African Studies Association. Houston, Texas. 1978.
Greene, P.A.
Innovative Approaches in Rural Women's Programmes in
Three African Countries: Kenya, Nigeria, Sierra Leone:
Case Studies. Rome: United Nations Food and Agriculture
Organization. 1985. 148p.
International Labour Organization (ILO)
Employment Problems of Rural Women in Kenya. Nairobi:
ILO. Economic Commission for Africa. 1981.
Leonard, D.K.
Reaching the Peasant Farmer: Organization Theory and
Practice in Kenya. Chicago: University of Chicago Press.
1977.
Leonard, D.K. and Kimenya, P. and Muzaale, P. and Ngugi, D.
and Oyugi, W.
An Evaluation of the Components Needed to Improve the
Performance of Kenya's Agricultural Extension Service.
Nairobi, Kenya: Ministry of Agriculture. 1982.
Lewis, Barbara C.
"The Impact of Development Policies on Women." (In) Hay,
Margaret J. and Stichter, Sharon (eds.). African Women
South of the Sahara. New York: Longman. 1984. pp.
170-187.
Merryman, Nancy H.
"Economy and Ecological Stress: Household Strategies of
Transitional Somali Pastoralists in Northern Kenya."
Ph.D Dissertation: Northwestern University. Evanston,
Illinois. 1984. 338p.
Mickelwait, Donald R. and Riegelman, Mary Ann and Sweet,
Charles F.
Women in Rural Development: A Survey of the Roles of
Women in Ghana, Lesotho, Kenya, Nigeria... Boulder,
Colorado: Westview Press. 1976. 224p.
Mohan, P.C.
"Of the Women, By the Women, For Everybody: A Goat
Project in Kenya." Ideas and Action Bulletin #144 1981.

Monstead, Mette
The Changing Division of Labour Within Rural Families in
Kenya. Copenhagen, Denmark: Centre for Development
Research. 1977.
Monstead, Mette
The Changing Division of Labour Within Rural Families in

Kenya. Nairobi: University of Nairobi. Centre for
Development Research. 1976.
Monsted, Mette
   "The Changing Division of Labor Within Rural Families in
   Kenya." (In) Caldwell, John C. (ed.). The Persistence
   of High Fertility: Population Prospects in the Third
   World. Canberra, Australia: Australian National
   University. 1977. pp. 259-312.
Monsted, Mette
   Women's Groups in Rural Kenya and Their Role in
   Development. Copenhagen, Denmark: Centre for Development
   Research. CDR Paper A/78/2. June, 1978.
Moock, P.R.
   "Efficiency of Women as Farm Managers: Kenya." American
   Journal of Agricultural Economics. Volume 58 #5
   December, 1976. pp. 831-835.
Mutiso, Roberta M.
   Career Role/Family Role Conflict Among Women Agricultural
   Extension Officers in Kenya. Nairobi: University of
   Nairobi. 1978.
Muzale, P. and Leonard, D.K.
   Women'a Groups and Extension in Kenya: Their Impact on
   Food Production and Malnutrition in Baringo, Busia and
   Taita Taveta. Nairobi, Kenya: Ministry of Agriculture.
   1982.
Ojiambo, Julia
   "Women and Development in Kenya." Paper Presented at the
   15th World Conference of the Society for International
   Development. Amsterdam, Netherlands. Nov. 28-Dec. 3,
   1976. 17p.
Okeyo, Achola P.
   "Daughters of the Lakes and Rivers: Colonization and the
   Land Rights of Luo Women." (In) Etienne, Mona and
   Leacook, Eleanor (eds.). Women and Colonization:
   Anthropological Perspectives. New York: Praeger
   Publishers. 1980. pp. 186-213.
Ombina, O. and May, Nicky
   "Progress Through Piggeries and Prejudice in Kenya."
   Community Development Journal. Volume 20 #3 1985. pp.
   191-194.
Pala, Achola O.
   "Changes in Economy and Ideology: A Study of Joluo of
   Kenya With Special Reference to Women." Ph.D
   Dissertation: Harvard University. Department of
   Anthropology. Cambridge, Massachusetts. 1977.
Pala, Achola O.
   Women and Development: An Overview on Kenya. Paper
   Presented at the Seminiar on Women in Rural Development.
   Washington, D.C.: American Council on Education.
   Overseas Liaison Committee. April 21-23, 1976.
Pala, Achola O. and Krystall, Abigail
   Women in Rural Development. Nairobi: University of
   Nairobi. Bureau of Education Research. 1978.

Pala, Achola O.
    Women's Access to Land and Their Role in Agriculture and
    Decision-Making on the Farm: Experiences of Joluo of
    Kenya. Nairobi: University of Nairobi. Institute For
    Development Studies. Discussion Paper #263. 1978. 22p.
Pala, Achola O.
    "Women's Access to Land and Their Role in Agriculture and
    Decision-Making on the Farm: Experiences of the Joluo of
    Kenya." Journal of Eastern African Research and
    Development. Volume 13 1983. pp. 69-87.
Smock, Audrey C.
    "Measuring Rural Women's Economic Roles and Contributions
    in Kenya." Studies in Family Planning. Volume 10 #11/12
    November-December, 1979. pp. 385-390.
Staudt, Kathleen A.
    "Agricultural Policy, Political Power, and Women Farmers
    in Western Kenya." Ph.D Dissertation: University of
    Wisconsin-Madison. Madison, Wisconsin. 1976. 422p.
Staudt, Kathleen A.
    Inequities in the Delivery of Services to a Female Farm
    Clientele: Some Implications for Policy. Nairobi, Kenya:
    University of Nairobi. Institute for Development
    Studies. IDS Discussion Paper #247. 1977.
Thrupp. Lori-Ann
    "Women, Wood and Work: In Kenya and Beyond." Unasylva.
    Volume 36 #146 1984.
Ventura, Dias
    "Modernisation, Production Organization and Rural Women
    in Kenya." (In) Ahmed, Iftikhar (ed.). Technology and
    Rural Women: Conceptual and Empirical Issues. Boston:
    George Allen and Unwin. 1985. pp. 157-210.
Wanjala, Esther
    "Kenya." ISIS Women's World. #4 December, 1984.
Whiting, Martha and Krystall, Abigail
    The Impact of Rural Water Supply Projects on Women.
    Nairobi: University of Nairobi. Bureau of Educational
    Research. 1979.
Wienpahl, Jan
    "Women's Roles in Livestock Production Among the Turkana
    of Kenya." Research in Economic Anthropology. Volume 6
    1984. pp. 193-215.

ARTS

Campbell, C.A. and Eastman, C.M.
    "Ngoma: Swahili Adult Song Performance in Context."
    Ethnomusicology. Volume 28 #3 1984. pp. 467-493.
Thiong'o, Ngugi W.
    "Women in Cultural Work: The Fate of Kamiriithu People's
    Theatre in Kenya." Development Dialogue. #1/2 1982.
    pp. 115-133.

BIBLIOGRAPHIES

Bifani, Patricia
    The Impact of Development on Women in Kenya: An Annotated
    Bibliography. Nairobi: UNICEF. 1982. 38p.
Chandler, Dale and Thairu, R.W.
    Women of Kenya: An Annotated Bibliography. Nairobi:
    Women's Bureau of the Ministry of Housing and Social
    Services. 1977.

CULTURAL ROLES

Adu-Bobie, Gemma
    "The Role of Rendille Women in the Nomadic Society."
    Bulletin of the Regional Office for Science and
    Technology for Africa. Volume 18 #2 1983. pp. 30-32.
Ahlberg, B.M.
    The Rural Water Supply (RWS) Programme in Kenya: Its
    Impact on Women. Stockholm, Sweden: Swedish
    International Development Agency (SIDA). October, 1983.
    21p.
Anderson, Mary B.
    "Kenya: Egerton College." (In) Overholt, Catherine and
    Anderson, Mary B. and Cloud, Kathleen and Austin, James
    (eds.). Gender Roles in Development Projects: A Case
    Book. West Hartford, Connecticut: Kumarian Press. 1985.
    pp. 185-213.
Anderson, Mary B.
    "Kenya: Kitui District Arid and Semi-Arid Lands Project."
    (In) Overholt, Catherine and Anderson, Mary B. and Cloud,
    Kathleen and Austin, James E. (eds.). Gender Roles in
    Development Projects: A Case Book. West Hartford,
    Connecticut: Kumarian Press. 1985. pp. 309-326.
Anker, Richard and Knowles, James C.
    Population Growth, Employment and Economic Demographic
    Interactions in Kenya: Bachue-Kenya. New York: St.
    Martin's Press. 1983. 735p.
Anonymous
    Women in Kenya. Nairobi: Kenya Central Bureau of
    Statistics. 1978.
Arungu-Olende, Rose
    "Kenya: Not Just Literacy, But Wisdom." (In) Morgan,
    Robin (ed.). Sisterhood is Global. Garden City, New
    York: Anchor Books. 1984. pp. 389-398.
Ayiemba, Elias H.
    "Intercensal Fertility Change in Kenya: A Study of
    Regional Differentials Between 1969-1979." PIDSA
    Abstracts. Volume 5 #1 December, 1982. pp. 5-22.
Barnes, Carolyn
    "Differentiation by Sex Among Small Scale Farming
    Households in Kenya." Rural Africana. #15-16 1983. pp.
    41-64.

Beaman, Anne C.
"Women's Participation in Pastoral Economy: Income Maximization Among the Rendille." Nomadic Peoples. Volume 12 1983. pp. 20-25.

Bifani, Patricia and Adagala, Kavetsa and Kariuki, Patricia W.
The Impact of Development of Women in Kenya: A Methodological Approach. Nairobi: UNICEF. 1982. 118p.

Brainard, J.M.
"Herders to Farmers: The Effects of Settlement on the Demography of the Turkana Population of Kenya." Ph.D Dissertation: State University of New York. Binghampton, New York. 1981. 356p.

Brantley, Cynthia
"An Historical Perspective of the Giriama and Witchcraft Control." Africa. Volume 49 #2 1979. pp. 112-133.

Broche-Due, Vigdis
Women at the Backstage of Development: A Socio-Anthropological Case Study From Katilu Irrigation Scheme, Turkana, Kenya. Rome: United Nations Food and Agriculture Organization. 1983.

Bujra, Janet M.
"Proletarianization and the 'Informal Economy': A Case Study From Nairobi." African Urban Studies. #47 1978. pp. 47-66.

Bujra, Janet M.
"Women 'Entrepreneurs' in Early Nairobi." (In) Sumner, Colin (ed.). Crime, Justice and Underdevelopment. London: Heineman. Cambridge Studies in Criminology. #46. 1982.

Campbell, C.A. and Eastman, C.M.
"Ngoma: Swahili Adult Song Performance in Context." Ethnomusicology. Volume 28 #3 1984. pp. 467-493.

Caron, James W.
Effects of Infant Characteristics on Caretaking Responsiveness Among the Gusii. Boston: Harvard University. Harvard Graduate School of Education. 1982. 128p.

Ciancanelli, Penelope
"Exchange, Reproduction and Sex Subordination Among the Kikuyu of East Africa." Review of Radical Political Economics. Volume 12 #2 Summer, 1980. pp. 25-36.

Clark, Carolyn M.
"Land and Food, Women and Power, in 19th Century Kikuyu." Africa. Volume 50 #4 1980. pp. 357-370.

Clark, Mari H.
"Women-Headed Households and Poverty: Insights From Kenya." Signs. Volume 10 #2 Winter, 1984. pp. 338-354.

Cochrane, J.
"Women as Guardians of the Tribe in Ngugi Novels." Critical Perspectives. Volume 13 1984. pp. 90-100.

Cochrane, Judith
    "Women as the Guardians of the Tribe in Ngugi's Novels."
    ACLALS Bulletin. Volume 4 #5 1977. pp. 1-11.
Curtin, Patricia R.
    "Weddings in Lamu, Kenya: An Example of Social and
    Economic Change." Cahiers d'Etudes Africaines. Volume
    24 #2 1984. pp. 131-155.
Davison, J.
    "Achievements and Constraints Among Rural Kenyan Women: A
    Case Study." Journal of Eastern African Research and
    Development. Volume 15 1985. pp. 268-279.
Davison, Jean
    "Voices From Mutira: Education in the Lives of Rural
    Gikuyu Women." Ph.D Dissertation: Stanford University.
    Stanford, California. 1985. 422p.
Donley, L.
    "Eighteenth Century Lamu Weddings." Kenya Past and
    Present. # 11 1979. pp. 3-11.
Dow, Thomas E. and Werner, Linda H.
    "Family Size and Family Planning in Kenya: Continuity and
    Change in Metropolitan and Rural Attitudes." Studies in
    Family Planning. Volume 12 #6-7 June-July, 1981. pp.
    272-277.
Dow, Thomas E. and Werner, Linda H.
    "Modern, Transitional, and Traditional Demographic and
    Contraceptive Patterns Among Kenyan Women." Studies in
    Family Planning. Volume 13 #1 January, 1982. pp.
    12-23.
Dow, Thomas E. and Werner, Linda H.
    A Note on Modern, Transitional and Traditional
    Demographic and Contraceptive Patterns Among Kenyan
    Women, 1977-1978. Nairobi: University of Nairobi.
    Population Studies and Research Institute. January,
    1981. 29p.
Dow, Thomas E. and Werner, Linda H.
    Continuity and Change in Metropolitan and Rural Attitudes
    Towards Family Size and Family Planning in Kenya Between
    1966/67-1977/78. Nairobi: University of Nairobi.
    Population Studies and Research Institute. February,
    1981. 17p.
Eastman, C.M.
    "Waungwana na Wanawake: Muslim Ethnicity and Sexual
    Segregation in Coastal Kenya." Journal of Multilingual
    and Multicultural Development. Volume 5 #2 1984. pp.
    97-112.
Emereuwaonu, Ernest U.
    "Marital Fertility, Desired Family Size, Communication
    Channel and Modern Reproductive Values in an African
    City." Ph.D Dissertation: University of California Los
    Angeles. Los Angeles, California. 1977. 216p.
Ensminger, J.
    "Theoretical Perspectives on Pastoral Women: Feminist
    Critiques." Nomadic Peoples. #16 1984. pp. 59-71.

"Mother Africa and the Heroic Whore: Female Images in
'Petals of Blood'." (In) Wylie, Hal (ed.). Contemporary
African Literature. Washington, D.C.: Three Continents.
Feldman, Rayah
"Women's Groups and Women's Subordination: An Analysis of
Policies Towards Rural Women in Kenya." Review of
African Political Economy. #27/28 1983. pp. 67-85.
Ferry, Benoit and Page, Hilary J.
The Proximate Differentials of Fertility and Their Effect
on Fertility Patterns: An Illustrative Analysis Applied
to Kenya. Voorburg, Netherlands: International
Statistical Institute. WFS Scientific Reports #71.
Fjellman, Stephen M.
"The Akamba Domestic Cycle as Markovian Process."
American Ethnologist. Volume 4 #4 November, 1977. pp.
Gachukia, Eddah W.
"Mothers Role in Rural Kenya." Ekistics. Volume 45 #272
September-October, 1978. pp. 356-357.
Gakuo, Mumbi
"The Kenyan Women and Situation and Strategies for
Improvement." Women's Studies International Forum.
Volume 8 #4 1985. pp. 373-379.
Gatara, Timothy H.
"The Influence of Religion and Education on Current
Family Size and Fertility Preference in Kenya." Ph.D
Dissertation: Florida State University. Tallahassee,
Gold, Alice
"Women in Agricultural Change: The Nandi in the 19th
Century." Paper Presented at the Annual Meeting of the
African Studies Association. Houston, Texas. 1978.
Gomm, Roger
"Bargaining From Weakness: Spirit Possession on the South
Kenya Coast." (In) Tiffany, Sharon W. (ed.). Women and
Society: An Anthropological Reader. St. Albans, Vermont:
Eden Press. 1979. pp. 120-144.
Gorfain, Phyllis and Glazier, Jack
"Sexual Symbolism, Origins and the Ogre in Mbeere,
Kenya." Journal of American Folklore. Volume 91 #362
October-December, 1978. pp. 925-946.
Greeley, Edward H.
"Men and Fertility Regulation in Southern Meru: A Case
Study From the Kenya Highlands." Ph.D Dissertation:
Catholic University of America. Washington, D.C. 1977.
Gupta, Anirudha
"Illusion of Progress: The Women of Kenya." (In)
Phadnis, Urmila and Malani, Indira (eds.). Women of the

World: Ilusion and Reality. New Delhi, India: Vikas
Publishing House Ltd. 1980. pp. 245-259.

Gutto, Shadrack B.
"The Legal Status of Women in Kenya: Paternalism and
Inequality." Fletcher Forum. Volume 1 Fall, 1976. pp.
62-82.

Gutto, Shadrack B.
The Status of Women in Kenya: A Study of Paternalism,
Inequality and Under Privilege. Nairobi: University of
Nairobi. Institute for Development Studies. Discussion
Paper #235. April, 1976. 76p.

Harris, Joan
"Women in Kenya: Revolution or Evolution?" Africa
Report. Volume 30 #2 March-April, 1985. pp. 30-32.

Hay, Margaret J.
"Luo Women and Economic Change During the Colonial
Period." (In) Hafkin, Margaret J. and Bay, Edna G.
(eds.). Women in Africa: Studies in Social and Economic
Change. Stanford, California: Stanford University
Press. 1976. pp. 87-109.

Hay, Margaret J.
"Women as Owners, Occupants and Managers of Property in
Colonial Western Kenya." (In) Hay, Margaret J. and
Wright, Marcia (eds.). African Women and the Law:
Historical Perspectives. Boston: Boston University.
African Studies Center. Boston University Papers on
Africa. Volume 7. 1982. pp. 110-123.

Hollander, Roberta B.
"Out of Tradition: The Position of Women in Kenya and
Tanzania During the Pre-Colonial, Colonial and Post
Independence Eras." Ph.D Dissertation: The American
University. Washington, D.C. 1979. 399p.

Hull, Valerie and Simpson, Mayling
Breastfeeding, Child Health and Child Spacing:
Cross-Cultural Perspectives. Dover, New Hampshire: Croom
Helm. 1985. 216p.

Jackson, Kennell A.
"The Family Entity and Famine Among the 19th Century
Akamba of Kenya: Social Responses to Environmental
Stress." Journal of Family History. Volume 1 Winter,
1976. pp. 192-215.

Kabwegyere, Tarsis
"Determinants of Fertility: A Discussion of Change in the
Family Among the Akamba of Kenya." (In) Caldwell, John
C. (ed.). The Persistence of High Fertility: Population
Prospects in the Third World. Canberra, Australia:
Australian National University. Volume One. 1977. pp.
189-222.

Kamau, G.K. and Ojwang, J.B.
"Law and Witchcraft: A Review Article." Kenya Historical
Review. Volume 6 1978. pp. 146-160.

Kangi, M.W.
"Some Factors Affecting Urban-Rural Fertility

Differentials in Kenya: A Case Study of Nairobi and Central Province." Kenyan Geographer. Volume 4 #1/2 1982. pp. 29-49.

Kanyiri, Elisha M.
"The Socioeconomic and Demographic Factors Influencing Contraceptive Behavior in Kenya." Ph.D Dissertation: Florida State University. Tallahassee, Florida. 1984. 143p.

Kelley, Allen C. and Swartz, Caroline
"The Impact of Family Structure on Microeconomic Decision Making in Developing Countries: A Case Study of Nuclear and Extended Families in Urban Kenya." (In) International Union for the Scientific Study of Population (IUSSP). Economic and Demographic Change: Issues for the 1980's: Proceedings of the Conference on Economic and Demographic Change, 1978. Liege, Belgium: (IUSSP). Volume One. Helsinki, Finland. 1979. pp. 361-375.

Kenya. Ministry of Finance and Economic Planning
"Continuity and Change in Metropolitan and Rural Attitudes Towards Family Size and Family Planning in Kenya Between 1966/1967 and 1977/1978." Social Perspectives. Volume 5 #1 December, 1980. 8p.

Kenya. Ministry of Finance and Economic Planning
"Demographic and Contraceptive Patterns Among Kenyan Women: 1977-1978." Social Perspectives. Volume 6 #2 April, 1981. 16p.

Kenya. Ministry of Finance and Economic Planning
"Modernization, Birth Spacing and Marital Fertility in Kenya." Social Perspectives. Volume 6 #5 September, 1981. 12p

Kenya. Ministry of Finance and Economic Planning
Women in Kenya, Social Perspectives. Nairobi: The Ministry. Central Bureau of Statistics. 1978. 62p.

Kenya. Ministry of Finance and Economic Planning.
"Women in Kenya." Social Perspectives. Volume 3 #3 April, 1978.

Kershaw, Greet
"The Changing Roles of Men and Women in the Kikuyu Family by Socioeconomic Strata." Rural Africana. Volume 29 Winter, 1976. pp. 173-194.

Kershaw, Greet
"The Changing Roles of Men and Women in the Kikuyu Family by Socioeconomic Strata." Rural Africana. Volume 29 Winter, 1976. pp. 173-194.

Kettel, Bonnie
"Gender and Class in Tugen-Kalenjin Social Organization." Paper Presented at the Annual Meeting of the African Studies Association. Bloomington, Indiana. October 21-24, 1981.

Kipury, N.
"Engagement and Marriage Among the Massai." Kenya Past and Present. #9 1978. pp. 38-42.

Komma, Toru
"The Women's Self Help Association Movement Among the
Kipsigis of Kenya." (In) Wada, S. and Eguchi, P.K.
(eds.). Africa 3. Osaka, Japan: National Museum of
Ethnology. Senri Ethnological Studies #15. 1984. pp.
145-186.

Komma, Toru
"The Women's Self-Help Association Movement Among the
Kipsigis of Kenya." Senri Ethnological Studies. Volume
15 1984. pp. 145-186.

Kongstad, P. and Monsted, Mette
Family, Labour and Trade in Western Kenya. Uppsala,
Sweden: Scandinavian Institute of African Studies. 1980.

Kosgei, Sally J.
Kipsigis Women and the Colonial Economy. Nairobi:
University of Nairobi. Department of History. 1979.
17p.

Kramer, Joyce M.
"Production and Reproduction at Various Levels of
Participation in the Modern World System: An Analysis of
the Effects of Urbanization on Fertility for Twelve
Communities in Kenya." Ph.D Dissertation: University of
North Carolina. Chapel Hill, North Carolina. 1980.
371p.

Kune, J.B.
"Machakos Project Studies: Agents Affecting Health of
Mother and Child in a Rural Area of Kenya. XV. The
Economic Setting at the Household Level." Tropical and
Geographical Medicine. Volume 31 #3 September, 1979.
pp. 441-457.

Kuria, Gibson K.
"The African or Customary Marriage in Kenya Law Today."
Paper Presented at the Conference on Conceptualizing the
Household. Cambridge, Massachusetts: Harvard University.
November, 1984.

Lakhani, S.A. and Jansen, A.A.
"Opinions About Breastfeeding Amongst Middle Income
African and Indian Women in Nairobi." East African
Medical Journal. Volume 61 #4 1984. pp. 266-271.

Langley, Myrtle S.
"Spirit Possession, Exorcism and Social Context: An
Anthropological Perspective With Theological
Implications." Churchman. Volume 94 #3 1980. pp.
226-245.

LeVine, Robert A.
"Influences of Women's Schooling on Maternal Behavior in
the Third World." Comparative Education Review. Volume
24 #2 Part Two June, 1980. pp. S78-S105.

LeVine, Sarah
"Dreams of Young Gusii Women: A Context Analysis."
Ethnology. Volume 21 #1 January, 1986. pp. 63-77.

LeVine, Sarah and LeVine, Robert A.
    Mothers and Wives: Gusii Women of East Africa. Chicago:
    University of Chicago Press. 1979. 391p.
LeVine, Sarah and Pfeifer, G.
    "Separation and Individualization in an African Society:
    The Developmental Tasks of the Gusii Married Women."
    Psychiatry. Volume 45 #1 February, 1982. pp. 61-75.
Lesthaeghe, Ron J. and Vanderhoeft, C. and Becker, Stan and
Kibet, M.
    Individual and Contextual Effects of Female Education on
    the Kenya Marital Fertility Transition. Brussels,
    Belgium: Vrije Universiteit Brussel. Interuniversity
    Programme in Demography. IPD Working Paper #1983-9.
    1983. 19p.
Lesthaeghe, Ron J. and Eelens, Frank
    Social Organization and Reproductive Regimes: Lessons
    From Sub-Saharan Africa and Historical Western Europe.
    Brussels, Belgium: Vrije Universiteit Brussel.
    Interuniversity Programme in Demography. IDP Working
    Paper #1985-1. 1985. 64p.
Likimani, Muthoni G.
    Women of Kenya: Fifteen Years of Independence. Nairobi:
    Likamani. 1979. 76p.
Lindsay, Beverly
    "Issues Confronting Professional African Women:
    Illustrations From Kenya." (In) Lindsay, Beverly (ed.).
    Comparative Perspectives of Third World Women: The Impact
    of Race, Sex and Class. New York: Praeger Publishers.
    1980. pp. 78-95.
Llewelyn-Davies, Melissa
    "Two Contexts of Solidarity Among Pastoral Maasai Women."
    (In) Caplan, P. and Bujra, J. (eds.). Women United,
    Women Divided: Female Solidarity in Cross-Cultural
    Perspective. Bloomington, Indiana: Indiana University
    Press. 1978. pp. 206-237.
Llewelyn-Davies, Melissa
    "Women, Warriors and Patriarchs." (In) Ortner, Sherry B.
    and Whitehead, Harriet (eds.). Sexual Meanings.
    Cambridge, New York: Cambridge University Press. 1981.
    pp. 330-358.
Lura, Russell P.
    "Population Change in Kericho District, Kenya: An Example
    of Fertility Increase in Africa." African Studies
    Review. Volume 28 #1 March, 1985. pp. 45-56.
Maina, Rose and Muchai, V.W. and Gutto, S.B.O.
    "Law and the Status of Women in Kenya." (In) Columbia
    Human Rights Law Review (eds.). Law and the Status of
    Women: An International Symposium. New York: United
    Nations. Centre for Social Development and Humanitarian
    Affairs. 1977. pp. 185-206.
Mbevi, Grace
    "Child Marriage and Early Teenage Childbirth." Paper
    Presented at the Seminar on Traditional Practices

Affecting the Health of Women and Children: Female
Circumcision, Childhood Marriage, Nutritional Taboos,
etc. Alexandria, Egypt: World Health Organization.
Eastern Mediterranean Regional Office. Khartoum, Sudan.
February 10-15, 1979.

Mbughuni, Patricia
"The Image of Women in Kiswahili Prose Fiction."
Kiswahili. Volume 49 #1 1982. pp. 15-24.

Mbughuni, Patricia
"The Image of Women in Kiswahili Prose Fiction." Paper
Presented at the Workshop on Women's Studies and
Development. Dar-es-Salaam, Tanzania: University of
Dar-es-Salaam. Bureau of Resource Assessment and Land
Use Planning. Paper #26. September 24-29, 1979. 14p.

Mbulu, J.
Women and the Family. Nairobi: Ministry of
Transportation and Communications. Roads and Aerodromes
Department. 1981.

McAdoo, Harriette P.
"Extended Family Involvement and Roles of Urban Kenyan
Women." Paper Presented at the "Women in the African
Diaspora: An Interdisciplinary Perspective Research
Conference. Washington, D.C.: Howard University. June,
1983.

Merryman, Nancy H.
"Economy and Ecological Stress: Household Strategies of
Transitional Somali Pastoralists in Northern Kenya."
Ph.D Dissertation: Northwestern University. Evanston,
Illinois. 1984. 338p.

Mhloyi, Marvellous M.
"Fertility Determinants: A Comparative Study Of Kenya and
Lesotho." Ph.D Dissertation: University of Pennsylvania.
Philadelphia, Pennsylvania. 1984. 342p.

Mkangi, George C.
"Education, Poverty and Fertility Among the Wataita of
Kenya." (In) Epstein, T. Scarlett and Jackson, Darrell
(eds.). The Feasibility of Fertility Planning. Oxford,
England: Pergamon Press. 1977. pp. 173-182.

Monstead, Mette
The Changing Division of Labour Within Rural Families in
Kenya. Copenhagen, Denmark: Centre for Development
Research. 1977.

Monstead, Mette
The Changing Division of Labour Within Rural Families in
Kenya. Nairobi: University of Nairobi. Centre for
Development Research. 1976.

Monsted, Mette
"The Changing Division of Labor Within Rural Families in
Kenya." (In) Caldwell, John C. (ed.). The Persistence
of High Fertility: Population Prospects in the Third
World. Canberra, Australia: Australian National
University. 1977. pp. 259-312.

Mosley, W. Henry and Werner, Linda H.
   Some Determinants of Marital Fertility in Kenya: A Birth
   Interval Analysis From the 1978 Kenya Fertility Survey.
   Nairobi: University of Nairobi. Population Studies and
   Research Institute. Central Bureau of Statistics.
   Unpublished. 1980.
Mosley, W. Henry and Werner, Linda H. and Becker, Stan
   The Dynamics of Birth Spacing and Marital Fertility in
   Kenya. Voorburg, Netherlands: International Statistical
   Institute. World Fertility Survey. Scientific Reports
   #30. August, 1982. 30p.
Mott, Frank L. and Shapiro, D.
   "Seasonal Variations in Labor Force Activity and
   Intrahousehold Substitution of Labor in Rural Kenya."
   Journal of Developing Areas. Volume 18 #4 July, 1984.
   pp. 449-463.
Mott, S.H.
   "A Note on the Determinants of Breastfeeding Durations in
   an African Country." Social Biology. Volume 31
   Fall/Winter, 1984. pp. 279-289.
Mott, Susan H.
   "A Note on the Determinants of Breastfeeding Durations in
   an African Country." Social Biology. Volume 31 #3-4
   Fall-Winter, 1984. pp. 279-289.
Munroe, Ruth H. and Shimmin, Harold S. and Munroe, Robert L.
(eds.)
   "Gender Understanding and Sex Role Preference in Four
   Countries." Developmental Psychology. Volume 20 July,
   1984. pp. 673-682.
Murray, Joselyn
   "The Church Missionary Society and the 'Female
   Circumcision' Issue in Kenya, 1929-1932." Journal of
   Religion in Africa. Volume 8 #2 1976. pp. 92-104.
Mutungi, O.K.
   Legal Aspects of Witchcraft in East Africa: With
   Particular Reference to Kenya. Nairobi: East African
   Literature Bureau. 1977. 144p.
Mwaniki, N. and Marasha, M. and Mati, J.K.G. and Mwaniki,
M.K. (eds.)
   Surgical Contraception in Sub-Saharan Africa:
   Proceedings. Nairobi: University of Nairobi. Paper
   Presented at a Conference May 8-13, 1977. Sponsored by
   the Pathfinder Fund. Chestnut Hill, Massachusetts.
   1979. 182p.
Mwaria, Cheryl B.
   "Rural-Urban Labor Migration and Family Arrangements
   Among the Kamba." (In) Robinson, Pearl T. and Skinner,
   Elliott (eds.). Transformation and Resiliency in Africa.
   Washington, D.C.: Howard University Press. 1983. pp.
   29-43.
Nagashima, Nobuhiro
   "A Note on Marriage and Affinal Relationship Among the

Iteso of Kenya, With Special Reference to Ivan Karp's
Proposition." Hitotsubaski Journal of Social Studies.
Volume 12 November, 1980. pp. 25-46.
Nagashima, Nobuhiro
"Bridewealth Among the Iteso of Kenya: A Further Note on
Their Affinal Relationship and its Historical Change."
Hitotsubashi Journal of Social Studies. Volume 14
August, 1982. pp. 14-26.
Nelson, Nici
"Dependence and Independence: Female Household Heads in
Mathare Valley, A Squatter Community in Nairobi, Kenya."
Ph.D Dissertation: University of London. School of
Oriental and African Studies. London, England. 1977.
Nelson, Nici
"Female-Centered Families: Changing Patterns of Marriage
and Family Among Buzaa Brewers of Mathari Valley."
African Urban Studies. #3 Winter, 1978. pp. 85-103.
Nelson, Nici
"How Women and Men Get By: The Sexual Division of Labour
in the Informal Sector of a Nairobi Squatter Settlement."
(In) Bromley, Ray and Gerry, Chris (eds.). Casual Work
and Poverty in Third World Cities. New York: John Wiley
and Sons. 1979. pp. 283-302.
Nelson, Nici
"Is Fostering of Children on the Increase in Central
Kenya? Parental Strategies in a Situation of Accelerating
Urbanization and Economic Stratification." Paper
Presented at the Conference on the History of the Family
in Africa. London: Cambridge University. School of
Oriental and African Studies. September, 1981.
Nelson, Nici
"Women Must Help Each Other: The Operation of Peasant
Networks Among Buzaa Beer Brewers in Mathare Valley,
Kenya." (In) Caplan, Patricia and Bujra, Janet M.
(eds.). Women United, Women Divided. Bloomington,
Indiana: Indiana University Press. 1978. pp. 77-98.
Newman, James L. and Lura, Russell P.
"Fertility Control in Africa." Geographical Review.
Volume 73 #4 October, 1983. pp. 396-406.
Njau, Rebeka
Kenya Women Heroes and Their Mystical Power. Nairobi,
Kenya: Risk Publications. 1984.
Njoki, Margaret
"Female Circumcision in Kenya." Paper Presented at the
Seminar on Traditional Practices Affecting the Health of
Women and Children. World Conference for the United
Nations Decade for Women. New York: United Nations.
Copenhagen, Denmark. July 14-30, 1980.
Njoki, Margaret
"Traditional Practices in Relation to Childbirth in
Kenya." Paper Presented at the Seminar on Traditional
Practices Affecting the Health of Women and Children.

World Conference of the United Nations Decade for Women.
New York: United Nations. Copenhagen, Denmark. July
14-30, 1980.

Njoki, Margaret
"Traditional Practices in Relation to Childbirth in
Kenya." Paper Presented at the Seminar on Traditional
Practices Affecting the Health of Women and Children:
Female Circumcision, Childhood Marriage, Nutritional
Taboos, etc. Alexandria, Egypt: World Health
Organization. Eastern Mediterranean Regional Office.
Khartoum, Sudan. February 10-15, 1979.

Njuki, Caroline W.
"Problems of Access to Women's Education in Kenya." Ph.D
Dissertation: University of Pittsburgh. Pittsburgh,
Pennsylvania. 1982. 181p.

Nyonyntono, Rebecca M.
"Poverty and the Changing Family in the African Context."
Paper Presented at the Seminar on the Changing Family in
the African Context, Maseru, Lesotho, 1983. Paris:
United Nations Educational, Scientific and Cultural
Organization. 1984. 23p.

Oboler, Regina S.
"Is the Female Husband A Man? Woman/Woman Marriage Among
the Nandi of Kenya." Ethnology. Volume 19 #1 January,
1980. pp. 69-88.

Oboler, Regina S.
The Economic Rights of Nandi Women. Nairobi: University
of Nairobi. Institute of Development Studies. Working
Paper #328. November, 1977.

Oboler, Regina S.
"Women, Men, Property and Change in Nandi District,
Kenya." Ph.D Dissertation: Temple University.
Philadelphia, Pennsylvania. 1982. 492p.

Oboler, Regina S.
Women, Power and Economic Change: The Nandi of Kenya.
Stanford, California: Stanford University Press. 1985.
368p.

Okeyo, Achola P.
"Daughters of the Lakes and Rivers: Colonization and the
Land Rights of Luo Women." (In) Etienne, Mona and
Leacook, Eleanor (eds.). Women and Colonization:
Anthropological Perspectives. New York: Praeger
Publishers. 1980. pp. 186-213.

Olusanya, P.O.
The Demographic, Health, Economic and Social Impact of
Family Planning in Selected African Countries. Addis
Ababa, Ethiopia: United Nations Economic Commission for
Africa. ECA/PD/1985-9. March, 1985. 97p.

Ombina, O. and May, Nicky
"Progress Through Piggeries and Prejudice in Kenya."
Community Development Journal. Volume 20 #3 1985. pp.
191-194.

KENYA

Pala, Achola O.
    "Women Power in Kenya: Raising Funds and Awareness."
    Ceres. Volume 11 #2 March-April, 1978. pp. 43-46.
Pala, Achola O.
    Women's Access to Land and Their Role in Agriculture and
    Decision-Making on the Farm: Experiences of Joluo of
    Kenya. Nairobi: University of Nairobi. Institute For
    Development Studies. Discussion Paper #263. 1978. 22p.
Pala, Achola O.
    "Women's Access to Land and Their Role in Agriculture and
    Decision-Making on the Farm: Experiences of the Joluo of
    Kenya." Journal of Eastern African Research and
    Development. Volume 13 1983. pp. 69-87.
Pala, Achola O.
    A Preliminary Survey of Avenues for and Constraints of
    Women's Involvement in the Development Process in Kenya.
    Nairobi: University of Nairobi. Institute of Development
    Studies. Discussion Paper #218. 1976.
Parker, C.
    "How to Be/Treat a Lady in Swahili Culture: An Expression
    of Ideal." Ba Shiru. Volume 8 #2 1977. pp. 37-45.
Parkin, David
    "Kind Bridewealth and Hard Cash: Eventing a Structure."
    (In) Comaroff, J.L. (ed.). The Meaning of Marriage
    Payments. New York: Academic Press. 1980. pp. 197-220.
Potash, Betty
    "Some Aspects of Marital Stability in a Rural Luo
    Community." Africa. Volume 48 #4 1978. pp. 380-397.
Presley, Cora A.
    Kikuyu Women as Wage Labourers: 1919-1960. Nairobi:
    University of Nairobi. Department of History. Staff
    Seminar. Paper #24. 1978. 20p.
Presley, Cora A.
    "Labor Unrest Among Kikuyu Women in Colonial Kenya."
    Paper Presented at the Annual Meeting of the African
    Studies Association. Paper #100. Bloomington, Indiana.
    October 21-24, 1981.
Reining, Priscilla (ed.)
    Village Women: Their Changing Lives and Fertility:
    Studies in Kenya. Mexico and the Philippines. Washington,
    D.C.: American Association for the Advancement of
    Science. AAAS Publication #77-6. 1977. 273p.
Riria, J.V.N.
    "What Kenyan Women Want." Journal of Eastern African
    Research and Development. Volume 13 1983. pp. 55-68.
Russell, Joan
    "Women's Narration: Performance and the Marking of Verbal
    Aspects." (In) Maw, Joan and Parkin, David (eds.).
    Swahili Language and Society. Wien, West Germany:
    Institute fur Afrikanistik und Agytologie der University
    Wien. 1984. pp. 89-105.

Santilli, Kathy
"Kikuyu Women in the Mau Mau Revolt: A Closer Look."
Ufahamu. Volume 8 #1 1977. pp. 143-174.

Schulpen, T.W.
"Machakos Project Studies. Agents Affecting Health of
Mother and Child in a Rural Area of Kenya. XIX. The
Utilization of Health Services in a Rural Area of Kenya."
Tropical and Geographical Medicine. Volume 32 #4
December, 1980. pp. 340-349.

Seeley, Janet
"'We Have the Healing Power...': Independent Churches and
Women in Urban Kenya." Cambridge Anthropology. Volume 9
#2 1984. pp. 58-70.

Shepherd, Gilliam M.
Lesbians In Mombasa: A Healthy Response to Female
Socialization? 1977.

Smock, Audrey C.
"Measuring Rural Women's Economic Roles and Contributions
in Kenya." Studies in Family Planning. Volume 10 #11/12
November-December, 1979. pp. 385-390.

Smock, Audrey C.
Women's Education and Roles in Kenya. Nairobi:
University of Nairobi. Institute of Development Studies.
Working Paper #316. July, 1977.

Staudt, Kathleen A.
"Administrative Resources, Political Patrons, and
Redressing Sexual Inequities: A Case From Western Kenya."
Journal of Developing Areas. Volume 12 #4 July, 1978.
pp. 399-414.

Staudt, Kathleen A.
"Agricultural Policy, Political Power, and Women Farmers
in Western Kenya." Ph.D Dissertation: University of
Wisconsin-Madison. Madison, Wisconsin. 1976. 422p.

Staudt, Kathleen A.
"Rural Women Leaders: Late Colonial and Contemporary
Contexts." Rural Africana. #3 Winter, 1978. pp. 5-21.

Staudt, Kathleen A.
"Sex, Ethnic and Class Consciousness in Western Kenya."
Paper Presented at the Annual Meeting of the African
Studies Association. Paper #97. Baltimore, Maryland.
1978.

Staudt, Kathleen A.
"Sex, Ethnic and Class Consciousness in Western Kenya."
Comparative Politics. Volume 14 #2 1982. pp. 149-168.

Stichter, Sharon B.
Women and the Labor Force in Kenya, 1895-1964. Nairobi:
University of Nairobi. Institute for Development
Studies. Discussion Paper #258. 1977. 26p.

Stichter, Sharon B.
Women in the Labor Force in Kenya: Some Effects on Their
Family Roles. Boston: University of Massachusetts.
1978.

Stichter, Sharon B.
   "Women in the Urban Labor Force in Kenya." Paper
   Presented to the Wellesley Conference on Women and
   Development. Wellesley, Massachusetts: Wellesley
   College. Wellesley Center for Research on Women. June,
   1976.
Strobel, Margaret A.
   Muslim Women in Mombasa, 1890-1975. New Haven,
   Connecticut: Yale University Press. 1979. 258p.
Strobel, Margaret A.
   "Slavery and Reproductive Labor in Mombasa." (In)
   Robertson, Claire C. and Klein, Martin A. (eds.). Women
   and Slavery in Africa. Madison, Wisconsin: University of
   Wisconsin Press. 1983. pp. 111-129.
Swartz, Audrey R. and Swartz, Marc J.
   "Women's Power and Its Sources Among the Swahili of
   Mombasa." Paper Presented at the Annual Meeting of the
   African Studies Association. Paper #93. Los Angeles,
   California. 1979. 9p.
Swartz, Marc J.
   "The Isolation of Men and the Happiness of Women: Sources
   and Use of Power in Swahili Marital Relationships."
   Journal of Anthropological Research. Volume 38 #1
   Spring, 1982. pp. 26-44.
Thadani, Veena N.
   Social Relations and Geographic Mobility: Male and Female
   Migration in Kenya. New York: Population Council.
   Center for Policy Studies. Working Paper #85. June,
   1982. 67p.
Thadani, Veena N.
   "The Forgotten Factor in Social Change: The Case of Women
   in Nairobi, Kenya." Ph.D Dissertation: Bryn Mawr
   College. Bryn Mawr, Pennsylvania. 1976. 259p.
Thadani, Veena N.
   "Women in Nairobi: The Paradox of Urban Progress."
   African Urban Studies. #3 Winter, 1978.
Thiong'o, Ngugi W.
   "Women in Cultural Work: The Fate of Kamiriithu People's
   Theatre in Kenya." Development Dialogue. #1/2 1982.
   pp. 115-133.
United Nations Economic Commission for Africa (UNECA)
   Nuptiality and Fertility (A Comparative Analysis of WFS
   Data). Addis Ababa, Ethiopia: UNECA. African Population
   Studies Series #5. 1983. 96p.
Van Ginneken, J.K. and Muller, A.S. and Blok, P.G. and
Omondi, Odhiambo
   "Agents Affecting Health of Mother and Child in a Rural
   Area of Kenya. XVII: Population Growth in 1974-1978."
   Tropical and Geographical Medicine. Volume 32 #2 June,
   1980. pp. 174-180.
Van Ginneken, J.K. and Voorhoeve, A.M. and Omondi, Odhiambo
and Muller, A.S.
   "Agents Affecting Health of Mother and Child in a Rural

Area of Kenya. XVIII: Fertility, Mortality and Migration
in 1975-1978." Tropical and Geographical Medicine.
Volume 32 #2 1980. pp. 183-188.

Voorhoeve, A.M.
"Machakos Project Studies. Agents Affecting Health of
Mother and Child in A Rural Area of Kenya. XXI.
Antenatal and Delivery Care." Tropical and Geographical
Medicine. Volume 34 #1 March, 1982. pp. 91-101.

Voorhoeve, A.M.
"Machakos Project Studies: Agents Affecting Health of
Mother and Child in a Rural Area of Kenya. XVI. The
Outcome of Pregnancy." Tropical and Geographical
Medicine. Volume 31 #4 December, 1979. pp. 607-627.

Waife, Ronald S. and Burkhart, Marianne (eds.)
The Nonphysician and Family Health in Sub-Saharan Africa:
Proceedings of a Conference, Freetown, Sierra Leone,
September 1-4, 1980. Chestnut Hill, Massachusetts:
Pathfinder Fund. 1981. 141p.

Waller, R.D.
"Interaction and Identity on the Periphery--The
Trans-Mara Maasai." International Journal of African
Historical Studies. Volume 17 #2 1984. pp. 243-284.

White, Luise S.
"A Colonial State and an African Petty Bourgeoisie:
Prostitution, Property and Class Struggle in Nairobi,
1936-1940." (In) Cooper, Frederick (ed.). Struggle for
the City: Migrant Labour, Capital, and the State in Urban
Africa. Beverly Hills, California: Sage Publications.
African Modernization and Development Series #8. 1983.
pp. 167-194.

White, Luise S.
"A History of Prostitution in Nairobi, Kenya. c.
1900-1952." Ph.D Dissertation: University of Cambridge.
London, England. 1983.

White, Luise S.
"Women's Domestic Labor in Colonial Kenya: Prostitution
in Nairobi, 1909-1950." Brookline, Massachusetts: Boston
University. African Studies Center. Working Paper #30.
1980. 26p.

Whiting, Beatrice B.
"Changing Life Styles in Kenya." Daedalus. Volume 106
#2 Spring, 1977. pp. 211-226.

Whiting, Beatrice B.
"Woman's Role in Social Change: Education and the Kikuyu
of Kenya." Cultural Survival Quarterly. Volume 8 #2
Summer, 1984. pp. 43-45.

Whiting, Martha and Krystall, Abigail
The Impact of Rural Water Supply Projects on Women.
Nairobi: University of Nairobi. Bureau of Educational
Research. 1979.

Wienpahl, Jan
"Women's Roles in Livestock Production Among the Turkana

of Kenya." Research in Economic Anthropology. Volume 6
1984. pp. 193-215.
Wilson, G.M.
"A Study of Prostitution in Mombasa." (In) Muga, Erasto.
Studies in Prostitution: East, West and South Africa,
Zaire and Nevada. Nairobi: Kenya Literature Bureau.
1980. pp. 130-141.

DEVELOPMENT AND TECHNOLOGY

Ahlberg, B.M.
The Rural Water Supply (RWS) Programme in Kenya: Its
Impact on Women. Stockholm, Sweden: Swedish
International Development Agency (SIDA). October, 1983.
21p.
Akerele, Olubanke
Women Workers in Ghana, Kenya, Zambia: A Comparative
Analysis of Women's Employment in the Modern Wage
Sector. Addis Ababa, Ethiopia: United Nations Economic
Commission for Africa. African Training and Research
Center for Women. 1979. 109p.
Anderson, Mary B.
"Kenya: Egerton College." (In) Overholt, Catherine and
Anderson, Mary B. and Cloud, Kathleen and Austin, James
(eds.). Gender Roles in Development Projects: A Case
Book. West Hartford, Connecticut: Kumarian Press. 1985.
pp. 185-213.
Anderson, Mary B.
"Kenya: Kitui District Arid and Semi-Arid Lands Project."
(In) Overholt, Catherine and Anderson, Mary B. and Cloud,
Kathleen and Austin, James E. (eds.). Gender Roles in
Development Projects: A Case Book. West Hartford,
Connecticut: Kumarian Press. 1985. pp. 309-326.
Anonymous
"The Women Sing of Harambee." Agenda. Volume 1 #2
February, 1978. pp. 15-18.
Anonymous
Women in Kenya. Nairobi: Kenya Central Bureau of
Statistics. 1978.
Bifani, Patricia and Adagala, Kavetsa and Kariuki,
Patricia W.
The Impact of Development of Women in Kenya: A
Methodological Approach. Nairobi: UNICEF. 1982. 118p.
Bifani, Patricia
The Impact of Development on Women in Kenya: An Annotated
Bibliography. Nairobi: UNICEF. 1982. 38p.
Broche-Due, Vigdis
Women at the Backstage of Development: A
Socio-Anthropological Case Study From Katilu Irigation
Scheme, Turkana, Kenya. Rome: United Nations Food and
Agriculture Organization. 1983.

Clark, Noreen
  Education for Development and the Rural Women. New York:
  World Education Inc. Volume One--A Review of Theory and
  Principles With Emphasis on Kenya and the Philippines.
  1979. 66p.
Davison, J.
  "Achievements and Constraints Among Rural Kenyan Women: A
  Case Study." Journal of Eastern African Research and
  Development. Volume 15 1985. pp. 268-279.
Feldman, Rayah
  "Women's Groups and Women's Subordination: An Analysis of
  Policies Towards Rural Women in Kenya." Review of
  African Political Economy. #27/28 1983. pp. 67-85.
Feldman, Rayah
  Employment Problems of Rural Women in Kenya. Addis
  Ababa, Ethiopia: International Labour Office. JASPA.
  1981.
Gachukia, Eddah W.
  "Mothers Role in Rural Kenya." Ekistics. Volume 45 #272
  September-October, 1978. pp. 356-357.
Gachukia, Eddah W.
  "Women's Self-Help Efforts for Water Supply in Kenya."
  Appropriate Technology. Volume 9 #3 1982. pp. 19-21.
Gachukia, Eddah W.
  "Women's Self-Help Efforts for Water Supply in Kenya: The
  Important Role of NGO Support." Assignment Children.
  Volume 45/46 Spring, 1979. pp. 167-174.
Gakuo, Mumbi
  "The Kenyan Women and Situation and Strategies for
  Improvement." Women's Studies International Forum.
  Volume 8 #4 1985. pp. 373-379.
Getechah, W.
  "The Role of Women in Rural Water Development in Kenya."
  (In) International Development Research Centre (IDRC).
  Rural Water Supply in Developing Countries. A Workshop
  on Training, Zomba, Malawi, August 5-12, 1980. Ottawa,
  Canada: IDRC. 1981. pp. 85-88.
Greene, P.A.
  Innovative Approaches in Rural Women's Programmes in
  Three African Countries: Kenya, Nigeria, Sierra Leone:
  Case Studies. Rome: United Nations Food and Agriculture
  Organization. 1985. 148p.
Gupta, Anirudha
  "Illusion of Progress: The Women of Kenya." (In)
  Phadnis, Urmila and Malani, Indira (eds.). Women of the
  World: Ilusion and Reality. New Delhi, India: Vikas
  Publishing House Ltd. 1980. pp. 245-259.
Gutto, Shadrack B.
  "The Legal Status of Women in Kenya: Paternalism and
  Inequality." Fletcher Forum. Volume 1 Fall, 1976. pp.
  62-82.
Gutto, Shadrack B.
  The Status of Women in Kenya: A Study of Paternalism,

Inequality and Under Privilege. Nairobi: University of
Nairobi. Institute for Development Studies. Discussion
Paper #235. April, 1976. 76p.

Hay, Margaret J.
"Luo Women and Economic Change During the Colonial
Period." (In) Hafkin, Margaret J. and Bay, Edna G.
(eds.). Women in Africa: Studies in Social and Economic
Change. Stanford, California: Stanford University
Press. 1976. pp. 87-109.

International Labour Organization (ILO)
Employment Problems of Rural Women in Kenya. Nairobi:
ILO. Economic Commission for Africa. 1981.

Kayongo-Male, Diana
"Problems and Prospects of Integrating Women into
Development Planning and Process in Kenya." Journal of
Eastern African Research and Development. Volume 15
1985. pp. 280-296.

Kenya. Ministry of Finance and Economic Planning
Women in Kenya, Social Perspectives. Nairobi: The
Ministry. Central Bureau of Statistics. 1978. 62p.

Kenya. Ministry of Finance and Economic Planning.
"Women in Kenya." Social Perspectives. Volume 3 #3
April, 1978.

Leonard, D.K.
Reaching the Peasant Farmer: Organization Theory and
Practice in Kenya. Chicago: University of Chicago Press.
1977.

Leonard, D.K. and Kimenya, P. and Muzaale, P. and Ngugi, D.
and Oyugi, W.
An Evaluation of the Components Needed to Improve the
Performance of Kenya's Agricultural Extension Service.
Nairobi, Kenya: Ministry of Agriculture. 1982.

Lewis, Barbara C.
"The Impact of Development Policies on Women." (In) Hay,
Margaret J. and Stichter, Sharon (eds.). African Women
South of the Sahara. New York: Longman. 1984. pp.
170-187.

Likimani, Muthoni G.
Women of Kenya: Fifteen Years of Independence. Nairobi:
Likamani. 1979. 76p.

Lindsay, Beverly
"An Examination of Education, Social Change and National
Development Policy: The Case of Kenyan Women." (In)
Women and Politics in 20th Century Africa and Asia.
Williamsburg, Virginia: College of William and Mary.
Anthropology Department. Studies in Third World
Societies. #16. June, 1981. pp. 29-48.

Mickelwait, Donald R. and Riegelman, Mary Ann and Sweet,
Charles F.
Women in Rural Development: A Survey of the Roles of
Women in Ghana, Lesotho, Kenya, Nigeria... Boulder,
Colorado: Westview Press. 1976. 224p.

Mohan, P.C.
   "Of the Women, By the Women, For Everybody: A Goat
   Project in Kenya." Ideas and Action Bulletin #144 1981.

Monsted, Mette
   Women's Groups in Rural Kenya and Their Role in
   Development. Copenhagen, Denmark: Centre for Development
   Research. CDR Paper A/78/2. June, 1978.
Moock, P.R.
   "Efficiency of Women as Farm Managers: Kenya." American
   Journal of Agricultural Economics. Volume 58 #5
   December, 1976. pp. 831-835.
Mott, Susan H.
   "Modernization and Fertility Orientation in Kenya." Ph.D
   Dissertation: Ohio State University. Columbus, Ohio.
   1982. 165p.
Munene, Fibi
   "Women in Africa: A Kenyan Perspective." Africa Report.
   Volume 22 #1 January-February, 1977. pp. 18-20.
Nelson, Nici
   "Is Fostering of Children on the Increase in Central
   Kenya? Parental Strategies in a Situation of Accelerating
   Urbanization and Economic Stratification." Paper
   Presented at the Conference on the History of the Family
   in Africa. London: Cambridge University. School of
   Oriental and African Studies. September, 1981.
Nyonyntono, Rebecca M.
   Women as Agents of Change in Developing Countries: The
   Case of Kenya. Nairobi: University of Nairobi. 1982.
Ojiambo, Julia
   "Women and Development in Kenya." Paper Presented at the
   15th World Conference of the Society for International
   Development. Amsterdam, Netherlands. Nov. 28-Dec. 3,
   1976. 17p.
Ombina, O. and May, Nicky
   "Progress Through Piggeries and Prejudice in Kenya."
   Community Development Journal. Volume 20 #3 1985. pp.
   191-194.
Opondo, Diana
   "A Women's Group in Kenya and its Struggle to Obtain
   Credit." Assignment Children. Volume 49/50 Spring,
   1980. pp. 127-140.
Pala, Achola O.
   "Changes in Economy and Ideology: A Study of Joluo of
   Kenya With Special Reference to Women." Ph.D
   Dissertation: Harvard University. Department of
   Anthropology. Cambridge, Massachusetts. 1977.
Pala, Achola O.
   Women and Development: An Overview on Kenya. Paper
   Presented at the Seminiar on Women in Rural Development.
   Washington, D.C.: American Council on Education.
   Overseas Liaison Committee. April 21-23, 1976.

Pala, Achola O. and Krystall, Abigail
    Women in Rural Development. Nairobi: University of
    Nairobi. Bureau of Education Research. 1978.
Pala, Achola O.
    A Preliminary Survey of Avenues for and Constraints of
    Women's Involvement in the Development Process in Kenya.
    Nairobi: University of Nairobi. Institute of Development
    Studies. Discussion Paper #218. 1976.
Palmer, Ingrid
    "New Official Ideas on Women and Development." Institute
    for Development Studies. Volume 10 #3 1979. pp. 42-53.
Riria Ouko, J.V.N.
    "Women Organizations in Kenya." Journal of Eastern
    African Research and Development. Volume 15 1985. pp.
    188-197.
Riria, J.V.N.
    "What Kenyan Women Want." Journal of Eastern African
    Research and Development. Volume 13 1983. pp. 55-68.
Smock, Audrey C.
    "Measuring Rural Women's Economic Roles and Contributions
    in Kenya." Studies in Family Planning. Volume 10 #11/12
    November-December, 1979. pp. 385-390.
Staudt, Kathleen A.
    "Agricultural Policy, Political Power, and Women Farmers
    in Western Kenya." Ph.D Dissertation: University of
    Wisconsin-Madison. Madison, Wisconsin. 1976. 422p.
Staudt, Kathleen A.
    Inequities in the Delivery of Services to a Female Farm
    Clientele: Some Implications for Policy. Nairobi, Kenya:
    University of Nairobi. Institute for Development
    Studies. IDS Discussion Paper #247. 1977.
Strobel, Margaret A.
    "From Lelemamato Lobbying: Women's Associations in
    Mombasa, Kenya." (In) Hafkin, N.J. and Bay, E.G. (eds.).
    Women in Africa: Studies in Social and Economic Change.
    Stanford, California: Stanford University Press. 1976.
    pp. 183-211.
Thadani, Veena N.
    "The Forgotten Factor in Social Change: The Case of Women
    in Nairobi, Kenya." Ph.D Dissertation: Bryn Mawr
    College. Bryn Mawr, Pennsylvania. 1976. 259p.
Thrupp. Lori-Ann
    "Women, Wood and Work: In Kenya and Beyond." Unasylva.
    Volume 36 #146 1984.
U.S. Department of Commerce. Bureau of the Census
    Illustrative Statistics on Women in Development in
    Selected Developing Countries. Washington, D.C.: U.S.
    Department of Commerce. 1982. 24p.
Ventura, Dias
    "Modernisation, Production Organization and Rural Women
    in Kenya." (In) Ahmed, Iftikhar (ed.). Technology and
    Rural Women: Conceptual and Empirical Issues. Boston:
    George Allen and Unwin. 1985. pp. 157-210.

Wachtel, Eleanor and Wachtel, Andy
Women's Co-Operative Enterprise in Nakuru. Nairobi:
University of Nairobi. Institute for Development
Studies. Discussion Paper #250. 1977. 18p.
Wanjala, Esther
"Kenya." ISIS Women's World. #4 December, 1984.
Wasow, Bernard
"The Working Age Sex Ratio and Job Search Migration in
Kenya." Journal of Developing Areas. Volume 15 #3
April, 1981. pp. 435-444.
Whiting, Martha and Krystall, Abigail
The Impact of Rural Water Supply Projects on Women.
Nairobi: University of Nairobi. Bureau of Educational
Research. 1979.

ECONOMICS

Ahlberg, B.M.
The Rural Water Supply (RWS) Programme in Kenya: Its
Impact on Women. Stockholm, Sweden: Swedish
International Development Agency (SIDA). October, 1983.
21p.
Akerele, Olubanke
Women Workers in Ghana, Kenya, Zambia: A Comparative
Analysis of Women's Employment in the Modern Wage
Sector. Addis Ababa, Ethiopia: United Nations Economic
Commission for Africa. African Training and Research
Center for Women. 1979. 109p.
Anderson, Mary B.
"Kenya: Egerton College." (In) Overholt, Catherine and
Anderson, Mary B. and Cloud, Kathleen and Austin, James
(eds.). Gender Roles in Development Projects: A Case
Book. West Hartford, Connecticut: Kumarian Press. 1985.
pp. 185-213.
Anker, Richard and Knowles, James C.
"A Micro Analysis of Female Labour Force Participation in
Kenya." (In) Standing, G. And Sheehan, G. (eds.).
Labour Force Participation in Low Income Countries.
Geneva: International Labour Organization. 1978.
Anker, Richard and Knowles, James C.
Population Growth, Employment and Economic Demographic
Interactions in Kenya: Bachue-Kenya. New York: St.
Martin's Press. 1983. 735p.
Anonymous
Women in Kenya. Nairobi: Kenya Central Bureau of
Statistics. 1978.
Bifani, Patricia and Adagala, Kavetsa and Kariuki, Patricia
W.
The Impact of Development of Women in Kenya: A
Methodological Approach. Nairobi: UNICEF. 1982. 118p.
Bujra, Janet M.
"Proletarianization and the 'Informal Economy': A Case

Study From Nairobi." African Urban Studies. #47 1978.
pp. 47-66.
Bujra, Janet M.
"Women 'Entrepreneurs' in Early Nairobi." (In) Sumner,
Colin (ed.). Crime, Justice and Underdevelopment.
London: Heineman. Cambridge Studies in Criminology.
#46. 1982.
Butterfield, Cynthia
Women and the Modern Wage Sector: A Study of Female
Participation in Commercial Banks and Finance Companies
in Nairobi. Nairobi: University of Nairobi. Institute
for Development Studies. Discussion Paper 256. 1977.
28p.
Buzzard, Shirley
"Women's Status and Wage Employment in Kisumu, Kenya."
Ph.D Dissertation: American University. Washington D.C.
1982. 289p.
Clark, Mari H.
"Women-Headed Households and Poverty: Insights From
Kenya." Signs. Volume 10 #2 Winter, 1984. pp.
338-354.
Gakuo, Mumbi
"The Kenyan Women and Situation and Strategies for
Improvement." Women's Studies International Forum.
Volume 8 #4 1985. pp. 373-379.
Greene, P.A.
Innovative Approaches in Rural Women's Programmes in
Three African Countries: Kenya, Nigeria, Sierra Leone:
Case Studies. Rome: United Nations Food and Agriculture
Organization. 1985. 148p.
Gupta, Anirudha
"Illusion of Progress: The Women of Kenya." (In)
Phadnis, Urmila and Malani, Indira (eds.). Women of the
World: Ilusion and Reality. New Delhi, India: Vikas
Publishing House Ltd. 1980. pp. 245-259.
Hay, Margaret J.
"Luo Women and Economic Change During the Colonial
Period." (In) Hafkin, Margaret J. and Bay, Edna G.
(eds.). Women in Africa: Studies in Social and Economic
Change. Stanford, California: Stanford University
Press. 1976. pp. 87-109.
International Labour Organization (ILO)
Employment Problems of Rural Women in Kenya. Nairobi:
ILO. Economic Commission for Africa. 1981.
Kabwegyere, Tarsis
"Determinants of Fertility: A Discussion of Change in the
Family Among the Akamba of Kenya." (In) Caldwell, John
C. (ed.). The Persistence of High Fertility: Population
Prospects in the Third World. Canberra, Australia:
Australian National University. Volume One. 1977. pp.
189-222.

Kanyiri, Elisha M.
    "The Socioeconomic and Demographic Factors Influencing
    Contraceptive Behavior in Kenya." Ph.D Dissertation:
    Florida State University. Tallahassee, Florida. 1984.
    143p.
Kayongo-Male, Diana
    "Problems and Prospects of Integrating Women into
    Development Planning and Process in Kenya." Journal of
    Eastern African Research and Development. Volume 15
    1985. pp. 280-296.
Kelley, Allen C. and Swartz, Caroline
    "The Impact of Family Structure on Microeconomic Decision
    Making in Developing Countries: A Case Study of Nuclear
    and Extended Families in Urban Kenya." (In)
    International Union for the Scientific Study of
    Population (IUSSP). Economic and Demographic Change:
    Issues for the 1980's: Proceedings of the Conference on
    Economic and Demographic Change, 1978. Liege, Belgium:
    (IUSSP). Volume One. Helsinki, Finland. 1979. pp.
    361-375.
Kenya. Ministry of Finance and Economic Planning
    Women in Kenya, Social Perspectives. Nairobi: The
    Ministry. Central Bureau of Statistics. 1978. 62p.
Kenya. Ministry of Finance and Economic Planning.
    "Women in Kenya." Social Perspectives. Volume 3 #3
    April, 1978.
Kershaw, Greet
    "The Changing Roles of Men and Women in the Kikuyu Family
    by Socioeconomic Strata." Rural Africana. Volume 29
    Winter, 1976. pp. 173-194.
Kershaw, Greet
    "The Changing Roles of Men and Women in the Kikuyu Family
    by Socioeconomic Strata." Rural Africana. Volume 29
    Winter, 1976. pp. 173-194.
Kneerim, Jill
    Village Women Organize: The Mraru Bus Service. New York:
    Carnegie Corporation. Volume One of the Seeds Pamphlet
    Series #3. 1980. 20p.
Knotts, Mary A.
    "The Social and Economic Factors Associated With the
    Rural-Urban Migration of Kenyan Women." Ph.D
    Dissertation: Johns Hopkins University. Baltimore,
    Maryland. 1977. 306p.
Komma, Toru
    "The Women's Self-Help Association Movement Among the
    Kipsigis of Kenya." Senri Ethnological Studies. Volume
    15 1984. pp. 145-186.
Kosgei, Sally J.
    Kipsigis Women and the Colonial Economy. Nairobi:
    University of Nairobi. Department of History. 1979.
    17p.
Kune, J.B.
    "Machakos Project Studies: Agents Affecting Health of

Mother and Child in a Rural Area of Kenya. XV. The
Economic Setting at the Household Level." Tropical and
Geographical Medicine. Volume 31 #3 September, 1979.
pp. 441-457.

Lewis, Barbara C.
"The Impact of Development Policies on Women." (In) Hay,
Margaret J. and Stichter, Sharon (eds.). African Women
South of the Sahara. New York: Longman. 1984. pp.
170-187.

Likimani, Muthoni G.
Women of Kenya: Fifteen Years of Independence. Nairobi:
Likamani. 1979. 76p.

Lindsay, Beverly
"An Examination of Education, Social Change and National
Development Policy: The Case of Kenyan Women." (In)
Women and Politics in 20th Century Africa and Asia.
Williamsburg, Virginia: College of William and Mary.
Anthropology Department. Studies in Third World
Societies. #16. June, 1981. pp. 29-48.

Lindsay, Beverly
"Career Aspirations of Kenyan Women." Journal of Negro
Education. Volume 49 #4 Fall, 1980. pp. 432-440.

Lindsay, Beverly
"Comparative Perspectives of Kenya Women on Career
Choices." International Education Journal. Volume 5 #2
1976. pp. 15-32.

Lindsay, Beverly
"Issues Confronting Professional African Women:
Illustrations From Kenya." (In) Lindsay, Beverly (ed.).
Comparative Perspectives of Third World Women: The Impact
of Race, Sex and Class. New York: Praeger Publishers.
1980. pp. 78-95.

Mickelwait, Donald R. and Riegelman, Mary Ann and Sweet,
Charles F.
Women in Rural Development: A Survey of the Roles of
Women in Ghana, Lesotho, Kenya, Nigeria... Boulder,
Colorado: Westview Press. 1976. 224p.

Mkangi, George C.
"Education, Poverty and Fertility Among the Wataita of
Kenya." (In) Epstein, T. Scarlett and Jackson, Darrell
(eds.). The Feasibility of Fertility Planning. Oxford,
England: Pergamon Press. 1977. pp. 173-182.

Mohan, P.C.
"Of the Women, By the Women, For Everybody: A Goat
Project in Kenya." Ideas and Action Bulletin #144 1981.

Monsted, Mette
Women's Groups in Rural Kenya and Their Role in
Development. Copenhagen, Denmark: Centre for Development
Research. CDR Paper A/78/2. June, 1978.

Moock, P.R.
"Efficiency of Women as Farm Managers: Kenya." American
Journal of Agricultural Economics. Volume 58 #5
December, 1976. pp. 831-835.

Mott, Frank L. and Shapiro, D.
"Seasonal Variations in Labor Force Activity and
Intrahousehold Substitution of Labor in Rural Kenya."
Journal of Developing Areas. Volume 18 #4 July, 1984.
pp. 449-463.
Munene, Fibi
"Women in Africa: A Kenyan Perspective." Africa Report.
Volume 22 #1 January-February, 1977. pp. 18-20.
Mwaria, Cheryl B.
"Rural-Urban Labor Migration and Family Arrangements
Among the Kamba." (In) Robinson, Pearl T. and Skinner,
Elliott (eds.). Transformation and Resiliency in Africa.
Washington, D.C.: Howard University Press. 1983. pp.
29-43.
Nelson, Nici
"Is Fostering of Children on the Increase in Central
Kenya? Parental Strategies in a Situation of Accelerating
Urbanization and Economic Stratification." Paper
Presented at the Conference on the History of the Family
in Africa. London: Cambridge University. School of
Oriental and African Studies. September, 1981.
Nyonyntono, Rebecca M.
"Poverty and the Changing Family in the African Context."
Paper Presented at the Seminar on the Changing Family in
the African Context, Maseru, Lesotho, 1983. Paris:
United Nations Educational, Scientific and Cultural
Organization. 1984. 23p.
Nyonyntono, Rebecca M.
Women as Agents of Change in Developing Countries: The
Case of Kenya. Nairobi: University of Nairobi. 1982.
Oboler, Regina S.
Women, Power and Economic Change: The Nandi of Kenya.
Stanford, California: Stanford University Press. 1985.
368p.
Ogutu, M.A.
"The Changing Role of Women in the Commercial History of
Busia District in Kenya, 1900-1983." Journal of Eastern
African Research and Development. Volume 15 1985. pp.
56-73.
Ojiambo, Julia
"Women and Development in Kenya." Paper Presented at the
15th World Conference of the Society for International
Development. Amsterdam, Netherlands. Nov. 28-Dec. 3,
1976. 17p.
Opondo, Diana
"A Women's Group in Kenya and its Struggle to Obtain
Credit." Assignment Children. Volume 49/50 Spring,
1980. pp. 127-140.
Pala, Achola O.
"Changes in Economy and Ideology: A Study of Joluo of
Kenya With Special Reference to Women." Ph.D
Dissertation: Harvard University. Department of
Anthropology. Cambridge, Massachusetts. 1977.

Pala, Achola O.
Women and Development: An Overview on Kenya. Paper
Presented at the Seminiar on Women in Rural Development.
Washington, D.C.: American Council on Education.
Overseas Liaison Committee. April 21-23, 1976.
Pala, Achola O. and Krystall, Abigail
Women in Rural Development. Nairobi: University of
Nairobi. Bureau of Education Research. 1978.
Pala, Achola O.
Women's Access to Land and Their Role in Agriculture and
Decision-Making on the Farm: Experiences of Joluo of
Kenya. Nairobi: University of Nairobi. Institute For
Development Studies. Discussion Paper #263. 1978. 22p.
Pala, Achola O.
"Women's Access to Land and Their Role in Agriculture and
Decision-Making on the Farm: Experiences of the Joluo of
Kenya." Journal of Eastern African Research and
Development. Volume 13 1983. pp. 69-87.
Pala, Achola O.
A Preliminary Survey of Avenues for and Constraints of
Women's Involvement in the Development Process in Kenya.
Nairobi: University of Nairobi. Institute of Development
Studies. Discussion Paper #218. 1976.
Palmer, Ingrid
"New Official Ideas on Women and Development." Institute
for Development Studies. Volume 10 #3 1979. pp. 42-53.
Smock, Audrey C.
"Measuring Rural Women's Economic Roles and Contributions
in Kenya." Studies in Family Planning. Volume 10 #11/12
November-December, 1979. pp. 385-390.
Staudt, Kathleen A.
"Agricultural Policy, Political Power, and Women Farmers
in Western Kenya." Ph.D Dissertation: University of
Wisconsin-Madison. Madison, Wisconsin. 1976. 422p.
Staudt, Kathleen A.
Inequities in the Delivery of Services to a Female Farm
Clientele: Some Implications for Policy. Nairobi, Kenya:
University of Nairobi. Institute for Development
Studies. IDS Discussion Paper #247. 1977.
Stichter, Sharon B.
Women and the Labor Force in Kenya, 1895-1964. Nairobi:
University of Nairobi. Institute for Development
Studies. Discussion Paper #258. 1977. 26p.
Stichter, Sharon B.
"Women in the Urban Labor Force in Kenya." Paper
Presented to the Wellesley Conference on Women and
Development. Wellesley, Massachusetts: Wellesley
College. Wellesley Center for Research on Women. June,
1976.
Strobel, Margaret A.
"From Lelemamato Lobbying: Women's Associations in
Mombasa, Kenya." (In) Hafkin, N.J. and Bay, E.G. (eds.).
Women in Africa: Studies in Social and Economic Change.

Stanford, California: Stanford University Press. 1976.
pp. 183-211.
Thadani, Veena N.
Social Relations and Geographic Mobility: Male and Female
Migration in Kenya. New York: Population Council.
Center for Policy Studies. Working Paper #85. June,
1982. 67p.
Thadani, Veena N.
"Women in Nairobi: The Paradox of Urban Progress."
African Urban Studies. #3 Winter, 1978.
United Nations Economic Commission for Africa (UNECA)
Women Workers in Ghana-Kenya-Zambia: A Comparative
Analysis of Women's Employment in the Modern Wage
Sector. Addis Ababa, Ethiopia: UNECA. 1979.
Ventura, Dias
"Modernisation, Production Organization and Rural Women
in Kenya." (In) Ahmed, Iftikhar (ed.). Technology and
Rural Women: Conceptual and Empirical Issues. Boston:
George Allen and Unwin. 1985. pp. 157-210.
Wachtel, Eleanor
"Minding Her Own Business: Women Shopkeepers in Nakuru,
Kenya." African Urban Notes. Volume 2 #2 Spring, 1976.
pp. 27-42.
Wachtel, Eleanor and Wachtel, Andy
Women's Co-Operative Enterprise in Nakuru. Nairobi:
University of Nairobi. Institute for Development
Studies. Discussion Paper #250. 1977. 18p.
Wanjala, Esther
"Kenya." ISIS Women's World. #4 December, 1984.
Wasow, Bernard
"The Working Age Sex Ratio and Job Search Migration in
Kenya." Journal of Developing Areas. Volume 15 #3
April, 1981. pp. 435-444.

EDUCATION AND TRAINING

Anderson, Mary B.
"Kenya: Egerton College." (In) Overholt, Catherine and
Anderson, Mary B. and Cloud, Kathleen and Austin, James
(eds.). Gender Roles in Development Projects: A Case
Book. West Hartford, Connecticut: Kumarian Press. 1985.
pp. 185-213.
Anker, Richard and Knowles, James C.
Population Growth, Employment and Economic Demographic
Interactions in Kenya: Bachue-Kenya. New York: St.
Martin's Press. 1983. 735p.
Clark, Noreen
Education for Development and the Rural Women. New York:
World Education Inc. Volume One--A Review of Theory and
Principles With Emphasis on Kenya and the Philippines.
1979. 66p.

Davison, Jean
    "Voices From Mutira: Education in the Lives of Rural
    Gikuyu Women." Ph.D Dissertation: Stanford University.
    Stanford, California. 1985. 422p.
Emereuwaonu, Ernest U.
    "Determinants of Fertility: A Regression Analysis of
    Kenya Data." Genus. Volume 40 #3/4 July-December,
    1984. pp. 77-96.
Gatara, Timothy H.
    "The Influence of Religion and Education on Current
    Family Size and Fertility Preference in Kenya." Ph.D
    Dissertation: Florida State University. Tallahassee,
    Florida. 1982. 152p.
Greene, P.A.
    Innovative Approaches in Rural Women's Programmes in
    Three African Countries: Kenya, Nigeria, Sierra Leone:
    Case Studies. Rome: United Nations Food and Agriculture
    Organization. 1985. 148p.
Kenya. Ministry of Finance and Economic Planning
    Educational Characteristics and Their Relationship to
    Fertility for a Selected Area of Kenya. Nairobi: The
    Ministry. Central Bureau of Statistics. Demographic
    Working Paper #3. June, 1976. 10p.
Komma, Toru
    "The Women's Self Help Association Movement Among the
    Kipsigis of Kenya." (In) Wada, S. and Eguchi, P.K.
    (eds.). Africa 3. Osaka, Japan: National Museum of
    Ethnology. Senri Ethnological Studies #15. 1984. pp.
    145-186.
Krystall, Abigail
    The Education of Women Since Independence. Nairobi:
    University of Kenya. Bureau of Educational Research
    Paper. 1976. pp. 2-24.
LeVine, Robert A.
    "Influences of Women's Schooling on Maternal Behavior in
    the Third World." Comparative Education Review. Volume
    24 #2 Part Two June, 1980. pp. S78-S105.
Leonard, D.K.
    Reaching the Peasant Farmer: Organization Theory and
    Practice in Kenya. Chicago: University of Chicago Press.
    1977.
Leonard, D.K. and Kimenya, P. and Muzaale, P. and Ngugi, D.
and Oyugi, W.
    An Evaluation of the Components Needed to Improve the
    Performance of Kenya's Agricultural Extension Service.
    Nairobi, Kenya: Ministry of Agriculture. 1982.
Lesthaeghe, Ron J. and Vanderhoeft, C. and Becker, Stan and
Kibet, M.
    Individual and Contextual Effects of Education on
    Proximate Fertility Determinants and Life Time Fertility
    in Kenya. Brussels, Belgium: Vrije Universiteit Brussel.
    Interuniversity Programme in Demography. IDS Working
    Paper #1983-2. 1983. 67p.

Lesthaeghe, Ron J. and Vanderhoeft, C. and Becker, Stan and
Kibet, M.
    Individual and Contextual Effects of Female Education on
    the Kenya Marital Fertility Transition. Brussels,
    Belgium: Vrije Universiteit Brussel. Interuniversity
    Programme in Demography. IPD Working Paper #1983-9.
    1983. 19p.
Lindsay, Beverly
    "An Examination of Education, Social Change and National
    Development Policy: The Case of Kenyan Women." (In)
    Women and Politics in 20th Century Africa and Asia.
    Williamsburg, Virginia: College of William and Mary.
    Anthropology Department. Studies in Third World
    Societies. #16. June, 1981. pp. 29-48.
Lindsay, Beverly
    "Career Aspirations of Kenyan Women." Journal of Negro
    Education. Volume 49 #4 Fall, 1980. pp. 432-440.
Lindsay, Beverly
    "Comparative Perspectives of Kenya Women on Career
    Choices." International Education Journal. Volume 5 #2
    1976. pp. 15-32.
Lura, Russell P.
    "Population Change in Kericho District, Kenya: An Example
    of Fertility Increase in Africa." African Studies
    Review. Volume 28 #1 March, 1985. pp. 45-56.
Mkangi, George C.
    "Education, Poverty and Fertility Among the Wataita of
    Kenya." (In) Epstein, T. Scarlett and Jackson, Darrell
    (eds.). The Feasibility of Fertility Planning. Oxford,
    England: Pergamon Press. 1977. pp. 173-182.
Mott, Susan H.
    "Modernization and Fertility Orientation in Kenya." Ph.D
    Dissertation: Ohio State University. Columbus, Ohio.
    1982. 165p.
Munene, Fibi
    "Women in Africa: A Kenyan Perspective." Africa Report.
    Volume 22 #1 January-February, 1977. pp. 18-20.
Musyoki, Rachel N.
    "Education and Desired Family Size: A Study of Kenyan
    Youth." Ph.D Dissertation: Florida State University.
    Tallahassee, Florida. 1983. 196p.
Muzale, P. and Leonard, D.K.
    Women's Groups and Extension in Kenya: Their Impact on
    Food Production and Malnutrition in Baringo, Busia and
    Taita Taveta. Nairobi, Kenya: Ministry of Agriculture.
    1982.
Njuki, Caroline W.
    "Problems of Access to Women's Education in Kenya." Ph.D
    Dissertation: University of Pittsburgh. Pittsburgh,
    Pennsylvania. 1982. 181p.
Pala, Achola O.
    "Women and Development: An Overview on Kenya." Paper
    Presented at the Seminiar on Women in Rural Development.

Washington, D.C.: American Council on Education.
Overseas Liaison Committee. April 21-23, 1976.

Pala, Achola O.
A Preliminary Survey of Avenues for and Constraints of
Women's Involvement in the Development Process in Kenya.
Nairobi: University of Nairobi. Institute of Development
Studies. Discussion Paper #218. 1976.

Riria, J.V.N.
"What Kenyan Women Want." Journal of Eastern African
Research and Development. Volume 13 1983. pp. 55-68.

Smock, Audrey C.
Women's Education and Roles in Kenya. Nairobi:
University of Nairobi. Institute of Development Studies.
Working Paper #316. July, 1977.

Whiting, Beatrice B.
"Woman's Role in Social Change: Education and the Kikuyu
of Kenya." Cultural Survival Quarterly. Volume 8 #2
Summer, 1984. pp. 43-45.

EMPLOYMENT AND LABOR

Akerele, Olubanke
Women Workers in Ghana, Kenya, Zambia: A Comparative
Analysis of Women's Employment in the Modern Wage
Sector. Addis Ababa, Ethiopia: United Nations Economic
Commission for Africa. African Training and Research
Center for Women. 1979. 109p.

Anderson, Mary B.
"Kenya: Egerton College." (In) Overholt, Catherine and
Anderson, Mary B. and Cloud, Kathleen and Austin, James
(eds.). Gender Roles in Development Projects: A Case
Book. West Hartford, Connecticut: Kumarian Press. 1985.
pp. 185-213.

Anker, Richard and Knowles, James C.
"A Micro Analysis of Female Labour Force Participation in
Kenya." (In) Standing, G. And Sheehan, G. (eds.).
Labour Force Participation in Low Income Countries.
Geneva: International Labour Organization. 1978.

Anker, Richard and Knowles, James C.
Population Growth, Employment and Economic Demographic
Interactions in Kenya: Bachue-Kenya. New York: St.
Martin's Press. 1983. 735p.

Anonymous
"The Women Sing of Harambee." Agenda. Volume 1 #2
February, 1978. pp. 15-18.

Bifani, Patricia and Adagala, Kavetsa and Kariuki, Patricia
W.
The Impact of Development of Women in Kenya: A
Methodological Approach. Nairobi: UNICEF. 1982. 118p.

Bujra, Janet M.
"Women 'Entrepreneurs' in Early Nairobi." (In) Sumner,
Colin (ed.). Crime, Justice and Underdevelopment.

London: Heineman. Cambridge Studies in Criminology.
#46. 1982.
Bujra, Janet M.
"Women 'Entrepreneurs' of Early Nairobi." (In) Summer,
C. (ed.). Crime, Justice and Underdevelopment. London:
Heinemann. 1982.
Butterfield, Cynthia
Women and the Modern Wage Sector: A Study of Female
Participation in Commercial Banks and Finance Companies
in Nairobi. Nairobi: University of Nairobi. Institute
for Development Studies. Discussion Paper 256. 1977.
28p.
Buzzard, Shirley
"Women's Status and Wage Employment in Kisumu, Kenya."
Ph.D Dissertation: American University. Washington D.C.
1982. 289p.
Cooper, Frederick
From Slaves to Squatters: Plantation Labor and
Agriculture in Zanzibar and Coastal Kenya, 1890-1925.
New Haven, Connecticut: Yale University Press. 1980.
328p.
Feldman, Rayah
Employment Problems of Rural Women in Kenya. Addis
Ababa, Ethiopia: International Labour Office. JASPA.
1981.
Kanyiri, Elisha M.
"The Socioeconomic and Demographic Factors Influencing
Contraceptive Behavior in Kenya." Ph.D Dissertation:
Florida State University. Tallahassee, Florida. 1984.
143p.
Kayongo-Male, Diana
"Problems and Prospects of Integrating Women into
Development Planning and Process in Kenya." Journal of
Eastern African Research and Development. Volume 15
1985. pp. 280-296.
Kneerim, Jill
Village Women Organize: The Mraru Bus Service. New York:
Carnegie Corporation. Volume One of the Seeds Pamphlet
Series #3. 1980. 20p.
Knotts, Mary A.
"The Social and Economic Factors Associated With the
Rural-Urban Migration of Kenyan Women." Ph.D
Dissertation: Johns Hopkins University. Baltimore,
Maryland. 1977. 306p.
Komma, Toru
"The Women's Self-Help Association Movement Among the
Kipsigis of Kenya." Senri Ethnological Studies. Volume
15 1984. pp. 145-186.
Kongstad, P. and Monsted, Mette
Family, Labour and Trade in Western Kenya. Uppsala,
Sweden: Scandinavian Institute of African Studies. 1980.

Leonard, D.K. and Kimenya, P. and Muzaale, P. and Ngugi, D. and Oyugi, W.
An Evaluation of the Components Needed to Improve the Performance of Kenya's Agricultural Extension Service. Nairobi, Kenya: Ministry of Agriculture. 1982.

Lewis, Barbara C.
"The Impact of Development Policies on Women." (In) Hay, Margaret J. and Stichter, Sharon (eds.). African Women South of the Sahara. New York: Longman. 1984. pp. 170-187.

Lindsay, Beverly
"Career Aspirations of Kenyan Women." Journal of Negro Education. Volume 49 #4 Fall, 1980. pp. 432-440.

Lindsay, Beverly
"Comparative Perspectives of Kenya Women on Career Choices." International Education Journal. Volume 5 #2 1976. pp. 15-32.

Mickelwait, Donald R. and Riegelman, Mary Ann and Sweet, Charles F.
Women in Rural Development: A Survey of the Roles of Women in Ghana, Lesotho, Kenya, Nigeria... Boulder, Colorado: Westview Press. 1976. 224p.

Mohan, P.C.
"Of the Women, By the Women, For Everybody: A Goat Project in Kenya." Ideas and Action Bulletin #144 1981.

Monstead, Mette
The Changing Division of Labour Within Rural Families in Kenya. Copenhagen, Denmark: Centre for Development Research. 1977.

Monstead, Mette
The Changing Division of Labour Within Rural Families in Kenya. Nairobi: University of Nairobi. Centre for Development Research. 1976.

Monsted, Mette
"The Changing Division of Labor Within Rural Families in Kenya." (In) Caldwell, John C. (ed.). The Persistence of High Fertility: Population Prospects in the Third World. Canberra, Australia: Australian National University. 1977. pp. 259-312.

Moock, P.R.
"Efficiency of Women as Farm Managers: Kenya." American Journal of Agricultural Economics. Volume 58 #5 December, 1976. pp. 831-835.

Mott, Frank L. and Shapiro, D.
"Seasonal Variations in Labor Force Activity and Intrahousehold Substitution of Labor in Rural Kenya." Journal of Developing Areas. Volume 18 #4 July, 1984. pp. 449-463.

Mutiso, Roberta M.
Career Role/Family Role Conflict Among Women Agricultural Extension Officers in Kenya. Nairobi: University of Nairobi. 1978.

Muzale, P. and Leonard, D.K.
   Women'a Groups and Extension in Kenya: Their Impact on
   Food Production and Malnutrition in Baringo, Busia and
   Taita Taveta. Nairobi, Kenya: Ministry of Agriculture.
   1982.
Mwaria, Cheryl B.
   "Rural-Urban Labor Migration and Family Arrangements
   Among the Kamba." (In) Robinson, Pearl T. and Skinner,
   Elliott (eds.). Transformation and Resiliency in Africa.
   Washington, D.C.: Howard University Press. 1983. pp.
   29-43.
Nelson, Nici
   "How Women and Men Get By: The Sexual Division of Labour
   in the Informal Sector of a Nairobi Squatter Settlement."
   (In) Bromley, Ray and Gerry, Chris (eds.). Casual Work
   and Poverty in Third World Cities. New York: John Wiley
   and Sons. 1979. pp. 283-302.
Nyonyntono, Rebecca M.
   Women as Agents of Change in Developing Countries: The
   Case of Kenya. Nairobi: University of Nairobi. 1982.
Ogutu, M.A.
   "The Changing Role of Women in the Commercial History of
   Busia District in Kenya, 1900-1983." Journal of Eastern
   African Research and Development. Volume 15 1985. pp.
   56-73.
Ojiambo, Julia
   "Women and Development in Kenya." Paper Presented at the
   15th World Conference of the Society for International
   Development. Amsterdam, Netherlands. Nov. 28-Dec. 3,
   1976. 17p.
Pala, Achola O. and Krystall, Abigail
   Women in Rural Development. Nairobi: University of
   Nairobi. Bureau of Education Research. 1978.
Palmer, Ingrid
   "New Official Ideas on Women and Development." Institute
   for Development Studies. Volume 10 #3 1979. pp. 42-53.
Presley, Cora A.
   Kikuyu Women as Wage Labourers: 1919-1960. Nairobi:
   University of Nairobi. Department of History. Staff
   Seminar. Paper #24. 1978. 20p.
Smock, Audrey C.
   Women's Education and Roles in Kenya. Nairobi:
   University of Nairobi. Institute of Development Studies.
   Working Paper #316. July, 1977.
Stichter, Sharon B.
   Women and the Labor Force in Kenya, 1895-1964. Nairobi:
   University of Nairobi. Institute for Development
   Studies. Discussion Paper #258. 1977. 26p.
Stichter, Sharon B.
   Women in the Labor Force in Kenya: Some Effects on Their
   Family Roles. Boston: University of Massachusetts. 1978.
Stichter, Sharon B.
   "Women in the Urban Labor Force in Kenya." Paper

Presented to the Wellesley Conference on Women and
Development. Wellesley, Massachusetts: Wellesley
College. Wellesley Center for Research on Women. June,
1976.
Strobel, Margaret A.
"Slavery and Reproductive Labor in Mombasa." (In)
Robertson, Claire C. and Klein, Martin A. (eds.). Women
and Slavery in Africa. Madison, Wisconsin: University of
Wisconsin Press. 1983. pp. 111-129.
Thadani, Veena N.
Social Relations and Geographic Mobility: Male and Female
Migration in Kenya. New York: Population Council.
Center for Policy Studies. Working Paper #85. June,
1982. 67p.
Thadani, Veena N.
"Women in Nairobi: The Paradox of Urban Progress."
African Urban Studies. #3 Winter, 1978.
Thrupp. Lori-Ann
"Women, Wood and Work: In Kenya and Beyond." Unasylva.
Volume 36 #146 1984.
United Nations Economic Commission for Africa (UNECA)
Women Workers in Ghana-Kenya-Zambia: A Comparative
Analysis of Women's Employment in the Modern Wage
Sector. Addis Ababa, Ethiopia: UNECA. 1979.
Ventura, Dias
"Modernisation, Production Organization and Rural Women
in Kenya." (In) Ahmed, Iftikhar (ed.). Technology and
Rural Women: Conceptual and Empirical Issues. Boston:
George Allen and Unwin. 1985. pp. 157-210.
Wachtel, Eleanor
"Minding Her Own Business: Women Shopkeepers in Nakuru,
Kenya." African Urban Notes. Volume 2 #2 Spring, 1976.
pp. 27-42.
Wanjala, Esther
"Kenya." ISIS Women's World. #4 December, 1984.
Wasow, Bernard
"The Working Age Sex Ratio and Job Search Migration in
Kenya." Journal of Developing Areas. Volume 15 #3
April, 1981. pp. 435-444.
White, Luise S.
"A Colonial State and an African Petty Bourgeoisie:
Prostitution, Property and Class Struggle in Nairobi,
1936-1940." (In) Cooper, Frederick (ed.). Struggle for
the City: Migrant Labour, Capital, and the State in Urban
Africa. Beverly Hills, California: Sage Publications.
African Modernization and Development Series #8. 1983.
pp. 167-194.
White, Luise S.
"A History of Prostitution in Nairobi, Kenya. c.
1900-1952." Ph.D Dissertation: University of Cambridge.
London, England. 1983.
White, Luise S.
Women's Domestic Labor in Colonial Kenya: Prostitution in

Nairobi, 1909-1950. Brookline, Massachusetts: Boston
University. African Studies Center. Working Paper #30.
1980. 26p.
Whiting, Martha and Krystall, Abigail
The Impact of Rural Water Supply Projects on Women.
Nairobi: University of Nairobi. Bureau of Educational
Research. 1979.
Wilson, G.M.
"A Study of Prostitution in Mombasa." (In) Muga, Erasto.
Studies in Prostitution: East, West and South Africa,
Zaire and Nevada. Nairobi: Kenya Literature Bureau.
1980. pp. 130-141.

EQUALITY AND LIBERATION

Harris, Joan
"Women in Kenya: Revolution or Evolution?" Africa
Report. Volume 30 #2 March-April, 1985. pp. 30-32.
Riria, J.V.N.
"What Kenyan Women Want." Journal of Eastern African
Research and Development. Volume 13 1983. pp. 55-68.
Staudt, Kathleen A.
"Administrative Resources, Political Patrons, and
Redressing Sexual Inequities: A Case From Western Kenya."
Journal of Developing Areas. Volume 12 #4 July, 1978.
pp. 399-414.

FAMILY LIFE

Eastman, C.M.
"Waungwana na Wanawake: Muslim Ethnicity and Sexual
Segregation in Coastal Kenya." Journal of Multilingual
and Multicultural Development. Volume 5 #2 1984. pp.
97-112.
Gatara, Timothy H.
"The Influence of Religion and Education on Current
Family Size and Fertility Preference in Kenya." Ph.D
Dissertation: Florida State University. Tallahassee,
Florida. 1982. 152p.
Jackson, Kennell A.
"The Family Entity and Famine Among the 19th Century
Akamba of Kenya: Social Responses to Environmental
Stress." Journal of Family History. Volume 1 Winter,
1976. pp. 192-215.
Kabwegyere, Tarsis and Mbula, J.
A Case of the Akamba of Eastern Kenya. Canberra,
Australia: Australian National University. Department of
Demography. Changing African Family Project. Monograph
Series #5. 1979. 100p.
Kelley, Allen C. and Swartz, Caroline
"The Impact of Family Structure on Microeconomic Decision

Making in Developing Countries: A Case Study of Nuclear and Extended Families in Urban Kenya." (In) International Union for the Scientific Study of Population (IUSSP). Economic and Demographic Change: Issues for the 1980's: Proceedings of the Conference on Economic and Demographic Change, 1978. Liege, Belgium: (IUSSP). Volume One. Helsinki, Finland. 1979. pp. 361-375.

Kershaw, Greet
"The Changing Roles of Men and Women in the Kikuyu Family by Socioeconomic Strata." Rural Africana. Volume 29 Winter, 1976. pp. 173-194.

Knotts, Mary A.
"The Social and Economic Factors Associated With the Rural-Urban Migration of Kenyan Women." Ph.D Dissertation: Johns Hopkins University. Baltimore, Maryland. 1977. 306p.

Kongstad, P. and Monsted, Mette
Family, Labour and Trade in Western Kenya. Uppsala, Sweden: Scandinavian Institute of African Studies. 1980.

Kune, J.B.
"Machakos Project Studies: Agents Affecting Health of Mother and Child in a Rural Area of Kenya. XV. The Economic Setting at the Household Level." Tropical and Geographical Medicine. Volume 31 #3 September, 1979. pp. 441-457.

Kuria, Gibson K.
"The African or Customary Marriage in Kenya Law Today." Paper Presented at the Conference on Conceptualizing the Household. Cambridge, Massachusetts: Harvard University. November, 1984.

LeVine, Robert A.
"Influences of Women's Schooling on Maternal Behavior in the Third World." Comparative Education Review. Volume 24 #2 Part Two June, 1980. pp. S78-S105.

Maina, Rose and Muchai, V.W. and Gutto, S.B.O.
"Law and the Status of Women in Kenya." (In) Columbia Human Rights Law Review (eds.). Law and the Status of Women: An International Symposium. New York: United Nations. Centre for Social Development and Humanitarian Affairs. 1977. pp. 185-206.

Mbulu, J.
Women and the Family. Nairobi: Ministry of Transportation and Communications. Roads and Aerodromes Department. 1981.

McAdoo, Harriette P.
"Extended Family Involvement and Roles of Urban Kenyan Women." Paper Presented at the Women in the African Diaspora: An Interdisciplinary Perspective Research Conference. Washington, D.C.: Howard University. June, 1983.

Merryman, Nancy H.
"Economy and Ecological Stress: Household Strategies of

Transitional Somali Pastoralists in Northern Kenya."
Ph.D Dissertation: Northwestern University. Evanston,
Illinois. 1984. 338p.
Monstead, Mette
The Changing Division of Labour Within Rural Families in
Kenya. Copenhagen, Denmark: Centre for Development
Research. 1977.
Monstead, Mette
The Changing Division of Labour Within Rural Families in
Kenya. Nairobi: University of Nairobi. Centre for
Development Research. 1976.
Monsted, Mette
"The Changing Division of Labor Within Rural Families in
Kenya." (In) Caldwell, John C. (ed.). The Persistence
of High Fertility: Population Prospects in the Third
World. Canberra, Australia: Australian National
University. 1977. pp. 259-312.
Mott, Frank L. and Shapiro, D.
"Seasonal Variations in Labor Force Activity and
Intrahousehold Substitution of Labor in Rural Kenya."
Journal of Developing Areas. Volume 18 #4 July, 1984.
pp. 449-463.
Mutiso, Roberta M.
Career Role/Family Role Conflict Among Women Agricultural
Extension Officers in Kenya. Nairobi: University of
Nairobi. 1978.
Mwaria, Cheryl B.
"Rural-Urban Labor Migration and Family Arrangements
Among the Kamba." (In) Robinson, Pearl T. and Skinner,
Elliott (eds.). Transformation and Resiliency in Africa.
Washington, D.C.: Howard University Press. 1983. pp.
29-43.
Nelson, Nici
"Dependence and Independence: Female Household Heads in
Mathare Valley, A Squatter Community in Nairobi, Kenya."
Ph.D Dissertation: University of London. School of
Oriental and African Studies. London, England. 1977.
Nelson, Nici
"Female-Centered Families: Changing Patterns of Marriage
and Family Among Buzaa Brewers of Mathari Valley."
African Urban Studies. #3 Winter, 1978. pp. 85-103.
Nelson, Nici
"Is Fostering of Children on the Increase in Central
Kenya? Parental Strategies in a Situation of Accelerating
Urbanization and Economic Stratification." Paper
Presented at the Conference on the History of the Family
in Africa. London: Cambridge University. School of
Oriental and African Studies. September, 1981.
Nyonyntono, Rebecca M.
"Poverty and the Changing Family in the African Context."
Paper Presented at the Seminar on the Changing Family in
the African Context, Maseru, Lesotho, 1983. Paris:

United Nations Educational, Scientific and Cultural
Organization. 1984. 23p.
Reining, Priscilla (ed.)
Village Women: Their Changing Lives and Fertility:
Studies in Kenya. Mexico and the Philippines.
Washington, D.C.: American Association for the
Advancement of Science. AAAS Publication #77-6. 1977.
273p.
Schulpen, T.W.
"Machakos Project Studies. Agents Affecting Health of
Mother and Child in a Rural Area of Kenya. XIX. The
Utilization of Health Services in a Rural Area of Kenya."
Tropical and Geographical Medicine. Volume 32 #4
December, 1980. pp. 340-349.
Stichter, Sharon B.
Women in the Labor Force in Kenya: Some Effects on Their
Family Roles. Boston: University of Massachusetts.
1978.
Stichter, Sharon B.
"Women in the Urban Labor Force in Kenya." Paper
Presented to the Wellesley Conference on Women and
Development. Wellesley, Massachusetts: Wellesley
College. Wellesley Center for Research on Women. June,
1976.
Thadani, Veena N.
Social Relations and Geographic Mobility: Male and Female
Migration in Kenya. New York: Population Council.
Center for Policy Studies. Working Paper #85. June,
1982. 67p.
Voorhoeve, A.M.
"Machakos Project Studies. Agents Affecting Health of
Mother and Child in A Rural Area of Kenya. XXI.
Antenatal and Delivery Care." Tropical and Geographical
Medicine. Volume 34 #1 March, 1982. pp. 91-101.
Voorhoeve, A.M.
"Machakos Project Studies: Agents Affecting Health of
Mother and Child in a Rural Area of Kenya. XVI. The
Outcome of Pregnancy." Tropical and Geographical
Medicine. Volume 31 #4 December, 1979. pp. 607-627.
Wanjala, Esther
"Kenya." ISIS Women's World. #4 December, 1984.
Whiting, Beatrice B.
"Woman's Role in Social Change: Education and the Kikuyu
of Kenya." Cultural Survival Quarterly. Volume 8 #2
Summer, 1984. pp. 43-45.

FAMILY PLANNING AND CONTRACEPTION

Aggarwal, V.P. and Mati, J.K.G.
"Epidemiology of Induced Abortion in Nairobi, Kenya."
Journal of Obstetrics and Gynaecology of Eastern and
Central Africa. Volume 1 #2 June, 1982. pp. 54-57.

Ayiemba, Elias H.
"Intercensal Fertility Change in Kenya: A Study of
Regional Differentials Between 1969-1979." PIDSA
Abstracts. Volume 5 #1 December, 1982. pp. 5-22.

Diepenhorst, M.J.
Population Problems and Family Planning in Five
Countries: A Transcultural Reconnaissance. Amsterdam,
Netherlands: Koninklijk Instituut Voor de Tropen. 1982.
228p.

Dow, Thomas E. and Werner, Linda H.
"Family Size and Family Planning in Kenya: Continuity and
Change in Metropolitan and Rural Attitudes." Studies in
Family Planning. Volume 12 #6-7 June-July, 1981. pp.
272-277.

Dow, Thomas E. and Werner, Linda H.
"Modern, Transitional, and Traditional Demographic and
Contraceptive Patterns Among Kenyan Women." Studies in
Family Planning. Volume 13 #1 January, 1982. pp.
12-23.

Dow, Thomas E. and Werner, Linda H.
"Perceptions of Family Planning Among Rural Kenyan
Women." Studies in Family Planning. Volume 14 #2
February, 1983. pp. 35-43.

Dow, Thomas E. and Werner, Linda H.
A Note on Modern, Transitional and Traditional
Demographic and Contraceptive Patterns Among Kenyan
Women, 1977-1978. Nairobi: University of Nairobi.
Population Studies and Research Institute. January,
1981. 29p.

Dow, Thomas E. and Werner, Linda H.
Continuity and Change in Metropolitan and Rural Attitudes
Towards Family Size and Family Planning in Kenya Between
1966/67-1977/78. Nairobi: University of Nairobi.
Population Studies and Research Institute. February,
1981. 17p.

Emereuwaonu, Ernest U.
"Determinants of Fertility: A Regression Analysis of
Kenya Data." Genus. Volume 40 #3/4 July-December,
1984. pp. 77-96.

Emereuwaonu, Ernest U.
"Marital Fertility, Desired Family Size, Communication
Channel and Modern Reproductive Values in an African
City." Ph.D Dissertation: University of California Los
Angeles. Los Angeles, California. 1977. 216p.

Eraj, Yusuf A.
"Integration of Family Planning and Maternal and Child
Health Services: Problems of and the Safeguards
Required." (In) International Planned Parenthood
Federation (IPPF). Proceedings of the IPPF Africa
Regional Conference. London: IPPF. 1977. pp. 103-107.

Ferry, Benoit and Page, Hilary J.
The Proximate Differentials of Fertility and Their Effect
on Fertility Patterns: An Illustrative Analysis Applied

to Kenya. Voorburg, Netherlands: International Statistical Institute. WFS Scientific Reports #71. December, 1984. 54p.

Gachuhi, J. Mugo
"African Youth." (In) International Planned Parenthood Federation (IPPF). Proceedings of the IPPF Africa Regional Conference. London: IPPF. 1977. pp. 192-224.

Hull, Valerie and Simpson, Mayling
Breastfeeding, Child Health and Child Spacing: Cross-Cultural Perspectives. Dover, New Hampshire: Croom Helm. 1985. 216p.

Kabwegyere, Tarsis
"Determinants of Fertility: A Discussion of Change in the Family Among the Akamba of Kenya." (In) Caldwell, John C. (ed.). The Persistence of High Fertility: Population Prospects in the Third World. Canberra, Australia: Australian National University. Volume One. 1977. pp. 189-222.

Kabwegyere, Tarsis and Mbula, J.
A Case of the Akamba of Eastern Kenya. Canberra, Australia: Australian National University. Department of Demography. Changing African Family Project. Monograph Series #5. 1979. 100p.

Kangi, M.W.
"Some Factors Affecting Urban-Rural Fertility Differentials in Kenya: A Case Study of Nairobi and Central Province." Kenyan Geographer. Volume 4 #1/2 1982. pp. 29-49.

Kanyiri, Elisha M.
"The Socioeconomic and Demographic Factors Influencing Contraceptive Behavior in Kenya." Ph.D Dissertation: Florida State University. Tallahassee, Florida. 1984. 143p.

Kenya. Ministry of Finance and Economic Planning
"Continuity and Change in Metropolitan and Rural Attitudes Towards Family Size and Family Planning in Kenya Between 1966/1967 and 1977/1978." Social Perspectives. Volume 5 #1 December, 1980. 8p.

Kenya. Ministry of Finance and Economic Planning
"Demographic and Contraceptive Patterns Among Kenyan Women: 1977-1978." Social Perspectives. Volume 6 #2 April, 1981. 16p.

Kenya. Ministry of Finance and Economic Planning
"Modernization, Birth Spacing and Marital Fertility in Kenya." Social Perspectives. Volume 6 #5 September, 1981. 12p

Kenya. Ministry of Finance and Economic Planning
Educational Characteristics and Their Relationship to Fertility for a Selected Area of Kenya. Nairobi: The Ministry. Central Bureau of Statistics. Demographic Working Paper #3. June, 1976. 10p.

Lesthaeghe, Ron J. and Vanderhoeft, C. and Becker, Stan and
Kibet, M.
    Individual and Contextual Effects of Education on
    Proximate Fertility Determinants and Life Time Fertility
    in Kenya. Brussels, Belgium: Vrije Universiteit Brussel.
    Interuniversity Programme in Demography. IDS Working
    Paper #1983-2. 1983. 67p.
Lesthaeghe, Ron J. and Vanderhoeft, C. and Becker, Stan and
Kibet, M.
    Individual and Contextual Effects of Female Education on
    the Kenya Marital Fertility Transition. Brussels,
    Belgium: Vrije Universiteit Brussel. Interuniversity
    Programme in Demography. IPD Working Paper #1983-9.
    1983. 19p.
Lesthaeghe, Ron J. and Eelens, Frank
    Social Organization and Reproductive Regimes: Lessons
    From Sub-Saharan Africa and Historical Western Europe.
    Brussels, Belgium: Vrije Universiteit Brussel.
    Interuniversity Programme in Demography. IDP Working
    Paper #1985-1. 1985. 64p.
Mhloyi, Marvellous M.
    "Fertility Determinants: A Comparative Study Of Kenya and
    Lesotho." Ph.D Dissertation: University of Pennsylvania.
    Philadelphia, Pennsylvania. 1984. 342p.
Mosley, W. Henry and Werner, Linda H.
    Some Determinants of Marital Fertility in Kenya: A Birth
    Interval Analysis From the 1978 Kenya Fertility Survey.
    Nairobi: University of Nairobi. Population Studies and
    Research Institute. Central Bureau of Statistics.
    Unpublished. 1980.
Mosley, W. Henry and Werner, Linda H. and Becker, Stan
    The Dynamics of Birth Spacing and Marital Fertility in
    Kenya. Voorburg, Netherlands: International Statistical
    Institute. World Fertility Survey. Scientific Reports
    #30. August, 1982. 30p.
Mott, Susan H.
    "Modernization and Fertility Orientation in Kenya." Ph.D
    Dissertation: Ohio State University. Columbus, Ohio.
    1982. 165p.
Musyoki, Rachel N.
    "Education and Desired Family Size: A Study of Kenyan
    Youth." Ph.D Dissertation: Florida State University.
    Tallahassee, Florida. 1983. 196p.
Mwaniki, N. and Marasha, M. and Mati, J.K.G. and Mwaniki,
M.K. (eds.)
    Surgical Contraception in Sub-Saharan Africa:
    Proceedings. Nairobi: University of Nairobi. Paper
    Presented at a Conference May 8-13, 1977. Sponsored by
    the Pathfinder Fund. Chestnut Hill, Massachusetts.
    1979. 182p.
Newman, James L. and Lura, Russell P.
    "Fertility Control in Africa." Geographical Review.
    Volume 73 #4 October, 1983. pp. 396-406.

Olusanya, P.O.
    The Demographic, Health, Economic and Social Impact of
    Family Planning in Selected African Countries. Addis
    Ababa, Ethiopia: United Nations Economic Commission for
    Africa. ECA/PD/1985-9. March, 1985. 97p.
Richter, Kerry and Adlakha, Arjun
    The Effect of Infant and Child Mortality on Subsequent
    Fertility. Washington, D.C.: U.S. Department of
    Commerce. U.S. Bureau of the Census. Center for
    International Research. 1985.
Shepherd, Gilliam M.
    Responding to the Contraception Needs of the Rural
    People: Kenya, 1984. Oxford, England: OXFAM. 1984.
Smith, Susan E. and Radel, David
    "The KAP in Kenya: A Critical Look at Survey
    Methodology." (In) Marshall, John F. and Polgar, Steven
    (eds.). Culture, Natality and Family Planning. Chapel
    Hill, North Carolina: University of North Carolina.
    Carolina Population Center. 1976. pp. 263-287.
Smock, Audrey C.
    "Measuring Rural Women's Economic Roles and Contributions
    in Kenya." Studies in Family Planning. Volume 10 #11/12
    November-December, 1979. pp. 385-390.

FERTILITY AND INFERTILITY

Agbasi, Gabriel O.
    "Differential Fertility in Urban Kenya." Ph.D
    Dissertation: Fordham University. New York, New York.
    1977. 424p.
Amobi, Nnambi K.
    Microeconomic Determinants of Fertility in Kenya. New
    York: University of New York. 1980.
Anker, Richard and Knowles, James C.
    Fertility Determinants in Developing Countries: A Case
    Study of Kenya. Liege, Belgium: International Labour
    Office. World Employment Programme. 1982. 222p.
Anker, Richard and Knowles, James C.
    Population Growth, Employment and Economic Demographic
    Interactions in Kenya: Bachue-Kenya. New York: St.
    Martin's Press. 1983. 735p.
Anker, Richard
    "Problems of Interpretation and Specification in
    Analysing Fertility Differentials: Illustrated With
    Kenyan Survey Data." (In) Farooq, Ghazi M. and Simmons,
    George B. (eds.). Fertility in Developing Countries: An
    Economic Perspective on Research and Policy Issues. New
    York: St. Martin's Press. 1985. pp. 277-311.
Anker, Richard and Knowles, James C.
    Analysis of Fertility Differentials in Kenya. Geneva:
    International Labour Office. Employment and Development
    Department. 1977.

Ayiemba, Elias H.
    "Intercensal Fertility Change in Kenya: A Study of
    Regional Differentials Between 1969-1979." PIDSA
    Abstracts. Volume 5 #1 December, 1982. pp. 5-22.
Diepenhorst, M.J.
    Population Problems and Family Planning in Five
    Countries: A Transcultural Reconnaissance. Amsterdam,
    Netherlands: Koninklijk Instituut Voor de Tropen. 1982.
    228p.
Dow, Thomas E. and Werner, Linda H.
    "Family Size and Family Planning in Kenya: Continuity and
    Change in Metropolitan and Rural Attitudes." Studies in
    Family Planning. Volume 12 #6-7 June-July, 1981. pp.
    272-277.
Dow, Thomas E. and Werner, Linda H.
    "Prospects for Fertility Decline in Rural Kenya."
    Population and Development Review. Volume 9 #1 March,
    1983. pp. 77-97+.
Eelens, Frank
    Impact of Breast-Feeding on Infant and Child Mortality
    With Varying Incidence of Malaria--Evidence From the
    Kenya Fertility Survey, 1977-78. Brussels, Belgium:
    Vrije Universiteit Brussel. Interuniversity Programme in
    Demography. IDP Working Paper #1983-3. 1983. 29p.
Eelens, Frank and Donne, L.
    The Proximate Determinants of Fertility in Sub-Saharan
    Africa: A Factbook Based on the Results of the World
    Fertility Survey. Brussels, Belgium: Vrije Universiteit
    Brussel. Interuniversity Programme in Demography. IDP
    Working Paper #1985-3. 1985. 122p.
Emereuwaonu, Ernest U.
    "Determinants of Fertility: A Regression Analysis of
    Kenya Data." Genus. Volume 40 #3/4 July-December,
    1984. pp. 77-96.
Emereuwaonu, Ernest U.
    "Marital Fertility, Desired Family Size, Communication
    Channel and Modern Reproductive Values in an African
    City." Ph.D Dissertation: University of California Los
    Angeles. Los Angeles, California. 1977. 216p.
Faruqee, Rashid
    "Fertility and its Trend in Kenya." Rural Africana. #14
    Fall, 1982. pp. 25-48.
Ferry, Benoit and Page, Hilary J.
    The Proximate Differentials of Fertility and Their Effect
    on Fertility Patterns: An Illustrative Analysis Applied
    to Kenya. Voorburg, Netherlands: International
    Statistical Institute. WFS Scientific Reports #71.
    December, 1984. 54p.
Gatara, Timothy H.
    "The Influence of Religion and Education on Current
    Family Size and Fertility Preference in Kenya." Ph.D
    Dissertation: Florida State University. Tallahassee,
    Florida. 1982. 152p.

Greeley, Edward H.
"Men and Fertility Regulation in Southern Meru: A Case Study From the Kenya Highlands." Ph.D Dissertation: Catholic University of America. Washington, D.C. 1977. 273p.

Gyepi-Garbrah, Benjamin
Adolescent Fertility in Kenya. Boston: Pathfinder Fund. 1985. 62p.

Henin, Roushdi A. and Mwobobia, I.
"Fertility Differentials in Kenya: A Cross-Regional Study." (In) Cairo Demographic Centre (CDC). Determinants of Fertility in Some African and Asian Countries. Cairo: CDC. CDC Research Monograph Series #10. 1982. pp. 313-349.

Henin, Roushdi A. and Korten, Ailsa and Werner, Linda H.
Evaluation of Birth Histories: A Case Study of Kenya. Voorburg, Netherlands: International Statistical Institute. World Fertility Survey. Scientific Report #36. 1982. 31p.

International Statistical Institute (ISI)
The Kenya Fertility Survey, 1978: A Summary of Findings. Voorburg, Netherlands: ISI. World Fertility Survey Report #26. 1978. 14p.

Kabwegyere, Tarsis
"Determinants of Fertility: A Discussion of Change in the Family Among the Akamba of Kenya." (In) Caldwell, John C. (ed.). The Persistence of High Fertility: Population Prospects in the Third World. Canberra, Australia: Australian National University. Volume One. 1977. pp. 189-222.

Kabwegyere, Tarsis and Mbula, J.
A Case of the Akamba of Eastern Kenya. Canberra, Australia: Australian National University. Department of Demography. Changing African Family Project. Monograph Series #5. 1979. 100p.

Kalule-Sabiti, I.
"Bongaart's Proximate Determinants of Fertility Applied to Group Data From the Kenya Fertility Survey, 1977/78." Journal of Biosocial Science. Volume 16 #2 April, 1984. pp. 205-218.

Kangi, M.W.
"Some Factors Affecting Urban-Rural Fertility Differentials in Kenya: A Case Study of Nairobi and Central Province." Kenyan Geographer. Volume 4 #1/2 1982. pp. 29-49.

Kenya. Central Bureau of Statistics.
Kenya Contraceptive Prevalence Survey, 1984: First Report. Nairobi: Central Bureau of Statistics. December, 1984. 121pp.

Kenya. Ministry of Finance and Economic Planning
Kenya Fertility Survey 1977/78: First Report. Nairobi: The Ministry. Central Bureau of Statistics. 1980. 257p.

Kenya. Ministry of Finance and Economic Planning
    "Major Highlights of the Kenya Fertility Survey." Social
    Perspectives. Volume 4 #2 December, 1979. 12p.
Kenya. Ministry of Finance and Economic Planning
    "Modernization, Birth Spacing and Marital Fertility in
    Kenya." Social Perspectives. Volume 6 #5 September,
    1981. 12p
Kenya. Ministry of Finance and Economic Planning
    Educational Characteristics and Their Relationship to
    Fertility for a Selected Area of Kenya. Nairobi: The
    Ministry. Central Bureau of Statistics. Demographic
    Working Paper #3. June, 1976. 10p.
Kramer, Joyce M.
    "Production and Reproduction at Various Levels of
    Participation in the Modern World System: An Analysis of
    the Effects of Urbanization on Fertility for Twelve
    Communities in Kenya." Ph.D Dissertation: University of
    North Carolina. Chapel Hill, North Carolina. 1980.
    371p.
Larsen, Ulla
    A Comparative Study of the Levels and the Covariates of
    Sterility in Cameroon, Kenya and Sudan. Princeton, New
    Jersey: Princeton University. Office of Population
    Research. 1985.
Lesthaeghe, Ron J. and Vanderhoeft, C. and Becker, Stan and
Kibet, M.
    Individual and Contextual Effects of Education on
    Proximate Fertility Determinants and Life Time Fertility
    in Kenya. Brussels, Belgium: Vrije Universiteit Brussel.
    Interuniversity Programme in Demography. IDS Working
    Paper #1983-2. 1983. 67p.
Lesthaeghe, Ron J. and Vanderhoeft, C. and Becker, Stan and
Kibet, M.
    Individual and Contextual Effects of Female Education on
    the Kenya Marital Fertility Transition. Brussels,
    Belgium: Vrije Universiteit Brussel. Interuniversity
    Programme in Demography. IPD Working Paper #1983-9.
    1983. 19p.
Lesthaeghe, Ron J. and Eelens, Frank
    Social Organization and Reproductive Regimes: Lessons
    From Sub-Saharan Africa and Historical Western Europe.
    Brussels, Belgium: Vrije Universiteit Brussel.
    Interuniversity Programme in Demography. IDP Working
    Paper #1985-1. 1985. 64p.
Lura, Russell P.
    "Population Change in Kericho District, Kenya: An Example
    of Fertility Increase in Africa." African Studies
    Review. Volume 28 #1 March, 1985. pp. 45-56.
Mathews, T. and Mati, J.K.G. and Fomulu, J.N.
    "A Study of Infertility in Kenya: Results of
    Investigation of the Infertile Couple in Nairobi." East
    African Medical Journal. Volume 58 #4 April, 1981. pp.
    288-297.

Mhloyi, Marvellous M.
    "Fertility Determinants: A Comparative Study Of Kenya and
    Lesotho." Ph.D Dissertation: University of Pennsylvania.
    Philadelphia, Pennsylvania. 1984. 342p.
Mkangi, George C.
    "Education, Poverty and Fertility Among the Wataita of
    Kenya." (In) Epstein, T. Scarlett and Jackson, Darrell
    (eds.). The Feasibility of Fertility Planning. Oxford,
    England: Pergamon Press. 1977. pp. 173-182.
Mosley, W. Henry and Werner, Linda H.
    Some Determinants of Marital Fertility in Kenya: A Birth
    Interval Analysis From the 1978 Kenya Fertility Survey.
    Nairobi: University of Nairobi. Population Studies and
    Research Institute. Central Bureau of Statistics.
    Unpublished. 1980.
Mosley, W. Henry and Werner, Linda H. and Becker, Stan
    The Dynamics of Birth Spacing and Marital Fertility in
    Kenya. Voorburg, Netherlands: International Statistical
    Institute. World Fertility Survey. Scientific Reports
    #30. August, 1982. 30p.
Mott, Susan H.
    "Modernization and Fertility Orientation in Kenya." Ph.D
    Dissertation: Ohio State University. Columbus, Ohio.
    1982. 165p.
Newman, James L. and Lura, Russell P.
    "Fertility Control in Africa." Geographical Review.
    Volume 73 #4 October, 1983. pp. 396-406.
Reining, Priscilla (ed.)
    Village Women: Their Changing Lives and Fertility:
    Studies in Kenya. Mexico and the Philippines.
    Washington, D.C.: American Association for the
    Advancement of Science. AAAS Publication #77-6. 1977.
    273p.
Richter, Kerry and Adlakha, Arjun
    The Effect of Infant and Child Mortality on Subsequent
    Fertility. Washington, D.C.: U.S. Department of
    Commerce. U.S. Bureau of the Census. Center for
    International Research. 1985.
Sindiga, Isaac
    "The Persistence of High Fertility in Kenya." Social
    Science and Medicine. Volume 20 #1 1985. pp. 77-84.
Smith, Susan E. and Radel, David
    "The KAP in Kenya: A Critical Look at Survey
    Methodology." (In) Marshall, John F. and Polgar, Steven
    (eds.). Culture, Natality and Family Planning. Chapel
    Hill, North Carolina: University of North Carolina.
    Carolina Population Center. 1976. pp. 263-287.
United Nations Economic Commission for Africa (UNECA)
    Nuptiality and Fertility (A Comparative Analysis of WFS
    Data). Addis Ababa, Ethiopia: UNECA. African Population
    Studies Series #5. 1983. 96p.

Van Ginneken, J.K. and Voorhoeve, A.M. and Omondi, Odhiambo
and Muller, A.S.
    "Agents Affecting Health of Mother and Child in a Rural
    Area of Kenya. XVIII: Fertility, Mortality and Migration
    in 1975-1978." Tropical and Geographical Medicine.
    Volume 32 #2 1980. pp. 183-188.
Waltons, S.M. and Mati, J.K.G.
    "An Evaluation of Secondary Infertility in Kenya." East
    African Medical Journal. Volume 53 #6 June, 1976. pp.
    310-314.

HEALTH, NUTRITION AND MEDICINE

Aggarwal, V.P. and Mati, J.K.G.
    "Epidemiology of Induced Abortion in Nairobi, Kenya."
    Journal of Obstetrics and Gynaecology of Eastern and
    Central Africa. Volume 1 #2 June, 1982. pp. 54-57.
Aggarwal, V.P. and Mati, J.K.G.
    "Review of Abortions in Kenyatta National Hospital,
    Nairobi." East African Medical Journal. Volume 57 #2
    February, 1980. pp. 38-144.
Boerma, J.T.
    "Birth Interval, Mortality and Growth of Children in a
    Rural Area of Kenya." Journal of Biosocial Science.
    Volume 16 #4 October, 1984. pp. 475-486.
Brainard, J.M.
    "Herders to Farmers: The Effects of Settlement on the
    Demography of the Turkana Population of Kenya." Ph.D
    Dissertation: State University of New York. Binghampton,
    New York. 1981. 356p.
Dissevelt, A.G.
    "Integrated Maternal and Child Health Services. A Study
    at a Rural Health Centre in Kenya." Tropical and
    Geographic Medicine. Volume 32 #1 March, 1980. pp.
    57-69.
Eelens, Frank
    Impact of Breast-Feeding on Infant and Child Mortality
    With Varying Incidence of Malaria--Evidence From the
    Kenya Fertility Survey, 1977-78. Brussels, Belgium:
    Vrije Universiteit Brussel. Interuniversity Programme in
    Demography. IDP Working Paper #1983-3. 1983. 29p.
Eraj, Yusuf A.
    "Integration of Family Planning and Maternal and Child
    Health Services: Problems of and the Safeguards
    Required." (In) International Planned Parenthood
    Federation (IPPF). Proceedings of the IPPF Africa
    Regional Conference. London: IPPF. 1977. pp. 103-107.
Greeley, Edward H.
    "Men and Fertility Regulation in Southern Meru: A Case
    Study From the Kenya Highlands." Ph.D Dissertation:

Catholic University of America. Washington, D.C. 1977.
273p.

Hull, Valerie and Simpson, Mayling
Breastfeeding, Child Health and Child Spacing:
Cross-Cultural Perspectives. Dover, New Hampshire: Croom
Helm. 1985. 216p.

Jackson, Kennell A.
"The Family Entity and Famine Among the 19th Century
Akamba of Kenya: Social Responses to Environmental
Stress." Journal of Family History. Volume 1 Winter,
1976. pp. 192-215.

Jansen, A.A. and Kusin, Jane A. and Thiuri, B. and Lakhani,
S.A. and Tmannetje, W.
"Anthropometric Changes During Pregnancy in Rural African
Women." (Machakos Project Studies #24) Tropical and
Geographical Medicine. Volume 36 #1 1984. pp. 91-97.

Jansen, A.A. and Lakhani, S.A. and Tmannetje, W. and Kusin,
Jane A.
"Some Nutritional Aspects of Pregnancy in Rural Kenya."
East African Medical Journal. Volume 57 1980. pp.
97-104.

Kangi, M.W.
"Some Factors Affecting Urban-Rural Fertility
Differentials in Kenya: A Case Study of Nairobi and
Central Province." Kenyan Geographer. Volume 4 #1/2
1982. pp. 29-49.

Kenya. Central Bureau of Statistics.
Kenya Contraceptive Prevalence Survey, 1984: First
Report. Nairobi: Central Bureau of Statistics.
December, 1984. 121pp.

Komma, Toru
"The Women's Self Help Association Movement Among the
Kipsigis of Kenya." (In) Wada, S. and Eguchi, P.K.
(eds.). Africa 3. Osaka, Japan: National Museum of
Ethnology. Senri Ethnological Studies #15. 1984. pp.
145-186.

Kramer, Joyce M.
"Production and Reproduction at Various Levels of
Participation in the Modern World System: An Analysis of
the Effects of Urbanization on Fertility for Twelve
Communities in Kenya." Ph.D Dissertation: University of
North Carolina. Chapel Hill, North Carolina. 1980.
371p.

Kune, J.B.
"Machakos Project Studies: Agents Affecting Health of
Mother and Child in a Rural Area of Kenya. XV. The
Economic Setting at the Household Level." Tropical and
Geographical Medicine. Volume 31 #3 September, 1979.
pp. 441-457.

Kusin, J.A.
"Infant Nutrition and Growth in Relation to Maternal
Nutrition in Rural Kenya." Journal of Tropical
Pediatrics. Volume 31 #1 February, 1985. pp. 24-30.

Kusin, J.A.
  "Vitamin A Status of Pregnant and Lactating Women as
  Assessed by Serum Levels in Machakos Area, Kenya." East
  African Medical Journal. Volume 62 #7 July, 1985. pp.
  476-479.
Lakhani, S.
  "Practical Therapeutics: Present Day Hospital Practices
  Influencing Breastfeeding in Nairobi, Kenya." East
  African Medical Journal. Volume 61 #2 February, 1984.
  pp. 163-168.
Lakhani, S.A. and Jansen, A.A.
  "Opinions About Breastfeeding Amongst Middle Income
  African and Indian Women in Nairobi." East African
  Medical Journal. Volume 61 #4 1984. pp. 266-271.
Lakhani, S.A. and Jansen, A.A. and Lacko, W. and Sequeira,
E.
  "Suggested Reference Values for Serum Total Protein and
  Fractions of African and Indian Middle Class Urban Women
  and Newborns." East African Medical Journal. Volume 61
  #2 1984. pp. 128-132.
Larsen, Ulla
  A Comparative Study of the Levels and the Covariates of
  Sterility in Cameroon, Kenya and Sudan. Princeton, New
  Jersey: Princeton University. Office of Population
  Research. 1985.
Lee, Lily W. and Winikoff, Beverly and Laukaran, Virginia
and Bongaarts, John
  Explaining the Differential Effects of Breast-Feeding on
  Duration of Amenorrhea: Frequency and Patterns of
  Breast-Feeding. New York: Population Council. 1984.
Makokha, A.E.
  "Maternal Mortality: Kenyatta National Hospital
  1972-1977." East African Medical Journal. Volume 57 #7
  July, 1980. pp. 451-460.
Mathews, T. and Mati, J.K.G. and Fomulu, J.N.
  "A Study of Infertility in Kenya: Results of
  Investigation of the Infertile Couple in Nairobi." East
  African Medical Journal. Volume 58 #4 April, 1981. pp.
  288-297.
Mbevi, Grace
  "Child Marriage and Early Teenage Childbirth." Paper
  Presented at the Seminar on Traditional Practices
  Affecting the Health of Women and Children: Female
  Circumcision, Childhood Marriage, Nutritional Taboos,
  etc. Alexandria, Egypt: World Health Organization.
  Eastern Mediterranean Regional Office. Khartoum, Sudan.
  February 10-15, 1979.
Mhloyi, Marvellous M.
  "Fertility Determinants: A Comparative Study Of Kenya and
  Lesotho." Ph.D Dissertation: University of Pennsylvania.
  Philadelphia, Pennsylvania. 1984. 342p.
Mott, S.H.
  "A Note on the Determinants of Breastfeeding Durations in

an African Country." Social Biology. Volume 31
Fall/Winter, 1984. pp. 279-289.
Mott, Susan H.
"A Note on the Determinants of Breastfeeding Durations in
an African Country." Social Biology. Volume 31 #3-4
Fall-Winter, 1984. pp. 279-289.
Muganzi, Zibeon S.
"The Effect of Individual and Contextual Factors on
Infant Mortality in Kenya." Ph.D Dissertation: Florida
State University. Tallahassee, Florida. 1984. 172p.
Muller, A.S. and Ouma, J.H. and Mburu, F.M. and Blok, P.G.
"Agents Affecting Health of Mother and Child in a Rural
Area of Kenya." Tropical and Geographical Medicine.
Volume 29 #3 1977. pp. 291-302.
Murray, Joselyn
"The Church Missionary Society and the 'Female
Circumcision' Issue in Kenya, 1929-1932." Journal of
Religion in Africa. Volume 8 #2 1976. pp. 92-104.
Muzale, P. and Leonard, D.K.
Women's Groups and Extension in Kenya: Their Impact on
Food Production and Malnutrition in Baringo, Busia and
Taita Taveta. Nairobi, Kenya: Ministry of Agriculture.
1982.
Njoki, Margaret
"Female Circumcision in Kenya." Paper Presented at the
Seminar on Traditional Practices Affecting the Health of
Women and Children. World Conference for the United
Nations Decade for Women. New York: United Nations.
Copenhagen, Denmark. July 14-30, 1980.
Njoki, Margaret
"Traditional Practices in Relation to Childbirth in
Kenya." Paper Presented at the Seminar on Traditional
Practices Affecting the Health of Women and Children.
World Conference of the United Nations Decade for Women.
New York: United Nations. Copenhagen, Denmark.
July 14-30, 1980.
Njoki, Margaret
"Traditional Practices in Relation to Childbirth in
Kenya." Paper Presented at the Seminar on Traditional
Practices Affecting the Health of Women and Children:
Female Circumcision, Childhood Marriage, Nutritional
Taboos, etc. Alexandria, Egypt: World Health
Organization. Eastern Mediterranean Regional Office.
Khartoum, Sudan. February 10-15, 1979.
Olusanya, P.O.
The Demographic, Health, Economic and Social Impact of
Family Planning in Selected African Countries. Addis
Ababa, Ethiopia: United Nations Economic Commission for
Africa. ECA/PD/1985-9. March, 1985. 97p.
Plummer, F.A.
"Clinical and Microbilogical Studies of Genital Ulcers in
Kenyan Women." Sexually Transmited Diseases. Volume 12
#4 October-December, 1985. pp. 193-197.

Ramsay, V.P.
   "Vitamin Cofactor Saturation Indices for Riboflavin,
   Thiamin and Pyridoxine in Placental Tissues of Kenyan
   Women." American Journal of Clinical Nutrition. Volume
   37 June, 1983. pp. 969-973.
Richter, Kerry and Adlakha, Arjun
   The Effect of Infant and Child Mortality on Subsequent
   Fertility. Washington, D.C.: U.S. Department of
   Commerce. U.S. Bureau of the Census. Center for
   International Research. 1985.
Schulpen, T.W.
   "Machakos Project Studies. Agents Affecting Health of
   Mother and Child in a Rural Area of Kenya. XIX.   The
   Utilization of Health Services in a Rural Area of Kenya."
   Tropical and Geographical Medicine. Volume 32 #4
   December, 1980. pp. 340-349.
Shepherd, Gilliam M.
   Responding to the Contraception Needs of the Rural
   People: Kenya, 1984. Oxford, England: OXFAM. 1984.
Sindiga, Isaac
   "The Persistence of High Fertility in Kenya." Social
   Science and Medicine. Volume 20 #1 1985. pp. 77-84.
Van Ginneken, J.K. and Muller, A.S. and Blok, P.G. and
Omondi, Odhiambo
   "Agents Affecting Health of Mother and Child in a Rural
   Area of Kenya. XVII: Population Growth in 1974-1978."
   Tropical and Geographical Medicine. Volume 32 #2 June,
   1980. pp. 174-180.
Van Ginneken, J.K. and Voorhoeve, A.M. and Omondi, Odhiambo
and Muller, A.S.
   "Agents Affecting Health of Mother and Child in a Rural
   Area of Kenya. XVIII: Fertility, Mortality and Migration
   in 1975-1978." Tropical and Geographical Medicine.
   Volume 32 #2 1980. pp. 183-188.
Van Ginneken, J.K. and Muller, A.S.
   Maternal and Child Health in Rural Kenya: An
   Epidemiological Study. London: Croom Helm. 1984.   373p.
Van Steenbergen, W.M.
   "Lactation Performance of Mothers With Contrasting
   Nutritional Status in Rural Kenya." ACTA Paediatrica
   Scandinavica. Volume 72 #6 November, 1983. pp.
   805-810.
Voorhoeve, A.M.
   "Machakos Project Studies. Agents Affecting Health of
   Mother and Child in A Rural Area of Kenya. XXI.
   Antenatal and Delivery Care." Tropical and Geographical
   Medicine. Volume 34 #1 March, 1982. pp. 91-101.
Voorhoeve, A.M.
   "Machakos Project Studies: Agents Affecting Health of
   Mother and Child in a Rural Area of Kenya. XVI. The
   Outcome of Pregnancy." Tropical and Geographical
   Medicine. Volume 31 #4 December, 1979. pp. 607-627.

Waife, Ronald S. and Burkhart, Marianne (eds.)
The Nonphysician and Family Health in Sub-Saharan Africa:
Proceedings of a Conference, Freetown, Sierra Leone,
September 1-4, 1980. Chestnut Hill, Massachusetts:
Pathfinder Fund. 1981. 141p.
Waltons, S.M. and Mati, J.K.G.
"An Evaluation of Secondary Infertility in Kenya." East
African Medical Journal. Volume 53 #6 June, 1976. pp.
310-314.
Wanjala, S. and Murugu, N.M. and Mati, J.K.G.
"Mortality Due to Abortion at Kenyatta National Hospital,
1974-1983." CIBA Foundation Symposia. #115 1985. pp.
41-48.

HISTORY

Bujra, Janet M.
"Women 'Entrepreneurs' in Early Nairobi." (In) Sumner,
Colin (ed.). Crime, Justice and Underdevelopment.
London: Heineman. Cambridge Studies in Criminology.
#46. 1982.
Bujra, Janet M.
"Women 'Entrepreneurs' of Early Nairobi." (In) Summer,
C. (ed.). Crime, Justice and Underdevelopment. London:
Heinemann. 1982.
Clark, Carolyn M.
"Land and Food, Women and Power, in 19th Century Kikuyu."
Africa. Volume 50 #4 1980. pp. 357-370.
Cooper, Frederick
From Slaves to Squatters: Plantation Labor and
Agriculture in Zanzibar and Coastal Kenya, 1890-1925.
New Haven, Connecticut: Yale University Press. 1980.
328p.
Donley, L.
"Eighteenth Century Lamu Weddings." Kenya Past and
Present. # 11 1979. pp. 3-11.
Gold, Alice
"Women in Agricultural Change: The Nandi in the 19th
Century." Paper Presented at the Annual Meeting of the
African Studies Association. Houston, Texas. 1978.
Hay, Margaret J.
"Luo Women and Economic Change During the Colonial
Period." (In) Hafkin, Margaret J. and Bay, Edna G.
(eds.). Women in Africa: Studies in Social and Economic
Change. Stanford, California: Stanford University
Press. 1976. pp. 87-109.
Hay, Margaret J.
"Women as Owners, Occupants and Managers of Property in
Colonial Western Kenya." (In) Hay, Margaret J. and
Wright, Marcia (eds.). African Women and the Law:
Historical Perspectives. Boston: Boston University.

African Studies Center. Boston University Papers on Africa. Volume 7. 1982. pp. 110-123.

Hollander, Roberta B.
"Out of Tradition: The Position of Women in Kenya and Tanzania During the Pre-Colonial, Colonial and Post Independence Eras." Ph.D Dissertation: The American University. Washington, D.C. 1979. 399p.

Jackson, Kennell A.
"The Family Entity and Famine Among the 19th Century Akamba of Kenya: Social Responses to Environmental Stress." Journal of Family History. Volume 1 Winter, 1976. pp. 192-215.

Kamau, G.K. and Ojwang, J.B.
"Law and Witchcraft: A Review Article." Kenya Historical Review. Volume 6 1978. pp. 146-160.

Kosgei, Sally J.
Kipsigis Women and the Colonial Economy. Nairobi: University of Nairobi. Department of History. 1979. 17p.

Llewelyn-Davies, Melissa
"Women, Warriors and Patriarchs." (In) Ortner, Sherry B. and Whitehead, Harriet (eds.). Sexual Meanings. Cambridge, New York: Cambridge University Press. 1981. pp. 330-358.

Murray, Joselyn
"The Church Missionary Society and the 'Female Circumcision' Issue in Kenya, 1929-1932." Journal of Religion in Africa. Volume 8 #2 1976. pp. 92-104.

Ogutu, M.A.
"The Changing Role of Women in the Commercial History of Busia District in Kenya, 1900-1983." Journal of Eastern African Research and Development. Volume 15 1985. pp. 56-73.

Okeyo, Achola P.
"Daughters of the Lakes and Rivers: Colonization and the Land Rights of Luo Women." (In) Etienne, Mona and Leacook, Eleanor (eds.). Women and Colonization: Anthropological Perspectives. New York: Praeger Publishers. 1980. pp. 186-213.

Presley, Cora A.
Kikuyu Women as Wage Labourers: 1919-1960. Nairobi: University of Nairobi. Department of History. Staff Seminar. Paper #24. 1978. 20p.

Presley, Cora A.
"Labor Unrest Among Kikuyu Women in Colonial Kenya." Paper Presented at the Annual Meeting of the African Studies Association. Paper #100. Bloomington, Indiana. October 21-24, 1981.

Staudt, Kathleen A.
"Rural Women Leaders: Late Colonial and Contemporary Contexts." Rural Africana. #3 Winter, 1978. pp. 5-21.

Stichter, Sharon B.
Women and the Labor Force in Kenya, 1895-1964. Nairobi:

University of Nairobi. Institute for Development
Studies. Discussion Paper #258. 1977. 26p.
Strobel, Margaret A.
Muslim Women in Mombasa, 1890-1975. New Haven,
Connecticut: Yale University Press. 1979. 258p.
Strobel, Margaret A.
"Slavery and Reproductive Labor in Mombasa." (In)
Robertson, Claire C. and Klein, Martin A. (eds.). Women
and Slavery in Africa. Madison, Wisconsin: University of
Wisconsin Press. 1983. pp. 111-129.
Waller, R.D.
"Interaction and Identity on the Periphery--The
Trans-Mara Maasai." International Journal of African
Historical Studies. Volume 17 #2 1984. pp. 243-284.
White, Luise S.
"A Colonial State and an African Petty Bourgeoisie:
Prostitution, Property and Class Struggle in Nairobi,
1936-1940." (In) Cooper, Frederick (ed.). Struggle for
the City: Migrant Labour, Capital, and the State in Urban
Africa. Beverly Hills, California: Sage Publications.
African Modernization and Development Series #8. 1983.
pp. 167-194.
White, Luise S.
Women's Domestic Labor in Colonial Kenya: Prostitution in
Nairobi, 1909-1950. Brookline, Massachusetts: Boston
University. African Studies Center. Working Paper #30.
1980. 26p.

LAW AND LEGAL ISSUES

Gutto, Shadrack B.
"The Legal Status of Women in Kenya: Paternalism and
Inequality." Fletcher Forum. Volume 1 Fall, 1976. pp.
62-82.
Hay, Margaret J.
"Women as Owners, Occupants and Managers of Property in
Colonial Western Kenya." (In) Hay, Margaret J. and
Wright, Marcia (eds.). African Women and the Law:
Historical Perspectives. Boston: Boston University.
African Studies Center. Boston University Papers on
Africa. Volume 7. 1982. pp. 110-123.
Kamau, G.K. and Ojwang, J.B.
"Law and Witchcraft: A Review Article." Kenya Historical
Review. Volume 6 1978. pp. 146-160.
Kuria, Gibson K.
"The African or Customary Marriage in Kenya Law Today."
Paper Presented at the Conference on Conceptualizing the
Household. Cambridge, Massachusetts: Harvard University.
November, 1984.
Maina, Rose and Muchai, V.W. and Gutto, S.B.O.
"Law and the Status of Women in Kenya." (In) Columbia
Human Rights Law Review (eds.). Law and the Status of

Women: An International Symposium. New York: United
Nations. Centre for Social Development and Humanitarian
Affairs. 1977. pp. 185-206.
Mutungi, O.K.
Legal Aspects of Witchcraft in East Africa: With
Particular Reference to Kenya. Nairobi: East African
Literature Bureau. 1977. 144p.

LITERATURE

Cochrane, J.
"Women as Guardians of the Tribe in Ngugi Novels."
Critical Perspectives. Volume 13 1984. pp. 90-100.
Cochrane, Judith
"Women as the Guardians of the Tribe in Ngugi's Novels."
ACLALS Bulletin. Volume 4 #5 1977. pp. 1-11.
Evans, Jennifer
"Mother Africa and the Heroic Whore: Female Images in
'Petals of Blood'." (In) Wylie, Hal and Julien, Eileen
and Linnemann, Russell J. (eds.). Contemporary African
Literature. Washington, D.C.: Three Continents Press.
1983. pp. 57-65.
Mayes, Janis
"Ideology and the Image of Women: Kenyan Women in Novels
by Njau and Ngugi." Paper Presented at the 1981 African
Literature Association Conference. Baltimore, Maryland:
University of Maryland. African-American Studies
Department. 1981.
Mbughuni, Patricia
"The Image of Women in Kiswahili Prose Fiction."
Kiswahili. Volume 49 #1 1982. pp. 15-24.
Mbughuni, Patricia
"The Image of Women in Kiswahili Prose Fiction." Paper
Presented at the Workshop on Women's Studies and
Development. Dar-es-Salaam, Tanzania: University of
Dar-es-Salaam. Bureau of Resource Assessment and Land
Use Planning. Paper #26. September 24-29, 1979. 14p.
Nwankwo, Chimalum
"Women in Ngugi's Plays: From Passivity to Social
Responsibility." Ufahamu. Volume 14 #3 1985. pp.
85-92.
Nwankwo, Chimalum M.
"Women, Violence and the Quest for Social Justice in the
Works of Ngugi wa Thiong'o." Ph.D Dissertation:
University of Texas. Austin, Texas. 1982. 394p.
Parker, C.
"How to Be/Treat a Lady in Swahili Culture: An Expression
of Ideal." Ba Shiru. Volume 8 #2 1977. pp. 37-45.
Porter, Abioseh
"Ideology and the Image of Women in Njau and Ngugu."
Ariel: Review of International English Literature.
Volume 12 #3 July, 1981. pp. 61-74.

Senkoro, F.E.M.K.
"Silie Mwana Silie: Women in Kiswahili and Tanzanian
Lullabies." Paper Presented at the 1982 African
Literature Association Conference. Baltimore, Maryland:
University of Maryland. African and American Studies
Department. 1982.

MARITAL RELATIONS AND NUPTIALITY

Ciancanelli, Penelope
"Exchange, Reproduction and Sex Subordination Among the
Kikuyu of East Africa." Review of Radical Political
Economics. Volume 12 #2 Summer, 1980. pp. 25-36.
Curtin, Patricia R.
"Weddings in Lamu, Kenya: An Example of Social and
Economic Change." Cahiers d'Etudes Africaines. Volume
24 #2 1984. pp. 131-155.
Donley, L.
"Eighteenth Century Lamu Weddings." Kenya Past and
Present. # 11 1979. pp. 3-11.
Dow, Thomas E. and Werner, Linda H.
"Modern, Transitional, and Traditional Demographic and
Contraceptive Patterns Among Kenyan Women." Studies in
Family Planning. Volume 13 #1 January, 1982. pp.
12-23.
Dow, Thomas E. and Werner, Linda H.
"Perceptions of Family Planning Among Rural Kenyan
Women." Studies in Family Planning. Volume 14 #2
February, 1983. pp. 35-43.
Dow, Thomas E. and Werner, Linda H.
A Note on Modern, Transitional and Traditional
Demographic and Contraceptive Patterns Among Kenyan
Women, 1977-1978. Nairobi: University of Nairobi.
Population Studies and Research Institute. January,
1981. 29p.
Dow, Thomas E. and Werner, Linda H.
Continuity and Change in Metropolitan and Rural Attitudes
Towards Family Size and Family Planning in Kenya Between
1966/67-1977/78. Nairobi: University of Nairobi.
Population Studies and Research Institute. February,
1981. 17p.
Eastman, C.M.
"Waungwana na Wanawake: Muslim Ethnicity and Sexual
Segregation in Coastal Kenya." Journal of Multilingual
and Multicultural Development. Volume 5 #2 1984. pp.
97-112.
Emereuwaonu, Ernest U.
"Determinants of Fertility: A Regression Analysis of
Kenya Data." Genus. Volume 40 #3/4 July-December,
1984. pp. 77-96.
Emereuwaonu, Ernest U.
"Marital Fertility, Desired Family Size, Communication

Channel and Modern Reproductive Values in an African
City." Ph.D Dissertation: University of California Los
Angeles. Los Angeles, California. 1977. 216p.
Gatara, Timothy H.
"The Influence of Religion and Education on Current
Family Size and Fertility Preference in Kenya." Ph.D
Dissertation: Florida State University. Tallahassee,
Florida. 1982. 152p.
Kenya. Ministry of Finance and Economic Planning
"Continuity and Change in Metropolitan and Rural
Attitudes Towards Family Size and Family Planning in
Kenya Between 1966/1967 and 1977/1978." Social
Perspectives. Volume 5 #1 December, 1980. 8p.
Kenya. Ministry of Finance and Economic Planning
"Demographic and Contraceptive Patterns Among Kenyan
Women: 1977-1978." Social Perspectives. Volume 6 #2
April, 1981. 16p.
Kenya. Ministry of Finance and Economic Planning
"Modernization, Birth Spacing and Marital Fertility in
Kenya." Social Perspectives. Volume 6 #5 September,
1981. 12p
Kipury, N.
"Engagement and Marriage Among the Massai." Kenya Past
and Present. #9 1978. pp. 38-42.
Kuria, Gibson K.
"The African or Customary Marriage in Kenya Law Today."
Paper Presented at the Conference on Conceptualizing the
Household. Cambridge, Massachusetts: Harvard University.
November, 1984.
LeVine, Robert A.
"Influences of Women's Schooling on Maternal Behavior in
the Third World." Comparative Education Review. Volume
24 #2 Part Two June, 1980. pp. S78-S105.
LeVine, Sarah and LeVine, Robert A.
Mothers and Wives: Gusii Women of East Africa. Chicago:
University of Chicago Press. 1979. 391p.
LeVine, Sarah and Pfeifer, G.
"Separation and Individualization in an African Society:
The Developmental Tasks of the Gusii Married Women."
Psychiatry. Volume 45 #1 February, 1982. pp. 61-75.
Lesthaeghe, Ron J. and Vanderhoeft, C. and Becker, Stan and
Kibet, M.
Individual and Contextual Effects of Education on
Proximate Fertility Determinants and Life Time Fertility
in Kenya. Brussels, Belgium: Vrije Universiteit Brussel.
Interuniversity Programme in Demography. IDS Working
Paper #1983-2. 1983. 67p.
Lesthaeghe, Ron J. and Vanderhoeft, C. and Becker, Stan and
Kibet, M.
Individual and Contextual Effects of Female Education on
the Kenya Marital Fertility Transition. Brussels,
Belgium: Vrije Universiteit Brussel. Interuniversity

Programme in Demography. IPD Working Paper #1983-9.
1983. 19p.

Lura, Russell P.
"Population Change in Kericho District, Kenya: An Example
of Fertility Increase in Africa." African Studies
Review. Volume 28 #1 March, 1985. pp. 45-56.

Maina, Rose and Muchai, V.W. and Gutto, S.B.O.
"Law and the Status of Women in Kenya." (In) Columbia
Human Rights Law Review (eds.). Law and the Status of
Women: An International Symposium. New York: United
Nations. Centre for Social Development and Humanitarian
Affairs. 1977. pp. 185-206.

Mbevi, Grace
"Child Marriage and Early Teenage Childbirth." Paper
Presented at the Seminar on Traditional Practices
Affecting the Health of Women and Children: Female
Circumcision, Childhood Marriage, Nutritional Taboos,
etc. Alexandria, Egypt: World Health Organization.
Eastern Mediterranean Regional Office. Khartoum, Sudan.
February 10-15, 1979.

Monstead, Mette
The Changing Division of Labour Within Rural Families in
Kenya. Copenhagen, Denmark: Centre for Development
Research. 1977.

Monstead, Mette
The Changing Division of Labour Within Rural Families in
Kenya. Nairobi: University of Nairobi. Centre for
Development Research. 1976.

Monsted, Mette
"The Changing Division of Labor Within Rural Families in
Kenya." (In) Caldwell, John C. (ed.). The Persistence
of High Fertility: Population Prospects in the Third
World. Canberra, Australia: Australian National
University. 1977. pp. 259-312.

Mosley, W. Henry and Werner, Linda H.
Some Determinants of Marital Fertility in Kenya: A Birth
Interval Analysis From the 1978 Kenya Fertility Survey.
Nairobi: University of Nairobi. Population Studies and
Research Institute. Central Bureau of Statistics.
Unpublished. 1980.

Mosley, W. Henry and Werner, Linda H. and Becker, Stan
The Dynamics of Birth Spacing and Marital Fertility in
Kenya. Voorburg, Netherlands: International Statistical
Institute. World Fertility Survey. Scientific Reports
#30. August, 1982. 30p.

Nagashima, Nobuhiro
"A Note on Marriage and Affinal Relationship Among the
Iteso of Kenya, With Special Reference to Ivan Karp's
Proposition." Hitotsubaski Journal of Social Studies.
Volume 12 November, 1980. pp. 25-46.

Nagashima, Nobuhiro
"Bridewealth Among the Iteso of Kenya: A Further Note on
Their Affinal Relationship and its Historical Change."

Hitotsubashi Journal of Social Studies. Volume 14
   August, 1982. pp. 14-26.
Nelson, Nici
   "Female-Centered Families: Changing Patterns of Marriage
   and Family Among Buzaa Brewers of Mathari Valley."
   African Urban Studies. #3 Winter, 1978. pp. 85-103.
Nelson, Nici
   "How Women and Men Get By: The Sexual Division of Labour
   in the Informal Sector of a Nairobi Squatter Settlement."
   (In) Bromley, Ray and Gerry, Chris (eds.). Casual Work
   and Poverty in Third World Cities. New York: John Wiley
   and Sons. 1979. pp. 283-302.
Oboler, Regina S.
   "Is the Female Husband A Man? Woman/Woman Marriage Among
   the Nandi of Kenya." Ethnology. Volume 19 #1 January,
   1980. pp. 69-88.
Parkin, David
   "Kind Bridewealth and Hard Cash: Eventing a Structure."
   (In) Comaroff, J.L. (ed.). The Meaning of Marriage
   Payments. New York: Academic Press. 1980. pp. 197-220.
Potash, Betty
   "Some Aspects of Marital Stability in a Rural Luo
   Community." Africa. Volume 48 #4 1978. pp. 380-397.
Stichter, Sharon B.
   Women in the Labor Force in Kenya: Some Effects on Their
   Family Roles. Boston: University of Massachusetts.
   1978.
Swartz, Audrey R. and Swartz, Marc J.
   "Women's Power and Its Sources Among the Swahili of
   Mombasa." Paper Presented at the Annual Meeting of the
   African Studies Association. Paper #93. Los Angeles,
   California. 1979. 9p.
Swartz, Marc J.
   "The Isolation of Men and the Happiness of Women: Sources
   and Use of Power in Swahili Marital Relationships."
   Journal of Anthropological Research. Volume 38 #1
   Spring, 1982. pp. 26-44.
United Nations Economic Commission for Africa (UNECA)
   Nuptiality and Fertility (A Comparative Analysis of WFS
   Data). Addis Ababa, Ethiopia: UNECA. African Population
   Studies Series #5. 1983. 96p.

MIGRATION

Anker, Richard and Knowles, James C.
   Population Growth, Employment and Economic Demographic
   Interactions in Kenya: Bachue-Kenya. New York: St.
   Martin's Press. 1983. 735p.
Ensminger, J.
   "Theoretical Perspectives on Pastoral Women: Feminist
   Critiques." Nomadic Peoples. #16 1984. pp. 59-71.

Knotts, Mary A.
"The Social and Economic Factors Associated With the Rural-Urban Migration of Kenyan Women." Ph.D Dissertation: Johns Hopkins University. Baltimore, Maryland. 1977. 306p.

Mutiso, Roberta M.
Career Role/Family Role Conflict Among Women Agricultural Extension Officers in Kenya. Nairobi: University of Nairobi. 1978.

Mwaria, Cheryl B.
"Rural-Urban Labor Migration and Family Arrangements Among the Kamba." (In) Robinson, Pearl T. and Skinner, Elliott (eds.). Transformation and Resiliency in Africa. Washington, D.C.: Howard University Press. 1983. pp. 29-43.

Thadani, Veena N.
Social Relations and Geographic Mobility: Male and Female Migration in Kenya. New York: Population Council. Center for Policy Studies. Working Paper #85. June, 1982. 67p.

Van Ginneken, J.K. and Voorhoeve, A.M. and Omondi, Odhiambo and Muller, A.S.
"Agents Affecting Health of Mother and Child in a Rural Area of Kenya. XVIII: Fertility, Mortality and Migration in 1975-1978." Tropical and Geographical Medicine. Volume 32 #2 1980. pp. 183-188.

Wasow, Bernard
"The Working Age Sex Ratio and Job Search Migration in Kenya." Journal of Developing Areas. Volume 15 #3 April, 1981. pp. 435-444.

MISCELLANEOUS

Feldman, Rayah
"Women's Groups and Women's Subordination: An Analysis of Policies Towards Rural Women in Kenya." Review of African Political Economy. #27/28 1983. pp. 67-85.

Presley, Cora A.
"Labor Unrest Among Kikuyu Women in Colonial Kenya." Paper Presented at the Annual Meeting of the African Studies Association. Paper #100. Bloomington, Indiana. October 21-24, 1981.

White, Luise S.
"A Colonial State and an African Petty Bourgeoisie: Prostitution, Property and Class Struggle in Nairobi, 1936-1940." (In) Cooper, Frederick (ed.). Struggle for the City: Migrant Labour, Capital, and the State in Urban Africa. Beverly Hills, California: Sage Publications. African Modernization and Development Series #8. 1983. pp. 167-194.

White, Luise S.
"A History of Prostitution in Nairobi, Kenya. c.

1900-1952." Ph.D Dissertation: University of Cambridge.
London, England. 1983.
White, Luise S.
    Women's Domestic Labor in Colonial Kenya: Prostitution in
    Nairobi, 1909-1950. Brookline, Massachusetts: Boston
    University. African Studies Center. Working Paper #30.
    1980. 26p.
Wilson, G.M.
    "A Study of Prostitution in Mombasa." (In) Muga, Erasto.
    Studies in Prostitution: East, West and South Africa,
    Zaire and Nevada. Nairobi: Kenya Literature Bureau.
    1980. pp. 130-141.

NATIONALISM

Santilli, Kathy
    "Kikuyu Women in the Mau Mau Revolt: A Closer Look."
    Ufahamu. Volume 8 #1 1977. pp. 143-174.

ORGANIZATIONS

Davison, Jean
    "Voices From Mutira: Education in the Lives of Rural
    Gikuyu Women." Ph.D Dissertation: Stanford University.
    Stanford, California. 1985. 422p.
Gachukia, Eddah W.
    "Women's Self-Help Efforts for Water Supply in Kenya."
    Appropriate Technology. Volume 9 #3 1982. pp. 19-21.
Gachukia, Eddah W.
    "Women's Self-Help Efforts for Water Supply in Kenya: The
    Important Role of NGO Support." Assignment Children.
    Volume 45/46 Spring, 1979. pp. 167-174.
Kneerim, Jill
    Village Women Organize: The Mraru Bus Service. New York:
    Carnegie Corporation. Volume One of the Seeds Pamphlet
    Series #3. 1980. 20p.
Komma, Toru
    "The Women's Self Help Association Movement Among the
    Kipsigis of Kenya." (In) Wada, S. and Eguchi, P.K.
    (eds.). Africa 3. Osaka, Japan: National Museum of
    Ethnology. Senri Ethnological Studies #15. 1984. pp.
    145-186.
Komma, Toru
    "The Women's Self-Help Association Movement Among the
    Kipsigis of Kenya." Senri Ethnological Studies. Volume
    15 1984. pp. 145-186.
Monsted, Mette
    Women's Groups in Rural Kenya and Their Role in
    Development. Copenhagen, Denmark: Centre for Development
    Research. CDR Paper A/78/2. June, 1978.

Muzale, P. and Leonard, D.K.
   Women'a Groups and Extension in Kenya: Their Impact on
   Food Production and Malnutrition in Baringo, Busia and
   Taita Taveta. Nairobi, Kenya: Ministry of Agriculture.
   1982.
Nelson, Nici
   "Women Must Help Each Other: The Operation of Peasant
   Networks Among Buzaa Beer Brewers in Mathare Valley,
   Kenya." (In) Caplan, Patricia and Bujra, Janet M.
   (eds.). Women United, Women Divided. Bloomington,
   Indiana: Indiana University Press. 1978. pp. 77-98.
Opondo, Diana
   "A Women's Group in Kenya and its Struggle to Obtain
   Credit." Assignment Children. Volume 49/50 Spring,
   1980. pp. 127-140.
Pala, Achola O.
   "Women Power in Kenya: Raising Funds and Awareness."
   Ceres. Volume 11 #2 March-April, 1978. pp. 43-46.
Riria Ouko, J.V.N.
   "Women Organizations in Kenya." Journal of Eastern
   African Research and Development. Volume 15 1985. pp.
   188-197.
Strobel, Margaret A.
   "From Lelemamato Lobbying: Women's Associations in
   Mombasa, Kenya." (In) Hafkin, N.J. and Bay, E.G. (eds.).
   Women in Africa: Studies in Social and Economic Change.
   Stanford, California: Stanford University Press. 1976.
   pp. 183-211.
Wachtel, Eleanor and Wachtel, Andy
   Women's Co-Operative Enterprise in Nakuru. Nairobi:
   University of Nairobi. Institute for Development
   Studies. Discussion Paper #250. 1977. 18p.

POLITICS AND GOVERNMENT

Harris, Joan
   "Women in Kenya: Revolution or Evolution?" Africa
   Report. Volume 30 #2 March-April, 1985. pp. 30-32.
Hollander, Roberta B.
   "Out of Tradition: The Position of Women in Kenya and
   Tanzania During the Pre-Colonial, Colonial and Post
   Independence Eras." Ph.D Dissertation: The American
   University. Washington, D.C. 1979. 399p.
Likimani, Muthoni G.
   Women of Kenya: Fifteen Years of Independence. Nairobi:
   Likamani. 1979. 76p.
Lindsay, Beverly
   "An Examination of Education, Social Change and National
   Development Policy: The Case of Kenyan Women." (In)
   Women and Politics in 20th Century Africa and Asia.
   Williamsburg, Virginia: College of William and Mary.

Anthropology Department. Studies in Third World
Societies. #16. June, 1981. pp. 29-48.
Pala, Achola O.
"Women Power in Kenya: Raising Funds and Awareness."
Ceres. Volume 11 #2 March-April, 1978. pp. 43-46.
Palmer, Ingrid
"New Official Ideas on Women and Development." Institute
for Development Studies. Volume 10 #3 1979. pp. 42-53.
Santilli, Kathy
"Kikuyu Women in the Mau Mau Revolt: A Closer Look."
Ufahamu. Volume 8 #1 1977. pp. 143-174.
Staudt, Kathleen A.
"Administrative Resources, Political Patrons, and
Redressing Sexual Inequities: A Case From Western Kenya."
Journal of Developing Areas. Volume 12 #4 July, 1978.
pp. 399-414.
Staudt, Kathleen A.
"Agricultural Policy, Political Power, and Women Farmers
in Western Kenya." Ph.D Dissertation: University of
Wisconsin-Madison. Madison, Wisconsin. 1976. 422p.
Staudt, Kathleen A.
"Rural Women Leaders: Late Colonial and Contemporary
Contexts." Rural Africana. #3 Winter, 1978. pp. 5-21.
Staudt, Kathleen A.
"Sex, Ethnic and Class Consciousness in Western Kenya."
Paper Presented at the Annual Meeting of the African
Studies Association. Paper #97. Baltimore, Maryland.
1978.
Staudt, Kathleen A.
"Sex, Ethnic and Class Consciousness in Western Kenya."
Comparative Politics. Volume 14 #2 1982. pp. 149-168.
White, Luise S.
"A Colonial State and an African Petty Bourgeoisie:
Prostitution, Property and Class Struggle in Nairobi,
1936-1940." (In) Cooper, Frederick (ed.). Struggle for
the City: Migrant Labour, Capital, and the State in Urban
Africa. Beverly Hills, California: Sage Publications.
African Modernization and Development Series #8. 1983.
pp. 167-194.

RELIGION AND WITCHCRAFT

Brantley, Cynthia
"An Historical Perspective of the Giriama and Witchcraft
Control." Africa. Volume 49 #2 1979. pp. 112-133.
Gatara, Timothy H.
"The Influence of Religion and Education on Current
Family Size and Fertility Preference in Kenya." Ph.D
Dissertation: Florida State University. Tallahassee,
Florida. 1982. 152p.
Gomm, Roger
"Bargaining From Weakness: Spirit Possession on the South
Kenya Coast." (In) Tiffany, Sharon W. (ed.). Women and

Society: An Anthropological Reader. St. Albans, Vermont:
Eden Press. 1979. pp. 120-144.
Kamau, G.K. and Ojwang, J.B.
    "Law and Witchcraft: A Review Article." Kenya Historical
    Review. Volume 6 1978. pp. 146-160.
Langley, Myrtle S.
    "Spirit Possession, Exorcism and Social Context: An
    Anthropological Perspective With Theological
    Implications." Churchman. Volume 94 #3 1980. pp.
    226-245.
Murray, Joselyn
    "The Church Missionary Society and the 'Female
    Circumcision' Issue in Kenya, 1929-1932." Journal of
    Religion in Africa. Volume 8 #2 1976. pp. 92-104.
Mutungi, O.K.
    Legal Aspects of Witchcraft in East Africa: With
    Particular Reference to Kenya. Nairobi: East African
    Literature Bureau. 1977. 144p.
Seeley, Janet
    "'We Have the Healing Power...': Independent Churches and
    Women in Urban Kenya." Cambridge Anthropology. Volume 9
    #2 1984. pp. 58-70.
Strobel, Margaret A.
    Muslim Women in Mombasa, 1890-1975. New Haven,
    Connecticut: Yale University Press. 1979. 258p.

RESEARCH

Bifani, Patricia
    The Impact of Development on Women in Kenya: An Annotated
    Bibliography. Nairobi: UNICEF. 1982. 38p.
Chandler, Dale and Thairu, R.W.
    Women of Kenya: An Annotated Bibliography. Nairobi:
    Women's Bureau of the Ministry of Housing and Social
    Services. 1977.
Kayongo-Male, Diana
    "Problems and Prospects of Integrating Women into
    Development Planning and Process in Kenya." Journal of
    Eastern African Research and Development. Volume 15
    1985. pp. 280-296.
U.S. Department of Commerce. Bureau of the Census
    Illustrative Statistics on Women in Development in
    Selected Developing Countries. Washington, D.C.: U.S.
    Department of Commerce. 1982. 24p.

SEX ROLES

Adu-Bobie, Gemma
    "The Role of Rendille Women in the Nomadic Society."
    Bulletin of the Regional Office for Science and
    Technology for Africa. Volume 18 #2 1983. pp. 30-32.

Anderson, Mary B.
    "Kenya: Kitui District Arid and Semi-Arid Lands Project."
    (In) Overholt, Catherine and Anderson, Mary B. and Cloud,
    Kathleen and Austin, James E. (eds.). Gender Roles in
    Development Projects: A Case Book. West Hartford,
    Connecticut: Kumarian Press. 1985. pp. 309-326.
Arungu-Olende, Rose
    "Kenya: Not Just Literacy, But Wisdom." (In) Morgan,
    Robin (ed.). Sisterhood is Global. Garden City, New
    York: Anchor Books. 1984. pp. 389-398.
Barnes, Carolyn
    "Differentiation by Sex Among Small Scale Farming
    Households in Kenya." Rural Africana. #15-16 1983. pp.
    41-64.
Beaman, Anne C.
    "Women's Participation in Pastoral Economy: Income
    Maximization Among the Rendille." Nomadic Peoples.
    Volume 12 1983. pp. 20-25.
Caron, James W.
    Effects of Infant Characteristics on Caretaking
    Responsiveness Among the Gusii. Boston: Harvard
    University. Harvard Graduate School of Education. 1982.
    128p.
Ciancanelli, Penelope
    "Exchange, Reproduction and Sex Subordination Among the
    Kikuyu of East Africa." Review of Radical Political
    Economics. Volume 12 #2 Summer, 1980. pp. 25-36.
Clark, Carolyn M.
    "Land and Food, Women and Power, in 19th Century Kikuyu."
    Africa. Volume 50 #4 1980. pp. 357-370.
Clark, Mari H.
    "Women-Headed Households and Poverty: Insights From
    Kenya." Signs. Volume 10 #2 Winter, 1984. pp.
    338-354.
Eastman, C.M.
    "Waungwana na Wanawake: Muslim Ethnicity and Sexual
    Segregation in Coastal Kenya." Journal of Multilingual
    and Multicultural Development. Volume 5 #2 1984. pp.
    97-112.
Ensminger, J.
    "Theoretical Perspectives on Pastoral Women: Feminist
    Critiques." Nomadic Peoples. #16 1984. pp. 59-71.
Fjellman, Stephen M.
    "The Akamba Domestic Cycle as Markovian Process."
    American Ethnologist. Volume 4 #4 November, 1977. pp.
    69-713.
Gold, Alice
    "Women in Agricultural Change: The Nandi in the 19th
    Century." Paper Presented at the Annual Meeting of the
    African Studies Association. Houston, Texas. 1978.
Gutto, Shadrack B.
    "The Legal Status of Women in Kenya: Paternalism and

Inequality." Fletcher Forum. Volume 1 Fall, 1976. pp. 62-82.

Gutto, Shadrack B.
The Status of Women in Kenya: A Study of Paternalism, Inequality and Under Privilege. Nairobi: University of Nairobi. Institute for Development Studies. Discussion Paper #235. April, 1976. 76p.

Hollander, Roberta B.
"Out of Tradition: The Position of Women in Kenya and Tanzania During the Pre-Colonial, Colonial and Post Independence Eras." Ph.D Dissertation: The American University. Washington, D.C. 1979. 399p.

Kayongo-Male, Diana
"Problems and Prospects of Integrating Women into Development Planning and Process in Kenya." Journal of Eastern African Research and Development. Volume 15 1985. pp. 280-296.

Kenya. Central Bureau of Statistics.
Kenya Contraceptive Prevalence Survey, 1984: First Report. Nairobi: Central Bureau of Statistics. December, 1984. 121p.

Kershaw, Greet
"The Changing Roles of Men and Women in the Kikuyu Family by Socioeconomic Strata." Rural Africana. Volume 29 Winter, 1976. pp. 173-194.

Kershaw, Greet
"The Changing Roles of Men and Women in the Kikuyu Family by Socioeconomic Strata." Rural Africana. Volume 29 Winter, 1976. pp. 173-194.

Kettel, Bonnie
"Gender and Class in Tugen-Kalenjin Social Organization." Paper Presented at the Annual Meeting of the African Studies Association. Bloomington, Indiana. October 21-24, 1981.

Kune, J.B.
"Machakos Project Studies: Agents Affecting Health of Mother and Child in a Rural Area of Kenya. XV. The Economic Setting at the Household Level." Tropical and Geographical Medicine. Volume 31 #3 September, 1979. pp. 441-457.

Kuria, Gibson K.
"The African or Customary Marriage in Kenya Law Today." Paper Presented at the Conference on Conceptualizing the Household. Cambridge, Massachusetts: Harvard University. November, 1984.

LeVine, Sarah and LeVine, Robert A.
Mothers and Wives: Gusii Women of East Africa. Chicago: University of Chicago Press. 1979. 391p.

LeVine, Sarah and Pfeifer, G.
"Separation and Individualization in an African Society: The Developmental Tasks of the Gusii Married Women." Psychiatry. Volume 45 #1 February, 1982. pp. 61-75.

Llewelyn-Davies, Melissa
    "Two Contexts of Solidarity Among Pastoral Maasai Women."
    (In) Caplan, P. and Bujra, J. (eds.). Women United,
    Women Divided: Female Solidarity in Cross-Cultural
    Perspective. Bloomington, Indiana: Indiana University
    Press. 1978. pp. 206-237.
Llewelyn-Davies, Melissa
    "Women, Warriors and Patriarchs." (In) Ortner, Sherry B.
    and Whitehead, Harriet (eds.). Sexual Meanings.
    Cambridge, New York: Cambridge University Press. 1981.
    pp. 330-358.
Mbulu, J.
    Women and the Family. Nairobi: Ministry of
    Transportation and Communications. Roads and Aerodromes
    Department. 1981.
McAdoo, Harriette P.
    "Extended Family Involvement and Roles of Urban Kenyan
    Women." Paper Presented at the Women in the African
    Diaspora: An Interdisciplinary Perspective Research
    Conference. Washington, D.C.: Howard University. June,
    1983.
Monstead, Mette
    The Changing Division of Labour Within Rural Families in
    Kenya. Copenhagen, Denmark: Centre for Development
    Research. 1977.
Monstead, Mette
    The Changing Division of Labour Within Rural Families in
    Kenya. Nairobi: University of Nairobi. Centre for
    Development Research. 1976.
Monsted, Mette
    "The Changing Division of Labor Within Rural Families in
    Kenya." (In) Caldwell, John C. (ed.). The Persistence
    of High Fertility: Population Prospects in the Third
    World. Canberra, Australia: Australian National
    University. 1977. pp. 259-312.
Mott, Frank L. and Shapiro, D.
    "Seasonal Variations in Labor Force Activity and
    Intrahousehold Substitution of Labor in Rural Kenya."
    Journal of Developing Areas. Volume 18 #4 July, 1984.
    pp. 449-463.
Munroe, Ruth H. and Shimmin, Harold S. and Munroe, Robert L.
(eds.)
    "Gender Understanding and Sex Role Preference in Four
    Countries." Developmental Psychology. Volume 20 July,
    1984. pp. 673-682.
Mwaria, Cheryl B.
    "Rural-Urban Labor Migration and Family Arrangements
    Among the Kamba." (In) Robinson, Pearl T. and Skinner,
    Elliott (eds.). Transformation and Resiliency in Africa.
    Washington, D.C.: Howard University Press. 1983. pp.
    29-43.
Nelson, Nici
    "Dependence and Independence: Female Household Heads in

Mathare Valley, A Squatter Community in Nairobi, Kenya."
Ph.D Dissertation: University of London. School of
Oriental and African Studies. London, England. 1977.

Nelson, Nici
"Female-Centered Families: Changing Patterns of Marriage
and Family Among Buzaa Brewers of Mathari Valley."
African Urban Studies. #3 Winter, 1978. pp. 85-103.

Nelson, Nici
"How Women and Men Get By: The Sexual Division of Labour
in the Informal Sector of a Nairobi Squatter Settlement."
(In) Bromley, Ray and Gerry, Chris (eds.). Casual Work
and Poverty in Third World Cities. New York: John Wiley
and Sons. 1979. pp. 283-302.

Oboler, Regina S.
The Economic Rights of Nandi Women. Nairobi: University
of Nairobi. Institute of Development Studies. Working
Paper #328. November, 1977.

Oboler, Regina S.
"Women, Men, Property and Change in Nandi District,
Kenya." Ph.D Dissertation: Temple University.
Philadelphia, Pennsylvania. 1982. 492p.

Oboler, Regina S.
Women, Power and Economic Change: The Nandi of Kenya.
Stanford, California: Stanford University Press. 1985.
368p.

Ombina, O. and May, Nicky
"Progress Through Piggeries and Prejudice in Kenya."
Community Development Journal. Volume 20 #3 1985. pp.
191-194.

Pala, Achola O.
Women's Access to Land and Their Role in Agriculture and
Decision-Making on the Farm: Experiences of Joluo of
Kenya. Nairobi: University of Nairobi. Institute For
Development Studies. Discussion Paper #263. 1978. 22p.

Pala, Achola O.
"Women's Access to Land and Their Role in Agriculture and
Decision-Making on the Farm: Experiences of the Joluo of
Kenya." Journal of Eastern African Research and
Development. Volume 13 1983. pp. 69-87.

Reining, Priscilla (ed.)
Village Women: Their Changing Lives and Fertility:
Studies in Kenya. Mexico and the Philippines.
Washington, D.C.: American Association for the
Advancement of Science. AAAS Publication #77-6. 1977.
273p.

Smock, Audrey C.
"Measuring Rural Women's Economic Roles and Contributions
in Kenya." Studies in Family Planning. Volume 10 #11/12
November-December, 1979. pp. 385-390.

Smock, Audrey C.
Women's Education and Roles in Kenya. Nairobi:
University of Nairobi. Institute of Development Studies.
Working Paper #316. July, 1977.

Staudt, Kathleen A.
    "Agricultural Policy, Political Power, and Women Farmers
    in Western Kenya." Ph.D Dissertation: University of
    Wisconsin-Madison. Madison, Wisconsin. 1976. 422p.
Stichter, Sharon B.
    Women in the Labor Force in Kenya: Some Effects on Their
    Family Roles. Boston: University of Massachusetts.
    1978.
Swartz, Audrey R. and Swartz, Marc J.
    "Women's Power and Its Sources Among the Swahili of
    Mombasa." Paper Presented at the Annual Meeting of the
    African Studies Association. Paper #93. Los Angeles,
    California. 1979. 9p.
Swartz, Marc J.
    "The Isolation of Men and the Happiness of Women: Sources
    and Use of Power in Swahili Marital Relationships."
    Journal of Anthropological Research. Volume 38 #1
    Spring, 1982. pp. 26-44.
Thadani, Veena N.
    "The Forgotten Factor in Social Change: The Case of Women
    in Nairobi, Kenya." Ph.D Dissertation: Bryn Mawr
    College. Bryn Mawr, Pennsylvania. 1976. 259p.
Wienpahl, Jan
    "Women's Roles in Livestock Production Among the Turkana
    of Kenya." Research in Economic Anthropology. Volume 6
    1984. pp. 193-215.

SEXUAL MUTILATION/CIRCUMCISION

Murray, Joselyn
    "The Church Missionary Society and the 'Female
    Circumcision' Issue in Kenya, 1929-1932." Journal of
    Religion in Africa. Volume 8 #2 1976. pp. 92-104.
Njoki, Margaret
    "Female Circumcision in Kenya." Paper Presented at the
    Seminar on Traditional Practices Affecting the Health of
    Women and Children. World Conference for the United
    Nations Decade for Women. New York: United Nations.
    Copenhagen, Denmark. July 14-30, 1980.

SLAVERY

Cooper, Frederick
    From Slaves to Squatters: Plantation Labor and
    Agriculture in Zanzibar and Coastal Kenya, 1890-1925.
    New Haven, Connecticut: Yale University Press. 1980.
    328p.
Maina, Rose and Muchai, V.W. and Gutto, S.B.O.
    "Law and the Status of Women in Kenya." (In) Columbia
    Human Rights Law Review (eds.). Law and the Status of
    Women: An International Symposium. New York: United

Nations. Centre for Social Development and Humanitarian
Affairs. 1977. pp. 185-206.
Strobel, Margaret A.
"Slavery and Reproductive Labor in Mombasa." (In)
Robertson, Claire C. and Klein, Martin A. (eds.). Women
and Slavery in Africa. Madison, Wisconsin: University of
Wisconsin Press. 1983. pp. 111-129.

STATUS OF WOMEN

Buzzard, Shirley
"Women's Status and Wage Employment in Kisumu, Kenya."
Ph.D Dissertation: American University. Washington D.C.
1982. 289p.
Ciancanelli, Penelope
"Exchange, Reproduction and Sex Subordination Among the
Kikuyu of East Africa." Review of Radical Political
Economics. Volume 12 #2 Summer, 1980. pp. 25-36.
Gakuo, Mumbi
"The Kenyan Women and Situation and Strategies for
Improvement." Women's Studies International Forum.
Volume 8 #4 1985. pp. 373-379.
Gupta, Anirudha
"Illusion of Progress: The Women of Kenya." (In)
Phadnis, Urmila and Malani, Indira (eds.). Women of the
World: Ilusion and Reality. New Delhi, India: Vikas
Publishing House Ltd. 1980. pp. 245-259.
Gutto, Shadrack B.
"The Legal Status of Women in Kenya: Paternalism and
Inequality." Fletcher Forum. Volume 1 Fall, 1976. pp.
62-82.
Gutto, Shadrack B.
The Status of Women in Kenya: A Study of Paternalism,
Inequality and Under Privilege. Nairobi: University of
Nairobi. Institute for Development Studies. Discussion
Paper #235. April, 1976. 76p.
Harris, Joan
"Women in Kenya: Revolution or Evolution?" Africa
Report. Volume 30 #2 March-April, 1985. pp. 30-32.
Kenya. Ministry of Finance and Economic Planning
Women in Kenya, Social Perspectives. Nairobi: The
Ministry. Central Bureau of Statistics. 1978. 62p.
Likimani, Muthoni G.
"Women of Kenya: Fifteen Years of Independence. Nairobi:
Likamani. 1979. 76p.
Lindsay, Beverly
"An Examination of Education, Social Change and National
Development Policy: The Case of Kenyan Women." (In)
Women and Politics in 20th Century Africa and Asia.
Williamsburg, Virginia: College of William and Mary.
Anthropology Department. Studies in Third World
Societies. #16. June, 1981. pp. 29-48.

Lindsay, Beverly
   "Issues Confronting Professional African Women:
   Illustrations From Kenya." (In) Lindsay, Beverly (ed.).
   Comparative Perspectives of Third World Women: The Impact
   of Race, Sex and Class. New York: Praeger Publishers.
   1980. pp. 78-95.
Pala, Achola O.
   "Women Power in Kenya: Raising Funds and Awareness."
   Ceres. Volume 11 #2 March-April, 1978. pp. 43-46.
Reining, Priscilla (ed.)
   Village Women: Their Changing Lives and Fertility:
   Studies in Kenya. Mexico and the Philippines.
   Washington, D.C.: American Association for the
   Advancement of Science. AAAS Publication #77-6. 1977.
   273p.

URBANIZATION

Bujra, Janet M.
   "Proletarianization and the 'Informal Economy': A Case
   Study From Nairobi." African Urban Studies. #47 1978.
   pp. 47-66.
Kangi, M.W.
   "Some Factors Affecting Urban-Rural Fertility
   Differentials in Kenya: A Case Study of Nairobi and
   Central Province." Kenyan Geographer. Volume 4 #1/2
   1982. pp. 29-49.
Knotts, Mary A.
   "The Social and Economic Factors Associated With the
   Rural-Urban Migration of Kenyan Women." Ph.D
   Dissertation: Johns Hopkins University. Baltimore,
   Maryland. 1977. 306p.
Lakhani, S.A. and Jansen, A.A. and Lacko, W. and Sequeira,
E.
   "Suggested Reference Values for Serum Total Protein and
   Fractions of African and Indian Middle Class Urban Women
   and Newborns." East African Medical Journal. Volume 61
   #2 1984. pp. 128-132.
McAdoo, Harriette P.
   "Extended Family Involvement and Roles of Urban Kenyan
   Women." Paper Presented at the Women in the African
   Diaspora: An Interdisciplinary Perspective Research
   Conference. Washington, D.C.: Howard University. June,
   1983.
Mwaria, Cheryl B.
   "Rural-Urban Labor Migration and Family Arrangements
   Among the Kamba." (In) Robinson, Pearl T. and Skinner,
   Elliott (eds.). Transformation and Resiliency in Africa.
   Washington, D.C.: Howard University Press. 1983. pp.
   29-43.
Seeley, Janet
   "'We Have the Healing Power...': Independent Churches and

Women in Urban Kenya." Cambridge Anthropology. Volume 9 #2 1984. pp. 58-70.

Stichter, Sharon B.
"Women in the Urban Labor Force in Kenya." Paper Presented to the Wellesley Conference on Women and Development. Wellesley, Massachusetts: Wellesley College. Wellesley Center for Research on Women. June, 1976.

Thadani, Veena N.
"Women in Nairobi: The Paradox of Urban Progress." African Urban Studies. #3 Winter, 1978.

WOMEN AND THEIR CHILDREN

Brainard, J.M.
"Herders to Farmers: The Effects of Settlement on the Demography of the Turkana Population of Kenya." Ph.D Dissertation: State University of New York. Binghampton, New York. 1981. 356p.

Caron, James W.
Effects of Infant Characteristics on Caretaking Responsiveness Among the Gusii. Boston: Harvard University. Harvard Graduate School of Education. 1982. 128p.

Hull, Valerie and Simpson, Mayling
Breastfeeding, Child Health and Child Spacing: Cross-Cultural Perspectives. Dover, New Hampshire: Croom Helm. 1985. 216p.

Kune, J.B.
"Machakos Project Studies: Agents Affecting Health of Mother and Child in a Rural Area of Kenya. XV. The Economic Setting at the Household Level." Tropical and Geographical Medicine. Volume 31 #3 September, 1979. pp. 441-457.

Kusin, J.A.
"Infant Nutrition and Growth in Relation to Maternal Nutrition in Rural Kenya." Journal of Tropical Pediatrics. Volume 31 #1 February, 1985. pp. 24-30.

Mott, Susan H.
"A Note on the Determinants of Breastfeeding Durations in an African Country." Social Biology. Volume 31 #3-4 Fall-Winter, 1984. pp. 279-289.

Muganzi, Zibeon S.
"The Effect of Individual and Contextual Factors on Infant Mortality in Kenya." Ph.D Dissertation: Florida State University. Tallahassee, Florida. 1984. 172p.

Muller, A.S. and Ouma, J.H. and Mburu, F.M. and Blok, P.G.
"Agents Affecting Health of Mother and Child in a Rural Area of Kenya." Tropical and Geographical Medicine. Volume 29 #3 1977. pp. 291-302.

Seychelles

Benedict, Marion and Benedict, Burton
    Men, Women and Money in Seychelles. Berkeley,
    California: University of California Press. 1982. 250p.
Grainger, C.R.
    "The Age of Menarche in School Girls on Hahe,
    Seychelles." Transactions of the Royal Society of
    Tropical Medicine and Hygiene. Volume 74 #1 1980. pp.
    123-124.

Somalia

Adan, Amina H.
  "The Nomad Woman: Somalia." Paper Presented at the
  Seminar on Basic Education for Nomads. Nairobi: UNICEF.
  Eastern Africa Regional Office. Mogadishu, Somalia.
  April 1-9, 1978.
Dualeh, Raqiya H.
  "Female Circumcision in Somalia." Paper Presented at the
  Seminar on Traditional Practices Affecting the Health of
  Women and Children: Female Circumcision, Childhood
  Marriage, Nutritional Taboos, etc., Khartoum, Sudan.
  Alexandria, Egypt: World Health Organization. Eastern
  Mediterranean Regional Office. 1979.
Dualeh, Raqiya H.
  "Female Circumcision in Somalia." Paper Presented at the
  Seminar on Tradtional Practices Affecting the Health of
  Women and Children. World Conference of the United
  Nations Decade for Women, Copenhagen, Denmark, July
  14-30, 1980. New York: United Nations. 1980.
Forni, Elisabetta
  "Woman's New Role and Status in the Barawa Settlement."
  Paper Presented at the International Symposium on Somalia
  and the World. Mogadishu, Somalia. 1979. 6p.
Grassivaro, Gallo P.
  "Female Circumcision in Somalia: Anthropological Traits."
  Anthropologischer Anzeiger. Volume 43 #4 December,
  1985. pp. 311-326.
Ismail, Edna A.
  "Female Circumcision-Physical and Mental Complications."
  Paper Presented at the Seminar on Traditional Practices
  Affecting the Health of Women and Children: Female
  Circumcision, Childhood Marriage, Nutritional Taboos,
  etc., Khartoum, Sudan, February 10-15, 1979. Alexandria,
  Egypt: World Health Organization. Eastern Mediterranean
  Regional Office. 1979.

Ismail, Edna A.
   "Child Marriage and Early Teenage Childbirth." Paper
   Presented at the Seminar on Traditional Practices
   Affecting the Health of Women and Children: Female
   Circumcision, Childhood Marriage, Nutritional Taboos,
   etc., Khartoum, Sudan, 1979. Alexandria, Egypt: World
   Health Organization. Eastern Mediterranean Regional
   Office. 1979.
Ismail, Edna A.
   "Child Marriage and Early Teenage Childbirth." Paper
   Presented at the Seminar on Traditional Practices
   Affecting the Health of Women and Children, World
   Conference on the United Nations Decade for Women,
   Copenhagen, Denmark, July 14-30, 1980. New York: United
   Nations. 1980.
Ismail, Edna A.
   "Female Circumcision-Physical and Mental Complications."
   Paper Presented at the Seminar on Traditional Practices
   Affecting the Health of Women and Children. World
   Conference of the United Nations Decade for Women,
   Copenhagen, Denmark, July 14-30, 1980. New York: United
   Nations. 1980.
Langley, Myrtle S.
   "Spirit Possession, Exorcism and Social Context: An
   Anthropological Perspective With Theological
   Implications." Churchman. Volume 94 #3 1980. pp.
   226-245.
Okonkwo, J.I.
   "Naruddin Farah and the Changing Roles of Women." World
   Literature Today. Volume 58 #2 1984. pp. 215-221.
Otoo, S.N.A.
   Pharonic Circumcision in Somalia. Alexandria, Egypt:
   World Health Organization. Eastern Mediterranean
   Regional Office. Unpublished Report. 1976.
Pieters, Guy and Lowenfels, A.
   "Infibulation in the Horn of Africa." New York State
   Journal of Medicine. Volume 77 1977. pp. 729.
Slottved, Astrid
   "Role of Women in the Somali Revolution." Horn of
   Africa. Volume 2 #2 1979. pp. 15-21.
Somali Women's Democratic Organization
   "Somali Women." Report Delivered to the First Congress
   of the Somali Women's Democratic Organization.
   Mogadishu, Somalia: Somali Women's Democratic
   Organization. 1979. 34p.
Somalia. Ministry of Health.
   Fertility and Family Planning in Urban Somalia. Results
   of the Somali Family Health Survey in Five Cities, 1983.
   Mogadishu, Somalia: Ministry of Health. July, 1985.
   100p.
University of North Carolina
   The 1980-81 Somalia Fertility and Mortality Survey of
   Benadir, Bay and Lower Shebelle: A Summary of Results.

Chapel Hill, North Carolina: University of North
Carolina. International Program of Laboratories for
Population Statistics Summary. Series #4. December,
1981. 20p.
Warsame, M.
"Early Marriage and Teenage Deliveries in Somalia."
Paper Presented at the Seminar on Traditional Practices
Affecting the Health of Women and Childen: Female
Circumcision, Childhood Marriage, Nutritional Taboos,
etc., Khartoum, Sudan, February 10-15, 1979. Alexandria,
Egypt: World Health Organization. Eastern Mediterranean
Regional Office. 1979.
Warsame, M.
"Early Marriage and Teenage Deliveries in Somalia."
Paper Presented at the Seminar on Traditional Practices
Affecting the Health of Women and Children. World
Conference of the United Nations Decade for Women.
Copenhagen, Denmark, July 14-30, 1980.

Sudan

ABORTION

Rushwan, Hamid E. and Doodoh, A. and Chi, I-Cheng
    "Contraceptive Practice After Women Have Undergone
    'Spontaneous' Abortion in Indonesia and Sudan."
    International Journal of Gynaecology and Obstetrics.
    Volume 15 1977. pp. 241-249.
Rushwan, Hamid E.
    "Epidemiological Analysis and Reproductive
    Characteristics of Incomplete Abortion Patients in
    Khartoum, The Sudan." Journal of Biosocial Science.
    Volume 11 #1 January, 1979. pp. 65-76.
Rushwan, Hamid E. and Ferguson, J.G. and Bernard, Roger P.
    "Hospital Counseling in Khartoum: A Study of Factors
    Affecting Contraceptive Acceptance After Abortion."
    International Journal of Gynaecology and Obstetrics.
    Volume 15 #5 1978. pp. 440-443.
Rushwan, James G. and Bernard, Roger P.
    "Hospital Counseling in Khartoum: A Study of Factors
    Affecting Contraceptive Acceptance After Abortion."
    Paper Presented at the International Fertility Research
    Program. Chapel Hill, South Carolina: University of
    South Carolina. Pregnancy Termination Series #98. 1976.
    9p.

AGRICULTURE

Babiker, Abdel B. and El Din Abdu, Anwar S.
    "Rural Energy and the Environment: Impact of Women in
    Semi-Arid Sudan." (In) Baxter, Diana (ed.). Women and
    the Environment in the Sudan. Khartoum, Sudan:
    University of Khartoum. Institute for Environmental
    Studies. Environmental Research Paper Series #2.
    October, 1981. pp. 86-91a.

Badran, Margot
"Contamination in Practice." (In) Blair, Patricia W.
(ed.). Health Needs of the World's Poor Women.
Washington, D.C.: Equity Policy Center. 1981. pp.
98-101.
Baxter, Diana
"Women and Environment: A Downward Spiral." (In) Baxter,
Diana (ed.). Women and the Environment in the Sudan.
Khartoum, Sudan: University of Khartoum. Institute for
Environmental Studies. Environmental Research Paper
Series #2. October, 1981. pp. 1-9.
Baxter, Diana
Women and the Environment in the Sudan: Papers Presented
at the Workshop on Women and the Environment. Khartoum,
Sudan: University of Khartoum. Institute of
Environmental Studies. April 4-7, 1981. 142p.
Baxter, Diana (ed.).
Women and the Environment in the Sudan. Khartoum, Sudan:
University of Khartoum. Institute for Environmental
Studies. Environmental Research Paper Series #2.
October, 1981. 149p.
Bedri, Balghis Y.
"Pitfalls in Social Development: A Critical Review of a
Training Centre for Women." (In) Baxter, Diana (ed.).
Women and the Environment in the Sudan. Khartoum, Sudan:
University of Khartoum. Institute for Environmental
Studies. Environmental Research Paper Series #2.
October, 1981. pp. 36-40.
Berio, Ann
"Women as Nurturers: Present and Future." (In) Baxter,
Diana (ed.). Women and the Environment in the Sudan.
Khartoum, Sudan: University of Khartoum. Institute for
Environmental Studies. Environmental Research Paper
Series #2. October, 1981. pp. 130-136.
Bernal, V.
"Household Agricultural Production and Off-Farm Work in a
Sudan Village." Ph.D Dissertation: Northwestern
University. Evanston, Indiana. 1985.
Dey, Jennie M. and El Bagir, Ibrahim and Wagner, Albert
"The Rural Labour Market in the Eastern Region of Sudan."
Geneva: International Labour Office. Rural Employment
Policies Branch. 1983.
El Meheina, Rabab H.
"Food Production Projects for Rural Women." (In) Baxter,
Diana (ed.). Women and the Environment in the Sudan.
Khartoum, Sudan: University of Khartoum. Institute for
Environmental Studies. Environmental Research Paper
Series #2. October, 1981. pp. 111-112.
El Sayed, Mahasin K.
"Women's Role in Agriculture in Rural Khartoum Province."
(In) Baxter, Diana (ed.). Women and the Environment in
the Sudan. Khartoum, Sudan: University of Khartoum.

Institute for Environmental Studies. Environmental
Research Paper Series #2. October, 1981. pp. 113-119.
El-Bushra, Judy and Bekele, Abebech and Hammour, Fawzia
"Socio-Economic Development and Women's Changing Status."
(In) Baxter, Diana (ed.). Women and the Environment in
the Sudan. Khartoum, Sudan: University of Khartoum.
Institute for Environmental Studies. Environmental
Research Paper Series #2. October, 1981. pp. 8-16.
El-Sayyid, Mahasin K.
"Women's Role in Agriculture in Rural Khartoum Province."
Ph.D Dissertation: University of Khartoum. Khartoum,
Sudan. 1981.
El-Sayyid, Mahasin K.
"Women's Role in Agriculture in Rural Khartoum Province."
(In) Baxter, Diana (ed.). Women and the Environment in
the Sudan. Khartoum, Sudan: University of Khartoum.
Institute of Environmental Studies. Papers Presented at
the Workshop on Women and the Environment. April 4-7,
1981.
Fluehr-Lobban, Carolyn
"Women in Radical Political Movements in the Sudan."
Paper Presented at the Wellesley Conference on Women and
Development. Wellesley, Massachusetts: Wellesley
College. June 2-6, 1976.
Founou-Tchuigoua, B.
"De Facto Wage Earners in the Gezira Scheme." African
Development. Volume 8 #1 January-March, 1978. pp.
25-50.
Fruzzetti, L.
"Farm and Health: Rural Women in a Farming Community."
(In) Afshar, H. (ed.). Women, Work and Ideology in the
Third World. London: Tavistock. 1985. 37-65.
Gruenbaum, Ellen
Women's Labour in Subsistence Sector: The Case of the
Central Nuer Area of Jonglei Province. Unpublished
Paper. 1978.
Hassan, Kamil I.
"Women's Contribution to the Economy Through Agricultural
Work." (In) Baxter, Diana (ed.). Women and the
Environment in the Sudan. Khartoum, Sudan: University of
Khartoum. Institute for Environmental Studies.
Environmental Research Paper series #2. October, 1981.
pp. 107-110.
Ibrahim, Fouad N.
"The Role of Women Peasants in the Process of
Desertification in Western Sudan." Geojournal. Volume 6
#1 1982. pp. 25-30.
Ibrahim, Fouad N.
"The Role of Women in the Process of Desertification in
Western Sudan." (In) Baxter, Diana (ed.). Women and the
Environment in the Sudan. Khartoum, Sudan: University of
Khartoum. Institute for Environmental Studies.

Environmental Research Paper Series #2. October, 1981.
pp. 99-106.

Ibrahim, Suad A.
"Women's Role in Deforestation." (In) Baxter, Diana
(ed.). Women and the Environment in the Sudan.
Khartoum, Sudan: University of Khartoum. Institute for
Environmental Studies. Environmental Research Paper
Series #2. October, 1981. pp. 80-85.

Jahn, Samia A.
"Water Decade Projects for the Tropics Based on
Traditional Purification Methods of Sudanese Women."
(In) Baxter, Diana (ed.). Women and the Environment in
the Sudan. Khartoum, Sudan: University of Khartoum.
Institute for Environmental Studies. Environmental
Research Paper Series #2. October, 1981. pp. 49-57.

Khider, M.
"Women's Role in Agriculture in Rural Khartoum Province."
Ph.D Dissertation: University of Khartoum. Khartoum,
Sudan. 1981.

Murdock, Muneera S.
The Impact of Agricultural Development on a Pastoral
Society: The Shukriya of the Eastern Sudan. Washington,
D.C.: U.S. Department of State. U.S. Agency for
International Development. 1976. 54p.

Mustafa, Asha
"Women and Water in Western Kordofan." (In) Baxter,
Diana (ed.). Women and the Environment in the Sudan.
Khartoum, Sudan: University of Khartoum. Institute for
Environmental Studies. Environmental Research Paper
Series #2. October, 1981. pp. 67-69.

Russell, Annemarie
Report on the Situation of Women in the Target Villages
on the UNICEF Domestic Water Supply Project in Bahr el
Ghazal Province, Sudan. New York: United Nations.
UNICEF. 1979.

United Nations Economic Commission for Africa (UNECA)
Women and Cooperatives: Egypt, The Libyan Arab Jamahiriya
and the Sudan. Addis Ababa, Ethiopia: UNECA. Research
Series. 1980.

Villaume, Mary L.
"Alternative Technologies for Conservation and Food
Production in Southern Sudan." (In) Baxter, Diana (ed.).
Women and the Environment in the Sudan. Khartoum, Sudan:
University of Khartoum. Institute for Environmental
Studies. Environmental Research Paper Series #2.
October, 1981. pp. 120-124.

BIBLIOGRAPHIES

Women's Studies Documentation Unit
Women in Sudan: An Annotated Bibliography. Khartoum,
Sudan: University of Khartoum. Development Studies and

Research Centre. Women's Studies Documentation Unit.
1982. 28p.

CULTURAL ROLES

Abbas, Ibrahim and Kalule-Sabiti, I.
   The Proximate Determinates of Fertility in North Sudan.
   Voorburg, Netherlands: International Statistical
   Institute. WFS Scientific Report #73. June, 1985. 35p.
Abdalla, Raqiya
   Sisters in Affliction: Circumcision and Infibulation of
   Women in Africa. London: Zed Press. 1982. 122p.
Adam, Abbas Y.
   "Fertility and Prospects of Family Planning in the Three
   Towns." Sudan Journal of Population Studies. Volume 1
   #1 December, 1983. pp. 60-74.
Adam, Abbas Y.
   The Relation Between Nuptiality and Fertility in the
   Sudan. Khartoum, Sudan: Economic and Social Research
   Council, National Council for Research. Bulletin #98.
   August, 1983. 47p.
Adnan, Amal M. and Abu-Bakr, Salah
   "Postpartum Lactational Amenorrhoea as a Means of Family
   Planning in the Sudan: A Study of 500 Cases." Journal of
   Biosocial Science. Volume 15 #1 January, 1983. pp.
   9-23.
Ali, Mohamed A.
   "Education, Fertility and Development: An Overview."
   Economic and Social Research Council Bulletin. # 111
   April, 1984. 36p.
Ali, Nur and Mohammed, Nadia and Badri, Amira
   "Water Collection and Use: A Village Case Study." (In)
   Baxter, Diana (ed.). Women and the Environment in the
   Sudan. Khartoum, Sudan: University of Khartoum.
   Institute for Environmental Studies. Environmental
   Research Paper Series #2. October, 1981. pp. 58-63.
Anonymous
   "Sudan: Arab Women's Struggle." The Second Wave. Volume
   2 #2 1977.
Anonymous
   "Symposium on the Changing Status of Sudanese Women:
   Afhad University College for Women: Omdurman, Sudan,
   February 23-March 1, 1979." Resources for Feminist
   Research. Volume 9 #1 1980. pp. 81-94.
Aromasodu, M.C.
   "Traditional Practices Affecting the Health of Women in
   Pregnancy and Childbirth." Paper Presented at the
   Seminar on Traditional Practices Affecting the Health of
   Women and Children: Female Circumcision, Childhood
   Marriage, Nutritional Taboos, etc. Alexandria, Egypt:
   World Health Organization. Eastern Mediterranean
   Regional Office. Khartoum, Sudan. February 10-15, 1979.

Assaad, Fawzia
    "In Focus: The Sexual Mutilation of Women." World Health
    Forum: An International Journal of Health Development.
    Volume 3 #4 1982.
Aziz, F.
    "Gynecological and Obstetric Complications of Female
    Circumcision." International Journal of Gynaecology and
    Obstetrics. Volume 17 1980. pp. 560.
Baasher, Taha A.
    "Psycho-Social Aspects of Female Circumcision." Paper
    Presented at the Seminar on Traditional Practices
    Affecting the Health of Women and Children. World
    Conference of the United Nations Decade for Women. New
    York: United Nations. Copenhagen, Denmark. July 14-30,
    1980.
Baasher, Taha A.
    "Psychological Aspects of Female Circumcision." (In)
    World Health Organization (WHO). Traditional Practices
    Affecting the Health of Women and Children: Female
    Circumcision, Childhood Marriage, Nutritional Taboos,
    etc. Report of a Seminar. Alexandria, Egypt:
    WHO/Eastern Mediterranean Regional Office. Technical
    Publication #2. Khartoum, Sudan. 1979. pp. 71-105.
Baasher, Taha A.
    Psycho-Social Aspects of Female Circumcision." Paper
    Presented at the Seminar on Traditional Practices
    Affecting the Health of Women and Children: Female
    Circumcision, Childhood Marriage, Nutritional Taboos,
    etc. Alexandria, Egypt: World Health Organization.
    Eastern Mediterranean Regional Office. Khartoum, Sudan.
    February 10-15, 1979.
Babiker, Abdel B. and El Din Abdu, Anwar S.
    "Rural Energy and the Environment: Impact of Women in
    Semi-Arid Sudan." (In) Baxter, Diana (ed.). Women and
    the Environment in the Sudan. Khartoum, Sudan:
    University of Khartoum. Institute for Environmental
    Studies. Environmental Research Paper Series #2.
    October, 1981. pp. 86-91a.
Badri, Amina E. and Shabo, Mariam K. and Nujumi, Elhan E.
and Obeid, Marwa A. and Hassan, Majda M.
    "Income Generating Projects for Women: A Village Case
    Study." (In) Baxter, Diana (ed.). Women and the
    Environment in the Sudan. Khartoum, Sudan: University of
    Khartoum. Institute for Environmental Studies.
    Environmental Research Paper Series #2. October, 1981.
    pp. 30-35.
Badri, Gasim Y.
    "Child-Rearing Practices in the Sudan: Implications for
    Present Education." Ph.D Dissertation: University of
    California-Santa Barbara. Santa Barbara, California.
    1978. 238p.
Badri, Gasim Y.
    "Opinions About Female Circumcision." Paper Presented at
    the Seminar on Traditional Practices Affecting the Health

of Women and Children: Female Circumcision, Childhood
Marriage, Nutritional Taboos, etc. Alexandria, Egypt:
World Health Organization. Eastern Mediterranean
Regional Office. Khartoum, Sudan. February 10-15, 1979.
Badri, Gasim Y.
"Psycho-Social Aspects of Female Circumcision in the
Sudan." Paper Presented at the Seminar on Traditional
Practices Affecting the Health of Women and Children.
World Conference of the United Nations Decade for Women.
Copenhagen, Denmark. July 14-30, 1980.
Badri, Malik
"Sudanese Children's Concepts About Female Circumcision."
Paper Presented at the Seminar on Traditional Practices
Affecting the Health of Women and Children: Female
Circumcision, Childhood Marriage, Nutritional Taboos,
etc. Alexandria, Egypt: World Health Organization.
Eastern Mediteranean Regional Office. Khartoum, Sudan.
February 10-15, 1979.
Badri, Malik
"Sudanese Children's Concepts About Female Circumcision."
Paper Presented at the Seminar on Traditional Practices
Affecting the Health of Women and Children. World
Conference of the United Nations Decade for Women. New
York: United Nations. Copenhagen, Denmark. July 14-30,
1980.
Bakr, Salah A.
"Circumcision and Infibulation in Sudan." Paper
Presented at the Seminar on Traditional Practices
Affecting the Health of Women and Children: Female
Circumcision, Childhood Marriage, and Nutritional Taboos,
etc. Alexandria, Egypt: World Health Organization.
Eastern Mediterranean Regional Office. Khartoum, Sudan.
February 10-15, 1979.
Bakr, Salah A.
"Circumcision and Infibulation in the Sudan." Paper
Presented at the Seminar on Traditional Practices
Affecting the Health of Women and Children. World
Conference of the United Nations Decade for Women. New
York: United Nations. Copenhagen, Denamrk. July 14-30,
1980.
Bakri, Z.B. and Kameir, E.M.
"Aspects of Women's Political Participation in Sudan."
International Social Science Journal. Volume 35 #4 1983.
pp. 605-623.
Barnes-Dean, Virginia L.
"Clitoridectomy and Infibulation." Cultural Survival
Quarterly. Volume 9 #2 1985. pp. 26-30.
Baxter, Diana
"Women and Environment: A Downward Spiral." (In) Baxter,
Diana (ed.). Women and the Environment in the Sudan.
Khartoum, Sudan: University of Khartoum. Institute for
Environmental Studies. Environmental Research Paper
Series #2. October, 1981. pp. 1-9.

Baxter, Diana
Women and the Environment in the Sudan: Papers Presented
at the Workshop on Women and the Environment. Khartoum,
Sudan: University of Khartoum. Institute of
Environmental Studies. April 4-7, 1981. 142p.

Baxter, Diana (ed.).
Women and the Environment in the Sudan. Khartoum, Sudan:
University of Khartoum. Institute for Environmental
Studies. Environmental Research Paper Series #2.
October, 1981. 149p.

Bayoumi, Ahmed
"The Training and Activity of Village Midwives in the
Sudan." Tropical Doctor. Volume 6 #3 July, 1976. pp.
118-225.

Bella, H.
"The Village Midwives of the Sudan: An Enquiry into the
Availability and Quality of Maternity Care." Journal of
Tropical Pediatrics. Volume 30 #2 April, 1984. pp.
115-118.

Benson, Susan and Duffield, Mark
"Women's Work and Economic Change: The Hausa in Sudan and
in Nigeria." I.D.S. Bulletin. Volume 10 #9 June, 1979.
pp. 13-19.

Bernal, V.
"Household Agricultural Production and Off-Farm Work in a
Sudan Village." Ph.D Dissertation: Northwestern
University. Evanston, Indiana. 1985.

Boddy, J.
"Womb as Oasis: The Symbolic Context of Pharaonic
Circumcision in Rural Northern Sudan." American
Ethnologist. Volume 9 #4 November, 1982. pp. 682-698.

Burton, John F.
"Women and Men in Marriage: Some Atout Texts."
Anthropos. Volume 75 #5/6 1980. pp. 710-720.

Burton, John W.
"'The Moon is a Sheep': A Feminine Principle in Atout
Cosmology." Man. Volume 16 #3 September, 1981. pp.
441-450.

Burton, John W.
"Ghost Marriage and the Cattle Trade Among the Atout of
the Southern Sudan." Africa. Volume 48 #4 1978. pp.
398-405.

Burton, John W.
"Independence and the Status of Nilotic Women." Africa
Today. Volume 28 #2 2nd Quarter 1981. pp. 54-60.

Burton, John W.
"Nilotic Women: A Diachronic Perspective." Journal of
Modern African Studies. Volume 20 #3 1982. pp. 467-491.

Clark, Isobel and Diaz, Christina
"Circumcision: A Slow Change in Attitudes." Sudanow.
Volume 2 #3 March, 1977. pp. 43-45.

Cloudsley, Anne
Women of Omdurman: Life, Love and the Cult of Virginity.
London: Ethnographica Publishers. 1983. 184p.

Cloudsley, Anne
Women of the Sudan: Victims of Circumcision. Privately
Printed. Available From Author: 4 Craven Hill, London,
England. W2 3DS. 1980. 144p.
Constantinides, Pamela
"Women Heal Women: Spirit Possession and Sexual
Segregation in a Muslim Society." Social Science and
Medicine. Volume 21 #6 1985. pp. 685-692.
Cook, Robert
"Damage to Physical Health From Pharaonic Cicumcision of
Females--A Review of the Medical Literature." Paper
Presented at the Seminar on Traditional Practices
Affecting the Health of Women And Children: Female
Circumcision, Childhood Marriage, Nutritional Taboos,
etc. Alexandria, Egypt: World Health Organization.
Eastern Mediterranean Regional Office. Khartoum, Sudan.
1979.
Delmet, C.
"Islamization and Matriliny in the Dar-Fung, Sudan."
L'Homme. Volume 19 April-June, 1979. pp. 33-52.
Dodoo, Nii M.S.
"On the Micro-Level Decisions to Limit Fertility: A
Theoretical Framework and Econometric Estimation Using
Taiwan, Korea and Urban Sudan." Ph. D Dissertation:
University of Pennsylvania. Philadelphia, Pennsylvania.
1985. 165p.
El Awad Galal El Din, Mohamed
"The Rationality of High Fertility in Urban Sudan." (In)
Caldwell, John C. (ed.). The Persistence of High
Fertility: Population Prospects in the Third World.
Canberra, Australia: Australian National University.
Department of Demography. Volume Two. 1977. pp.
633-660.
El Awad alal el Din, Mohamed
"The Economic Value of Children in Rural Sudan." (In)
Caldwell, John C. (ed.). The Persistence of High
Fertility: Population Prospects in the Third World.
Canberra, Australia: Australian National University.
Department of Demography. Volume Two. 1977. pp.
617-632.
El Sadaawi, Nawal
"Circumcision of Girls." Paper Presented at the Seminar
on Tradtional Practices Affecting the Health of Women and
Children. World Conference of the United Nations Decade
for Women. New York: United Nations. Copenhagen,
Denmark. July 14-30, 1980.
El Sayed, M.
"Female Circumcision in Sudan." Paper Presented at the
Seminar on Traditional Practices Affecting the Health of
Women and Children. World Conference of the United
Nations Decade for Women. New York: United Nations.
Copenhagen, Denmark. July 14-30, 1980.

El Sayed, M.
"Female Circumcision in Sudan." Paper Presented at the
Seminar on Traditional Practices Affecting the Health of
Women and Children: Female Circumcision, Childhood
Marriage, Nutritional Taboos, etc. Alexandria, Egypt:
World Health Organization. Eastern Mediterranean
Regional Office. Khartoum, Sudan. February 10-15, 1979.

El Sayed, Mahasin K.
"Women's Role in Agriculture in Rural Khartoum Province."
(In) Baxter, Diana (ed.). Women and the Environment in
the Sudan. Khartoum, Sudan: University of Khartoum.
Institute for Environmental Studies. Environmental
Research Paper Series #2. October, 1981. pp. 113-119.

El-Bakri, Z.B. and Kameir, E.M. (eds.)
"Aspects of Women's Political Participation in Sudan."
International Social Science Journal. Volume 35 #4 1983.
pp. 605-624.

El-Bushra, Judy and Bekele, Abebech and Hammour, Fawzia
"Socio-Economic Development and Women's Changing Status."
(In) Baxter, Diana (ed.). Women and the Environment in
the Sudan. Khartoum, Sudan: University of Khartoum.
Institute for Environmental Studies. Environmental
Research Paper Series #2. October, 1981. pp. 8-16.

El-Dareer, Asma A.
"A Study of Prevalence and Epidemiology of Female
Circumcision in Sudan Today." Paper Presented at the
Seminar on Traditional Practices Affecting the Health of
Women and Children. World Conference of the United
Nations Decade for Women. New York: United Nations.
Copenhagen, Denmark. July 14-30, 1980.

El-Dareer, Asma A.
"A Study on Prevalence and Epidemiology of Female
Circumcision in Sudan Today." Paper Presented at the
Seminar on Tradtional Practices Affecting the Health of
Women and Children: Female Circumcision, Childhood
Marriage, Nutritional Taboos, etc. Alexandria, Egypt:
World Health Organization. Eastern Mediterranean
Regional Office. Khartoum, Sudan. February 10-15, 1979.

El-Dareer, Asma A.
"Attitudes of Sudanese People to the Practice of Female
Circumcision." International Journal of Epidemiology.
Volume 12 #2 June, 1983. pp. 138-144.

El-Dareer, Asma A.
"Female Circumcision and Current Preventive Efforts in
the Sudan." Paper Presented at the Annual Meeting of the
African Studies Association. Paper #25. Baltimore,
Maryland. 1978. 28p.

El-Dareer, Asma A.
Woman, Why Do You Weep? Circumcision and Its
Consequences. London: Zed Press. 1982. 130p.

El-Dareer, Asma A.
"Women and Health in the Sudan." Paper Presented at the
Annual Meeting of the African Studies Association. Paper
#26. Baltimore, Maryland. 1978. 25p.

El-Kashef, Samy and Youssef, Humam A.
"Household and Family in Rural Gezira, Sudan." (In)
Huzayyin, S.A. and Acsadi, G.T. (eds.). Family and
Marriage in Some African and Asiatic Countries. Cairo:
Cairo Demographic Centre. Research Monograph Series #6.
1976. pp. 161-174.

El-Nagar, S.
"The Zar." Sudanow. Volume 3 #1 January, 1978. pp.
65-67.

El-Sayyid, Mahasin K.
"Women's Role in Agriculture in Rural Khartoum Province."
Ph.D Dissertation: University of Khartoum. Khartoum,
Sudan. 1981.

El-Sayyid, Mahasin K.
"Women's Role in Agriculture in Rural Khartoum Province."
(In) Baxter, Diana (ed.). Women and the Environment in
the Sudan. Khartoum, Sudan: University of Khartoum.
Institute of Environmental Studies. Papers Presented at
the Workshop on Women and the Environment. April 4-7,
1981.

El-Tom, Abdul R. and Farah, Abdul-Aziz and Lauro, Donald and
Fenn, Thomas
Community and Individual Acceptance: Family Planning
Services in the Sudan. New York: Columbia University.
Center for Population and Family Health. Health Working
Paper Series #14. January, 1985. 47p.

Elmalik, Khitma H.
"Hazards of Water Use." (In) Baxter, Diana (ed.). Women
and the Environment in the Sudan. Khartoum, Sudan:
University of Khartoum. Institute for Environmental
Studies. Environmental Research Paper Series #2.
October, 1981. pp. 64-66.

Evans-Pritchard, E.E.
Witchcraft Oracles and Magic Among the Azande. Oxford,
England: Clarendon Press. 1976. 265p.

Evens, T.M.
"Mind, Logic and the Efficacy of the Nuer Incest
Prohibition." Man. Volume 18 #1 March, 1983. pp.
111-133.

Farah, Abdul-Aziz
"Child Mortality and its Correlates in Sudan." Ph.D
Dissertation: University of Pennsylvania. Philadelphia,
Pennsylvania. 1981. 282p.

Farah, Abdul-Aziz
"Influence of Child Mortality on Fertility Related
Attitudes and Behavior in Greater Khartoum." (In) Cairo
Demographic Centre (CDC). Determinants of Fertility in
Some African and Asian Countries. Cairo: CDC. CDC
Research Monograph Series #10. 1982. pp. 227-261.

Fluehr-Lobban, Carolyn
"Agitation for Change in the Sudan." (In) Schlegel,
Alice E. (ed.). Sexual Stratification: A Cross-Cultural
View. New York: Columbia University Press. 1977. pp.
127-143.

Fluehr-Lobban, Carolyn
    "Challenging Some Myths: Women in Shari's (Islamic) Law
    in the Sudan." Expedition. Volume 25 #3 Spring, 1983.
    pp. 32-39.
Fluehr-Lobban, Carolyn
    "Women in Radical Political Movements in the Sudan."
    Paper Presented at the Wellesley Conference on Women and
    Development. Wellesley, Massachusetts: Wellesley
    College. June 2-6, 1976.
Founou-Tchuigoua, B.
    "De Facto Wage Earners in the Gezira Scheme." African
    Development. Volume 8 #1 January-March, 1978. pp.
    25-50.
Fruzzetti, L.
    "Farm and Health: Rural Women in a Farming Community."
    (In) Afshar, H. (ed.). Women, Work and Ideology in the
    Third World. London: Tavistock. 1985. 37-65.
Gerais, Abdel S. and Omran, S. and Liao, Kharia F. and
Winston C.
    "A Comparative Study of Two Estrogen Dosages in Combined
    Oral Contraceptives Among Sudanese Women." International
    Journal of Gynaecology and Obstetrics. Volume 21 #6
    December, 1983. pp. 459-468.
Gilfoun, Nadia
    "A Women's Place?" Sudanow. Volume 2 #11 November,
    1977. pp. 26-32.
Gizuli, Shahwa
    "Current Programmes in Nutrition Education." (In)
    Baxter, Diana (ed.). Women and the Environment in the
    Sudan. Khartoum, Sudan: University of Khartoum.
    Institute for Environmental Studies. Environmental
    Research Paper Series #2. October, 1981. pp. 125-129.
Gore, Paul W.
    "How Stable are Marriages Among the Azande." Sudan
    Journal of Population. Volume 1 #1 December, 1983. pp.
    75-100.
Gore, Paul W.
    Population Decline in South-Western Sudan: The Case of
    the Azande. Khartoum, Sudan: University of Khartoum.
    Development Studies and Research Centre. DSRC Seminar
    Series Discussion Paper #27. January, 1983. 36p.
Gore, Paul W.
    "Socio-Cultural and Demographic Characteristics of a Low
    Fertility Population in South-Western Sudan: The Case of
    the Azande." Ph.D Dissertation: London School of
    Economics. London, England. 1981. 377p.
Gruenbaum, Ellen
    "The Movement Against Clitoridectomy and Infibulation in
    Sudan: Public Health Policy and the Women's Movement."
    Medical Anthropology Newsletter. Volume 13 #2 1982. pp.
    4-12.
Gruenbaum, Ellen
    Women's Labour in Subsistence Sector: The Case of the

Central Nuer Area of Jonglei Province. Unpublished
Paper. 1978.

Hakem, Ahmed M. and Hrbek, Ivan and Vercoutter, Jean
"The Matriarchs of Meroe: A Powerful Line of Queens Who
Ruled the Kushitic Empire." UNESCO Courier. Volume 32
#8/9 August-September, 1979. pp. 58-59.

Hall, Marjorie J. and Ismail, Bakhita A.
Sisters Under the Sun: The Story of Sudanese Women. New
York: Longman. 1982. 264p.

Hall, Marjorie J.
"The Position of Women in Egypt and the Sudan as
Reflected in Feminist Writing Since 1900." Ph.D
Dissertation: University of London. London, England.
1977. 369p.

Hammour, Fatima A.
"Women, Economic Backwardness and Education in the
Sudan." (In) Baxter, Diana (ed.). Women and the
Environment in the Sudan. Khartoum, Sudan: University of
Khartoum. Institute for Environmental Studies.
Environmental Research Paper Series #2. October, 1981.
pp. 23-24.

Hassan, Kamil I.
"Women's Contribution to the Economy Through Agricultural
Work." (In) Baxter, Diana (ed.). Women and the
Environment in the Sudan. Khartoum, Sudan: University of
Khartoum. Institute for Environmental Studies.
Environmental Research Paper series #2. October, 1981.
pp. 107-110.

Hutchinson, Sharon
"Relations Between the Sexes Among the Nuer: 1930."
Africa. Volume 50 #4 1980. pp. 371-388.

Ibrahim, Fouad N.
"The Role of Women Peasants in the Process of
Desertification in Western Sudan." Geojournal. Volume 6
#1 1982. pp. 25-30.

Ibrahim, Fouad N.
"The Role of Women in the Process of Desertification in
Western Sudan." (In) Baxter, Diana (ed.). Women and the
Environment in the Sudan. Khartoum, Sudan: University of
Khartoum. Institute for Environmental Studies.
Environmental Research Paper Series #2. October, 1981.
pp. 99-106.

Ibrahim, Suad A.
"Women's Role in Deforestation." (In) Baxter, Diana
(ed.). Women and the Environment in the Sudan.
Khartoum, Sudan: University of Khartoum. Institute for
Environmental Studies. Environmental Research Paper
Series #2. October, 1981. pp. 80-85.

Ismail, Ellen T.
Social Environment and Daily Routine of Sudanese Women: A
Case Study of Urban Middle Class Housewives. Berlin,
Germany: D. Reimer. 1982. 224p.

Jahn, Samia A.
    "Water Decade Projects for the Tropics Based on
    Traditional Purification Methods of Sudanese Women."
    (In) Baxter, Diana (ed.). Women and the Environment in
    the Sudan. Khartoum, Sudan: University of Khartoum.
    Institute for Environmental Studies. Environmental
    Research Paper Series #2. October, 1981. pp. 49-57.
Jalal el-Deen, Mohamed A.
    "Birth Control Trends and Preference for Male Children in
    Jordon and Sudan." Population Bulletin of ECWA. #22/23
    June-December, 1982. pp. 71-91.
Karrar, Gaafar
    "Population Planning for the Future." Sudanow. Volume 9
    #2 February, 1984. pp. 36-37.
Kertzer, David I. and Madison, Oker B.B.
    "Women's Age-Set Systems in Africa: The Lutuka of
    Southern Sudan." (In) Fry, Christine L. (ed.).
    Dimensions: Aging, Culture and Health. New York: Praeger
    Publishers. pp. 109-130. 1981.
Khalifa, Mona A.
    "Age Pattern of Fertility in Sudan." Journal of
    Biosocial Science. Volume 15 #3 July, 1983. pp.
    317-323.
Khalifa, Mona A.
    "Birth Control Practice in Khartoum." Egyptian
    Population and Family Planning Review. Volume 15 #1
    June, 1981. pp. 10-21.
Khalifa, Mona A.
    "Characterisitics and Attitudes of Family Planners in
    Khartoum, Sudan." Journal of Biosocial Science. Volume
    14 #1 January, 1982. pp. 7-16.
Khalifa, Mona A.
    Fertility Differentials in Urban Khartoum. Khartoum,
    Sudan: National Council for Research. Economic and
    Social Research Council. Bulletin #81. December, 1979.
    19p.
Khalifa, Mona A.
    "Fertility Differentials in a Moslem Society: A Case
    Study From Khartoum Province, Sudan." Ph.D Dissertation:
    London University. London, England. 1979. 359p.
Khalifa, Mona A.
    "Knowledge and Attitudes of Family Planning in Khartoum
    Province, Sudan." Egyptian Population and Family
    Planning Review. Volume 16 #1 June, 1982. pp. 20-38.
Khider, M.
    "Women's Role in Agriculture in Rural Khartoum Province."
    Ph.D Dissertation: University of Khartoum. Khartoum,
    Sudan. 1981.
Levy, Wendy and Bijleveld, Catrien
    "Workshop Against Circumcision: African Women Speak."
    Sudanow. Volume 9 #12 December, 1984. pp. 28-31.
Lightfoot-Klein, H.
    "Pharaonic Circumcision of Females in the Sudan."
    Medicine and Law. Volume 2 #4 1983. pp. 353-360.

Lowenstein, L.F.
  "Attitudes and Attitude Differences to Female Genital
  Mutilation in the Sudan: Is There a Change on the
  Horizon?" Social Science and Medicine. Volume 12 #5A
  September, 1978. pp. 417-421.
Magnarella, P.J.
  "Republican Brothers: A Reformist Movement in the Sudan."
  Muslim World. Volume 72 January, 1982. pp. 14-24.
Modawi, Osman
  "Traditional Practices in Child Health in Sudan." Paper
  Presented at the Seminar on Traditional Practices
  Affecting the Health of Women and Children. World
  Conference of the United Nations Decade for Women. New
  York: United Nations. Copenhagen, Denmark. July 14-30,
  1980.
Modawi, Osman
  "Traditional Practices in Childbirth in Sudan." Paper
  Presented at the Seminar on Traditional Practices
  Affecting the Health of Women and Children: Female
  Circumcision, Childhood Marriage, Nutritional Taboos,
  Etc. Alexandria, Egypt: World Health Organization.
  Eastern Mediterranean Regional Office. Khartoum, Sudan.
  1979.
Modawi, Suleiman
  "The Obstetrical and Gynaecological Aspects of Female
  Circumcision in the Sudan." Paper Presented at the
  Seminar on Traditional Practices Affecting the Health of
  Women and Children. World Conference of the United
  Nations Decade for Women. New York: United Nations.
  Copenhagen, Denmark. July 14-30, 1980.
Modawi, Suleiman
  "The Obstetrical and Gynaecological Aspects of Female
  Circumcision." Paper Presented at the Seminar on
  Traditional Practices Affecting the Health of Women and
  Children: Female Circumcision, Childhood Marriage,
  Nutritional Taboos, etc. Alexandria, Egypt: World Health
  Organization. Eastern Mediterranean Regional Office.
  Khartoum, Sudan. February 10-15, 1979.
Moharib, Samir R. (ed.)
  Fertility Norms in Sudan. Cairo: Cairo Demographic
  Centre. CDC Research Monograph Series #12. 1984. pp.
  235-264.
Muludiang, Venansio T.
  "Urbanization, Female Migration and Labor Utilization in
  Urban Sudan: The Case of the Southern Region." Ph.D
  Dissertation: Brown University. Providence, Rhode
  Island. 1983. 265p.
Murdock, Muneera S.
  The Impact of Agricultural Development on a Pastoral
  Society: The Shukriya of the Eastern Sudan. Washington,
  D.C.: U.S. Department of State. U.S. Agency for
  International Development. 1976. 54p.

Mustafa, Asha
"Women and Water in Western Kordofan." (In) Baxter,
Diana (ed.). Women and the Environment in the Sudan.
Khartoum, Sudan: University of Khartoum. Institute for
Environmental Studies. Environmental Research Paper
Series #2. October, 1981. pp. 67-69.
Mustafa, M.Y.
Fertility and Migration: A Preliminary Analysis of
Dynamics of Urban Growth. Khartoum, Sudan: National
Council for Research. Economic and Social Research
Council. Bulletin #91. February, 1981. 87p.
Naisho, Joyce
"Health Care for Women in the Sudan." World Health
Forum: An International Journal of Health Development.
Volume 3 #2 1982.
Naishom, Joyce
"Tradition and Other Constraints on Health Care for Women
in the Sudan." (In) Blair, Patricia W. (ed.). Health
Needs of the World's Poor Women. Washington, D.C.:
Equity Policy Center. 1981. pp. 76-77.
Nouri, Mohamed O.
"Fertility Differentials in the Democratic Republic of
the Sudan." Ph.D Dissertation: Mississippi State
University. Starksville, Mississippi. 1983. 264p.
Nur, Osman el-H. M.
"The Physiological Effect of Infant Mortality in
Reproductive Behavior in the Sudan." International
Journal of Gynaecology and Obstetrics. Volume 23 #2
April, 1985. pp. 143-147.
Ocholla-Ayayo, A.B.
"Marriage and Cattle Exchange Among the Nilotic Luo."
Paideuma. Volume 25 1979. pp. 173-193.
Osman, A.K.
"Dietary Practices and Aversions During Pregnancy and
Lactation Among Sudanese Women." Journal of Tropical
Pediatrics. Volume 31 #1 February, 1985. pp.16-20.
Osman, Ali K.
"Dietary Practices and Aversions During Pregnancy and
Lactation Among Sudanese Women." Paper Presented at the
Seminar on Traditional Practices Affecting the Health of
Women and Children. World Conference of the United
Nations Decade for Women. New York: United Nations.
Copenhagen, Denmark. July 14-30, 1980.
Osman, Ali K.
"Dietary Practices and Aversions During Pregnancy and
Lactation Among Sudanese Women." Paper Presented at the
Seminar on Traditional Practices Affecting the Health of
Women and Children: Female Circumcision, Childhood
Marriage, Nutritional Taboos, etc. Alexandria, Egypt:
World Health Organization. Eastern Mediterranean
Regional Office. Khartoum, Sudan. February 10-15, 1979.
Rushwan, Hamid E. and Doodoh, A. and Chi, I-Cheng
"Contraceptive Practice After Women Have Undergone
'Spontaneous' Abortion in Indonesia and Sudan."

International Journal of Gynaecology and Obstetrics.
Volume 15 1977. pp. 241-249.
Rushwan, Hamid E. and Ferguson, J.G. and Bernard, Roger P.
"Hospital Counseling in Khartoum: A Study of Factors
Affecting Contraceptive Acceptance After Abortion."
International Journal of Gynaecology and Obstetrics.
Volume 15 #5 1978. pp. 440-443.
Rushwan, James G. and Bernard, Roger P.
"Hospital Counseling in Khartoum: A Study of Factors
Affecting Contraceptive Acceptance After Abortion."
Paper Presented at the International Fertility Research
Program. Chapel Hill, South Carolina: University of
South Carolina. Pregnancy Termination Series #98. 1976.
9p.
Russell, Annemarie
Report on the Situation of Women in the Target Villages
on the UNICEF Domestic Water Supply Project in Bahr el
Ghazal Province, Sudan. New York: United Nations.
UNICEF. 1979.
Saghayroun, Atif A.R.
"Women's Status and Fertility in the Sudan." Ahfad
Journal. Volume 2 #1 June, 1985. pp. 46-52.
Sanderson, Lilian P.
Against the Mutilation of Women: The Struggle to End
Unnecessary Suffering. London: Ithaca Press. 1981.
117p.
Toubia, Nahid F.
"The Social and Political Implications of Female
Circumcision: The Case of the Sudan." (In) Fernea,
Elizabeth W. (ed.). Women and the Family in the Middle
East: New Voices of Change. Austin, Texas: University of
Texas Press. 1985. pp. 148-164.
United Nations Educational, Scientific and Cultural Organ.
Social Science Research and Women in the Arab World.
Paris: UNESCO. 1984. 175p.
Villaume, Mary L.
"Alternative Technologies for Conservation and Food
Production in Southern Sudan." (In) Baxter, Diana (ed.).
Women and the Environment in the Sudan. Khaartoum,
Sudan: University of Khartoum. Institute for
Environmental Studies. Environmental Research Paper
Series #2. October, 1981. pp. 120-124.
Wallace, Wendy
"The Birth Control Debate." Middle East. #108 October,
1983. pp. 53-54.
Young, William C.
"Cultural Change and Women's Work: The Sedentarization of
the Rashiidy Bedouin in the Sudan." Cultural Survival
Quarterly. Volume 8 #2 Summer, 1984. pp. 28-29.

DEVELOPMENT AND TECHNOLOGY

Ali, Mohamed A.
   "Education, Fertility and Development: An Overview."
   Economic and Social Research Council Bulletin. # 111
   April, 1984. 36p.
Badri, Amina E. and Shabo, Mariam K. and Nujumi, Elhan E.
and Obeid, Marwa A. and Hassan, Majda M.
   "Income Generating Projects for Women: A Village Case
   Study." (In) Baxter, Diana (ed.). Women and the
   Environment in the Sudan. Khartoum, Sudan: University of
   Khartoum. Institute for Environmental Studies.
   Environmental Research Paper Series #2. October, 1981.
   pp. 30-35.
Baxter, Diana
   "Women and Environment: A Downward Spiral." (In) Baxter,
   Diana (ed.). Women and the Environment in the Sudan.
   Khartoum, Sudan: University of Khartoum. Institute for
   Environmental Studies. Environmental Research Paper
   Series #2. October, 1981. pp. 1-9.
Baxter, Diana
   Women and the Environment in the Sudan: Papers Presented
   at the Workshop on Women and the Environment. Khartoum,
   Sudan: University of Khartoum. Institute of
   Environmental Studies. April 4-7, 1981. 142p.
Baxter, Diana (ed.).
   Women and the Environment in the Sudan. Khartoum, Sudan:
   University of Khartoum. Institute for Environmental
   Studies. Environmental Research Paper Series #2.
   October, 1981. 149p.
Bedri, Balghis Y.
   "Pitfalls in Social Development: A Critical Review of a
   Training Centre for Women." (In) Baxter, Diana (ed.).
   Women and the Environment in the Sudan. Khartoum, Sudan:
   University of Khartoum. Institute for Environmental
   Studies. Environmental Research Paper Series #2.
   October, 1981. pp. 36-40.
Berio, Ann
   "Women as Nurturers: Present and Future." (In) Baxter,
   Diana (ed.). Women and the Environment in the Sudan.
   Khartoum, Sudan: University of Khartoum. Institute for
   Environmental Studies. Environmental Research Paper
   Series #2. October, 1981. pp. 130-136.
Dey, Jennie M. and El Bagir, Ibrahim and Wagner, Albert
   The Rural Labour Market in the Eastern Region of Sudan.
   Geneva: International Labour Office. Rural Employment
   Policies Branch. 1983.
El Meheina, Rabab H.
   "Food Production Projects for Rural Women." (In) Baxter,
   Diana (ed.). Women and the Environment in the Sudan.
   Khartoum, Sudan: University of Khartoum. Institute for
   Environmental Studies. Environmental Research Paper
   Series #2. October, 1981. pp. 111-112.

SUDAN

El-Bushra, Judy and Bekele, Abebech and Hammour, Fawzia
"Socio-Economic Development and Women's Changing Status."
(In) Baxter, Diana (ed.). Women and the Environment in
the Sudan. Khartoum, Sudan: University of Khartoum.
Institute for Environmental Studies. Environmental
Research Paper Series #2. October, 1981. pp. 8-16.

El-Sayyid, Mahasin K.
"Women's Role in Agriculture in Rural Khartoum Province."
Ph.D Dissertation: University of Khartoum. Khartoum,
Sudan. 1981.

El-Sayyid, Mahasin K.
"Women's Role in Agriculture in Rural Khartoum Province."
(In) Baxter, Diana (ed.). Women and the Environment in
the Sudan. Khartoum, Sudan: University of Khartoum.
Institute of Environmental Studies. Papers Presented at
the Workshop on Women and the Environment. April 4-7,
1981.

El-Wassela, Negeya
A Study on Three Centres Catering for Women Training
Programs. Khartoum, Sudan: University of Khartoum.
Development Studies and Research Centre. 1980.

Fluehr-Lobban, Carolyn
"Agitation for Change in the Sudan." (In) Schlegel,
Alice E. (ed.). Sexual Stratification: A Cross-Cultural
View. New York: Columbia University Press. 1977. pp.
127-143.

Founou-Tchuigoua, B.
"De Facto Wage Earners in the Gezira Scheme." African
Development. Volume 8 #1 January-March, 1978. pp.
25-50.

Gore, Paul W.
Population Decline in South-Western Sudan: The Case of
the Azande. Khartoum, Sudan: University of Khartoum.
Development Studies and Research Centre. DSRC Seminar
Series Discussion Paper #27. January, 1983. 36p.

Gruenbaum, Ellen
Women's Labour in Subsistence Sector: The Case of the
Central Nuer Area of Jonglei Province. Unpublished
Paper. 1978.

Hammour, Fatima A.
"Women, Economic Backwardness and Education in the
Sudan." (In) Baxter, Diana (ed.). Women and the
Environment in the Sudan. Khartoum, Sudan: University of
Khartoum. Institute for Environmental Studies.
Environmental Research Paper Series #2. October, 1981.
pp. 23-24.

Jahn, Samia A.
"Water Decade Projects for the Tropics Based on
Traditional Purification Methods of Sudanese Women."
(In) Baxter, Diana (ed.). Women and the Environment in
the Sudan. Khartoum, Sudan: University of Khartoum.
Institute for Environmental Studies. Environmental
Research Paper Series #2. October, 1981. pp. 49-57.

137

Kashif-Badri, Hagga
  "The History, Development, Organization and Position of
  Women's Studies in the Sudan." (In) United Nations
  Educational, Scientific and Cultural Organization.
  Social Science Research and Women in the Arab World.
  Paris: UNESCO. 1984. pp. 94-112.
Kashif-Badri, Hagga
  "The History, Development, Organization and Position of
  Women's Studies in the Sudan." Paper Presented at the
  Meeting of Arab Women Researchers on the Development of
  Research in the Social Sciences on Women in the Arab
  World. Paris: United Nations Educational, Scientific and
  Cultural Organization. Tunis, Tunisia. 1982. 17p.
Murdock, Muneera S.
  The Impact of Agricultural Development on a Pastoral
  Society: The Shukriya of the Eastern Sudan. Washington,
  D.C.: U.S. Department of State. U.S. Agency for
  International Development. 1976. 54p.
Pasquet, Marie-Ange
  "Women in the Economic Environment: A Comparison of Two
  Co-Operatives." (In) Baxter, Diana (ed.). Women and the
  Environment in the Sudan. Khartoum, Sudan: University of
  Khartoum. Institute for Environmental Studies.
  Environmental Research Paper Series #2. October, 1981.
  pp. 25-29.
Russell, Annemarie
  Report on the Situation of Women in the Target Villages
  on the UNICEF Domestic Water Supply Project in Bahr el
  Ghazal Province, Sudan. New York: United Nations.
  UNICEF. 1979.
Sadaty, Fahima Z.
  "Women and Their Environment: A General View." (In)
  Baxter, Diana (ed.). Women and the Environment in the
  Sudan. Khartoum, Sudan: University of Khartoum.
  Institute for Environmental Studies. Environmental
  Research Paper Series #2. October, 1981. pp. 17-22.
Snyder, M.
  "Women and Development." (In) El-Hassan, Ali M. (ed.).
  Growth, Employment and Equity in the Sudan. Khartoum,
  Sudan: University of Khartoum Press. 1977. pp. 237-238.
United Nations Economic Commission for Africa (UNECA)
  Report of a Workshop for Trainees of Rural Women Leaders:
  Khartoum. Addis Ababa, Ethiopia: UNECA. Workshop Report
  Series. 1977. 132p.
United Nations Economic Commission for Africa (UNECA)
  Women and Cooperatives: Egypt, The Libyan Arab Jamahiriya
  and the Sudan. Addis Ababa, Ethiopia: UNECA. Research
  Series. 1980.
Villaume, Mary L.
  "Alternative Technologies for Conservation and Food
  Production in Southern Sudan." (In) Baxter, Diana (ed.).
  Women and the Environment in the Sudan. Khartoum, Sudan:
  University of Khartoum. Institute for Environmental

Studies. Environmental Research Paper Series #2.
October, 1981. pp. 120-124.

ECONOMICS

Badri, Amina E. and Shabo, Mariam K. and Nujumi, Elhan E.
and Obeid, Marwa A. and Hassan, Majda M.
    "Income Generating Projects for Women: A Village Case
    Study." (In) Baxter, Diana (ed.). Women and the
    Environment in the Sudan. Khartoum, Sudan: University of
    Khartoum. Institute for Environmental Studies.
    Environmental Research Paper Series #2. October, 1981.
    pp. 30-35.
Bakri, Z.B. and Kameir, E.M.
    "Aspects of Women's Political Participation in Sudan."
    International Social Science Journal. Volume 35 #4 1983.
    pp. 605-623.
Baxter, Diana
    "Women and Environment: A Downward Spiral." (In) Baxter,
    Diana (ed.). Women and the Environment in the Sudan.
    Khartoum, Sudan: University of Khartoum. Institute for
    Environmental Studies. Environmental Research Paper
    Series #2. October, 1981. pp. 1-9.
Baxter, Diana (ed.).
    Women and the Environment in the Sudan. Khartoum, Sudan:
    University of Khartoum. Institute for Environmental
    Studies. Environmental Research Paper Series #2.
    October, 1981. 149p.
Bedri, Balghis Y.
    "Pitfalls in Social Development: A Critical Review of a
    Training Centre for Women." (In) Baxter, Diana (ed.).
    Women and the Environment in the Sudan. Khartoum, Sudan:
    University of Khartoum. Institute for Environmental
    Studies. Environmental Research Paper Series #2.
    October, 1981. pp. 36-40.
Benson, Susan and Duffield, Mark
    "Women's Work and Economic Change: The Hausa in Sudan and
    in Nigeria." I.D.S. Bulletin. Volume 10 #9 June, 1979.
    pp. 13-19.
Berio, Ann
    "Women as Nurturers: Present and Future." (In) Baxter,
    Diana (ed.). Women and the Environment in the Sudan.
    Khartoum, Sudan: University of Khartoum. Institute for
    Environmental Studies. Environmental Research Paper
    Series #2. October, 1981. pp. 130-136.
El-Bakri, Z.B. and Kameir, E.M. (eds.)
    "Aspects of Women's Political Participation in Sudan."
    International Social Science Journal. Volume 35 #4 1983.
    pp. 605-624.
El-Bushra, Judy and Bekele, Abebech and Hammour, Fawzia
    "Socio-Economic Development and Women's Changing Status."
    (In) Baxter, Diana (ed.). Women and the Environment in

the Sudan. Khartoum, Sudan: University of Khartoum. Institute for Environmental Studies. Environmental Research Paper Series #2. October, 1981. pp. 8-16.

Hassan, Kamil I.
"Women's Contribution to the Economy Through Agricultural Work." (In) Baxter, Diana (ed.). Women and the Environment in the Sudan. Khartoum, Sudan: University of Khartoum. Institute for Environmental Studies. Environmental Research Paper series #2. October, 1981. pp. 107-110.

Muludiang, Venansio T.
"Urbanization, Female Migration and Labor Utilization in Urban Sudan: The Case of the Southern Region." Ph.D Dissertation: Brown University. Providence, Rhode Island. 1983. 265p.

Pasquet, Marie-Ange
"Women in the Economic Environment: A Comparison of Two Co-Operatives." (In) Baxter, Diana (ed.). Women and the Environment in the Sudan. Khartoum, Sudan: University of Khartoum. Institute for Environmental Studies. Environmental Research Paper Series #2. October, 1981. pp. 25-29.

Sadaty, Fahima Z.
"Women and Their Environment: A General View." (In) Baxter, Diana (ed.). Women and the Environment in the Sudan. Khartoum, Sudan: University of Khartoum. Institute for Environmental Studies. Environmental Research Paper Series #2. October, 1981. pp. 17-22.

Snyder, M.
"Women and Development." (In) El-Hassan, Ali M. (ed.). Growth, Employment and Equity in the Sudan. Khartoum, Sudan: University of Khartoum Press. 1977. pp. 237-238.

United Nations Economic Commission for Africa (UNECA)
Report of a Workshop for Trainees of Rural Women Leaders: Khartoum. Addis Ababa, Ethiopia: UNECA. Workshop Report Series. 1977. 132p.

United Nations Economic Commission for Africa (UNECA)
Women and Cooperatives: Egypt, The Libyan Arab Jamahiriya and the Sudan. Addis Ababa, Ethiopia: UNECA. Research Series. 1980.

Young, William C.
"Cultural Change and Women's Work: The Sedentarization of the Rashiidy Bedouin in the Sudan." Cultural Survival Quarterly. Volume 8 #2 Summer, 1984. pp. 28-29.

EDUCATION AND TRAINING

Ali, Mohamed A.
"Education, Fertility and Development: An Overview." Economic and Social Research Council Bulletin. # 111 April, 1984. 36p.

Badri, Amina E. and Shabo, Mariam K. and Nujumi, Elhan E.
and Obeid, Marwa A. and Hassan, Majda M.
    "Income Generating Projects for Women: A Village Case
    Study." (In) Baxter, Diana (ed.). Women and the
    Environment in the Sudan. Khartoum, Sudan: University of
    Khartoum. Institute for Environmental Studies.
    Environmental Research Paper Series #2. October, 1981.
    pp. 30-35.
Badri, Amina E.
    "Sudan: Women's Studies--A New Village Stove." (In)
    Morgan, Robin (ed.). Sisterhood is Global. Garden City,
    New York: Anchor Books. 1984. pp. 644-654.
Badri, Gasim Y.
    "Child-Rearing Practices in the Sudan: Implications for
    Present Education." Ph.D Dissertation: University of
    California-Santa Barbara. Santa Barbara, California.
    1978. 238p.
Bakri, Z.B. and Kameir, E.M.
    "Aspects of Women's Political Participation in Sudan."
    International Social Science Journal. Volume 35 #4 1983.
    pp. 605-623.
Bedri, Balghis Y.
    "Pitfalls in Social Development: A Critical Review of a
    Training Centre for Women." (In) Baxter, Diana (ed.).
    Women and the Environment in the Sudan. Khartoum, Sudan:
    University of Khartoum. Institute for Environmental
    Studies. Environmental Research Paper Series #2.
    October, 1981. pp. 36-40.
El Meheina, Rabab H.
    "Food Production Projects for Rural Women." (In) Baxter,
    Diana (ed.). Women and the Environment in the Sudan.
    Khartoum, Sudan: University of Khartoum. Institute for
    Environmental Studies. Environmental Research Paper
    Series #2. October, 1981. pp. 111-112.
El Sayed, Mahasin K.
    "Women's Role in Agriculture in Rural Khartoum Province."
    (In) Baxter, Diana (ed.). Women and the Environment in
    the Sudan. Khartoum, Sudan: University of Khartoum.
    Institute for Environmental Studies. Environmental
    Research Paper Series #2. October, 1981. pp. 113-119.
Eyben, Rosalind and Kartunnen, Maryatta
    "Skills Training for Girls and Women." Paper Presented
    at the Ahfad Symposium on the Changing Status of Women in
    the Sudan. Omdurman, Sudan: Ahfad University College for
    Women. 1978.
Gizuli, Shahwa
    "Current Programmes in Nutrition Education." (In)
    Baxter, Diana (ed.). Women and the Environment in the
    Sudan. Khartoum, Sudan: University of Khartoum.
    Institute for Environmental Studies. Environmental
    Research Paper Series #2. October, 1981. pp. 125-129.
Hammour, Fatima A.
    "Women, Economic Backwardness and Education in the
    Sudan." (In) Baxter, Diana (ed.). Women and the

Environment in the Sudan. Khartoum, Sudan: University of
Khartoum. Institute for Environmental Studies.
Environmental Research Paper Series #2. October, 1981.
pp. 23-24.
Kashif-Badri, Hagga
"The History, Development, Organization and Position of
Women's Studies in the Sudan." (In) United Nations
Educational, Scientific and Cultural Organization.
Social Science Research and Women in the Arab World.
Paris: UNESCO. 1984. pp. 94-112.
Kashif-Badri, Hagga
"The History, Development, Organization and Position of
Women's Studies in the Sudan." Paper Presented at the
Meeting of Arab Women Researchers on the Development of
Research in the Social Sciences on Women in the Arab
World. Paris: United Nations Educational, Scientific and
Cultural Organization. Tunis, Tunisia. 1982. 17p.
Moharib, Samir R. (ed.)
Fertility Norms in Sudan. Cairo: Cairo Demographic
Centre. CDC Research Monograph Series #12. 1984. pp.
235-264.
Pasquet, Marie-Ange
"Women in the Economic Environment: A Comparison of Two
Co-Operatives." (In) Baxter, Diana (ed.). Women and the
Environment in the Sudan. Khartoum, Sudan: University of
Khartoum. Institute for Environmental Studies.
Environmental Research Paper Series #2. October, 1981.
pp. 25-29.

EMPLOYMENT AND LABOR

Ali, Nur and Mohammed, Nadia and Badri, Amira
"Water Collection and Use: A Village Case Study." (In)
Baxter, Diana (ed.). Women and the Environment in the
Sudan. Khartoum, Sudan: University of Khartoum.
Institute for Environmental Studies. Environmental
Research Paper Series #2. October, 1981. pp. 58-63.
Babiker, Abdel B. and El Din Abdu, Anwar S.
"Rural Energy and the Environment: Impact of Women in
Semi-Arid Sudan." (In) Baxter, Diana (ed.). Women and
the Environment in the Sudan. Khartoum, Sudan:
University of Khartoum. Institute for Environmental
Studies. Environmental Research Paper Series #2.
October, 1981. pp. 86-91a.
Baxter, Diana
"Women and Environment: A Downward Spiral." (In) Baxter,
Diana (ed.). Women and the Environment in the Sudan.
Khartoum, Sudan: University of Khartoum. Institute for
Environmental Studies. Environmental Research Paper
Series #2. October, 1981. pp. 1-9.
Baxter, Diana
Women and the Environment in the Sudan: Papers Presented

at the Workshop on Women and the Environment. Khartoum,
Sudan: University of Khartoum. Institute of
Environmental Studies. April 4-7, 1981. 142p.

Baxter, Diana (ed.).
Women and the Environment in the Sudan. Khartoum, Sudan:
University of Khartoum. Institute for Environmental
Studies. Environmental Research Paper Series #2.
October, 1981. 149p.

Benson, Susan and Duffield, Mark
"Women's Work and Economic Change: The Hausa in Sudan and
in Nigeria." I.D.S. Bulletin. Volume 10 #9 June, 1979.
pp. 13-19.

Berio, Ann
"Women as Nurturers: Present and Future." (In) Baxter,
Diana (ed.). Women and the Environment in the Sudan.
Khartoum, Sudan: University of Khartoum. Institute for
Environmental Studies. Environmental Research Paper
Series #2. October, 1981. pp. 130-136.

Bernal, V.
"Household Agricultural Production and Off-Farm Work in a
Sudan Village." Ph.D Dissertation: Northwestern
University. Evanston, Indiana. 1985.

Dey, Jennie M. and El Bagir, Ibrahim and Wagner, Albert
The Rural Labour Market in the Eastern Region of Sudan.
Geneva: International Labour Office. Rural Employment
Policies Branch. 1983.

El Sayed, Mahasin K.
"Women's Role in Agriculture in Rural Khartoum Province."
(In) Baxter, Diana (ed.). Women and the Environment in
the Sudan. Khartoum, Sudan: University of Khartoum.
Institute for Environmental Studies. Environmental
Research Paper Series #2. October, 1981. pp. 113-119.

El-Bakri, Z.B. and Kameir, E.M. (eds.)
"Aspects of Women's Political Participation in Sudan."
International Social Science Journal. Volume 35 #4 1983.
pp. 605-624.

El-Bushra, Judy and Bekele, Abebech and Hammour, Fawzia
"Socio-Economic Development and Women's Changing Status."
(In) Baxter, Diana (ed.). Women and the Environment in
the Sudan. Khartoum, Sudan: University of Khartoum.
Institute for Environmental Studies. Environmental
Research Paper Series #2. October, 1981. pp. 8-16.

El-Sayyid, Mahasin K.
"Women's Role in Agriculture in Rural Khartoum Province."
Ph.D Dissertation: University of Khartoum. Khartoum,
Sudan. 1981.

El-Sayyid, Mahasin K.
"Women's Role in Agriculture in Rural Khartoum Province."
(In) Baxter, Diana (ed.). Women and the Environment in
the Sudan. Khartoum, Sudan: University of Khartoum.
Institute of Environmental Studies. Papers Presented at
the Workshop on Women and the Environment. April 4-7,
1981.

El-Wassela, Negeya
    A Study on Three Centres Catering for Women Training
    Programs. Khartoum, Sudan: University of Khartoum.
    Development Studies and Research Centre. 1980.
Eyben, Rosalind and Kartunnen, Maryatta
    "Skills Training for Girls and Women." Paper Presented
    at the Ahfad Symposium on the Changing Status of Women in
    the Sudan. Omdurman, Sudan: Ahfad University College for
    Women. 1978.
Founou-Tchuigoua, B.
    "De Facto Wage Earners in the Gezira Scheme." African
    Development. Volume 8 #1 January-March, 1978. pp.
    25-50.
Gruenbaum, Ellen
    Women's Labour in Subsistence Sector: The Case of the
    Central Nuer Area of Jonglei Province. Unpublished
    Paper. 1978.
Hammour, Fatima A.
    "Women, Economic Backwardness and Education in the
    Sudan." (In) Baxter, Diana (ed.). Women and the
    Environment in the Sudan. Khartoum, Sudan: University of
    Khartoum. Institute for Environmental Studies.
    Environmental Research Paper Series #2. October, 1981.
    pp. 23-24.
Hassan, Kamil I.
    "Women's Contribution to the Economy Through Agricultural
    Work." (In) Baxter, Diana (ed.). Women and the
    Environment in the Sudan. Khartoum, Sudan: University of
    Khartoum. Institute for Environmental Studies.
    Environmental Research Paper Series #2. October, 1981.
    pp. 107-110.
Ibrahim, Fouad N.
    "The Role of Women in the Process of Desertification in
    Western Sudan." (In) Baxter, Diana (ed.). Women and the
    Environment in the Sudan. Khartoum, Sudan: University of
    Khartoum. Institute for Environmental Studies.
    Environmental Research Paper Series #2. October, 1981.
    pp. 99-106.
Kashif-Badri, Hagga
    "The History, Development, Organization and Position of
    Women's Studies in the Sudan." (In) United Nations
    Educational, Scientific and Cultural Organization.
    Social Science Research and Women in the Arab World.
    Paris: UNESCO. 1984. pp. 94-112.
Kashif-Badri, Hagga
    "The History, Development, Organization and Position of
    Women's Studies in the Sudan." Paper Presented at the
    Meeting of Arab Women Researchers on the Development of
    Research in the Social Sciences on Women in the Arab
    World. Paris: United Nations Educational, Scientific and
    Cultural Organization. Tunis, Tunisia. 1982. 17p.
Khider, M.
    "Women's Role in Agriculture in Rural Khartoum Province."

Ph.D Dissertation: University of Khartoum. Khartoum,
Sudan. 1981.
Moharib, Samir R. (ed.)
Fertility Norms in Sudan. Cairo: Cairo Demographic
Centre. CDC Research Monograph Series #12. 1984. pp.
235-264.
Muludiang, Venansio T.
"Urbanization, Female Migration and Labor Utilization in
Urban Sudan: The Case of the Southern Region." Ph.D
Dissertation: Brown University. Providence, Rhode
Island. 1983. 265p.
Sadaty, Fahima Z.
"Women and Their Environment: A General View." (In)
Baxter, Diana (ed.). Women and the Environment in the
Sudan. Khartoum, Sudan: University of Khartoum.
Institute for Environmental Studies. Environmental
Research Paper Series #2. October, 1981. pp. 17-22.
Snyder, M.
"Women and Development." (In) El-Hassan, Ali M. (ed.).
Growth, Employment and Equity in the Sudan. Khartoum,
Sudan: University of Khartoum Press. 1977. pp. 237-238.
Young, William C.
"Cultural Change and Women's Work: The Sedentarization of
the Rashiidy Bedouin in the Sudan." Cultural Survival
Quarterly. Volume 8 #2 Summer, 1984. pp. 28-29.

EQUALITY AND LIBERATION

Snyder, M.
"Women and Development." (In) El-Hassan, Ali M. (ed.).
Growth, Employment and Equity in the Sudan. Khartoum,
Sudan: University of Khartoum Press. 1977. pp. 237-238.

FAMILY LIFE

Ali, Nur and Mohammed, Nadia and Badri, Amira
"Water Collection and Use: A Village Case Study." (In)
Baxter, Diana (ed.). Women and the Environment in the
Sudan. Khartoum, Sudan: University of Khartoum.
Institute for Environmental Studies. Environmental
Research Paper Series #2. October, 1981. pp. 58-63.
Badri, Gasim Y.
"Child-Rearing Practices in the Sudan: Implications for
Present Education." Ph.D Dissertation: University of
California-Santa Barbara. Santa Barbara, California.
1978. 238p.
Baxter, Diana
"Women and Environment: A Downward Spiral." (In) Baxter,
Diana (ed.). Women and the Environment in the Sudan.
Khartoum, Sudan: University of Khartoum. Institute for
Environmental Studies. Environmental Research Paper
Series #2. October, 1981. pp. 1-9.

Benson, Susan and Duffield, Mark
    "Women's Work and Economic Change: The Hausa in Sudan and
    in Nigeria." I.D.S. Bulletin. Volume 10 #9 June, 1979.
    pp. 13-19.
Burton, John F.
    "Women and Men in Marriage: Some Atout Texts."
    Anthropos. Volume 75 #5/6 1980. pp. 710-720.
Delmet, C.
    "Islamization and Matriliny in the Dar-Fung, Sudan."
    L'Homme. Volume 19 April-June, 1979. pp. 33-52.
El-Kashef, Samy and Youssef, Humam A.
    "Household and Family in Rural Gezira, Sudan." (In)
    Huzayyin, S.A. and Acsadi, G.T. (eds.). Family and
    Marriage in Some African and Asiatic Countries. Cairo:
    Cairo Demographic Centre. Research Monograph Series #6.
    1976. pp. 161-174.
Gilfoun, Nadia
    "A Women's Place?" Sudanow. Volume 2 #11 November,
    1977. pp. 26-32.
Ismail, Ellen T.
    Social Environment and Daily Routine of Sudanese Women: A
    Case Study of Urban Middle Class Housewives. Berlin,
    Germany: D. Reimer. 1982. 224p.
Mustafa, M.Y.
    Fertility and Migration: A Preliminary Analysis of
    Dynamics of Urban Growth. Khartoum, Sudan: National
    Council for Research. Economic and Social Research
    Council. Bulletin #91. February, 1981. 87p.
Saghayroun, Atif A.R.
    "Women's Status and Fertility in the Sudan." Ahfad
    Journal. Volume 2 #1 June, 1985. pp. 46-52.
Young, William C.
    "Cultural Change and Women's Work: The Sedentarization of
    the Rashiidy Bedouin in the Sudan." Cultural Survival
    Quarterly. Volume 8 #2 Summer, 1984. pp. 28-29.

FAMILY PLANNING AND CONTRACEPTION

Abbas, Ibrahim and Kalule-Sabiti, I.
    The Proximate Determinates of Fertility in North Sudan.
    Voorburg, Netherlands: International Statistical
    Institute. WFS Scientific Report #73. June, 1985. 35p.
Adam, Abbas Y.
    "Fertility and Prospects of Family Planning in the Three
    Towns." Sudan Journal of Population Studies. Volume 1
    #1 December, 1983. pp. 60-74.
Adam, Abbas Y.
    The Relation Between Nuptiality and Fertility in the
    Sudan. Khartoum, Sudan: Economic and Social Research
    Council, National Council for Research. Bulletin #98.
    August, 1983. 47p.

Adnan, Amal M. and Abu-Bakr, Salah
"Postpartum Lactational Amenorrhoea as a Means of Family
Planning in the Sudan: A Study of 500 Cases." Journal of
Biosocial Science. Volume 15 #1 January, 1983. pp.
9-23.
Dodoo, Nii M.S.
"On the Micro-Level Decisions to Limit Fertility: A
Theoretical Framework and Econometric Estimation Using
Taiwan, Korea and Urban Sudan." Ph. D Dissertation:
University of Pennsylvania. Philadelphia, Pennsylvania.
1985. 165p.
El Awad Galal El Din, Mohamed
"The Rationality of High Fertility in Urban Sudan." (In)
Caldwell, John C. (ed.). The Persistence of High
Fertility: Population Prospects in the Third World.
Canberra, Australia: Australian National University.
Department of Demography. Volume Two. 1977. pp.
633-660.
El-Tom, Abdul R. and Farah, Abdul-Aziz and Lauro, Donald and
Fenn, Thomas
Community and Individual Acceptance: Family Planning
Services in the Sudan. New York: Columbia University.
Center for Population and Family Health. Health Working
Paper Series #14. January, 1985. 47p.
Farah, Abdul-Aziz
"Influence of Child Mortality on Fertility Related
Attitudes and Behavior in Greater Khartoum." (In) Cairo
Demographic Centre (CDC). Determinants of Fertility in
Some African and Asian Countries. Cairo: CDC. CDC
Research Monograph Series #10. 1982. pp. 227-261.
Farid, Samir
"Fertility Patterns in the Arab Region." International
Family Planning Perspectives. Volume 10 #4 December,
1984. pp. 119-125.
Gerais, Abdel S. and Omran, S. and Liao, Kharia F. and
Winston C.
"A Comparative Study of Two Estrogen Dosages in Combined
Oral Contraceptives Among Sudanese Women." International
Journal of Gynaecology and Obstetrics. Volume 21 #6
December, 1983. pp. 459-468.
Jalal el-Deen, Mohamed A.
"Birth Control Trends and Preference for Male Children in
Jordon and Sudan." Population Bulletin of ECWA. #22/23
June-December, 1982. pp. 71-91.
Karrar, Gaafar
"Population Planning for the Future." Sudanow. Volume 9
#2 February, 1984. pp. 36-37.
Khalifa, Mona A.
"Age Pattern of Fertility in Sudan." Journal of
Biosocial Science. Volume 15 #3 July, 1983. pp.
317-323.
Khalifa, Mona A.
"Birth Control Practice in Khartoum." Egyptian

Population and Family Planning Review. Volume 15 #1
June, 1981. pp. 10-21.
Khalifa, Mona A.
"Characterisitics and Attitudes of Family Planners in
Khartoum, Sudan." Journal of Biosocial Science. Volume
14 #1 January, 1982. pp. 7-16.
Khalifa, Mona A.
Fertility Differentials in Urban Khartoum. Khartoum,
Sudan: National Council for Research. Economic and
Social Research Council. Bulletin #81. December, 1979.
19p.
Khalifa, Mona A.
"Fertility Differentials in a Moslem Society: A Case
Study From Khartoum Province, Sudan." Ph.D Dissertation:
London University. London, England. 1979. 359p.
Khalifa, Mona A.
"Knowledge and Attitudes of Family Planning in Khartoum
Province, Sudan." Egyptian Population and Family
Planning Review. Volume 16 #1 June, 1982. pp. 20-38.
Nouri, Mohamed O.
"Fertility Differentials in the Democratic Republic of
the Sudan." Ph.D Dissertation: Mississippi State
University. Starksville, Mississippi. 1983. 264p.
Nur, Osman el-H. M.
Infant and Child Mortality and its Effect on Reproductive
Behavior in the Northern Provinces of Sudan. Wad Medani,
Sudan: University of Gezira. Faculty of Economics and
Rural Development. Population Studies Center. PSC
Research Report. 1983. 68p.
Nur, Osman el-H. M.
"The Physiological Effect of Infant Mortality in
Reproductive Behavior in the Sudan." International
Journal of Gynaecology and Obstetrics. Volume 23 #2
April, 1985. pp. 143-147.
Rushwan, Hamid E. and Doodoh, A. and Chi, I-Cheng
"Contraceptive Practice After Women Have Undergone
'Spontaneous' Abortion in Indonesia and Sudan."
International Journal of Gynaecology and Obstetrics.
Volume 15 1977. pp. 241-249.
Rushwan, Hamid E. and Ferguson, J.G. and Bernard, Roger P.
"Hospital Counseling in Khartoum: A Study of Factors
Affecting Contraceptive Acceptance After Abortion."
International Journal of Gynaecology and Obstetrics.
Volume 15 #5 1978. pp. 440-443.
Rushwan, James G. and Bernard, Roger P.
"Hospital Counseling in Khartoum: A Study of Factors
Affecting Contraceptive Acceptance After Abortion."
Paper Presented at the International Fertility Research
Program. Chapel Hill, South Carolina: University of
South Carolina. Pregnancy Termination Series #98. 1976.
9p.

Wallace, Wendy
    "The Birth Control Debate." Middle East. #108 October,
    1983. pp. 53-54.

FERTILITY AND INFERTILITY

Abbas, Ibrahim and Kalule-Sabiti, I.
    The Proximate Determinates of Fertility in North Sudan.
    Voorburg, Netherlands: International Statistical
    Institute. WFS Scientific Report #73. June, 1985. 35p.
Adam, Abbas Y.
    "Fertility and Prospects of Family Planning in the Three
    Towns." Sudan Journal of Population Studies. Volume 1
    #1 December, 1983. pp. 60-74.
Adam, Abbas Y.
    The Relation Between Nuptiality and Fertility in the
    Sudan. Khartoum, Sudan: Economic and Social Research
    Council, National Council for Research. Bulletin #98.
    August, 1983. 47p.
Ali, Mohamed A.
    "Education, Fertility and Development: An Overview."
    Economic and Social Research Council Bulletin. # 111
    April, 1984. 36p.
Dodoo, Nii M.S.
    "On the Micro-Level Decisions to Limit Fertility: A
    Theoretical Framework and Econometric Estimation Using
    Taiwan, Korea and Urban Sudan." Ph. D Dissertation:
    University of Pennsylvania. Philadelphia, Pennsylvania.
    1985. 165p.
Eelens, Frank and Donne, L.
    The Proximate Determinants of Fertility in Sub-Saharan
    Africa: A Factbook Based on the Results of the World
    Fertility Survey. Brussels, Belgium: Vrije Universiteit
    Brussel. Interuniversity Programme in Demography. IDP
    Working Paper #1985-3. 1985. 122p.
El Awad Galal El Din, Mohamed
    "The Rationality of High Fertility in Urban Sudan." (In)
    Caldwell, John C. (ed.). The Persistence of High
    Fertility: Population Prospects in the Third World.
    Canberra, Australia: Australian National University.
    Department of Demography. Volume Two. 1977. pp.
    633-660.
Farah, Abdul-Aziz
    "Influence of Child Mortality on Fertility Related
    Attitudes and Behavior in Greater Khartoum." (In) Cairo
    Demographic Centre (CDC). Determinants of Fertility in
    Some African and Asian Countries. Cairo: CDC. CDC
    Research Monograph Series #10. 1982. pp. 227-261.
Farid, Samir
    "Fertility Patterns in the Arab Region." International
    Family Planning Perspectives. Volume 10 #4 December,
    1984. pp. 119-125.

Gore, Paul W.
   Population Decline in South-Western Sudan: The Case of
   the Azande. Khartoum, Sudan: University of Khartoum.
   Development Studies and Research Centre. DSRC Seminar
   Series Discussion Paper #27. January, 1983. 36p.
Gore, Paul W.
   "Socio-Cultural and Demographic Characteristics of a Low
   Fertility Population in South-Western Sudan: The Case of
   the Azande." Ph.D Dissertation: London School of
   Economics. London, England. 1981. 377p.
International Statistical Institute (ISI)
   The Sudan Fertility Survey, 1979: A Summary of Findings.
   Voorburg, Netherlands: ISI. World Fertility Survey
   Report #36. 1982. 17p.
International Statistical Institute (ISI)
   The Sudan Fertility Survey, 1979: A Summary of Findings.
   Voorburg, Netherlands: ISI. World Fertility Survey
   Report #36. 1982. 17p.
Khalifa, Mona A.
   "Age Pattern of Fertility in Sudan." Journal of
   Biosocial Science. Volume 15 #3 July, 1983. pp.
   317-323.
Khalifa, Mona A.
   Fertility Differentials in Urban Khartoum. Khartoum,
   Sudan: National Council for Research. Economic and
   Social Research Council. Bulletin #81. December, 1979.
   19p.
Khalifa, Mona A.
   "Fertility Differentials in a Moslem Society: A Case
   Study From Khartoum Province, Sudan." Ph.D Dissertation:
   London University. London, England. 1979. 359p.
Larsen, Ulla
   A Comparative Study of the Levels and the Covariates of
   Sterility in Cameroon, Kenya and Sudan. Princeton, New
   Jersey: Princeton University. Office of Population
   Research. 1985.
Moharib, Samir R. (ed.)
   Fertility Norms in Sudan. Cairo: Cairo Demographic
   Centre. CDC Research Monograph Series #12. 1984. pp.
   235-264.
Mustafa, M.Y.
   Fertility and Migration: A Preliminary Analysis of
   Dynamics of Urban Growth. Khartoum, Sudan: National
   Council for Research. Economic and Social Research
   Council. Bulletin #91. February, 1981. 87p.
Nouri, Mohamed O.
   "Fertility Differentials in the Democratic Republic of
   the Sudan." Ph.D Dissertation: Mississippi State
   University. Starksville, Mississippi. 1983. 264p.
Nur, Osman el-H. M.
   Infant and Child Mortality and its Effect on Reproductive
   Behavior in the Northern Provinces of Sudan. Wad Medani,
   Sudan: University of Gezira. Faculty of Economics and

Rural Development. Population Studies Center. PSC
Research Report. 1983. 68p.
Saghayroun, Atif A.R.
"Women's Status and Fertility in the Sudan." Ahfad
Journal. Volume 2 #1 June, 1985. pp. 46-52.
Sudan. Department of Statistics
The Sudan Fertility Survey, 1979: Principle Report.
Khartoum, Sudan: Department of Statistics. Two Volumes.
1982. 1001p.
Sudan. Ministry of Health
Infant and Early Childhood Mortality in Relation to
Fertility Patterns: Report on an Ad-Hoc Survey in Greater
Khartoum and in the Blue Nile, Kassala and Kordofan
Provinces, 1974-1976. Khartoum, Sudan: Ministry of
Health. 1981. 165p.

HEALTH, NUTRITION AND MEDICINE

Abbas, Ibrahim and Kalule-Sabiti, I.
The Proximate Determinates of Fertility in North Sudan.
Voorburg, Netherlands: International Statistical
Institute. WFS Scientific Report #73. June, 1985. 35p.
Abdalla, Raqiya
Sisters in Affliction: Circumcision and Infibulation of
Women in Africa. London: Zed Press. 1982. 122p.
Adnan, Amal M. and Abu-Bakr, Salah
"Postpartum Lactational Amenorrhoea as a Means of Family
Planning in the Sudan: A Study of 500 Cases." Journal of
Biosocial Science. Volume 15 #1 January, 1983. pp.
9-23.
Aromasodu, M.C.
"Traditional Practices Affecting the Health of Women in
Pregnancy and Childbirth." Paper Presented at the
Seminar on Traditional Practices Affecting the Health of
Women and Children: Female Circumcision, Childhood
Marriage, Nutritional Taboos, etc. Alexandria, Egypt:
World Health Organization. Eastern Mediterranean
Regional Office. Khartoum, Sudan. February 10-15, 1979.
Assaad, Fawzia
"In Focus: The Sexual Mutilation of Women." World Health
Forum: An International Journal of Health Development.
Volume 3 #4 1982.
Attallah, N.L.
"Age at Menarche of Schoolgirls in Khartoum." Annals of
Human Biology. Volume 10 #2 March-April, 1983. pp.
185-188.
Aziz, F.
"Gynecological and Obstetric Complications of Female
Circumcision." International Journal of Gynaecology and
Obstetrics. Volume 17 1980. pp. 560.
Baasher, Taha A.
"Psycho-Social Aspects of Female Circumcision." Paper

Presented at the Seminar on Traditional Practices
Affecting the Health of Women and Children. World
Conference of the United Nations Decade for Women. New
York: United Nations. Copenhagen, Denmark. July 14-30,
1980.
Baasher, Taha A.
"Psychological Aspects of Female Circumcision." (In)
World Health Organization (WHO). Traditional Practices
Affecting the Health of Women and Children: Female
Circumcision, Childhood Marriage, Nutritional Taboos,
etc. Report of a Seminar. Alexandria, Egypt:
WHO/Eastern Mediterranean Regional Office. Technical
Publication #2. Khartoum, Sudan. 1979. pp. 71-105.
Baasher, Taha A.
Psycho-Social Aspects of Female Circumcision." Paper
Presented at the Seminar on Traditional Practices
Affecting the Health of Women and Children: Female
Circumcision, Childhood Marriage, Nutritional Taboos,
etc. Alexandria, Egypt: World Health Organization.
Eastern Mediterranean Regional Office. Khartoum, Sudan.
February 10-15, 1979.
Badran, Margot
"Contamination in Practice." (In) Blair, Patricia W.
(ed.). Health Needs of the World's Poor Women.
Washington, D.C.: Equity Policy Center. 1981. pp.
98-101.
Badri, Gasim Y.
"Child-Rearing Practices in the Sudan: Implications for
Present Education." Ph.D Dissertation: University of
California-Santa Barbara. Santa Barbara, California.
1978. 238p.
Badri, Gasim Y.
"Opinions About Female Circumcision." Paper Presented at
the Seminar on Traditional Practices Affecting the Health
of Women and Children: Female Circumcision, Childhood
Marriage, Nutritional Taboos, etc. Alexandria, Egypt:
World Health Organization. Eastern Mediterranean
Regional Office. Khartoum, Sudan. February 10-15, 1979.
Badri, Gasim Y.
"Psycho-Social Aspects of Female Circumcision in the
Sudan." Paper Presented at the Seminar on Traditional
Practices Affecting the Health of Women and Children.
World Conference of the United Nations Decade for Women.
Copenhagen, Denmark. July 14-30, 1980.
Badri, Malik
"Sudanese Children's Concepts About Female Circumcision."
Paper Presented at the Seminar on Traditional Practices
Affecting the Health of Women and Children: Female
Circumcision, Childhood Marriage, Nutritional Taboos,
etc. Alexandria, Egypt: World Health Organization.
Eastern Mediteranean Regional Office. Khartoum, Sudan.
February 10-15, 1979.

Badri, Malik
"Sudanese Children's Concepts About Female Circumcision."
Paper Presented at the Seminar on Traditional Practices
Affecting the Health of Women and Children. World
Conference of the United Nations Decade for Women. New
York: United Nations. Copenhagen, Denmark. July 14-30,
1980.
Bakr, Salah A.
"Circumcision and Infibulation in Sudan." Paper
Presented at the Seminar on Traditional Practices
Affecting the Health of Women and Children: Female
Circumcision, Childhood Marriage, and Nutritional Taboos,
etc. Alexandria, Egypt: World Health Organization.
Eastern Mediterranean Regional Office. Khartoum, Sudan.
February 10-15, 1979.
Bakr, Salah A.
"Circumcision and Infibulation in the Sudan." Paper
Presented at the Seminar on Traditional Practices
Affecting the Health of Women and Children. World
Conference of the United Nations Decade for Women. New
York: United Nations. Copenhagen, Denamrk. July 14-30,
1980.
Barnes-Dean, Virginia L.
"Clitoridectomy and Infibulation." Cultural Survival
Quarterly. Volume 9 #2 1985. pp. 26-30.
Bayoumi, Ahmed
"The Training and Activity of Village Midwives in the
Sudan." Tropical Doctor. Volume 6 #3 July, 1976. pp.
118-225.
Bella, H.
"The Village Midwives of the Sudan: An Enquiry into the
Availability and Quality of Maternity Care." Journal of
Tropical Pediatrics. Volume 30 #2 April, 1984. pp.
115-118.
Boddy, J.
"Womb as Oasis: The Symbolic Context of Pharaonic
Circumcision in Rural Northern Sudan." American
Ethnologist. Volume 9 #4 November, 1982. pp. 682-698.
Clark, Isobel and Diaz, Christina
"Circumcision: A Slow Change in Attitudes." Sudanow.
Volume 2 #3 March, 1977. pp. 43-45.
Cloudsley, Anne
Women of the Sudan: Victims of Circumcision. Privately
Printed. Available From Author: 4 Craven Hill, London,
England. W2 3DS. 1980. 144p.
Constantinides, Pamela
"Women Heal Women: Spirit Possession and Sexual
Segregation in a Muslim Society." Social Science and
Medicine. Volume 21 #6 1985. pp. 685-692.
Cook, Robert
"Damage to Physical Health From Pharaonic Cicumcision of
Females--A Review of the Medical Literature." Paper
Presented at the Seminar on Traditional Practices

Affecting the Health of Women And Children: Female
Circumcision, Childhood Marriage, Nutritional Taboos,
etc. Alexandria, Egypt: World Health Organization.
Eastern Mediterranean Regional Office. Khartoum, Sudan.
1979.
El Dareer, A.A.
"Complications of Female Circumcision in the Sudan."
Tropical Doctor. Volume 13 #3 July, 1983. pp. 131-133.
El Dareer, A.A.
"Epidemiology of Female Circumcision in the Sudan."
Tropical Doctor. Volume 13 #1 January, 1983. pp.
41-45.
El Sadaawi, Nawal
"Circumcision of Girls." Paper Presented at the Seminar
on Tradtional Practices Affecting the Health of Women and
Children. World Conference of the United Nations Decade
for Women. New York: United Nations. Copenhagen,
Denmark. July 14-30, 1980.
El Sayed, M.
"Female Circumcision in Sudan." Paper Presented at the
Seminar on Traditional Practices Affecting the Health of
Women and Children. World Conference of the United
Nations Decade for Women. New York: United Nations.
Copenhagen, Denmark. July 14-30, 1980.
El Sayed, M.
"Female Circumcision in Sudan." Paper Presented at the
Seminar on Traditional Practices Affecting the Health of
Women and Children: Female Circumcision, Childhood
Marriage, Nutritional Taboos, etc. Alexandria, Egypt:
World Health Organization. Eastern Mediterranean
Regional Office. Khartoum, Sudan. February 10-15, 1979.
El-Dareer, Asma A.
"A Study of Prevalence and Epidemiology of Female
Circumcision in Sudan Today." Paper Presented at the
Seminar on Traditional Practices Affecting the Health of
Women and Children. World Conference of the United
Nations Decade for Women. New York: United Nations.
Copenhagen, Denmark. July 14-30, 1980.
El-Dareer, Asma A.
"A Study on Prevalence and Epidemiology of Female
Circumcision in Sudan Today." Paper Presented at the
Seminar on Tradtional Practices Affecting the Health of
Women and Children: Female Circumcision, Childhood
Marriage, Nutritional Taboos, etc. Alexandria, Egypt:
World Health Organization. Eastern Mediterranean
Regional Office. Khartoum, Sudan. February 10-15, 1979.
El-Dareer, Asma A.
"Attitudes of Sudanese People to the Practice of Female
Circumcision." International Journal of Epidemiology.
Volume 12 #2 June, 1983. pp. 138-144.
El-Dareer, Asma A.
"Female Circumcision and Current Preventive Efforts in
the Sudan." Paper Presented at the Annual Meeting of the

African Studies Association. Paper #25. Baltimore, Maryland. 1978. 28p.

El-Dareer, Asma A.
Woman, Why Do You Weep? Circumcision and Its Consequences. London: Zed Press. 1982. 130p.

El-Dareer, Asma A.
"Women and Health in the Sudan." Paper Presented at the Annual Meeting of the African Studies Association. Paper #26. Baltimore, Maryland. 1978. 25p.

El-Tom, Abdul R. and Farah, Abdul-Aziz and Lauro, Donald and Fenn, Thomas
Community and Individual Acceptance: Family Planning Services in the Sudan. New York: Columbia University. Center for Population and Family Health. Health Working Paper Series #14. January, 1985. 47p.

Farah, Abdul-Aziz
"Child Mortality and its Correlates in Sudan." Ph.D Dissertation: University of Pennsylvania. Philadelphia, Pennsylvania. 1981. 282p.

Farah, Abdul-Aziz
"Influence of Child Mortality on Fertility Related Attitudes and Behavior in Greater Khartoum." (In) Cairo Demographic Centre (CDC). Determinants of Fertility in Some African and Asian Countries. Cairo: CDC. CDC Research Monograph Series #10. 1982. pp. 227-261.

Fruzzetti, L.
"Farm and Health: Rural Women in a Farming Community." (In) Afshar, H. (ed.). Women, Work and Ideology in the Third World. London: Tavistock. 1985. 37-65.

Gerais, Abdel S. and Omran, S. and Liao, Kharia F. and Winston C.
"A Comparative Study of Two Estrogen Dosages in Combined Oral Contraceptives Among Sudanese Women." International Journal of Gynaecology and Obstetrics. Volume 21 #6 December, 1983. pp. 459-468.

Gizuli, Shahwa
"Current Programmes in Nutrition Education." (In) Baxter, Diana (ed.). Women and the Environment in the Sudan. Khartoum, Sudan: University of Khartoum. Institute for Environmental Studies. Environmental Research Paper Series #2. October, 1981. pp. 125-129.

Gore, Paul W.
Population Decline in South-Western Sudan: The Case of the Azande. Khartoum, Sudan: University of Khartoum. Development Studies and Research Centre. DSRC Seminar Series Discussion Paper #27. January, 1983. 36p.

Gore, Paul W.
"Socio-Cultural and Demographic Characteristics of a Low Fertility Population in South-Western Sudan: The Case of the Azande." Ph.D Dissertation: London School of Economics. London, England. 1981. 377p.

Gruenbaum, Ellen
"The Movement Against Clitoridectomy and Infibulation in

Sudan: Public Health Policy and the Women's Movement."
Medical Anthropology Newsletter. Volume 13 #2 1982. pp.
4-12.

International Statistical Institute (ISI)
The Sudan Fertility Survey, 1979: A Summary of Findings.
Voorburg, Netherlands: ISI. World Fertility Survey
Report #36. 1982. 17p.

Kertzer, David I. and Madison, Oker B.B.
"Women's Age-Set Systems in Africa: The Lutuka of
Southern Sudan." (In) Fry, Christine L. (ed.).
Dimensions: Aging, Culture and Health. New York: Praeger
Publishers. pp. 109-130. 1981.

Khalifa, Mona A.
"Characterisitics and Attitudes of Family Planners in
Khartoum, Sudan." Journal of Biosocial Science. Volume
14 #1 January, 1982. pp. 7-16.

Larsen, Ulla
A Comparative Study of the Levels and the Covariates of
Sterility in Cameroon, Kenya and Sudan. Princeton, New
Jersey: Princeton University. Office of Population
Research. 1985.

Levy, Wendy and Bijleveld, Catrien
"Workshop Against Circumcision: African Women Speak."
Sudanow. Volume 9 #12 December, 1984. pp. 28-31.

Lightfoot-Klein, H.
"Pharaonic Circumcision of Females in the Sudan."
Medicine and Law. Volume 2 #4 1983. pp. 353-360.

Lowenstein, L.F.
"Attitudes and Attitude Differences to Female Genital
Mutilation in the Sudan: Is There a Change on the
Horizon?" Social Science and Medicine. Volume 12 #5A
September, 1978. pp. 417-421.

Modawi, Osman
"Traditional Practices in Child Health in Sudan." Paper
Presented at the Seminar on Traditional Practices
Affecting the Health of Women and Children. World
Conference of the United Nations Decade for Women. New
York: United Nations. Copenhagen, Denmark. July 14-30,
1980.

Modawi, Osman
"Traditional Practices in Childbirth in Sudan." Paper
Presented at the Seminar on Traditional Practices
Affecting the Health of Women and Children: Female
Circumcision, Childhood Marriage, Nutritional Taboos,
Etc. Alexandria, Egypt: World Health Organization.
Eastern Mediterranean Regional Office. Khartoum, Sudan.
1979.

Modawi, Suleiman
"The Obstetrical and Gynaecological Aspects of Female
Circumcision in the Sudan." Paper Presented at the
Seminar on Traditional Practices Affecting the Health of
Women and Children. World Conference of the United

Nations Decade for Women. New York: United Nations.
Copenhagen, Denmark. July 14-30, 1980.
Modawi, Suleiman
    "The Obstetrical and Gynaecological Aspects of Female
    Circumcision." Paper Presented at the Seminar on
    Traditional Practices Affecting the Health of Women and
    Children: Female Circumcision, Childhood Marriage,
    Nutritional Taboos, etc. Alexandria, Egypt: World Health
    Organization. Eastern Mediterranean Regional Office.
    Khartoum, Sudan. February 10-15, 1979.
Naisho, Joyce
    "Health Care for Women in the Sudan." World Health
    Forum: An International Journal of Health Development.
    Volume 3 #2 1982.
Naishom, Joyce
    "Tradition and Other Constraints on Health Care for Women
    in the Sudan." (In) Blair, Patricia W. (ed.). Health
    Needs of the World's Poor Women. Washington, D.C.:
    Equity Policy Center. 1981. pp. 76-77.
Nur, Osman el-H. M.
    Infant and Child Mortality and its Effect on Reproductive
    Behavior in the Northern Provinces of Sudan. Wad Medani,
    Sudan: University of Gezira. Faculty of Economics and
    Rural Development. Population Studies Center. PSC
    Research Report. 1983. 68p.
Nur, Osman el-H. M.
    "The Physiological Effect of Infant Mortality in
    Reproductive Behavior in the Sudan." International
    Journal of Gynaecology and Obstetrics. Volume 23 #2
    April, 1985. pp. 143-147.
Omer, E.E.
    "Seroepidemiological Survey of Chlamydial Genital
    Infections in Khartoum, Sudan." Genitourinary Medicine.
    Volume 61 #4 August, 1985. pp. 261-263.
Osman, A.K.
    "Dietary Practices and Aversions During Pregnancy and
    Lactation Among Sudanese Women." Journal of Tropical
    Pediatrics. Volume 31 #1 February, 1985. pp.16-20.
Osman, Ali K.
    "Dietary Practices and Aversions During Pregnancy and
    Lactation Among Sudanese Women." Paper Presented at the
    Seminar on Traditional Practices Affecting the Health of
    Women and Children. World Conference of the United
    Nations Decade for Women. New York: United Nations.
    Copenhagen, Denmark. July 14-30, 1980.
Osman, Ali K.
    "Dietary Practices and Aversions During Pregnancy and
    Lactation Among Sudanese Women." Paper Presented at the
    Seminar on Traditional Practices Affecting the Health of
    Women and Children: Female Circumcision, Childhood
    Marriage, Nutritional Taboos, etc. Alexandria, Egypt:
    World Health Organization. Eastern Mediterranean
    Regional Office. Khartoum, Sudan. February 10-15, 1979.

Rushwan, Hamid E. and Doodoh, A. and Chi, I-Cheng
    "Contraceptive Practice After Women Have Undergone
    'Spontaneous' Abortion in Indonesia and Sudan."
    International Journal of Gynaecology and Obstetrics.
    Volume 15 1977. pp. 241-249.
Rushwan, Hamid E.
    "Epidemiological Analysis and Reproductive
    Characteristics of Incomplete Abortion Patients in
    Khartoum, The Sudan." Journal of Biosocial Science.
    Volume 11 #1 January, 1979. pp. 65-76.
Rushwan, Hamid E. and Ferguson, J.G. and Bernard, Roger P.
    "Hospital Counseling in Khartoum: A Study of Factors
    Affecting Contraceptive Acceptance After Abortion."
    International Journal of Gynaecology and Obstetrics.
    Volume 15 #5 1978. pp. 440-443.
Rushwan, James G. and Bernard, Roger P.
    "Hospital Counseling in Khartoum: A Study of Factors
    Affecting Contraceptive Acceptance After Abortion."
    Paper Presented at the International Fertility Research
    Program. Chapel Hill, South Carolina: University of
    South Carolina. Pregnancy Termination Series #98. 1976.
    9p.
Sanderson, Lilian P.
    Against the Mutilation of Women: The Struggle to End
    Unnecessary Suffering. London: Ithaca Press. 1981.
    117p.
Sudan. Department of Statistics
    The Sudan Fertility Survey, 1979: Principle Report.
    Khartoum, Sudan: Department of Statistics. Two Volumes.
    1982. 1001p.
Sudan. Ministry of Health
    Infant and Early Childhood Mortality in Relation to
    Fertility Patterns: Report on an Ad-Hoc Survey in Greater
    Khartoum and in the Blue Nile, Kassala and Kordofan
    Provinces, 1974-1976. Khartoum, Sudan: Ministry of
    Health. 1981. 165p.
Toubia, Nahid F.
    "The Social and Political Implications of Female
    Circumcision: The Case of the Sudan." (In) Fernea,
    Elizabeth W. (ed.). Women and the Family in the Middle
    East: New Voices of Change. Austin, Texas: University of
    Texas Press. 1985. pp. 148-164.
Wallace, Wendy
    "Sudan--The Real Village Health Workers." UNICEF News.
    Volume 122 1985. pp. 28-29.

HISTORY

Hakem, Ahmed M. and Hrbek, Ivan and Vercoutter, Jean
    "The Matriarchs of Meroe: A Powerful Line of Queens Who
    Ruled the Kushitic Empire." UNESCO Courier. Volume 32
    #8/9 August-September, 1979. pp. 58-59.

LAW AND LEGAL ISSUES

Fluehr-Lobban, Carolyn
"Challenging Some Myths: Women in Shari's (Islamic) Law
in the Sudan." Expedition. Volume 25 #3 Spring, 1983.
pp. 32-39.

LITERATURE

Hall, Marjorie J.
"The Position of Women in Egypt and the Sudan as
Reflected in Feminist Writing Since 1900." Ph.D
Dissertation: University of London. London, England.
1977. 369p.

MARITAL RELATIONS AND NUPTIALITY

Adam, Abbas Y.
"Fertility and Prospects of Family Planning in the Three
Towns." Sudan Journal of Population Studies. Volume 1
#1 December, 1983. pp. 60-74.
Adam, Abbas Y.
The Relation Between Nuptiality and Fertility in the
Sudan. Khartoum, Sudan: Economic and Social Research
Council, National Council for Research. Bulletin #98.
August, 1983. 47p.
Adnan, Amal M. and Abu-Bakr, Salah
"Postpartum Lactational Amenorrhoea as a Means of Family
Planning in the Sudan: A Study of 500 Cases." Journal of
Biosocial Science. Volume 15 #1 January, 1983. pp.
9-23.
Burton, John F.
"Women and Men in Marriage: Some Atout Texts."
Anthropos. Volume 75 #5/6 1980. pp. 710-720.
Burton, John W.
"Ghost Marriage and the Cattle Trade Among the Atout of
the Southern Sudan." Africa. Volume 48 #4 1978. pp.
398-405.
Delmet, C.
"Islamization and Matriliny in the Dar-Fung, Sudan."
L'Homme. Volume 19 April-June, 1979. pp. 33-52.
El Awad alal el Din, Mohamed
"The Economic Value of Children in Rural Sudan." (In)
Caldwell, John C. (ed.). The Persistence of High
Fertility: Population Prospects in the Third World.
Canberra, Australia: Australian National University.
Department of Demography. Volume Two. 1977. pp.
617-632.
El-Kashef, Samy and Youssef, Humam A.
"Household and Family in Rural Gezira, Sudan." (In)
Huzayyin, S.A. and Acsadi, G.T. (eds.). Family and

Marriage in Some African and Asiatic Countries. Cairo:
Cairo Demographic Centre. Research Monograph Series #6.
1976. pp. 161-174.
Farid, Samir
"Fertility Patterns in the Arab Region." International
Family Planning Perspectives. Volume 10 #4 December,
1984. pp. 119-125.
Gilfoun, Nadia
"A Women's Place?" Sudanow. Volume 2 #11 November,
1977. pp. 26-32.
Gore, Paul W.
"How Stable are Marriages Among the Azande." Sudan
Journal of Population. Volume 1 #1 December, 1983. pp.
75-100.
Ismail, Ellen T.
Social Environment and Daily Routine of Sudanese Women: A
Case Study of Urban Middle Class Housewives. Berlin,
Germany: D. Reimer. 1982. 224p.
Khalifa, Mona A.
"Birth Control Practice in Khartoum." Egyptian
Population and Family Planning Review. Volume 15 #1
June, 1981. pp. 10-21.
Moharib, Samir R. (ed.)
Fertility Norms in Sudan. Cairo: Cairo Demographic
Centre. CDC Research Monograph Series #12. 1984. pp.
235-264.
Mustafa, M.Y.
Fertility and Migration: A Preliminary Analysis of
Dynamics of Urban Growth. Khartoum, Sudan: National
Council for Research. Economic and Social Research
Council. Bulletin #91. February, 1981. 87p.
Ocholla-Ayayo, A.B.
"Marriage and Cattle Exchange Among the Nilotic Luo."
Paideuma. Volume 25 1979. pp. 173-193.
Rushwan, Hamid E. and Ferguson, J.G. and Bernard, Roger P.
"Hospital Counseling in Khartoum: A Study of Factors
Affecting Contraceptive Acceptance After Abortion."
International Journal of Gynaecology and Obstetrics.
Volume 15 #5 1978. pp. 440-443.
Rushwan, James G. and Bernard, Roger P.
"Hospital Counseling in Khartoum: A Study of Factors
Affecting Contraceptive Acceptance After Abortion."
Paper Presented at the International Fertility Research
Program. Chapel Hill, South Carolina: University of
South Carolina. Pregnancy Termination Series #98. 1976.
9p.
Wallace, Wendy
"The Birth Control Debate." Middle East. #108 October,
1983. pp. 53-54.

SUDAN

MIGRATION

Muludiang, Venansio T.
"Urbanization, Female Migration and Labor Utilization in Urban Sudan: The Case of the Southern Region." Ph.D Dissertation: Brown University. Providence, Rhode Island. 1983. 265p.
Mustafa, M.Y.
Fertility and Migration: A Preliminary Analysis of Dynamics of Urban Growth. Khartoum, Sudan: National Council for Research. Economic and Social Research Council. Bulletin #91. February, 1981. 87p.

MISCELLANEOUS

Badri, Amina E.
Integrated Welfare Programmes for Rural Women: A Suggested Approach to the Sudan. Khartoum, Sudan: University of Khartoum. Second Population Conference. 1982.

ORGANIZATIONS

Badri, Amina E.
"Sudan: Women's Studies--A New Village Stove." (In) Morgan, Robin (ed.). Sisterhood is Global. Garden City, New York: Anchor Books. 1984. pp. 644-654.
Pasquet, Marie-Ange
"Women in the Economic Environment: A Comparison of Two Co-Operatives." (In) Baxter, Diana (ed.). Women and the Environment in the Sudan. Khartoum, Sudan: University of Khartoum. Institute for Environmental Studies. Environmental Research Paper Series #2. October, 1981. pp. 25-29.
Sidahmed, Awatif
"We Don't Deny S.W.U.'s Inadequacy." Sudanow. Volume 6 #1 January, 1981. pp. 41-42.
United Nations Economic Commission for Africa (UNECA)
Women and Cooperatives: Egypt, The Libyan Arab Jamahiriya and the Sudan. Addis Ababa, Ethiopia: UNECA. Research Series. 1980.

POLITICS AND GOVERNMENT

Badri, Amina E.
Integrated Welfare Programmes for Rural Women: A Suggested Approach to the Sudan. Khartoum, Sudan: University of Khartoum. Second Population Conference. 1982.

161

Bakri, Z.B. and Kameir, E.M.
    "Aspects of Women's Political Participation in Sudan."
    International Social Science Journal. Volume 35 #4 1983.
    pp. 605-623.
El-Bakri, Z.B. and Kameir, E.M. (eds.)
    "Aspects of Women's Political Participation in Sudan."
    International Social Science Journal. Volume 35 #4 1983.
    pp. 605-624.
Fluehr-Lobban, Carolyn
    "Women in Radical Political Movements in the Sudan."
    Paper Presented at the Wellesley Conference on Women and
    Development. Wellesley, Massachusetts: Wellesley
    College. June 2-6, 1976.
Magnarella, P.J.
    "Republican Brothers: A Reformist Movement in the Sudan."
    Muslim World. Volume 72 January, 1982. pp. 14-24.
Sidahmed, Awatif
    "We Don't Deny S.W.U.'s Inadequacy." Sudanow. Volume 6
    #1 January, 1981. pp. 41-42.
United Nations Economic Commission for Africa (UNECA)
    Report of a Workshop for Trainees of Rural Women Leaders:
    Khartoum. Addis Ababa, Ethiopia: UNECA. Workshop Report
    Series. 1977. 132p.

RELIGION AND WITCHCRAFT

Barnes-Dean, Virginia L.
    "Clitoridectomy and Infibulation." Cultural Survival
    Quarterly. Volume 9 #2 1985. pp. 26-30.
Boddy, J.
    "Womb as Oasis: The Symbolic Context of Pharaonic
    Circumcision in Rural Northern Sudan." American
    Ethnologist. Volume 9 #4 November, 1982. pp. 682-698.
Burton, John W.
    "'The Moon is a Sheep': A Feminine Principle in Atout
    Cosmology." Man. Volume 16 #3 September, 1981. pp.
    441-450.
Burton, John W.
    "Ghost Marriage and the Cattle Trade Among the Atout of
    the Southern Sudan." Africa. Volume 48 #4 1978. pp.
    398-405.
Cloudsley, Anne
    Women of Omdurman: Life, Love and the Cult of Virginity.
    London: Ethnographica Publishers. 1983. 184p.
Constantinides, Pamela
    "Women Heal Women: Spirit Possession and Sexual
    Segregation in a Muslim Society." Social Science and
    Medicine. Volume 21 #6 1985. pp. 685-692.
Cook, Robert
    "Damage to Physical Health From Pharaonic Cicumcision of
    Females--A Review of the Medical Literature." Paper
    Presented at the Seminar on Traditional Practices

Affecting the Health of Women And Children: Female
Circumcision, Childhood Marriage, Nutritional Taboos,
etc. Alexandria, Egypt: World Health Organization.
Eastern Mediterranean Regional Office. Khartoum, Sudan.
1979.

Delmet, C.
"Islamization and Matriliny in the Dar-Fung, Sudan."
L'Homme. Volume 19 April-June, 1979. pp. 33-52.

El Awad Galal El Din, Mohamed
"The Rationality of High Fertility in Urban Sudan." (In)
Caldwell, John C. (ed.). The Persistence of High
Fertility: Population Prospects in the Third World.
Canberra, Australia: Australian National University.
Department of Demography. Volume Two. 1977. pp.
633-660.

El Sadaawi, Nawal
"Circumcision of Girls." Paper Presented at the Seminar
on Tradtional Practices Affecting the Health of Women and
Children. World Conference of the United Nations Decade
for Women. New York: United Nations. Copenhagen,
Denmark. July 14-30, 1980.

El Sayed, M.
"Female Circumcision in Sudan." Paper Presented at the
Seminar on Traditional Practices Affecting the Health of
Women and Children. World Conference of the United
Nations Decade for Women. New York: United Nations.
Copenhagen, Denmark. July 14-30, 1980.

El Sayed, M.
"Female Circumcision in Sudan." Paper Presented at the
Seminar on Traditional Practices Affecting the Health of
Women and Children: Female Circumcision, Childhood
Marriage, Nutritional Taboos, etc. Alexandria, Egypt:
World Health Organization. Eastern Mediterranean
Regional Office. Khartoum, Sudan. February 10-15, 1979.

El-Nagar, S.
"The Zar." Sudanow. Volume 3 #1 January, 1978. pp.
65-67.

Evans-Pritchard, E.E.
Witchcraft Oracles and Magic Among the Azande. Oxford,
England: Clarendon Press. 1976. 265p.

Evens, T.M.
"Mind, Logic and the Efficacy of the Nuer Incest
Prohibition." Man. Volume 18 #1 March, 1983. pp.
111-133.

Fluehr-Lobban, Carolyn
"Challenging Some Myths: Women in Shari's (Islamic) Law
in the Sudan." Expedition. Volume 25 #3 Spring, 1983.
pp. 32-39.

Khalifa, Mona A.
"Fertility Differentials in a Moslem Society: A Case
Study From Khartoum Province, Sudan." Ph.D Dissertation:
London University. London, England. 1979. 359p.

Magnarella, P.J.
    "Republican Brothers: A Reformist Movement in the Sudan."
    Muslim World. Volume 72 January, 1982. pp. 14-24.

RESEARCH

Kashif-Badri, Hagga
    "The History, Development, Organization and Position of
    Women's Studies in the Sudan." (In) United Nations
    Educational, Scientific and Cultural Organization.
    Social Science Research and Women in the Arab World.
    Paris: UNESCO. 1984. pp. 94-112.
Kashif-Badri, Hagga
    "The History, Development, Organization and Position of
    Women's Studies in the Sudan." Paper Presented at the
    Meeting of Arab Women Researchers on the Development of
    Research in the Social Sciences on Women in the Arab
    World. Paris: United Nations Educational, Scientific and
    Cultural Organization. Tunis, Tunisia. 1982. 17p.
United Nations Educational, Scientific and Cultural Organ.
    Social Science Research and Women in the Arab World.
    Paris: UNESCO. 1984. 175p.
Women's Studies Documentation Unit
    Women in Sudan: An Annotated Bibliography. Khartoum,
    Sudan: University of Khartoum. Development Studies and
    Research Centre. Women's Studies Documentation Unit.
    1982. 28p.

SEX ROLES

Ali, Nur and Mohammed, Nadia and Badri, Amira
    "Water Collection and Use: A Village Case Study." (In)
    Baxter, Diana (ed.). Women and the Environment in the
    Sudan. Khartoum, Sudan: University of Khartoum.
    Institute for Environmental Studies. Environmental
    Research Paper Series #2. October, 1981. pp. 58-63.
Anonymous
    "Sudan: Arab Women's Struggle." The Second Wave. Volume
    2 #2 1977.
Anonymous
    "Symposium on the Changing Status of Sudanese Women:
    Afhad University College for Women: Omdurman, Sudan,
    February 23-March 1, 1979." Resources for Feminist
    Research. Volume 9 #1 1980. pp. 81-94.
Babiker, Abdel B. and El Din Abdu, Anwar S.
    "Rural Energy and the Environment: Impact of Women in
    Semi-Arid Sudan." (In) Baxter, Diana (ed.). Women and
    the Environment in the Sudan. Khartoum, Sudan:
    University of Khartoum. Institute for Environmental
    Studies. Environmental Research Paper Series #2.
    October, 1981. pp. 86-91a.

Badri, Amina E. and Shabo, Mariam K. and Nujumi, Elhan E.
and Obeid, Marwa A. and Hassan, Majda M.
"Income Generating Projects for Women: A Village Case
Study." (In) Baxter, Diana (ed.). Women and the
Environment in the Sudan. Khartoum, Sudan: University of
Khartoum. Institute for Environmental Studies.
Environmental Research Paper Series #2. October, 1981.
pp. 30-35.

Badri, Gasim Y.
"Child-Rearing Practices in the Sudan: Implications for
Present Education." Ph.D Dissertation: University of
California-Santa Barbara. Santa Barbara, California.
1978. 238p.

Baxter, Diana
"Women and Environment: A Downward Spiral." (In) Baxter,
Diana (ed.). Women and the Environment in the Sudan.
Khartoum, Sudan: University of Khartoum. Institute for
Environmental Studies. Environmental Research Paper
Series #2. October, 1981. pp. 1-9.

Baxter, Diana (ed.).
"Women and the Environment in the Sudan." Khartoum,
Sudan: University of Khartoum. Institute for
Environmental Studies. Environmental Research Paper
Series #2. October, 1981. 149p.

Bayoumi, Ahmed
"The Training and Activity of Village Midwives in the
Sudan." Tropical Doctor. Volume 6 #3 July, 1976. pp.
118-225.

Bernal, V.
"Household Agricultural Production and Off-Farm Work in a
Sudan Village." Ph.D Dissertation: Northwestern
University. Evanston, Indiana. 1985.

Burton, John W.
"Independence and the Status of Nilotic Women." Africa
Today. Volume 28 #2 2nd Quarter 1981. pp. 54-60.

Constantinides, Pamela
"Women Heal Women: Spirit Possession and Sexual
Segregation in a Muslim Society." Social Science and
Medicine. Volume 21 #6 1985. pp. 685-692.

Dey, Jennie M. and El Bagir, Ibrahim and Wagner, Albert
The Rural Labour Market in the Eastern Region of Sudan.
Geneva: International Labour Office. Rural Employment
Policies Branch. 1983.

El Sayed, Mahasin K.
"Women's Role in Agriculture in Rural Khartoum Province."
(In) Baxter, Diana (ed.). Women and the Environment in
the Sudan. Khartoum, Sudan: University of Khartoum.
Institute for Environmental Studies. Environmental
Research Paper Series #2. October, 1981. pp. 113-119.

El-Bushra, Judy and Bekele, Abebech and Hammour, Fawzia
"Socio-Economic Development and Women's Changing Status."
(In) Baxter, Diana (ed.). Women and the Environment in
the Sudan. Khartoum, Sudan: University of Khartoum.

Institute for Environmental Studies. Environmental
Research Paper Series #2. October, 1981. pp. 8-16.

El-Kashef, Samy and Youssef, Humam A.
"Household and Family in Rural Gezira, Sudan." (In)
Huzayyin, S.A. and Acsadi, G.T. (eds.). Family and
Marriage in Some African and Asiatic Countries. Cairo:
Cairo Demographic Centre. Research Monograph Series #6.
1976. pp. 161-174.

El-Sayyid, Mahasin K.
"Women's Role in Agriculture in Rural Khartoum Province."
Ph.D Dissertation: University of Khartoum. Khartoum,
Sudan. 1981.

El-Sayyid, Mahasin K.
"Women's Role in Agriculture in Rural Khartoum Province."
(In) Baxter, Diana (ed.). Women and the Environment in
the Sudan. Khartoum, Sudan: University of Khartoum.
Institute of Environmental Studies. Papers Presented at
the Workshop on Women and the Environment. April 4-7,
1981.

Elmalik, Khitma H.
"Hazards of Water Use." (In) Baxter, Diana (ed.). Women
and the Environment in the Sudan. Khartoum, Sudan:
University of Khartoum. Institute for Environmental
Studies. Environmental Research Paper Series #2.
October, 1981. pp. 64-66.

Fluehr-Lobban, Carolyn
"Agitation for Change in the Sudan." (In) Schlegel,
Alice E. (ed.). Sexual Stratification: A Cross-Cultural
View. New York: Columbia University Press. 1977. pp.
127-143.

Fluehr-Lobban, Carolyn
"Challenging Some Myths: Women in Shari's (Islamic) Law
in the Sudan." Expedition. Volume 25 #3 Spring, 1983.
pp. 32-39.

Fruzzetti, L.
"Farm and Health: Rural Women in a Farming Community."
(In) Afshar, H. (ed.). Women, Work and Ideology in the
Third World. London: Tavistock. 1985. 37-65.

Gilfoun, Nadia
"A Women's Place?" Sudanow. Volume 2 #11 November,
1977. pp. 26-32.

Gruenbaum, Ellen
"Women's Labour in Subsistence Sector: The Case of the
Central Nuer Area of Jonglei Province." Unpublished
Paper. 1978.

Hammour, Fatima A.
"Women, Economic Backwardness and Education in the
Sudan." (In) Baxter, Diana (ed.). Women and the
Environment in the Sudan. Khartoum, Sudan: University of
Khartoum. Institute for Environmental Studies.
Environmental Research Paper Series #2. October, 1981.
pp. 23-24.

SUDAN

SUDAN

Hassan, Kamil I.
  "Women's Contribution to the Economy Through Agricultural Work." (In) Baxter, Diana (ed.). Women and the Environment in the Sudan. Khartoum, Sudan: University of Khartoum. Institute for Environmental Studies. Environmental Research Paper series #2. October, 1981. pp. 107-110.
Hutchinson, Sharon
  "Relations Between the Sexes Among the Nuer: 1930." Africa. Volume 50 #4 1980. pp. 371-388.
Ibrahim, Fouad N.
  "The Role of Women in the Process of Desertification in Western Sudan." (In) Baxter, Diana (ed.). Women and the Environment in the Sudan. Khartoum, Sudan: University of Khartoum. Institute for Environmental Studies. Environmental Research Paper Series #2. October, 1981. pp. 99-106.
Ibrahim, Suad A.
  "Women's Role in Deforestation." (In) Baxter, Diana (ed.). Women and the Environment in the Sudan. Khartoum, Sudan: University of Khartoum. Institute for Environmental Studies. Environmental Research Paper Series #2. October, 1981. pp. 80-85.
Ismail, Ellen T.
  Social Environment and Daily Routine of Sudanese Women: A Case Study of Urban Middle Class Housewives. Berlin, Germany: D. Reimer. 1982. 224p.
Jahn, Samia A.
  "Water Decade Projects for the Tropics Based on Traditional Purification Methods of Sudanese Women." (In) Baxter, Diana (ed.). Women and the Environment in the Sudan. Khartoum, Sudan: University of Khartoum. Institute for Environmental Studies. Environmental Research Paper Series #2. October, 1981. pp. 49-57.
Kertzer, David I. and Madison, Oker B.B.
  "Women's Age-Set Systems in Africa: The Lutuka of Southern Sudan." (In) Fry, Christine L. (ed.). Dimensions: Aging, Culture and Health. New York: Praeger Publishers. pp. 109-130. 1981.
Khider, M.
  "Women's Role in Agriculture in Rural Khartoum Province." Ph.D Dissertation: University of Khartoum. Khartoum, Sudan. 1981.
Modawi, Osman
  "Traditional Practices in Child Health in Sudan." Paper Presented at the Seminar on Traditional Practices Affecting the Health of Women and Children. World Conference of the United Nations Decade for Women. New York: United Nations. Copenhagen, Denmark. July 14-30, 1980.
Modawi, Osman
  "Traditional Practices in Childbirth in Sudan." Paper Presented at the Seminar on Traditional Practices

167

Affecting the Health of Women and Children: Female
Circumcision, Childhood Marriage, Nutritional Taboos,
Etc. Alexandria, Egypt: World Health Organization.
Eastern Mediterranean Regional Office. Khartoum, Sudan.
1979.
Murdock, Muneera S.
The Impact of Agricultural Development on a Pastoral
Society: The Shukriya of the Eastern Sudan. Washington,
D.C.: U.S. Department of State. U.S. Agency for
International Development. 1976. 54p.
Mustafa, Asha
"Women and Water in Western Kordofan." (In) Baxter,
Diana (ed.). Women and the Environment in the Sudan.
Khartoum, Sudan: University of Khartoum. Institute for
Environmental Studies. Environmental Research Paper
Series #2. October, 1981. pp. 67-69.
Naishom, Joyce
"Tradition and Other Constraints on Health Care for Women
in the Sudan." (In) Blair, Patricia W. (ed.). Health
Needs of the World's Poor Women. Washington, D.C.:
Equity Policy Center. 1981. pp. 76-77.
Ocholla-Ayayo, A.B.
"Marriage and Cattle Exchange Among the Nilotic Luo."
Paideuma. Volume 25 1979. pp. 173-193.
Russell, Annemarie
Report on the Situation of Women in the Target Villages
on the UNICEF Domestic Water Supply Project in Bahr el
Ghazal Province, Sudan. New York: United Nations.
UNICEF. 1979.
Saghayroun, Atif A.R.
"Women's Status and Fertility in the Sudan." Ahfad
Journal. Volume 2 #1 June, 1985. pp. 46-52.
Snyder, M.
"Women and Development." (In) El-Hassan, Ali M. (ed.).
Growth, Employment and Equity in the Sudan. Khartoum,
Sudan: University of Khartoum Press. 1977. pp. 237-238.
Villaume, Mary L.
"Alternative Technologies for Conservation and Food
Production in Southern Sudan." (In) Baxter, Diana (ed.).
Women and the Environment in the Sudan. Khaartoum,
Sudan: University of Khartoum. Institute for
Environmental Studies. Environmental Research Paper
Series #2. October, 1981. pp. 120-124.
Young, William C.
"Cultural Change and Women's Work: The Sedentarization of
the Rashiidy Bedouin in the Sudan." Cultural Survival
Quarterly. Volume 8 #2 Summer, 1984. pp. 28-29.

SEXUAL MUTILATION/CIRCUMCISION

Abdalla, Raqiya
Sisters in Affliction: Circumcision and Infibulation of
Women in Africa. London: Zed Press. 1982. 122p.

Assaad, Fawzia
"In Focus: The Sexual Mutilation of Women." World Health
Forum: An International Journal of Health Development.
Volume 3 #4 1982.
Aziz, F.
"Gynecological and Obstetric Complications of Female
Circumcision." International Journal of Gynaecology and
Obstetrics. Volume 17 1980. pp. 560.
Baasher, Taha A.
"Psycho-Social Aspects of Female Circumcision." Paper
Presented at the Seminar on Traditional Practices
Affecting the Health of Women and Children. World
Conference of the United Nations Decade for Women. New
York: United Nations. Copenhagen, Denmark. July 14-30,
1980.
Baasher, Taha A.
"Psychological Aspects of Female Circumcision." (In)
World Health Organization (WHO). Traditional Practices
Affecting the Health of Women and Children: Female
Circumcision, Childhood Marriage, Nutritional Taboos,
etc. Report of a Seminar. Alexandria, Egypt:
WHO/Eastern Mediterranean Regional Office. Technical
Publication #2. Khartoum, Sudan. 1979. pp. 71-105.
Baasher, Taha A.
Psycho-Social Aspects of Female Circumcision." Paper
Presented at the Seminar on Traditional Practices
Affecting the Health of Women and Children: Female
Circumcision, Childhood Marriage, Nutritional Taboos,
etc. Alexandria, Egypt: World Health Organization.
Eastern Mediterranean Regional Office. Khartoum, Sudan.
February 10-15, 1979.
Badri, Gasim Y.
"Opinions About Female Circumcision." Paper Presented at
the Seminar on Traditional Practices Affecting the Health
of Women and Children: Female Circumcision, Childhood
Marriage, Nutritional Taboos, etc. Alexandria, Egypt:
World Health Organization. Eastern Mediterranean
Regional Office. Khartoum, Sudan. February 10-15, 1979.
Badri, Gasim Y.
"Psycho-Social Aspects of Female Circumcision in the
Sudan." Paper Presented at the Seminar on Traditional
Practices Affecting the Health of Women and Children.
World Conference of the United Nations Decade for Women.
Copenhagen, Denmark. July 14-30, 1980.
Badri, Malik
"Sudanese Children's Concepts About Female Circumcision."
Paper Presented at the Seminar on Traditional Practices
Affecting the Health of Women and Children: Female
Circumcision, Childhood Marriage, Nutritional Taboos,
etc. Alexandria, Egypt: World Health Organization.
Eastern Mediteranean Regional Office. Khartoum, Sudan.
February 10-15, 1979.

SUDAN

Badri, Malik
"Sudanese Children's Concepts About Female Circumcision."
Paper Presented at the Seminar on Traditional Practices
Affecting the Health of Women and Children. World
Conference of the United Nations Decade for Women. New
York: United Nations. Copenhagen, Denmark. July 14-30,
1980.

Bakr, Salah A.
"Circumcision and Infibulation in Sudan." Paper
Presented at the Seminar on Traditional Practices
Affecting the Health of Women and Children: Female
Circumcision, Childhood Marriage, and Nutritional Taboos,
etc. Alexandria, Egypt: World Health Organization.
Eastern Mediterranean Regional Office. Khartoum, Sudan.
February 10-15, 1979.

Bakr, Salah A.
"Circumcision and Infibulation in the Sudan." Paper
Presented at the Seminar on Traditional Practices
Affecting the Health of Women and Children. World
Conference of the United Nations Decade for Women. New
York: United Nations. Copenhagen, Denamrk. July 14-30,
1980.

Barnes-Dean, Virginia L.
"Clitoridectomy and Infibulation." Cultural Survival
Quarterly. Volume 9 #2 1985. pp. 26-30.

Boddy, J.
"Womb as Oasis: The Symbolic Context of Pharaonic
Circumcision in Rural Northern Sudan." American
Ethnologist. Volume 9 #4 November, 1982. pp. 682-698.

Clark, Isobel and Diaz, Christina
"Circumcision: A Slow Change in Attitudes." Sudanow.
Volume 2 #3 March, 1977. pp. 43-45.

Cloudsley, Anne
Women of Omdurman: Life, Love and the Cult of Virginity.
London: Ethnographica Publishers. 1983. 184p.

Cloudsley, Anne
Women of the Sudan: Victims of Circumcision. Privately
Printed. Available From Author: 4 Craven Hill, London,
England. W2 3DS. 1980. 144p.

Cook, Robert
"Damage to Physical Health From Pharaonic Cicumcision of
Females--A Review of the Medical Literature." Paper
Presented at the Seminar on Traditional Practices
Affecting the Health of Women And Children: Female
Circumcision, Childhood Marriage, Nutritional Taboos,
etc. Alexandria, Egypt: World Health Organization.
Eastern Mediterranean Regional Office. Khartoum, Sudan.
1979.

El Dareer, A.A.
"Complications of Female Circumcision in the Sudan."
Tropical Doctor. Volume 13 #3 July, 1983. pp. 131-133.

El Dareer, A.A.
"Epidemiology of Female Circumcision in the Sudan."

Tropical Doctor. Volume 13 #1 January, 1983. pp. 41-45.

El Sadaawi, Nawal
"Circumcision of Girls." Paper Presented at the Seminar on Tradtional Practices Affecting the Health of Women and Children. World Conference of the United Nations Decade for Women. New York: United Nations. Copenhagen, Denmark. July 14-30, 1980.

El Sayed, M.
"Female Circumcision in Sudan." Paper Presented at the Seminar on Traditional Practices Affecting the Health of Women and Children. World Conference of the United Nations Decade for Women. New York: United Nations. Copenhagen, Denmark. July 14-30, 1980.

El Sayed, M.
"Female Circumcision in Sudan." Paper Presented at the Seminar on Traditional Practices Affecting the Health of Women and Children: Female Circumcision, Childhood Marriage, Nutritional Taboos, etc. Alexandria, Egypt: World Health Organization. Eastern Mediterranean Regional Office. Khartoum, Sudan. February 10-15, 1979.

El-Dareer, Asma A.
"A Study of Prevalence and Epidemiology of Female Circumcision in Sudan Today." Paper Presented at the Seminar on Traditional Practices Affecting the Health of Women and Children. World Conference of the United Nations Decade for Women. New York: United Nations. Copenhagen, Denmark. July 14-30, 1980.

El-Dareer, Asma A.
"A Study on Prevalence and Epidemiology of Female Circumcision in Sudan Today." Paper Presented at the Seminar on Tradtional Practices Affecting the Health of Women and Children: Female Circumcision, Childhood Marriage, Nutritional Taboos, etc. Alexandria, Egypt: World Health Organization. Eastern Mediterranean Regional Office. Khartoum, Sudan. February 10-15, 1979.

El-Dareer, Asma A.
"Attitudes of Sudanese People to the Practice of Female Circumcision." International Journal of Epidemiology. Volume 12 #2 June, 1983. pp. 138-144.

El-Dareer, Asma A.
"Female Circumcision and Current Preventive Efforts in the Sudan." Paper Presented at the Annual Meeting of the African Studies Association. Paper #25. Baltimore, Maryland. 1978. 28p.

El-Dareer, Asma A.
Woman, Why Do You Weep? Circumcision and Its Consequences. London: Zed Press. 1982. 130p.

El-Dareer, Asma A.
"Women and Health in the Sudan." Paper Presented at the Annual Meeting of the African Studies Association. Paper #26. Baltimore, Maryland. 1978. 25p.

Gruenbaum, Ellen
  "The Movement Against Clitoridectomy and Infibulation in
  Sudan: Public Health Policy and the Women's Movement."
  Medical Anthropology Newsletter. Volume 13 #2 1982. pp.
  4-12.
Hall, Marjorie J. and Ismail, Bakhita A.
  Sisters Under the Sun: The Story of Sudanese Women. New
  York: Longman. 1982. 264p.
Levy, Wendy and Bijleveld, Catrien
  "Workshop Against Circumcision: African Women Speak."
  Sudanow. Volume 9 #12 December, 1984. pp. 28-31.
Lightfoot-Klein, H.
  "Pharaonic Circumcision of Females in the Sudan."
  Medicine and Law. Volume 2 #4 1983. pp. 353-360.
Lowenstein, L.F.
  "Attitudes and Attitude Differences to Female Genital
  Mutilation in the Sudan: Is There a Change on the
  Horizon?" Social Science and Medicine. Volume 12 #5A
  September, 1978. pp. 417-421.
Modawi, Suleiman
  "The Obstetrical and Gynaecological Aspects of Female
  Circumcision in the Sudan." Paper Presented at the
  Seminar on Traditional Practices Affecting the Health of
  Women and Children. World Conference of the United
  Nations Decade for Women. New York: United Nations.
  Copenhagen, Denmark. July 14-30, 1980.
Modawi, Suleiman
  "The Obstetrical and Gynaecological Aspects of Female
  Circumcision." Paper Presented at the Seminar on
  Traditional Practices Affecting the Health of Women and
  Children: Female Circumcision, Childhood Marriage,
  Nutritional Taboos, etc. Alexandria, Egypt: World Health
  Organization. Eastern Mediterranean Regional Office.
  Khartoum, Sudan. February 10-15, 1979.
Sanderson, Lilian P.
  Against the Mutilation of Women: The Struggle to End
  Unnecessary Suffering. London: Ithaca Press. 1981.
  117p.
Toubia, Nahid F.
  "The Social and Political Implications of Female
  Circumcision: The Case of the Sudan." (In) Fernea,
  Elizabeth W. (ed.). Women and the Family in the Middle
  East: New Voices of Change. Austin, Texas: University of
  Texas Press. 1985. pp. 148-164.

STATUS OF WOMEN

Anonymous
  "Symposium on the Changing Status of Sudanese Women:
  Afhad University College for Women: Omdurman, Sudan,
  February 23-March 1, 1979." Resources for Feminist
  Research. Volume 9 #1 1980. pp. 81-94.

Bakri, Z.B. and Kameir, E.M.
    "Aspects of Women's Political Participation in Sudan."
    International Social Science Journal. Volume 35 #4 1983.
    pp. 605-623.
Baxter, Diana
    "Women and Environment: A Downward Spiral." (In) Baxter,
    Diana (ed.). Women and the Environment in the Sudan.
    Khartoum, Sudan: University of Khartoum. Institute for
    Environmental Studies. Environmental Research Paper
    Series #2. October, 1981. pp. 1-9.
Baxter, Diana (ed.).
    Women and the Environment in the Sudan. Khartoum, Sudan:
    University of Khartoum. Institute for Environmental
    Studies. Environmental Research Paper Series #2.
    October, 1981. 149p.
Burton, John W.
    "Independence and the Status of Nilotic Women." Africa
    Today. Volume 28 #2 2nd Quarter 1981. pp. 54-60.
El Meheina, Rabab H.
    "Food Production Projects for Rural Women." (In) Baxter,
    Diana (ed.). Women and the Environment in the Sudan.
    Khartoum, Sudan: University of Khartoum. Institute for
    Environmental Studies. Environmental Research Paper
    Series #2. October, 1981. pp. 111-112.
El-Bushra, Judy and Bekele, Abebech and Hammour, Fawzia
    "Socio-Economic Development and Women's Changing Status."
    (In) Baxter, Diana (ed.). Women and the Environment in
    the Sudan. Khartoum, Sudan: University of Khartoum.
    Institute for Environmental Studies. Environmental
    Research Paper Series #2. October, 1981. pp. 8-16.
Eyben, Rosalind and Kartunnen, Maryatta
    "Skills Training for Girls and Women." Paper Presented
    at the Ahfad Symposium on the Changing Status of Women in
    the Sudan. Omdurman, Sudan: Ahfad University College for
    Women. 1978.
Gruenbaum, Ellen
    "The Movement Against Clitoridectomy and Infibulation in
    Sudan: Public Health Policy and the Women's Movement."
    Medical Anthropology Newsletter. Volume 13 #2 1982. pp.
    4-12.
Hall, Marjorie J. and Ismail, Bakhita A.
    Sisters Under the Sun: The Story of Sudanese Women. New
    York: Longman. 1982. 264p.
Kashif-Badri, Hagga
    "The History, Development, Organization and Position of
    Women's Studies in the Sudan." (In) United Nations
    Educational, Scientific and Cultural Organization.
    Social Science Research and Women in the Arab World.
    Paris: UNESCO. 1984. pp. 94-112.
Kashif-Badri, Hagga
    "The History, Development, Organization and Position of
    Women's Studies in the Sudan." Paper Presented at the
    Meeting of Arab Women Researchers on the Development of
    Research in the Social Sciences on Women in the Arab

World. Paris: United Nations Educational, Scientific and
Cultural Organization. Tunis, Tunisia. 1982. 17p.
Sadaty, Fahima Z.
"Women and Their Environment: A General View." (In)
Baxter, Diana (ed.). Women and the Environment in the
Sudan. Khartoum, Sudan: University of Khartoum.
Institute for Environmental Studies. Environmental
Research Paper Series #2. October, 1981. pp. 17-22.
Saghayroun, Atif A.R.
"Women's Status and Fertility in the Sudan." Ahfad
Journal. Volume 2 #1 June, 1985. pp. 46-52.

URBANIZATION

El Awad Galal El Din, Mohamed
"The Rationality of High Fertility in Urban Sudan." (In)
Caldwell, John C. (ed.). The Persistence of High
Fertility: Population Prospects in the Third World.
Canberra, Australia: Australian National University.
Department of Demography. Volume Two. 1977. pp.
633-660.
Khalifa, Mona A.
Fertility Differentials in Urban Khartoum. Khartoum,
Sudan: National Council for Research. Economic and
Social Research Council. Bulletin #81. December, 1979.
19p.
Muludiang, Venansio T.
"Urbanization, Female Migration and Labor Utilization in
Urban Sudan: The Case of the Southern Region." Ph.D
Dissertation: Brown University. Providence, Rhode
Island. 1983. 265p.
Mustafa, M.Y.
Fertility and Migration: A Preliminary Analysis of
Dynamics of Urban Growth. Khartoum, Sudan: National
Council for Research. Economic and Social Research
Council. Bulletin #91. February, 1981. 87p.

WOMEN AND THEIR CHILDREN

Aromasodu, M.C.
"Traditional Practices Affecting the Health of Women in
Pregnancy and Childbirth." Paper Presented at the
Seminar on Traditional Practices Affecting the Health of
Women and Children: Female Circumcision, Childhood
Marriage, Nutritional Taboos, etc. Alexandria, Egypt:
World Health Organization. Eastern Mediterranean
Regional Office. Khartoum, Sudan. February 10-15, 1979.
Badri, Gasim Y.
"Child-Rearing Practices in the Sudan: Implications for
Present Education." Ph.D Dissertation: University of

California-Santa Barbara.   Santa Barbara, California.
1978.   238p.

El Awad alal el Din, Mohamed
"The Economic Value of Children in Rural Sudan."   (In)
Caldwell, John C. (ed.).   The Persistence of High
Fertility: Population Prospects in the Third World.
Canberra, Australia: Australian National University.
Department of Demography.   Volume Two.   1977.   pp.
617-632.

Tanzania

ABORTION

Caplan, Patricia
"Development Policies in Tanzania--Some Implications for
Women." (In) Nelson, Nici (ed.). African Women in the
Developing World. Totowa, New Jersey: Frank Cass. 1981.
pp. 98-108.
Hathi, Jee T.
"Medical Factors Associated With Abortions at Muhumbili
Medical Centre (June, 1978)." Paper Presented at the
Workshop on Women's Studies and Development.
Dar-es-Salaam, Tanzania: University of Tanzania. Bureau
of Resource Assessment and Land Use Planning. Paper #41.
September 24-29, 1979. 7p.
Sackak, Najma
"Creating Employment Opportunites for Rural Women: Case
Study of Dodoma Rural District." Paper Presented at the
Workshop on Women's Studies and Development.
Dar-es-Salaam, Tanzania: University of Dar-es-Salaam.
Bureau of Resource Assessment and Land Use Planning.
Paper #6. September 24-29, 1979. 18p.

AGRICULTURE

Alopaeus-Stahl, Dorrit
"Tanzanian Women Activities and Development Cooperation."
Dar-es-Salaam, Tanzania: Swedish International
Development Agency. May, 1979.
Bader, Zinnat
"Social Conditions of the Peasant Women in Zanzibar and
Pemba." Paper Presented at the Workshop on Women's
Studies and Development. Dar-es-Salaam, Tanzania:
University of Dar-es-Salaam. Bureau of Resource
Assessment and Land Use Planning. Paper #18. September
24-29, 1979.

Brain, James L.
"Less Than Second Class: Women in Rural Settlement
Schemes in Tanzania." (In) Hafkin, N.J. and Bay, Edna
(eds.). Women in Africa: Studies in Social and Economic
Change. Stanford, California: Stanford University Press.
1976. pp. 265-282.
Bryceson, Deborah F.
Peasant Food Production and Food Supply in Relation to
the Historical Development of Commoditiy Production in
Pre-Colonial and Colonial Tanganyika. Dar-es-Salaam,
Tanzania: Bureau of Resource Assessment and Land Use
Planning. Service Paper #78/3. 1978. 41p.
Bryceson, Deborah F. and Mbilinyi, Marjorie J.
"The Changing Role of Tanzanian Women in Production: From
Peasants to Proletarians." Paper Presented at the Sussex
University Conference on Women and Subordination.
Sussex, England: University of Sussex. September, 1978.
Bryceson, Deborah F.
"The Proletarianization of Women in Tanzania." Review of
African Political Economy. #17 January-April, 1980.
pp. 4-27.
Bryceson, Deborah F.
"The Proletarianization of Women in Tanzania." Paper
Presented at the Workshop on Women's Studies and
Development. Dar-es-Salaam, Tanzania: University of
Dar-es-Salaam. Bureau of Resource Assessment and Land
Use Planning. Paper #2. September 24-29, 1979. 45p.
Caplan, Patricia
"Development Policies in Tanzania--Some Implications for
Women." Journal of Development. Volume 17 #3 April,
1981. pp. 98-108.
Chale, Freda U. and Generose, Ngonyani
"Report on a Survey of Cooperative Income Generating
Projects for Women and its Impact on the Welfare of
Children and the Family." Paper Presented at the
Workshop on Women's Studies and Development.
Dar-es-Salaam, Tanzania: University of Dar-es-Salaam.
Bureau of Resource Assessment and Land Use Planning.
Paper #24. September 24-29, 1979. 42p.
Chale, Freda U.
"Women's Programmes and the Role of a Rural Woman in
Tanzania." Paper Presented at the Workshop on Population
Life Education Project in Integrated Rural Development.
Arusha, Tanzania: Arusha Technical School. January 1-25,
1979.
Cooper, Frederick
From Slaves to Squatters: Plantation Labor and
Agriculture in Zanzibar and Coastal Kenya, 1890-1925.
New Haven, Connecticut: Yale University Press. 1980.
328p.
Croll, E.J.
"Women in Rural Production and Reproduction in the Soviet

Union, China, Cuba and Tanzania." Signs. Volume 7 #2 Winter, 1981. pp. 375-399.

Due, Jean M.
"Intra-Household Gender Issues in Farming Systems in Tanzania, Zambia and Malawi." (In) Poats, Susan V. and Schmink, Marianne and Spring, Anita (eds.). Gender Issues in Farming Systems Research and Extension. Boulder, Colorado: Westview Press. 1980. pp. 331-344.

Due, Jean M. and Anandajayasekeram
Women and Productivity in Two Contrasting Farming Areas of Tanzania. Dar es Salaam, Tanzania: University of Dar es Salaam. Bean/Cowpea CRSP Project Report #228. Urbana, Illinois: University of Illinois-Urbana-Champaign. Department of Agricultural Economics. July, 1982.

Fortmann, Louise P.
"Women and Agricultural Development." (In) Kim, K.S. and Mabele, R. and Schultheis, M.J. (eds.). Papers on the Political Economy of Tanzania. Nairobi: Heinemann Educational. 1979.

Fortmann, Louise P.
Women and Tanzanian Agricultural Development. Dar-es-Salaam, Tanzania: University of Dar-es-Salaam. Economic Research Bureau. Paper #77.4. Mimeo. 1977. 24p.

Fortmann, Louise P.
"Women's Work in a Communal Setting: The Tanzanian Policy of Ujamaa." Paper Presented at the Conference on Women and Work in Africa. Urbana, Illinois: University of Illinois-Urbana. Mimeo. April 28-May 1, 1979.

Fortmann, Louise P.
"Women's Work in a Communal Setting: The Tanzanian Policy of Ujamaa." (In) Bay, Edna (ed.). Women in Work in Africa. Boulder, Colorado: Westview Press. 1982. pp. 191-205.

Geiger, Susan
"Umoja wa Wanawake wa Tanzania and the Needs of the Rural Poor." African Studies Review. Volume 25 #2/3 July-September, 1982. pp. 45-65.

Hamdani, Salha
"Peasantry and the Peasant Women in Tanzania: The Luguru Case." Paper Presented at the Workshop on Women's Studies and Development. Dar-es-Salaam, Tanzania: University of Dar-es-Salaam. Bureau of Resource Assessment and Land Use Planning. Paper #8. September 24-29, 1979. 9p.

Henn, Jeanne K.
"Who Benefits From Peasant Women's Work? Insights From a Modes of Production Analysis." Paper Presented at the Workshop on Women's Studies and Development. Dar-es-Salaam: University of Dar-es-Salaam. Bureau of Resource Assessment and Land Use Planning. Paper #29. September 24-29, 1979. 19p.

Kamuzora, C. Lwechungura
"High Fertility and the Demand for Labour in Peasant
Economies: The Case of Bukoba District, Tanzania."
Development and Change. Volume 15 #1 January, 1984.
pp. 105-124.

Kocher, James E.
Rural Development and Fertility Change in Northeastern
Tanzania. Cambridge, Massachusetts: Harvard University.
Harvard Institute for International Development. 1977.

Kocher, James E.
Rural Development and Fertility Change in Tropical
Africa: Evidence From Tanzania. East Lansing, Michigan:
Michigan State University. Department of Agricultural
Economics. Africana Rural Economy Paper #19. 1979.
95p.

Kocher, James E.
Rural Development, Health, Mortality and Fertility in
Rural Northeastern Tanzania. Cambridge, Massachusetts:
Harvard University. Harvard Institute for International
Development. 1980. 123p.

Kocher, James E.
Socioeconomic Development and Fertility Change in Rural
Africa. Cambridge, Massachusetts: Harvard University.
Harvard Institute for International Development.
Development Discussion Paper #16. 1976. 22p.

Ladner, Joyce A.
"Tanzanian Women in Nation Building." (In) Steady,
Filomina C. (ed.). The Black Woman Cross-Culturally.
Cambridge, Massachusetts: Schenkman Publications. 1981.
pp. 107-118.

Madsen, Birgit
Women's Mobilization and Integration in Development: A
Village Case Study From Tanzania. Copenhagen, Denmark:
Centre for Development Research. CDR Research Report #3.
1984. 95p.

Mbilinyi, M.
Women in the Rural Development of Mbeya Region. Dar es
Salaam, Tanzania: Ministry of Agriculture/U.N. FAO.
Mbeya RIDEP Project. 1982.

Mbilinyi, Marjorie J.
"Wife, Slave and Subject of the King: The Oppression of
Women in the Shambala Kingdom." Tanzania Notes and
Records. #88-89. 1982. pp. 1-13.

Mbilinyi, Marjorie J.
"Women in Agricultural Production in West Bagamoyo,
Tanzania." Paper Presented at a Workshop on Women in
Agricultural Development in Eastern and Southern Africa.
Nairobi: Ford Foundation. April, 1980.

Mbilinyi, Marjorie J.
Women: Producers and Reproducers in Peasant Production.
Dar-es-Salaam, Tanzania: University of Dar-es-Salaam.
Economic Research Bureau. Occasional Paper #77.3. 1977.
39p.

McHenry, Dean E.
    "Communal Farming in Tanzania: A Comparison of Male and
    Female Participants." African Studies Review. Volume 25
    #4 December, 1982. pp. 49-64.
Muro, Asseny
    "The Study of Women's Position in Peasant Production and
    Their Education and Training: A Case Study of Diozile I
    Village in Bagomoyo District." M.A. Thesis: University
    of Dar-es-Salaam. Dar-es-Salaam, Tanzania. June, 1979.
Muro, Asseny
    "Women in Agricultural Production and Their Education and
    Training: A Case Study of Diozile I Village in Bagamoyo
    District." Paper Presented at the Workshop on Women's
    Studies and Development. Dar-es-Salaam, Tanzania:
    University of Dar-es-Salaam. Bureau of Resource
    Assessment and Land Use Planning. Paper #11. September
    24-29, 1979. 42p.
Ngalula, Theresia K.
    "Women as a Productive Force in the Tanzanian Rural
    Society: A Case Study of Buhongwa Village in Mwanza
    District." M.A. Thesis: University of Dar-es-Salaam.
    Department of Sociology. Dar-es-Salaam, Tanzania. 1977.
    113p.
O'Brien, M.
    "The Maize Grinding Mill at Sinon." Community
    Development Journal. Volume 20 #3 1985. pp. 189-191.
Oomen-Myin, Marie A.
    "The Involvement of Rural Women in Village Development in
    Tanzania." Convergence. Volume 16 #2 1983. pp. 59-69.
Rogers, Susan G.
    "Efforts Toward Women's Development in Tanzania: Gender
    Rhetoric vs. Gender Realities." Women and Politics.
    Volume 2 #4 Winter, 1982. pp. 23-41.
Swantz, Marja-Liisa
    Women's Creative Role in Development in Tanzania.
    Helsinki, Finland: University of Helsinki. 1982.
Swantz, Marja-Liisa.
    Strain and Strength Among Peasant Women in Tanzania.
    Dar-es-Salaam, Tanzania: University of Dar-es-Salaam.
    Bureau of Resource Assessment and Land Use Planning.
    Research Paper #49. May, 1977. 81p.
Tobisson, Eva
    Women, Work, Food and Nutrition in Nyamwigura Village,
    Mara Region, Tanzania. Dar-es-Salaam, Tanzania: Tanzania
    Food and Nutrition Centre. Report #548. July, 1980.
    127p.
Wiley, Liz
    "Tanzania: The Arusha Planning and Village Development
    Project." (In) Overholt, Catherine and Anderson, Mary B.
    and Cloud, Kathleen and Austin, James E. (eds.). Gender
    Roles in Development Projects: A Case Book. Hartford,
    Connecticut: Kumarian Press. 1985. pp. 163-184.

Wylie, Liz
    Women and Development: A Case Study of Ten Tanzania
    Villages. Arusha, Tanzania: Arusha Planning and Village
    Development Project. 1981.

ARTS

Lihamba, Amandina
    "The Image of Women in the Performing Arts." Paper
    Presented at the Workshop on Women's Studies and
    Development. Dar-es-Salaam, Tanzania: University of
    Dar-es-Salaam. Bureau of Resource Assessment and Land
    Use Planning. Paper 46. September 24-29, 1979. 28p.
Mlama, Penina
    "The Role of Women in Culture Reproduction: The Case of
    Tanzanian Art and Literature." Paper Presented at the
    Workshop on Women's Studies and Development.
    Dar-es-Salaam, Tanzania: University of Dar-es-Salaam.
    Bureau of Resource Assessment and Land Use Planning.
    Paper #17. September 24-29, 1979. 14p.

BIBLIOGRAPHIES

Mascarenhas, Ophelia and Mbilinyi, Marjorie J.
    Women and Development in Tanzania: An Annotated
    Bibliography. Addis Ababa, Ethiopia: United Nations
    Economic Commission for Africa. African Training and
    Research Centre for Women. Bibliography Series #2.
    1980. 135p.
Mascarenhas, Ophelia and Mbilinyi, Marjorie J.
    Women in Tanzania: An Analytical Bibliography. Uppsala,
    Sweden: Scandinavian Institute for African Studies.
    1983. 256p.

CULTURAL ROLES

Abrahams, R.G.
    "Aspects of the Distribution Between the Sexes in
    Nyamwezi and Some Other African Systems of Kinship and
    Marriage." (In) LaFontaine, J.S. (ed.). Sex and Age as
    Principles of Social Differentiation. New York: Academic
    Press. 1978. pp. 67-88.
Alopaeus-Stahl, Dorrit
    Tanzanian Women Activities and Development Cooperation.
    Dar-es-Salaam, Tanzania: Swedish International
    Development Agency. May, 1979.
Alpers, E.A.
    "Female Subculture in Nineteenth Century Zanzibar: The
    Kitimiri Spirit Possession Cult." Paper Presented at the
    Symposium on African Women: Historical Dimensions.

University of Santa Clara. Santa Clara, California. May
15-16, 1981.
Anonymous
"Tanzania: The New Women and Traditional Norms in
Tanzania." IDOC Bulletin. #50-51 December, 1976.
Asayehgn, Desta
Role of Women in Tanzania: Their Access to Education and
Participation in the Labour Force. Paris: International
Institute for Educational Planning(IIEP). 1979. 31p.
Bader, Zinnat
"Social Conditions of the Peasant Women in Zanzibar and
Pemba." Paper Presented at the Workshop on Women's
Studies and Development. Dar-es-Salaam, Tanzania:
University of Dar-es-Salaam. Bureau of Resource
Assessment and Land Use Planning. Paper #18. September
24-29, 1979.
Balisidya, M.L.
"The Image of the Woman in Tanzanian Oral Literature: A
Survey." Kiswahili. Volume 49 #2 1982. pp. 1-31.
Brain, James L.
"Down to Gentility: Women in Tanzania." Sex Roles: A
Journal of Research. Volume 4 #5 October, 1978. pp.
695-715.
Brain, James L.
"Less Than Second Class: Women in Rural Settlement
Schemes in Tanzania." (In) Hafkin, N.J. and Bay, Edna
(eds.). Women in Africa: Studies in Social and Economic
Change. Stanford, California: Stanford University Press.
1976. pp. 265-282.
Brain, James L.
"Witchcraft and Development." African Affairs. Volume
81 #324 July, 1982. pp. 371-384.
Bryceson, Deborah F.
"Notes on the Educational Potential of Mass Media
Vis-a-Vis Women's Roles in Tanzanian Society." Paper
Presented at the Workshop on Women's Studies and
Development. Dar-es-Salaam, Tanzania: University of
Dar-es-Salaam. Bureau of Resource Assessment and Land
Use Planning. Paper #23. September 24-29, 1979. 10p.
Bryceson, Deborah F. and Mbilinyi, Marjorie J.
"The Changing Role of Tanzanian Women in Production: From
Peasants to Proletarians." Paper Presented at the Sussex
University Conference on Women and Subordination.
Sussex, England: University of Sussex. September, 1978.
Bryceson, Deborah F. and Mbilinyi, Marjorie J.
The Changing Roles of Women in Production: From Peasants
to Proletarians. Dar-es-Salaam, Tanzania: University of
Dar-es-Salaam. History Department. 1978.
Caplan, A.P.
"Boys' Circumcision and Girls' Puberty Rites Among the
Swahili of Mafia Island, Tanzania." Africa. Volume 46
#1 1976. pp. 21-33.

Caplan, Patricia
"Gender, Ideology and Modes of Production on the Coast of East Africa." Paideuma. Volume 28 1982. pp. 29-43.

Caplan, Patricia
"Spirit Possession: A Means of Curing on Mafia Island, Tanzania." Kenya Past and Present. #10 1979. pp. 41-44.

Chijumba, Beat J.
"Attitudes of Tanzanian Husbands Toward the Employment of their Wives." Africa Development. Volume 8 #2 1983. pp. 74-85.

Croll, E.J.
"Women in Rural Production and Reproduction in the Soviet Union, China, Cuba and Tanzania." Signs. Volume 7 #2 Winter, 1981. pp. 375-399.

Due, Jean M.
"Intra-Household Gender Issues in Farming Systems in Tanzania, Zambia and Malawi." (In) Poats, Susan V. and Schmink, Marianne and Spring, Anita (eds.). Gender Issues in Farming Systems Research and Extension. Boulder, Colorado: Westview Press. 1980. pp. 331-344.

Due, Jean M. and Anandajayasekeram
Women and Productivity in Two Contrasting Farming Areas of Tanzania. Dar es Salaam, Tanzania: University of Dar es Salaam. Bean/Cowpea CRSP Project Report #228. Urbana, Illinois: University of Illinois-Urbana-Champaign. Department of Agricultural Economics. July, 1982.

Ewbank, Douglas C.
"Indicators of Fertility Levels in Tanzania: Differentials and Trends in Reported Poverty and Childlessness." Paper Presented at the Annual Meeting of the Population Association of America. St. Louis, Missouri. April 21-23, 1977.

Ewbank, Douglas C.
Indicators of Fertility Levels in Tanzania: Differentials and Trends in Reported Poverty and Childlessness. Boston: Harvard School of Public Health. Department of Population Sciences. 1977.

Findley, Sally E. and Orr, Ann C.
"A Suggested Framework for Analysing Urban-Rural Fertility Differentials With an Illustration of the Tanzanian Case." Paper Presented at the Annual Meeting of the Population Association of America. Atlanta, Georgia. April, 1978.

Findley, Sally E.
"A Suggested Framework for Analysis of Urban-Rural Fertility Differentials With an Illustration of the Tanzanian Case." Population and Environment. Volume 3 #3/4 Fall-Winter, 1980. pp. 237-261.

Findley, Sally E. and Orr, Ann C.
Patterns of Urban-Rural Fertility Differentials in Developing Countries: A Suggested Framework. Washington,

D.C.: U.S. Department of State. U.S. Agency for
International Development. September, 1978. 242p.
Flanagan, William G.
"The Extended Family as an Agent in Urbanization: A
Survey of Men and Women Working in Dar-es-Salaam,
Tanzania." Ph.D Dissertation: University of
Connecticut-Storrs. Storrs, Connecticut. 1977. 234p.
Fortmann, Louise P.
"Women and Agricultural Development." (In) Kim, K.S. and
Mabele, R. and Schultheis, M.J. (eds.). Papers on the
Political Economy of Tanzania. Nairobi: Heinemann
Educational. 1979.
Fortmann, Louise P.
Women and Tanzanian Agricultural Development.
Dar-es-Salaam, Tanzania: University of Dar-es-Salaam.
Economic Research Bureau. Paper #77.4. Mimeo. 1977.
24p.
Hathi, Jee T.
"Medical Factors Associated With Abortions at Muhumbili
Medical Centre (June, 1978)." Paper Presented at the
Workshop on Women's Studies and Development.
Dar-es-Salaam, Tanzania: University of Tanzania. Bureau
of Resource Assessment and Land Use Planning. Paper #41.
September 24-29, 1979. 7p.
Hollander, Roberta B.
"Out of Tradition: The Position of Women in Kenya and
Tanzania During the Pre-Colonial, Colonial and Post
Independence Eras." Ph.D Dissertation: The American
University. Washington, D.C. 1979. 399p.
Kamuzora, C. Lwechungura
"High Fertility and the Demand for Labour in Peasant
Economies: The Case of Bukoba District, Tanzania."
Development and Change. Volume 15 #1 January, 1984.
pp. 105-124.
Kasulamemba, Sylvia
"Problems of Working Women: The Case of Dar-es-Salaam
City Council." Paper Presented at the Workshop on
Women's Studies and Development. Dar-es-Salaam,
Tanzania: University of Dar-es-Salaam. Bureau of
Resource Assessment and Land Use Planning. Paper #9.
September 24-29, 1979. 4p.
Kikopa, Jane R.
"Human Rights: The Position of Women and Children in
Tanzania." Paper Presented at the Workshop on Women's
Studies and Development. Dar-es-Salaam, Tanzania:
University of Dar-es-Salaam. Bureau of Resource
Assessment and Land Use Planning. Paper #33. September
24-29, 1979. 11p.
Kikopa, Jane R.
Law and the Status of Women in Tanzania. Addis Ababa,
Ethiopia: United Nations Economic Commission for Africa.
African Training and Research Centre for Women. Research
Series. 1981. 108p.

Kimaryo, Scholastica
"Implication for Women's Status and Position of Structural Changes in Tanzanian Society." Paper Presented at the Meeting of Experts on the History of Women's Contributions to National Liberation Struggles and Their Roles and Needs During Reconstruction in Newly Independent Countries of Africa. Paris: United Nations Educational, Scientific and Cultural Organization. Bissau, Guinea-Bissau. 1983. 17p.

Klima, George
"Jural Relations Between the Sexes Among the Barabaig." (In) Tiffany, Sharon W (ed.). Women and Society: An Anthropological Reader. St. Albans, Vermont: Eden Press. 1979. pp. 145-162.

Kocher, James E.
"A Micro-Economic Analysis of the Determinants of Human Fertility in Rural Northeastern Tanzania." Ph.D Dissertation: Michigan State University. Department of Agricultural Economics. East Lansing, Michigan. 1976. 279p.

Kocher, James E.
Rural Development and Fertility Change in Northeastern Tanzania. Cambridge, Massachusetts: Harvard University. Harvard Institute for International Development. 1977.

Kocher, James E.
Rural Development and Fertility Change in Tropical Africa: Evidence From Tanzania. East Lansing, Michigan: Michigan State University. Department of Agricultural Economics. Africana Rural Economy Paper #19. 1979. 95p.

Kocher, James E.
Rural Development, Health, Mortality and Fertility in Rural Northeastern Tanzania. Cambridge, Massachusetts: Harvard University. Harvard Institute for International Development. 1980. 123p.

Kocher, James E.
Socioeconomic Development and Fertility Change in Rural Africa. Cambridge, Massachusetts: Harvard University. Harvard Institute for International Development. Development Discussion Paper #16. 1976. 22p.

Kocher, James E.
"Socioeconomic Development and Fertility Change in Rural Africa." Food Research Institute Studies. Volume 16 #2 1977. pp. 63-73.

Koda, Bertha
"Liberation of Women in Tanzania." Maji Maji. #35 1978. pp, 54-61.

Kokuhirwa, Hilda N.
"Village Women and Nonformal Education in Tanzania: Factors Affecting Participation." Ph.D Dissertation: University of Massachusetts. Amherst, Massachusetts. 1982. 260p.

Larsen, Lorne E.
"Problems in the Study of Witchcraft Eradication
Movements in Southern Tanzania." Ufahamu. Volume 6 #3
1976. pp. 88-100.
Lihamba, Amandina
The Image of Women in the Performing Arts. Paper
Presented at the Workshop on Women's Studies and
Development. Dar-es-Salaam, Tanzania: University of
Dar-es-Salaam. Bureau of Resource Assessment and Land
Use Planning. Paper 46. September 24-29, 1979. 28p.
Luhanga, Emily
"Law and the Status of Women in Tanzania." Paper
Presented at the Workshop on Women's Status and
Development. Dar-es-Salaam, Tanzania: University of
Dar-es-Salaam. Bureau of Resource Assessment and Land
Use Planning. Paper #36. September 24-29, 1979. 7p.
Madsen, Birgit
Women's Mobilization and Integration in Development: A
Village Case Study From Tanzania. Copenhagen, Denmark:
Centre for Development Research. CDR Research Report #3.
1984. 95p.
Matteru, May
"The Image of Women in Tanzanian Oral Literature." Paper
Presented at the Workshop on Women's Studies and
Development. Dar-es-Salaam, Tanzania: University of
Dar-es-Salaam. Bureau of Resource Assessment and Land
Use Planning. Paper #22. September 24-29, 1979. 26p.
Mbilinyi, Marjorie J.
"The Political Practices of Peasant Women in Tanzania."
Paper Presented at the 12th World Congress of the
International Political Science Association. Rio de
Janeiro, Brazil. 1982.
Mbilinyi, Marjorie J.
The Problem of Sexuality and Fertility Among Female
Youth. Dar-es-Salaam, Tanzania: University of
Dar-es-Salaam. Institute of Development Studies. 1979.
30p.
Mbilinyi, Marjorie J.
The Social Transformation of the Shambaa Kingdom and the
Changing Position of Women. Dar-es-Salaam, Tanzania:
University of Dar-es-Salaam. Southern African
Universities--Social Science Conference. June 23-27,
1979.
Mbilinyi, Marjorie J.
"The Social Transformation of the Shambaa Kingdom and the
Changing Position of Women." Paper Presented at the
Workshop on Women's Studies and Development.
Dar-es-Salaam, Tanzania: University of Dar-es-Salaam.
Bureau of Resource Assessment and Land Use Planning.
Paper #7. September 24-29, 1979. 37p.
Mbilinyi, Marjorie J.
"Wife, Slave and Subject of the King: The Oppression of

Women in the Shambala Kingdom." Tanzania Notes and
Records. #88-89. 1982. pp. 1-13.

Mbilinyi, Marjorie J.
"Women in Agricultural Production in West Bagamoyo,
Tanzania." Paper Presented at a Workshop on Women in
Agricultural Development in Eastern and Southern Africa.
Nairobi: Ford Foundation. April, 1980.

Mbilinyi, Marjorie J.
Women: Producers and Reproducers in Peasant Production.
Dar-es-Salaam, Tanzania: University of Dar-es-Salaam.
Economic Research Bureau. Occasional Paper #77.3. 1977.
39p.

McHenry, Dean E.
"Communal Farming in Tanzania: A Comparison of Male and
Female Participants." African Studies Review. Volume 25
#4 December, 1982. pp. 49-64.

Mcharo, N.E.
Literacy: A Tool for the Development of Rural Women in
Tanzania. Dar-es-Salaam, Tanzania: Institute of Adult
Education. Studies in Adult Education #27. 1977. 17p.

Mgaya, Mary
"Women Workers in a Factory in Tanzania." Paper
Presented at the Workshop on Women's Studies and
Development. Dar-es-Salaam, Tanzania: University of
Dar-es-Salaam. Bureau of Resource Assessment and Land
Use Planning. Paper #1. September 24-29, 1979. 9p.

Mlama, Penina
"The Role of Women in Culture Reproduction: The Case of
Tanzanian Art and Literature." Paper Presented at the
Workshop on Women's Studies and Development.
Dar-es-Salaam, Tanzania: University of Dar-es-Salaam.
Bureau of Resource Assessment and Land Use Planning.
Paper #17. September 24-29, 1979. 14p.

Muro, Asseny
"The Study of Women's Position in Peasant Production and
Their Education and Training: A Case Study of Diozile I
Village in Bagomoyo District." M.A. Thesis: University
of Dar-es-Salaam. Dar-es-Salaam, Tanzania. June, 1979.

Muro, Asseny
"Women in Agricultural Production and Their Education and
Training: A Case Study of Diozile I Village in Bagamoyo
District." Paper Presented at the Workshop on Women's
Studies and Development. Dar-es-Salaam, Tanzania:
University of Dar-es-Salaam. Bureau of Resource
Assessment and Land Use Planning. Paper #11. September
24-29, 1979. 42p.

Muro, M.
"The Controversy Over Bride Price and Polygamy: New Laws
on Marriage and Maternity Leave." Tanzania Notes and
Records. #83 1978. pp. 133-137.

Muze, Siphiwe
"Family Life Education: A Growing Need in Tanzania."
Paper Presented at the Workshop on Women's Studies and

Development. Dar-es-Salaam, Tanzania: University of
Dar-es-Salaam. Bureau of Resource Assessment and Land
Use Planning. Paper #21. September 24-29, 1979. 4p.
Namfua, Pelad P.
"Polygyny in Tanzania: Its Determinants and Effect on
Fertility." Ph.D Dissertation: Johns Hopkins University.
Baltimore, Maryland. 1982. 233p.
Ngalula, Theresia K.
"Domestic Labour and Property Ownership: A Case Study of
Buhongwa Village in Mwanza District." Paper Presented at
the Workshop on Women's Studies and Development.
Dar-es-Salaam, Tanzania: University of Dar-es-Salaam.
Bureau of Resource Assessment and Land Use Planning.
Paper #13. September 24-29, 1979. 10p.
Ngalula, Theresia K.
"Women as a Productive Force in the Tanzanian Rural
Society: A Case Study of Buhongwa Village in Mwanza
District." M.A. Thesis: University of Dar-es-Salaam.
Department of Sociology. Dar-es-Salaam, Tanzania. 1977.
113p.
O'Brien, M.
"The Maize Grinding Mill at Sinon." Community
Development Journal. Volume 20 #3 1985. pp. 189-191.
Ohadike, Patrick O.
"A Case Study of the Determinants of Family-Household
Size in African Development." (In) Oppong, C. and Adaba,
G and Bekombo-Priso, M. and Mogey, J. (eds.). Marriage,
Fertility and Parenthood in West Africa. Canberra,
Australia: Australian National University. Department of
Demography. Volume One. 1978. pp. 381-398.
Rogers, Susan G.
"Efforts Toward Women's Development in Tanzania: Gender
Rhetoric vs. Gender Realities." (In) Staudt, Kathleen A.
and Jaquette, Jane S. (eds.). Women in Developing
Countries: A Policy Focus. New York: Haworth Press.
1983. pp. 23-41.
Rogers, Susan G.
"Efforts Toward Women's Development in Tanzania: Gender
Rhetoric vs. Gender Realities." Women and Politics.
Volume 2 #4 Winter, 1982. pp. 23-41.
Sawyerr, Akilagpa
"Judicial Manipulation of Customary Family Law in
Tanzania." (In) Roberts, Simon (ed.). Law and the
Family in Africa. Hague, Netherlands: Mouton. 1977.
pp. 115-128.
Sekatawa, Emmanuel K.
"Compensating Mechanisms in the Nuptiality-Fertility
Relationship: Evidence From Tanzania, 1973." Ph.D
Dissertation: University of Pennsylvania. Philadelphia,
Pennsylvania. 1981. 241p.
Sekatawa, Emmanuel K.
Mechanisms Affecting the Link Between Nuptiality and
Fertility: Tanzania, 1973. Philadelphia, Pennsylvania:

University of Pennsylvania. Population Studies Center.
African Demography Program Working Paper #6. June, 1981.
19p.
Sembajwe, I.S.L.
"The Effect of the Changing Position of Women on Family,
Size and Child Survival in the United Republic of
Tanzania." (In) International Labour Office (ILO).
Final Report on the National Seminar on Population and
Development in the United Republic of Tanzania. Geneva:
ILO. 1980.
Singleton, Michael
"Obsession With Possession." Pro Mundi Vita Africa
Dossier. #4 July-August, 1977. pp. 2-34.
Swantz, Marja-Liisa
"Church and the Changing Role of Women in Tanzania."
(In) Fashole-Luke, Edward. Christianity in Independent
Africa. London: R. Collings. 1978. pp. 136-150.
Swantz, Marja-Liisa
"Free Women of Bukoba." (In) Sundkler, Bengt and
Wahlstrom, Per-Ake (eds.). Vision and Service: Papers in
Honor of Babbro Johansson. Uppsala, Sweden: Scandinavian
Institute of African Studies and the Swedish Institute of
Missionary Research. 1977. pp. 99-107.
Swantz, Marja-Liisa.
Strain and Strength Among Peasant Women in Tanzania.
Dar-es-Salaam, Tanzania: University of Dar-es-Salaam.
Bureau of Resource Assessment and Land Use Planning.
Research Paper #49. May, 1977. 81p.
Tobisson, Eva
Women, Work, Food and Nutrition in Nyamwigura Village,
Mara Region, Tanzania. Dar-es-Salaam, Tanzania: Tanzania
Food and Nutrition Centre. Report #548. July, 1980.
127p.
Turshen, Meredith
The Political Ecology of Disease in Tanzania. New
Brunswick, New Jersey: Rutgers University Press. 1984.
259p.
United Nations Economic Commission for Africa (UNECA)
"The Relationship Between Changing Roles and Status of
Women and Childbearing and Child Survival in Tanzania."
Paper Presented at the National Seminar on Population and
Development. Addis Ababa, Ethiopia: UNECA. Arusha,
Tanzania. 1980.
Vourela, Ulla
"Women's Role in Production and Reproduction: Some
Reflections on Relationships Between Men and Women in
Tanzania and Finland." Paper Presented at the Workshop
on Women's Studies and Development. Dar-es-Salaam,
Tanzania: University of Dar-es-Salaam. Bureau of
Resource Assessment and Land Use Planning. Paper #28.
September 24-29, 1979. 19p.
Wada, Shonei
"Female Initiation Rites of the Iraqw and the Gorowa."

Senri Ethnological Studies. Volume 15 1984. pp. 187-196.
Wiley, Liz
"Tanzania: The Arusha Planning and Village Development Project." (In) Overholt, Catherine and Anderson, Mary B. and Cloud, Kathleen and Austin, James E. (eds.). Gender Roles in Development Projects: A Case Book. Hartford, Connecticut: Kumarian Press. 1985. pp. 163-184.
Willis, Roy G.
"Executive Women and the Emergence of Female Class Consciousness: The Case of Fipa." Anthropology. Volume 4 #1 1980. pp. 1-10.
Wilson, Monica H.
For Men and Elders--Changes in the Relations of Generations and of Men and Women Among the Nyakyusa-Ngonde People, 1875-1971. New York: Africana Publishing Company. 1977. 209p.
Wright, Marcia
"Family Community and Women as Reflected in 'Die Safwa' by Elise Kootz-Kretschmer." (In) Sundkler, Bengt and Wahlstrom, Per-Ake (eds.). Vision and Service: Papers in Honour of Babbro Johansson. Uppsala, Sweden: Scandinavian Institute of African Studies and the Swedish Institute of Missionary Research. 1977. pp. 108-116.
Wylie, Liz
Women and Development: A Case Study of Ten Tanzania Villages. Arusha, Tanzania: Arusha Planning and Village Development Project. 1981.

DEVELOPMENT AND TECHNOLOGY

Alopaeus-Stahl, Dorrit
Tanzanian Women Activities and Development Cooperation. Dar-es-Salaam, Tanzania: Swedish International Development Agency. May, 1979.
Alpers, E.A.
"Ordinary Household Chores--Ritual and Power in a 19th Century Swahili Women's Spirit Possession Cult." International Journal of African Historical Studies. Volume 17 #4 1984. pp. 677-702.
Bader, Zinnat
"Social Conditions of the Peasant Women in Zanzibar and Pemba." Paper Presented at the Workshop on Women's Studies and Development. Dar-es-Salaam, Tanzania: University of Dar-es-Salaam. Bureau of Resource Assessment and Land Use Planning. Paper #18. September 24-29, 1979.
Brain, James L.
"Less Than Second Class: Women in Rural Settlement Schemes in Tanzania." (In) Hafkin, N.J. and Bay, Edna (eds.). Women in Africa: Studies in Social and Economic

Change. Stanford, California: Stanford University Press.
1976. pp. 265-282.

Brain, James L.
"Witchcraft and Development." African Affairs. Volume
81 #324 July, 1982. pp. 371-384.

Bryceson, Deborah F.
Peasant Food Production and Food Supply in Relation to
the Historical Development of Commoditiy Production in
Pre-Colonial and Colonial Tanganyika. Dar-es-Salaam,
Tanzania: Bureau of Resource Assessment and Land Use
Planning. Service Paper #78/3. 1978. 41p.

Bryceson, Deborah F. and Majma, Sachak
Proceedings of the Workshop on Women's Studies and
Development. Dar-es-Salaam, Tanzania: University of
Dar-es-Salaam. September, 1979. 85p.

Bryceson, Deborah F. and Mbilinyi, Marjorie J.
The Changing Roles of Women in Production: From Peasants
to Proletarians. Dar-es-Salaam, Tanzania: University of
Dar-es-Salaam. History Department. 1978.

Bryceson, Deborah F.
"The Proletarianization of Women in Tanzania." Review of
African Political Economy. #17 January-April, 1980.
pp. 4-27.

Bryceson, Deborah F.
"The Proletarianization of Women in Tanzania." Paper
Presented at the Workshop on Women's Studies and
Development. Dar-es-Salaam, Tanzania: University of
Dar-es-Salaam. Bureau of Resource Assessment and Land
Use Planning. Paper #2. September 24-29, 1979. 45p.

Caplan, Patricia
"Development Policies in Tanzania--Some Implications for
Women." (In) Nelson, Nici (ed.). African Women in the
Developing World. Totowa, New Jersey: Frank Cass. 1981.
pp. 98-108.

Caplan, Patricia
"Development Policies in Tanzania--Some Implications for
Women." Journal of Development. Volume 17 #3 April,
1981. pp. 98-108.

Chale, Freda U. and Generose, Ngonyani
"Report on a Survey of Cooperative Income Generating
Projects for Women and its Impact on the Welfare of
Children and the Family." Paper Presented at the
Workshop on Women's Studies and Development.
Dar-es-Salaam, Tanzania: University of Dar-es-Salaam.
Bureau of Resource Assessment and Land Use Planning.
Paper #24. September 24-29, 1979. 42p.

Chale, Freda U.
"Women's Programmes and the Role of a Rural Woman in
Tanzania." Paper Presented at the Workshop on Population
Life Education Project in Integrated Rural Development.
Arusha, Tanzania: Arusha Technical School. January 1-25,
1979.

Chengelela, Rustica
"Adult Education's Impact on Women." Paper Presented at
the Workshop on Women's Studies and Development.
Dar-es-Salaam, Tanzania: University of Dar-es-Salaam.
Bureau of Resource Assessment and Land Use Plannning.
Paper #16. September 24-29, 1979. 10p.

Chiume, Kanyama
"Women in a Developing Tanzania." African Women.
November-December, 1977. pp. 60-61.

Croll, E.J.
"Women in Rural Production and Reproduction in the Soviet
Union, China, Cuba and Tanzania." Signs. Volume 7 #2
Winter, 1981. pp. 375-399.

Fleuret, A.
"The Role of Women in Rural Markets: Lushoto, Tanzania."
Paper Presented at the First Women and Anthropology
Symposium. Sacramento, California. March, 1977.

Fortmann, Louise P.
"Women and Agricultural Development." (In) Kim, K.S. and
Mabele, R. and Schultheis, M.J. (eds.). Papers on the
Political Economy of Tanzania. Nairobi: Heinemann
Educational. 1979.

Fortmann, Louise P.
Women and Tanzanian Agricultural Development.
Dar-es-Salaam, Tanzania: University of Dar-es-Salaam.
Economic Research Bureau. Paper #77.4. Mimeo. 1977.
24p.

Fortmann, Louise P.
"Women's Work in a Communal Setting: The Tanzanian Policy
of Ujamaa." Paper Presented at the Conference on Women
and Work in Africa. Urbana, Illinois: University of
Illinois-Urbana. Mimeo. April 28-May 1, 1979.

Fortmann, Louise P.
"Women's Work in a Communal Setting: The Tanzanian Policy
of Ujamaa." (In) Bay, Edna (ed.). Women in Work in
Africa. Boulder, Colorado: Westview Press. 1982. pp.
191-205.

Geiger, Susan
"Umoja wa Wanawake wa Tanzania and the Needs of the Rural
Poor." African Studies Review. Volume 25 #2/3
July-September, 1982. pp. 45-65.

Hamdani, Salha
"Peasantry and the Peasant Women in Tanzania: The Luguru
Case." Paper Presented at the Workshop on Women's
Studies and Development. Dar-es-Salaam, Tanzania:
University of Dar-es-Salaam. Bureau of Resource
Assessment and Land Use Planning. Paper #8. September
24-29, 1979. 9p.

Henn, Jeanne K.
"Who Benefits From Peasant Women's Work? Insights From a
Modes of Production Analysis." Paper Presented at the
Workshop on Women's Studies and Development.
Dar-es-Salaam: University of Dar-es-Salaam. Bureau of

Resource Assessment and Land Use Planning. Paper #29.
September 24-29, 1979. 19p.
Huth, Mary J.
"Female Participation and Status in Tanzania's Urban
Labor Market." Paper Presented at the Annual Meeting of
the North Central Sociological Association. University
of Dayton. Dayton, Ohio. 1985.
Internation Co-Operative Alliance
Report on the Evaluation of the ICA Women Co-Operative
Education and Other Activities Project Moshi, ICA.
Moshi, Tanzania: ICA. Regional Office for East and
Central Africa. 1980.
Johnson, Willene
"The Study of Economic Activities of Women in Urban
Tanzania." Ph.D Dissertation: Columbia University. New
York, New York. 1983. 156p.
Kamuzora, C. Lwechungura
"High Fertility and the Demand for Labour in Peasant
Economies: The Case of Bukoba District, Tanzania."
Development and Change. Volume 15 #1 January, 1984.
pp. 105-124.
Kimaryo, Scholastica
"Implication for Women's Status and Position of
Structural Changes in Tanzanian Society." Paper
Presented at the Meeting of Experts on the History of
Women's Contributions to National Liberation Struggles
and Their Roles and Needs During Reconstruction in Newly
Independent Countries of Africa. Paris: United Nations
Educational, Scientific and Cultural Organization.
Bissau, Guinea-Bissau. 1983. 17p.
Kocher, James E.
Rural Development and Fertility Change in Northeastern
Tanzania. Cambridge, Massachusetts: Harvard University.
Harvard Institute for International Development. 1977.
Kocher, James E.
Rural Development and Fertility Change in Tropical
Africa: Evidence From Tanzania. East Lansing, Michigan:
Michigan State University. Department of Agricultural
Economics. Africana Rural Economy Paper #19. 1979.
95p.
Kocher, James E.
Rural Development, Health, Mortality and Fertility in
Rural Northeastern Tanzania. Cambridge, Massachusetts:
Harvard University. Harvard Institute for International
Development. 1980. 123p.
Kocher, James E.
Socioeconomic Development and Fertility Change in Rural
Africa. Cambridge, Massachusetts: Harvard University.
Harvard Institute for International Development.
Development Discussion Paper #16. 1976. 22p.
Kocher, James E.
"Socioeconomic Development and Fertility Change in Rural

Africa." Food Research Institute Studies. Volume 16 #2
1977. pp. 63-73.
Koda, Bertha
"The Role of UWT in Rural Development." Paper Presented
at the Workshop on Women's Studies and Development.
Dar-es-Salaam, Tanzania: University of Dar-es-Salaam.
Bureau of Resource Assessment and Land Use Planning.
Paper #19. September 24-29, 1979. 8p.
Kokuhirwa, Hilda N.
The Role of Education in Mobilizing Women for Development
in Tanzania. Amherst, Massachusetts: University of
Massachusetts. Center for International Education.
School of Education. May, 1978. 39p.
Ladner, Joyce A.
"Tanzanian Women in Nation Building." (In) Steady,
Filomina C. (ed.). The Black Woman Cross-Culturally.
Cambridge, Massachusetts: Schenkman Publications. 1981.
pp. 107-118.
Lowe, Linda T.
"The Urban Woman Worker in Dar-es-Salaam." African Urban
Notes. Volume 2 #3 Fall-Winter, 1976. pp. 11-19.
Luhanga, Emily
"Law and the Status of Women in Tanzania." Paper
Presented at the Workshop on Women's Status and
Development. Dar-es-Salaam, Tanzania: University of
Dar-es-Salaam. Bureau of Resource Assessment and Land
Use Planning. Paper #36. September 24-29, 1979. 7p.
Madsen, Birgit
Women's Mobilization and Integration in Development: A
Village Case Study From Tanzania. Copenhagen, Denmark:
Centre for Development Research. CDR Research Report #3.
1984. 95p.
Mascarenhas, Ophelia and Mbilinyi, Marjorie J.
Women and Development in Tanzania: An Annotated
Bibliography. Addis Ababa, Ethiopia: United Nations
Economic Commission for Africa. African Training and
Research Centre for Women. Bibliography Series #2.
1980. 135p.
Mbilinyi, Marjorie J.
Women in the Rural Development of Mbeya Region. Dar es
Salaam, Tanzania: Ministry of Agriculture/U.N. FAO.
Mbeya RIDEP Project. 1982.
Mbilinyi, Marjorie J.
The Liberation of Women in the Context of Tanzania.
Dar-es-Salaam, Tanzania: University of Dar-es-Salaam.
Papers in Education and Development. #4. October, 1977.
pp. 1-26.
Mbilinyi, Marjorie J.
"Women in Agricultural Production in West Bagamoyo,
Tanzania." Paper Presented at a Workshop on Women in
Agricultural Development in Eastern and Southern Africa.
Nairobi: Ford Foundation. April, 1980.

Mbilinyi, Marjorie J.
    Women: Producers and Reproducers in Peasant Production.
    Dar-es-Salaam, Tanzania: University of Dar-es-Salaam.
    Economic Research Bureau. Occasional Paper #77.3. 1977.
    39p.
McHenry, Dean E.
    "Communal Farming in Tanzania: A Comparison of Male and
    Female Participants." African Studies Review. Volume 25
    #4 December, 1982. pp. 49-64.
Mcharo, N.E.
    Literacy: A Tool for the Development of Rural Women in
    Tanzania. Dar-es-Salaam, Tanzania: Institute of Adult
    Education. Studies in Adult Education #27. 1977. 17p.
Meghji, Zakia
    "The Development of Women in Wage Labour: The Case of
    Industries in Moshi District." M.A. Thesis: University
    of Dar es Salaam. Dar es Salaam, Tanzania. 1977.
Mgaya, Mary
    "Women Workers in a Factory in Tanzania." Paper
    Presented at the Workshop on Women's Studies and
    Development. Dar-es-Salaam, Tanzania: University of
    Dar-es-Salaam. Bureau of Resource Assessment and Land
    Use Planning. Paper #1. September 24-29, 1979. 9p.
Muro, Asseny
    "Education and Training of Women for Employment: The Case
    of Mainland Tanzania." Paper Presented at the Highlevel
    Workshop on Development and Participation of Women.
    Arusha, Tanzania: East and Southern Africa Management
    Institute. 1982.
Muro, Asseny
    "The Study of Women's Position in Peasant Production and
    Their Education and Training: A Case Study of Diozile I
    Village in Bagomoyo District." M.A. Thesis: University
    of Dar-es-Salaam. Dar-es-Salaam, Tanzania. June, 1979.
Muro, Asseny
    "Women in Agricultural Production and Their Education and
    Training: A Case Study of Diozile I Village in Bagamoyo
    District." Paper Presented at the Workshop on Women's
    Studies and Development. Dar-es-Salaam, Tanzania:
    University of Dar-es-Salaam. Bureau of Resource
    Assessment and Land Use Planning. Paper #11. September
    24-29, 1979. 42p.
Ngalula, Theresia K.
    "Women as a Productive Force in the Tanzanian Rural
    Society: A Case Study of Buhongwa Village in Mwanza
    District." M.A. Thesis: University of Dar-es-Salaam.
    Department of Sociology. Dar-es-Salaam, Tanzania. 1977.
    113p.
O'Brien, M.
    "The Maize Grinding Mill at Sinon." Community
    Development Journal. Volume 20 #3 1985. pp. 189-191.
Olekambaine, Priscilla
    "Women and Education in Tanzania." Paper Presented at

the Workshop on Women's Studies and Development.
Dar-es-Salaam, Tanzania: University of Dar-es-Salaam.
Bureau of Resource Assessment and Land Use Planning.
Paper #30. September 24-29, 1979. 9p.

Oomen-Myin, Marie A.
"The Involvement of Rural Women in Village Development in
Tanzania." Convergence. Volume 16 #2 1983. pp. 59-69.

Rogers, Susan G.
"Efforts Toward Women's Development in Tanzania: Gender
Rhetoric vs. Gender Realities." (In) Staudt, Kathleen A.
and Jaquette, Jane S. (eds.). Women in Developing
Countries: A Policy Focus. New York: Haworth Press.
1983. pp. 23-41.

Rogers, Susan G.
"Efforts Toward Women's Development in Tanzania: Gender
Rhetoric vs. Gender Realities." Women and Politics.
Volume 2 #4 Winter, 1982. pp. 23-41.

Sackak, Najma
"Creating Employment Opportunites for Rural Women: Case
Study of Dodoma Rural District." Paper Presented at the
Workshop on Women's Studies and Development.
Dar-es-Salaam, Tanzania: University of Dar-es-Salaam.
Bureau of Resource Assessment and Land Use Planning.
Paper #6. September 24-29, 1979. 18p.

Shields, Nwanganga G.
Women in the Urban Labor Markets of Africa: The Case of
Tanzania. Washington, D.C.: World Bank. Staff Working
Paper #380. April, 1980. 138p.

Sijaona, S.T.
"Women's Projects in Urban Areas: Dar-es-Salaam City."
Paper Presented at the Workshop on Women's Studies and
Development. Dar-es-Salaam, Tanzania: University of
Dar-es-Salaam. Bureau of Resource Assessment and Land
Use Planning. Paper #10. September 24-29, 1979. 9p.

Swantz, Marja-Liisa
Women in Development: A Creative Role Denied? The Case
of Tanzania. New York: St. Martin's Press. 1985. 170p.

Swantz, Marja-Liisa
Women's Creative Role in Development in Tanzania.
Helsinki, Finland: University of Helsinki. 1982.

Swantz, Marja-Liisa.
Strain and Strength Among Peasant Women in Tanzania.
Dar-es-Salaam, Tanzania: University of Dar-es-Salaam.
Bureau of Resource Assessment and Land Use Planning.
Research Paper #49. May, 1977. 81p.

U.S. Department of Commerce. Bureau of the Census
Illustrative Statistics on Women in Development in
Selected Developing Countries. Washington, D.C.: U.S.
Department of Commerce. 1982. 24p.

United Nations Economic Commission for Africa (UNECA)
Training and Employment Opportunities for Out-of-School
Girls in the City of Dar-es-Salaam: A Planner's Point of
View. Addis Ababa, Ethiopia: UNECA. 1981.

Virji, Parin
   "Summary of the Labour Turnover at Friendship Textile
   Mill in 1978 With Special Reference to Women Workers."
   Paper Presented at the Workshop on Women's Studies and
   Development. Dar-es-Salaam, Tanzania: University of
   Dar-es-Salaam. Bureau of Resource Assessment and Land
   Use Planning. Paper #3. September 24-29, 1979. 8p.
Wiley, Liz
   "Tanzania: The Arusha Planning and Village Development
   Project." (In) Overholt, Catherine and Anderson, Mary B.
   and Cloud, Kathleen and Austin, James E. (eds.). Gender
   Roles in Development Projects: A Case Book. Hartford,
   Connecticut: Kumarian Press. 1985. pp. 163-184.
Wylie, Liz
   Women and Development: A Case Study of Ten Tanzania
   Villages. Arusha, Tanzania: Arusha Planning and Village
   Development Project. 1981.

ECONOMICS

Alopaeus-Stahl, Dorrit
   Tanzanian Women Activities and Development Cooperation.
   Dar-es-Salaam, Tanzania: Swedish International
   Development Agency. May, 1979.
Asayehgn, Desta
   Role of Women in Tanzania: Their Access to Education and
   Participation in the Labour Force. Paris: International
   Institute for Educational Planning(IIEP). 1979. 31p.
Brain, James L.
   "Less Than Second Class: Women in Rural Settlement
   Schemes in Tanzania." (In) Hafkin, N.J. and Bay, Edna
   (eds.). Women in Africa: Studies in Social and Economic
   Change. Stanford, California: Stanford University Press.
   1976. pp. 265-282.
Bryceson, Deborah F.
   Peasant Food Production and Food Supply in Relation to
   the Historical Development of Commoditiy Production in
   Pre-Colonial and Colonial Tanganyika. Dar-es-Salaam,
   Tanzania: Bureau of Resource Assessment and Land Use
   Planning. Service Paper #78/3. 1978. 41p.
Bryceson, Deborah F. and Majma, Sachak
   Proceedings of the Workshop on Women's Studies and
   Development. Dar-es-Salaam, Tanzania: University of
   Dar-es-Salaam. September, 1979. 85p.
Bryceson, Deborah F. and Mbilinyi, Marjorie J.
   The Changing Roles of Women in Production: From Peasants
   to Proletarians. Dar-es-Salaam, Tanzania: University of
   Dar-es-Salaam. History Department. 1978.

Bryceson, Deborah F.
"The Proletarianization of Women in Tanzania." Review of African Political Economy. #17 January-April, 1980. pp. 4-27.

Bryceson, Deborah F.
"The Proletarianization of Women in Tanzania." Paper Presented at the Workshop on Women's Studies and Development. Dar-es-Salaam, Tanzania: University of Dar-es-Salaam. Bureau of Resource Assessment and Land Use Planning. Paper #2. September 24-29, 1979. 45p.

Caplan, Patricia
"Development Policies in Tanzania--Some Implications for Women." (In) Nelson, Nici (ed.). African Women in the Developing World. Totowa, New Jersey: Frank Cass. 1981. pp. 98-108.

Caplan, Patricia
"Development Policies in Tanzania--Some Implications for Women." Journal of Development. Volume 17 #3 April, 1981. pp. 98-108.

Caplan, Patricia
"Gender, Ideology and Modes of Production on the Coast of East Africa." Paideuma. Volume 28 1982. pp. 29-43.

Chale, Freda U. and Generose, Ngonyani
"Report on a Survey of Cooperative Income Generating Projects for Women and its Impact on the Welfare of Children and the Family." Paper Presented at the Workshop on Women's Studies and Development. Dar-es-Salaam, Tanzania: University of Dar-es-Salaam. Bureau of Resource Assessment and Land Use Planning. Paper #24. September 24-29, 1979. 42p.

Chale, Freda U.
"Women's Programmes and the Role of a Rural Woman in Tanzania." Paper Presented at the Workshop on Population Life Education Project in Integrated Rural Development. Arusha, Tanzania: Arusha Technical School. January 1-25, 1979.

Chijumba, Beat J.
"Attitudes of Tanzanian Husbands Toward the Employment of their Wives." Africa Development. Volume 8 #2 1983. pp. 74-85.

Chiume, Kanyama
"Women in a Developing Tanzania." African Women. November-December, 1977. pp. 60-61.

Croll, E.J.
"Women in Rural Production and Reproduction in the Soviet Union, China, Cuba and Tanzania." Signs. Volume 7 #2 Winter, 1981. pp. 375-399.

Due, Jean M.
"Intra-Household Gender Issues in Farming Systems in Tanzania, Zambia and Malawi." (In) Poats, Susan V. and Schmink, Marianne and Spring, Anita (eds.). Gender Issues in Farming Systems Research and Extension. Boulder, Colorado: Westview Press. 1980. pp. 331-344.

Fleuret, A.
"The Role of Women in Rural Markets: Lushoto, Tanzania."
Paper Presented at the First Women and Anthropology
Symposium. Sacramento, California. March, 1977.

Fortmann, Louise P.
"Women and Agricultural Development." (In) Kim, K.S. and
Mabele, R. and Schultheis, M.J. (eds.). Papers on the
Political Economy of Tanzania. Nairobi: Heinemann
Educational. 1979.

Fortmann, Louise P.
Women and Tanzanian Agricultural Development.
Dar-es-Salaam, Tanzania: University of Dar-es-Salaam.
Economic Research Bureau. Paper #77.4. Mimeo. 1977.
24p.

Fortmann, Louise P.
"Women's Work in a Communal Setting: The Tanzanian Policy
of Ujamaa." Paper Presented at the Conference on Women
and Work in Africa. Urbana, Illinois: University of
Illinois-Urbana. Mimeo. April 28-May 1, 1979.

Fortmann, Louise P.
"Women's Work in a Communal Setting: The Tanzanian Policy
of Ujamaa." (In) Bay, Edna (ed.). Women in Work in
Africa. Boulder, Colorado: Westview Press. 1982. pp.
191-205.

Geiger, Susan
"Umoja wa Wanawake wa Tanzania and the Needs of the Rural
Poor." African Studies Review. Volume 25 #2/3
July-September, 1982. pp. 45-65.

Hamdani, Salha
"Peasantry and the Peasant Women in Tanzania: The Luguru
Case." Paper Presented at the Workshop on Women's
Studies and Development. Dar-es-Salaam, Tanzania:
University of Dar-es-Salaam. Bureau of Resource
Assessment and Land Use Planning. Paper #8. September
24-29, 1979. 9p.

Henn, Jeanne K.
"Who Benefits From Peasant Women's Work? Insights From a
Modes of Production Analysis." Paper Presented at the
Workshop on Women's Studies and Development.
Dar-es-Salaam: University of Dar-es-Salaam. Bureau of
Resource Assessment and Land Use Planning. Paper #29.
September 24-29, 1979. 19p.

Huth, Mary J.
"Female Participation and Status in Tanzania's Urban
Labor Market." Paper Presented at the Annual Meeting of
the North Central Sociological Association. University
of Dayton. Dayton, Ohio. 1985.

Johnson, Willene
"The Study of Economic Activities of Women in Urban
Tanzania." Ph.D Dissertation: Columbia University. New
York, New York. 1983. 156p.

Kimaryo, Scholastica
"Implication for Women's Status and Position of

Structural Changes in Tanzanian Society." Paper
Presented at the Meeting of Experts on the History of
Women's Contributions to National Liberation Struggles
and Their Roles and Needs During Reconstruction in Newly
Independent Countries of Africa. Paris: United Nations
Educational, Scientific and Cultural Organization.
Bissau, Guinea-Bissau. 1983. 17p.

Kocher, James E.
Socioeconomic Development and Fertility Change in Rural
Africa. Cambridge, Massachusetts: Harvard University.
Harvard Institute for International Development.
Development Discussion Paper #16. 1976. 22p.

Kocher, James E.
"Socioeconomic Development and Fertility Change in Rural
Africa." Food Research Institute Studies. Volume 16 #2
1977. pp. 63-73.

Ladner, Joyce A.
"Tanzanian Women in Nation Building." (In) Steady,
Filomina C. (ed.). The Black Woman Cross-Culturally.
Cambridge, Massachusetts: Schenkman Publications. 1981.
pp. 107-118.

Lowe, Linda T.
"The Urban Woman Worker in Dar-es-Salaam." African Urban
Notes. Volume 2 #3 Fall-Winter, 1976. pp. 11-19.

Madsen, Birgit
Women's Mobilization and Integration in Development: A
Village Case Study From Tanzania. Copenhagen, Denmark:
Centre for Development Research. CDR Research Report #3.
1984. 95p.

Mbilinyi, Marjorie J.
Women in the Rural Development of Mbeya Region. Dar es
Salaam, Tanzania: Ministry of Agriculture/U.N. FAO.
Mbeya RIDEP Project. 1982.

Mbilinyi, Marjorie J.
"Women in Agricultural Production in West Bagamoyo,
Tanzania." Paper Presented at a Workshop on Women in
Agricultural Development in Eastern and Southern Africa.
Nairobi: Ford Foundation. April, 1980.

Mbilinyi, Marjorie J.
Women: Producers and Reproducers in Peasant Production.
Dar-es-Salaam, Tanzania: University of Dar-es-Salaam.
Economic Research Bureau. Occasional Paper #77.3. 1977.
39p.

McHenry, Dean E.
"Communal Farming in Tanzania: A Comparison of Male and
Female Participants." African Studies Review. Volume 25
#4 December, 1982. pp. 49-64.

Meghji, Zakia
"The Development of Women in Wage Labour: The Case of
Industries in Moshi District." M.A. Thesis: University
of Dar es Salaam. Dar es Salaam, Tanzania. 1977.

Mgaya, Mary
"Women Workers in a Factory in Tanzania." Paper

Presented at the Workshop on Women's Studies and
Development. Dar-es-Salaam, Tanzania: University of
Dar-es-Salaam. Bureau of Resource Assessment and Land
Use Planning. Paper #1. September 24-29, 1979. 9p.

Muro, Asseny
"The Study of Women's Position in Peasant Production and
Their Education and Training: A Case Study of Diozile I
Village in Bagomoyo District." M.A. Thesis: University
of Dar-es-Salaam. Dar-es-Salaam, Tanzania. June, 1979.

Muro, Asseny
"Women in Agricultural Production and Their Education and
Training: A Case Study of Diozile I Village in Bagamoyo
District." Paper Presented at the Workshop on Women's
Studies and Development. Dar-es-Salaam, Tanzania:
University of Dar-es-Salaam. Bureau of Resource
Assessment and Land Use Planning. Paper #11. September
24-29, 1979. 42p.

Ngalula, Theresia K.
"Women as a Productive Force in the Tanzanian Rural
Society: A Case Study of Buhongwa Village in Mwanza
District." M.A. Thesis: University of Dar-es-Salaam.
Department of Sociology. Dar-es-Salaam, Tanzania. 1977.
113p.

Oomen-Myin, Marie A.
"The Involvement of Rural Women in Village Development in
Tanzania." Convergence. Volume 16 #2 1983. pp. 59-69.

Rogers, Susan G.
"Efforts Toward Women's Development in Tanzania: Gender
Rhetoric vs. Gender Realities." (In) Staudt, Kathleen A.
and Jaquette, Jane S. (eds.). Women in Developing
Countries: A Policy Focus. New York: Haworth Press.
1983. pp. 23-41.

Rogers, Susan G.
"Efforts Toward Women's Development in Tanzania: Gender
Rhetoric vs. Gender Realities." Women and Politics.
Volume 2 #4 Winter, 1982. pp. 23-41.

Sackak, Najma
"Creating Employment Opportunites for Rural Women: Case
Study of Dodoma Rural District." Paper Presented at the
Workshop on Women's Studies and Development.
Dar-es-Salaam, Tanzania: University of Dar-es-Salaam.
Bureau of Resource Assessment and Land Use Planning.
Paper #6. September 24-29, 1979. 18p.

Shields, Nwanganga G.
Women in the Urban Labor Markets of Africa: The Case of
Tanzania. Washington, D.C.: World Bank. Staff Working
Paper #380. April, 1980. 138p.

Sijaona, S.T.
"Women's Projects in Urban Areas: Dar-es-Salaam City."
Paper Presented at the Workshop on Women's Studies and
Development. Dar-es-Salaam, Tanzania: University of
Dar-es-Salaam. Bureau of Resource Assessment and Land
Use Planning. Paper #10. September 24-29, 1979. 9p.

Swantz, Marja-Liisa
  Women in Development: A Creative Role Denied? The Case
  of Tanzania. New York: St. Martin's Press. 1985. 170p.
Swantz, Marja-Liisa
  Women's Creative Role in Development in Tanzania.
  Helsinki, Finland: University of Helsinki. 1982.
Tadesse, Zenebeworke
  "An Overview on Women's Organizations in Africa: The Case
  of Ethiopia, Mozambique and Tanzania." Paper Presented
  at the 9th World Conference of Sociology. Uppsala,
  Sweden. 1978.
Tadesse, Zenebeworke
  An Oveview on the Role of Women's Organizations in
  Africa: Case Study of Ethiopia, Zambia, Mozambique and
  Tanzania. Lusaka, Zambia: P/O Box RW 514. 1978.
Wiley, Liz
  "Tanzania: The Arusha Planning and Village Development
  Project." (In) Overholt, Catherine and Anderson, Mary B.
  and Cloud, Kathleen and Austin, James E. (eds.). Gender
  Roles in Development Projects: A Case Book. Hartford,
  Connecticut: Kumarian Press. 1985. pp. 163-184.
Willis, Roy G.
  "Executive Women and the Emergence of Female Class
  Consciousness: The Case of Fipa." Anthropology. Volume
  4 #1 1980. pp. 1-10.

EDUCATION AND TRAINING

Asayehgn, Desta
  Role of Women in Tanzania: Their Access to Education and
  Participation in the Labour Force. Paris: International
  Institute for Educational Planning(IIEP). 1979. 31p.
Balisidya, M.L.
  "The Image of the Woman in Tanzanian Oral Literature: A
  Survey." Kiswahili. Volume 49 #2 1982. pp. 1-31.
Bryceson, Deborah F.
  "Notes on the Educational Potential of Mass Media
  Vis-a-Vis Women's Roles in Tanzanian Society." Paper
  Presented at the Workshop on Women's Studies and
  Development. Dar-es-Salaam, Tanzania: University of
  Dar-es-Salaam. Bureau of Resource Assessment and Land
  Use Planning. Paper #23. September 24-29, 1979. 10p.
Bryceson, Deborah F. and Majma, Sachak
  Proceedings of the Workshop on Women's Studies and
  Development. Dar-es-Salaam, Tanzania: University of
  Dar-es-Salaam. September, 1979. 85p.
Chale, Freda U.
  "Women's Programmes and the Role of a Rural Woman in
  Tanzania." Paper Presented at the Workshop on Population
  Life Education Project in Integrated Rural Development.
  Arusha, Tanzania: Arusha Technical School. January 1-25,
  1979.

Chengelela, Rustica
"Adult Education's Impact on Women." Paper Presented at
the Workshop on Women's Studies and Development.
Dar-es-Salaam, Tanzania: University of Dar-es-Salaam.
Bureau of Resource Assessment and Land Use Plannning.
Paper #16. September 24-29, 1979. 10p.

Geiger, Susan
"Umoja wa Wanawake wa Tanzania and the Needs of the Rural
Poor." African Studies Review. Volume 25 #2/3
July-September, 1982. pp. 45-65.

Internation Co-Operative Alliance
Report on the Evaluation of the ICA Women Co-Operative
Education and Other Activities Project Moshi, ICA.
Moshi, Tanzania: ICA. Regional Office for East and
Central Africa. 1980.

Koda, Bertha
"The Role of UWT in Rural Development." Paper Presented
at the Workshop on Women's Studies and Development.
Dar-es-Salaam, Tanzania: University of Dar-es-Salaam.
Bureau of Resource Assessment and Land Use Planning.
Paper #19. September 24-29, 1979. 8p.

Kokuhirwa, Hilda N.
The Role of Education in Mobilizing Women for Development
in Tanzania. Amherst, Massachusetts: University of
Massachusetts. Center for International Education.
School of Education. May, 1978. 39p.

Kokuhirwa, Hilda N.
"Village Women and Nonformal Education in Tanzania:
Factors Affecting Participation." Ph.D Dissertation:
University of Massachusetts. Amherst, Massachusetts.
1982. 260p.

Matteru, May
"The Image of Women in Tanzanian Oral Literature." Paper
Presented at the Workshop on Women's Studies and
Development. Dar-es-Salaam, Tanzania: University of
Dar-es-Salaam. Bureau of Resource Assessment and Land
Use Planning. Paper #22. September 24-29, 1979. 26p.

Mbilinyi, Marjorie J.
"The Creation of Women Oriented Education Programmes in
Colonial Tanganyika and Zanzibar (1920-1964)." Paper
Presented at the 1984 Meeting of the International
Sociological Association. Sociology of Education
Research Section. Paris, France. August, 1984.

Mbilinyi, Marjorie J.
The Liberation of Women in the Context of Tanzania.
Dar-es-Salaam, Tanzania: University of Dar-es-Salaam.
Papers in Education and Development. #4. October, 1977.
pp. 1-26.

Mcharo, N.E.
Literacy: A Tool for the Development of Rural Women in
Tanzania. Dar-es-Salaam, Tanzania: Institute of Adult
Education. Studies in Adult Education #27. 1977. 17p.

Mlama, Penina
"The Role of Women in Culture Reproduction: The Case of Tanzanian Art and Literature." Paper Presented at the Workshop on Women's Studies and Development. Dar-es-Salaam, Tanzania: University of Dar-es-Salaam. Bureau of Resource Assessment and Land Use Planning. Paper #17. September 24-29, 1979. 14p.

Muro, Asseny
"Education and Training of Women for Employment: The Case of Mainland Tanzania." Paper Presented at the Highlevel Workshop on Development and Participation of Women. Arusha, Tanzania: East and Southern Africa Management Institute. 1982.

Muro, Asseny
"The Study of Women's Position in Peasant Production and Their Education and Training: A Case Study of Diozile I Village in Bagomoyo District." M.A. Thesis: University of Dar-es-Salaam. Dar-es-Salaam, Tanzania. June, 1979.

Muro, Asseny
"Women in Agricultural Production and Their Education and Training: A Case Study of Diozile I Village in Bagomoyo District." Paper Presented at the Workshop on Women's Studies and Development. Dar-es-Salaam, Tanzania: University of Dar-es-Salaam. Bureau of Resource Assessment and Land Use Planning. Paper #11. September 24-29, 1979. 42p.

Olekambaine, Priscilla
"Women and Education in Tanzania." Paper Presented at the Workshop on Women's Studies and Development. Dar-es-Salaam, Tanzania: University of Dar-es-Salaam. Bureau of Resource Assessment and Land Use Planning. Paper #30. September 24-29, 1979. 9p.

Tadesse, Zenebeworke
"An Overview on Women's Organizations in Africa: The Case of Ethiopia, Mozambique and Tanzania." Paper Presented at the 9th World Conference of Sociology. Uppsala, Sweden. 1978.

Tadesse, Zenebeworke
An Oveview on the Role of Women's Organizations in Africa: Case Study of Ethiopia, Zambia, Mozambique and Tanzania. Lusaka, Zambia: P/O Box RW 514. 1978.

EMPLOYMENT AND LABOR

Alopaeus-Stahl, Dorrit
Tanzanian Women Activities and Development Cooperation. Dar-es-Salaam, Tanzania: Swedish International Development Agency. May, 1979.

Asayehgn, Desta
Role of Women in Tanzania: Their Access to Education and Participation in the Labour Force. Paris: International Institute for Educational Planning(IIEP). 1979. 31p.

Brain, James L.
  "Less Than Second Class: Women in Rural Settlement
  Schemes in Tanzania." (In) Hafkin, N.J. and Bay, Edna
  (eds.). Women in Africa: Studies in Social and Economic
  Change. Stanford, California: Stanford University Press.
  1976. pp. 265-282.
Bryceson, Deborah F. and Mbilinyi, Marjorie J.
  The Changing Roles of Women in Production: From Peasants
  to Proletarians. Dar-es-Salaam, Tanzania: University of
  Dar-es-Salaam. History Department. 1978.
Bryceson, Deborah F.
  "The Proletarianization of Women in Tanzania." Review of
  African Political Economy. #17 January-April, 1980.
  pp. 4-27.
Bryceson, Deborah F.
  "The Proletarianization of Women in Tanzania." Paper
  Presented at the Workshop on Women's Studies and
  Development. Dar-es-Salaam, Tanzania: University of
  Dar-es-Salaam. Bureau of Resource Assessment and Land
  Use Planning. Paper #2. September 24-29, 1979. 45p.
Caplan, Patricia
  "Development Policies in Tanzania--Some Implications for
  Women." (In) Nelson, Nici (ed.). African Women in the
  Developing World. Totowa, New Jersey: Frank Cass. 1981.
  pp. 98-108.
Caplan, Patricia
  "Development Policies in Tanzania--Some Implications for
  Women." Journal of Development. Volume 17 #3 April,
  1981. pp. 98-108.
Chale, Freda U. and Generose, Ngonyani
  "Report on a Survey of Cooperative Income Generating
  Projects for Women and its Impact on the Welfare of
  Children and the Family." Paper Presented at the
  Workshop on Women's Studies and Development.
  Dar-es-Salaam, Tanzania: University of Dar-es-Salaam.
  Bureau of Resource Assessment and Land Use Planning.
  Paper #24. September 24-29, 1979. 42p.
Chijumba, Beat J.
  "Attitudes of Tanzanian Husbands Toward the Employment of
  their Wives." Africa Development. Volume 8 #2 1983.
  pp. 74-85.
Chiume, Kanyama
  "Women in a Developing Tanzania." African Women.
  November-December, 1977. pp. 60-61.
Cooper, Frederick
  From Slaves to Squatters: Plantation Labor and
  Agriculture in Zanzibar and Coastal Kenya, 1890-1925.
  New Haven, Connecticut: Yale University Press. 1980.
  328p.
Croll, E.J.
  "Women in Rural Production and Reproduction in the Soviet
  Union, China, Cuba and Tanzania." Signs. Volume 7 #2
  Winter, 1981. pp. 375-399.

Due, Jean M.
"Intra-Household Gender Issues in Farming Systems in
Tanzania, Zambia and Malawi." (In) Poats, Susan V. and
Schmink, Marianne and Spring, Anita (eds.). Gender
Issues in Farming Systems Research and Extension.
Boulder, Colorado: Westview Press. 1980. pp. 331-344.
Flanagan, William G.
"The Extended Family as an Agent in Urbanization: A
Survey of Men and Women Working in Dar-es-Salaam,
Tanzania." Ph.D Dissertation: University of
Connecticut-Storrs. Storrs, Connecticut. 1977. 234p.
Fleuret, A.
"The Role of Women in Rural Markets: Lushoto, Tanzania."
Paper Presented at the First Women and Anthropology
Symposium. Sacramento, California. March, 1977.
Fortmann, Louise P.
"Women and Agricultural Development." (In) Kim, K.S. and
Mabele, R. and Schultheis, M.J. (eds.). Papers on the
Political Economy of Tanzania. Nairobi: Heinemann
Educational. 1979.
Fortmann, Louise P.
Women and Tanzanian Agricultural Development.
Dar-es-Salaam, Tanzania: University of Dar-es-Salaam.
Economic Research Bureau. Paper #77.4. Mimeo. 1977.
24p.
Fortmann, Louise P.
"Women's Work in a Communal Setting: The Tanzanian Policy
of Ujamaa." Paper Presented at the Conference on Women
and Work in Africa. Urbana, Illinois: University of
Illinois-Urbana. Mimeo. April 28-May 1, 1979.
Fortmann, Louise P.
"Women's Work in a Communal Setting: The Tanzanian Policy
of Ujamaa." (In) Bay, Edna (ed.). Women in Work in
Africa. Boulder, Colorado: Westview Press. 1982. pp.
191-205.
Hamdani, Salha
"Peasantry and the Peasant Women in Tanzania: The Luguru
Case." Paper Presented at the Workshop on Women's
Studies and Development. Dar-es-Salaam, Tanzania:
University of Dar-es-Salaam. Bureau of Resource
Assessment and Land Use Planning. Paper #8. September
24-29, 1979. 9p.
Henn, Jeanne K.
"Who Benefits From Peasant Women's Work? Insights From a
Modes of Production Analysis." Paper Presented at the
Workshop on Women's Studies and Development.
Dar-es-Salaam: University of Dar-es-Salaam. Bureau of
Resource Assessment and Land Use Planning. Paper #29.
September 24-29, 1979. 19p.
Huth, Mary J.
"Female Participation and Status in Tanzania's Urban
Labor Market." Paper Presented at the Annual Meeting of

the North Central Sociological Association. University of Dayton. Dayton, Ohio. 1985.

Johnson, Willene
"The Study of Economic Activities of Women in Urban Tanzania." Ph.D Dissertation: Columbia University. New York, New York. 1983. 156p.

Kamuzora, C. Lwechungura
"High Fertility and the Demand for Labour in Peasant Economies: The Case of Bukoba District, Tanzania." Development and Change. Volume 15 #1 January, 1984. pp. 105-124.

Kasulamemba, Sylvia
"Problems of Working Women: The Case of Dar-es-Salaam City Council." Paper Presented at the Workshop on Women's Studies and Development. Dar-es-Salaam, Tanzania: University of Dar-es-Salaam. Bureau of Resource Assessment and Land Use Planning. Paper #9. September 24-29, 1979. 4p.

Kimaryo, Scholastica
"Implication for Women's Status and Position of Structural Changes in Tanzanian Society." Paper Presented at the Meeting of Experts on the History of Women's Contributions to National Liberation Struggles and Their Roles and Needs During Reconstruction in Newly Independent Countries of Africa. Paris: United Nations Educational, Scientific and Cultural Organization. Bissau, Guinea-Bissau. 1983. 17p.

Koda, Bertha
"Liberation of Women in Tanzania." Maji Maji. #35 1978. pp. 54-61.

Lowe, Linda T.
"The Urban Woman Worker in Dar-es-Salaam." African Urban Notes. Volume 2 #3 Fall-Winter, 1976. pp. 11-19.

Madsen, Birgit
Women's Mobilization and Integration in Development: A Village Case Study From Tanzania. Copenhagen, Denmark: Centre for Development Research. CDR Research Report #3. 1984. 95p.

Mbilinyi, Marjorie J.
Women in the Rural Development of Mbeya Region. Dar es Salaam, Tanzania: Ministry of Agriculture/U.N. FAO. Mbeya RIDEP Project. 1982.

Mbilinyi, Marjorie J.
"Women in Agricultural Production in West Bagamoyo, Tanzania." Paper Presented at a Workshop on Women in Agricultural Development in Eastern and Southern Africa. Nairobi: Ford Foundation. April, 1980.

Mbilinyi, Marjorie J.
Women: Producers and Reproducers in Peasant Production. Dar-es-Salaam, Tanzania: University of Dar-es-Salaam. Economic Research Bureau. Occasional Paper #77.3. 1977. 39p.

McHenry, Dean E.
"Communal Farming in Tanzania: A Comparison of Male and Female Participants." African Studies Review. Volume 25 #4 December, 1982. pp. 49-64.

Meghji, Zakia
"The Development of Women in Wage Labour: The Case of Industries in Moshi District." M.A. Thesis: University of Dar es Salaam. Dar es Salaam, Tanzania. 1977.

Mgaya, Mary
"Women Workers in a Factory in Tanzania." Paper Presented at the Workshop on Women's Studies and Development. Dar-es-Salaam, Tanzania: University of Dar-es-Salaam. Bureau of Resource Assessment and Land Use Planning. Paper #1. September 24-29, 1979. 9p.

Mukurasi, Laeticia
"Factors Hindering the Participation of Women in Decision Making at Senior Levels in the Civil Service and Parastatal Organizations." Paper Presented at the Annual Manpower Manager's Symposium. Arusha, Tanzania: East and Southern Africa Management Institute. 1984.

Muro, Asseny
"Education and Training of Women for Employment: The Case of Mainland Tanzania." Paper Presented at the Highlevel Workshop on Development and Participation of Women. Arusha, Tanzania: East and Southern Africa Management Institute. 1982.

Muro, Asseny
"The Study of Women's Position in Peasant Production and Their Education and Training: A Case Study of Diozile I Village in Bagomoyo District." M.A. Thesis: University of Dar-es-Salaam. Dar-es-Salaam, Tanzania. June, 1979.

Muro, Asseny
"Women in Agricultural Production and Their Education and Training: A Case Study of Diozile I Village in Bagamoyo District." Paper Presented at the Workshop on Women's Studies and Development. Dar-es-Salaam, Tanzania: University of Dar-es-Salaam. Bureau of Resource Assessment and Land Use Planning. Paper #11. September 24-29, 1979. 42p.

Ngalula, Theresia K.
"Women as a Productive Force in the Tanzanian Rural Society: A Case Study of Buhongwa Village in Mwanza District." M.A. Thesis: University of Dar-es-Salaam. Department of Sociology. Dar-es-Salaam, Tanzania. 1977. 113p.

O'Brien, M.
"The Maize Grinding Mill at Sinon." Community Development Journal. Volume 20 #3 1985. pp. 189-191.

Oomen-Myin, Marie A.
"The Involvement of Rural Women in Village Development in Tanzania." Convergence. Volume 16 #2 1983. pp. 59-69.

Rogers, Susan G.
"Efforts Toward Women's Development in Tanzania: Gender

Rhetoric vs. Gender Realities." (In) Staudt, Kathleen A. and Jaquette, Jane S. (eds.). Women in Developing Countries: A Policy Focus. New York: Haworth Press. 1983. pp. 23-41.

Sackak, Najma
"Creating Employment Opportunites for Rural Women: Case Study of Dodoma Rural District." Paper Presented at the Workshop on Women's Studies and Development. Dar-es-Salaam, Tanzania: University of Dar-es-Salaam. Bureau of Resource Assessment and Land Use Planning. Paper #6. September 24-29, 1979. 18p.

Shields, Nwanganga G.
Women in the Urban Labor Markets of Africa: The Case of Tanzania. Washington, D.C.: World Bank. Staff Working Paper #380. April, 1980. 138p.

Sijaona, S.T.
"Women's Projects in Urban Areas: Dar-es-Salaam City." Paper Presented at the Workshop on Women's Studies and Development. Dar-es-Salaam, Tanzania: University of Dar-es-Salaam. Bureau of Resource Assessment and Land Use Planning. Paper #10. September 24-29, 1979. 9p.

Swantz, Marja-Liisa
Women in Development: A Creative Role Denied? The Case of Tanzania. New York: St. Martin's Press. 1985. 170p.

Swantz, Marja-Liisa
Women's Creative Role in Development in Tanzania. Helsinki, Finland: University of Helsinki. 1982.

Swantz, Marja-Liisa.
Strain and Strength Among Peasant Women in Tanzania. Dar-es-Salaam, Tanzania: University of Dar-es-Salaam. Bureau of Resource Assessment and Land Use Planning. Research Paper #49. May, 1977. 81p.

Tobisson, Eva
Women, Work, Food and Nutrition in Nyamwigura Village, Mara Region, Tanzania. Dar-es-Salaam, Tanzania: Tanzania Food and Nutrition Centre. Report #548. July, 1980. 127p.

United Nations Economic Commission for Africa (UNECA)
Training and Employment Opportunities for Out-of-School Girls in the City of Dar-es-Salaam: A Planner's Point of View. Addis Ababa, Ethiopia: UNECA. 1981.

Virji, Parin
"Summary of the Labour Turnover at Friendship Textile Mill in 1978 With Special Reference to Women Workers." Paper Presented at the Workshop on Women's Studies and Development. Dar-es-Salaam, Tanzania: University of Dar-es-Salaam. Bureau of Resource Assessment and Land Use Planning. Paper #3. September 24-29, 1979. 8p.

Wylie, Liz
Women and Development: A Case Study of Ten Tanzania Villages. Arusha, Tanzania: Arusha Planning and Village Development Project. 1981.

EQUALITY AND LIBERATION

Anonymous
"Tanzania: The New Women and Traditional Norms in
Tanzania." IDOC Bulletin. #50-51 December, 1976.
Bryceson, Deborah F. and Majma, Sachak
Proceedings of the Workshop on Women's Studies and
Development. Dar-es-Salaam, Tanzania: University of
Dar-es-Salaam. September, 1979. 85p.
Kikopa, Jane R.
"Human Rights: The Position of Women and Children in
Tanzania." Paper Presented at the Workshop on Women's
Studies and Development. Dar-es-Salaam, Tanzania:
University of Dar-es-Salaam. Bureau of Resource
Assessment and Land Use Planning. Paper #33. September
24-29, 1979. 11p.
Koda, Bertha
"Liberation of Women in Tanzania." Maji Maji. #35 1978.
pp. 54-61.
Mbilinyi, Marjorie J.
The Liberation of Women in the Context of Tanzania.
Dar-es-Salaam, Tanzania: University of Dar-es-Salaam.
Papers in Education and Development. #4. October, 1977.
pp. 1-26.

FAMILY LIFE

Bader, Zinnat
"Social Conditions of the Peasant Women in Zanzibar and
Pemba." Paper Presented at the Workshop on Women's
Studies and Development. Dar-es-Salaam, Tanzania:
University of Dar-es-Salaam. Bureau of Resource
Assessment and Land Use Planning. Paper #18. September
24-29, 1979.
Chale, Freda U. and Generose, Ngonyani
"Report on a Survey of Cooperative Income Generating
Projects for Women and its Impact on the Welfare of
Children and the Family." Paper Presented at the
Workshop on Women's Studies and Development.
Dar-es-Salaam, Tanzania: University of Dar-es-Salaam.
Bureau of Resource Assessment and Land Use Planning.
Paper #24. September 24-29, 1979. 42p.
Chengelela, Rustica
"Adult Education's Impact on Women." Paper Presented at
the Workshop on Women's Studies and Development.
Dar-es-Salaam, Tanzania: University of Dar-es-Salaam.
Bureau of Resource Assessment and Land Use Plannning.
Paper #16. September 24-29, 1979. 10p.
Due, Jean M.
"Intra-Household Gender Issues in Farming Systems in
Tanzania, Zambia and Malawi." (In) Poats, Susan V. and
Schmink, Marianne and Spring, Anita (eds.). Gender

Issues in Farming Systems Research and Extension.
Boulder, Colorado: Westview Press. 1980. pp. 331-344.
Flanagan, William G.
"The Extended Family as an Agent in Urbanization: A
Survey of Men and Women Working in Dar-es-Salaam,
Tanzania." Ph.D Dissertation: University of
Connecticut-Storrs. Storrs, Connecticut. 1977. 234p.
Kasulamemba, Sylvia
"Problems of Working Women: The Case of Dar-es-Salaam
City Council." Paper Presented at the Workshop on
Women's Studies and Development. Dar-es-Salaam,
Tanzania: University of Dar-es-Salaam. Bureau of
Resource Assessment and Land Use Planning. Paper #9.
September 24-29, 1979. 4p.
Kokuhirwa, Hilda N.
"Village Women and Nonformal Education in Tanzania:
Factors Affecting Participation." Ph.D Dissertation:
University of Massachusetts. Amherst, Massachusetts.
1982. 260p.
Mbilinyi, Marjorie J.
The Social Transformation of the Shambaa Kingdom and the
Changing Position of Women. Dar-es-Salaam, Tanzania:
University of Dar-es-Salaam. Southern African
Universities--Social Science Conference. June 23-27,
1979.
Mbilinyi, Marjorie J.
"The Social Transformation of the Shambaa Kingdom and the
Changing Position of Women." Paper Presented at the
Workshop on Women's Studies and Development.
Dar-es-Salaam, Tanzania: University of Dar-es-Salaam.
Bureau of Resource Assessment and Land Use Planning.
Paper #7. September 24-29, 1979. 37p.
Muze, Siphiwe
"Family Life Education: A Growing Need in Tanzania."
Paper Presented at the Workshop on Women's Studies and
Development. Dar-es-Salaam, Tanzania: University of
Dar-es-Salaam. Bureau of Resource Assessment and Land
Use Planning. Paper #21. September 24-29, 1979. 4p.
Ngalula, Theresia K.
"Domestic Labour and Property Ownership: A Case Study of
Buhongwa Village in Mwanza District." Paper Presented at
the Workshop on Women's Studies and Development.
Dar-es-Salaam, Tanzania: University of Dar-es-Salaam.
Bureau of Resource Assessment and Land Use Planning.
Paper #13. September 24-29, 1979. 10p.
Ohadike, Patrick O.
"A Case Study of the Determinants of Family-Household
Size in African Development." (In) Oppong, C. and Adaba,
G and Bekombo-Priso, M. and Mogey, J. (eds.). Marriage,
Fertility and Parenthood in West Africa. Canberra,
Australia: Australian National University. Department of
Demography. Volume One. 1978. pp. 381-398.

TANZANIA

Sawyerr, Akilagpa
  "Judicial Manipulation of Customary Family Law in
  Tanzania." (In) Roberts, Simon (ed.). Law and the
  Family in Africa. Hague, Netherlands: Mouton. 1977.
  pp. 115-128.
Sembajwe, I.S.L.
  "The Effect of the Changing Position of Women on Family,
  Size and Child Survival in the United Republic of
  Tanzania." (In) International Labour Office (ILO).
  Final Report on the National Seminar on Population and
  Development in the United Republic of Tanzania. Geneva:
  ILO. 1980.
United Nations Economic Commission for Africa (UNECA)
  The Relationship Between Changing Roles and Status of
  Women and Childbearing and Child Survival in Tanzania.
  Paper Presented at the National Seminar on Population and
  Development. Addis Ababa, Ethiopia: UNECA. Arusha,
  Tanzania. 1980.
Wright, Marcia
  "Family Community and Women as Reflected in 'Die Safwa'
  by Elise Kootz-Kretschmer." (In) Sundkler, Bengt and
  Wahlstrom, Per-Ake (eds.). Vision and Service: Papers in
  Honour of Babbro Johansson. Uppsala, Sweden:
  Scandinavian Institute of African Studies and the Swedish
  Institute of Missionary Research. 1977. pp. 108-116.

FAMILY PLANNING AND CONTRACEPTION

Ewbank, Douglas C.
  "Indicators of Fertility Levels in Tanzania:
  Differentials and Trends in Reported Poverty and
  Childlessness." Paper Presented at the Annual Meeting of
  the Population Association of America. St. Louis,
  Missouri. April 21-23, 1977.
Ewbank, Douglas C.
  "Indicators of Fertility Levels in Tanzania:
  Differentials and Trends in Reported Poverty and
  Childlessness." Boston: Harvard School of Public Health.
  Department of Population Sciences. 1977.
Findley, Sally E. and Orr, Ann C.
  "A Suggested Framework for Analysing Urban-Rural
  Fertility Differentials With an Illustration of the
  Tanzanian Case." Paper Presented at the Annual Meeting
  of the Population Association of America. Atlanta,
  Georgia. April, 1978.
Findley, Sally E.
  "A Suggested Framework for Analysis of Urban-Rural
  Fertility Differentials With an Illustration of the
  Tanzanian Case." Population and Environment. Volume 3
  #3/4 Fall-Winter, 1980. pp. 237-261.
Findley, Sally E. and Orr, Ann C.
  Patterns of Urban-Rural Fertility Differentials in

Developing Countries: A Suggested Framework. Washington,
D.C.: U.S. Department of State. U.S. Agency for
International Development. September, 1978. 242p.
Kocher, James E.
"A Micro-Economic Analysis of the Determinants of Human
Fertility in Rural Northeastern Tanzania." Ph.D
Dissertation: Michigan State University. Department of
Agricultural Economics. East Lansing, Michigan. 1976.
279p.
Kocher, James E.
"Rural Development and Fertility Change in Northeastern
Tanzania." Cambridge, Massachusetts: Harvard University.
Harvard Institute for International Development. 1977.
Kocher, James E.
Rural Development and Fertility Change in Tropical
Africa: Evidence From Tanzania. East Lansing, Michigan:
Michigan State University. Department of Agricultural
Economics. Africana Rural Economy Paper #19. 1979.
95p.
Kocher, James E.
Socioeconomic Development and Fertility Change in Rural
Africa. Cambridge, Massachusetts: Harvard University.
Harvard Institute for International Development.
Development Discussion Paper #16. 1976. 22p.
Kocher, James E.
"Socioeconomic Development and Fertility Change in Rural
Africa." Food Research Institute Studies. Volume 16 #2
1977. pp. 63-73.
Mbilinyi, Marjorie J.
The Problem of Sexuality and Fertility Among Female
Youth. Dar-es-Salaam, Tanzania: University of
Dar-es-Salaam. Institute of Development Studies. 1979.
30p.
Ohadike, Patrick O.
"A Case Study of the Determinants of Family-Household
Size in African Development." (In) Oppong, C. and Adaba,
G. and Bekombo-Priso, M. and Mogey, J. (eds.). Marriage,
Fertility and Parenthood in West Africa. Canberra,
Australia: Australian National University. Department of
Demography. Volume One. 1978. pp. 381-398.
Sekatawa, Emmanuel K.
"Compensating Mechanisms in the Nuptiality-Fertility
Relationship: Evidence From Tanzania, 1973." Ph.D
Dissertation: University of Pennsylvania. Philadelphia,
Pennsylvania. 1981. 241p.
Sekatawa, Emmanuel K.
Mechanisms Affecting the Link Between Nuptiality and
Fertility: Tanzania, 1973. Philadelphia, Pennsylvania:
University of Pennsylvania. Population Studies Center.
African Demography Program Working Paper #6. June, 1981.
19p.
Sembajwe, I.S.L.
"The Effect of the Changing Position of Women on Family,

Size and Child Survival in the United Republic of
Tanzania." (In) International Labour Office (ILO).
Final Report on the National Seminar on Population and
Development in the United Republic of Tanzania. Geneva:
ILO. 1980.

FERTILITY AND INFERTILITY

Ewbank, Douglas C.
  "Indicators of Fertility Levels in Tanzania:
  Differentials and Trends in Reported Poverty and
  Childlessness." Paper Presented at the Annual Meeting of
  the Population Association of America. St. Louis,
  Missouri. April 21-23, 1977.
Ewbank, Douglas C.
  Indicators of Fertility Levels in Tanzania: Differentials
  and Trends in Reported Poverty and Childlessness.
  Boston: Harvard School of Public Health. Department of
  Population Sciences. 1977.
Findley, Sally E. and Orr, Ann C.
  "A Suggested Framework for Analysing Urban-Rural
  Fertility Differentials With an Illustration of the
  Tanzanian Case." Paper Presented at the Annual Meeting
  of the Population Association of America. Atlanta,
  Georgia. April, 1978.
Findley, Sally E.
  "A Suggested Framework for Analysis of Urban-Rural
  Fertility Differentials With an Illustration of the
  Tanzanian Case." Population and Environment. Volume 3
  #3/4 Fall-Winter, 1980. pp. 237-261.
Findley, Sally E. and Orr, Ann C.
  Patterns of Urban-Rural Fertility Differentials in
  Developing Countries: A Suggested Framework. Washington,
  D.C.: U.S. Department of State. U.S. Agency for
  International Development. September, 1978. 242p.
Kamuzora, C. Lwechungura
  "High Fertility and the Demand for Labour in Peasant
  Economies: The Case of Bukoba District, Tanzania."
  Development and Change. Volume 15 #1 January, 1984.
  pp. 105-124.
Kocher, James E.
  "A Micro-Economic Analysis of the Determinants of Human
  Fertility in Rural Northeastern Tanzania." Ph.D
  Dissertation: Michigan State University. Department of
  Agricultural Economics. East Lansing, Michigan. 1976.
  279p.
Kocher, James E.
  Rural Development and Fertility Change in Northeastern
  Tanzania. Cambridge, Massachusetts: Harvard University.
  Harvard Institute for International Development. 1977.
Kocher, James E.
  Rural Development and Fertility Change in Tropical

Africa: Evidence From Tanzania. East Lansing, Michigan:
Michigan State University. Department of Agricultural
Economics. Africana Rural Economy Paper #19. 1979.
95p.
Kocher, James E.
Rural Development, Health, Mortality and Fertility in
Rural Northeastern Tanzania. Cambridge, Massachusetts:
Harvard University. Harvard Institute for International
Development. 1980. 123p.
Kocher, James E.
Socioeconomic Development and Fertility Change in Rural
Africa. Cambridge, Massachusetts: Harvard University.
Harvard Institute for International Development.
Development Discussion Paper #16. 1976. 22p.
Kocher, James E.
"Socioeconomic Development and Fertility Change in Rural
Africa." Food Research Institute Studies. Volume 16 #2
1977. pp. 63-73.
Mbilinyi, Marjorie J.
The Problem of Sexuality and Fertility Among Female
Youth. Dar-es-Salaam, Tanzania: University of
Dar-es-Salaam. Institute of Development Studies. 1979.
30p.
Namfua, Pelad P.
"Polygyny in Tanzania: Its Determinants and Effect on
Fertility." Ph.D Dissertation: Johns Hopkins University.
Baltimore, Maryland. 1982. 233p.
Ohadike, Patrick O.
"A Case Study of the Determinants of Family-Household
Size in African Development." (In) Oppong, C. and Adaba,
G. and Bekombo-Priso, M. and Mogey, J. (eds.). Marriage,
Fertility and Parenthood in West Africa. Canberra,
Australia: Australian National University. Department of
Demography. Volume One. 1978. pp. 381-398.
Sekatawa, Emmanuel K.
"Compensating Mechanisms in the Nuptiality-Fertility
Relationship: Evidence From Tanzania, 1973." Ph.D
Dissertation: University of Pennsylvania. Philadelphia,
Pennsylvania. 1981. 241p.
Sekatawa, Emmanuel K.
Mechanisms Affecting the Link Between Nuptiality and
Fertility: Tanzania, 1973. Philadelphia, Pennsylvania:
University of Pennsylvania. Population Studies Center.
African Demography Program Working Paper #6. June, 1981.
19p.

HEALTH, NUTRITION AND MEDICINE

Arkutu, A.A.
"A Clinical Study of Maternal Age and Parturition in 2791
Tanzanian Primiparae." International Journal of

Gynaecology and Obstetrics. Volume 16 1978. pp.
128-131.

Arkutu, A.A.
"Pregnancy and Labor in Tanzanian Primigravidae Aged 15
Years and Under." International Journal of Gynaecology
and Obstetrics. Volume 16 #2 1979. pp. 128-131.

Armon, P.J.
"Maternal Deaths in the Kilimanjaro Region of Tanzania."
Transactions of the Royal Society of Tropical Medicine
and Hygiene. Volume 73 #3 1979. pp. 284-288.

Caplan, Patricia
"Spirit Possession: A Means of Curing on Mafia Island,
Tanzania." Kenya Past and Present. #10 1979. pp.
41-44.

Ewbank, Douglas C.
"Indicators of Fertility Levels in Tanzania:
Differentials and Trends in Reported Poverty and
Childlessness." Paper Presented at the Annual Meeting of
the Population Association of America. St. Louis,
Missouri. April 21-23, 1977.

Ewbank, Douglas C.
Indicators of Fertility Levels in Tanzania: Differentials
and Trends in Reported Poverty and Childlessness.
Boston: Harvard School of Public Health. Department of
Population Sciences. 1977.

Gill, H.S. and Mtimavalye, L.A.
"Prevalence of Toxoplasma Antibodies in Pregnant African
Women in Tanzania." African Journal of Medicine and
Medical Science. Volume 11 #4 December, 1982. pp.
167-170.

Hart, R.H.
"Maternal and Child Health Services in Tanzania."
Tropical Doctor. Volume 7 #4 October, 1977. pp.
179-185.

Hathi, Jee T.
"Medical Factors Associated With Abortions at Muhumbili
Medical Centre (June, 1978)." Paper Presented at the
Workshop on Women's Studies and Development.
Dar-es-Salaam, Tanzania: University of Tanzania. Bureau
of Resource Assessment and Land Use Planning. Paper #41.
September 24-29, 1979. 7p.

Kocher, James E.
"A Micro-Economic Analysis of the Determinants of Human
Fertility in Rural Northeastern Tanzania." Ph.D
Dissertation: Michigan State University. Department of
Agricultural Economics. East Lansing, Michigan. 1976.
279p.

Kocher, James E.
Rural Development, Health, Mortality and Fertility in
Rural Northeastern Tanzania. Cambridge, Massachusetts:
Harvard University. Harvard Institute for International
Development. 1980. 123p.

Mtimavalye, L.A. and Lisasi, D. and Ntuyabaliwe, W.K.
    "Maternal Mortality in Dar-es-Salaam, Tanzania,
    1974-1977." East African Medical Journal. Volume 57 #2
    February, 1980. pp. 111-118.
Reese, M.C.
    "Meeting Maternal and Child Health Care Needs in
    Tanzania." International Nursing Review. Volume 25 #1
    January-February, 1978.
Tobisson, Eva
    Women, Work, Food and Nutrition in Nyamwigura Village,
    Mara Region, Tanzania. Dar-es-Salaam, Tanzania: Tanzania
    Food and Nutrition Centre. Report #548. July, 1980.
    127p.
Turshen, Meredith
    The Political Ecology of Disease in Tanzania. New
    Brunswick, New Jersey: Rutgers University Press. 1984.
    259p.
United Nations Economic Commission for Africa (UNECA)
    "The Relationship Between Changing Roles and Status of
    Women and Childbearing and Child Survival in Tanzania."
    Paper Presented at the National Seminar on Population and
    Development. Addis Ababa, Ethiopia: UNECA. Arusha,
    Tanzania. 1980.

HISTORY

Alpers, E.A.
    "Female Subculture in Nineteenth Century Zanzibar: The
    Kitimiri Spirit Possession Cult." Paper Presented at the
    Symposium on African Women: Historical Dimensions.
    University of Santa Clara. Santa Clara, California. May
    15-16, 1981.
Alpers, E.A.
    "Ordinary Household Chores--Ritual and Power in a 19th
    Century Swahili Women's Spirit Possession Cult."
    International Journal of African Historical Studies.
    Volume 17 #4 1984. pp. 677-702.
Bryceson, Deborah F.
    Peasant Food Production and Food Supply in Relation to
    the Historical Development of Commoditiy Production in
    Pre-Colonial and Colonial Tanganyika. Dar-es-Salaam,
    Tanzania: Bureau of Resource Assessment and Land Use
    Planning. Service Paper #78/3. 1978. 41p.
Cooper, Frederick
    From Slaves to Squatters: Plantation Labor and
    Agriculture in Zanzibar and Coastal Kenya, 1890-1925.
    New Haven, Connecticut: Yale University Press. 1980.
    328p.
Hollander, Roberta B.
    "Out of Tradition: The Position of Women in Kenya and
    Tanzania During the Pre-Colonial, Colonial and Post

Independence Eras." Ph.D Dissertation: The American
University. Washington, D.C. 1979. 399p.
Mbilinyi, Marjorie J.
    "The Creation of Women Oriented Education Programmes in
    Colonial Tanganyika and Zanzibar (1920-1964)." Paper
    Presented at the 1984 Meeting of the International
    Sociological Association. Sociology of Education
    Research Section. Paris, France. August, 1984.
Mbilinyi, Marjorie J.
    The Social Transformation of the Shambaa Kingdom and the
    Changing Position of Women. Dar-es-Salaam, Tanzania:
    University of Dar-es-Salaam. Southern African
    Universities--Social Science Conference. June 23-27,
    1979.
Mbilinyi, Marjorie J.
    "The Social Transformation of the Shambaa Kingdom and the
    Changing Position of Women." Paper Presented at the
    Workshop on Women's Studies and Development.
    Dar-es-Salaam, Tanzania: University of Dar-es-Salaam.
    Bureau of Resource Assessment and Land Use Planning.
    Paper #7. September 24-29, 1979. 37p.
Mbilinyi, Marjorie J.
    "Wife, Slave and Subject of the King: The Oppression of
    Women in the Shambala Kingdom." Tanzania Notes and
    Records. #88-89. 1982. pp. 1-13.
Rogers, Susan G.
    "Anti-Colonial Protest in Africa: A Female Strategy
    Reconsidered." Heresies. Volume 3 #1 1980. pp. 22-27.

LAW AND LEGAL ISSUES

Kikopa, Jane R.
    Law and the Status of Women in Tanzania. Addis Ababa,
    Ethiopia: United Nations Economic Commission for Africa.
    African Training and Research Centre for Women. Research
    Series. 1981. 108p.
Klima, George
    "Jural Relations Between the Sexes Among the Barabaig."
    (In) Tiffany, Sharon W (ed.). Women and Society: An
    Anthropological Reader. St. Albans, Vermont: Eden Press.
    1979. pp. 145-162.
Luhanga, Emily
    "Law and the Status of Women in Tanzania." Paper
    Presented at the Workshop on Women's Status and
    Development. Dar-es-Salaam, Tanzania: University of
    Dar-es-Salaam. Bureau of Resource Assessment and Land
    Use Planning. Paper #36. September 24-29, 1979. 7p.
Muro, M.
    "The Controversy Over Bride Price and Polygamy: New Laws
    on Marriage and Maternity Leave." Tanzania Notes and
    Records. #83 1978. pp. 133-137.

Sawyerr, Akilagpa
  "Judicial Manipulation of Customary Family Law in
  Tanzania." (In) Roberts, Simon (ed.). Law and the
  Family in Africa. Hague, Netherlands: Mouton. 1977.
  pp. 115-128.

LITERATURE

Balisidya, M.L.
  "The Image of the Woman in Tanzanian Oral Literature: A
  Survey." Kiswahili. Volume 49 #2 1982. pp. 1-31.
Matteru, May
  "The Image of Women in Tanzanian Oral Literature." Paper
  Presented at the Workshop on Women's Studies and
  Development. Dar-es-Salaam, Tanzania: University of
  Dar-es-Salaam. Bureau of Resource Assessment and Land
  Use Planning. Paper #22. September 24-29, 1979. 26p.
Mlama, Penina
  "The Role of Women in Culture Reproduction: The Case of
  Tanzanian Art and Literature." Paper Presented at the
  Workshop on Women's Studies and Development.
  Dar-es-Salaam, Tanzania: University of Dar-es-Salaam.
  Bureau of Resource Assessment and Land Use Planning.
  Paper #17. September 24-29, 1979. 14p.
Senkoro, F.E.M.K.
  "Silie Mwana Silie: Women in Kiswahili and Tanzanian
  Lullabies." Paper Presented at the 1982 African
  Literature Association Conference. Baltimore, Maryland:
  University of Maryland. African and American Studies
  Department. 1982.

MARITAL RELATIONS AND NUPTIALITY

Abrahams, R.G.
  "Aspects of the Distribution Between the Sexes in
  Nyamwezi and Some Other African Systems of Kinship and
  Marriage." (In) LaFontaine, J.S. (ed.). Sex and Age as
  Principles of Social Differentiation. New York: Academic
  Press. 1978. pp. 67-88.
Brain, James L.
  "Down to Gentility: Women in Tanzania." Sex Roles: A
  Journal of Research. Volume 4 #5 October, 1978. pp.
  695-715.
Chijumba, Beat J.
  "Attitudes of Tanzanian Husbands Toward the Employment of
  their Wives." Africa Development. Volume 8 #2 1983.
  pp. 74-85.
Ewbank, Douglas C.
  "Indicators of Fertility Levels in Tanzania:
  Differentials and Trends in Reported Poverty and
  Childlessness." Paper Presented at the Annual Meeting of

the Population Association of America. St. Louis,
Missouri. April 21-23, 1977.
Ewbank, Douglas C.
    Indicators of Fertility Levels in Tanzania: Differentials
    and Trends in Reported Poverty and Childlessness.
    Boston: Harvard School of Public Health. Department of
    Population Sciences. 1977.
Flanagan, William G.
    "The Extended Family as an Agent in Urbanization: A
    Survey of Men and Women Working in Dar-es-Salaam,
    Tanzania." Ph.D Dissertation: University of
    Connecticut-Storrs. Storrs, Connecticut. 1977. 234p.
Kasulamemba, Sylvia
    "Problems of Working Women: The Case of Dar-es-Salaam
    City Council." Paper Presented at the Workshop on
    Women's Studies and Development. Dar-es-Salaam,
    Tanzania: University of Dar-es-Salaam. Bureau of
    Resource Assessment and Land Use Planning. Paper #9.
    September 24-29, 1979. 4p.
Klima, George
    "Jural Relations Between the Sexes Among the Barabaig."
    (In) Tiffany, Sharon W (ed.). Women and Society: An
    Anthropological Reader. St. Albans, Vermont: Eden Press.
    1979. pp. 145-162.
Kokuhirwa, Hilda N.
    "Village Women and Nonformal Education in Tanzania:
    Factors Affecting Participation." Ph.D Dissertation:
    University of Massachusetts. Amherst, Massachusetts.
    1982. 260p.
Muro, M.
    "The Controversy Over Bride Price and Polygamy: New Laws
    on Marriage and Maternity Leave." Tanzania Notes and
    Records. #83 1978. pp. 133-137.
Muze, Siphiwe
    "Family Life Education: A Growing Need in Tanzania."
    Paper Presented at the Workshop on Women's Studies and
    Development. Dar-es-Salaam, Tanzania: University of
    Dar-es-Salaam. Bureau of Resource Assessment and Land
    Use Planning. Paper #21. September 24-29, 1979. 4p.
Namfua, Pelad P.
    "Polygyny in Tanzania: Its Determinants and Effect on
    Fertility." Ph.D Dissertation: Johns Hopkins University.
    Baltimore, Maryland. 1982. 233p.
Ngalula, Theresia K.
    "Domestic Labour and Property Ownership: A Case Study of
    Buhongwa Village in Mwanza District." Paper Presented at
    the Workshop on Women's Studies and Development.
    Dar-es-Salaam, Tanzania: University of Dar-es-Salaam.
    Bureau of Resource Assessment and Land Use Planning.
    Paper #13. September 24-29, 1979. 10p.
Ohadike, Patrick O.
    "A Case Study of the Determinants of Family-Household

Size in African Development." (In) Oppong, C. and Adaba,
G. and Bekombo-Priso, M. and Mogey, J. (eds.). Marriage,
Fertility and Parenthood in West Africa. Canberra,
Australia: Australian National University. Department of
Demography. Volume One. 1978. pp. 381-398.

Sawyerr, Akilagpa
"Judicial Manipulation of Customary Family Law in
Tanzania." (In) Roberts, Simon (ed.). Law and the
Family in Africa. Hague, Netherlands: Mouton. 1977.
pp. 115-128.

Sekatawa, Emmanuel K.
"Compensating Mechanisms in the Nuptiality-Fertility
Relationship: Evidence From Tanzania, 1973." Ph.D
Dissertation: University of Pennsylvania. Philadelphia,
Pennsylvania. 1981. 241p.

Sekatawa, Emmanuel K.
Mechanisms Affecting the Link Between Nuptiality and
Fertility: Tanzania, 1973. Philadelphia, Pennsylvania:
University of Pennsylvania. Population Studies Center.
African Demography Program Working Paper #6. June, 1981.
19p.

Sembajwe, I.S.L.
"The Effect of the Changing Position of Women on Family,
Size and Child Survival in the United Republic of
Tanzania." (In) International Labour Office (ILO).
Final Report on the National Seminar on Population and
Development in the United Republic of Tanzania. Geneva:
ILO. 1980.

Vourela, Ulla
"Women's Role in Production and Reproduction: Some
Reflections on Relationships Between Men and Women in
Tanzania and Finland." Paper Presented at the Workshop
on Women's Studies and Development. Dar-es-Salaam,
Tanzania: University of Dar-es-Salaam. Bureau of
Resource Assessment and Land Use Planning. Paper #28.
September 24-29, 1979. 19p.

Wilson, Monica H.
For Men and Elders--Changes in the Relations of
Generations and of Men and Women Among the
Nyakyusa-Ngonde People, 1875-1971. New York: Africana
Publishing Company. 1977. 209p.

MASS MEDIA

Bryceson, Deborah F.
"Notes on the Educational Potential of Mass Media
Vis-a-Vis Women's Roles in Tanzanian Society." Paper
Presented at the Workshop on Women's Studies and
Development. Dar-es-Salaam, Tanzania: University of
Dar-es-Salaam. Bureau of Resource Assessment and Land
Use Planning. Paper #23. September 24-29, 1979. 10p.

Kyaruzi, Agnes
"Women's Image in Mass Media: Newspapers." Paper
Presented at the Workshop on Women's Studies and
Development. Dar-es-Salaam, Tanzania: University of
Dar-es-Salaam. Bureau of Resource Assessment and Land
Use Planning. Paper #45. September 24-29, 1979. 4p.

Mwenda, Deborah
"The Women's Image in the Tanzanian Mass Media: Radio."
Paper Presented at the Workshop on Women's Studies and
Development. Dar-es-Salaam, Tanzania: University of
Dar-es-Salaam. Bureau of Resource Assessment and Land
Use Planning. Paper #38. September 24-29, 1979. 5p.

MISCELLANEOUS

Kocher, James E.
Rural Development, Health, Mortality and Fertility in
Rural Northeastern Tanzania. Cambridge, Massachusetts:
Harvard University. Harvard Institute for International
Development. 1980. 123p.

Mtimavalye, L.A. and Lisasi, D. and Ntuyabaliwe, W.K.
"Maternal Mortality in Dar-es-Salaam, Tanzania,
1974-1977." East African Medical Journal. Volume 57 #2
February, 1980. pp. 111-118.

NATIONALISM

Ladner, Joyce A.
"Tanzanian Women in Nation Building." (In) Steady,
Filomina C. (ed.). The Black Woman Cross-Culturally.
Cambridge, Massachusetts: Schenkman Publications. 1981.
pp. 107-118.

Rogers, Susan G.
"Anti-Colonial Protest in Africa: A Female Strategy
Reconsidered." Heresies. Volume 3 #1 1980. pp. 22-27.

ORGANIZATIONS

Alopaeus-Stahl, Dorrit
Tanzanian Women Activities and Development Cooperation.
Dar-es-Salaam, Tanzania: Swedish International
Development Agency. May, 1979.

Koda, Bertha
"The Role of UWT in Rural Development." Paper Presented
at the Workshop on Women's Studies and Development.
Dar-es-Salaam, Tanzania: University of Dar-es-Salaam.
Bureau of Resource Assessment and Land Use Planning.
Paper #19. September 24-29, 1979. 8p.

Mukurasi, Laeticia
"Factors Hindering the Participation of Women in Decision

Making at Senior Levels in the Civil Service and
Parastatal Organizations." Paper Presented at the Annual
Manpower Manager's Symposium. Arusha, Tanzania: East and
Southern Africa Management Institute. 1984.
Tadesse, Zenebeworke
"An Overview on Women's Organizations in Africa: The Case
of Ethiopia, Mozambique and Tanzania." Paper Presented
at the 9th World Conference of Sociology. Uppsala,
Sweden. 1978.
Tadesse, Zenebeworke
An Oveview on the Role of Women's Organizations in
Africa: Case Study of Ethiopia, Zambia, Mozambique and
Tanzania. Lusaka, Zambia: P/O Box RW 514. 1978.

POLITICS AND GOVERNMENT

Anonymous
"Tanzania: The New Women and Traditional Norms in
Tanzania." IDOC Bulletin. #50-51 December, 1976.
Gabba, Anna
"Women in Diplomacy: Tenacity a Virtue-Dorah." Tanzania
News Review. May-June, 1979.
Hollander, Roberta B.
"Out of Tradition: The Position of Women in Kenya and
Tanzania During the Pre-Colonial, Colonial and Post
Independence Eras." Ph.D Dissertation: The American
University. Washington, D.C. 1979. 399p.
Kikopa, Jane R.
"Human Rights: The Position of Women and Children in
Tanzania." Paper Presented at the Workshop on Women's
Studies and Development. Dar-es-Salaam, Tanzania:
University of Dar-es-Salaam. Bureau of Resource
Assessment and Land Use Planning. Paper #33. September
24-29, 1979. 11p.
Ladner, Joyce A.
"Tanzanian Women in Nation Building." (In) Steady,
Filomina C. (ed.). The Black Woman Cross-Culturally.
Cambridge, Massachusetts: Schenkman Publications. 1981.
pp. 107-118.
Mbilinyi, Marjorie J.
"The Political Practices of Peasant Women in Tanzania."
Paper Presented at the 12th World Congress of the
International Political Science Association. Rio de
Janeiro, Brazil. 1982.
Mukurasi, Laeticia
"Factors Hindering the Participation of Women in Decision
Making at Senior Levels in the Civil Service and
Parastatal Organizations." Paper Presented at the Annual
Manpower Manager's Symposium. Arusha, Tanzania: East and
Southern Africa Management Institute. 1984.
Sackak, Najma
"Creating Employment Opportunites for Rural Women: Case

Study of Dodoma Rural District." Paper Presented at the
Workshop on Women's Studies and Development.
Dar-es-Salaam, Tanzania: University of Dar-es-Salaam.
Bureau of Resource Assessment and Land Use Planning.
Paper #6. September 24-29, 1979. 18p.
Swantz, Marja-Liisa
Women in Development: A Creative Role Denied? The Case
of Tanzania. New York: St. Martin's Press. 1985. 170p.
Turshen, Meredith
The Political Ecology of Disease in Tanzania. New
Brunswick, New Jersey: Rutgers University Press. 1984.
259p.

RELIGION AND WITCHCRAFT

Alpers, E.A.
"Female Subculture in Nineteenth Century Zanzibar: The
Kitimiri Spirit Possession Cult." Paper Presented at the
Symposium on African Women: Historical Dimensions.
University of Santa Clara. Santa Clara, California. May
15-16, 1981.
Alpers, E.A.
"Ordinary Household Chores--Ritual and Power in a 19th
Century Swahili Women's Spirit Possession Cult."
International Journal of African Historical Studies.
Volume 17 #4 1984. pp. 677-702.
Brain, James L.
"Witchcraft and Development." African Affairs. Volume
81 #324 July, 1982. pp. 371-384.
Caplan, A.P.
"Boys' Circumcision and Girls' Puberty Rites Among the
Swahili of Mafia Island, Tanzania." Africa. Volume 46
#1 1976. pp. 21-33.
Caplan, Patricia
"Spirit Possession: A Means of Curing on Mafia Island,
Tanzania." Kenya Past and Present. #10 1979. pp.
41-44.
Larsen, Lorne E.
"Problems in the Study of Witchcraft Eradication
Movements in Southern Tanzania." Ufahamu. Volume 6 #3
1976. pp. 88-100.
Singleton, Michael
"Obsession With Possession." Pro Mundi Vita Africa
Dossier. #4 July-August, 1977. pp. 2-34.
Sundkler, Bengt and Wahlstrom, Per-Ake (eds.)
Vision and Service: Papers in Honor of Babbro Johansson.
Uppsala, Sweden: Scandinavian Institute of African
Studies and the Swedish Institute of Missionary
Research. 1977. 161p.
Swantz, Marja-Liisa
"Church and the Changing Role of Women in Tanzania."

(In) Fashole-Luke, Edward. Christianity in Independent
Africa. London: R. Collings. 1978. pp. 136-150.
Swantz, Marja-Liisa
    "Free Women of Bukoba." (In) Sundkler, Bengt and
    Wahlstrom, Per-Ake (eds.). Vision and Service: Papers in
    Honor of Babbro Johansson. Uppsala, Sweden: Scandinavian
    Institute of African Studies and the Swedish Institute of
    Missionary Research. 1977. pp. 99-107.
Wright, Marcia
    "Family Community and Women as Reflected in 'Die Safwa'
    by Elise Kootz-Kretschmer." (In) Sundkler, Bengt and
    Wahlstrom, Per-Ake (eds.). Vision and Service: Papers in
    Honour of Babbro Johansson. Uppsala, Sweden:
    Scandinavian Institute of African Studies and the Swedish
    Institute of Missionary Research. 1977. pp. 108-116.

RESEARCH

Due, Jean M.
    "Intra-Household Gender Issues in Farming Systems in
    Tanzania, Zambia and Malawi." (In) Poats, Susan V. and
    Schmink, Marianne and Spring, Anita (eds.). Gender
    Issues in Farming Systems Research and Extension.
    Boulder, Colorado: Westview Press. 1980. pp. 331-344.
Mascarenhas, Ophelia and Mbilinyi, Marjorie J.
    Women and Development in Tanzania: An Annotated
    Bibliography. Addis Ababa, Ethiopia: United Nations
    Economic Commission for Africa. African Training and
    Research Centre for Women. Bibliography Series #2.
    1980. 135p.
Mascarenhas, Ophelia and Mbilinyi, Marjorie J.
    Women in Tanzania: An Analytical Bibliography. Uppsala,
    Sweden: Scandinavian Institute for African Studies.
    1983. 256p.
U.S. Department of Commerce. Bureau of the Census
    Illustrative Statistics on Women in Development in
    Selected Developing Countries. Washington, D.C.: U.S.
    Department of Commerce. 1982. 24p.

SEX ROLES

Abrahams, R.G.
    "Aspects of the Distribution Between the Sexes in
    Nyamwezi and Some Other African Systems of Kinship and
    Marriage." (In) LaFontaine, J.S. (ed.). Sex and Age as
    Principles of Social Differentiation. New York: Academic
    Press. 1978. pp. 67-88.
Alpers, E.A.
    "Ordinary Household Chores--Ritual and Power in a 19th
    Century Swahili Women's Spirit Possession Cult."

International Journal of African Historical Studies.
Volume 17 #4 1984. pp. 677-702.
Anonymous
  "Tanzania: The New Women and Traditional Norms in
  Tanzania." IDOC Bulletin. #50-51 December, 1976.
Asayehgn, Desta
  Role of Women in Tanzania: Their Access to Education and
  Participation in the Labour Force. Paris: International
  Institute for Educational Planning(IIEP). 1979. 31p.
Bader, Zinnat
  "Social Conditions of the Peasant Women in Zanzibar and
  Pemba." Paper Presented at the Workshop on Women's
  Studies and Development. Dar-es-Salaam, Tanzania:
  University of Dar-es-Salaam. Bureau of Resource
  Assessment and Land Use Planning. Paper #18. September
  24-29, 1979.
Brain, James L.
  "Less Than Second Class: Women in Rural Settlement
  Schemes in Tanzania." (In) Hafkin, N.J. and Bay, Edna
  (eds.). Women in Africa: Studies in Social and Economic
  Change. Stanford, California: Stanford University Press.
  1976. pp. 265-282.
Bryceson, Deborah F.
  "Notes on the Educational Potential of Mass Media
  Vis-a-Vis Women's Roles in Tanzanian Society." Paper
  Presented at the Workshop on Women's Studies and
  Development. Dar-es-Salaam, Tanzania: University of
  Dar-es-Salaam. Bureau of Resource Assessment and Land
  Use Planning. Paper #23. September 24-29, 1979. 10p.
Bryceson, Deborah F. and Mbilinyi, Marjorie J.
  "The Changing Role of Tanzanian Women in Production: From
  Peasants to Proletarians." Paper Presented at the Sussex
  University Conference on Women and Subordination.
  Sussex, England: University of Sussex. September, 1978.
Bryceson, Deborah F. and Mbilinyi, Marjorie J.
  The Changing Roles of Women in Production: From Peasants
  to Proletarians. Dar-es-Salaam, Tanzania: University of
  Dar-es-Salaam. History Department. 1978.
Caplan, Patricia
  "Gender, Ideology and Modes of Production on the Coast of
  East Africa." Paideuma. Volume 28 1982. pp. 29-43.
Chale, Freda U.
  "Women's Programmes and the Role of a Rural Woman in
  Tanzania." Paper Presented at the Workshop on Population
  Life Education Project in Integrated Rural Development.
  Arusha, Tanzania: Arusha Technical School. January 1-25,
  1979.
Chengelela, Rustica
  "Adult Education's Impact on Women." Paper Presented at
  the Workshop on Women's Studies and Development.
  Dar-es-Salaam, Tanzania: University of Dar-es-Salaam.
  Bureau of Resource Assessment and Land Use Plannning.
  Paper #16. September 24-29, 1979. 10p.

TANZANIA

Chijumba, Beat J.
"Attitudes of Tanzanian Husbands Toward the Employment of their Wives." Africa Development. Volume 8 #2 1983. pp. 74-85.
Croll, E.J.
"Women in Rural Production and Reproduction in the Soviet Union, China, Cuba and Tanzania." Signs. Volume 7 #2 Winter, 1981. pp. 375-399.
Due, Jean M.
"Intra-Household Gender Issues in Farming Systems in Tanzania, Zambia and Malawi." (In) Poats, Susan V. and Schmink, Marianne and Spring, Anita (eds.). Gender Issues in Farming Systems Research and Extension. Boulder, Colorado: Westview Press. 1980. pp. 331-344.
Due, Jean M. and Anandajayasekeram
"Women and Productivity in Two Contrasting Farming Areas of Tanzania." Dar es Salaam, Tanzania: University of Dar es Salaam. Bean/Cowpea CRSP Project Report #228. Urbana, Illinois: University of Illinois-Urbana-Champaign. Department of Agricultural Economics. July, 1982.
Fortmann, Louise P.
"Women's Work in a Communal Setting: The Tanzanian Policy of Ujamaa." Paper Presented at the Conference on Women and Work in Africa. Urbana, Illinois: University of Illinois-Urbana. Mimeo. April 28-May 1, 1979.
Fortmann, Louise P.
"Women's Work in a Communal Setting: The Tanzanian Policy of Ujamaa." (In) Bay, Edna (ed.). Women in Work in Africa. Boulder, Colorado: Westview Press. 1982. pp. 191-205.
Hamdani, Salha
"Peasantry and the Peasant Women in Tanzania: The Luguru Case." Paper Presented at the Workshop on Women's Studies and Development. Dar-es-Salaam, Tanzania: University of Dar-es-Salaam. Bureau of Resource Assessment and Land Use Planning. Paper #8. Setember 24-29, 1979. 9p.
Henn, Jeanne K.
"Who Benefits From Peasant Women's Work? Insights From a Modes of Production Analysis." Paper Presented at the Workshop on Women's Studies and Development. Dar-es-Salaam: University of Dar-es-Salaam. Bureau of Resource Assessment and Land Use Planning. Paper #29. September 24-29, 1979. 19p.
Hollander, Roberta B.
"Out of Tradition: The Position of Women in Kenya and Tanzania During the Pre-Colonial, Colonial and Post Independence Eras." Ph.D Dissertation: The American University. Washington, D.C. 1979. 399p.
Kamuzora, C. Lwechungura
"High Fertility and the Demand for Labour in Peasant Economies: The Case of Bukoba District, Tanzania."

227

Development and Change. Volume 15 #1 January, 1984.
pp. 105-124.
Kikopa, Jane R.
Law and the Status of Women in Tanzania. Addis Ababa,
Ethiopia: United Nations Economic Commission for Africa.
African Training and Research Centre for Women. Research
Series. 1981. 108p.
Kimaryo, Scholastica
"Implication for Women's Status and Position of
Structural Changes in Tanzanian Society." Paper
Presented at the Meeting of Experts on the History of
Women's Contributions to National Liberation Struggles
and Their Roles and Needs During Reconstruction in Newly
Independent Countries of Africa. Paris: United Nations
Educational, Scientific and Cultural Organization.
Bissau, Guinea-Bissau. 1983. 17p.
Klima, George
"Jural Relations Between the Sexes Among the Barabaig."
(In) Tiffany, Sharon W (ed.). Women and Society: An
Anthropological Reader. St. Albans, Vermont: Eden Press.
1979. pp. 145-162.
Kocher, James E.
Rural Development and Fertility Change in Northeastern
Tanzania. Cambridge, Massachusetts: Harvard University.
Harvard Institute for International Development. 1977.
Kocher, James E.
Rural Development and Fertility Change in Tropical
Africa: Evidence From Tanzania. East Lansing, Michigan:
Michigan State University. Department of Agricultural
Economics. Africana Rural Economy Paper #19. 1979.
95p.
Kocher, James E.
Rural Development, Health, Mortality and Fertility in
Rural Northeastern Tanzania. Cambridge, Massachusetts:
Harvard University. Harvard Institute for International
Development. 1980. 123p.
Kocher, James E.
Socioeconomic Development and Fertility Change in Rural
Africa. Cambridge, Massachusetts: Harvard University.
Harvard Institute for International Development.
Development Discussion Paper #16. 1976. 22p.
Kocher, James E.
"Socioeconomic Development and Fertility Change in Rural
Africa." Food Research Institute Studies. Volume 16 #2
1977. pp. 63-73.
Koda, Bertha
"Liberation of Women in Tanzania." Maji Maji. #35 1978.
pp. 54-61.
Mbilinyi, Marjorie J.
The Liberation of Women in the Context of Tanzania.
Dar-es-Salaam, Tanzania: University of Dar-es-Salaam.
Papers in Education and Development. #4. October, 1977.
pp. 1-26.

Mbilinyi, Marjorie J.
    The Social Transformation of the Shambaa Kingdom and the
    Changing Position of Women. Dar-es-Salaam, Tanzania:
    University of Dar-es-Salaam. Southern African
    Universities--Social Science Conference. June 23-27,
    1979.
Mbilinyi, Marjorie J.
    "The Social Transformation of the Shambaa Kingdom and the
    Changing Position of Women." Paper Presented at the
    Workshop on Women's Studies and Development.
    Dar-es-Salaam, Tanzania: University of Dar-es-Salaam.
    Bureau of Resource Assessment and Land Use Planning.
    Paper #7. September 24-29, 1979. 37p.
Mbilinyi, Marjorie J.
    "Wife, Slave and Subject of the King: The Oppression of
    Women in the Shambala Kingdom." Tanzania Notes and
    Records. #88-89. 1982. pp. 1-13.
Mbilinyi, Marjorie J.
    Women in Agricultural Production in West Bagamoyo,
    Tanzania. Paper Presented at a Workshop on Women in
    Agricultural Development in Eastern and Southern Africa.
    Nairobi: Ford Foundation. April, 1980.
Mbilinyi, Marjorie J.
    Women: Producers and Reproducers in Peasant Production.
    Dar-es-Salaam, Tanzania: University of Dar-es-Salaam.
    Economic Research Bureau. Occasional Paper #77.3. 1977.
    39p.
McHenry, Dean E.
    "Communal Farming in Tanzania: A Comparison of Male and
    Female Participants." African Studies Review. Volume 25
    #4 December, 1982. pp. 49-64.
Meghji, Zakia
    "The Development of Women in Wage Labour: The Case of
    Industries in Moshi District." M.A. Thesis: University
    of Dar es Salaam. Dar es Salaam, Tanzania. 1977.
Mlama, Penina
    "The Role of Women in Culture Reproduction: The Case of
    Tanzanian Art and Literature." Paper Presented at the
    Workshop on Women's Studies and Development.
    Dar-es-Salaam, Tanzania: University of Dar-es-Salaam.
    Bureau of Resource Assessment and Land Use Planning.
    Paper #17. September 24-29, 1979. 14p.
Mukurasi, Laeticia
    "Factors Hindering the Participation of Women in Decision
    Making at Senior Levels in the Civil Service and
    Parastatal Organizations." Paper Presented at the Annual
    Manpower Manager's Symposium. Arusha, Tanzania: East and
    Southern Africa Management Institute. 1984.
Muro, Asseny
    "The Study of Women's Position in Peasant Production and
    Their Education and Training: A Case Study of Diozile I
    Village in Bagomoyo District." M.A. Thesis: University
    of Dar-es-Salaam. Dar-es-Salaam, Tanzania. June, 1979.

Muro, Asseny
"Women in Agricultural Production and Their Education and
Training: A Case Study of Diozile I Village in Bagamoyo
District." Paper Presented at the Workshop on Women's
Studies and Development. Dar-es-Salaam, Tanzania:
University of Dar-es-Salaam. Bureau of Resource
Assessment and Land Use Planning. Paper #11. September
24-29, 1979. 42p.

Muro, M.
"The Controversy Over Bride Price and Polygamy: New Laws
on Marriage and Maternity Leave." Tanzania Notes and
Records. #83 1978. pp. 133-137.

Namfua, Pelad P.
"Polygyny in Tanzania: Its Determinants and Effect on
Fertility." Ph.D Dissertation: Johns Hopkins University.
Baltimore, Maryland. 1982. 233p.

Ngalula, Theresia K.
"Domestic Labour and Property Ownership: A Case Study of
Buhongwa Village in Mwanza District." Paper Presented at
the Workshop on Women's Studies and Development.
Dar-es-Salaam, Tanzania: University of Dar-es-Salaam.
Bureau of Resource Assessment and Land Use Planning.
Paper #13. September 24-29, 1979. 10p.

Ngalula, Theresia K.
"Women as a Productive Force in the Tanzanian Rural
Society: A Case Study of Buhongwa Village in Mwanza
District." M.A. Thesis: University of Dar-es-Salaam.
Department of Sociology. Dar-es-Salaam, Tanzania. 1977.
113p.

O'Brien, M.
"The Maize Grinding Mill at Sinon." Community
Development Journal. Volume 20 #3 1985. pp. 189-191.

Oomen-Myin, Marie A.
"The Involvement of Rural Women in Village Development in
Tanzania." Convergence. Volume 16 #2 1983. pp. 59-69.

Rogers, Susan G.
"Efforts Toward Women's Development in Tanzania: Gender
Rhetoric vs. Gender Realities." (In) Staudt, Kathleen A.
and Jaquette, Jane S. (eds.). Women in Developing
Countries: A Policy Focus. New York: Haworth Press.
1983. pp. 23-41.

Rogers, Susan G.
"Efforts Toward Women's Development in Tanzania: Gender
Rhetoric vs. Gender Realities." Women and Politics.
Volume 2 #4 Winter, 1982. pp. 23-41.

Sekatawa, Emmanuel K.
"Compensating Mechanisms in the Nuptiality-Fertility
Relationship: Evidence From Tanzania, 1973." Ph.D
Dissertation: University of Pennsylvania. Philadelphia,
Pennsylvania. 1981. 241p.

Sekatawa, Emmanuel K.
Mechanisms Affecting the Link Between Nuptiality and
Fertility: Tanzania, 1973. Philadelphia, Pennsylvania:

University of Pennsylvania. Population Studies Center.
   African Demography Program Working Paper #6. June, 1981.
   19p.
Sembajwe, I.S.L.
   "The Effect of the Changing Position of Women on Family,
   Size and Child Survival in the United Republic of
   Tanzania." (In) International Labour Office (ILO).
   Final Report on the National Seminar on Population and
   Development in the United Republic of Tanzania. Geneva:
   ILO. 1980.
Swantz, Marja-Liisa
   Women in Development: A Creative Role Denied? The Case
   of Tanzania. New York: St. Martin's Press. 1985. 170p.
Swantz, Marja-Liisa.
   Strain and Strength Among Peasant Women in Tanzania.
   Dar-es-Salaam, Tanzania: University of Dar-es-Salaam.
   Bureau of Resource Assessment and Land Use Planning.
   Research Paper #49. May, 1977. 81p.
Tobisson, Eva
   Women, Work, Food and Nutrition in Nyamwigura Village,
   Mara Region, Tanzania. Dar-es-Salaam, Tanzania: Tanzania
   Food and Nutrition Centre. Report #548. July, 1980.
   127p.
United Nations Economic Commission for Africa (UNECA)
   "The Relationship Between Changing Roles and Status of
   Women and Childbearing and Child Survival in Tanzania."
   Paper Presented at the National Seminar on Population and
   Development. Addis Ababa, Ethiopia: UNECA. Arusha,
   Tanzania. 1980.
Vourela, Ulla
   "Women's Role in Production and Reproduction: Some
   Reflections on Relationships Between Men and Women in
   Tanzania and Finland." Paper Presented at the Workshop
   on Women's Studies and Development. Dar-es-Salaam,
   Tanzania: University of Dar-es-Salaam. Bureau of
   Resource Assessment and Land Use Planning. Paper #28.
   September 24-29, 1979. 19p.
Wilson, Monica H.
   For Men and Elders--Changes in the Relations of
   Generations and of Men and Women Among the
   Nyakyusa-Ngonde People, 1875-1971. New York: Africana
   Publishing Company. 1977. 209p.

SEXUAL MUTILATION/CIRCUMCISION

Caplan, A.P.
   "Boys' Circumcision and Girls' Puberty Rites Among the
   Swahili of Mafia Island, Tanzania." Africa. Volume 46
   #1 1976. pp. 21-33.

SLAVERY

Cooper, Frederick
    From Slaves to Squatters: Plantation Labor and
    Agriculture in Zanzibar and Coastal Kenya, 1890-1925.
    New Haven, Connecticut: Yale University Press. 1980.
    328p.
Mbilinyi, Marjorie J.
    "Wife, Slave and Subject of the King: The Oppression of
    Women in the Shambala Kingdom." Tanzania Notes and
    Records. #88-89. 1982. pp. 1-13.

STATUS OF WOMEN

Anonymous
    "Tanzania: The New Women and Traditional Norms in
    Tanzania." IDOC Bulletin. #50-51 December, 1976.
Bryceson, Deborah F. and Majma, Sachak
    Proceedings of the Workshop on Women's Studies and
    Development. Dar-es-Salaam, Tanzania: University of
    Dar-es-Salaam. September, 1979. 85p.
Huth, Mary J.
    "Female Participation and Status in Tanzania's Urban
    Labor Market." Paper Presented at the Annual Meeting of
    the North Central Sociological Association. University
    of Dayton. Dayton, Ohio. 1985.
Kikopa, Jane R.
    Law and the Status of Women in Tanzania. Addis Ababa,
    Ethiopia: United Nations Economic Commission for Africa.
    African Training and Research Centre for Women. Research
    Series. 1981. 108p.
Luhanga, Emily
    "Law and the Status of Women in Tanzania." Paper
    Presented at the Workshop on Women's Status and
    Development. Dar-es-Salaam, Tanzania: University of
    Dar-es-Salaam. Bureau of Resource Assessment and Land
    Use Planning. Paper #36. September 24-29, 1979. 7p.
Rogers, Susan G.
    "Anti-Colonial Protest in Africa: A Female Strategy
    Reconsidered." Heresies. Volume 3 #1 1980. pp. 22-27.
Sembajwe, I.S.L.
    "The Effect of the Changing Position of Women on Family,
    Size and Child Survival in the United Republic of
    Tanzania." (In) International Labour Office (ILO).
    Final Report on the National Seminar on Population and
    Development in the United Republic of Tanzania. Geneva:
    ILO. 1980.
United Nations Economic Commission for Africa (UNECA)
    "The Relationship Between Changing Roles and Status of
    Women and Childbearing and Child Survival in Tanzania."
    Paper Presented at the National Seminar on Population and

Development. Addis Ababa, Ethiopia: UNECA. Arusha, Tanzania. 1980.
Willis, Roy G.
"Executive Women and the Emergence of Female Class Consciousness: The Case of Fipa." Anthropology. Volume 4 #1 1980. pp. 1-10.

URBANIZATION

Findley, Sally E. and Orr, Ann C.
"A Suggested Framework for Analysing Urban-Rural Fertility Differentials With an Illustration of the Tanzanian Case." Paper Presented at the Annual Meeting of the Population Association of America. Atlanta, Georgia. April, 1978.
Findley, Sally E.
"A Suggested Framework for Analysis of Urban-Rural Fertility Differentials With an Illustration of the Tanzanian Case." Population and Environment. Volume 3 #3/4 Fall-Winter, 1980. pp. 237-261.
Findley, Sally E. and Orr, Ann C.
Patterns of Urban-Rural Fertility Differentials in Developing Countries: A Suggested Framework. Washington, D.C.: U.S. Department of State. U.S. Agency for International Development. September, 1978. 242p.
Flanagan, William G.
"The Extended Family as an Agent in Urbanization: A Survey of Men and Women Working in Dar-es-Salaam, Tanzania." Ph.D Dissertation: University of Connecticut-Storrs. Storrs, Connecticut. 1977. 234p.
Huth, Mary J.
"Female Participation and Status in Tanzania's Urban Labor Market." Paper Presented at the Annual Meeting of the North Central Sociological Association. University of Dayton. Dayton, Ohio. 1985.
Johnson, Willene
"The Study of Economic Activities of Women in Urban Tanzania." Ph.D Dissertation: Columbia University. New York, New York. 1983. 156p.
Lowe, Linda T.
"The Urban Woman Worker in Dar-es-Salaam." African Urban Notes. Volume 2 #3 Fall-Winter, 1976. pp. 11-19.
Shields, Nwanganga G.
Women in the Urban Labor Markets of Africa: The Case of Tanzania. Washington, D.C.: World Bank. Staff Working Paper #380. April, 1980. 138p.
Sijaona, S.T.
"Women's Projects in Urban Areas: Dar-es-Salaam City." Paper Presented at the Workshop on Women's Studies and Development. Dar-es-Salaam, Tanzania: University of Dar-es-Salaam. Bureau of Resource Assessment and Land Use Planning. Paper #10. September 24-29, 1979. 9p.

WOMEN AND THEIR CHILDREN

Chale, Freda U. and Generose, Ngonyani
"Report on a Survey of Cooperative Income Generating
Projects for Women and its Impact on the Welfare of
Children and the Family." Paper Presented at the
Workshop on Women's Studies and Development.
Dar-es-Salaam, Tanzania: University of Dar-es-Salaam.
Bureau of Resource Assessment and Land Use Planning.
Paper #24. September 24-29, 1979. 42p.
Kasulamemba, Sylvia
"Problems of Working Women: The Case of Dar-es-Salaam
City Council." Paper Presented at the Workshop on
Women's Studies and Development. Dar-es-Salaam,
Tanzania: University of Dar-es-Salaam. Bureau of
Resource Assessment and Land Use Planning. Paper #9.
September 24-29, 1979. 4p.
Kikopa, Jane R.
"Human Rights: The Position of Women and Children in
Tanzania." Paper Presented at the Workshop on Women's
Studies and Development. Dar-es-Salaam, Tanzania:
University of Dar-es-Salaam. Bureau of Resource
Assessment and Land Use Planning. Paper #33. September
24-29, 1979. 11p.
Kimaryo, Scholastica
"Implication for Women's Status and Position of
Structural Changes in Tanzanian Society." Paper
Presented at the Meeting of Experts on the History of
Women's Contributions to National Liberation Struggles
and Their Roles and Needs During Reconstruction in Newly
Independent Countries of Africa. Paris: United Nations
Educational, Scientific and Cultural Organization.
Bissau, Guinea-Bissau. 1983. 17p.
United Nations Economic Commission for Africa (UNECA)
"The Relationship Between Changing Roles and Status of
Women and Childbearing and Child Survival in Tanzania."
Paper Presented at the National Seminar on Population and
Development. Addis Ababa, Ethiopia: UNECA. Arusha,
Tanzania. 1980.

Uganda

Abrahams, R.
   "A Modern Witch-Hunt Among the Lango of Uganda."
   Cambridge Anthropology. Volume 10 #1 1985. pp. 32-44.
Akello, Grace
   Self Twice Removed: Ugandan Women. London: Change.
   1982. 19p.
Arya, O.P. and Taber, S.R. and Nsanze, H.
   "Gonorrhea and Female Infertility in Rural Uganda."
   American Journal of Obstetrics and Gynecology. Volume
   138 #7 Pt. 2 December 1, 1980. pp. 929-932.
Barnes, Virginia L.
   Changes in Crop Mixtures and Their Relationship to Gender
   Role Changes Among the Lugbara. Cambridge,
   Massachusetts: Harvard University. Joint Harvard/MIT
   Group. Working Paper #2. 1984.
Casale, Dorothy M.
   "Women, Power, and Change in Lugbara (Uganda) Cosmology:
   A Re-Interpretation." Anthropos. Volume 77 #3/4 1982.
   pp. 385-396.
Cox, J.L.
   "Psychiatric Morbidity and Pregnancy: Controlled Study of
   263 Semi-Rural Ugandan Women." British Journal of
   Psychiatry. Volume 134 April, 1979. pp. 401-405.
Duza, M. Badrud and Omiat, John
   "Nuptiality and Fertility in Tororo, Uganda." (In)
   Huzayyin, S.A. and Acsadi, G.T. (eds.). Family and
   Marriage in Some African and Asiatic Countries. Cairo:
   Cairo Demographic Centre. CDC Research Monograph Series
   #6. 1976. pp. 199-221.
Heyneman, Stephen P.
   "Influences on Academic Achievement: A Comparison of
   Results From Uganda and More Industrialized Societies."
   Sociology of Education. Volume 49 1976. pp. 200-210.

Katumba, Rebecca
   "Rural Education in Uganda." Africa Women. #26 1980.
   pp. 62-63.
Katumba, Rebecca
   "The Plight of the Women of Karamoja." Africa Women.
   #32 1981. pp. 10-11.
Kibuka, E.P.
   "The Changing Family in the Africa Context: The Uganda
   Case." Paper Presented at the Seminar on the Changing
   Family in the African Context, Maseru, Lesotho, 1983.
   Paris: United Nations Educational, Scientific and
   Cultural Organization. 1984. 29p.
Kigozi, Dorcus
   Women/Sexism/The Feminist Movement. A Roster of Material
   at the Makere Institute of Social Research Library.
   Kampala, Uganda: Makere Institute of Social Research
   Library. 1977. 10p.
Kilbride, Philip L. and Kilbride, Janet E.
   "Socialization for High Positive Affect Between Mother
   and Infant Among the Baganda of Uganda." Ethos. Volume
   11 #4 Winter, 1983. pp. 232-245.
Kisekka, Mere N.
   "The Identification and Use of Indicators of Women's
   Participation in Socio-Economic Development in the
   Context of Nigeria and Uganda." Paper Presented at the
   Meeting of Experts on the Indicators of Women's
   Participation in Socio-Economic Development. Paris:
   United Nations Educational, Scientific and Cultural
   Organization. 1980. 52p.
Maitum, Mary I.D.
   "Women, the Law and Convention: A Ugandan Perspective."
   Journal of Eastern African Research and Development.
   Volume 15 1985. pp. 151-164.
Mandeville, Elizabeth
   "Poverty, Work and the Financing of Single Women in
   Kampala." Africa. Volume 49 #1 1979. pp. 42-52.
Ntozi, James P.
   "Patterns of Fertility for Africans in Uganda Between
   1948 and 1969." Zeitschrift Fur
   Bevolkerungswissen-Schaft. Volume 4 #3 1978. pp.
   297-318.
Obbo, Christine S.
   Town Migration is Not for Women: African Women's Struggle
   for Economic Independence. London: Zed Press. 1980.
   329p.
Opolot, J.A.
   "Childrearing and Child Care in Uganda." Journal of
   Social Psychology. Volume 106 October, 1978. pp.
   123-124.
Princess Elizabeth of Toro
   African Princess: The Story of Princess Elizabth of Toro.
   London: Hamish Hamilton. 1983. 219p.

Robertson, A.F. and Hughes, C.A.
    "The Family Farm in Uganda." Development and Change.
    Volume 9 1978. pp. 415-438.
Robins, Catherine
    "Conversion, Life Crises and Stability Among Women in the
    East African Revival." (In) Jules-Rosette, Bennetta.
    The New Religions of Africa. Norwood, New Jersey: Ablex
    Publishing Corp. 1979. pp. 185-202.
Sembajwe, Israel S.
    "Socio-Cultural Supports for High Fertility in Buganda."
    (In) Ruzicka, Lado T. (ed.). Proceedings of the
    Conference on the Economics and Social Supports for High
    Fertility, November 16-18, 1976. Canberra, Australia:
    Australian National University. Development Studies
    Center. 1977. pp. 135-154.
Thompson, Richard W.
    "Fertility Aspirations and Modernization in Urban Uganda:
    A Case of Resilient Cultural Values." Urban
    Anthropology. Volume 7 #2 Summer, 1978. pp. 155-170.
Tiffany, Sharon W.
    Women, Work and Motherhood: The Power of Female Sexuality
    in the Workplace. Englewood Cliffs, New Jersey:
    Prentice-Hall. 1982. 148p.
United Nations Educational, Scientific and Cultural Organ.
    Women and Development: Indicators of Their Changing
    Role. Paris: UNESCO. Socio-Economic Studies #3. 1981.
    112p.

General Subject Bibliography— Southern Africa

AGRICULTURE

Deheusch, L.
    "The Good Usage of Wives and Cattle-Transformation of
    Marriage in Southern Africa." L'Homme. Volume 23 #4
    1983.
Germain, Adrienne
    "Research on Women in Agricultural Production in Eastern
    and Southern Africa." Paper Presented at a Workshop on
    Women in Agricultural Production in Eastern and Southern
    Africa. Nairobi, Kenya. April 9-11, 1980.
Guenther, Mathias G.
    "Bushman Hunters as Farm Labourers." Canadian Journal of
    African Studies. Volume 11 #2 1977.
Matsepe, Ivy F.
    "Underdevelopment and African Women." Journal of
    Southern African Affairs. Volume 2 #2 April, 1977. pp.
    135-143.
Matsepe-Casaburri, Ivy F.
    "Underdevelopment and African Women." Paper Presented at
    the Conference of the Southern Africa Research Group.
    College Park, Maryland: Southern Africa Research Group.
    September, 1976.
Mies, M.
    "Consequences of Capitalist Penetration for Women's
    Subsistence Reproduction." Paper Presented at the
    Seminar on Underdevelopment and Subsistence Production in
    South East Africa. April, 1978.
Murray, Colin G.
    "Migrant Labour and Changing Family Structure in the
    Rural Periphery of Southern Africa." Journal of Southern
    African Studies. Volume 6 #2 1980. pp. 139-156.
Palmer, Ingrid
    The Impact of Male Out-Migration on Women in Farming.
    West Hartford, Connecticut: Kumarian Press. 1985. 78p.

BIBLIOGRAPHIES

Anonymous
"Women in Southern Africa: Bibliography." Africa Report.
Volume 28 #2 March-April, 1983. pp. 54-55.
Durban Women's Bibliography Group
Women in Southern Africa: A Bibliography. Durban, South
Africa: The Group. 1985. 107p.
Moody, Elizabeth J.
Women and Development: A Select Bibliography. Pretoria,
South Africa: Africa Institute of South Africa.
Occasional Papers #43. 1979. 28p.
Wadsworth, Gail M.
Women in Development: A Bibliography of Materials
Available in the Library and Documentation Centre,
Eastern and Southern African Management Institute.
Arusha, Tanzania: Eastern and Southern African Management
Institute. Library and Documentation Centre. February,
1982. 106p.

CULTURAL ROLES

Anonymous
"Southern African Women Speak Out." Africa Report.
Volume 28 #2 March-April, 1983. pp. 15-19.
Catchpole, David R.
"The Fearful Silence of the Women at the Tomb: A Study in
Markan Theology." Journal of Theology for Southern
Africa. #18 March, 1977. pp. 3-10.
Deheusch, L.
"The Good Usage of Wives and Cattle-Transformation of
Marriage in Southern Africa." L'Homme. Volume 23 #4
1983.
Edwards, Felicity
"The Doctrine of God and the Feminine Principle."
Journal of Theology for Southern Africa. #37 December,
1981. pp. 23-37.
Ensor, Linda and Cooper, Carole
The African Women's Handbook on the Law. Johannesburg:
South African Institute of Race Relations. 1980. 41p.
Erasto, Muga
Studies in Prostitution: East, West and South Africa,
Zaire and Nevada. Nairobi: Kenya Literature Bureau.
1980.
Germain, Adrienne
"Research on Women in Agricultural Production in Eastern
and Southern Africa." Paper Presented at a Workshop on
Women in Agricultural Production in Eastern and Southern
Africa. Nairobi, Kenya. April 9-11, 1980.
Guenther, Mathias G.
"Bushman Hunters as Farm Labourers." Canadian Journal of
African Studies. Volume 11 #2 1977.

Igbinovia, Patrick E.
    "Prostitution in Black Africa." International Journal of
    Women's Studies. Volume 7 #5 November-December, 1984.
    pp. 430-449.
Jules-Rosette, Bennetta
    "Changing Aspects of Women's Initiation in Southern
    Africa: An Exploratory Study." Canadian Journal of
    African Studies. Volume 13 #3 1980. pp. 389-406.
Konie, Gwendoline
    "Women in Southern Africa: Gaining Political Power."
    Africa Report. Volume 28 #2 March-April, 1983. pp.
    11-14.
Kuper, Adam
    "Cousin Marriage Among the Thembu?" African Affairs.
    Volume 40 #1 1981. pp. 41-42.
Kuper, Adam
    "Symbolic Dimensions of the Southern Bantu Homestead."
    Africa. Volume 50 #1 1980. pp. 8-23.
MacGaffey, Wyatt
    "Lineage Structure, Marriage and the Family Amongst the
    Central Bantu." Journal of African History. Volume 24
    #2 1983. pp. 173-187.
Matsepe-Casaburri, Ivy F.
    "Underdevelopment and African Women." Paper Presented at
    the Conference of the Southern Africa Research Group.
    College Park, Maryland: Southern Africa Research Group.
    September, 1976.
Matsepe-Casaburri, Ivy F.
    "Women in Southern Africa: Legacy of Exclusion." Africa
    Report. Volume 28 #2 March-April, 1983. pp. 7-10.
McFadden, Patricia
    "Women Workers in Southern Africa." Journal of African
    Marxists. #4 September, 1983. pp. 54-62.
Muchena, Olivia N.
    "Women in Southern Africa: Are Women Integrated Into
    Development?" Africa Report. Volume 28 #2 March-April,
    1983. pp. 4-6.
Murray, Colin G.
    "Migrant Labour and Changing Family Structure in the
    Rural Periphery of Southern Africa." Journal of Southern
    African Studies. Volume 6 #2 1980. pp. 139-156.
O'Brien, Denise
    "Female Husbands in Southern Bantu." (In) Schlegal, A.
    (ed.). Sexual Stratification: A Cross-Cultural View.
    New York: Columbia University Press. 1977. pp. 109-126.
Palmer, Ingrid
    The Impact of Male Out-Migration on Women in Farming.
    West Hartford, Connecticut: Kumarian Press. 1985. 78p.
Schierling, Marla J.
    "Primeval Women: A Yahwistic View of Women in Genesis
    1-11:9." Journal of Theology for Southern Africa. #42
    March, 1983.

Thelejane, T.S.
  "An African Girl and an African Woman in a Changing
  World." Paper Presented at the Seminar on the Changing
  Family in the African Context, Maseru, Lesotho, 1983.
  Paris: United Nations Educational, Scientific and
  Cultural Organization. 1984. 24p.
Uba, Sam
  "Women Put the Case for Southern African Liberation."
  New African Development. March, 1977.
Watson, D.S.
  "The Mutual Recognition of Ordained Ministries." Journal
  of Theology for Southern Africa. #23 June, 1978. pp.
  56-70.

DEVELOPMENT AND TECHNOLOGY

Bifani, Patricia
  "Women and Development in Africa: A Tentative Approach
  Through Scenario Building." Journal of Eastern African
  Research and Development. Volume 15 1985. pp. 245-267.
Elias, Misrak
  Training for Development Planning and Women, an African
  Perspective: Report on the Second Training Programme.
  Arusha, Tanzania: Eastern and Southern Africa Management
  Institute. April 5-May 14, 1982. 55p.
Elias, Misrak
  Training for Development Planning and Women: An African
  Perspective. Arusha, Tanzania: Eastern and Southern
  African Management Institute. Annual Report and Report
  of the First Training Programme. September 16,
  1980-September 15, 1981. 1981.
Germain, Adrienne
  "Research on Women in Agricultural Production in Eastern
  and Southern Africa." Paper Presented at a Workshop on
  Women in Agricultural Production in Eastern and Southern
  Africa. Nairobi, Kenya. April 9-11, 1980.
Matsepe, Ivy F.
  "Underdevelopment and African Women." Journal of
  Southern African Affairs. Volume 2 #2 April, 1977. pp.
  135-143.
Matsepe-Casaburri, Ivy F.
  "Underdevelopment and African Women." Paper Presented at
  the Conference of the Southern Africa Research Group.
  College Park, Maryland: Southern Africa Research Group.
  September, 1976.
Matsepe-Casaburri, Ivy F.
  Uneven Development and Political Consciousness Among
  African Women in Southern Africa. Lusaka, Zambia: United
  Nations Institute on Namibia. 1978.
Moody, Elizabeth J.
  Women and Development: A Select Bibliography. Pretoria,

South Africa: Africa Institute of South Africa.
Occasional Papers #43. 1979. 28p.

Moody, Elize
   "Women: An Underrated Development Source." South African
   Journal of African Affairs. Volume 9 #2 1979. pp.
   64-71.

Muchena, Olivia N.
   "Women in Southern Africa: Are Women Integrated Into
   Development?" Africa Report. Volume 28 #2 March-April,
   1983. pp. 4-6.

Uba, Sam
   "Women Put the Case for Southern African Liberation."
   New African Development. March, 1977.

United Nations
   Measures of Assistance for Women in Southern Africa.
   Paper Presented at the United Nations World Conference of
   the United Nations Decade for Women: Equality,
   Development and Peace. New York: United Nations.
   Copenhagen, Denmark. July 14-30, 1980. 34p.

United Nations Secretary-General
   "Measures of Assistance for Women in Southern Africa:
   Report of the Secretary General." Paper Presented at the
   World Conference of the United Nations Decade for Women.
   New York: United Nations. Copenhagen, Denmark. July
   14-30, 1980.

Van der Horst, Sheila T.
   Women as an Economic Force in Southern Africa.
   Rondebosch, South Africa: University of Cape Town. Abe
   Bailey Institute of Interracial Studies #18. 1977.

Wadsworth, Gail M.
   Women in Development: A Bibliography of Materials
   Available in the Library and Documentation Centre,
   Eastern and Southern African Management Institute.
   Arusha, Tanzania: Eastern and Southern African Management
   Institute. Library and Documentation Centre. February,
   1982. 106p.

ECONOMICS

Bifani, Patricia
   "Women and Development in Africa: A Tentative Approach
   Through Scenario Building." Journal of Eastern African
   Research and Development. Volume 15 1985. pp. 245-267.

Matsepe, Ivy F.
   "Underdevelopment and African Women." Journal of
   Southern African Affairs. Volume 2 #2 April, 1977. pp.
   135-143.

Matsepe-Casaburri, Ivy F.
   "Underdevelopment and African Women." Paper Presented at
   the Conference of the Southern Africa Research Group.
   College Park, Maryland: Southern Africa Research Group.
   September, 1976.

McFadden, Patricia
    "Women Workers in Southern Africa." Journal of African
    Marxists. #4 September, 1983. pp. 54-62.
Mies, M.
    "Consequences of Capitalist Penetration for Women's
    Subsistence Reproduction." Paper Presented at the
    Seminar on Underdevelopment and Subsistence Production in
    South East Africa. April, 1978.
Moody, Elize
    "Women: An Underrated Development Source." South African
    Journal of African Affairs. Volume 9 #2 1979. pp.
    64-71.
Muchena, Olivia N.
    "Women in Southern Africa: Are Women Integrated Into
    Development?" Africa Report. Volume 28 #2 March-April,
    1983. pp. 4-6.
Murray, Colin G.
    "Migrant Labour and Changing Family Structure in the
    Rural Periphery of Southern Africa." Journal of Southern
    African Studies. Volume 6 #2 1980. pp. 139-156.
Palmer, Ingrid
    The Impact of Male Out-Migration on Women in Farming.
    West Hartford, Connecticut: Kumarian Press. 1985. 78p.
Van der Horst, Sheila T.
    Women as an Economic Force in Southern Africa.
    Rondebosch, South Africa: University of Cape Town. Abe
    Bailey Institute of Interracial Studies #18. 1977.

EDUCATION AND TRAINING

Elias, Misrak
    Training for Development Planning and Women, an African
    Perspective: Report on the Second Training Programme.
    Arusha, Tanzania: Eastern and Southern Africa Management
    Institute. April 5-May 14, 1982. 55p.
Elias, Misrak
    Training for Development Planning and Women: An African
    Perspective. Arusha, Tanzania: Eastern and Southern
    African Management Institute. Annual Report and Report
    of the First Training Programme. September 16,
    1980-September 15, 1981. 1981.
Muriuki, Margaret N.
    "The Role of Women in African Librarianship: The Next 25
    Years." Paper Presented at the Standing Conference of
    Eastern, Central and Southern African Libraries. Lusaka,
    Zambia. October 4-9, 1976.
Robertson, Claire
    "A Growing Dilemma: Women and Change in African and
    Primary Education, 1958-1980." Journal of Eastern
    African Research and Development. Volume 15 1985. pp.
    14-35.

GENERAL SUBJECT BIBLIOGRAPHY--SOUTHERN AFRICA

Thelejane, T.S.
    "An African Girl and an African Woman in a Changing
    World." Paper Presented at the Seminar on the Changing
    Family in the African Context, Maseru, Lesotho, 1983.
    Paris: United Nations Educational, Scientific and
    Cultural Organization. 1984. 24p.
United Nations
    Measures of Assistance for Women in Southern Africa.
    Paper Presented at the United Nations World Conference of
    the United Nations Decade for Women: Equality,
    Development and Peace. New York: United Nations.
    Copenhagen, Denmark. July 14-30, 1980. 34p.
United Nations Secretary-General
    "Measures of Assistance for Women in Southern Africa:
    Report of the Secretary General." Paper Presented at the
    World Conference of the United Nations Decade for Women.
    New York: United Nations. Copenhagen, Denmark. July
    14-30, 1980.

EMPLOYMENT AND LABOR

Guenther, Mathias G.
    "Bushman Hunters as Farm Labourers." Canadian Journal of
    African Studies. Volume 11 #2 1977.
Hein, Catherine R.
    Factory Employment, Marriage and Fertility: The Case of
    Mauritian Women. Geneva: International Labour
    Organization. World Employment Programme Research
    Working Paper #118. June, 1982. 57p.
Igbinovia, Patrick E.
    "Prostitution in Black Africa." International Journal of
    Women's Studies. Volume 7 #5 November-December, 1984.
    pp. 430-449.
McFadden, Patricia
    "Women Workers in Southern Africa." Journal of African
    Marxists. #4 September, 1983. pp. 54-62.
Mies, M.
    "Consequences of Capitalist Penetration for Women's
    Subsistence Reproduction." Paper Presented at the
    Seminar on Underdevelopment and Subsistence Production in
    South East Africa. April, 1978.
Moody, Elize
    "Women: An Underrated Development Source." South African
    Journal of African Affairs. Volume 9 #2 1979. pp.
    64-71.
Muriuki, Margaret N.
    "The Role of Women in African Librarianship: The Next 25
    Years." Paper Presented at the Standing Conference of
    Eastern, Central and Southern African Libraries. Lusaka,
    Zambia. October 4-9, 1976.
Murray, Colin G.
    "Migrant Labour and Changing Family Structure in the

244

Rural Periphery of Southern Africa." Journal of Southern
African Studies. Volume 6 #2 1980. pp. 139-156.
Palmer, Ingrid
The Impact of Male Out-Migration on Women in Farming.
West Hartford, Connecticut: Kumarian Press. 1985. 78p.
United Nations
Measures of Assistance for Women in Southern Africa.
Paper Presented at the United Nations World Conference of
the United Nations Decade for Women: Equality,
Development and Peace. New York: United Nations.
Copenhagen, Denmark. July 14-30, 1980. 34p.
Van der Horst, Sheila T.
Women as an Economic Force in Southern Africa.
Rondebosch, South Africa: University of Cape Town. Abe
Bailey Institute of Interracial Studies #18. 1977.

EQUALITY AND LIBERATION

Anonymous
"Southern African Women Speak Out." Africa Report.
Volume 28 #2 March-April, 1983. pp. 15-19.
Leland, Stephanie and Mutasa, Joyce and Willard, Fran
Women in Southern Africa: Struggles and Achievements--The
U.N. Decade for Women Diary, July, 1985/86. London:
Feminist International for Peace and Food. 1985. 120p.
Matsepe, Ivy F.
"Underdevelopment and African Women." Journal of
Southern African Affairs. Volume 2 #2 April, 1977. pp.
135-143.
Matsepe, Ivy F.
"Women in the Struggle for Liberation." (In) Wiley,
David and Isaacman, Allen (eds.). Southern Africa:
Society, Economy and Liberation. East Lansing, Michigan:
Michigan State University. African Studies Center.
1981.

FAMILY LIFE

Hein, Catherine R.
Factory Employment, Marriage and Fertility: The Case of
Mauritian Women. Geneva: International Labour
Organization. World Employment Programme Research
Working Paper #118. June, 1982. 57p.
Kuper, Adam
"Symbolic Dimensions of the Southern Bantu Homestead."
Africa. Volume 50 #1 1980. pp. 8-23.
MacGaffey, Wyatt
"Lineage Structure, Marriage and the Family Amongst the
Central Bantu." Journal of African History. Volume 24
#2 1983. pp. 173-187.

Murray, Colin G.
    "Migrant Labour and Changing Family Structure in the
    Rural Periphery of Southern Africa." Journal of Southern
    African Studies. Volume 6 #2 1980. pp. 139-156.
Thelejane, T.S.
    "An African Girl and an African Woman in a Changing
    World." Paper Presented at the Seminar on the Changing
    Family in the African Context, Maseru, Lesotho, 1983.
    Paris: United Nations Educational, Scientific and
    Cultural Organization. 1984. 24p.

FAMILY PLANNING AND CONTRACEPTION

Uba, Sam
    "Women Put the Case for Southern African Liberation."
    New African Development. March, 1977.

FERTILITY AND INFERTILITY

Hein, Catherine R.
    Factory Employment, Marriage and Fertility: The Case of
    Mauritian Women. Geneva: International Labour
    Organization. World Employment Programme Research
    Working Paper #118. June, 1982. 57p.

HISTORY

MacGaffey, Wyatt
    "Lineage Structure, Marriage and the Family Amongst the
    Central Bantu." Journal of African History. Volume 24
    #2 1983. pp. 173-187.
Matsepe-Casaburri, Ivy F.
    "Women in Southern Africa: Legacy of Exclusion." Africa
    Report. Volume 28 #2 March-April, 1983. pp. 7-10.

LAW AND LEGAL ISSUES

Ensor, Linda and Cooper, Carole
    The African Women's Handbook on the Law. Johannesburg:
    South African Institute of Race Relations. 1980. 41p.
Thomas, Rosalind
    "The Law in Southern Africa: Justice for All?" Africa
    Report. Volume 30 #2 March-April, 1985. pp. 59-63.

LITERATURE

Ngcobo, Lauretta
    "Four Women Writers in Africa Today." South African
    Outlook. Volume 114 #1355 May, 1984. pp. 64-69.

MARITAL RELATIONS AND NUPTIALITY

Deheusch, L.
"The Good Usage of Wives and Cattle-Transformation of Marriage in Southern Africa." L'Homme. Volume 23 #4 1983.

Hein, Catherine R.
Factory Employment, Marriage and Fertility: The Case of Mauritian Women. Geneva: International Labour Organization. World Employment Programme Research Working Paper #118. June, 1982. 57p.

Kuper, Adam
"Cousin Marriage Among the Thembu?" African Affairs. Volume 40 #1 1981. pp. 41-42.

MacGaffey, Wyatt
"Lineage Structure, Marriage and the Family Amongst the Central Bantu." Journal of African History. Volume 24 #2 1983. pp. 173-187.

Murray, Colin G.
"Migrant Labour and Changing Family Structure in the Rural Periphery of Southern Africa." Journal of Southern African Studies. Volume 6 #2 1980. pp. 139-156.

O'Brien, Denise
"Female Husbands in Southern Bantu." (In) Schlegal, A. (ed.). Sexual Stratification: A Cross-Cultural View. New York: Columbia University Press. 1977. pp. 109-126.

Palmer, Ingrid
The Impact of Male Out-Migration on Women in Farming. West Hartford, Connecticut: Kumarian Press. 1985. 78p.

MASS MEDIA

Isaacs, Gayla C.
"Women in Southern Africa: The Media and the Ideal Woman." Africa Report. Volume 28 #2 March-April, 1983. pp. 48-51.

MIGRATION

Murray, Colin G.
"Migrant Labour and Changing Family Structure in the Rural Periphery of Southern Africa." Journal of Southern African Studies. Volume 6 #2 1980. pp. 139-156.

Palmer, Ingrid
The Impact of Male Out-Migration on Women in Farming. West Hartford, Connecticut: Kumarian Press. 1985. 78p.

GENERAL SUBJECT BIBLIOGRAPHY--SOUTHERN AFRICA

MISCELLANEOUS

Erasto, Muga
    Studies in Prostitution: East, West and South Africa,
    Zaire and Nevada. Nairobi: Kenya Literature Bureau.
    1980.
Igbinovia, Patrick E.
    "Prostitution in Black Africa." International Journal of
    Women's Studies. Volume 7 #5 November-December, 1984.
    pp. 430-449.
Muriuki, Margaret N.
    "The Role of Women in African Librarianship: The Next 25
    Years." Paper Presented at the Standing Conference of
    Eastern, Central and Southern African Libraries. Lusaka,
    Zambia. October 4-9, 1976.

NATIONALISM

Anonymous
    "Southern African Women Speak Out." Africa Report.
    Volume 28 #2 March-April, 1983. pp. 15-19.
Matsepe, Ivy F.
    "Women in the Struggle for Liberation." (In) Wiley,
    David and Isaacman, Allen (eds.). Southern Africa:
    Society, Economy and Liberation. East Lansing, Michigan:
    Michigan State University. African Studies Center.
    1981.
Uba, Sam
    "Women Put the Case for Southern African Liberation."
    New African Development. March, 1977.

POLITICS AND GOVERNMENT

Anonymous
    "Southern African Women Speak Out." Africa Report.
    Volume 28 #2 March-April, 1983. pp. 15-19.
Konie, Gwendoline
    "Women in Southern Africa: Gaining Political Power."
    Africa Report. Volume 28 #2 March-April, 1983. pp.
    11-14.
Matsepe, Ivy F.
    "Underdevelopment and African Women." Journal of
    Southern African Affairs. Volume 2 #2 April, 1977. pp.
    135-143.
Matsepe, Ivy F.
    "Women in the Struggle for Liberation." (In) Wiley,
    David and Isaacman, Allen (eds.). Southern Africa:
    Society, Economy and Liberation. East Lansing, Michigan:
    Michigan State University. African Studies Center.
    1981.

248

Matsepe-Casaburri, Ivy F.
Uneven Development and Political Consciousness Among
African Women in Southern Africa. Lusaka, Zambia: United
Nations Institute on Namibia. 1978.

RELIGION AND WITCHCRAFT

Catchpole, David R.
"The Fearful Silence of the Women at the Tomb: A Study in
Markan Theology." Journal of Theology for Southern
Africa. #18 March, 1977. pp. 3-10.
Edwards, Felicity
"The Doctrine of God and the Feminine Principle."
Journal of Theology for Southern Africa. #37 December,
1981. pp. 23-37.
Jules-Rosette, Bennetta
"Changing Aspects of Women's Initiation in Southern
Africa: An Exploratory Study." Canadian Journal of
African Studies. Volume 13 #3 1980. pp. 389-406.
Schierling, Marla J.
"Primeval Women: A Yahwistic View of Women in Genesis
1-11:9." Journal of Theology for Southern Africa. #42
March, 1983.
Watson, D.S.
"The Mutual Recognition of Ordained Ministries." Journal
of Theology for Southern Africa. #23 June, 1978. pp.
56-70.

RESEARCH

Anonymous
"Women in Southern Africa: Bibliography." Africa Report.
Volume 28 #2 March-April, 1983. pp. 54-55.
Bifani, Patricia
"Women and Development in Africa: A Tentative Approach
Through Scenario Building." Journal of Eastern African
Research and Development. Volume 15 1985. pp. 245-267.
Germain, Adrienne
"Research on Women in Agricultural Production in Eastern
and Southern Africa." Paper Presented at a Workshop on
Women in Agricultural Production in Eastern and Southern
Africa. Nairobi, Kenya. April 9-11, 1980.
Leland, Stephanie and Mutasa, Joyce and Willard, Fran
Women in Southern Africa: Struggles and Achievements--The
U.N. Decade for Women Diary, July, 1985/86. London:
Feminist International for Peace and Food. 1985. 120p.
Moody, Elizabeth J.
Women and Development: A Select Bibliography. Pretoria,
South Africa: Africa Institute of South Africa.
Occasional Papers #43. 1979. 28p.

Wadsworth, Gail M.
  Women in Development: A Bibliography of Materials
  Available in the Library and Documentation Centre,
  Eastern and Southern African Management Institute.
  Arusha, Tanzania: Eastern and Southern African Management
  Institute. Library and Documentation Centre. February,
  1982. 106p.

SEX ROLES

Deheusch, L.
  "The Good Usage of Wives and Cattle-Transformation of
  Marriage in Southern Africa." L'Homme. Volume 23 #4
  1983.
Edwards, Felicity
  "The Doctrine of God and the Feminine Principle."
  Journal of Theology for Southern Africa. #37 December,
  1981. pp. 23-37.
Igbinovia, Patrick E.
  Prostitution in Black Africa. International Journal of
  Women's Studies. Volume 7 #5 November-December, 1984.
  pp. 430-449.
Kuper, Adam
  "Cousin Marriage Among the Thembu?" African Affairs.
  Volume 40 #1 1981. pp. 41-42.
Kuper, Adam
  "Symbolic Dimensions of the Southern Bantu Homestead."
  Africa. Volume 50 #1 1980. pp. 8-23.
MacGaffey, Wyatt
  "Lineage Structure, Marriage and the Family Amongst the
  Central Bantu." Journal of African History. Volume 24
  #2 1983. pp. 173-187.
O'Brien, Denise
  "Female Husbands in Southern Bantu." (In) Schlegal, A.
  (ed.). Sexual Stratification: A Cross-Cultural View.
  New York: Columbia University Press. 1977. pp. 109-126.

STATUS OF WOMEN

Anonymous
  "Southern African Women Speak Out." Africa Report.
  Volume 28 #2 March-April, 1983. pp. 15-19.
Konie, Gwendoline
  "Women in Southern Africa: Gaining Political Power."
  Africa Report. Volume 28 #2 March-April, 1983. pp.
  11-14.
Matsepe, Ivy F.
  "Women in the Struggle for Liberation." (In) Wiley,
  David and Isaacman, Allen (eds.). Southern Africa:
  Society, Economy and Liberation. East Lansing, Michigan:

Michigan State University. African Studies Center.
   1981.
Matsepe-Casaburri, Ivy F.
   "Women in Southern Africa: Legacy of Exclusion." Africa
   Report. Volume 28 #2 March-April, 1983. pp. 7-10.
Thelejane, T.S.
   "An African Girl and an African Woman in a Changing
   World." Paper Presented at the Seminar on the Changing
   Family in the African Context, Maseru, Lesotho, 1983.
   Paris: United Nations Educational, Scientific and
   Cultural Organization. 1984. 24p.

NATIONS OF
SOUTHERN AFRICA

Angola

Anonymous
   "Women's Emancipation Part of a Class Struggle." (In)
   U.S. Joint Publications Research Service. Translations
   on Sub-Saharan Africa #1673 (Translation of an Article
   in Journal de Angola, August 15, 1976). Springield,
   Virginia: National Technical Information Service. 1976.
   pp. 6-10.
Jules-Rosette, Bennetta
   The New Religions of Africa. Norwood, New Jersey: Ablex
   Publishing Corp. 1979. 248p.
Kinsman, Margaret
   "Beasts of Burden: The Subordination of Southern Tswana
   Women, ca. 1800-1840." Journal of Southern African
   Studies. Volume 10 #1 1983. pp. 39-54.
Lee, Richard B.
   The !Kung San: Men, Women and Work in a Foraging
   Society. Cambridge, New York: Cambridge University
   Press. 1979. 526p.
Organization of Angolan Women
   Angolan Women Building the Future: From National
   Liberation to Women's Emancipation. London: Zed Press.
   Third World Series. Translated by Marga Holness. 1984.
   151p.
Urdang, Stephanie
   The Liberation of Women as a Necessity for the Successful
   Revolution in Guinea-Bissau, Mozambique and Angola.
   Waltham, Massachusetts: Brandeis University. African
   Studies Association. 1977.

Botswana

AGRICULTURE

Bettles, F.M.
    Women's Access to Agricultural Extension Services in
    Botswana. Gaborone, Botswana: Ministry of Agriculture.
    1980.
Bond, C.A.
    Discussion Paper on Agricultural Extension for Women.
    Gaborone, Botswana: Botswana Ministry of Agriculture.
    1977. 6p.
Botswana. Ministry of Agriculture
    Report on the Involvement of Women in the Integrated
    Farming Pilot Project. Gaborone, Botswana: Ministry of
    Agriculture. Department of Field Services. 1976. 10p.
Date-Bah, Eugenia and Stevens, Yvette
    "Rural Women in Africa and Technological Change: Some
    Issues." Labour and Society. Volume 6 #2 April-June,
    1981. pp. 149-162.
Fortmann, Louise P.
    "Economic Status and Women's Participation in
    Agriculture: A Botswana Case Study." Rural Sociology.
    Volume 49 #3 August, 1984. pp. 452-464.
Fortmann, Louise P.
    Who Plows: The Effect of Economic Status on Women's
    Participation in Agriculture in Botswana. Madison,
    Wisconsin. Mimeo. 1983. 40p.
Fortmann, Louise P.
    Women's Agriculture in a Cattle Economy. Ithaca, New
    York: Cornell University. Center for International
    Studies. Gaborone, Botswana: Botswana Ministry of
    Agriculture. 1981. 33p.
Fortmann, Louise P.
    Women's Involvement in High Risk Arable Agriculture: The
    Botswana Case. Gaborone, Botswana: Botswana Ministry of

Agriculture. Paper Prepared for the Ford Foundation
Workshop on Women in Agriculture in Eastern and Southern
Africa. Nairobi, Kenya. 1980.

Guyer, Jane I.
"Women in the Rural Economy: Contemporary Variations."
(In) Hay, Margaret J. and Stichter, Sharon (eds.).
African Women South of the Sahara. New York: Longman.
1984. pp. 19-32.

Horn, Nancy and Nkambule-Kanyima, Brenda
Resource Guide: Women in Agriculture in Botswana. East
Lansing, Michigan: Bean/Cowpea CRSP (Collaborative
Research Support Program. 1984.

Kerven, Carol
National Migration Study: Urban and Rural Female
Headed-Households' Dependence on Agriculture. Gaborone,
Botswana: Central Statistics Office. National Migration
Study. Issue Paper #4. 1979. 65p.

Kossoudji, Sherrie and Mueller, Eva
"The Economic and Demographic Status of Female-Headed
Households in Rural Botswana." Economic Development and
Cultural Change. Volume 31 #4 July, 1983. pp. 831-859.

Peters, Pauline E.
"Household Management in Botswana: Cattle Crops and Wage
Labor." Paper Presented at a Conference in Bellagio,
Lake Como, Italy. 1984.

Wikan, G.
"Development and Women in Botswana." Norsk Geografisk
Tidsskrift. Volume 38 #2 1984. pp. 129-134.

Yates, Leslie M.
"Integration of Women in Development in Southern Africa:
An Evaluation With Recommendations for U.S. AID Programs
in Botswana, Lesotho and Zambia." Sadex.
November-December, 1979. pp. 1-15.

Yates, Leslie M.
Integration of Women in Development in Zambia, Botswana
and Lesotho: AID's Efforts. Washington, D.C.: U.S.
Department of State. U.S. Agency for International
Development. Southern Africa Development Analysis.
1978. 92p.

BIBLIOGRAPHIES

Henderson, Francene I.
Women in Botswana: An Annotated Bibliography. Gaborone,
Botswana: University of Botswana and Swaziland. National
Institute of Development and Cultural Research.
Documentation Unit Working Bibliography #4. March, 1981.
20p.

CULTURAL ROLES

Alverson, Hoyt
    Mind in the Heart of Darkness: Value and Self-Idenity
    Among the Tswana of Southern Africa. New Haven,
    Connecticut: Yale University Press. 1978. 299p.
Aromasodu, M.C.
    "Traditional Practices Affecting the Health of Women in
    Pregnancy and Childbirth." Paper Presented at the
    Seminar on Traditional Practices Affecting the Health of
    Women and Children. World Conference of the United
    Nations Decade for Women. Copenhagen, Denmark. July
    14-30, 1980.
Barnard, Alan
    "Sex Roles Among the Nharo Bushmen of Botswana." Africa.
    Volume 50 #2 1980. pp. 115-124.
Bentley, G.R.
    "Hunter-Gatherer Energetics and Fertility: A Reassessment
    of !Kung San." Human Ecology. Volume 13 March, 1985.
    pp. 79-109.
Brown, Barbara B.
    "Impact of Male Labour Migration on Women in Botswana."
    African Affairs. Volume 82 #328 July, 1983. pp.
    367-388.
Brown, Barbara B.
    "The Impact of Male Labor Migration on Women in
    Botswana." Paper Presented at the Annual Meeting of the
    African Studies Association. Paper #19. Bloomington,
    Indiana. October 21-24, 1981.
Brown, Barbara B.
    Women, Migrant Labor and Social Change in Botswana.
    Boston: Boston University. African Studies Center.
    Working Paper in African Studies. #41. 1980. 21p.
Bryant, Coralie
    "Women Migrants, Urbanization and Social Change: The
    Botswana Case." Paper Presented at the American
    Political Science Association Annual Meeting.
    Washington, D.C. September, 1977.
Chernichovsky, Dov
    "Socioeconomic Correlates of Fertility Behavior in Rural
    Botswana." Genus. Volume 40 #3-4 July-December, 1984.
    pp. 129-146.
Chernichovsky, Dov
    Socioeconomic Correlates of Fertility Behavior in Rural
    Botswana. Washington, D.C.: World Bank. Mimeo. May,
    1979.
Collier, J.F. and Rosaldo, M.Z.
    "Politics and Gender in Simple Societies." (In) Ortner,
    Sherry B. and Whitehead, Harriet (eds.). Sexual
    Meanings. New York: Cambridge University Press. 1981.
    pp. 275-329.
Comaroff, John L.
    "Bridewealth and the Control of Ambiguity in a Tswana

Chiefdom." (In) Comaroff, J.L. (ed.). The Meaning of
Marriage Payments. New York: Academic Press. 1980. pp.
161-195.

Comaroff, John L. and Roberts, S.
"Marriage and Extra-Marital Sexuality: The Dialectics of
Legal Change Among the Kgatla." Journal of African Law.
Volume 21 #1 1977. pp. 97-123.

Comaroff, John L.
"The Management of Marriage in Tswana Chiefdom." (In)
Krige, E.J. and Comaroff, J.L. (eds.). Essays on African
Marriage in Southern Africa. Cape Town, South Africa:
Wetton. 1981.

Cooper, David
Rural Urban Migration and Female Headed Households in
Botswana Towns: Case Study of Unskilled Women Workers and
Female Self Employment in a Site and Service Area,
Selebi-Phikwe. Gaborone, Botswana: Central Statistical
Office. Mimeograph. March, 1979.

Cooper, David
"Rural-Urban Migration of Female-Headed Households in
Botswana Towns." (In) Kerven, Carol (ed.). Workshop on
Migration Research. Gaborone, Botswana: Central
Statistics Office. Ministry of Finance and Development
Planning. 1979.

Date-Bah, Eugenia and Stevens, Yvette
"Rural Women in Africa and Technological Change: Some
Issues." Labour and Society. Volume 6 #2 April-June,
1981. pp. 149-162.

De Villiers, F.
"Ideal Family Size in a Rural Tswana Population." South
African Medical Journal. Volume 63 #15 April, 1983.
pp. 573-574.

Du Pradal, Pia
A Report on Attitudes Towards Family Planning and Family
Size in Botswana. Gaborone, Botswana: University of
Botswana. National Institute of Development Research and
Documentation. March, 1983. 81p.

Fortmann, Louise P.
Who Plows: The Effect of Economic Status on Women's
Participation in Agriculture in Botswana. Madison,
Wisconsin. Mimeo. 1983. 40p.

Fortmann, Louise P.
Women's Involvement in High Risk Arable Agriculture: The
Botswana Case. Gaborone, Botswana: Botswana Ministry of
Agriculture. Paper Prepared for the Ford Foundation
Workshop on Women in Agriculture in Eastern and Southern
Africa. Nairobi, Kenya. 1980.

Griffiths, Anne
"Support for Women With Dependent Children Under the
Customary System of the Bakwena and the Roman-Dutch
Common and Statutory Law of Botswana." Journal of Legal
Pluralism and Unofficial Law. #22 1984. pp. 1-16.

Guyer, Jane I.
"Women in the Rural Economy: Contemporary Variations."
(In) Hay, Margaret J. and Stichter, Sharon (eds.).
African Women South of the Sahara. New York: Longman.
1984. pp. 19-32.

Henderson, Francene I.
Women in Botswana: An Annotated Bibliography. Gaborone,
Botswana: University of Botswana and Swaziland. National
Institute of Development and Cultural Research.
Documentation Unit Working Bibliography #4. March, 1981.
20p.

Horn, Nancy and Nkambule-Kanyima, Brenda
Resource Guide: Women in Agriculture in Botswana. East
Lansing, Michigan: Bean/Cowpea CRSP (Collaborative
Research Support Program. 1984.

Izzard, Wendy
"Migrants and Mothers: Case Studies From Botswana."
Journal of Southern African Studies. Volume 11 #2 1985.
pp. 258-280.

Izzard, Wendy
"Preliminary Ideas on the Rural-Urban Migration of Female
Headed Households Within Botswana." (In) Kerven, Carol
(ed.). Workshop on Migration Research. Gaborone,
Botswana: Ministry of Finance and Development Planning.
Central Statistics Office. 1979.

Izzard, Wendy
Rural-Urban Migration of Women in Botswana: Final
Fieldwork Report. Gaborone, Botswana: Ministry of
Finance and Development Planning. Central Statistics
Office. Rural Sociology Unit. August, 1979. 50p.

Izzard, Wendy
"The Impact of Migration on the Roles of Women." (In)
Botswana. Ministry of Finance and Development Planning.
Migration in Botswana: Patterns, Causes and Consequences.
Gaborone, Botswana: The Ministry. Central Statistics
Office. 1982. pp.657-718.

Kerven, Carol
National Migration Study: Urban and Rural Female
Headed-Households' Dependence on Agriculture. Gaborone,
Botswana: Central Statistics Office. National Migration
Study. Issue Paper #4. 1979. 65p.

Kinsman, Margaret
"Beasts of Burden: The Subordination of Southern Tswana
Women, ca. 1800-1840." Journal of Southern African
Studies. Volume 10 #1 1983. pp. 39-54.

Konner, M.J.
"Maternal Care, Infant Behavior and Development Among the
!Kung." (In) Lee, R.B. and DeVore, I. (eds.). Kalahari
Hunter-Gatherers, Studies of the !Kung San and Their
Neighbors. Cambridge, Massachusetts: Harvard University
Press. 1976. pp. 218-246.

Konner, M.J. and Worthman, C.
"Nursing Frequencies, Gonadal Function and Birth-Spacing

Among the !Kung Hunter-Gatherers." Science. Volume 207
February 15, 1980. pp. 788-791.
Kossoudji, Sherrie and Mueller, Eva
"The Economic and Demographic Status of Female-Headed
Households in Rural Botswana." Economic Development and
Cultural Change. Volume 31 #4 July, 1983. pp. 831-859.
Kreysler, J.
Some Aspects of Women, Health and Nutrition, With Special
Reference to Kgatleng District and Serowe Village.
Gaborone, Botswana: Ministry of Health. Unpublished
Paper. 1978.
Lagerwerf, Levy
'They Pray for You...': Independent Churches and Women in
Botswana. Leiden, Netherlands: Interuniversitaic
Instituut Voor Missiologie en Oecumenica. IIMO Research
Pamphlet #6. 1982. 135p.
Larson, Thomas J.
"Sorcery and Witchcraft of the Hambukushu of Ngamiland."
Anthropos. Volume 75 #3/4 1980. pp. 416-432.
Larson, Thomas J.
"Hambukushu Girls' Puberty Rites." Botswana Notes and
Records. Volume 11 1979. pp. 33-36.
Lee, Richard
"Politics, Sexual and Non-Sexual, in an Egalitarian
Society (With Special Reference to the !Kung)." (In)
Leacock, E. and Lee, Richard (eds.). Politics and
History in Band Societies. Cambridge, England: Cambridge
University Press. 1982. pp. 37-59.
Lee, Richard B.
The !Kung San: Men, Women and Work in a Foraging Society.
Cambridge, New York: Cambridge University Press. 1979.
526p.
Manyeneng, W.G. and Khulumani, P. and Larson, M.K. and Way,
Ann A.
Botswana Family Health Survey, 1984. Gaborone, Botswana:
Ministry of Health. Family Health Division. July, 1985.
245p.
Molokomme, Athaliah
"Marriage: What Every Woman Wants or a Declaration of
'Civil Death'? Some Legal Aspects of the Status of
Married Women in Botswana." Pula. Volume 4 #1 1984.
pp. 70-79.
Motshologane, S.R.
"Influence of Urbanization on the Role and Status of
Husband and Wife in the Tswana Family." South African
Journal of Sociology. Volume 17 April, 1978. pp.
83-90.
Mueller, Eva
"Household Structure, Time Use, and Income Distribution
in Rural Botswana." Paper Presented at the Annual
Meeting of the Population Association of America.
Philadelphia, Pennsylvania. April 27, 1979.

Otaala, Barnabas
   "The Changing Family in a Changing World: The Botswana
   Case." Paper Presented at the Seminar on the Changing
   Family in the African Context, Maseru, Lesotho, 1983.
   Paris: United Nations Educational, Scientific and
   Cultural Organization. 1984. 17p.
Peters, Pauline E.
   "Gender, Developmental Cycles and Historical Process: a
   Critique of Recent Research on Women in Botswana."
   Journal of Southern African Studies. Volume 10 #1 1983.
   pp. 100-122.
Peters, Pauline E.
   "Gender, Developmental Cycles, and Historical Process: A
   Critique of Recent Research on Women in Botswana."
   Journal of Southern African Studies. Volume 10 #1
   October, 1983. pp. 100-122.
Peters, Pauline E.
   "Household Management in Botswana: Cattle Crops and Wage
   Labor." Paper Presented at a Conference in Bellagio,
   Lake Como, Italy. 1984.
Peters, Pauline E.
   "Women in Botswana." Journal of Southern African
   Studies. Volume 11 #1 October, 1984. pp. 150-153.
Roberts, Simon
   "The Kgatla Marriage: Concepts of Validity." (In)
   Roberts, Simon (ed.). Law and the Family in Africa.
   Hague, Netherlands: Mouton. 1977. pp. 241-260.
Sanders, A.J.G.M.
   "Ten Years of the Botswana Matrimonial Causes Act:
   Further Proposals for Divorce Reform." Journal of
   African Law. Volume 26 #2 Autumn, 1982. pp. 163-176.
Schapera, I.
   "Some Notes on Tswana Bogadi." Journal of African Law.
   Volume 22 #2 1978. pp. 112-124.
Selolwane, Onalenna
   "Domestic Workers in Botswana." Women in Southern
   African History. #2 May, 1983. pp. 33-38.
Shostak, Marjorie
   "A !Kung Women's Memories of Childhood." (In) Lee,
   Richard B. and DeVore, I. (eds.). Kalahari
   Hunter-Gatherers: Studies of the !Kung San and Their
   Neighbors. Cambridge, Massachusetts: Harvard University
   Press. 1976. pp. 246-277.
Shostak, Marjorie
   Nisa, the Life and Words of a !Kung Woman. New York:
   Vintage Books. 1983. 402p.
Stephens, Betsy
   Family Planning Follow-Up Study. Gaborone, Botswana:
   University College of Botswana and Swaziland. National
   Institute for Research in Development and African
   Studies. Documentation Unit. Discussion Paper #5.
   July, 1977. 61p.

Tiffany, Sharon W.
   Women, Work and Motherhood: The Power of Female Sexuality
   in the Workplace. Englewood Cliffs, New Jersey:
   Prentice-Hall. 1982. 148p.
Volkman, Toby A.
   The San in Transition: Volume One: A Guide to N!Ai, the
   Story of a !Kung Woman. Cambridge, Massachusetts:
   Documentary Educational Resources. 1982. 56p.
Wilmsen, Edwin N.
   "Studies in Diet, Nutrition and Fertility Among a Group
   of Kalahari Bushmen in Botswana." Social Science
   Information. Volume 21 #1 1982. pp. 95-125.
Wilmsen, Edwin N.
   Diet and Fertility Among the Kalahari Bushmen. Waltham,
   Massachusetts: Boston University. African Studies
   Center. Working Paper #14. 1979.

DEVELOPMENT AND TECHNOLOGY

Bettles, F.M.
   Women's Access to Agricultural Extension Services in
   Botswana. Gaborone, Botswana: Ministry of Agriculture.
   1980.
Bond, C.A.
   Discussion Paper on Agricultural Extension for Women.
   Gaborone, Botswana: Botswana Ministry of Agriculture.
   1977. 6p.
Botswana. Ministry of Agriculture
   Report on the Involvement of Women in the Integrated
   Farming Pilot Project. Gaborone, Botswana: Ministry of
   Agriculture. Department of Field Services. 1976. 10p.
Date-Bah, Eugenia and Stevens, Yvette
   "Rural Women in Africa and Technological Change: Some
   Issues." Labour and Society. Volume 6 #2 April-June,
   1981. pp. 149-162.
Fortmann, Louise P.
   "Economic Status and Women's Participation in
   Agriculture: A Botswana Case Study." Rural Sociology.
   Volume 49 #3 August, 1984. pp. 452-464.
Fortmann, Louise P.
   Women's Agriculture in a Cattle Economy. Ithaca, New
   York: Cornell University. Center for International
   Studies. Gaborone, Botswana: Botswana Ministry of
   Agriculture. 1981. 33p.
Fortmann, Louise P.
   Women's Involvement in High Risk Arable Agriculture: The
   Botswana Case. Gaborone, Botswana: Botswana Ministry of
   Agriculture. Paper Prepared for the Ford Foundation
   Workshop on Women in Agriculture in Eastern and Southern
   Africa. Nairobi, Kenya. 1980.
Guyer, Jane I.
   "Women in the Rural Economy: Contemporary Variations."

(In) Hay, Margaret J. and Stichter, Sharon (eds.).
African Women South of the Sahara. New York: Longman.
1984. pp. 19-32.

Henderson, Francene I.
Women in Botswana: An Annotated Bibliography. Gaborone,
Botswana: University of Botswana and Swaziland. National
Institute of Development and Cultural Research.
Documentation Unit Working Bibliography #4. March, 1981.
20p.

Horn, Nancy and Nkambule-Kanyima, Brenda
Resource Guide: Women in Agriculture in Botswana. East
Lansing, Michigan: Bean/Cowpea CRSP (Collaborative
Research Support Program. 1984.

Kaha, Ulla
Voluntary Women's Organizations in Botswana. Gaborone,
Botswana: Swedish International Development Agency.
Mimeo. 1979.

Kerven, Carol
"Academics, Practitioners and All Kinds of Women in
Development: A Reply to Peters." Journal of Southern
African Studies. Volume 10 #2 April, 1984. pp.
259-268.

Motsete, Ruth K.
The Role of Women's Organizations in Development in
Botswana. Addis Ababa, Ethiopia: United Nations Economic
Commission for Africa. African Training and Research
Centre for Women. Occasional Papers Series #M82-707.
March, 1982. 11p.

Peters, Pauline E.
"Gender, Developmental Cycles and Historical Process: a
Critique of Recent Research on Women in Botswana."
Journal of Southern African Studies. Volume 10 #1 1983.
pp. 100-122.

Peters, Pauline E.
"Gender, Developmental Cycles, and Historical Process: A
Critique of Recent Research on Women in Botswana."
Journal of Southern African Studies. Volume 10 #1
October, 1983. pp. 100-122.

Peters, Pauline E.
"Women in Botswana." Journal of Southern African
Studies. Volume 11 #1 October, 1984. pp. 150-153.

Van De Wall-Bake, Titia and De Jager, Thea
Boiteko/Serowe and Itekeng: A Socio-Economic Study of Two
Projects in Botswana Involving Women in Low-Income
Households. Gaborone, Botswana: University College of
Botswana. Working Paper #30. May, 1980. 62p.

Wikan, G.
"Development and Women in Botswana." Norsk Geografisk
Tidsskrift. Volume 38 #2 1984. pp. 129-134.

Yates, Leslie M.
"Integration of Women in Development in Southern Africa:
An Evaluation With Recommendations for U.S. AID Programs

BOTSWANA

in Botswana, Lesotho and Zambia." Sadex.
November-December, 1979. pp. 1-15.
Yates, Leslie M.
Integration of Women in Development in Zambia, Botswana
and Lesotho: AID's Efforts. Washington, D.C.: U.S.
Department of State. U.S. Agency for International
Development. Southern Africa Development Analysis.
1978. 92p.

DIVORCE

Sanders, A.J.G.M.
"Ten Years of the Botswana Matrimonial Causes Act:
Further Proposals for Divorce Reform." Journal of
African Law. Volume 26 #2 Autumn, 1982. pp. 163-176.

ECONOMICS

Brown, Barbara B.
"Impact of Male Labour Migration on Women in Botswana."
African Affairs. Volume 82 #328 July, 1983. pp.
367-388.
Brown, Barbara B.
"The Impact of Male Labor Migration on Women in
Botswana." Paper Presented at the Annual Meeting of the
African Studies Association. Paper #19. Bloomington,
Indiana. October 21-24, 1981.
Brown, Barbara B.
Women, Migrant Labor and Social Change in Botswana.
Boston: Boston University. African Studies Center.
Working Paper in African Studies. #41. 1980. 21p.
Bryant, Coralie
"Women Migrants, Urbanization and Social Change: The
Botswana Case." Paper Presented at the American
Political Science Association Annual Meeting.
Washington, D.C. September, 1977.
Cooper, David
Rural Urban Migration and Female Headed Households in
Botswana Towns: Case Study of Unskilled Women Workers and
Female Self Employment in a Site and Service Area,
Selebi-Phikwe. Gaborone, Botswana: Central Statistical
Office. Mimeograph. March, 1979.
Cooper, David
"Rural-Urban Migration of Female-Headed Households in
Botswana Towns." (In) Kerven, Carol (ed.). Workshop on
Migration Research. Gaborone, Botswana: Central
Statistics Office. Ministry of Finance and Development
Planning. 1979.
Fortmann, Louise P.
"Economic Status and Women's Participation in

Agriculture: A Botswana Case Study." Rural Sociology.
Volume 49 #3 August, 1984. pp. 452-464.

Fortmann, Louise P.
Who Plows: The Effect of Economic Status on Women's
Participation in Agriculture in Botswana. Madison,
Wisconsin. Mimeo. 1983. 40p.

Fortmann, Louise P.
Women's Agriculture in a Cattle Economy. Ithaca, New
York: Cornell University. Center for International
Studies. Gaborone, Botswana: Botswana Ministry of
Agriculture. 1981. 33p.

Guyer, Jane I.
"Women in the Rural Economy: Contemporary Variations."
(In) Hay, Margaret J. and Stichter, Sharon (eds.).
African Women South of the Sahara. New York: Longman.
1984. pp. 19-32.

Horn, Nancy and Nkambule-Kanyima, Brenda
Resource Guide: Women in Agriculture in Botswana. East
Lansing, Michigan: Bean/Cowpea CRSP (Collaborative
Research Support Program. 1984.

Izzard, Wendy
"Migrants and Mothers: Case Studies From Botswana."
Journal of Southern African Studies. Volume 11 #2 1985.
pp. 258-280.

Izzard, Wendy
"Preliminary Ideas on the Rural-Urban Migration of Female
Headed Households Within Botswana." (In) Kerven, Carol
(ed.). Workshop on Migration Research. Gaborone,
Botswana: Ministry of Finance and Development Planning.
Central Statistics Office. 1979.

Izzard, Wendy
Rural-Urban Migration of Women in Botswana: Final
Fieldwork Report. Gaborone, Botswana: Ministry of
Finance and Development Planning. Central Statistics
Office. Rural Sociology Unit. August, 1979. 50p.

Izzard, Wendy
"The Impact of Migration on the Roles of Women." (In)
Botswana. Ministry of Finance and Development Planning.
Migration in Botswana: Patterns, Causes and Consequences.
Gaborone, Botswana: The Ministry. Central Statistics
Office. 1982. pp.657-718.

Kaha, Ulla
Voluntary Women's Organizations in Botswana. Gaborone,
Botswana: Swedish International Development Agency.
Mimeo. 1979.

Kerven, Carol
"Academics, Practitioners and All Kinds of Women in
Development: A Reply to Peters." Journal of Southern
African Studies. Volume 10 #2 April, 1984. pp.
259-268.

Kerven, Carol
National Migration Study: Urban and Rural Female
Headed-Households' Dependence on Agriculture. Gaborone,

Botswana: Central Statistics Office. National Migration
Study. Issue Paper #4. 1979. 65p.
Kossoudji, Sherrie and Mueller, Eva
"The Economic and Demographic Status of Female-Headed
Households in Rural Botswana." Economic Development and
Cultural Change. Volume 31 #4 July, 1983. pp. 831-859.
Motsete, Ruth K.
The Role of Women's Organizations in Development in
Botswana. Addis Ababa, Ethiopia: United Nations Economic
Commission for Africa. African Training and Research
Centre for Women. Occasional Papers Series #M82-707.
March, 1982. 11p.
Mueller, Eva
"Household Structure, Time Use, and Income Distribution
in Rural Botswana." Paper Presented at the Annual
Meeting of the Population Association of America.
Philadelphia, Pennsylvania. April 27, 1979.
Van De Wall-Bake, Titia and De Jager, Thea
Boiteko/Serowe and Itekeng: A Socio-Economic Study of Two
Projects in Botswana Involving Women in Low-Income
Households. Gaborone, Botswana: University College of
Botswana. Working Paper #30. May, 1980. 62p.
Wikan, G.
"Development and Women in Botswana." Norsk Geografisk
Tidsskrift. Volume 38 #2 1984. pp. 129-134.
Yates, Leslie M.
"Integration of Women in Development in Southern Africa:
An Evaluation With Recommendations for U.S. AID Programs
in Botswana, Lesotho and Zambia." Sadex.
November-December, 1979. pp. 1-15.
Yates, Leslie M.
Integration of Women in Development in Zambia, Botswana
and Lesotho: AID's Efforts. Washington, D.C.: U.S.
Department of State. U.S. Agency for International
Development. Southern Africa Development Analysis.
1978. 92p.

EDUCATION AND TRAINING

Bettles, F.M.
Women's Access to Agricultural Extension Services in
Botswana. Gaborone, Botswana: Ministry of Agriculture.
1980.
Bond, C.A.
Discussion Paper on Agricultural Extension for Women.
Gaborone, Botswana: Botswana Ministry of Agriculture.
1977. 6p.
Botswana. Ministry of Agriculture
Report on the Involvement of Women in the Integrated
Farming Pilot Project. Gaborone, Botswana: Ministry of
Agriculture. Department of Field Services. 1976. 10p.

Brown, Barbara
  "Girls Achievement in School in Botswana." Botswana
  Notes and Records. Volume 12 1980. pp. 35-40.
Chernichovsky, Dov
  "Socioeconomic Correlates of Fertility Behavior in Rural
  Botswana." Genus. Volume 40 #3-4 July-December, 1984.
  pp. 129-146.
Chernichovsky, Dov
  Socioeconomic Correlates of Fertility Behavior in Rural
  Botswana. Washington, D.C.: World Bank. Mimeo. May,
  1979.
Kerven, Carol
  "Academics, Practitioners and All Kinds of Women in
  Development: A Reply to Peters." Journal of Southern
  African Studies. Volume 10 #2 April, 1984. pp.
  259-268.
Otaala, Barnabas
  "The Changing Family in a Changing World: The Botswana
  Case." Paper Presented at the Seminar on the Changing
  Family in the African Context, Maseru, Lesotho, 1983.
  Paris: United Nations Educational, Scientific and
  Cultural Organization. 1984. 17p.

EMPLOYMENT AND LABOR

Brown, Barbara B.
  "Impact of Male Labour Migration on Women in Botswana."
  African Affairs. Volume 82 #328 July, 1983. pp.
  367-388.
Brown, Barbara B.
  "The Impact of Male Labor Migration on Women in
  Botswana." Paper Presented at the Annual Meeting of the
  African Studies Association. Paper #19. Bloomington,
  Indiana. October 21-24, 1981.
Brown, Barbara B.
  Women, Migrant Labor and Social Change in Botswana.
  Boston: Boston University. African Studies Center.
  Working Paper in African Studies. #41. 1980. 21p.
Bryant, Coralie
  "Women Migrants, Urbanization and Social Change: The
  Botswana Case." Paper Presented at the American
  Political Science Association Annual Meeting.
  Washington, D.C. September, 1977.
Cooper, David
  Rural Urban Migration and Female Headed Households in
  Botswana Towns: Case Study of Unskilled Women Workers and
  Female Self Employment in a Site and Service Area,
  Selebi-Phikwe. Gaborone, Botswana: Central Statistical
  Office. Mimeograph. March, 1979.
Cooper, David
  "Rural-Urban Migration of Female-Headed Households in
  Botswana Towns." (In) Kerven, Carol (ed.). Workshop on

Migration Research. Gaborone, Botswana: Central
Statistics Office. Ministry of Finance and Development
Planning. 1979.

Date-Bah, Eugenia and Stevens, Yvette
"Rural Women in Africa and Technological Change: Some
Issues." Labour and Society. Volume 6 #2 April-June,
1981. pp. 149-162.

Guyer, Jane I.
"Women in the Rural Economy: Contemporary Variations."
(In) Hay, Margaret J. and Stichter, Sharon (eds.).
African Women South of the Sahara. New York: Longman.
1984. pp. 19-32.

Horn, Nancy and Nkambule-Kanyima, Brenda
Resource Guide: Women in Agriculture in Botswana. East
Lansing, Michigan: Bean/Cowpea CRSP (Collaborative
Research Support Program. 1984.

Izzard, Wendy
"Migrants and Mothers: Case Studies From Botswana."
Journal of Southern African Studies. Volume 11 #2 1985.
pp. 258-280.

Izzard, Wendy
"Preliminary Ideas on the Rural-Urban Migration of Female
Headed Households Within Botswana." (In) Kerven, Carol
(ed.). Workshop on Migration Research. Gaborone,
Botswana: Ministry of Finance and Development Planning.
Central Statistics Office. 1979.

Izzard, Wendy
Rural-Urban Migration of Women in Botswana: Final
Fieldwork Report. Gaborone, Botswana: Ministry of
Finance and Development Planning. Central Statistics
Office. Rural Sociology Unit. August, 1979. 50p.

Izzard, Wendy
"The Impact of Migration on the Roles of Women." (In)
Botswana. Ministry of Finance and Development Planning.
Migration in Botswana: Patterns, Causes and Consequences.
Gaborone, Botswana: The Ministry. Central Statistics
Office. 1982. pp.657-718.

Lee, Richard B.
The !Kung San: Men, Women and Work in a Foraging Society.
Cambridge, New York: Cambridge University Press. 1979.
526p.

Otaala, Barnabas
"The Changing Family in a Changing World: The Botswana
Case." Paper Presented at the Seminar on the Changing
Family in the African Context, Maseru, Lesotho, 1983.
Paris: United Nations Educational, Scientific and
Cultural Organization. 1984. 17p.

Peters, Pauline E.
"Household Management in Botswana: Cattle Crops and Wage
Labor." Paper Presented at a Conference in Bellagio,
Lake Como, Italy. 1984.

Selolwane, Onalenna
"Domestic Workers in Botswana." Women in Southern
African History. #2 May, 1983. pp. 33-38.
Tiffany, Sharon W.
Women, Work and Motherhood: The Power of Female Sexuality
in the Workplace. Englewood Cliffs, New Jersey:
Prentice-Hall. 1982. 148p.
Van De Wall-Bake, Titia and De Jager, Thea
Boiteko/Serowe and Itekeng: A Socio-Economic Study of Two
Projects in Botswana Involving Women in Low-Income
Households. Gaborone, Botswana: University College of
Botswana. Working Paper #30. May, 1980. 62p.

FAMILY LIFE

Brown, Barbara B.
"Impact of Male Labour Migration on Women in Botswana."
African Affairs. Volume 82 #328 July, 1983. pp.
367-388.
Brown, Barbara B.
"The Impact of Male Labor Migration on Women in
Botswana." Paper Presented at the Annual Meeting of the
African Studies Association. Paper #19. Bloomington,
Indiana. October 21-24, 1981.
Brown, Barbara B.
Women, Migrant Labor and Social Change in Botswana.
Boston: Boston University. African Studies Center.
Working Paper in African Studies. #41. 1980. 21p.
Bryant, Coralie
"Women Migrants, Urbanization and Social Change: The
Botswana Case." Paper Presented at the American
Political Science Association Annual Meeting.
Washington, D.C. September, 1977.
Chernichovsky, Dov
"Socioeconomic Correlates of Fertility Behavior in Rural
Botswana." Genus. Volume 40 #3-4 July-December, 1984.
pp. 129-146.
Chernichovsky, Dov
Socioeconomic Correlates of Fertility Behavior in Rural
Botswana. Washington, D.C.: World Bank. Mimeo. May,
1979.
Cooper, David
Rural Urban Migration and Female Headed Households in
Botswana Towns: Case Study of Unskilled Women Workers and
Female Self Employment in a Site and Service Area,
Selebi-Phikwe. Gaborone, Botswana: Central Statistical
Office. Mimeograph. March, 1979.
Cooper, David
"Rural-Urban Migration of Female-Headed Households in
Botswana Towns." (In) Kerven, Carol (ed.). Workshop on
Migration Research. Gaborone, Botswana: Central

Statistics Office. Ministry of Finance and Development Planning. 1979.

De Villiers, F.
"Ideal Family Size in a Rural Tswana Population." South African Medical Journal. Volume 63 #15 April, 1983. pp. 573-574.

Du Pradal, Pia
A Report on Attitudes Towards Family Planning and Family Size in Botswana. Gaborone, Botswana: University of Botswana. National Institute of Development Research and Documentation. March, 1983. 81p.

Izzard, Wendy
"Migrants and Mothers: Case Studies From Botswana." Journal of Southern African Studies. Volume 11 #2 1985. pp. 258-280.

Izzard, Wendy
"Preliminary Ideas on the Rural-Urban Migration of Female Headed Households Within Botswana." (In) Kerven, Carol (ed.). Workshop on Migration Research. Gaborone, Botswana: Ministry of Finance and Development Planning. Central Statistics Office. 1979.

Izzard, Wendy
Rural-Urban Migration of Women in Botswana: Final Fieldwork Report. Gaborone, Botswana: Ministry of Finance and Development Planning. Central Statistics Office. Rural Sociology Unit. August, 1979. 50p.

Izzard, Wendy
"The Impact of Migration on the Roles of Women." (In) Botswana. Ministry of Finance and Development Planning. Migration in Botswana: Patterns, Causes and Consequences. Gaborone, Botswana: The Ministry. Central Statistics Office. 1982. pp.657-718.

Kerven, Carol
National Migration Study: Urban and Rural Female Headed-Households' Dependence on Agriculture. Gaborone, Botswana: Central Statistics Office. National Migration Study. Issue Paper #4. 1979. 65p.

Kossoudji, Sherrie and Mueller, Eva
"The Economic and Demographic Status of Female-Headed Households in Rural Botswana." Economic Development and Cultural Change. Volume 31 #4 July, 1983. pp. 831-859.

Motshologane, S.R.
"Influence of Urbanization on the Role and Status of Husband and Wife in the Tswana Family." South African Journal of Sociology. Volume 17 April, 1978. pp. 83-90.

Mueller, Eva
"Household Structure, Time Use, and Income Distribution in Rural Botswana." Paper Presented at the Annual Meeting of the Population Association of America. Philadelphia, Pennsylvania. April 27, 1979.

Otaala, Barnabas
"The Changing Family in a Changing World: The Botswana

Case." Paper Presented at the Seminar on the Changing
Family in the African Context, Maseru, Lesotho, 1983.
Paris: United Nations Educational, Scientific and
Cultural Organization. 1984. 17p.
Peters, Pauline E.
"Gender, Developmental Cycles, and Historical Process: A
Critique of Recent Research on Women in Botswana."
Journal of Southern African Studies. Volume 10 #1
October, 1983. pp. 100-122.
Peters, Pauline E.
"Household Management in Botswana: Cattle Crops and Wage
Labor." Paper Presented at a Conference in Bellagio,
Lake Como, Italy. 1984.
Peters, Pauline E.
"Women in Botswana." Journal of Southern African
Studies. Volume 11 #1 October, 1984. pp. 150-153.
Selolwane, Onalenna
"Domestic Workers in Botswana." Women in Southern
African History. #2 May, 1983. pp. 33-38.
Tiffany, Sharon W.
Women, Work and Motherhood: The Power of Female Sexuality
in the Workplace. Englewood Cliffs, New Jersey:
Prentice-Hall. 1982. 148p.

FAMILY PLANNING AND CONTRACEPTION

Chernichovsky, Dov
"Socioeconomic Correlates of Fertility Behavior in Rural
Botswana." Genus. Volume 40 #3-4 July-December, 1984.
pp. 129-146.
Chernichovsky, Dov
Socioeconomic Correlates of Fertility Behavior in Rural
Botswana. Washington, D.C.: World Bank. Mimeo. May,
1979.
Cook, Sheila
Evaluation of Family Planning Programmes: An Example From
Botswana. London: International Planned Parenthood
Federation. Evaluation and Social Sciences Department.
1976. 13p.
De Villiers, F.
"Ideal Family Size in a Rural Tswana Population." South
African Medical Journal. Volume 63 #15 April, 1983.
pp. 573-574.
Du Pradal, Pia
A Report on Attitudes Towards Family Planning and Family
Size in Botswana. Gaborone, Botswana: University of
Botswana. National Institute of Development Research and
Documentation. March, 1983. 81p.
Konner, M.J. and Worthman, C.
"Nursing Frequencies, Gonadal Function and Birth-Spacing
Among the !Kung Hunter-Gatherers." Science. Volume 207
February 15, 1980. pp. 788-791.

Stephens, Betsy
    "Family Planning Follow-Up Study." Gaborone, Botswana:
    University College of Botswana and Swaziland. National
    Institute for Research in Development and African
    Studies. Documentation Unit. Discussion Paper #5.
    July, 1977. 61p.

FERTILITY AND INFERTILITY

Abdelraman, Mohammed A.
    Study of Age-Sex Composition and Some Estimates of
    Fertility and Mortality Levels for Botswana. Legon,
    Ghana: Regional Institute for Population Studies
    Newsletter. #12. January, 1979. pp. 12-21.
Bentley, G.R.
    "Hunter-Gatherer Energetics and Fertility: A Reassessment
    of !Kung San." Human Ecology. Volume 13 March, 1985.
    pp. 79-109.
Chernichovsky, Dov
    "Socioeconomic Correlates of Fertility Behavior in Rural
    Botswana." Genus. Volume 40 #3-4 July-December, 1984.
    pp. 129-146.
Chernichovsky, Dov
    Socioeconomic Correlates of Fertility Behavior in Rural
    Botswana. Washington, D.C.: World Bank. Mimeo. May,
    1979.
Wilmsen, Edwin N.
    "Studies in Diet, Nutrition and Fertility Among a Group
    of Kalahari Bushmen in Botswana." Social Science
    Information. Volume 21 #1 1982. pp. 95-125.
Wilmsen, Edwin N.
    Diet and Fertility Among the Kalahari Bushmen. Waltham,
    Massachusetts: Boston University. African Studies
    Center. Working Paper #14. 1979.

HEALTH, NUTRITION AND MEDICINE

Aromasodu, M.C.
    "Traditional Practices Affecting the Health of Women in
    Pregnancy and Childbirth." Paper Presented at the
    Seminar on Traditional Practices Affecting the Health of
    Women and Children. World Conference of the United
    Nations Decade for Women. Copenhagen, Denmark. July
    14-30, 1980.
Cook, Sheila
    Evaluation of Family Planning Programmes: An Example From
    Botswana. London: International Planned Parenthood
    Federation. Evaluation and Social Sciences Department.
    1976. 13p.

Konner, M.J.
    "Maternal Care, Infant Behavior and Development Among the
    !Kung." (In) Lee, R.B. and DeVore, I. (eds.). Kalahari
    Hunter-Gatherers, Studies of the !Kung San and Their
    Neighbors. Cambridge, Massachusetts: Harvard University
    Press. 1976. pp. 218-246.
Konner, M.J. and Worthman, C.
    "Nursing Frequencies, Gonadal Function and Birth-Spacing
    Among the !Kung Hunter-Gatherers." Science. Volume 207
    February 15, 1980. pp. 788-791.
Kreysler, J.
    Some Aspects of Women, Health and Nutrition, With Special
    Reference to Kgatleng District and Serowe Village.
    Gaborone, Botswana: Ministry of Health. Unpublished
    Paper. 1978.
Manyeneng, W.G. and Khulumani, P. and Larson, M.K. and Way,
Ann A.
    Botswana Family Health Survey, 1984. Gaborone, Botswana:
    Ministry of Health. Family Health Division. July, 1985.
    245p.
Otaala, Barnabas
    "The Changing Family in a Changing World: The Botswana
    Case." Paper Presented at the Seminar on the Changing
    Family in the African Context, Maseru, Lesotho, 1983.
    Paris: United Nations Educational, Scientific and
    Cultural Organization. 1984. 17p.
Stephens, Betsy
    Family Planning Follow-Up Study. Gaborone, Botswana:
    University College of Botswana and Swaziland. National
    Institute for Research in Development and African
    Studies. Documentation Unit. Discussion Paper #5.
    July, 1977. 61p.
Wilmsen, Edwin N.
    "Studies in Diet, Nutrition and Fertility Among a Group
    of Kalahari Bushmen in Botswana." Social Science
    Information. Volume 21 #1 1982. pp. 95-125.
Wilmsen, Edwin N.
    Diet and Fertility Among the Kalahari Bushmen. Waltham,
    Massachusetts: Boston University. African Studies
    Center. Working Paper #14. 1979.

HISTORY

Kinsman, Margaret
    "Beasts of Burden: The Subordination of Southern Tswana
    Women, ca. 1800-1840." Journal of Southern African
    Studies. Volume 10 #1 1983. pp. 39-54.
Peters, Pauline E.
    "Gender, Developmental Cycles and Historical Process: a
    Critique of Recent Research on Women in Botswana."
    Journal of Southern African Studies. Volume 10 #1 1983.
    pp. 100-122.

LAW AND LEGAL ISSUES

Comaroff, John L. and Roberts, S.
"Marriage and Extra-Marital Sexuality: The Dialectics of
Legal Change Among the Kgatla." Journal of African Law.
Volume 21 #1 1977. pp. 97-123.
Griffiths, Anne
"Support for Women With Dependent Children Under the
Customary System of the Bakwena and the Roman-Dutch
Common and Statutory Law of Botswana." Journal of Legal
Pluralism and Unofficial Law. #22 1984. pp. 1-16.
Molokomme, Athaliah
"Marriage: What Every Woman Wants or a Declaration of
'Civil Death'? Some Legal Aspects of the Status of
Married Women in Botswana." Pula. Volume 4 #1 1984.
pp. 70-79.
Roberts, Simon
"The Kgatla Marriage: Concepts of Validity." (In)
Roberts, Simon (ed.). Law and the Family in Africa.
Hague, Netherlands: Mouton. 1977. pp. 241-260.
Sanders, A.J.G.M.
"Ten Years of the Botswana Matrimonial Causes Act:
Further Proposals for Divorce Reform." Journal of
African Law. Volume 26 #2 Autumn, 1982. pp. 163-176.
Schapera, I.
"Some Notes on Tswana Bogadi." Journal of African Law.
Volume 22 #2 1978. pp. 112-124.

MARITAL RELATIONS AND NUPTIALITY

Brown, Barbara B.
"Impact of Male Labour Migration on Women in Botswana."
African Affairs. Volume 82 #328 July, 1983. pp.
367-388.
Chernichovsky, Dov
"Socioeconomic Correlates of Fertility Behavior in Rural
Botswana." Genus. Volume 40 #3-4 July-December, 1984.
pp. 129-146.
Chernichovsky, Dov
Socioeconomic Correlates of Fertility Behavior in Rural
Botswana. Washington, D.C.: World Bank. Mimeo. May,
1979.
Comaroff, John L.
"Bridewealth and the Control of Ambiguity in a Tswana
Chiefdom." (In) Comaroff, J.L. (ed.). The Meaning of
Marriage Payments. New York: Academic Press. 1980. pp.
161-195.
Comaroff, John L. and Roberts, S.
"Marriage and Extra-Marital Sexuality: The Dialectics of
Legal Change Among the Kgatla." Journal of African Law.
Volume 21 #1 1977. pp. 97-123.

Comaroff, John L.
  "The Management of Marriage in Tswana Chiefdom." (In)
  Krige, E.J. and Comaroff, J.L. (eds.). Essays on African
  Marriage in Southern Africa. Cape Town, South Africa:
  Wetton. 1981.
Du Pradal, Pia
  A Report on Attitudes Towards Family Planning and Family
  Size in Botswana. Gaborone, Botswana: University of
  Botswana. National Institute of Development Research and
  Documentation. March, 1983. 81p.
Izzard, Wendy
  Rural-Urban Migration of Women in Botswana: Final
  Fieldwork Report. Gaborone, Botswana: Ministry of
  Finance and Development Planning. Central Statistics
  Office. Rural Sociology Unit. August, 1979. 50p.
Molokomme, Athaliah
  "Marriage: What Every Woman Wants or a Declaration of
  'Civil Death'? Some Legal Aspects of the Status of
  Married Women in Botswana." Pula. Volume 4 #1 1984.
  pp. 70-79.
Motshologane, S.R.
  "Influence of Urbanization on the Role and Status of
  Husband and Wife in the Tswana Family." South African
  Journal of Sociology. Volume 17 April, 1978. pp.
  83-90.
Roberts, Simon
  "The Kgatla Marriage: Concepts of Validity." (In)
  Roberts, Simon (ed.). Law and the Family in Africa.
  Hague, Netherlands: Mouton. 1977. pp. 241-260.
Sanders, A.J.G.M.
  "Ten Years of the Botswana Matrimonial Causes Act:
  Further Proposals for Divorce Reform." Journal of
  African Law. Volume 26 #2 Autumn, 1982. pp. 163-176.
Stephens, Betsy
  Family Planning Follow-Up Study. Gaborone, Botswana:
  University College of Botswana and Swaziland. National
  Institute for Research in Development and African
  Studies. Documentation Unit. Discussion Paper #5.
  July, 1977. 61p.

MIGRATION

Brown, Barbara B.
  "Impact of Male Labour Migration on Women in Botswana."
  African Affairs. Volume 82 #328 July, 1983. pp.
  367-388.
Brown, Barbara B.
  "The Impact of Male Labor Migration on Women in
  Botswana." Paper Presented at the Annual Meeting of the
  African Studies Association. Paper #19. Bloomington,
  Indiana. October 21-24, 1981.

Brown, Barbara B.
    Women, Migrant Labor and Social Change in Botswana.
    Boston: Boston University. African Studies Center.
    Working Paper in African Studies. #41. 1980. 21p.
Bryant, Coralie
    "Women Migrants, Urbanization and Social Change: The
    Botswana Case." Paper Presented at the American
    Political Science Association Annual Meeting.
    Washington, D.C. September, 1977.
Cooper, David
    Rural Urban Migration and Female Headed Households in
    Botswana Towns: Case Study of Unskilled Women Workers and
    Female Self Employment in a Site and Service Area,
    Selebi-Phikwe. Gaborone, Botswana: Central Statistical
    Office. Mimeograph. March, 1979.
Cooper, David
    "Rural-Urban Migration of Female-Headed Households in
    Botswana Towns." (In) Kerven, Carol (ed.). Workshop on
    Migration Research. Gaborone, Botswana: Central
    Statistics Office. Ministry of Finance and Development
    Planning. 1979.
Izzard, Wendy
    "Migrants and Mothers: Case Studies From Botswana."
    Journal of Southern African Studies. Volume 11 #2 1985.
    pp. 258-280.
Izzard, Wendy
    "Preliminary Ideas on the Rural-Urban Migration of
    Female-Headed Households Within Botswana." (In) Kerven,
    Carol (ed.). Workshop on Migration Research. Gaborone,
    Botswana: Ministry of Finance and Development Planning.
    Central Statistics Office. 1979.
Izzard, Wendy
    Rural-Urban Migration of Women in Botswana: Final
    Fieldwork Report. Gaborone, Botswana: Ministry of
    Finance and Development Planning. Central Statistics
    Office. Rural Sociology Unit. August, 1979. 50p.
Izzard, Wendy
    "The Impact of Migration on the Roles of Women." (In)
    Botswana. Ministry of Finance and Development Planning.
    Migration in Botswana: Patterns, Causes and Consequences.
    Gaborone, Botswana: The Ministry. Central Statistics
    Office. 1982. pp.657-718.
Kerven, Carol
    National Migration Study: Urban and Rural Female
    Headed-Households' Dependence on Agriculture. Gaborone,
    Botswana: Central Statistics Office. National Migration
    Study. Issue Paper #4. 1979. 65p.

MISCELLANEOUS

Abdelraman, Mohammed A.
    Study of Age-Sex Composition and Some Estimates of

Fertility and Mortality Levels for Botswana. Legon, Ghana: Regional Institute for Population Studies Newsletter. #12. January, 1979. pp. 12-21.

ORGANIZATIONS

Kaha, Ulla
    Voluntary Women's Organizations in Botswana. Gaborone, Botswana: Swedish International Development Agency. Mimeo. 1979.
Motsete, Ruth K.
    The Role of Women's Organizations in Development in Botswana. Addis Ababa, Ethiopia: United Nations Economic Commission for Africa. African Training and Research Centre for Women. Occasional Papers Series #M82-707. March, 1982. 11p.

POLITICS AND GOVERNMENT

Collier, J.F. and Rosaldo, M.Z.
    "Politics and Gender in Simple Societies." (In) Ortner, Sherry B. and Whitehead, Harriet (eds.). Sexual Meanings. New York: Cambridge University Press. 1981. pp. 275-329.
Griffiths, Anne
    "Support for Women With Dependent Children Under the Customary System of the Bakwena and the Roman-Dutch Common and Statutory Law of Botswana." Journal of Legal Pluralism and Unofficial Law. #22 1984. pp. 1-16.
Lee, Richard
    "Politics, Sexual and Non-Sexual, in an Egalitarian Society (With Special Reference to the !Kung)." (In) Leacock, E. and Lee, Richard (eds.). Politics and History in Band Societies. Cambridge, England: Cambridge University Press. 1982. pp. 37-59.
Yates, Leslie M.
    "Integration of Women in Development in Southern Africa: An Evaluation With Recommendations for U.S. AID Programs in Botswana, Lesotho and Zambia." Sadex. November-December, 1979. pp. 1-15.
Yates, Leslie M.
    Integration of Women in Development in Zambia, Botswana and Lesotho: AID's Efforts. Washington, D.C.: U.S. Department of State. U.S. Agency for International Development. Southern Africa Development Analysis. 1978. 92p.

RELIGION AND WITCHCRAFT

Lagerwerf, Levy
    'They Pray for You...': Independent Churches and Women in
    Botswana. Leiden, Netherlands: Interuniversitaic
    Instituut Voor Missiologie en Oecumenica. IIMO Research
    Pamphlet #6. 1982. 135p.
Larson, Thomas J.
    "Sorcery and Witchcraft of the Hambukushu of Ngamiland."
    Anthropos. Volume 75 #3/4 1980. pp. 416-432.
Larson, Thomas J.
    "Hambukushu Girls' Puberty Rites." Botswana Notes and
    Records. Volume 11 1979. pp. 33-36.

RESEARCH

Henderson, Francene I.
    Women in Botswana: An Annotated Bibliography. Gaborone,
    Botswana: University of Botswana and Swaziland. National
    Institute of Development and Cultural Research.
    Documentation Unit Working Bibliography #4. March, 1981.
    20p.
Horn, Nancy and Nkambule-Kanyima, Brenda
    Resource Guide: Women in Agriculture in Botswana. East
    Lansing, Michigan: Bean/Cowpea CRSP (Collaborative
    Research Support Program. 1984.
Peters, Pauline E.
    "Gender, Developmental Cycles and Historical Process: a
    Critique of Recent Research on Women in Botswana."
    Journal of Southern African Studies. Volume 10 #1 1983.
    pp. 100-122.
Peters, Pauline E.
    "Gender, Developmental Cycles, and Historical Process: A
    Critique of Recent Research on Women in Botswana."
    Journal of Southern African Studies. Volume 10 #1
    October, 1983. pp. 100-122.
Yates, Leslie M.
    "Integration of Women in Development in Southern Africa:
    An Evaluation With Recommendations for U.S. AID Programs
    in Botswana, Lesotho and Zambia." Sadex.
    November-December, 1979. pp. 1-15.

SEX ROLES

Alverson, Hoyt
    Mind in the Heart of Darkness: Value and Self-Idenity
    Among the Tswana of Southern Africa. New Haven,
    Connecticut: Yale University Press. 1978. 299p.
Aromasodu, M.C.
    "Traditional Practices Affecting the Health of Women in
    Pregnancy and Childbirth." Paper Presented at the

Seminar on Traditional Practices Affecting the Health of
Women and Children. World Conference of the United
Nations Decade for Women. Copenhagen, Denmark. July
14-30, 1980.
Barnard, Alan
"Sex Roles Among the Nharo Bushmen of Botswana." Africa.
Volume 50 #2 1980. pp. 115-124.
Botswana. Ministry of Agriculture
Report on the Involvement of Women in the Integrated
Farming Pilot Project. Gaborone, Botswana: Ministry of
Agriculture. Department of Field Services. 1976. 10p.
Brown, Barbara B.
"Impact of Male Labour Migration on Women in Botswana."
African Affairs. Volume 82 #328 July, 1983. pp.
367-388.
Brown, Barbara B.
"The Impact of Male Labor Migration on Women in
Botswana." Paper Presented at the Annual Meeting of the
African Studies Association. Paper #19. Bloomington,
Indiana. October 21-24, 1981.
Collier, J.F. and Rosaldo, M.Z.
"Politics and Gender in Simple Societies." (In) Ortner,
Sherry B. and Whitehead, Harriet (eds.). Sexual
Meanings. New York: Cambridge University Press. 1981.
pp. 275-329.
Comaroff, John L. and Roberts, S.
"Marriage and Extra-Marital Sexuality: The Dialectics of
Legal Change Among the Kgatla." Journal of African Law.
Volume 21 #1 1977. pp. 97-123.
Cooper, David
Rural Urban Migration and Female Headed Households in
Botswana Towns: Case Study of Unskilled Women Workers and
Female Self Employment in a Site and Service Area,
Selebi-Phikwe. Gaborone, Botswana: Central Statistical
Office. Mimeograph. March, 1979.
Cooper, David
"Rural-Urban Migration of Female-Headed Households in
Botswana Towns." (In) Kerven, Carol (ed.). Workshop on
Migration Research. Gaborone, Botswana: Central
Statistics Office. Ministry of Finance and Development
Planning. 1979.
Date-Bah, Eugenia and Stevens, Yvette
"Rural Women in Africa and Technological Change: Some
Issues." Labour and Society. Volume 6 #2 April-June,
1981. pp. 149-162.
Fortmann, Louise P.
"Economic Status and Women's Participation in
Agriculture: A Botswana Case Study." Rural Sociology.
Volume 49 #3 August, 1984. pp. 452-464.
Fortmann, Louise P.
Who Plows: The Effect of Economic Status on Women's
Participation in Agriculture in Botswana. Madison,
Wisconsin. Mimeo. 1983. 40p.

Guyer, Jane I.
    "Women in the Rural Economy: Contemporary Variations."
    (In) Hay, Margaret J. and Stichter, Sharon (eds.).
    African Women South of the Sahara. New York: Longman.
    1984. pp. 19-32.
Horn, Nancy and Nkambule-Kanyima, Brenda
    Resource Guide: Women in Agriculture in Botswana. East
    Lansing, Michigan: Bean/Cowpea CRSP (Collaborative
    Research Support Program. 1984.
Izzard, Wendy
    "Migrants and Mothers: Case Studies From Botswana."
    Journal of Southern African Studies. Volume 11 #2 1985.
    pp. 258-280.
Izzard, Wendy
    "Preliminary Ideas on the Rural-Urban Migration of
    Female-Headed Households Within Botswana." (In) Kerven,
    Carol (ed.). Workshop on Migration Research. Gaborone,
    Botswana: Ministry of Finance and Development Planning.
    Central Statistics Office. 1979.
Izzard, Wendy
    "The Impact of Migration on the Roles of Women." (In)
    Botswana. Ministry of Finance and Development Planning.
    Migration in Botswana: Patterns, Causes and Consequences.
    Gaborone, Botswana: The Ministry. Central Statistics
    Office. 1982. pp.657-718.
Kerven, Carol
    National Migration Study: Urban and Rural Female
    Headed-Households' Dependence on Agriculture. Gaborone,
    Botswana: Central Statistics Office. National Migration
    Study. Issue Paper #4. 1979. 65p.
Kinsman, Margaret
    "Beasts of Burden: The Subordination of Southern Tswana
    Women, ca. 1800-1840." Journal of Southern African
    Studies. Volume 10 #1 1983. pp. 39-54.
Konner, M.J.
    "Maternal Care, Infant Behavior and Development Among the
    !Kung." (In) Lee, R.B. and DeVore, I. (eds.). Kalahari
    Hunter-Gatherers, Studies of the !Kung San and Their
    Neighbors. Cambridge, Massachusetts: Harvard University
    Press. 1976. pp. 218-246.
Kossoudji, Sherrie and Mueller, Eva
    "The Economic and Demographic Status of Female-Headed
    Households in Rural Botswana." Economic Development and
    Cultural Change. Volume 31 #4 July, 1983. pp. 831-859.
Lee, Richard B.
    The !Kung San: Men, Women and Work in a Foraging Society.
    Cambridge, New York: Cambridge University Press. 1979.
    526p.
Motshologane, S.R.
    "Influence of Urbanization on the Role and Status of
    Husband and Wife in the Tswana Family." South African
    Journal of Sociology. Volume 17 April, 1978. pp.
    83-90.

Mueller, Eva
    "Household Structure, Time Use, and Income Distribution
    in Rural Botswana." Paper Presented at the Annual
    Meeting of the Population Association of America.
    Philadelphia, Pennsylvania. April 27, 1979.
Otaala, Barnabas
    "The Changing Family in a Changing World: The Botswana
    Case." Paper Presented at the Seminar on the Changing
    Family in the African Context, Maseru, Lesotho, 1983.
    Paris: United Nations Educational, Scientific and
    Cultural Organization. 1984. 17p.
Peters, Pauline E.
    "Gender, Developmental Cycles and Historical Process: a
    Critique of Recent Research on Women in Botswana."
    Journal of Southern African Studies. Volume 10 #1 1983.
    pp. 100-122.
Peters, Pauline E.
    "Gender, Developmental Cycles, and Historical Process: A
    Critique of Recent Research on Women in Botswana."
    Journal of Southern African Studies. Volume 10 #1
    October, 1983. pp. 100-122.
Peters, Pauline E.
    "Household Management in Botswana: Cattle Crops and Wage
    Labor." Paper Presented at a Conference in Bellagio,
    Lake Como, Italy. 1984.
Roberts, Simon
    "The Kgatla Marriage: Concepts of Validity." (In)
    Roberts, Simon (ed.). Law and the Family in Africa.
    Hague, Netherlands: Mouton. 1977. pp. 241-260.
Selolwane, Onalenna
    "Domestic Workers in Botswana." Women in Southern
    African History. #2 May, 1983. pp. 33-38.
Shostak, Marjorie
    "A !Kung Women's Memories of Childhood." (In) Lee,
    Richard B. and DeVore, I. (eds.). Kalahari
    Hunter-Gatherers: Studies of the !Kung San and Their
    Neighbors. Cambridge, Massachusetts: Harvard University
    Press. 1976. pp. 246-277.
Shostak, Marjorie
    Nisa, the Life and Words of a !Kung Woman. New York:
    Vintage Books. 1983. 402p.
Tiffany, Sharon W.
    Women, Work and Motherhood: The Power of Female Sexuality
    in the Workplace. Englewood Cliffs, New Jersey:
    Prentice-Hall. 1982. 148p.
Volkman, Toby A.
    The San in Transition: Volume One: A Guide to N!Ai, the
    Story of a !Kung Woman. Cambridge, Massachusetts:
    Documentary Educational Resources. 1982. 56p.

STATUS OF WOMEN

Brown, Barbara B.
  Women, Migrant Labor and Social Change in Botswana.
  Boston: Boston University. African Studies Center.
  Working Paper in African Studies. #41. 1980. 21p.
Fortmann, Louise P.
  "Economic Status and Women's Participation in
  Agriculture: A Botswana Case Study." Rural Sociology.
  Volume 49 #3 August, 1984. pp. 452-464.
Molokomme, Athaliah
  "Marriage: What Every Woman Wants or a Declaration of
  'Civil Death'? Some Legal Aspects of the Status of
  Married Women in Botswana." Pula. Volume 4 #1 1984.
  pp. 70-79.
Motshologane, S.R.
  "Influence of Urbanization on the Role and Status of
  Husband and Wife in the Tswana Family." South African
  Journal of Sociology. Volume 17 April, 1978. pp.
  83-90.
Otaala, Barnabas
  "The Changing Family in a Changing World: The Botswana
  Case." Paper Presented at the Seminar on the Changing
  Family in the African Context, Maseru, Lesotho, 1983.
  Paris: United Nations Educational, Scientific and
  Cultural Organization. 1984. 17p.
Peters, Pauline E.
  "Gender, Developmental Cycles, and Historical Process: A
  Critique of Recent Research on Women in Botswana."
  Journal of Southern African Studies. Volume 10 #1
  October, 1983. pp. 100-122.

URBANIZATION

Bryant, Coralie
  "Women Migrants, Urbanization and Social Change: The
  Botswana Case." Paper Presented at the American
  Political Science Association Annual Meeting.
  Washington, D.C. September, 1977.
Cooper, David
  Rural Urban Migration and Female Headed Households in
  Botswana Towns: Case Study of Unskilled Women Workers and
  Female Self Employment in a Site and Service Area,
  Selebi-Phikwe. Gaborone, Botswana: Central Statistical
  Office. Mimeograph. March, 1979.
Cooper, David
  "Rural-Urban Migration of Female-Headed Households in
  Botswana Towns." (In) Kerven, Carol (ed.). Workshop on
  Migration Research. Gaborone, Botswana: Central
  Statistics Office. Ministry of Finance and Development
  Planning. 1979.

Izzard, Wendy
  "Preliminary Ideas on the Rural-Urban Migration of
  Female-Headed Households Within Botswana." (In) Kerven,
  Carol (ed.). Workshop on Migration Research. Gaborone,
  Botswana: Ministry of Finance and Development Planning.
  Central Statistics Office. 1979.
Izzard, Wendy
  Rural-Urban Migration of Women in Botswana: Final
  Fieldwork Report. Gaborone, Botswana: Ministry of
  Finance and Development Planning. Central Statistics
  Office. Rural Sociology Unit. August, 1979. 50p.
Kerven, Carol
  National Migration Study: Urban and Rural Female
  Headed-Households' Dependence on Agriculture. Gaborone,
  Botswana: Central Statistics Office. National Migration
  Study. Issue Paper #4. 1979. 65p.
Motshologane, S.R.
  "Influence of Urbanization on the Role and Status of
  Husband and Wife in the Tswana Family." South African
  Journal of Sociology. Volume 17 April, 1978. pp.
  83-90.

WOMEN AND THEIR CHILDREN

Griffiths, Anne
  "Support for Women With Dependent Children Under the
  Customary System of the Bakwena and the Roman-Dutch
  Common and Statutory Law of Botswana." Journal of Legal
  Pluralism and Unofficial Law. #22 1984. pp. 1-16.
Izzard, Wendy
  "Migrants and Mothers: Case Studies From Botswana."
  Journal of Southern African Studies. Volume 11 #2 1985.
  pp. 258-280.
Konner, M.J.
  "Maternal Care, Infant Behavior and Development Among the
  !Kung." (In) Lee, R.B. and DeVore, I. (eds.). Kalahari
  Hunter-Gatherers, Studies of the !Kung San and Their
  Neighbors. Cambridge, Massachusetts: Harvard University
  Press. 1976. pp. 218-246.
Tiffany, Sharon W.
  Women, Work and Motherhood: The Power of Female Sexuality
  in the Workplace. Englewood Cliffs, New Jersey:
  Prentice-Hall. 1982. 148p.

Comoro Islands

Lambek, Michael
    "Virgin Marriage and the Autonomy of Women in Mayotte."
    Signs. Volume 9 #2 Winter, 1983. pp. 264-281.
Ottenheimer, M.
    "Some Problems and Prospects in Residence and Marriage."
    American Anthropologist. Volume 86 June, 1984. pp.
    351-358.
Shepherd, Gilliam M.
    "Two Marriage Forms in the Comoro Islands: An
    Investigation." Africa. Volume 47 #4 1977. pp.
    344-359.

Lesotho

AGRICULTURE

Butler, Lorna
   "Lesotho Farming Systems: A Closer Look at Women Farm
   Managers and the Problems of Subsistence Production."
   Paper Presented at the Eleventh International Congress of
   Anthropological and Ethnographical Sciences. Vancouver,
   British Columbia. 1983.
Gay, Judy S.
   "Wage Employment in Rural Basotho Women: A Case Study."
   South African Labour Bulletin. Volume 6 #4 November,
   1980. pp. 40-57.
Gay, Judy S.
   Women and Development in Lesotho. Maseru, Lesotho: U.S.
   Agency for International Development. 1982. 84p.
Janelid, Ingrid
   Promoting the Participation of Women in Rural
   Development. Report on Mission to Lesotho. Rome: United
   Nations Food and Agriculture Organization. September,
   1977.
Madland, M.
   Women in Agriculture. Maseru, Lesotho: Thaba Bosiu Rural
   Development Planning and Evaluation Unit. 1977.
Mickelwait, Donald R. and Riegelman, Mary Ann and Sweet,
Charles F.
   Women in Rural Development: A Survey of the Roles of
   Women in Ghana, Lesotho, Kenya, Nigeria... Boulder,
   Colorado: Westview Press. 1976. 224p.
Safilios-Rothschild, Constantina
   The Persistence of Women's Invisibility in Agriculture:
   Theoretical and Policy Lessons From Lesotho and Sierra
   Leone. New York: Population Council. Center for Policy
   Studies. Working Paper #88. September, 1982. 31p.
Safilios-Rothschild, Constantina
   "The Persistence of Women's Invisibility in Agriculture:

Theoretical and Policy Lessons From Lesotho and Sierra
Leone." Economic Development and Cultural Change.
Volume 33 #2 January, 1985. pp. 299-317.
Wykstra, Ronald A.
Farm Labor in Lesotho: Scarcity or Surplus? Fort
Collins, Colorado: Colorado State University. Economics
Department. LASA (Lesotho Agricultural Sector Analysis
Project) Discussion Paper Series #5. September, 1978.
42p.
Yates, Leslie M.
"Integration of Women in Development in Southern Africa:
An Evaluation With Recommendations for U.S. AID Programs
in Botswana, Lesotho and Zambia." Sadex.
November-December, 1979. pp. 1-15.
Yates, Leslie M.
Integration of Women in Development in Zambia, Botswana
and Lesotho: AID's Efforts. Washington, D.C.: U.S.
Department of State. U.S. Agency for International
Development. Southern Africa Development Analysis.
1978. 92p.

BIBLIOGRAPHIES

Anonymous
The Role of Women in Lesotho's Development: An Annotated
Bibliography. Maseru, Lesotho: National University of
Lesotho. Institute of Southern African Studies. 1983.

CULTURAL ROLES

Anonymous
"South Africa and Lesotho: Three Lesbian Conversations."
Connexions. #3 Winter, 1982.
Gay, Judith S.
"'Mummies and Babies' and Friend and Lovers in Lesotho."
Cambridge Anthropology. Volume 5 #3 1979. pp. 32-61.
Gay, Judith S.
"Basotho Women's Options: A Study of Marital Careers in
Rural Lesotho." Ph.D. Dissertation: University of
Cambridge. Cambridge, England. 1980.
Gay, Judy S.
"Basotho Women as Migrant Workers." Paper Presented at
the Seminar on Women and Development. Sussex, England:
University of Sussex. May 16, 1979.
Gay, Judy S.
"Women Without Men: Female Social Networks in a Male
Controlled Society." (In) Lesotho. Ministry of Planning
and Statistics. Lesotho Fertility Survey. Maseru,
Lesotho: Central Bureau of Statistics. 1981.
Gordon, Elizabeth
"An Analysis of the Impact of Labour Migration on the

Lives of Women in Lesotho." Journal of Development Studies. Volume 17 #3 April, 1981. pp. 59-76.

Gordon, Elizabeth
"Proposals for Easing the Plight of Migrant Workers Families in Lesotho." (In) Bohning, W.R. (ed.). Black Migration to South Africa: A Selection of Policy Oriented Research. Geneva: International Labour Office. 1981.

Gordon, Elizabeth
The Women Left Behind: A Study of Wives of the Migrant Workers of Lesotho. Geneva: International Labour Office. World Employment Programme Research Working Paper. December, 1978. 110p.

Gordon, Elizabeth
"An Analysis of the Impact of Labour Migration on the Lives of Women in Lesotho." (In) Nelson, Nici (ed.). African Women in the Development Process. Totowa, New Jersey: Frank Cass. 1981. pp. 59-76.

Janelid, Ingrid
Promoting the Participation of Women in Rural Development. Report on Mission to Lesotho. Rome: United Nations Food and Agriculture Organization. September, 1977.

Kimane, I.
"Images of Basotho Women in Society: Their Contribution to Development." Journal of Eastern African Research and Development. Volume 15 1985. pp. 180-187.

Lesthaeghe, Ron J. and Eelens, Frank
Social Organization and Reproductive Regimes: Lessons From Sub-Saharan Africa and Historical Western Europe. Brussels, Belgium: Vrije Universiteit Brussel. Interuniversity Programme in Demography. IDP Working Paper #1985-1. 1985. 64p.

Low, Allan
"From Farm-Homestead Theory to Rural Development Policy in Lesotho and Swaziland." (In) de Vletter, Fion (ed.). Labour Migration and Agricultural Development in Southern Africa. Rome: United Nations Food and Agriculture Organization. 1982.

Madland, M.
Women in Agriculture. Maseru, Lesotho: Thaba Bosiu Rural Development Planning and Evaluation Unit. 1977.

Malahleha, Gwen M.
"Contradictions and Ironies: Women of Lesotho." off our backs. Volume 15 March, 1985. pp. 8-9.

Mamashela, M.
"Women and Development in Africa: With Special Reference to the Legal Disabilities of Married Women in Lesotho." Journal of Eastern African Research and Development. Volume 15 1985. pp. 165-170.

Maqutu, W.C.
"Lesotho's African Marriage is Not a 'Customary Union'." Comparative and International Law Journal of Southern Africa. Volume 16 #3 November, 1983. pp. 374-382.

Mhloyi, Marvellous M.
"Fertility Determinants: A Comparative Study Of Kenya and Lesotho." Ph.D Dissertation: University of Pennsylvania. Philadelphia, Pennsylvania. 1984. 342p.

Molise, Ngoakoane M.
Nuptiality Patterns and Differentials in Lesotho. Cairo: Cairo Demographic Centre. CDC Research Monograph Series #12. 1984. pp. 399-422.

Mpiti, A.M. and Kalule-Sabiti, I.
The Proximate Determinants of Fertility in Lesotho. Voorburg, Netherlands: International Statistical Institute. World Fertility Survey Reports #78. July, 1985. 44p.

Mueller, Martha B.
"Women and Men in Rural Lesotho: The Periphery of the Periphery." Ph.D Dissertation: Brandeis University. Waltham, Massachusetts. 1977. 385p.

Mueller, Martha B.
"Women and Men, Power and Powerless in Lesotho." (In) Wellesley Editorial Committee. Women and National Development: The Complexities of Change. Chicago: University of Chicago Press. 1977. pp. 154-166.

Mueller, Martha B.
"Women and Men, Power and Powerlessness in Lesotho." Signs. Volume 3 #1 Autumn, 1977. pp. 154-166.

Murray, Colin G.
"The Symbolism and Politics of Bohadi: Household Recruitment and Marriage by Instalment in Lesotho." (In) Krige, E.J. and Comaroff, J.L. (eds.). Essays on African Marriage in Southern Africa. Cape Town, South Africa: Juta. 1981.

Murray, Colin G.
Families Divided: The Impact of Migration in Lesotho. Cambridge, New York: Cambridge University Press. African Studies Studies #29. 1981. 219p.

Murray, Colin G.
"Keeping House in Lesotho: A Study on the Impact of Oscillating Migration." Ph.D Dissertation: Cambridge University. Cambridge, New York. 1976. 350p.

Murray, Colin G.
"Marital Strategy in Lesotho: The Redistribution of Migrant Earnings." African Studies. Volume 35 #2 1976. pp. 99-122.

Murray, Colin G.
"Sotho Fertility Symbolism." African Studies. Volume 39 #1 1980. pp. 65-76.

Murray, Colin G.
"The High Price of Bridewealth. Migrant Labour and the Position of Women in Lesotho." Journal of African Law. Volume 21 #1 1977. pp. 79-96.

Murray, Colin G.
"The Work of Men, Women and the Ancestors: Social Reproduction in the Periphery of South Africa." (In)

Wallman, Sandra (ed.). Social Anthropology of Work. New
York: Academic Press. 1979. pp. 337-363.

Olusanya, P.O.
The Demographic, Health, Economic and Social Impact of
Family Planning in Selected African Countries. Addis
Ababa, Ethiopia: United Nations Economic Commission for
Africa. ECA/PD/1985-9. March, 1985. 97p.

Poulter, Sebastian
Family Law and Litigation in Basotho Society. Oxford,
England: Clarendon Press. 1976. 361p.

Poulter, Sebastian
"Marriage, Divorce and Legitimacy in Lesotho." Journal
of African Law. Volume 21 #1 Spring, 1977. pp. 66-78.

Poulter, Sebastian
"The Choice of Law Dilemma in Lesotho: Some Criteria for
Decision Making in Family Law." (In) Roberts, Simon
(ed.). Law and the Family in Africa. Hague,
Netherlands: Mouton. 1977. pp. 169-182.

Rubens, Bernice
"The Gold Widows." ISIS International Bulletin. #9
Autumn, 1978. pp. 18-21.

Safilios-Rothschild, Constantina
The Persistence of Women's Invisibility in Agriculture:
Theoretical and Policy Lessons From Lesotho and Sierra
Leone. New York: Population Council. Center for Policy
Studies. Working Paper #88. September, 1982. 31p.

Safilios-Rothschild, Constantina
"The Persistence of Women's Invisibility in Agriculture:
Theoretical and Policy Lessons From Lesotho and Sierra
Leone." Economic Development and Cultural Change.
Volume 33 #2 January, 1985. pp. 299-317.

Sebatane, E. Molapi
"The Family in Lesotho: Perspectives on its Changing Life
and Structure." Paper Presented at the Seminar on the
Changing Family in the African Context, Maseru,
Lesotho, 1983. Paris: United Nations Educational,
Scientific and Cultural Organization. 1984. 24p.

United Nations Economic Commission for Africa (UNECA)
Nuptiality and Fertility (A Comparative Analysis of WFS
Data). Addis Ababa, Ethiopia: UNECA. African Population
Studies Series #5. 1983. 96p.

Wilkinson, R.C.
"Migration in Lesotho: Some Comparative Aspects With
Particular Reference to the Role of Women." Geography.
Volume 68 #300 Part Three June, 1982. pp. 208-224.

DEVELOPMENT AND TECHNOLOGY

Anonymous
"Mohair Industry on the Rise: Women in Lesotho Spin
Mohair Yarn, Boosting Income and a Vital National
Industry." Agenda. Volume 2 #7 September, 1979. pp.
7-10.

Anonymous
    The Role of Women in Lesotho's Development: An Annotated
    Bibliography. Maseru, Lesotho: National University of
    Lesotho. Institute of Southern African Studies. 1983.
Butler, Lorna
    "Lesotho Farming Systems: A Closer Look at Women Farm
    Managers and the Problems of Subsistence Production."
    Paper Presented at the Eleventh International Congress of
    Anthropological and Ethnographical Sciences. Vancouver,
    British Columbia. 1983.
Gay, Judy S.
    Women and Development in Lesotho. Maseru, Lesotho: U.S.
    Agency for International Development. 1982. 84p.
Janelid, Ingrid
    Promoting the Participation of Women in Rural
    Development. Report on Mission to Lesotho. Rome: United
    Nations Food and Agriculture Organization. September,
    1977.
Kimane, I.
    "Images of Basotho Women in Society: Their Contribution
    to Development." Journal of Eastern African Research and
    Development. Volume 15 1985. pp. 180-187.
Madland, M.
    Women in Agriculture. Maseru, Lesotho: Thaba Bosiu Rural
    Development Planning and Evaluation Unit. 1977.
Mamashela, M.
    "Women and Development in Africa: With Special Reference
    to the Legal Disabilities of Married Women in Lesotho."
    Journal of Eastern African Research and Development.
    Volume 15 1985. pp. 165-170.
Mickelwait, Donald R. and Riegelman, Mary Ann and Sweet,
Charles F.
    Women in Rural Development: A Survey of the Roles of
    Women in Ghana, Lesotho, Kenya, Nigeria... Boulder,
    Colorado: Westview Press. 1976. 224p.
Mueller, Martha B.
    "Women and Men, Power and Powerless in Lesotho." (In)
    Wellesley Editorial Committee. Women and National
    Development: The Complexities of Change. Chicago:
    University of Chicago Press. 1977. pp. 154-166.
Mueller, Martha B.
    "Women and Men, Power and Powerlessness in Lesotho."
    Signs. Volume 3 #1 Autumn, 1977. pp. 154-166.
Safilios-Rothschild, Constantina
    The Persistence of Women's Invisibility in Agriculture:
    Theoretical and Policy Lessons From Lesotho and Sierra
    Leone. New York: Population Council. Center for Policy
    Studies. Working Paper #88. September, 1982. 31p.
Safilios-Rothschild, Constantina
    "The Persistence of Women's Invisibility in Agriculture:
    Theoretical and Policy Lessons From Lesotho and Sierra
    Leone." Economic Development and Cultural Change.
    Volume 33 #2 January, 1985. pp. 299-317.

Yates, Leslie M.
  "Integration of Women in Development in Southern Africa:
  An Evaluation With Recommendations for U.S. AID Programs
  in Botswana, Lesotho and Zambia." Sadex.
  November-December, 1979. pp. 1-15.
Yates, Leslie M.
  Integration of Women in Development in Zambia, Botswana
  and Lesotho: AID's Efforts. Washington, D.C.: U.S.
  Department of State. U.S. Agency for International
  Development. Southern Africa Development Analysis.
  1978. 92p.

DIVORCE

Poulter, Sebastian
  "Marriage, Divorce and Legitimacy in Lesotho." Journal
  of African Law. Volume 21 #1 Spring, 1977. pp. 66-78.

ECONOMICS

Anonymous
  "Mohair Industry on the Rise: Women in Lesotho Spin
  Mohair Yarn, Boosting Income and a Vital National
  Industry." Agenda. Volume 2 #7 September, 1979. pp.
  7-10.
Anonymous
  The Role of Women in Lesotho's Development: An Annotated
  Bibliography. Maseru, Lesotho: National University of
  Lesotho. Institute of Southern African Studies. 1983.
Butler, Lorna
  "Lesotho Farming Systems: A Closer Look at Women Farm
  Managers and the Problems of Subsistence Production."
  Paper Presented at the Eleventh International Congress of
  Anthropological and Ethnographical Sciences. Vancouver,
  British Columbia. 1983.
Cobbe, Louise B.
  "Women's Income Generation and Informal Learning in
  Lesotho: A Policy-Related Ethnography." Ph.D
  Dissertation: Florida State University. Tallahassee,
  Florida. 1985. 308p.
Gay, Judy S.
  "Basotho Women Migrants: A Case Study." IDS Bulletin.
  Volume 11 #4 1980.
Gay, Judy S.
  "Basotho Women as Migrant Workers." Paper Presented at
  the Seminar on Women and Development. Sussex, England:
  University of Sussex. May 16, 1979.
Gay, Judy S.
  "Wage Employment in Rural Basotho Women: A Case Study."
  South African Labour Bulletin. Volume 6 #4 November,
  1980. pp. 40-57.

Gay, Judy S.
"Women Without Men: Female Social Networks in a Male
Controlled Society." (In) Lesotho. Ministry of Planning
and Statistics. Lesotho Fertility Survey. Maseru,
Lesotho: Central Bureau of Statistics. 1981.

Gordon, Elizabeth
The Women Left Behind: A Study of Wives of the Migrant
Workers of Lesotho. Geneva: International Labour Office.
World Employment Programme Research Working Paper.
December, 1978. 110p.

Gordon, Elizabeth
"An Analysis of the Impact of Labour Migration on the
Lives of Women in Lesotho." (In) Nelson, Nici (ed.).
African Women in the Development Process. Totowa, New
Jersey: Frank Cass. 1981. pp. 59-76.

Low, Allan
"From Farm-Homestead Theory to Rural Development Policy
in Lesotho and Swaziland." (In) de Vletter, Fion (ed.).
Labour Migration and Agricultural Development in Southern
Africa. Rome: United Nations Food and Agriculture
Organization. 1982.

Mickelwait, Donald R. and Riegelman, Mary Ann and Sweet,
Charles F.
Women in Rural Development: A Survey of the Roles of
Women in Ghana, Lesotho, Kenya, Nigeria... Boulder,
Colorado: Westview Press. 1976. 224p.

Murray, Colin G.
Families Divided: The Impact of Migration in Lesotho.
Cambridge, New York: Cambridge University Press. African
Studies Studies #29. 1981. 219p.

Murray, Colin G.
"Keeping House in Lesotho: A Study on the Impact of
Oscillating Migration." Ph.D Dissertation: Cambridge
University. Cambridge, New York. 1976. 350p.

Murray, Colin G.
"The High Price of Bridewealth. Migrant Labour and the
Position of Women in Lesotho." Journal of African Law.
Volume 21 #1 1977. pp. 79-96.

Murray, Colin G.
"The Work of Men, Women and the Ancestors: Social
Reproduction in the Periphery of South Africa." (In)
Wallman, Sandra (ed.). Social Anthropology of Work. New
York: Academic Press. 1979. pp. 337-363.

Safilios-Rothschild, Constantina
The Persistence of Women's Invisibility in Agriculture:
Theoretical and Policy Lessons From Lesotho and Sierra
Leone. New York: Population Council. Center for Policy
Studies. Working Paper #88. September, 1982. 31p.

Safilios-Rothschild, Constantina
"The Persistence of Women's Invisibility in Agriculture:
Theoretical and Policy Lessons From Lesotho and Sierra
Leone." Economic Development and Cultural Change.
Volume 33 #2 January, 1985. pp. 299-317.

Wilkinson, R.C.
    "Migration in Lesotho: Some Comparative Aspects With
    Particular Reference to the Role of Women." Geography.
    Volume 68 #300 Part Three June, 1982. pp. 208-224.
Wykstra, Ronald A.
    Farm Labor in Lesotho: Scarcity or Surplus? Fort
    Collins, Colorado: Colorado State University. Economics
    Department. LASA (Lesotho Agricultural Sector Analysis
    Project) Discussion Paper Series #5. September, 1978.
    42p.
Yates, Leslie M.
    "Integration of Women in Development in Southern Africa:
    An Evaluation With Recommendations for U.S. AID Programs
    in Botswana, Lesotho and Zambia." Sadex.
    November-December, 1979. pp. 1-15.
Yates, Leslie M.
    Integration of Women in Development in Zambia, Botswana
    and Lesotho: AID's Efforts. Washington, D.C.: U.S.
    Department of State. U.S. Agency for International
    Development. Southern Africa Development Analysis.
    1978. 92p.

EDUCATION AND TRAINING

Cobbe, Louise B.
    "Women's Income Generation and Informal Learning in
    Lesotho: A Policy-Related Ethnography." Ph.D
    Dissertation: Florida State University. Tallahassee,
    Florida. 1985. 308p.
Sebatane, E. Molapi
    "The Family in Lesotho: Perspectives on its Changing Life
    and Structure." Paper Presented at the Seminar on the
    Changing Family in the African Context, Maseru,
    Lesotho, 1983. Paris: United Nations Educational,
    Scientific and Cultural Organization. 1984. 24p.

EMPLOYMENT AND LABOR

Anonymous
    "Mohair Industry on the Rise: Women in Lesotho Spin
    Mohair Yarn, Boosting Income and a Vital National
    Industry." Agenda. Volume 2 #7 September, 1979. pp.
    7-10.
Cobbe, Louise B.
    "Women's Income Generation and Informal Learning in
    Lesotho: A Policy-Related Ethnography." Ph.D
    Dissertation: Florida State University. Tallahassee,
    Florida. 1985. 308p.
Gay, Judith S.
    "Basotho Women's Options: A Study of Marital Careers in
    Rural Lesotho." Ph.D. Dissertation: University of
    Cambridge. Cambridge, England. 1980.

Gay, Judy S.
"Basotho Women Migrants: A Case Study." IDS Bulletin.
Volume 11 #4 1980.
Gay, Judy S.
"Basotho Women as Migrant Workers." Paper Presented at
the Seminar on Women and Development. Sussex, England:
University of Sussex. May 16, 1979.
Gay, Judy S.
"Wage Employment in Rural Basotho Women: A Case Study."
South African Labour Bulletin. Volume 6 #4 November,
1980. pp. 40-57.
Gordon, Elizabeth
"An Analysis of the Impact of Labour Migration on the
Lives of Women in Lesotho." Journal of Development
Studies. Volume 17 #3 April, 1981. pp. 59-76.
Gordon, Elizabeth
The Women Left Behind: A Study of Wives of the Migrant
Workers of Lesotho. Geneva: International Labour Office.
World Employment Programme Research Working Paper.
December, 1978. 110p.
Gordon, Elizabeth
An Analysis of the Impact of Labour Migration on the
Lives of Women in Lesotho. (In) Nelson, Nici (ed.).
African Women in the Development Process. Totowa, New
Jersey: Frank Cass. 1981. pp. 59-76.
Kimane, I.
"Images of Basotho Women in Society: Their Contribution
to Development." Journal of Eastern African Research and
Development. Volume 15 1985. pp. 180-187.
Low, Allan
"From Farm-Homestead Theory to Rural Development Policy
in Lesotho and Swaziland." (In) de Vletter, Fion (ed.).
Labour Migration and Agricultural Development in Southern
Africa. Rome: United Nations Food and Agriculture
Organization. 1982.
Mickelwait, Donald R. and Riegelman, Mary Ann and Sweet,
Charles F.
Women in Rural Development: A Survey of the Roles of
Women in Ghana, Lesotho, Kenya, Nigeria... Boulder,
Colorado: Westview Press. 1976. 224p.
Murray, Colin G.
"The Effects of Migrant Labour: A Review of the Evidence
in Lesotho." South African Labour Bulletin. Volume 6 #4
November, 1980.
Murray, Colin G.
Families Divided: The Impact of Migration in Lesotho.
Cambridge, New York: Cambridge University Press. African
Studies Studies #29. 1981. 219p.
Murray, Colin G.
"Keeping House in Lesotho: A Study on the Impact of
Oscillating Migration." Ph.D Dissertation: Cambridge
University. Cambridge, New York. 1976. 350p.

Murray, Colin G.
"The High Price of Bridewealth. Migrant Labour and the
Position of Women in Lesotho." Journal of African Law.
Volume 21 #1 1977. pp. 79-96.
Murray, Colin G.
"The Work of Men, Women and the Ancestors: Social
Reproduction in the Periphery of South Africa." (In)
Wallman, Sandra (ed.). Social Anthropology of Work. New
York: Academic Press. 1979. pp. 337-363.
Rubens, Bernice
"The Gold Widows." ISIS International Bulletin. #9
Autumn, 1978. pp. 18-21.
Sebatane, E. Molapi
"The Family in Lesotho: Perspectives on its Changing Life
and Structure." Paper Presented at the Seminar on the
Changing Family in the African Context, Maseru,
Lesotho, 1983. Paris: United Nations Educational,
Scientific and Cultural Organization. 1984. 24p.
Wilkinson, R.C.
"Migration in Lesotho: Some Comparative Aspects With
Particular Reference to the Role of Women." Geography.
Volume 68 #300 Part Three June, 1982. pp. 208-224.
Wykstra, Ronald A.
Farm Labor in Lesotho: Scarcity or Surplus? Fort
Collins, Colorado: Colorado State University. Economics
Department. LASA (Lesotho Agricultural Sector Analysis
Project) Discussion Paper Series #5. September, 1978.
42p.

FAMILY LIFE

Gay, Judy S.
"Basotho Women's Options: A Study of Marital Careers in
Rural Lesotho." Ph.D. Dissertation: University of
Cambridge. Cambridge, England. 1980.
Gay, Judy S.
"Basotho Women Migrants: A Case Study." IDS Bulletin.
Volume 11 #4 1980.
Gay, Judy S.
"Basotho Women as Migrant Workers." Paper Presented at
the Seminar on Women and Development. Sussex, England:
University of Sussex. May 16, 1979.
Gordon, Elizabeth
"An Analysis of the Impact of Labour Migration on the
Lives of Women in Lesotho." Journal of Development
Studies. Volume 17 #3 April, 1981. pp. 59-76.
Gordon, Elizabeth
"Proposals for Easing the Plight of Migrant Workers
Families in Lesotho." (In) Bohning, W.R. (ed.). Black
Migration to South Africa: A Selection of Policy Oriented
Research. Geneva: International Labour Office. 1981.

Gordon, Elizabeth
   The Women Left Behind: A Study of Wives of the Migrant
   Workers of Lesotho. Geneva: International Labour Office.
   World Employment Programme Research Working Paper.
   December, 1978. 110p.
Gordon, Elizabeth
   An Analysis of the Impact of Labour Migration on the
   Lives of Women in Lesotho. (In) Nelson, Nici (ed.).
   African Women in the Development Process. Totowa, New
   Jersey: Frank Cass. 1981. pp. 59-76.
Makenete, S.T.
   "Possible Impact of Child Spacing on Basotho Health."
   Paper Presented at the National Conference on Population
   Management as a Factor in Development Including Family
   Planning. Maseru, Lesotho. April 26-29, 1979.
Murray, Colin G.
   "The Effects of Migrant Labour: A Review of the Evidence
   in Lesotho." South African Labour Bulletin. Volume 6 #4
   November, 1980.
Murray, Colin G.
   Families Divided: The Impact of Migration in Lesotho.
   Cambridge, New York: Cambridge University Press. African
   Studies Studies #29. 1981. 219p.
Murray, Colin G.
   "Keeping House in Lesotho: A Study on the Impact of
   Oscillating Migration." Ph.D Dissertation: Cambridge
   University. Cambridge, New York. 1976. 350p.
Murray, Colin G.
   "Marital Strategy in Lesotho: The Redistribution of
   Migrant Earnings." African Studies. Volume 35 #2 1976.
   pp. 99-122.
Murray, Colin G.
   "The High Price of Bridewealth. Migrant Labour and the
   Position of Women in Lesotho." Journal of African Law.
   Volume 21 #1 1977. pp. 79-96.
Poulter, Sebastian
   Family Law and Litigation in Basotho Society. Oxford,
   England: Clarendon Press. 1976. 361p.
Poulter, Sebastian
   Legal Dualism in Lesotho: A Study of the Choice of Law in
   Question in Family Matters. Morija, Lesotho: Morija
   Sesuto Book Depot. 1979. 126p.
Poulter, Sebastian
   "The Choice of Law Dilemma in Lesotho: Some Criteria for
   Decision Making in Family Law." (In) Roberts, Simon
   (ed.). Law and the Family in Africa. Hague,
   Netherlands: Mouton. 1977. pp. 169-182.
Rubens, Bernice
   "The Gold Widows." ISIS International Bulletin. #9
   Autumn, 1978. pp. 18-21.
Sebatane, E. Molapi
   "The Family in Lesotho: Perspectives on its Changing Life
   and Structure." Paper Presented at the Seminar on the

Changing Family in the African Context, Maseru,
Lesotho,1983. Paris: United Nations Educational,
Scientific and Cultural Organization. 1984. 24p.
Wilkinson, R.C.
"Migration in Lesotho: Some Comparative Aspects With
Particular Reference to the Role of Women." Geography.
Volume 68 #300 Part Three June, 1982. pp. 208-224.

FAMILY PLANNING AND CONTRACEPTION

Franks, James A. and Minnis, Robert L.
Maternal and Child Health/Family Planning Project for the
Kingdom of Lesotho, Southern Africa: Final Report. Santa
Cruz, California: University of California, Santa Cruz.
1977. 457p.
Lesthaeghe, Ron J. and Eelens, Frank
Social Organization and Reproductive Regimes: Lessons
From Sub-Saharan Africa and Historical Western Europe.
Brussels, Belgium: Vrije Universiteit Brussel.
Interuniversity Programme in Demography. IDP Working
Paper #1985-1. 1985. 64p.
Makenete, S.T.
"Possible Impact of Child Spacing on Basotho Health."
Paper Presented at the National Conference on Population
Management as a Factor in Development Including Family
Planning. Maseru, Lesotho. April 26-29, 1979.
Mhloyi, Marvellous M.
"Fertility Determinants: A Comparative Study Of Kenya and
Lesotho." Ph.D Dissertation: University of Pennsylvania.
Philadelphia, Pennsylvania. 1984. 342p.
Olusanya, P.O.
The Demographic, Health, Economic and Social Impact of
Family Planning in Selected African Countries. Addis
Ababa, Ethiopia: United Nations Economic Commission for
Africa. ECA/PD/1985-9. March, 1985. 97p.

FERTILITY AND INFERTILITY

Eelens, Frank and Donne, L.
The Proximate Determinants of Fertility in Sub-Saharan
Africa: A Factbook Based on the Results of the World
Fertility Survey. Brussels, Belgium: Vrije Universiteit
Brussel. Interuniversity Programme in Demography. IDP
Working Paper #1985-3. 1985. 122p.
International Statistical Institute (ISI)
The Lesotho Fertility Survey, 1977: A Summary of
Findings. Voorburg, Netherlands: ISI. World Fertility
Survey Report #34. 1981. 12p.
Lesotho. Central Bureau of Statistics
Lesotho Fertility Survey, 1977: First Report. Maseru,
Lesotho: Central Bureau of Statistics. 1981.

Lesthaeghe, Ron J. and Eelens, Frank
  Social Organization and Reproductive Regimes: Lessons
  From Sub-Saharan Africa and Historical Western Europe.
  Brussels, Belgium: Vrije Universiteit Brussel.
  Interuniversity Programme in Demography. IDP Working
  Paper #1985-1. 1985. 64p.
Mhloyi, Marvellous M.
  "Fertility Determinants: A Comparative Study Of Kenya and
  Lesotho." Ph.D Dissertation: University of Pennsylvania.
  Philadelphia, Pennsylvania. 1984. 342p.
Mpiti, A.M. and Kalule-Sabiti, I.
  The Proximate Determinants of Fertility in Lesotho.
  Voorburg, Netherlands: International Statistical
  Institute. World Fertility Survey Reports #78. July,
  1985. 44p.
United Nations Economic Commission for Africa (UNECA)
  Nuptiality and Fertility (A Comparative Analysis of WFS
  Data). Addis Ababa, Ethiopia: UNECA. African Population
  Studies Series #5. 1983. 96p.

HEALTH, NUTRITION AND MEDICINE

Franks, James A. and Minnis, Robert L.
  Maternal and Child Health/Family Planning Project for the
  Kingdom of Lesotho, Southern Africa: Final Report. Santa
  Cruz, California: University of California, Santa Cruz.
  1977. 457p.
Makenete, S.T.
  "Possible Impact of Child Spacing on Basotho Health."
  Paper Presented at the National Conference on Population
  Management as a Factor in Development Including Family
  Planning. Maseru, Lesotho. April 26-29, 1979.
Martin, P.M. and Hill, G.B.
  "Cervical Cancer in Relation to Tobacco and Alcohol
  Consumption in Lesotho, Southern Africa." Cancer
  Detection and Prevention. Volume 7 #2 1984. pp.
  109-115.
Mhloyi, Marvellous M.
  "Fertility Determinants: A Comparative Study Of Kenya and
  Lesotho." Ph.D Dissertation: University of Pennsylvania.
  Philadelphia, Pennsylvania. 1984. 342p.
Mpiti, A.M. and Kalule-Sabiti, I.
  The Proximate Determinants of Fertility in Lesotho.
  Voorburg, Netherlands: International Statistical
  Institute. World Fertility Survey Reports #78. July,
  1985. 44p.
Olusanya, P.O.
  The Demographic, Health, Economic and Social Impact of
  Family Planning in Selected African Countries. Addis
  Ababa, Ethiopia: United Nations Economic Commission for
  Africa. ECA/PD/1985-9. March, 1985. 97p.

HISTORY

Sweetman, David
    "Mmanthatisi of the Sotho." (In) Sweetman, David. Women
    Leaders in African History. London: Heineman. African
    Historical Biographies. 1984. pp. 55-63.

LAW AND LEGAL ISSUES

Mamashela, M.
    "Women and Development in Africa: With Special Reference
    to the Legal Disabilities of Married Women in Lesotho."
    Journal of Eastern African Research and Development.
    Volume 15 1985. pp. 165-170.
Maqutu, W.C.
    "Lesotho's African Marriage is Not a 'Customary Union'."
    Comparative and International Law Journal of Southern
    Africa. Volume 16 #3 November, 1983. pp. 374-382.
Maqutu, W.C.M.
    "Current Problems and Conflicts in the Marriage Law of
    Lesotho." Comparative and International Law Journal of
    Southern Africa. Volume 12 #2 July, 1979. pp. 176-187.
Poulter, Sebastian
    Family Law and Litigation in Basotho Society. Oxford,
    England: Clarendon Press. 1976. 361p.
Poulter, Sebastian
    Legal Dualism in Lesotho: A Study of the Choice of Law in
    Question in Family Matters. Morija, Lesotho: Morija
    Sesuto Book Depot. 1979. 126p.
Poulter, Sebastian
    "Marriage, Divorce and Legitimacy in Lesotho." Journal
    of African Law. Volume 21 #1 Spring, 1977. pp. 66-78.
Poulter, Sebastian
    "The Choice of Law Dilemma in Lesotho: Some Criteria for
    Decision Making in Family Law." (In) Roberts, Simon
    (ed.). Law and the Family in Africa. Hague,
    Netherlands: Mouton. 1977. pp. 169-182.

MARITAL RELATIONS AND NUPTIALITY

Gay, Judith S.
    "Basotho Women's Options: A Study of Marital Careers in
    Rural Lesotho." Ph.D. Dissertation: University of
    Cambridge. Cambridge, England. 1980.
Gordon, Elizabeth
    "An Analysis of the Impact of Labour Migration on the
    Lives of Women in Lesotho." Journal of Development
    Studies. Volume 17 #3 April, 1981. pp. 59-76.
Gordon, Elizabeth
    "Proposals for Easing the Plight of Migrant Workers
    Families in Lesotho." (In) Bohning, W.R. (ed.). Black

Migration to South Africa: A Selection of Policy Oriented Research. Geneva: International Labour Office. 1981.

Gordon, Elizabeth
The Women Left Behind: A Study of Wives of the Migrant Workers of Lesotho. Geneva: International Labour Office. World Employment Programme Research Working Paper. December, 1978. 110p.

Gordon, Elizabeth
"An Analysis of the Impact of Labour Migration on the Lives of Women in Lesotho." (In) Nelson, Nici (ed.). African Women in the Development Process. Totowa, New Jersey: Frank Cass. 1981. pp. 59-76.

Low, Allan
"From Farm-Homestead Theory to Rural Development Policy in Lesotho and Swaziland." (In) de Vletter, Fion (ed.). Labour Migration and Agricultural Development in Southern Africa. Rome: United Nations Food and Agriculture Organization. 1982.

Makenete, S.T.
"Possible Impact of Child Spacing on Basotho Health." Paper Presented at the National Conference on Population Management as a Factor in Development Including Family Planning. Maseru, Lesotho. April 26-29, 1979.

Mamashela, M.
"Women and Development in Africa: With Special Reference to the Legal Disabilities of Married Women in Lesotho." Journal of Eastern African Research and Development. Volume 15 1985. pp. 165-170.

Maqutu, W.C.
"Lesotho's African Marriage is Not a 'Customary Union'." Comparative and International Law Journal of Southern Africa. Volume 16 #3 November, 1983. pp. 374-382.

Maqutu, W.C.M.
"Current Problems and Conflicts in the Marriage Law of Lesotho." Comparative and International Law Journal of Southern Africa. Volume 12 #2 July, 1979. pp. 176-187.

Molise, Ngoakoane M.
Nuptiality Patterns and Differentials in Lesotho. Cairo: Cairo Demographic Centre. CDC Research Monograph Series #12. 1984. pp. 399-422.

Mpiti, A.M. and Kalule-Sabiti, I.
The Proximate Determinants of Fertility in Lesotho. Voorburg, Netherlands: International Statistical Institute. World Fertility Survey Reports #78. July, 1985. 44p.

Mueller, Martha B.
"Women and Men in Rural Lesotho: The Periphery of the Periphery." Ph.D Dissertation: Brandeis University. Waltham, Massachusetts. 1977. 385p.

Murray, Colin
"The Symbolism and Politics of Bohadi: Household Recruitment and Marriage by Instalment in Lesotho." (In) Krige, E.J. and Comaroff, J.L. (eds.). Essays on African

Marriage in Southern Africa. Cape Town, South Africa:
Juta. 1981.

Murray, Colin G.
Families Divided: The Impact of Migration in Lesotho.
Cambridge, New York: Cambridge University Press. African
Studies Studies #29. 1981. 219p.

Murray, Colin G.
"Marital Strategy in Lesotho: The Redistribution of
Migrant Earnings." African Studies. Volume 35 #2 1976.
pp. 99-122.

Poulter, Sebastian
"Marriage, Divorce and Legitimacy in Lesotho." Journal
of African Law. Volume 21 #1 Spring, 1977. pp. 66-78.

Sebatane, E. Molapi
"The Family in Lesotho: Perspectives on its Changing Life
and Structure." Paper Presented at the Seminar on the
Changing Family in the African Context, Maseru,
Lesotho, 1983. Paris: United Nations Educational,
Scientific and Cultural Organization. 1984. 24p.

United Nations Economic Commission for Africa (UNECA)
Nuptiality and Fertility (A Comparative Analysis of WFS
Data). Addis Ababa, Ethiopia: UNECA. African Population
Studies Series #5. 1983. 96p.

MIGRATION

Gay, Judy S.
"Basotho Women Migrants: A Case Study." IDS Bulletin.
Volume 11 #4 1980.

Gay, Judy S.
"Basotho Women as Migrant Workers." Paper Presented at
the Seminar on Women and Development. Sussex, England:
University of Sussex. May 16, 1979.

Gay, Judy S.
"Women Without Men: Female Social Networks in a Male
Controlled Society." (In) Lesotho. Ministry of Planning
and Statistics. Lesotho Fertility Survey. Maseru,
Lesotho: Central Bureau of Statistics. 1981.

Gordon, Elizabeth
"An Analysis of the Impact of Labour Migration on the
Lives of Women in Lesotho." Journal of Development
Studies. Volume 17 #3 April, 1981. pp. 59-76.

Gordon, Elizabeth
"Proposals for Easing the Plight of Migrant Workers
Families in Lesotho." (In) Bohning, W.R. (ed.). Black
Migration to South Africa: A Selection of Policy Oriented
Research. Geneva: International Labour Office. 1981.

Gordon, Elizabeth
"An Analysis of the Impact of Labour Migration on the
Lives of Women in Lesotho." (In) Nelson, Nici (ed.).
African Women in the Development Process. Totowa, New
Jersey: Frank Cass. 1981. pp. 59-76.

Low, Allan
    "From Farm-Homestead Theory to Rural Development Policy
    in Lesotho and Swaziland." (In) de Vletter, Fion (ed.).
    Labour Migration and Agricultural Development in Southern
    Africa. Rome: United Nations Food and Agriculture
    Organization. 1982.
Murray, Colin G.
    "The Effects of Migrant Labour: A Review of the Evidence
    in Lesotho." South African Labour Bulletin. Volume 6 #4
    November, 1980.
Murray, Colin G.
    Families Divided: The Impact of Migration in Lesotho.
    Cambridge, New York: Cambridge University Press. African
    Studies Studies #29. 1981. 219p.
Murray, Colin G.
    "Keeping House in Lesotho: A Study on the Impact of
    Oscillating Migration." Ph.D Dissertation: Cambridge
    University. Cambridge, New York. 1976. 350p.
Murray, Colin G.
    "Marital Strategy in Lesotho: The Redistribution of
    Migrant Earnings." African Studies. Volume 35 #2 1976.
    pp. 99-122.
Murray, Colin G.
    "The High Price of Bridewealth. Migrant Labour and the
    Position of Women in Lesotho." Journal of African Law.
    Volume 21 #1 1977. pp. 79-96.
Murray, Colin G.
    "The Work of Men, Women and the Ancestors: Social
    Reproduction in the Periphery of South Africa." (In)
    Wallman, Sandra (ed.). Social Anthropology of Work. New
    York: Academic Press. 1979. pp. 337-363.
Rubens, Bernice
    "The Gold Widows." ISIS International Bulletin. #9
    Autumn, 1978. pp. 18-21.
Sebatane, E. Molapi
    "The Family in Lesotho: Perspectives on its Changing Life
    and Structure." Paper Presented at the Seminar on the
    Changing Family in the African Context, Maseru, Lesotho.
    1983. Paris: United Nations Educational, Scientific and
    Cultural Organization. Maseru, Lesotho. 1984. 24p.
Wilkinson, R.C.
    "Migration in Lesotho: Some Comparative Aspects With
    Particular Reference to the Role of Women." Geography.
    Volume 68 #300 Part Three June, 1982. pp. 208-224.

MISCELLANEOUS

Anonymous
    "South Africa and Lesotho: Three Lesbian Conversations."
    Connexions. #3 Winter, 1982.

POLITICS AND GOVERNMENT

Anonymous
   The Role of Women in Lesotho's Development: An Annotated
   Bibliography. Maseru, Lesotho: National University of
   Lesotho. Institute of Southern African Studies. 1983.
Janelid, Ingrid
   Promoting the Participation of Women in Rural
   Development. Report on Mission to Lesotho. Rome: United
   Nations Food and Agriculture Organization. September,
   1977.
Sweetman, David
   "Mmanthatisi of the Sotho." (In) Sweetman, David. Women
   Leaders in African History. London: Heineman. African
   Historical Biographies. 1984. pp. 55-63.
Yates, Leslie M.
   "Integration of Women in Development in Southern Africa:
   An Evaluation With Recommendations for U.S. AID Programs
   in Botswana, Lesotho and Zambia." Sadex.
   November-December, 1979. pp. 1-15.
Yates, Leslie M.
   Integration of Women in Development in Zambia, Botswana
   and Lesotho: AID's Efforts. Washington, D.C.: U.S.
   Department of State. U.S. Agency for International
   Development. Southern Africa Development Analysis.
   1978. 92p.

RESEARCH

Yates, Leslie M.
   "Integration of Women in Development in Southern Africa:
   An Evaluation With Recommendations for U.S. AID Programs
   in Botswana, Lesotho and Zambia." Sadex.
   November-December, 1979. pp. 1-15.

SEX ROLES

Anonymous
   The Role of Women in Lesotho's Development: An Annotated
   Bibliography. Maseru, Lesotho: National University of
   Lesotho. Institute of Southern African Studies. 1983.
Gay, Judith S.
   "Basotho Women's Options: A Study of Marital Careers in
   Rural Lesotho." Ph.D. Dissertation: University of
   Cambridge. Cambridge, England. 1980.
Gay, Judy S.
   "Women Without Men: Female Social Networks in a Male
   Controlled Society." (In) Lesotho. Ministry of Planning
   and Statistics. Lesotho Fertility Survey. Maseru,
   Lesotho: Central Bureau of Statistics. 1981.

302

Gordon, Elizabeth
    "An Analysis of the Impact of Labour Migration on the
    Lives of Women in Lesotho." Journal of Development
    Studies. Volume 17 #3 April, 1981. pp. 59-76.
Gordon, Elizabeth
    "An Analysis of the Impact of Labour Migration on the
    Lives of Women in Lesotho." (In) Nelson, Nici (ed.).
    African Women in the Development Process. Totowa, New
    Jersey: Frank Cass. 1981. pp. 59-76.
Janelid, Ingrid
    Promoting the Participation of Women in Rural
    Development. Report on Mission to Lesotho. Rome: United
    Nations Food and Agriculture Organization. September,
    1977.
Kimane, I.
    "Images of Basotho Women in Society: Their Contribution
    to Development." Journal of Eastern African Research and
    Development. Volume 15 1985. pp. 180-187.
Low, Allan
    "From Farm-Homestead Theory to Rural Development Policy
    in Lesotho and Swaziland." (In) de Vletter, Fion (ed.).
    Labour Migration and Agricultural Development in Southern
    Africa. Rome: United Nations Food and Agriculture
    Organization. 1982.
Madland, M.
    Women in Agriculture. Maseru, Lesotho: Thaba Bosiu Rural
    Development Planning and Evaluation Unit. 1977.
Malahleha, Gwen M.
    "Contradictions and Ironies: Women of Lesotho." off our
    backs. Volume 15 March, 1985. pp. 8-9.
Mamashela, M.
    "Women and Development in Africa: With Special Reference
    to the Legal Disabilities of Married Women in Lesotho."
    Journal of Eastern African Research and Development.
    Volume 15 1985. pp. 165-170.
Maqutu, W.C.
    "Lesotho's African Marriage is Not a 'Customary Union'."
    Comparative and International Law Journal of Southern
    Africa. Volume 16 #3 November, 1983. pp. 374-382.
Mpiti, A.M. and Kalule-Sabiti, I.
    The Proximate Determinants of Fertility in Lesotho.
    Voorburg, Netherlands: International Statistical
    Institute. World Fertility Survey Reports #78. July,
    1985. 44p.
Mueller, Martha B.
    "Women and Men in Rural Lesotho: The Periphery of the
    Periphery." Ph.D Dissertation: Brandeis University.
    Waltham, Massachusetts. 1977. 385p.
Mueller, Martha B.
    "Women and Men, Power and Powerless in Lesotho." (In)
    Wellesley Editorial Committee. Women and National
    Development: The Complexities of Change. Chicago:
    University of Chicago Press. 1977. pp. 154-166.

Mueller, Martha B.
"Women and Men, Power and Powerlessness in Lesotho."
Signs. Volume 3 #1 Autumn, 1977. pp. 154-166.
Murray, Colin G.
"Keeping House in Lesotho: A Study on the Impact of
Oscillating Migration." Ph.D Dissertation: Cambridge
University. Cambridge, New York. 1976. 350p.
Murray, Colin G.
"Marital Strategy in Lesotho: The Redistribution of
Migrant Earnings." African Studies. Volume 35 #2 1976.
pp. 99-122.
Murray, Colin G.
"The High Price of Bridewealth. Migrant Labour and the
Position of Women in Lesotho." Journal of African Law.
Volume 21 #1 1977. pp. 79-96.
Murray, Colin G.
"The Work of Men, Women and the Ancestors: Social
Reproduction in the Periphery of South Africa." (In)
Wallman, Sandra (ed.). Social Anthropology of Work. New
York: Academic Press. 1979. pp. 337-363.
Rubens, Bernice
"The Gold Widows." ISIS International Bulletin. #9
Autumn, 1978. pp. 18-21.
Safilios-Rothschild, Constantina
The Persistence of Women's Invisibility in Agriculture:
Theoretical and Policy Lessons From Lesotho and Sierra
Leone. New York: Population Council. Center for Policy
Studies. Working Paper #88. September, 1982. 31p.
Safilios-Rothschild, Constantina
"The Persistence of Women's Invisibility in Agriculture:
Theoretical and Policy Lessons From Lesotho and Sierra
Leone." Economic Development and Cultural Change.
Volume 33 #2 January, 1985. pp. 299-317.
Wilkinson, R.C.
"Migration in Lesotho: Some Comparative Aspects With
Particular Reference to the Role of Women." Geography.
Volume 68 #300 Part Three June, 1982. pp. 208-224.

Madagascar

Bloch, Maurice
   "Marriage Amongst Equals: An Analysis of the Marriage
   Ceremony of the Merina of Madagascar." Man. Volume 13
   #1 March, 1978. pp. 21-33.
Bloch, Maurice
   "Death, Women and Power." (In) Bloch, M. and Parry, J.
   (eds.). Death and Regeneration of Life. Cambridge,
   England: Cambridge University Press. 1982. pp. 211-230.

Malawi

Bullough, C.H.
 "Analysis of Maternal Deaths in the Central Region of
 Malawi." East African Medical Journal. Volume 58 #1
 Janaury, 1981. pp. 25-36.
Butler, Lorna M.
 "Bases of Women's Influence in the Rural Malawian
 Domestic Group." Ph.D Dissertation: Washington State
 University. Pullman, Washington. 1976. 296p.
Chimwaza, B.M.
 "Factors Affecting Food and Nutrient Intake in Dowa West,
 Central Malawi." Paper Presented at the Workshop on the
 Role of Women and Home Economics in Rural Development in
 Africa, Alexandria, Egypt, October 17, 1983. Rome:
 United Nations Food and Agricultural Organization.
 1983. 13p.
Chipande, G.
 The Position of Women in Malawi and the Role of
 UNICEF-Aided Projects: An Appraisal. Lilongwe, Malawi:
 University of Malawi. 1985.
Due, Jean M.
 "Intra-Household Gender Issues in Farming Systems in
 Tanzania, Zambia and Malawi." (In) Poats, Susan V. and
 Schmink, Marianne and Spring, Anita (eds.). Gender
 Issues in Farming Systems Research and Extension.
 Boulder, Colorado: Westview Press. 1980. pp. 331-344.
Evans, J.
 "Women's Involvement in the Seasonal Credit Programmes in
 the Phalombe Rural Development Project." Paper Presented
 at the National Credit Seminar. Chintheche, Malawi.
 1983.
Evans, J.
 Phalombe Rural Development Project, Women's Programmes
 Programme Plan. Lilongwe, Malawi: Blantyre Agricultural
 Development Division. 1981.

Evans, J.E.
   Rural Women's Agricultural Extension Programmes in
   Phlombe Rural Development. Lilongwe, Malawi: Malawi
   Ministry of Agriculture. Working Document on the
   Base-Line Survey, Phase I. 1981.
Hirschmann, David and Vaughan, Megan
   "Food Production and Income Generation in a Matrilineal
   Society: Rural Women in Zomba, Malawi." Journal of
   Southern African Studies. Volume 10 #1 October, 1983.
   pp. 86-99.
Hirschmann, David
   "Bureaucracy and Rural Women: Illustrations From Malawi."
   Rural Africana. #21 Winter, 1985. pp. 51-64.
Hirschmann, David
   Women Farmers of Malawi: Food Production in the Zomba
   District. Berkeley, California: University of California
   Press. Institute Of International Studies. Research
   Series #58. 1984. 142p.
Hirschmann, David
   Women, Planning and Policy in Malawi. Addis Ababa,
   Ethiopia: United Nations Economic Commission for Africa.
   1984. 54p.
Hirschmann, David
   Women's Participation in Malawi's Local Councils and
   District Development Committees. East Lansing, Michigan:
   Michigan State University. Women in International
   Development. Working Paper #98. 1985. 17p.
Lamba, Isaac C.
   "African Women's Education in Malawi, 1875-1952."
   Journal of Education Administration and History. Volume
   14 #1 1982. pp. 46-54.
Malawi Ministry of Agriculture (MOA)
   Reaching Female Farmers Through Male Extension Workers.
   Lilongwe, Malawi: MOA. Extension Circular 2/83. 1983.
Mandala, Elias
   "Capitalism, Kinship and Gender in the Lower Tchiri
   (Shire) Valley of Malawi, 1860-1960: An Alternative
   Theoretical Framework." African Economic History.
   Volume 13 1984. pp. 137-170.
Mandala, Elias
   "Peasant Cotton Agriculture, Gender, and
   Inter-Generational Relationships: The Lower Tchiri
   (Shire) Valley of Malawi, 1906-1940." African Studies
   Review. Volume 25 #2/3 July-September, 1982. pp.
   26-44.
National Asso. of Negro Business and Prof. Women's Clubs
   African Women Small Entrepreneurs in Senegal, The Gambia,
   Sierra Leone, Cameroon and Malawi: Prefeasibility Study
   for Providing Assistance. Washington, D.C.: NANBPA.
   1977. 82p.
Phiri, Kings M.
   "Some Changes in the Matrilineal Family System Among the

Chewa of Malawi Since the 19th Century." Journal of
African History. Volume 24 #2 1983. pp. 257-274.
Spens, M.T.
Reaching Women Farmers in a British Aided Project in
Malawi: Some Preliminary Findings. London: Overseas
Development Administration. 1985.
Spring, Anita and Smith, C. and Kayuni, F.
Women Farmers in Malawi, Their Contributions to
Agriculture and Participation in Development Projects.
Lilongwe, Malawi: U.S. Agency for International
Development. Women in Development Office. 1983.
Spring, Anita
Profiles of Men and Women Smallholder Farmers in the
Lilongwe Rural Development Project, Malawi. Final
Report. Washington, D.C.: U.S. Agency for International
Development. Office of Women in Development. March,
1984. 144p.
Spring, Anita
"Women in Agricultural Development Projects in Malawi:
Making Gender Free Development Work." (In) Gallin, Rita
and Spring, Anita (eds.). Women Creating Wealth:
Transforming Economic Development. Washington, D.C.:
Association for Women in Development. 1985. pp. 71-75.
Spring, Anita
Adopting CIMMYT Farming Systems Survey Guidelines to the
Malawian Situation. Lilongwe, Malawi: Women in
Agricultural Development Project. Report #5. 1982.
Spring, Anita
"Reaching Female Farmers Through Male Extension Workers
in Malawi." (In) Food and Agriculture Organization
(FAO). 1985 Training for Agriculture and Rural
Development. Rome: FAO. FAO Economic and Social
Development Series #38. 1985. pp. 11-22.
Spring, Anita and Smith, C. and Kayuni, F.
Karonga Farmer Survey. Lilongwe, Malawi: Women in
Agricultural Development Project. Report #12. 1982.
Spring, Anita
"Women in Agricultural Development in Malawi." Paper
Presented at the 11th International Congress of
Anthropological and Ethnographic Sciences. Vancouver,
British Columbia: Canada. 1983.
Spring, Anita and Smith, C. and Kayuni, F.
Studies in Agricultural Constraints Facing Women Farmers
in Phalombe Rural Development Project. Lilongwe, Malawi:
Women in Agricultural Development Project. Report #19.
1983.
Spring, Anita
"The Women in Agricultural Development Projects in
Malawi: Making Gender Free Development Work." Paper
Presented at the Annual Meeting of the African Studies
Association. Los Angeles, California. October 27, 1984.

United Nations Economic Commission for Africa (UNECA)
Women, Planning and Policy in Malawi. (Draft). Addis
Ababa, Ethiopia: UNECA.   Research Series. 1982.
Vaughan, Megan
"Which Family? Problems in the Reconstruction of the
History of the Family as an Economic and Cultural Unit."
Journal of African History. Volume 24 #2 1983. pp.
275-283.
Wilson, Monica H.
For Men and Elders--Changes in the Relations of
Generations and of Men and Women Among the
Nyakyusa-Ngonde People, 1875-1971. New York: Africana
Publishing Company. 1977. 209p.

Mauritius

Brass, W.
   "Impact of the Family Planning Programme on Fertility in
   Mauritius." IPPF Medical Bulletin. Volume 10 #4
   August, 1976. pp. 1-2.
Chung, Ah-Fong
   "Menstruation--Taboos and Practices in Mauritius." ISIS
   International Bulletin. #20 1981.
Fam, Murman L.
   "The Need for an Independent Women's Movement in
   Mauritius." (In) Davies, M. (ed.). Third World-Second
   Sex: Women's Struggles and National Liberation. Third
   World Women Speak Out. London: Zed Press. 1983. pp.
   186-193.
Hanoomanjee, Esther
   "Application of Methods of Measuring the Impact of Family
   Planning Programmes on Fertility: The Case of
   Mauritius." (In) United Nations. Department of
   International Economic and Social Affairs. Evaluation of
   the Impact of Family Planning Programmes on Fertility.
   New York: United Nations. Population Studies #76. 1982.
   pp. 89-113.
Hein, Catherine R.
   "Family Planning in Mauritius: A National Survey."
   Studies in Family Planning. Volume 8 #12 December,
   1977. pp. 316-320.
Hein, Catherine R.
   "Jobs for the Girls: Export Manufacturing in Mauritius."
   International Labour Review. Volume 123 #2 March-April,
   1984. pp. 251-265.
Mauritius. Ministry of Health.
   Survey on Fertility Patterns Among Women Aged Under 25
   Years in the Island of Mauritius. Port Louis, Mauritius:
   The Ministry. Family Planning, Maternal Health and Child
   Health Division. December, 1980. 26p.

Mehta, S.R.
   "Maternal and Child Health and Family Planning in an
   Island Village Locality." Journal of Family Welfare.
   Volume 28 #4 June, 1982. pp. 66-77.
Olusanya, P.O.
   The Demographic, Health, Economic and Social Impact of
   Family Planning in Selected African Countries. Addis
   Ababa, Ethiopia: United Nations Economic Commission for
   Africa. ECA/PD/1985-9. March, 1985. 97p.
United Nations Economic Commission for Africa (UNECA)
   Analysis of Fertility Data From 1972 Population Census of
   Mauritius. Addis Ababa, Ethiopia: UNECA. 1979. 125p.
Xenos, Christos
   Fertility Change in Mauritius and the Impact of Family
   Planning Programmes. Port Louis, Mauritius: Mauritius
   Ministry of Health. 1977. 445p.

Mozambique

Alpers, E.A.
   "State, Merchant Capital, and Gender Relations in
   Southern Mozambique to the End of the 19th Century."
   African Economic History. Volume 13 1984. pp. 23-55.
Anonymous
   "Mozambican Women: The Struggle Continues." Union Wage.
   #41 May-June, 1977. pp. 12.
Anonymous
   "Mozambique: Women in FRELIMO." IDOC Bulletin. #50/51
   December, 1976.
Beidelman, T.O.
   "Women and Men in Two East African Societies." (In)
   Karp, I. and Bird, C.S. (eds.). Exploration in African
   Systems of Thought. Bloomington, Indiana: Indiana
   University Press. 1980. pp. 143-164.
Binford, Martha B.
   "Julia: An East African Diviner." (In) Falk, Nancy A.
   and Gross, Rita M. (eds.). Unspoken Worlds: Women's
   Religious Lives in Non-Western Cultures. San Francisco,
   California: Harper and Row Publishers. 1980. pp. 3-21.
De Heusch, Luc
   "Heat, Physiology and Cosmogony: Rites de Passage Among
   the Thonga." (In) Karp, Ivan and Bird, Charles S.
   (eds.). Explorations in African Systems of Thought.
   Bloomington, Indiana: University of Indiana Press. 1980.
   pp. 27-43.
Hansen, H. and Hansen, R. and Gjerstad, O. and Sarazin, C.
   "The Organization of Mozambican Women." Journal of
   Eastern African Research and Development. Volume 15
   1985. pp. 230-244.
Hill, Sylvia
   "Lessons From the Mozambican Women's Struggle."

TransAfrica Forum. Volume 2 #1 Summer, 1982. pp.
77-90.
Isaacman, Allen
   "A Luta Continua: Women and Liberation in Mozambique."
   (In) Allen, C. and Williams, G. (eds.). Subsaharan
   Africa. London: Macmillan. Sociology of Developing
   Societies Series. 1982. pp. 62-65.
Isaacman, Allen and Isaacman, Barbara
   "The Role of Womem in the Liberation of Mozambique."
   Ufahamu. Volume 13 #2/3 1984. pp. 128-185.
Isaacman, Barbara and Stephen, June
   Mozambique: Women, the Law and Agrarian Reform. Addis
   Ababa, Ethiopia: United Nations Economic Commission for
   Africa. African Training and Research Centre for
   Women/Ford Foundation Research Series. 1980. 148p.
Jelley, D.
   "Preventive Health Care for Mothers and Children. A
   Study in Mozambique." Journal of Tropical Medicine and
   Hygiene. Volume 86 #6 December, 1983. pp. 229-236.
Kruks, Sonia and Wisner, B.
   "The State, the Party and the Female Peasantry in
   Mozambique." Journal of Southern African Studies.
   Volume 11 #1 1984. pp. 106-127.
Kruks, Sonia
   "Mozambique: Some Reflections on the Struggle for Women's
   Emancipation." Frontiers. Volume 7 #2 1983. pp. 32-41.
Machel, S.M.
   "The Women Question and Social Emancipation: Samora on
   the Woman Question and Social Emancipation." Maji Maji.
   #33 1978. pp. 42-48.
Mundondo, Mabel
   "Mozambican Women's Role in the Revolution." Africa
   Women. #3 1976.
Murphy, D.
   "Training Programme for Rural Midwives of Mozambique."
   Tropical Doctor. Volume 15 #3 July, 1985. pp. 146-147.
Rodriguez, A.
   "Mozambican Women After the Revolution." (In) Davies, M.
   (ed.). Third World-Second Sex: Women's Struggles and
   National Liberation. Third World Women Speak Out.
   London: Zed Press. 1983. pp. 127-134.
South West Africa People's Organization (SWAPO)
   Study Tours of Namibian Women to Mozambique and the Congo
   and the SWAPO Women's Council Workshop: Namibia. Paris:
   United Nations Educational, Scientific and Cultural
   Organization. Lusaka, Zambia. November 26, 1981. 34p.
Tadesse, Zenebeworke
   An Oveview on the Role of Women's Organizations in
   Africa: Case Study of Ethiopia, Zambia, Mozambique and
   Tanzania. Lusaka, Zambia: P/O Box RW 514. 1978.
Tadesse, Zenebeworke
   "An Overview on Women's Organizations in Africa: The Case

of Ethiopia, Mozambique and Tanzania." Paper Presented
at the 9th World Conference of Sociology. Uppsala,
Sweden. 1978.
Urdang, Stephanie
The Liberation of Women as a Necessity for the Successful
Revolution in Guinea-Bissau, Mozambique and Angola.
Waltham, Massachusetts: Brandeis University. African
Studies Association. 1977.
Urdang, Stephanie
"Precondition for Victory: Women's Liberation in
Mozambique and Guinea-Bissau." Issue. Volume 8 #1
Spring, 1978. pp 25-31.
Urdang, Stephanie
"Women in Mozambique: Rural Transformations: Women in the
New Society." Africa Report. Volume 30 #2 March-April,
1985. pp. 66-70.
Urdang, Stephanie
"The Last Transition?: Women and Development in
Mozambique." Review of African Political Economy.
#27/28 1984. pp. 8-32.
Vail, L. and White, L.
"Tawani, Machambero! Forced Cotton and Rice Growing on
the Zambezi." Journal of African History. Volume 19 #1
1978. pp. 239-263.
Webster, D.
"Divorce and Ephemeral Alliance Among the Chopi." (In)
Krige, E.J. and Comaroff, J.L. (eds.). Essays on African
Marriage in Southern Africa. Capetown, South Africa:
Wetton. 1981.
Welch, Gita H.
"Transforming the Foundations of Family Law in the Course
of the Mozambican Revolution." Journal of Southern
African Studies. Volume 12 #1 October, 1985. pp.
60-74.
White, Susan
"Women and Underdevelopment in Mozambique." Canadian
Dimension. Volume 14 #6 1980. pp. 38-41.
Young, Sherilynn
"Fertility and Famine: Women's Agricultural History in
Southern Mozambique." (In) Palmer, Robin and Parsons,
Neil (eds.). The Roots of Rural Poverty in Central and
Southern Africa. Berkeley, California: University of
California Press. 1977. pp. 66-81.

Namibia

Collins, Carole
    This is the Time: Interview With Two Namibian Women.
    Chicago: Committee for African Liberation. 1977. 27p.
Collins, Carole
    "SWAPO Images of a Future Society: Women in Namibia."
    Issue. Volume 7 #4 Winter, 1977. pp. 39-43.
Cronje, Gillian and Cronje, Suzanne
    The Workers of Namibia. London: International Defense
    and Aid Fund for Southern Africa. 1979. 135p.
Hishongwa, Ndentala
    Women of Namibia: The Changing Role of Namibian Women
    From Traditional Precolonial Times to Present. London:
    International Defense and Aid Fund Publications. 1984.
    103p.
International Defense and Aid Fund (IDAF) and United Nations
Centre Against Apartheid
    To Honour Women's Day: Profiles of Leading Women in the
    South African and Namibian Liberation Struggles. London:
    IDAF/U.N. Centre Against Apartheid. 1981. 56p.
International Defense and Aid Fund for Southern Africa
    From You Have Struck a Rock: Women and Political
    Repression in Southern Africa. London: IDAFSA. 1980.
Konner, M.J.
    "Maternal Care, Infant Behavior and Development Among the
    !Kung." (In) Lee, R.B. and DeVore, I. (eds.). Kalahari
    Hunter-Gatherers, Studies of the !Kung San and Their
    Neighbors. Cambridge, Massachusetts: Harvard University
    Press. 1976. pp. 218-246.
Lapchick, Richard
    The Role of Women in the Struggle for Liberation in
    Zimbabwe, Namibia and South Africa. New York: United
    Nations. July, 1980. 37p.

Lapchick, Richard E. and Urdang, Stephanie
    Oppression and Resistance: The Struggle of Women in
    Southern Africa. Westport, Connecticut: Greenwood Press.
    Contributions in Women's Studies. #29. 1982. 234p.
Lee, Richard B.
    The !Kung San: Men, Women and Work in a Foraging Society.
    Cambridge, New York: Cambridge University Press. 1979.
    526p.
Matsepe-Casaburri, Ivy F.
    "Changing Roles and Needs of Women in South Africa and
    Namibia." Paper Presented at the World Conference for
    the United Nations Decade for Women. New York: United
    Nations. Copenhagen, Denmark. July 14-30, 1980.
Murray-Hudson, A.
    "SWAPO: Solidarity With Our Sisters." Review of African
    Political Economy. #27/28 1984. pp. 120-125.
Musialele, E.
    "Women in Namibia: The Only Way to Free Ourselves." (In)
    Davies, M. (ed.). Third World-Second Sex: Women's
    Struggles and National Liberation. Third World Women
    Speak Out. London: Zed Press. 1983. pp. 83-89.
Ntsoaki
    "Namibia: The Struggle With the Struggle." Vanguard. #4
    1979. pp. 36-42.
South West Africa People's Organization (SWAPO)
    "Namibian Women in the Struggle for National Liberation,
    Independence and Reconstruction." Paper Presented at the
    Meeting of Experts on the History of Women's Contribution
    to National Liberation Struggles and Their Roles and
    Needs During Reconstruction in Newly Independent
    Countries of Africa. Paris: United Nations Educational,
    Scientific and Cultural Organization. Bissau,
    Guinea-Bissau. 1983. 44p.
South West Africa People's Organization (SWAPO)
    Study Tours of Namibian Women to Mozambique and the Congo
    and the SWAPO Women's Council Workshop: Namibia. Paris:
    United Nations Educational, Scientific and Cultural
    Organization. Lusaka, Zambia. November 26, 1981. 34p.
South West Africa People's Organization Women's Council
    "The Namibian Women on the March." Nambia Today. Volume
    4 #3/4 1980. pp. 23-27.
United Nations
    "The Effects of Apartheid on the Status of Women in South
    Africa and Namibia." Paper Presented at the United
    Nations World Conference of the United Nations Decade for
    Women: Equality, Development and Peace. New York: United
    Nations. Copenhagen, Denmark. 1980. 37p.
United Nations
    The Effects of Apartheid on the Status of Women in South
    Africa, Namibia and Southern Rhodesia. New York: United
    Nations. 1978.
United Nations Secretary General
    "The Role of Women in the Struggle for Liberation in

Zimbabwe, Namibia and South Africa: Report to the
Secretary General." Paper Presented at the World
Conference of the United Nations Decade for Women. New
York: United Nations. Copenhagen, Denmark. July 14-30,
1980.

South Africa

ABORTION

Bloch, B.
"The Abortion and Sterilization Act of 1975: Experience
of the Johannesburg Hospital Pregnancy Advisory Service."
South African Medical Journal. Volume 53 #21 May 27,
1978. pp. 861-864.

Dommisse, J.
"The South African Gynaecologist's Attitude to the
Present Abortion Law." South African Medical Journal.
Volume 57 #25 June, 1980. pp. 1044-1045.

Drower, S.J. and Nash, E.S.
"Therapeutic Abortion on Psychiatric Ground. Part One: A
Local Study." South African Medical Journal. Volume 54
#15 October 7, 1978. pp. 604-608.

Drower, Sandra J.
"A Survey of Patients Referred for Therapeutic Abortion
on Psychiatric Grounds in a Cape Town Provincial
Hospital." Ph.D. Dissertation: University of Cape Town.
Cape Town, South Africa. 1977.

Kopenhager, T. and Kort, H. and Bloch, B.
"An Analysis of the First 200 Legal Abortions of the
Johannesburg General Hospital." South African Medical
Journal. Volume 53 #21 May, 1978. pp. 858-860.

Kunst, J. and Meiring, R.
"Abortion Law--A Need for Reform." De Rebus. # 198
June, 1984. pp. 264-266.

Mark, G.
"A Follow Up Study of Therapeutic Abortions: A Social
Work Perspective." M.A. Thesis: University of South
Africa. Pretoria, South Africa. 1981.

Marks, Shula
"Ruth First: A Tribute." Journal of Southern African
Studies. Volume 10 #1 1983. pp. 123+.

McCafferty, S.
    An Analysis of Abortion on Mental Health Grounds Within
    the South African Context. Durban, South Africa:
    University of Natal. L.L.B. Research Project. 1980.
Nash, E.S. and Navias, M.
    "Therapeutic Abortion on Psychiatric Grounds. Part III:
    Implementing the Abortion and Sterilization Act
    (1975-1981)." South African Medical Journal. Volume 63
    #17 April 23, 1983. pp. 639-644.
Nash, E.S. and Navias, M.
    Termination of Pregnancy on Psychiatric Grounds, Part
    Three: Implementing the Abortion and Sterilization Act
    (1975-1981). Cape Town, South Africa: Hospital Services,
    Cape Provincial Administration. 1982.
Sandler, S.W.
    "Spontaneous Abortion in Perspective: A Seven Year
    Study." South African Medical Journal. Volume 52 #1
    December 31, 1977. pp. 115, 118.
Schmidt, Elizabeth S.
    "Women of South Africa Speak." Africa Today. Volume 31
    #2 1984. pp. 52-54.
Van Niekerk, G.
    "Psychiatric Aspects of Therapeutic Abortion." South
    African Medical Journal. Volume 55 #11 March, 1979.
    pp. 421-424.
Westmore, Jean
    Abortion in South Africa and Attitudes of Natal Medical
    Practitioners Towards South African Abortion Legislation.
    Durban, South Africa: University of Natal. Centre for
    Applied Social Sciences and Abortion Reform Action Group.
    1977. 76p.

AGRICULTURE

Anonymous
    "Women: The Family Food Producers in South Africa."
    Apartheid Bulletin. #126 1978.
Egan, Siobhan
    "Black Women in South African Agriculture: An
    Introductory Study of Life and Labour in the
    Countryside." B.A. Honors Dissertation: University of
    Natal. Durban, South Africa. 1983.
Guyer, Jane I.
    "Women in the Rural Economy: Contemporary Variations."
    (In) Hay, Margaret J. and Stichter, Sharon (eds.).
    African Women South of the Sahara. New York: Longman.
    1984. pp. 19-32.
Harries, Jane
    "Women in Production in the Ciskei." B.A. Honors
    Dissertation: University of Cape Town. Cape Town, South
    Africa. 1979.

Matsetela, Ted
    "The Life Story of Nkgono MmaPooe: Aspects of
    Sharecropping and Proletatrianisation in the Northern
    Orange Free State, 1890-1930." (In) Marks, Shula and
    Rathbone, Richard (eds.). Industrialization and Social
    Change in South Africa: African Class Formation, Culture
    and Consciousness, 1870-1930. London: Longman. 1982.
Nene, Daphne S.
    "Women Caught in Between: The Case of Rural Women in
    KwaZulu." Paper Presented to the Women's Studies
    Symposium, University of Transkei. Umtata, South Africa:
    University of Transkei. March, 1984.
Nene, Daphne S.
    The Role and Potential of Black Women's Voluntary
    Associations in Development: The Case of KwaZulu and
    Natal. Kwa Dlangezwa, South Africa: University of
    Zululand. Publications of the University of Zululand.
    Series B #19. 1982. 74p.
Yawitch, Joanne
    "Women and Squatting: A Winterveld Case Study." (In)
    University of Witwatersrand. Working Papers in Southern
    African Studies. Johannesburg: University of the
    Witwatersrand. May, 1979. pp. 199-227.

APARTHEID AND RACE RELATIONS

Africa Bureau
    The Status of Black Women in South Africa. London:
    Africa Bureau. Document Paper #21. 1979.
African National Congress (ANC)
    'Apartheid--You Shall Be Crushed': Women's Fight Against
    Apartheid. Lusaka, Zambia: ANC. 1981. 32p.
Anonymous
    The Effects of Apartheid on the Status of Women in South
    Africa. New York: United Nations. Centre Against
    Apartheid. Notices and Documents. 1978. 26p.
Anonymous
    "Effects of Apartheid on the Status of Women in South
    Africa." Objective Justice. Volume 10 #1 Spring, 1978.

Anonymous
    "Effects of Apartheid on the Status of Women in Southern
    Africa." Paper Presented at the World Conference of the
    United Nations Decade for Women, Copenhagen, Denmark,
    July 14-30, 1980. New York: United Nations. 1980.
Anonymous
    "South African Women." Sechaba. August, 1979. pp.
    19-21.
Anonymous
    "Women Under Apartheid." U.N. Chronicle. Volume 19
    July, 1982. pp. 40-41.
Anonymous
    Women Under Apartheid: In Photographs and Text. London:

International Defense and Aid Fund for Southern Africa.
1982. 120p.
Anonymous
"Women and Apartheid." Objective Justice. Volume 12 #1
August, 1980. pp. 25-48.
Anonymous
"Women: The Family Food Producers in South Africa."
Apartheid Bulletin. #126 1978.
Baard, Francis
"Banishment and Jail." (In) National Union of South
African Students (NUSAS). NUSAS Conference on Women.
Cape Town, South Africa: NUSAS Women's Directive. 1983.
Beall, J.
"Unwanted Guests: Indian Women in the Context of
Indentured Immigration to the Natal." Paper Presented to
the Conference Commemorating the 150th Anniversary of
Indian Indentured Immigration and the Abolition of
Slaves. Moka, Mauritius. October, 1984.
Beall, J.D.
"Class, Race and Gender: The Political Economy of Women
in Colonial Natal." M.A. Thesis: University of Natal.
Durban, South Africa. 1982.
Beinart, William
"Amafelandawonye (the Diehards), Rural Popular Protest
and Women's Movements in Herschel District, South Africa
in the 1920's." Paper Presented at the History Workshop.
Johannesburg: University of the Witwatersrand. January,
1984.
Boddington, Erica
"Domestic Labour in the Western Cape." Paper Presented
to the Conference on Economic Development and Racial
Domination. Bellville, South Africa: University of
Western Cape. October, 1984.
Boddington, Erica
"Domestic Service: Changing Relations of Class
Domination, 1841-1948." M.A. Thesis: University of Cape
Town. Cape Town, South Africa. 1983.
Brown, Barbara B.
The Political Economy of Population Policy in South
Africa. Boston: Boston University. African Studies
Center. African Studies Working Paper #71. 1983. 15p.
Cachalia, Amina
"Indian Women in Resistance." Paper Presented at the
National Union of South African Students (NUSAS)
Conference on Women, July, 1982. Johannesburg:
University of Witwatersrand. NUSAS Women's Directive.
1983.
Cape Town. City Engineer. Technical Management Services
Mitchells Plain Survey of Coloured Females. Cape Town,
South Africa: City Engineers. March, 1979.
Cock, Jacklyn
"Black and White Women: A Socio-Historical Study of
Domestic Workers and Their Employers in the Eastern

Cape." Ph.D Dissertation: Rhodes University.
Grahamstown, South Africa. 1979.
Cock, Jacklyn
"Domestic Service: Apartheid's Deep South." South
African Outlook. Volume 111 #1301 November, 1979. pp.
165-168.
Cooper, C. and Ensor, Linda
African Woman's Handbook on the Law. Johannesburg: South
African Institute of Race Relations. 1980. 41p.
Dawber, Aneene
"Transvaal Women Organise." Work in Progress. Volume 34
1984. pp. 30-31.
De Villiers, Richard
"The Resistance to the Extension of Passes to Women,
1954-1960." Paper Presented to the African Studies
Institute Post Graduate Seminar. Johannesburg:
University of the Witwatersrand. September 24, 1979.
Demissic, Fassil
"Double Burden: African Women Under Apartheid." Ufahamu.
Volume 14 #3 1985. pp. 52-77.
Duncan, Sheena
"Women Under Apartheid: African Women and the Pass Laws."
(In) National Union of South African Students Law
Directive and Law Students Council. Law in South Africa:
Lifting the Veil. Cape Town, South Africa: NAUSA. 1981.
pp. 54-63.
Federal Council of the National Party of South Africa
Women, Our Silent Soldiers. Bloemfontein, South Africa:
Federal Council of the National Party of South Africa.
August, 1978.
Flepp, Caroline
"Women Under Apartheid; A Triple Oppression." UNESCO
Courier. Volume 38 #4 April, 1985. pp. 14-15.
Gaitskell, Deborah and Kimble, Judy
"Class, Race and Gender: Domestic Workers in South
Africa." Review of African Political Economy. #27/28
1983. pp. 86-108.
Ginwala, Frene and Mashiane, Shirley
"Women and Apartheid: Black South African Women Stand on
the Lowest Rung of the Ladder of Oppression." UNESCO
Courier. Volume 33 #7 July, 1980. pp. 13-17.
Goodwin, June
Cry Amandla: South African Women and the Question of
Power. New York: Holmes and Meier. 1984. 225p.
Griessel, Annette
"CATAPAW (Cape Association to Abolish Passes for African
Women) and the Anti-Pass Campaign in Cape Town in the
Fifties." (In) Cooper, Linda and Kaplan, Dave (eds.).
Selected Research Papers on Aspects of Organization in
the Western Cape. Cape Town, South Africa: University of
Cape Town. Department of Economic History. 1982.
Gwazela, Sindiswa
"The Female Target: Behind Prison Bars in South Africa."

Resources for Feminist Research. Volume 14   December, 1985. pp. 23-25.

Hamilton, Carolyn A.
"A Fragment of the Jigsaw: Authority and Labour Control Amongst the Early 19th Century Northern Nguni." B.A. Honors Dissertation: University of the Witwatersrand. Johannesburg, South Africa. 1980.

Hermer, Carol
The Diary of Maria Tholo. Johannesburg: Raven Press. 1980.

Intern. Defence and Aid Fund for Southern Africa (IDAF)
You Have Struck a Rock: Women and Political Repression in Southern Africa. London: IDAF. 1980. 24p.

Kimmons, Leona
"Women in South Africa--Agony and Struggle." Wree-View. Fall, 1976. pp. 1-5.

Kuzwayo, Ellen
Call Me Woman. London: Women's Press. 1985. 266p.

Lamula, Promise
"Women Under Apartheid." ISIS Women's World. #4 December, 1984.

Landis, Elizabeth
"African Women Under Apartheid." ISIS International Bulletin. #9 Autumn, 1978. pp. 7-11.

Lapchick, Richard E.
"The Role of Women in the Struggle Against Apartheid in South Africa." (In) Steady, Filomina C. (ed.). The Black Woman Cross-Culturally. Cambridge, Massachusetts: Schenkman Publishing. 1981. pp. 231-261.

Lapchick, Richard E. and Urdang, Stephanie
"The Effects of Apartheid on the Status of Women in Employment in South Africa." Paper Presented at the World Conference of the United Nations Decade for Women, Copenhagen, Denmark, July 14-30, 1980. New York: United Nations. 40p.

Lipman, Beata
We Make Freedom: Women in South Africa Speak. Boston: Pandora Press. 1984. 141p.

Locke, M.
"Sexism and Racism: Obstacles to Development of Black Women in South Africa." (In) Fowlkes, D.L. and McClure, C.S. (eds.). Feminist Visions: Toward a Transformation of the Liberal Arts Curriculum. University, Alabama: University of Alabama Press. 1984. pp. 119-129.

Lotter, Johann M. and Van Tonder, J.L.
Certain Aspects of Human Fertility in Rural Bophuthatswana. Pretoria, South Africa: South African Human Sciences Research Council. Institute for Sociological, Demographic and Criminological Research. Report #S-54. 1978. 53p.

Matsepe-Casaburri, Ivy F.
"Cheap Labour Policies and Their Implications for African Women in South Africa." Paper Presented at a Conference

on Women's Development. Sussex, England: University of Sussex. 1978.

Meer, Fatima
Women in the Apartheid Society. New York: United Nations. U.N. Centre Against Apartheid. April, 1985. 31p.

Nkabinde, C.
"The Legal Position of African Women in Employment." IPST Bulletin (University of Zululand). Volume 12 1978. pp. 27-32.

Ntantala, Phyllis
An African Tragedy: The Black Woman Under Apartheid. Detroit, Michigan: Agascha Productions. 1976. 137p.

Plaatje, S.T.
"The Mote and the Beam: An Epic on Sex-Relationship 'Twixt White and Black in British South Africa." English in Africa. Volume 3 #2 September, 1976. pp. 85-92.

Poinsette, Cheryl
"Black Women Under Apartheid: An Introduction." Harvard Women's Law Journal. Volume 8 Spring, 1985. pp. 93-119.

Preston-Whyte, Eleanor
"Race Attitudes and Behavior: The Case of Domestic Employment in White South African Homes." (In) Orkin, F.M. and Welz, S.E. (eds.). Society in Southern Africa, 1975-1978: Proceedings of the Association for Sociology in Southern Africa. Johannesburg: ASSA. 1979.

Preston-Whyte, Eleanor and Nene, Sibongile
Where the Formal Sector is not the Answer: Women and Poverty in Rural KwaZulu. Rondebosch, South Africa: University of Cape Town. SALDRU, School of Economics. Carnegie Conference Paper #235. 1984. 49p.

Preston-Whyte, Eleanor M.
"Race Attitudes and Behavior: The Case of Domestic Employment in White South African Homes." African Studies. Volume 35 #2 1976. pp. 71-90.

Ridd, Rosemary
"Where Women Must Dominate: Response to Oppression in A South African Urban Community." (In) Ardener, Shirley (ed.). Women and Space: Ground Rules and Social Maps. New York: St. Martin's Press. 1981. pp. 187-204.

Riekert, Julian
"Race, Sex and the Law in Colonial Natal." Journal of Natal and Zulu History. Volume 6 1983. pp. 82, 97.

Roscani, Luisa
"Qwa Qwa - Relocation and Survival: The Effects of Relocation on Women." B.Soc.Sci. Thesis: University of Natal. Durban, South Africa. 1983.

Ross, R.
"Sexuality and Slavery at the Cape in the Eighteenth Century." (In) University of London (eds.). The Societies of Southern Africa in the Nineteenth and

Twentieth Centuries. London: University of London.
Institute of Commonwealth Studies. Seminar Papers.
Volume 8 #22. 1977.

Russell, Kathryn
"The Internal Relation Between Production and
Reproduction: Reflections on the Manipulation of Family
Life in South Africa." Journal of Social Philosophy.
Volume 15 Summer, 1984. pp. 14-25.

Schreiner, J.A.
"Organising Women in the Liberation Struggle." (In)
National Union of South African Students (NUSAS). NUSAS
Conference on Women, University of the Witwatersrand,
July, 1982. Cape Town, South Africa: NUSAS Women's
Directive. 1983.

Sikakane, Joyce
A Widow in Soweto. London: International Defense and Aid
Fund for Southern Africa. 1977. 80p.

Sikakane, Joyce
"Women Under Apartheid." Paper Presented at a Conference
Sponsored by the British Anti-Apartheid Movement.
London, England. April, 1976.

United Nations
The Plight of Black Women in Apartheid South Africa. New
York: United Nations. Department of Public Information.
1981. 35p.

United Nations
International Conference on Women and Apartheid Report.
New York: United Nations. 1982. 38p.

United Nations
The Effects of Apartheid on the Status of Women in
Southern Africa. New York: United Nations. July, 1980.

United Nations
"The Effects of Apartheid on the Status of Women in South
Africa and Namibia." Paper Presented at the United
Nations World Conference of the United Nations Decade for
Women: Equality, Development and Peace, Copenhagen,
Denmark. New York: United Nations. 1980. 37p.

United Nations
The Effects of Apartheid on the Status of Women in South
Africa, Namibia and Southern Rhodesia. New York: United
Nations. 1978.

United Nations Centre Against Apartheid
"The Effects of Apartheid on the Status of Women in South
Africa." Black Scholar. Volume 10 #1 September, 1978.
pp. 11-21.

United Nations Centre Against Apartheid
African Women and Apartheid in Labour Matters. New York:
United Nations Centre Against Apartheid. Notes and
Documents Series #20/80. July, 1980. 13p.

United Nations Centre Against Apartheid
Mrs. Winnie Mandela: Profile in Courage and Defiance. New
York: United Nations Centre Against Apartheid. February,
1978.

United Nations Economic Commission for Africa (UNECA)
Apartheid and the Status of Women. Addis Ababa,
Ethiopia: UNECA. Regional Prepatory Meeting of the UNECA
Second Regional Conference for the Integration of Women
in Development, Lusaka, Zambia. December 3-7, 1979.

Unterhalter, Beryl
"Women in Struggle--South Africa." Third World
Quarterly. Volume 5 #4 1983. pp. 886-893.

Unterholter, Elaine
"South Africa: Women in Struggle." Third World
Quarterly. Volume 5 #4 1983. pp. 886-893.

Van Vuuren, Nancy
Women Against Apartheid: The Fight for Freedom in South
Africa, 1920-1975. Palo Alto, California: R and E
Research Association. 1979. 133p.

Vaughan, Iris
The Diary of Iris Vaughan. Cape Town, South Africa:
Howard Timmins. 1982. 62p.

Walker, Cherryl
"Women and Politics: The Anti-Pass Campaign of the
1950's." Paper Presented at the University of Cape Town
Summer School. Cape Town, South Africa: University of
Cape Town. 1979.

Wells, J.
"Interview With Josie Palmer." South African Institute
of Race Relations Journal. October, 1977.

Wells, Julia C.
"Women's Resistance to Passes in Bloemfontein During the
Inter-War Period." Africa Perspective. Volume 15
Autumn, 1980. pp. 16-35.

Wells, Julia C.
"The History of Black Women's Struggle Against Pass Laws
in South Africa, 1900-1960." Ph.D Dissertation: Columbia
University. New York, New York. 1982. 414p.

Wells, Julia C.
"Why Women Rebel: A Comparative Study of South African
Women's Resistance in Bloemfontein (1913) and
Johannesburg (1958)." Journal of Southern African
Studies. Volume 10 #1 October, 1983. pp. 55-70.

Wells, Julia C.
"Passes and Bypasses: Freedom of Movement for African
Women Under the Urban Areas Act of South Africa." (In)
Hays, Margaret J. and Wright, Marcia (eds.). African
Women and the Law: Historical Perspectives. Boston:
Boston University. African Studies Center. Boston
University Papers on Africa. Volume Seven. 1982. pp.
125-150.

World Health Organization (WHO)
Health Implications of Apartheid on Women. Geneva: WHO.
1979.

Yawitch, Joanne
"Rural Natal 1959: The Women's Riots." Africa
Perspective. Volume 5 1977. pp. 1-17.

Yawitch, Joanne
  "Apartheid and Family Life." Work in Progress. Volume
  27 1983. pp. 40-42.
Yawitch, Joanne
  Tightening the Noose: African Women and Influx Control in
  South Africa, 1950-1980. Rondebosch, South Africa:
  University of Cape Town. SALDRU. School of Economics.
  Carnegie Conference Paper #82. 1984. 36p.
Yawitch, Joanne
  "Tightening the Noose: African Women and Influx Control
  in South Africa, 1950-1980." Paper Presented to the
  Association for Sociology in Southern Africa.
  Johannesburg: University of the Witwatersrand. 1984.

ARTS

Gunner, E.
  "Songs of Innocence and Experience: Women as Composers
  and Performers of Izibongo, Zulu Praise Poetry."
  Research in African Literatures. Volume 10 #2 Fall,
  1979. pp. 239-267.
Gunner, Elizabeth
  "Women as Composers and Performers of Zulu Praise Poetry:
  Some Praise Poems." (In) University of York. Centre for
  Southern African Studies (ed.). Southern African
  Research in Progress. York, England: University of York.
  Collected Papers Volume 3. 1978. pp. 1-17.
Johnston, Thomas F.
  "Levirate Practices of the Shangana-Tsonga, Seen Through
  Widows Ritual Songs." Folklore. Volume 94 #1 1983. pp.
  66-74.
Joseph, Rosemary
  "Zulu Women's Music." African Music. Volume 6 #3 1983.
  pp. 53-89.
Krause, Richard A.
  The Clay Sleeps: An Ethnoarchaeological Study of Three
  African Potters. University, Alabama: University of
  Alabama Press. 1985. 203p.
Van Coeverden de Groot, H.A.
  "The Duration of Normal Labour in Cape Town Whites."
  South African Medical Journal. Volume 54 #27 December
  30, 1978. pp. 1125-1129.

BIBLIOGRAPHIES

Durban Women's Bibliography Group
  Women in Southern Africa: A Bibliography. Durban, South
  Africa: The Group. 1985. 107p.

CULTURAL ROLES

Alverson, Hoyt
    Mind in the Heart of Darkness: Value and Self-Idenity
    Among the Tswana of Southern Africa. New Haven,
    Connecticut: Yale University Press. 1978. 299p.
Anonymous
    The Effects of Apartheid on the Status of Women in South
    Africa. New York: United Nations. Centre Against
    Apartheid. Notices and Documents. 1978. 26p.
Anonymous
    "Effects of Apartheid on the Status of Women in South
    Africa." Objective Justice. Volume 10 #1 Spring, 1978.

Anonymous
    "Effects of Apartheid on the Status of Women in Southern
    Africa." Paper Presented at the World Conference of the
    United Nations Decade for Women, Copenhagen, Denmark,
    July 14-30, 1980. New York: United Nations. 1980.
Anonymous
    "'I Opened the Road for You': Dora Tamana and South
    Africa." ISIS International Bulletin. #21 1981.
Anonymous
    Laundry, Liquor and 'Playing Ladish': African Women in
    Johannesburg, 1903-1939. London: University of London.
    Centre of International and Area Studies. South African
    Social History Workshop. Unpublished. June, 1978.
Anonymous
    "South African Women." Sechaba. August, 1979. pp.
    19-21.
Anonymous
    "Women Under Apartheid." U.N. Chronicle. Volume 19
    July, 1982. pp. 40-41.
Anonymous
    Women Under Apartheid: In Photographs and Text. London:
    International Defense and Aid Fund for Southern Africa.
    1982. 120p.
Anonymous
    "Women and Changing Relations of Control." (In) South
    African Research Service (eds.). South Africa Review:
    Same Foundations New Facades. Johannesburg: Raven.
    1983. pp. 278-299.
Anonymous
    "General Questions on the Position of Black Women in
    South Africa: An Interview With Sheena Duncan, August,
    1979." Africa Perspective. Volume 15 August, 1980.
    pp. 56-69.
Anonymous
    "Sudan: Arab Women's Struggle." The Second Wave. Volume
    2 #2 1977.
Anonymous
    "Women: The Family Food Producers in South Africa."
    Apartheid Bulletin. #126 1978.

SOUTH AFRICA

Anonymous
"South Africa and Lesotho: Three Lesbian Conversations."
Connexions. #3 Winter, 1982.
Anonymous
"South Africa: A Bulletin From Within." (In) Morgan,
Robin (ed.). Sisterhood is Global. Garden City, New
York: Anchor Books. 1984. pp. 618-620.
Arenson, Paul and Moizen, Inga
"Women Office Cleaners on Night Shift: A Report on the
Study of the Effects on Night-Shift Work on the Health
and Social Conditions of Women Office Cleaners in Some
Johannesburg Office Blocks." South African Labour
Bulletin. Volume 9 #3 December, 1983. pp. 74-81.
Baartman, D.
"Traditional and Modern Approaches to the Health Care of
the Pregnant Woman in Xhosa Society." M.A. Thesis:
University of South Africa. Pretoria, South Africa.
1983.
Barling, Julian and Lanham, W.
"Beliefs Regarding the Consequences of Birth Control
Among Black, Colored, Indian and White South Africans."
Journal of Social Psychology. Volume 105 Part One June,
1978. pp. 149-150.
Barling, Julian and Fincham, Frank
"Locus of Control Beliefs in Male and Female Indian and
White School Children in South Africa." Journal of
Crosscultural Psychology. Volume 9 June, 1978. pp.
227-236.
Barling, Julian
"Multidimensional Locus of Control Beliefs Among English
Speaking South African Mothers." Journal of Social
Psychology. Volume 111 1st Quarter June, 1980. pp.
139-140.
Barrett, Jane
"Knitmore: A Study in the Relationship Between Sex and
Class." B.A. Honors Dissertation: University of the
Witwatersrand. Johannesburg, South Africa. 1981.
Beall, J.
"Unwanted Guests: Indian Women in the Context of
Indentured Immigation to the Natal." Paper Presented to
the Conference Commemorating the 150th Anniversary of
Indian Indentured Immigration and the Abolition of
Slaves. Moka, Mauritius. October, 1984.
Beall, J.D.
"Changing Function and Status of Women in Zululand,
1818-1879." Paper Presented to the Development Studies
Research Group. Pietermarizburg, South Africa:
University of Natal. 1982.
Beall, J.D.
"The Changing Role and Status of African Women in the
Political Economy of Colonial Natal." Paper Presented at
the 13th Annual Congress of the Association of
Sociologists of Southern Africa. 1982.

329

SOUTH AFRICA

Beall, J.D.
"The Function and Status of African Women in the Social and Economic Life of Natal and Zululand, 1818-1879." B.A. Honors Dissertation: University of Natal. Durban, South Africa. 1981.
Beavon, K. and Rogerson, C.
"The Changing Role of Women in the Informal Sector of South Africa." (In) Drakakissmith, D. (ed.). Urbanization in the Developing World. London: Croom Helm. 1980.
Becken, Hans-Jurgen
"Give Me Water, Women of Samaria: The Pilgrimage of Southern African Blacks in the 1980's." Journal of Religion in Africa. Volume 14 #2 1983. pp. 115-129.
Becker, Ruth
"The Sexual Division of Labour and its Implications for Trade Union Organization: A Case Study." B.A. Honors Dissertation: University of the Witwatersrand. Johannesburg, South Africa. 1983.
Behardien, Gadaja and Lehulere, K. and Shaw, Anita
Domestic Workers in Poverty. Rondebosch, South Africa: University of Cape Town. SALDRU. School of Economics. Carnegie Conference Paper #114. 1984. 76p.
Behr, D.
"Women and Work, in Psychological Perspective." Journal of the University of Durban-Westville. Volume 2 #4 1976. pp. 9-18.
Bekker, J.C.
Marriage, Money, Property and the Law: A Guide to the Legal and Financial Consequences of a Marriage Between Africans. Durban/Pretoria, South Africa: Butterworths. 1983. 53p.
Bekker, J.C.
"Grounds for Divorce in African Customary Marriages." Comparative and International Law Journal of Southern Africa. Volume 9 #3 November, 1976. pp. 346-355.
Berger, Iris
Sources of Class Consciousness: The Experience of Women Workers in South Africa, 1973-1980. Boston: Boston University. African Studies Center. Working Paper #55. 1982. 27p.
Berger, Iris
"Sources of Class Consciousness: South African Women in Recent Labor Struggles." International Journal of African Historical Studies. Volume 16 #1 1983. pp. 49-66.
Berning, G.
"The Status and Position of Black Women in Natal Between 1845 and 1891." B.A.Honors Dissertation: University of Natal. Pietermaritzburg, South Africa. 1980.
Bhana, Kastoor
"Indian Parents and Their Youth: Some Perceived and

Actual Differences." South African Journal of Sociology.
Volume 15 #3 August, 1984. pp. 124-128.
Blakeley, Brian L.
"Women and Imperialism: The Colonial Office and Female
Emigration to South Africa, 1901-1910." Albion. Volume
13 #2 1981. pp. 131-149.
Bloch, B. and Davies, A.H.
"Evaluation of a Combined Oestrogen-Progestogen
Injectable Contraceptive." South African Medical
Journal. Volume 53 #21 May 27, 1978. pp. 846-847.
Bozzoli, Belinda
"Migrant Women and South African Social Change:
Biographical Approaches to Social Analysis." African
Studies. Volume 44 #1 1985. pp. 87-96.
Bozzoli, Belinda
"Women's Work: The Story of Mrs. S." (In) National Union
of South African Students (NUSAS). NUSAS Conference on
Women. Cape Town, South Africa: NUSAS Women's Directive.
1983.
Bradshaw, Evelyn
The Use of Tobacco and Alcoholic Beverages by Male and
Female Xhosa in Transkei in Relation to Cancer of the
Oesophagus. Grahamstown, South Africa: Rhodes
University. Institute of Social and Economic Research.
Occasional Paper #27. 1983. 46p.
Brindley, Marianne
"Old Women in Zulu Culture: The Old Woman and
Childbirth." South African Journal of Ethnology. Volume
8 #3 1985. pp. 98-108.
Brindley, Marianne
"The Role of the Old Women in the Zulu Culture." Ph.D
Dissertation: University of Zululand. Kwa-Dlangezwa,
South Africa. 1982.
Bromberger, Norman and Gandor, Mark
"Economic and Demographic Functioning of Rural Households
in the Mahlabatini District Kwazulu." Social Dynamics.
Volume 10 #2 June, 1984. pp. 20-37.
Brown, Barbara B.
The Political Economy of Population Policy in South
Africa. Boston: Boston University. African Studies
Center. African Studies Working Paper #71. 1983. 15p.
Budlender, Debbie and Meintjes, Sheila and Schreiner, Jenny
"Women and Resistance in South Africa: A Review Article."
Journal of Southern African Studies. Volume 10 #1
October, 1983. pp. 131+.
Burman, Sandra
"Divorce and the Disadvantaged." (In) Hirschon, Renbee
(ed.). Women and Property, Women as Property. London:
Croom Helm. Oxford Women's Series. 1984.
Burman, Sandra B.
"Roman Dutch Family Law for Africans: The Black Divorce
Court in Action." Acta Juridica. 1983. pp. 171-190.

Burman, Sandra B. and Barry, J.
    Divorce and Deprivation in South Africa. Rondebosch,
    South Africa: University of Cape Town. SALDRU, School of
    Economics. Carnegie Conference Paper #87. 1984. 54p.
Cachalia, Amina
    "Indian Women in Resistance." Paper Presented at the
    National Union of South African Students (NUSAS)
    Conference on Women, July, 1982. Johannesburg:
    University of Witwatersrand. NUSAS Women's Directive.
    1983.
Carstens, Peter
    "The Socio-Economic Context of Initiation Ceremonies
    Among Two Southern African Peoples." Canadian Journal of
    African Studies. Volume 16 #3 1982. pp. 502-522.
Chabaku, Motlalepula
    "'We Carry the Cross Close to Us': A South African Woman
    Talks About Her Land and Her Faith." Sojourners. Volume
    9 #7 July, 1980. pp. 16-18.
Chabaku, Motlalepula
    "Southern Africa: Going Up the Mountain." (In) Morgan,
    Robin (ed.). Sisterhood is Global. Garden City, New
    York: Anchor Books. 1984. pp. 600-617.
Cheetham, R.W. and Rzadkowolski, A. and Rataemane, S.
    "Psychiatric Disorders of the Puerperium in South African
    Women of Nguni Origin--A Pilot Study." South African
    Medical Journal. Volume 60 #13 September 26, 1981. pp
    502-506.
Chetty, Romila
    "The Changing Family: A Study of the Indian Family in
    South Africa." South African Journal of Sociology.
    Volume 11 #2 September, 1980. pp.26-39.
Chetty, Thiagaraj D.
    Job Satisfaction on Indian Married Women in the Clothing
    Manufacturing Industry in Durban and its Effects on the
    Interpersonal Family Relationships. Durban, South
    Africa: University of Durban-Westville. Institute for
    Social and Economic Research. 1983. 130p.
Church, J.
    "A New Dispensation for Black Women?: A Note on Act 6 of
    1981 (KwaZulu)." Comparative and International Law
    Journal of Southern Africa. Volume 16 #1 1983. pp.
    100-102.
Church, Joan
    "Marriage and Human Rights: A Note on the Bophuthatswana
    Marriage Act." Codicillus. Volume 22 #2 1981. pp.
    220-266.
Cock, Jacklyn
    "Childcare and the Working Mother" Africa Perspective.
    Volume 26 1985. pp. 29-60.
Cock, Jacklyn
    Maids and Madams: A Study in the Politics of
    Exploitation. Johannesburg: Raven Press. 1980. 410p.

Cock, Jacklyn
"Disposable Nannies: Domestic Servants in the Political
Economy of South Africa." Review of African Political
Economy. #21 May-September, 1981. pp. 63-83.
Cock, Jacklyn
"The Missionary Articulation of Sexual Ideology and the
Initial Incorporation of Black Women Into Wage Labour."
Africa Perspective. Volume 13 1979. pp. 16-26.
Cock, Jacklyn
"Black and White Women: A Socio-Historical Study of
Domestic Workers and Their Employers in the Eastern
Cape." Ph.D Dissertation: Rhodes University.
Grahamstown, South Africa. 1979.
Cooper, C. and Ensor, Linda
African Woman's Handbook on the Law. Johannesburg: South
African Institute of Race Relations. 1980. 41p.
Crause, H.L. and Botha, P.M.C.
Prostitution: An Analysis of the Social System Centered
in the Harbour Area of Port Elizabeth by Night. Port
Elizabeth, South Africa: University of Port Elizabeth.
Youth Research Project Publication #3. 1977.
De Haas, Mary
"Changing Patterns of Black Marriage and Divorce in
Durban." M.Soc.Sci. Thesis: University of Natal.
Durban, South Africa. 1984.
Dlamini, C.R.
"The Transformation of a Customary Marriage in Zulu Law."
Comparative and International Law Journal of Southern
Africa. Volume 16 #3 November, 1983. pp. 383-392.
Dlamini, C.R.M.
"A Juridical Analysis and Critical Evaluation of Ilobolo
in a Changing Zulu Society." L.L.D Dissertation:
University of Zululand. Kwa-Dlangezwa, South Africa.
1983.
Drower, S.J. and Nash, E.S.
"Therapeutic Abortion on Psychiatric Ground. Part One: A
Local Study." South African Medical Journal. Volume 54
#15 October 7, 1978. pp. 604-608.
Duckitt, J.H.
"Psychological Factors Related to Subjective Health
Perception Among Elderly Women." Humanitas. Volume 9 #4
1983. pp. 441-449.
Duncan, Sheena
"Aspects of Family Breakdown." Work in Progress. Volume
27. 1983. pp. 36-38.
Egan, Siobhan
"Black Women in South African Agriculture: An
Introductory Study of Life and Labour in the
Countryside." B.A. Honors Dissertation: University of
Natal. Durban, South Africa. 1983.
El-Attar, M. and Nouri, Mohamed O.
"Socioeconomic Characteristics and Fertility Level in the
Sudan." (In) American Statistical Association (ASA).

1983 Proceedings of the Social Statistics Section.
Washington, D.C.: ASA. 1983. pp. 407-411.
Erasmus, G.
"Decision-Making in Regard to the Use of Contraceptives
After Confinement: A Study Among Urban Black Women."
South African Journal of Sociology. Volume 15 #2 May,
1984. pp. 94-97.
Fagan, J.J.
"New Rights for Married Women." Social Work. Volume 20
#4 1984. pp. 200-201.
Farrand, Dorothy M. and Holdstock, T. Len
"Dreams of a Sangoma or Indigenous Healer." Journal of
African Studies. Volume 9 #2 Summer, 1982. pp. 68-75.
Federal Council of the National Party of South Africa
Women, Our Silent Soldiers. Bloemfontein, South Africa:
Federal Council of the National Party of South Africa.
August, 1978.
Fernihough, T.J. and Munoz, W.P. and Mahadeyo, I.
"The Role of Brucella Abortus in Spontaneous Abortion
Among the Black Population." South African Medical
Journal. Volume 68 #6 September 14, 1985. pp. 379-380.
Finlayson, Rosalie
"Hlonipha: The Women's Language of Avoidance Among the
Xhosa." Studies in African Linguistics. Supplement #8
December, 1981. pp. 25-28.
Fisher, F.
"Women in Pre-Capitalist Societies in South Africa."
Paper Presented at the University of Cape Town Summer
School. Cape Town, South Africa: University of Cape
Town. January, 1979.
Flepp, Caroline
"Women Under Apartheid; A Triple Oppression." UNESCO
Courier. Volume 38 #4 April, 1985. pp. 14-15.
Friedman, Annette
"The Relationship Between Religiosity and Morality in a
Group of Female College Students." B.A. Honors
Dissertation: University of the Witwatersrand.
Johannesburg, South Africa. 1978.
Fuchs, Jean R.
"One Parent Families: Some Special Implications of
Lone-Parenthood." M.A. Thesis: University of Cape Town.
Cape Town, South Africa. 1980.
Furman, S.N.
"Attitudes of Middle-Class Mothers to Breast-Feeding."
South African Medical Journal. Volume 56 1979. pp.
722-723.
Gaitskell, Deborah
"Housewives, Maids or Mothers: Some Contradictions of
Domesticity for Christian Women in Johannesburg,
1903-1939." Journal of African History. Volume 24 #2
1983. pp. 241-256.
Gaitskell, Deborah and Kimble, Judy
"Class, Race and Gender: Domestic Workers in South

Africa." Review of African Political Economy. #27/28 1983. pp. 86-108.

Gaitskell, Deborah
"Female Mission Initiatives: Black and White Women in Three Witwatersrand Churches, 1903-1939." Ph.D Dissertation: University of London. London, England. 1981.

Gaitskell, Deborah
"'Christian Compounds for Girls': Church Hostels for African Women in Johannesburg, 1907-1970." Journal of Southern African Studies. Volume 6 #1 October, 1979. pp. 44-69.

Gaitskell, Deborah
"'Wailing for Purity': Prayer Unions, African Mothers and Adolescent Daughters, 1912-1940." (In) Marks, S. and Rathbone, R. (eds.). Industrialization and Social Change in South Africa... 1870-1930. New York: Longman. 1982. 357p.

Gerdes, L.C.
"Personality Differences Between Men and Women in Marital Roles." Social Welfare and Pensions. Volume 12 #1 June, 1977. pp. 6-12.

Ginwala, Frene and Mashiane, Shirley
"Women and Apartheid: Black South African Women Stand on the Lowest Rung of the Ladder of Oppression." UNESCO Courier. Volume 33 #7 July, 1980. pp. 13-17.

Goodwin, June
Cry Amandla: South African Women and the Question of Power. New York: Holmes and Meier. 1984. 225p.

Gumede, M.V.
"Traditional Zulu Practitioners and Obstetric Medicine." South African Medical Journal. Volume 53 #21 May 27, 1978. pp. 823-825.

Gunner, E.
"Songs of Innocence and Experience: Women as Composers and Performers of Izibongo, Zulu Praise Poetry." Research in African Literatures. Volume 10 #2 Fall, 1979. pp. 239-267.

Gunner, Elizabeth
"Women as Composers and Performers of Zulu Praise Poetry: Some Praise Poems." (In) University of York. Centre for Southern African Studies (ed.). Southern African Research in Progress. York, England: University of York. Collected Papers Volume 3. 1978. pp. 1-17.

Hamilton, Carolyn A.
"A Fragment of the Jigsaw: Authority and Labour Control Amongst the Early 19th Century Northern Nguni." B.A. Honors Dissertation: University of the Witwatersrand. Johannesburg, South Africa. 1980.

Hampson, M.E.
"Factors Involved in the Acceptance of Voluntary Female Sterilization Among Indians in Natal." South African

Medical Journal. Volume 55 #18 April 28, 1979. pp.
719-721.

Hlophe, J.M.
"The KwaZula Act on the Code of Zulu Law, 6 of 1981--A
Guide to Intending Spouses and Some Comments on the
Custom of Lobolo." Comparative and International Law
Journal of Southern Africa. Volume 17 #2 July, 1984.
pp. 163-171.

International Defense and Aid Fund for Southern Africa
From You Have Struck a Rock: Women and Political
Repression in Southern Africa. London: IDAFSA. 1980.

Isaacs, Gayla C.
"The Media and the Ideal Woman." Africa Report. Volume
28 #2 March-April, 1983. pp. 48-51.

Johnston, Thomas F.
"Levirate Practices of the Shangana-Tsonga, Seen Through
Widows Ritual Songs." Folklore. Volume 94 #1 1983. pp.
66-74.

Joseph, Rosemary
"Zulu Women's Music." African Music. Volume 6 #3 1983.
pp. 53-89.

Katz, I.B. and Brenner, B.N. and Sarzin, B.
"Pregnancy in the Unwed White South African." South
African Medical Journal. Volume 52 #2 July 9, 1977.
pp. 79-81.

Kerr, A.J.
"Claims by South African Customary Union Widows and
Foreign Widows of Similar Unions in Respect of Loss of
Support on the Death of Their Husbands." Speculum Juris.
Volume 12 1983. pp. 37-44.

Kiern, Susan M.
"Convivial Sisterhood: Spirit Mediumship and Client-Core
Network Among Black South African Women." (In)
Hoch-Smith, J. and Spring, Anita (eds.). Women in Ritual
and Symbolic Roles. New York: Plenum Press. 1978. pp.
191-205.

Kiernan, J.P.
"Spouses and Partners: Marriage and Career Among Urban
Zulu Zionists." Urban Anthropology. Volume 8 #1
Spring, 1979. pp. 95-110.

Kimble, Judy and Unterhalter, Elaine
"We Opened the Road for You, You Must Go Forwards: ANC
Women's Struggles, 1912-1982." Feminist Review. Volume
12 1982. pp. 11-16.

Kimmons, Leona
"Women in South Africa--Agony and Struggle." Wree-View.
Fall, 1976. pp. 1-5.

Kinsman, Margaret
"Beasts of Burden: The Subordination of Southern Tswana
Women, ca. 1800-1840." Journal of Southern African
Studies. Volume 10 #1 1983. pp. 39-54.

Klugman, Barbara
"Maternity Rights and Benefits and Protective Legislation

at Work." South African Labour Bulletin. Volume 9 #3
1983. pp. 25-51.
Kotze, J.J.
"Marital Privilege and the Competence and Compellability
of Customary Law: Spouses as Witnesses Against Each
Other." South African Journal of Criminal Law and
Criminology. Volume 7 #2 1983. pp. 157-166.
Krause, Richard A.
The Clay Sleeps: An Ethnoarchaeological Study of Three
African Potters. University, Alabama: University of
Alabama Press. 1985. 203p.
Krige, Eileen J. and Comaroff, John L. (eds.).
Essays on African Marriage in Southern Africa. Cape
Town, South Africa: Wetton. 1981. 205p.
Krige, Eileen J.
"Women-Marriage, With Special Reference to the
Lovedu--Its Significance for the Definition of Marriage."
(In) Tiffany, Sharon W. (ed.). Women and Society: An
Anthropological Reader. St. Albans, Vermont: Eden Press.
1979. pp. 208-237.
Krige, Eileen J. and Krige, J.D.
The Realm of a Rain-Queen: A Study of the Pattern of
Lovedu Society. New York: AMS Press. 1978. 335p.
Krige, Eileen J.
"A Comparative Analysis of Marriage and Social Structure
Among the Southern Bantu." (In) Krige, Eileen J, and
Comaroff, J.L. (eds.). Essays on African Marriage in
Southern Africa. Cape Town, South Africa: Juta. 1981.
Krige, Eileen J.
"Lovedu Marriage and Social Change." (In) Krige, Eileen
J. and Comaroff, J.L. (eds.). Essays on African Marriage
in Southern Africa. Cape Town, South Africa: Juta.
1981.
Kubukeli, Pumla
"Women in Transkei." Paper Presented at the Women
Studies Symposium, University of Transkei. Umtata, South
Africa. March, 1984.
Kunene, Mazisi
Anthem of the Decades--A Zulu Epic Dedicated to the Women
of Africa. London: Heinemann. African Writers Series
#234. 1981. 312p.
Kuper, Adam
"Tied By Bridewealth: The Tsonga Case." (In) Krige, E.J.
and Comaroff, J.L. (eds.). Essays on African Marriage in
Southern Africa. Cape Town, South Africa: Juta. 1981.
Kuzwayo, Ellen
Call Me Woman. London: Women's Press. 1985. 266p.
Lamula, Promise
"Women Under Apartheid." ISIS Women's World. #4
December, 1984.
Landis, Elizabeth
"African Women Under Apartheid." ISIS International
Bulletin. #9 Autumn, 1978. pp. 7-11.

Lapchick, Richard E.
    "The Role of Women in the Struggle Against Apartheid in
    South Africa." (In) Steady, Filomina C. (ed.). The
    Black Woman Cross-Culturally. Cambridge, Massachusetts:
    Schenkman Publishing. 1981. pp. 231-261.
Lapchick, Richard E. and Urdang, Stephanie
    Oppression and Resistance: The Struggle of Women in
    Southern Africa. Westport, Connecticut: Greenwood Press.
    Contributions in Women's Studies. #29. 1982. 234p.
Lapchick, Richard E. and Urdang, Stephanie
    "The Effects of Apartheid on the Status of Women in
    Employment in South Africa." Paper Presented at the
    World Conference of the United Nations Decade for Women,
    Copenhagen, Denmark, July 14-30, 1980. New York: United
    Nations. 1980. 40p.
Larsen, J.V. and Msane, C.L. and Monkhe, M.C.
    "The Zulu Traditional Birth Attendant. An Evaluation of
    Her Attitudes and Techniques and Their Implications for
    Health Education." South African Medical Journal.
    Volume 63 #14 April 2, 1983. pp. 540-542.
Larsen, J.V. and Msane, C.L. and Monkhe, M.C.
    "The Fate of Women Who Deliver at Home in Rural Kwazulu:
    Assessment of the Place of Traditional Birth Attendents
    in the South African Health Services." South African
    Medical Journal. Volume 63 #14 April 2, 1983. pp.
    534-545.
Lawton, L.
    Working Women. Johannesburg: Raven Press. 1985.
Lipman, Beata
    We Make Freedom: Women in South Africa Speak. Boston:
    Pandora Press. 1984. 141p.
Locke, M.
    "Sexism and Racism: Obstacles to Development of Black
    Women in South Africa." (In) Fowlkes, D.L. and McClure,
    C.S. (eds.). Feminist Visions: Toward a Transformation
    of the Liberal Arts Curriculum. University, Alabama:
    University of Alabama Press. 1984. pp. 119-129.
Lotter, Johann M.
    "Socio-Economic Status and Fertility: The Emergence of
    New Trends Among White South Africans." Humanitas.
    Volume 4 #3 1978. pp. 323-325.
Lotter, Johann M.
    "Some Aspects of Indian Fertility in South Africa."
    Humanitas. Volume 3 #4 1976. pp. 419-426.
Lotter, Johann M.
    Attitudes of Black South African Men Towards Fertility
    and Family Planning. Pretoria, South Africa: South
    African Human Sciences Research Council. Institute for
    Sociological, Demographic and Criminological Research.
    Research Finding #S-N-96. 1977. 16p.
Lotter, Johann M. and Van Tonder, J.L.
    "Fertility and Family Planning Among Blacks in South

Africa: 1974." Pretoria, South Africa: Human Sciences
Research Council. Report No. S-39. 1976. 111p.
Lotter, Johann M. and Van Tonder, J.L.
Certain Aspects of Human Fertility in Rural
Bophuthatswana. Pretoria, South Africa: South African
Human Sciences Research Council. Institute for
Sociological, Demographic and Criminological Research.
Report #S-54. 1978. 53p.
Mackenzie, D.J.
"African Women and the Urbanization Process in Durban, c.
1920-1949." Paper Presented at the Workshop on African
Urban Life in Durban in the Twentieth Century. Durban,
South Africa: University of Natal. October, 1983.
Mackenzie, D.J.
"A Social History of African Women in Durban, 1920-1950."
M.Soc.Sci. Thesis: University of Natal. Durban, South
Africa. 1984.
Malveaux, J.
"You Have Struck a Rock--A Note on the Status of Black
Women in South Africa." Review of Black Political
Economy. Volume 14 #2/3 1985. pp. 277-284.
Manona, C.W.
"Marriage, Family Life and Migrancy in a Ciskei Village."
(In) Mayer, Philip (ed.). Black Villagers in an
Industrial Society: Anthropological Perspectives on
Labour Migration in South Africa. New York: Oxford
University Press. 1980.
Manyosi, Maud
"Working Women in South Africa." Sechaba. January,
1980. pp. 23-24.
Marks, Shula
"Ruth First: A Tribute." Journal of Southern African
Studies. Volume 10 #1 1983. pp. 123+.
Marwick, M.
"Household Composition and Marriage in a Witwatersrand
African Township." (In) Argyle,J. and Preston-Whyte, E.
(eds.). Social System and Tradition in Southern Africa.
Cape Town, South Africa: Oxford University Press. 1978.
pp. 36-54.
Matsepe-Casaburri, Ivy F.
Women and the Political Economy of Southern Africa.
Harare, Zimbabwe. 1982. 100+p.
Matsepe-Casaburri, Ivy F.
"Changing Roles and Needs of Women in South Africa and
Namibia." Paper Presented at the World Conference for
the United Nations Decade for Women, Copenhagen,
Denmark, July 14-30, 1980. New York: United Nations.
1980.
Mayne, Anne V. and Levett, Ann
"Feminism in South Africa." off our backs. Volume 7
April, 1977. pp. 4.
Meer, Fatima
Women in the Apartheid Society. New York: United

Nations. U.N. Centre Against Apartheid. April, 1985.
31p.

Meer, Fatima (ed.).
Black Women, Durban 1975: Case Studies of 85 Women at
Home and Work. Durban, South Africa: University of
Natal. Sociology Department. 1976.

Meer, Fatima (ed.).
Factory and Family: The Divided Lives of South Africa's
Women Workers. Durban, South Africa: Institute for Black
Research. 1984. 105p.

Middleton-Keirn, Susan
"Convivial Sisterhood: Spirit Mediumship and Client-Core
Network Among Black South African Women." (In)
Hoch-Smith, Judith and Spring, Anita (eds.). Women in
Ritual and Symbolic Roles. New York: Plenum Press.
1978. pp. 191-205.

Mitchell, L.
Tsonga Women: Changes in Production and Reproduction: A
Working Paper. Minneapolis, Minnesota: University of
Minnesota. African History Seminar. 1978.

Mitchell, Mozella G.
"Howard Thurman and Olice Schreiner: Post-Modern Marriage
Post-Mortem." Journal of Religious Thought. Volume 38
Spring-Summer, 1981. pp. 62-72.

Moeno, N.S.
"Illegitimacy in an African Urban Township in South
Africa: An Ethnographic Note." African Studies. Volume
36 #1 1977. pp. 43-48.

Mommsen, C.
"A Psychodiagnostic Study of a Selected Group of Women
Pregnant Out of Wedlock." M.A. Thesis: University of
Orange Free State. Bloemfontein, South Africa. 1978.

Moodley, S.P. and Jialai, I. and Modley, J. and Naicker,
R.S. and Marivate, M.
"Carbohydrate Metabolism in African Women With Twin
Pregnancy." Diabetes Care. Volume 7 #1
January-February, 1984. pp. 72-74.

Moody, Elize
"Women and Development in South Africa." Development:
South African ed. Volume 3 1976. pp. 26-29.

Nattrass, Nicoli
Street Trading in the Transkei: A Struggle Against
Poverty, Persecution, and Prosecution. Durban, South
Africa: University of Natal. Development Studies Unit.
Working Paper #7. 1984. 35p.

Nene, Daphne S.
"A Survey of African Women Petty Traders and
Self-Employed in Town and Country in South Africa." (In)
International Labour Organization (ILO). Rural
Development and Women in Africa. Geneva: ILO. 1984.
pp. 147-154.

Nene, Daphne S.
"Role Enactment of Rural Women: A Sociological

Exploratory Study of the Role Behavior and its
Implications for Rural Development." M.A. Thesis:
University of Zululand. Kwa-Dlangezwa, South Africa.
1983.

Nene, Daphne S.
"Women Caught in Between: The Case of Rural Women in
KwaZulu." Paper Presented to the Women's Studies
Symposium, University of Transkei. Umtata, South Africa:
University of Transkei. March, 1984.

Ngubane, Harriet
"Some Notions of 'Purity' and 'Impurity' Among the Zulu."
Africa. Volume 46 #3 1976.

Ngubane, Harriet
"Marriage, Affinity and the Ancestral Realm: Zulu
Marriage in Female Perspective." (In) Krige, E.J. and
Comaroff, J.L. (eds.). Essays on African Marriage in
Southern Africa. Cape Town, South Africa: Juta. 1981.

Nkabinde, C.
"The Legal Position of African Women in Employment."
IPST Bulletin (University of Zululand). Volume 12 1978.
pp. 27-32.

Ntantala, Phyllis
An African Tragedy: The Black Woman Under Apartheid.
Detroit, Michigan: Agascha Productions. 1976. 137p.

Olmesdahl, M.J.C.
"Marriage and Cohabitation: Cross-Cultural Comparisons."
(In) Eekelaar, J.M. and Katz, S.N. (eds.). Marriage and
Cohabitation in Contemporary Societies: Areas of Legal,
Social and Ethical Change: An International and
Interdisciplinary Study. Toronto, Canada: Butterworth.
1980.

Peart, Nicola S.
"Civil or Christian Marriage and Customary Unions: The
Legal Position of the Discarded Spouse and Children."
Comparative and International Law Journal of South
Africa. Volume 16 #1 1983. pp. 39-64.

Perold, Helene (ed.).
Working Women: A Portrait of South Africa's Black Women
Workers. Braamfontein, South Africa: Raven Press. 1985.
144p.

Plaatje, S.T.
"The Mote and the Beam: An Epic on Sex-Relationship
'Twixt White and Black in British South Africa." English
in Africa. Volume 3 #2 September, 1976. pp. 85-92.

Poinsette, Cheryl
"Black Women Under Apartheid: An Introduction." Harvard
Women's Law Journal. Volume 8 Spring, 1985. pp.
93-119.

Preston-Whyte, E.
"Female Headed Households and Development: Lessons of
Cross-Cultural Models for Research on Women in Southern
Africa." Paper Presented to the Women's Studies

Symposium. Umtata, South Africa: University of Transkei.
March, 1984.

Preston-Whyte, Eleanor and Nene, Sibongile
Where the Formal Sector is not the Answer: Women and
Poverty in Rural KwaZulu. Rondebosch, South Africa:
University of Cape Town. SALDRU, School of Economics.
Carnegie Conference Paper #235. 1984. 49p.

Preston-Whyte, Eleanor M.
"Race Attitudes and Behavior: The Case of Domestic
Employment in White South African Homes." African
Studies. Volume 35 #2 1976. pp. 71-90.

Preston-Whyte, Eleanor M.
"Families Without Marriage: A Zulu Caste Study." (In)
Argyle, W. and Preston-Whyte E. (eds.). Social Systems
and Tradition in Southern Africa. Capetown, South
Africa: Oxford University Press. 1978.

Radebe, M.D.
"A Study of Matrimonial Breakdown Among Urban Blacks."
M.A. Thesis: University of South Africa. Pretoria, South
Africa. 1978.

Ridd, Rosemary
"Where Women Must Dominate: Response to Oppression in A
South African Urban Community." (In) Ardener, Shirley
(ed.). Women and Space: Ground Rules and Social Maps.
New York: St. Martin's Press. 1981. pp. 187-204.

Riekert, Julian
"Race, Sex and the Law in Colonial Natal." Journal of
Natal and Zulu History. Volume 6 1983. pp. 82, 97.

Rivkin, Elizabeth T.
"The Black Woman in South Africa: An Azanian Profile."
(In) Steady, Filomina C. (ed.). The Black Woman
Cross-Culturally. Cambridge, Massachusetts: Schenkman
Publishing. 1981. pp. 215-230.

Roberts, Mary and Rip, M.R.
"Black Fertility Patterns-Cape Town and Ciskei." South
African Medical Journal. Volume 66 #13 September 29,
1984. pp. 481-484.

Robinson, Sally
"Women and Politics of Liberation in South Africa."
Ufahamu. Volume 6 #1 1976.

Roscani, Luisa
"Qwa Qwa - Relocation and Survival: The Effects of
Relocation on Women." B.Soc.Sci. Thesis: University of
Natal. Durban, South Africa. 1983.

Ross, Robert
"The Age at Marriage of White South Africans, 1700-1951."
(In) University of Edinburgh. African Historical
Demography: Proceedings of a Seminar Held in the Centre
of African Studies. Edinburgh, Scotland: University of
Edinburgh. Volume Two. April 24-25, 1981. pp. 487-498.

Ross, Robert
"Oppression, Sexuality and Slavery at the Cape of Good

Hope." Historical Reflections. Volume 6 #2 1979. pp. 421-433.

Ross, S.M. and Van Middelkoop, A. and Khoza, N.C.
"Breast Feeding Practices in a Black Community." South African Medical Journal. Volume 63 #1 January 1, 1983. pp. 23-25.

Roux, A.
"Family Planning Among A Group of Coloured Women." South African Medical Journal. Volume 65 #22 June 2, 1984. pp. 898-901.

Russell, Kathryn
"The Internal Relation Between Production and Reproduction: Reflections on the Manipulation of Family Life in South Africa." Journal of Social Philosophy. Volume 15 Summer, 1984. pp. 14-25.

Rycroft, David K.
"KaDinazulu (Princess) Constance Magogo: Profile." Africa Insight. Volume 15 #4 1985. pp. 244-247.

Saghayroun, Atif A.R.
"Feasibility of Fertility Control in Rural Areas in the Sudan." Economic and Social Research Council Bulletin. #99 September, 1983.

Saling, Michael M. and Cooke, Wendy-Lynne
"Cradling and Transport of Infants by South African Mothers: A Cross Cultural Study." Current Anthropology. Volume 25 #3 1984. pp. 333-335.

Sandler, S.W.
"Spontaneous Abortion in Perspective: A Seven Year Study." South African Medical Journal. Volume 52 #1 December 31, 1977. pp. 115, 118.

Schmidt, Elizabeth S.
"Women of South Africa Speak." Africa Today. Volume 31 #2 1984. pp. 52-54.

Schreiner, J.
"Divisions of Labour in the Manufacturing Industry in the Western Cape, 1950-1965, and the Implications for a Materialist Theory of Women's Subordination." African Studies Honors Paper: University of Cape Town. Cape Town, South Africa. 1981.

Schurink, Willem J. and Levinthal, Terri
"Business Women Exchanging Sex for Money: A Descriptive Survey." South African Journal of Sociology. Volume 14 #4 November, 1983. pp. 154-163.

Schweigart, M.A. and Mostert, W.P.
"The Motivation of Women to Accept Family Planning." Tydskrif vir Rasse-Aangeleenthede. Volume 28 #1/2 January-April, 1977. pp. 18-21.

Shingler, John P.
Women of East London, 1900-1979. East London, South Africa: Griffith Standard Co. 1980.

Showers, Kate
"A Note on Women, Conflict and Migrant Labour." South African Labour Bulletin. Volume 6 #4 November, 1980.

Shuenyane, Esline N.
"Non-Formal Education and Socialization of Pre-Adolescent Girls: An Analysis of Content." M.A. Thesis: University of the Witwatersrand. Johannesburg, South Africa. 1980.

Sibisi, Harriet N.
"How African Women Cope With Migrant Labor in South Africa." Signs. Volume 3 #1 Autumn, 1977. pp. 167-177.

Sibisi, Harriet N.
"How African Women Cope With Migrant Labor in South Africa." (In) Wellesley Editorial Committee. Women and National Development: The Complexities of Change. Chicago: University of Chicago Press. 1977. pp. 167-177.

Sibisi, Harriet N.
"Effects of Training for a Profession on Life Styles and Life-Changes of African Women in South Africa." Paper Presented to the Women in Development Section at the 15th World Conference of the Society for International Development, Amsterdam, Netherlands, November 28-December 3, 1976. 16p.

Sikakane, Joyce
A Widow in Soweto. London: International Defense and Aid Fund for Southern Africa. 1977. 80p.

Sikakane, Joyce
"Women Under Apartheid." Paper Presented at a Conference Sponsored by the British Anti-Apartheid Movement. London, England. April, 1976.

Sinclair, June
"The Financial Consequences of Divorce in South Africa: Judicial Determination or Private Ordering?" International and Comparative Law Quarterly. Volume 32 #4 1983. pp. 785-811.

Sinclair, June
"Marriage: Is it Still a Commitment for Life Entailing a Lifelong Duty of Support?" Acta Juridica. 1983. pp. 75-96.

Smedley, L.N.
"White Housewives: An Introductory Study." South African Journal of Sociology. Volume 17 April, 1978. pp. 61-72.

Snyman, Rita
"A Nurse Looks Back on the Seige of Ladysmith." Africana Notes and News. Volume 22 #5 March, 1977. pp. 180-194.

Snyman. I.
"Social, Cultural and Psychological Barriers to Reduction of Fertility." Royal Society of South Africa. Transactions. Volume 43 Part One 1978. pp. 85-89.

South African Congress of Trade Unions
Conditions of Working Women in South Africa. Dar-es-Salaam, Tanzania: South African Congress of Trade Unions. June, 1979.

Spies, S.B.
    "Women and the War." (In) Warwick, Peter (ed.). The
    South African War: The Anglo-Boer War, 1899-1902.
    London: Longman. 1980. pp. 161-185.
Spuy, Adelemarie V.
    "Inequitable Legal and Economic Aspects of the
    Discrimination Against Women, Especially Married Women in
    South Africa Today." Plural Societies. Volume 9 #1
    Spring, 1978. pp. 49-58.
Spuy, Adelmarie V.
    "South African Women: The Other Discrimination." Munger
    Africana Library Notes. July, 1978. pp. 1-15.
Staniland, H.
    "Some Aspects of Co-Habitation and Home Ownership."
    Natal University Law Review. Volume 2 #3 1979. pp.
    285-297.
Steyn, Anna F. and Uys, J.M.
    "The Changing Position of Black Women in South Africa."
    (In) Lupri, E. (ed.). The Changing Position of Women in
    Family and Society. Leiden, Netherlands: Brill. 1983.
    pp. 344-370.
Stillman, Eric D. and Shapiro, Colin M.
    "Scaling Sex Attitudes and Behavior in South Africa."
    Archives of Sexual Behavior. Volume 8 January, 1979.
    pp. 1-14.
Thetele, Constance B.
    "Women in South Africa: The WAAIC [Women's Association of
    African Independent Churches]." (In) Appiah-Kubi, Kofi
    and Torres, Sergio (eds.). African Theology in Route:
    Papers From the Pan African Conference of Third World
    Theologians, December 17-23, 1977, Accra, Ghana.
    Maryknoll, New York: Orbis Books. 1979. pp. 150-154.
Thomson, R.C.
    Some Discriminatory Laws and Their Effects on African
    Women. Cape Town, South Africa: National Union of South
    African Students (NUSAS). 1978.
Thomson, R.C.
    "Some Discriminatory Laws and Their Effects on African
    Women." Jure ac Legibus. Volume 3 1976. pp. 19-24.
Thornton, L.
    "Breastfeeding in South Africa: Social and Cultural
    Aspects and Strategies for Promotion." Curationis.
    Volume 7 #3 September, 1984. pp. 33-41.
United Nations
    The Plight of Black Women in Apartheid South Africa. New
    York: United Nations. Department of Public Information.
    1981. 35p.
United Nations
    International Conference on Women and Apartheid Report.
    New York: United Nations. 1982. 38p.
United Nations
    The Effects of Apartheid on the Status of Women in
    Southern Africa. New York: United Nations. July, 1980.

United Nations
"The Effects of Apartheid on the Status of Women in South Africa and Namibia." Paper Presented at the United Nations World Conference of the United Nations Decade for Women: Equality, Development and Peace, Copenhagen, Denmark. New York: United Nations. 1980. 37p.

United Nations Centre Against Apartheid
"The Effects of Apartheid on the Status of Women in South Africa." Black Scholar. Volume 10 #1 September, 1978. pp. 11-21.

United Nations Centre Against Apartheid
African Women and Apartheid in Labour Matters. New York: United Nations Centre Against Apartheid. Notes and Documents Series #20/80. July, 1980. 13p.

United Nations Economic Commission for Africa (UNECA)
Apartheid and the Status of Women. Paper Presented at the Regional Prepatory Meeting of the UNECA Second Regional Conference for the Integration of Women in Development, Lusaka, Zambia, December 3-7, 1979. Addis Ababa, Ethiopia: United Nations.

Unterhalter, Beryl
"Women in Struggle--South Africa." Third World Quarterly. Volume 5 #4 1983. pp. 886-893.

Unterholter, Elaine
"South Africa: Women in Struggle." Third World Quarterly. Volume 5 #4 1983. pp. 886-893.

Van Coeverden de Groot, H.A.
"Trends in Maternal Mortality in Cape Town, 1953-1977." Part One. South African Medical Journal. Volume 56 #14 September 29, 1979. pp. 547-552.

Van Coeverden de Groot, H.A.
"Trends in Maternal Mortality in Capetown, 1953-1977." Part Two. South African Medical Journal. Volume 57 #7 February 16, 1980. pp. 224-225.

Van Der Spuy, A.
"Inequitable Legal and Economic Aspects of the Discrimination Against Women, Especially Married Women in South Africa Today." Plural Societies. Volume 9 #1 Spring, 1978. pp. 49-58.

Van Der Vliet, Virginia N.
"Black Marriage: Expectations and Aspirations in an Urban Environment." M.A. Thesis: University of the Witwatersrand. Johannesburg, South Africa. 1982.

Van Heyningen, Elizabeth B.
"The Social Evil of the Cape Colony, 1868-1902: Prostitution and the Contagious Diseases Act." Journal of Southern African Studies. Volume 10 #2 1984. pp. 170-197.

Van Heyningen, Elizabeth B.
"Prostitution and the Contagious Diseases Act: The Social Evil in the Cape Colony, 1868-1902." (In) Saunders, Christopher (ed.). Studies in the History of Cape Town. Cape Town, South Africa: University of Cape Town. Centre

for African Studies and the History Department. Volume Five. 1984. pp. 80-124.

Van Onselen, Charles
"Prostitutes and Proletarians, 1886-1914." (In) Van Onselen, C. Studies in the Social and Economic History of the Witwatersrand, 1886-1914. New York: Longman. Volume One: New Babylon. 1982. pp. 103-143.

Van Regenmortel, P.J. and Van Harte, E.
Family Planning in the Greater Cape Town Area: A Background Study. Bellville, South Africa: University of the Western Cape. Institute for Social Development. October, 1977. 107p.

Van Tonder, J.L.
Fertility Survey 1981: Data Concerning the Coloured Population of South Africa. Pretoria, South Africa: Human Sciences Research Council. Institute for Sociological and Demographic Research. Report #S-120. 1984. 204p.

Van Vuuren, Nancy
Women Against Apartheid: The Fight for Freedom in South Africa, 1920-1975. Palo Alto, California: R and E Research Association. 1979. 133p.

Van Wyk, A.H.
"Matrimonial Property Systems in Comparative Perspective." Acta Juridica. 1983. pp. 53-74.

Van der Merwe, Sandra
"A Portrait of the South African Woman Manager." South African Journal of Business Management. Volume 10 #2 1979. pp. 57-64.

Verster, J.
Trend and Pattern of Fertility in Soweto: An Urban Bantu Community: A Report on the Fertility Sample Survey of the Bantu Population in Soweto. Braamfontein, South Africa: University of the Witwatersrand Press. 1979.

Walker, A.R.P. and Dison, E. and Walker, B.F.
"Dental Caries in South African Rural Black Women Who Had Large Families and Long Lactations." Journal of Tropical Medicine and Hygiene. Volume 86 #6 1983. pp. 201-205.

Walker, A.R.P. and Walker, B.F. and Jones, J. and Duvenhage, A. and Mia, F.P.
"Knowledge of Nutrition Among Housewives in Three South African Ethnic Groups." South African Medical Journal. Volume 62 #17 October 16, 1982. pp. 605-610.

Wells, Julia C.
"Why Women Rebel: A Comparative Study of South African Women's Resistance in Bloemfontein (1913) and Johannesburg (1958)." Journal of Southern African Studies. Volume 10 #1 October, 1983. pp. 55-70.

Whitelaw, D.A.
"Socio-Economic Status and Use of Contraceptives Among Unmarried Primigravidas in Cape Town." South African Medical Journal. Volume 64 #18 October 22, 1983. pp. 712-715.

Wilson, Monica
   "Xhosa Marriage in Historical Perspective." (In) Krige,
   Eileen J. and Comarof, J.L. (eds.). Essays on African
   Marriage in Southern Africa. Cape Town, South Africa:
   Juta. 1981.
World Health Organization (WHO)
   Health Implications of Apartheid on Women. Geneva: WHO.
   1979.
Wright, John
   "Control of Women's Labour in the Zulu Kingdom." (In)
   Peires, J.B. (ed.). Before and After Shaka: Papers in
   Nguni History. Grahamstown, South Africa: Rhodes
   University. Institute of Social and Economic Research.
   1983. pp. 82-99.
Yawitch, Joanne
   "Natal 1959: The Women's Protests." Paper Presented at
   the Conference on the History of Opposition in Southern
   Africa. Johannesburg: (Student's) Development Studies
   Group of the University of the Witwatersrand. January,
   1978. pp. 206-223.
Yawitch, Joanne
   Black Women in South Africa: Capitalism, Employment and
   Reproduction. Johannesburg: Africa Perspective
   Dissertation #2. 1980.
Yawitch, Joanne
   "Women and Squatting: A Winterveld Case Study." (In)
   University of Witwatersrand. Working Papers in Southern
   African Studies. Johannesburg: University of the
   Witwatersrand. May, 1979. pp. 199-227.
Zlotnik, Zia
   "Achievement Motivation, Self-Concept, Feminine Role
   Perception and Feminity in White Female University
   Students." B.A. Honors Dissertation: University of the
   Witwatersrand. Johannesburg, South Africa. 1982.

DEVELOPMENT AND TECHNOLOGY

Armstrong, Amanda
   "Micro-Technology and the Control of Women in the
   Office." South African Labour Bulletin. Volume 9 #3
   1983. pp. 53-73.
Beavon, K. and Rogerson, C.
   "The Changing Role of Women in the Informal Sector of
   South Africa." (In) Drakakissmith, D. (ed.).
   Urbanization in the Developing World. London: Croom
   Helm. 1980.
Guyer, Jane I.
   "Women in the Rural Economy: Contemporary Variations."
   (In) Hay, Margaret J. and Stichter, Sharon (eds.).
   African Women South of the Sahara. New York: Longman.
   1984. pp. 19-32.

Landis, Elizabeth
    "African Women Under Apartheid." ISIS International
    Bulletin. #9 Autumn, 1978. pp. 7-11.
Lipman, Beata
    We Make Freedom: Women in South Africa Speak. Boston:
    Pandora Press. 1984. 141p.
Locke, M.
    "Sexism and Racism: Obstacles to Development of Black
    Women in South Africa." (In) Fowlkes, D.L. and McClure,
    C.S. (eds.). Feminist Visions: Toward a Transformation
    of the Liberal Arts Curriculum. University, Alabama:
    University of Alabama Press. 1984. pp. 119-129.
Mariotti, Amelia
    "The Incorporation of African Women Into Wage Employment
    in South Africa, 1920-1970." Ph.D Dissertation:
    University of Connecticut, Storrs. Stoors, Connecticut.
    1980. 338p.
Mariotti, Amelia
    "Capitalist Development and State Policy in South Africa:
    African Women, the Family and the Price of Labour Power."
    Paper Presented at the Conference on African Women in
    History. Santa Clara, California: University of Santa
    Clara. 1981.
Matsepe, Ivy F.
    "African Women's Labor in the Political Economy of South
    Africa, 1880 -1970." Ph.D Dissertation: Rutgers
    University. New Brunswick, New Jersey. 1984. 327p.
Matsepe-Casaburri, Ivy F.
    Women and the Political Economy of Southern Africa.
    Harare, Zimbabwe. 1982. 100+p.
Matsepe-Casaburri, Ivy F.
    "Cheap Labour Policies and Their Implications for African
    Women in South Africa." Paper Presented at a Conference
    on Women's Development. Sussex, England: University of
    Sussex. 1978.
Matsepe-Casaburri, Ivy F.
    "Changing Roles and Needs of Women in South Africa and
    Namibia." Paper Presented at the World Conference for
    the United Nations Decade for Women, Copenhagen,
    Denmark, July 14-30, 1980. New York: United Nations.
    1980.
Moody, Elize
    "Women and Development in South Africa." Development:
    South African ed. Volume 3 1976. pp. 26-29.
Nene, Daphne S.
    "Role Enactment of Rural Women: A Sociological
    Exploratory Study of the Role Behavior and its
    Implications for Rural Development." M.A. Thesis:
    University of Zululand. Kwa-Dlangezwa, South Africa.
    1983.
Nene, Daphne S.
    The Role and Potential of Black Women's Voluntary
    Associations in Development: The Case of KwaZulu and

Natal. Kwa Dlangezwa, South Africa: University of
Zululand. Publications of the University of Zululand.
Series B #19. 1982. 74p.

Norton, A.B.
"The Future of Women in South African Banks." South
African Banker. Volume 74 #2 May, 1977. pp. 85-88.

Preston-Whyte, E.
"Female Headed Households and Development: Lessons of
Cross-Cultural Models for Research on Women in Southern
Africa." Paper Presented to the Women's Studies
Symposium. Umtata, South Africa: University of Transkei.
March, 1984.

Sibisi, Harriet N.
"Effects of Training for a Profession on Life Styles and
Life-Changes of African Women in South Africa." Paper
Presented to the Women in Development Section at the 15th
World Conference of the Society for International
Development. Amsterdam, Netherlands. Nov. 28-Dec. 3,
1976. 16p.

Smit, G.J.
"Capable Managers Needed: A Strategy for Developing
Women's Potential." South African Journal of Labor
Relations. September, 1978. pp. 3-8.

Smit, G.J.
"Capable Managers Needed: A Strategy for Developing
Women's Potential." South African Journal of Labour
Relations. Volume 2 #3 September, 1978. pp. 3-8.

Tredoux, M.
"The Female Earth Scientist in Southern Africa II."
Geological Society of South Africa Quarterly News
Bulletin. Volume 24 #2 1981. pp. 34-36.

Van der Merwe, Sandra
"A Portrait of the South African Woman Manager." South
African Journal of Business Management. Volume 10 #2
1979. pp. 57-64.

Yawitch, Joanne
Black Women in South Africa: Capitalism, Employment and
Reproduction. Johannesburg: Africa Perspective
Dissertation #2. 1980.

Yawitch, Joanne
Tightening the Noose: African Women and Influx Control in
South Africa, 1950-1980. Rondebosch, South Africa:
University of Cape Town. SALDRU. School of Economics.
Carnegie Conference Paper #82. 1984. 36p.

Yawitch, Joanne
"Tightening the Noose: African Women and Influx Control
in South Africa, 1950-1980." Paper Presented to the
Association for Sociology in Southern Africa.
Johannesburg: University of the Witwatersrand. 1984.

DIVORCE

Anonymous
Garment Workers Unite: The Story of the Transvaal Garment
Workers Union. Salt River, South Africa: Labour History
Group. 1983. 51p.
Barnard, A.H.
"An Evaluation of the Divorce Act 70 of 1979." Acta
Juridica. 1983. pp. 39-51.
Bekker, J.C.
"Grounds for Divorce in African Customary Marriages."
Comparative and International Law Journal of Southern
Africa. Volume 9 #3 November, 1976. pp. 346-355.
Burman, Sandra and Martine, Huvers
"Church Versus State: Divorce Legislation and Divided
South Africa." Journal of Southern African Studies.
Volume 12 #1 October, 1985. pp. 116-135.
Burman, Sandra
"Divorce and the Disadvantaged." (In) Hirschon, Renbee
(ed.). Women and Property, Women as Property. London:
Croom Helm. Oxford Women's Series. 1984.
Burman, Sandra B.
"Roman Dutch Family Law for Africans: The Black Divorce
Court in Action." Acta Juridica. 1983. pp. 171-190.
Burman, Sandra B. and Barry, J.
Divorce and Deprivation in South Africa. Rondebosch,
South Africa: University of Cape Town. SALDRU, School of
Economics. Carnegie Conference Paper #87. 1984. 54p.
De Haas, Mary
"Changing Patterns of Black Marriage and Divorce in
Durban." M.Soc.Sci. Thesis: University of Natal.
Durban, South Africa. 1984.
Kinsman, Margaret
"Beasts of Burden: The Subordination of Southern Tswana
Women, ca. 1800-1840." Journal of Southern African
Studies. Volume 10 #1 1983. pp. 39-54.
Kloppers, H.P. and Coertze, T.F.
Bantu Divorce Courts: Guide to Practice and Proceedure.
Cape Town, South Africa: Juta. Second Edition. 1976.
131p.
Pascoe, Flavia
The Marriage and Divorce Book. Cape Town, South Africa:
Tafelberg. 1978.
Peart, Nicola S.
"Civil or Christian Marriage and Customary Unions: The
Legal Position of the Discarded Spouse and Children."
Comparative and International Law Journal of South
Africa. Volume 16 #1 1983. pp. 39-64.
Sinclair, June
"The Financial Consequences of Divorce in South Africa:
Judicial Determination or Private Ordering?"
International and Comparative Law Quarterly. Volume 32
#4 1983. pp. 785-811.

Trengrove, J.J.
    "Divorce Law Reform." De Rebus. #200 August, 1984.
    pp. 353-358.

ECONOMICS

Africa Bureau
    The Status of Black Women in South Africa. London:
    Africa Bureau. Document Paper #21. 1979.
Allen, Vivien
    Lady Trader: A Biography of Mrs. Sarah Heckford. London:
    Collins. 1979. 243p.
Anonymous
    Women Workers. Durban, South Africa: Federation of South
    African Trade Unions. 1984.
Anonymous
    "A Tribute to Ruth First." Review of African Political
    Economy. #25 September-December, 1982. pp. 3-64.
Argyle, John
    "Some African Meat-Sellers in Durban." Paper Presented
    at the Workshop on African Urban Life in Durban in the
    Twentieth Century. Johannesburg: University of the
    Witwatersrand. October, 1983.
Beall, J.D.
    "The Changing Role and Status of African Women in the
    Political Economy of Colonial Natal." Paper Presented at
    the 13th Annual Congress of the Association of
    Sociologists of Southern Africa. 1982.
Beall, J.D.
    "Class, Race and Gender: The Political Economy of Women
    in Colonial Natal." M.A. Thesis: University of Natal.
    Durban, South Africa. 1982.
Beall, J.D.
    "The Function and Status of African Women in the Social
    and Economic Life of Natal and Zululand, 1818-1879."
    B.A. Honors Dissertation: University of Natal. Durban,
    South Africa. 1981.
Beavon, K. and Rogerson, C.
    "The Changing Role of Women in the Informal Sector of
    South Africa." (In) Drakakissmith, D. (ed.).
    Urbanization in the Developing World. London: Croom
    Helm. 1980.
Behardien, Gadaja and Lehulere, K. and Shaw, Anita
    Domestic Workers in Poverty. Rondebosch, South Africa:
    University of Cape Town. SALDRU. School of Economics.
    Carnegie Conference Paper #114. 1984. 76p.
Bekker, J.C.
    Marriage, Money, Property and the Law: A Guide to the
    Legal and Financial Consequences of a Marriage Between
    Africans. Durban/Pretoria, South Africa: Butterworths.
    1983. 53p.

Berger, Iris
Sources of Class Consciousness: The Experience of Women
Workers in South Africa, 1973-1980. Boston: Boston
University. African Studies Center. Working Paper #55.
1982. 27p.

Berger, Iris
"Sources of Class Consciousness: South African Women in
Recent Labor Struggles." International Journal of
African Historical Studies. Volume 16 #1 1983. pp.
49-66.

Berger, Iris
"Women in the South African Trade Union Movement." Ph.D
Dissertation: Boston University. Boston, Massachusetts.
1980.

Bird, A.
"Organising Women in South Africa: Trade Unions." Paper
Presented to the Association for Sociology in Southern
Africa. Johannesburg: University of the Witwatersrand.
1984.

Boddington, Erica
"Economic Discrimination Against Women in South Africa:
Case Studies Involving White Middle Class Women." B.A.
Honors Dissertation: University of Cape Town. Cape Town,
South Africa. 1977.

Bozzoli, Belinda
"Marxism, Feminism and South African Studies." Journal
of Southern African Studies. Volume 9 #2 April, 1983.
pp. 137-171.

Bozzoli, Belinda
"Migrant Women and South African Social Change:
Biographical Approaches to Social Analysis." African
Studies. Volume 44 #1 1985. pp. 87-96.

Brink, Elsabe
"'Maar 'n Klomp Factory Meide': The Role of the Female
Garment Workers in the Clothing Industry, Afrikaner
Family and Community on the Witwatersrand During the
1920's." Paper Presented at the History Workshop.
Johannesburg: University of the Witwatersrand. 1984.

Bromberger, Norman and Gandor, Mark
"Economic and Demographic Functioning of Rural Households
in the Mahlabatini District Kwazulu." Social Dynamics.
Volume 10 #2 June, 1984. pp. 20-37.

Brown, Barbara B.
The Political Economy of Population Policy in South
Africa. Boston: Boston University. African Studies
Center. African Studies Working Paper #71. 1983. 15p.

Bughwan, Devi
"Discrimination Against and Exploitation of Women in the
Work Place." Paper Presented to the Conference on Women
and the Economy. Joahnnesburg: Rand Afrikaans
University. September 22, 1980.

Carim, Shirene F.
"The Role of Women in the South African Trade Union
Movement." New York: United Nations. Centre Against

Apartheid. Notices and Documents Series #7/80. April,
1980. 15p.

Cock, Jacklyn
"The Missionary Articulation of Sexual Ideology and the
Initial Incorporation of Black Women Into Wage Labour."
Africa Perspective. Volume 13 1979. pp. 16-26.

Cock, Jacklyn
"The Plight of Domestic Servants." Sash. August,
1979.

Cock, Jacklyn
"Domestic Servants in the Poitical Economy of South
Africa." Africa Perspective. Volume 15 1980. pp.
42-53.

Du Toit, Bettie
Ukubamba Amadolo: Workers' Struggle in the South African
Textile Industry. London: Onyx Press. 1978. 145p.

Faurie, K.M.
Die Loonstruktuur van Gegradueerde Blanke Vroue in 1981:
The Wage Structure of White Female Graduates in 1981.
Pretoria, South Africa: Human Sciences Research Council.
1981.

Favis, M.
Black Women in the South African Economy. Durban, South
Africa. 1983.

Gaitskell, Deborah and Kimble, Judy
"Class, Race and Gender: Domestic Workers in South
Africa." Review of African Political Economy. #27/28
1983. pp. 86-108.

Gillard, Jillian
"Perpetuation of a Capitalist Patriarchy: The Ideological
Apparatus of the Women's Magazine in South Africa."
B.Soc.Sci Honors Dissertation: University of Cape Town.
Cape Town, South Africa. 1978.

Ginwala, Frene and Mashiane, Shirley
"Women and Apartheid: Black South African Women Stand on
the Lowest Rung of the Ladder of Oppression." UNESCO
Courier. Volume 33 #7 July, 1980. pp. 13-17.

Guyer, Jane I.
"Women in the Rural Economy: Contemporary Variations."
(In) Hay, Margaret J. and Stichter, Sharon (eds.).
African Women South of the Sahara. New York: Longman.
1984. pp. 19-32.

Hamblin, E.
"The Occupational Aspirations of Women in South Africa."
D.Comm. Thesis: Rand Afrikaans University. Johannesburg,
South Africa. 1980.

Klugman, Barbara
"The Political Economy of Population Control in South
Africa." B.A. Honors Dissertation: University of the
Witwatersrand. Johannesburg, South Africa. 1980.

Landis, Elizabeth
"African Women Under Apartheid." ISIS International
Bulletin. #9 Autumn, 1978. pp. 7-11.

Lapchick, Richard E.
  "The Role of Women in the Struggle Against Apartheid in
  South Africa." (In) Steady, Filomina C. (ed.). The
  Black Woman Cross-Culturally. Cambridge, Massachusetts:
  Schenkman Publishing. 1981. pp. 231-261.
Lapchick, Richard E. and Urdang, Stephanie
  "The Effects of Apartheid on the Status of Women in
  Employment in South Africa." Paper Presented at the
  World Conference of the United Nations Decade for Women,
  Copenhagen, Denmark, July 14-30, 1980. New York: United
  Nations. 40p.
Lawton, L.
  Working Women. Johannesburg: Raven Press. 1985.
Lipman, Beata
  We Make Freedom: Women in South Africa Speak. Boston:
  Pandora Press. 1984. 141p.
Lotter, Johann M.
  "Socio-Economic Status and Fertility: The Emergence of
  New Trends Among White South Africans." Humanitas.
  Volume 4 #3 1978. pp. 323-325.
Manyosi, Maud
  "Working Women in South Africa." Sechaba. January,
  1980. pp. 23-24.
Mariotti, Amelia
  "The Incorporation of African Women Into Wage Employment
  in South Africa, 1920-1970." Ph.D Dissertation:
  University of Connecticut, Storrs. Stoors, Connecticut.
  1980. 338p.
Mariotti, Amelia
  "Capitalist Development and State Policy in South Africa:
  African Women, the Family and the Price of Labour Power."
  Paper Presented at the Conference on African Women in
  History. Santa Clara, California: University of Santa
  Clara. 1981.
Matsepe, Ivy F.
  "African Women's Labor in the Political Economy of South
  Africa, 1880-1970." Ph.D Dissertation: Rutgers
  University. New Brunswick, New Jersey. 1984. 327p.
Matsepe-Casaburri, Ivy F.
  Women and the Political Economy of Southern Africa.
  Harare, Zimbabwe. 1982. 100+p.
Matsepe-Casaburri, Ivy F.
  "Cheap Labour Policies and Their Implications for African
  Women in South Africa." Paper Presented at a Conference
  on Women's Development. Sussex, England: University of
  Sussex. 1978.
Matsepe-Casaburri, Ivy F.
  "Changing Roles and Needs of Women in South Africa and
  Namibia." Paper Presented at the World Conference for
  the United Nations Decade for Women, Copenhagen,
  Denmark, July 14-30, 1980. New York: United Nations.
  1980.

Matsetela, Ted
   "The Life Story of Nkgono MmaPooe: Aspects of
   Sharecropping and Proletatrianisation in the Northern
   Orange Free State, 1890-1930." (In) Marks, Shula and
   Rathbone, Richard (eds.). Industrialization and Social
   Change in South Africa: African Class Formation, Culture
   and Consciousness, 1870-1930. London: Longman. 1982.
Meer, Fatima
   Black Women in Industry, 1983: 988 Interviews, A
   Preliminary Report Conducted With African, Indian and
   Coloured Women in the Greater Durban Metropolitan Area.
   Durban, South Africa: Institute for Black Research.
   Community and Labour Relations Research Group. 1983.
Mehta, Aasha
   "Black Women in Wage Labour: A Factory Study Into Levels
   of Class Consciousness." B.A. Honors Dissertation:
   University of Natal. Durban, South Africa. 1983.
Mokgethi, S.S. and Matau, M.
   Adaptation to Industrialization: The Black Woman in
   Industry. Pretoria, South Africa: Council for Scientific
   and Industrial Research. 1978.
Moody, Elize
   "Women and Development in South Africa." Development:
   South African ed. Volume 3 1976. pp. 26-29.
Mullins, Elizabeth A.
   "Working Women and the Dual Shift: A Case Study of a
   Sample of Women in the Laundry, Drycleaning and Dyeing
   Industry." B.A. Honors Dissertation: University of the
   Witwatesrand. Johannesburg, South Africa. 1982.
Mvubelo, Lucy
   "Women in Industry." South African Outlook. Volume 110
   #1257 February, 1976. pp. 26.
Nattrass, Nicoli
   Street Trading in the Transkei: A Struggle Against
   Poverty, Persecution, and Prosecution. Durban, South
   Africa: University of Natal. Development Studies Unit.
   Working Paper #7. 1984. 35p.
Nattrass, Nicoli
   Street Trading in Transkei: A Struggle Against Poverty,
   Persecution and Prosecution. Rondebosch, South Africa:
   University of Cape Town. SALDRU. School of Economics.
   Carnegie Conference Paper #237. 1984. 35p.
Nene, Daphne S.
   "A Survey of African Women Petty Traders and
   Self-Employed in Town and Country in South Africa." (In)
   International Labour Organization (ILO). Rural
   Development and Women in Africa. Geneva: ILO. 1984.
   pp. 147-154.
Nicol, Martin
   "'Joh'burg Hotheads!' and 'Gullible Children of Cape
   Town': The Transvaal Garment Workers' Union Assault on
   Low Wages in the Cape Town Clothing Industry, 1930-1931."

Paper Presented at the History Workshop, University of the Witwatersrand. Johannesburg, South Africa. 1984.

Norton, A.B.
"The Future of Women in South African Banks." South African Banker. Volume 74 #2 May, 1977. pp. 85-88.

Oosthuizen, J.M.
"The Wage Perceptions of Hourly-Paid Coloured Female Workers: A Comparative Study in Seven Secondary Industry Companies." M.A. Thesis: University of Port Elizabeth. Port Elizabeth, South Africa. 1979.

Ricketts, D.J.
"Trends in the Employment of Women in the Banking Industry." Paper Presented to the Conference on Women and the Economy. Johannesburg: Rand Afrikaans University. September, 1980.

Schurink, Willem J. and Levinthal, Terri
"Business Women Exchanging Sex for Money: A Descriptive Survey." South African Journal of Sociology. Volume 14 #4 November, 1983. pp. 154-163.

Shapiro, Janet
"Political and Economic Organization of Women in South Africa: The Limitations of a Notion of 'Sisterhood' as a Basis for Solidarity." Africa Perspective. Volume 15 Autumn, 1980. pp. 1-15.

Sibisi, Harriet N.
"Effects of Training for a Profession on Life Styles and Life-Changes of African Women in South Africa." Paper Presented to the Women in Development Section at the 15th World Conference of the Society for International Development, Amsterdam, Netherlands, Nov. 28-Dec. 3, 1976. 16p.

Smit, G.J.
"Capable Managers Needed: A Strategy for Developing Women's Potential." South African Journal of Labor Relations. September, 1978. pp. 3-8.

South African Congress of Trade Unions
Conditions of Working Women in South Africa. Dar-es-Salaam, Tanzania: South African Congress of Trade Unions. June, 1979.

Spuy, Adelemarie V.
"Inequitable Legal and Economic Aspects of the Discrimination Against Women, Especially Married Women in South Africa Today." Plural Societies. Volume 9 #1 Spring, 1978. pp. 49-58.

Spuy, Adelmarie V.
"South African Women: The Other Discrimination." Munger Africana Library Notes. July, 1978. pp. 1-15.

United Nations
The Plight of Black Women in Apartheid South Africa. New York: United Nations. Department of Public Information. 1981. 35p.

United Nations Centre Against Apartheid
"The Effects of Apartheid on the Status of Women in South

Africa." Black Scholar. Volume 10 #1 September, 1978. pp. 11-21.

United Nations Economic Commission for Africa (UNECA) Apartheid and the Status of Women. Addis Ababa, Ethiopia: UNECA. Regional Prepatory Meeting of the UNECA Second Regional Conference for the Integration of Women in Development. Lusaka, Zambia. December 3-7, 1979.

Urtel, Helga and Smit, Roberta
The Income Structure of Highly Qualified White Women on July 1, 1976. Pretoria, South Africa: South African Human Sciences Research Council. 1976. 28p.

Van Der Spuy, A.
"Inequitable Legal and Economic Aspects of the Discrimination Against Women, Especially Married Women in South Africa Today." Plural Societies. Volume 9 #1 Spring, 1978. pp. 49-58.

Van der Merwe, Sandra
"A Portrait of the South African Woman Manager." South African Journal of Business Management. Volume 10 #2 1979. pp. 57-64.

Wessels, D.M.
The Taxation of the Income of Married Women. Pretoria, South Africa: Institute of Manpower Research. 1977.

Wessels, D.M.
"Where are Women in South Africa's Labour Force?" Paper Presented to the Conference on Women and the Economy. Johannesburg: Rand Afrikaans University. September 22, 1980.

Wolmarans, Karen M.
The Wage Structure of Graduate White Women in 1979. Pretoria, South Africa: Human Sciences Research Council. Research Finding M-R-67. 1979. 50p.

Yawitch, Joanne
Black Women in South Africa: Capitalism, Employment and Reproduction. Johannesburg: Africa Perspective Dissertation #2. 1980.

Yawitch, Joanne
"Women and Squatting: A Winterveld Case Study." (In) University of Witwatersrand. Working Papers in Southern African Studies. Johannesburg: University of the Witwatersrand. May, 1979. pp. 199-227.

Yawitch, Joanne
"African Women and Labour Force Participation." Work in Progress. Volume 9 August, 1979. pp. 35-44.

Yawitch, Joanne
"The Incorporation of African Women Into Wage Labour, 1950-1980." South African Labour Bulletin. Volume 9 #3 December, 1983. pp. 82-92.

EDUCATION AND TRAINING

Austoker, Joyce
"Vocational Training for Girls." (In) Technical and
Vocational Education Foundation of South Africa.
Technical and Vocational Education in Southern Africa.
Johannesburg: The Foundation. 1981.

Flisher, A.J.
"The Development, Implementation and Evaluation of a
Training Program in Rape Crisis Intervention for Lay
Therapists: A Community Psychology Approach." M.Sc.
Thesis: University of Cape Town. Cape Town, South
Africa. 1981.

Friedman, M.
"Sexual Discrimination at a South African University With
Special Reference to Sexual Harassment." Paper Presented
at the Conference of the Association for Sociology in
Southern Africa. Johannesburg: University of the
Witwatersrand. 1984.

Locke, M.
"Sexism and Racism: Obstacles to Development of Black
Women in South Africa." (In) Fowlkes, D.L. and McClure,
C.S. (eds.). Feminist Visions: Toward a Transformation
of the Liberal Arts Curriculum. University, Alabama:
University of Alabama Press. 1984. pp. 119-129.

Lotter, Johann M.
"The Effect of Urbanization and Education on the
Fertility of Blacks in South Africa." Humanitas. Volume
4 #1 1977. pp. 21-28.

Matsepe-Casaburri, Ivy F.
"Changing Roles and Needs of Women in South Africa and
Namibia." Paper Presented at the World Conference for
the United Nations Decade for Women, Copenhagen,
Denmark, July 14-30, 1980. New York: United Nations.

Nene, Daphne S.
The Role and Potential of Black Women's Voluntary
Associations in Development: The Case of KwaZulu and
Natal. Kwa Dlangezwa, South Africa: University of
Zululand. Publications of the University of Zululand.
Series B #19. 1982. 74p.

Parle, Julie
"Mrs. Florence MacDonald and University Education for
Non-Europeans in Natal c.1936-1952." B.A. Honors
Dissertation: University of Natal. Durban, South Africa.
1983.

Shuenyane, Esline N.
"Non-Formal Education and Socialization of Pre-Adolescent
Girls: An Analysis of Content." M.A. Thesis: University
of the Witwatersrand. Johannesburg, South Africa.
1980.

Sibisi, Harriet N.
"Effects of Training for a Profession on Life Styles and
Life-Changes of African Women in South Africa." Paper

Presented to the Women in Development Section at the 15th
World Conference of the Society for International
Development. Amsterdam, Netherlands. Nov. 28-Dec. 3,
1976. 16p.

Smit, G.J.
"Capable Managers Needed: A Strategy for Developing
Women's Potential." South African Journal of Labor
Relations. September, 1978. pp. 3-8.

Smit, G.J.
"Development of the Managerial Potential of South African
Women." M.B.L. Thesis: University of South Africa.
Pretoria, South Africa. 1978. 282p.

Smit, G.J.
"Capable Managers Needed: A Strategy for Developing
Women's Potential." South African Journal of Labour
Relations. Volume 2 #3 September, 1978. pp. 3-8.

EMPLOYMENT AND LABOR

Anonymous
"'I Opened the Road for You': Dora Tamana and South
Africa." ISIS International Bulletin. #21 1981.

Anonymous
"Maggie Oewies Talks About the Domestic Workers
Association." South African Labour Bulletin. Volume 6
#1 1980. pp. 35-36.

Anonymous
"Women, Work and Health." Critical Health. Volume 9
1983. pp. 18-28.

Anonymous
"Interview With Lucy Mvubelo." South African Labour
Bulletin. Volume 5 #3 October, 1979. pp. 97-100.

Anonymous
Garment Workers Unite: The Story of the Transvaal Garment
Workers Union. Salt River, South Africa: Labour History
Group. 1983. 51p.

Anonymous
"Women and Trade Unions: An Interview With Lydia
Ngwenya." South African Labour Bulletin. Volume 8 #6
June, 1983. pp. 63-68.

Anonymous
"Women Health Workers." Critical Health. Volume 9 1983.
pp. 5-10.

Anonymous
Women Workers. Durban, South Africa: Federation of South
African Trade Unions. 1984.

Anonymous
"Women Workers, Maternity Benefits and Trade Unions."
Critical Health. Volume 9 1983. pp. 29-35.

Anonymous
"Organising Women?" Work in Progress. Volume 21
February, 1982. pp. 14-22.

Anonymous
"Organising Women in Trade Unions: A Panel Discussion."
(In) National Union of South African Students (NUSAS).
NUSAS Conference on Women. Cape Town, South Africa:
NUSAS. Women's Directive. 1983.

Anonymous
"Obituary: Peggy Dhlamini, A Leading Woman in the Worker
Struggle." South African Labour Bulletin. Volume 7 #6/7
1982. pp. 176-177.

Anonymous
"Profile of Junerose Nala." South African Labour
Bulletin. Volume 2 #9/10 May-June, 1976. pp. 117.

Anonymous
"Interview With Mavis Nhlapo, Secretary of the Women's
Secretariat." Sechaba. March, 1981. pp. 17-20.

Arenson, Paul and Moizen, Inga
"Women Office Cleaners on Night Shift: A Report on the
Study of the Effects on Night-Shift Work on the Health
and Social Conditions of Women Office Cleaners in Some
Johannesburg Office Blocks." South African Labour
Bulletin. Volume 9 #3 December, 1983. pp. 74-81.

Argyle, John
"Some African Meat-Sellers in Durban." Paper Presented
at the Workshop on African Urban Life in Durban in the
Twentieth Century. Johannesburg: University of the
Witwatersrand. October, 1983.

Armstrong, Amanda
"Micro-Technology and the Control of Women in the
Office." South African Labour Bulletin. Volume 9 #3
1983. pp. 53-73.

Austoker, Joyce
"Vocational Training for Girls." (In) Technical and
Vocational Education Foundation of South Africa.
Technical and Vocational Education in Southern Africa.
Johannesburg: The Foundation. 1981.

Beavon, K. and Rogerson, C.
"The Changing Role of Women in the Informal Sector of
South Africa." (In) Drakakissmith, D. (ed.).
Urbanization in the Developing World. London: Croom
Helm. 1980.

Becker, Ruth
"The Sexual Division of Labour and its Implications for
Trade Union Organization: A Case Study." B.A. Honors
Dissertation: University of the Witwatersrand.
Johannesburg, South Africa. 1983.

Behardien, Gadaja and Lehulere, K. and Shaw, Anita
Domestic Workers in Poverty. Rondebosch, South Africa:
University of Cape Town. SALDRU. School of Economics.
Carnegie Conference Paper #114. 1984. 76p.

Behr, D.
"Women and Work, in Psychological Perspective." Journal
of the University of Durban-Westville. Volume 2 #4 1976.
pp. 9-18.

Berger, Iris
Sources of Class Consciousness: The Experience of Women
Workers in South Africa, 1973-1980. Boston: Boston
University. African Studies Center. Working Paper #55.
1982. 27p.

Berger, Iris
"Sources of Class Consciousness: South African Women in
Recent Labor Struggles." International Journal of
African Historical Studies. Volume 16 #1 1983. pp.
49-66.

Berger, Iris
"Women in the South African Trade Union Movement." Ph.D
Dissertation: Boston University. Boston, Massachusetts.
1980.

Berger, Iris
"Garment Workers in the Transvaal: The Labour Process in
the Shaping of Ideology." Paper Presented at a
Conference on South Africa in the Comparative Study of
Class, Race and Nationalism. New York. 1982.

Bird, A.
"Organising Women in South Africa: Trade Unions." Paper
Presented to the Association for Sociology in Southern
Africa. Johannesburg: University of the Witwatersrand.
1984.

Boddington, Erica
"Domestic Labour in the Western Cape." Paper Presented
to the Conference on Economic Development and Racial
Domination. Bellville, South Africa: University of
Western Cape. October, 1984.

Boddington, Erica
"Domestic Service: Changing Relations of Class
Domination, 1841-1948." M.A. Thesis: University of Cape
Town. Cape Town, South Africa. 1983.

Bozzoli, Belinda
"Migrant Women and South African Social Change:
Biographical Approaches to Social Analysis." African
Studies. Volume 44 #1 1985. pp. 87-96.

Brink, Elsabe
"Plays, Poetry and Production: The Literature of the
Garment Workers." South African Labour Bulletin. Volume
9 #8 1984. pp. 32-53.

Brink, Elsabe
"'Maar 'n Klomp Factory Meide': The Role of the Female
Garment Workers in the Clothing Industry, Afrikaner
Family and Community on the Witwatersrand During the
1920's." Paper Presented at the History Workshop.
Johannesburg: University of the Witwatersrand. 1984.

Bughwan, Devi
"Discrimination Against and Exploitation of Women in the
Work Place." Paper Presented to the Conference on Women
and the Economy. Joahnnesburg: Rand Afrikaans
University. September 22, 1980.

Carim, Shirene F.
   "The Role of Women in the South African Trade Union
   Movement." New York: United Nations. Centre Against
   Apartheid. Notices and Documents Series #7/80. April,
   1980. 15p.
Chetty, Thiagaraj D.
   Job Satisfaction on Indian Married Women in the Clothing
   Manufacturing Industry in Durban and its Effects on the
   Interpersonal Family Relationships. Durban, South
   Africa: University of Durban-Westville. Institute for
   Social and Economic Research. 1983. 130p.
Cock, Jacklyn
   "Childcare and the Working Mother" Africa Perspective.
   Volume 26 1985. pp. 29-60.
Cock, Jacklyn
   Maids and Madams: A Study in the Politics of
   Exploitation. Johannesburg: Raven Press. 1980. 410p.
Cock, Jacklyn
   "Disposable Nannies: Domestic Servants in the Political
   Economy of South Africa." Review of African Political
   Economy. #21 May-September, 1981. pp. 63-83.
Cock, Jacklyn and Emdon, E.
   "Child Care and the Working Mother." Paper Presented to
   the Association for Sociology in Southern Africa.
   Johannesburg: University of the Witwatersrand. 1984.
Cock, Jacklyn and Emdon, E. and Klugman, B.
   Child Care and the Working Mother: A Sociological
   Investigation of a Sample of Urban African Women.
   Rondebosch, South Africa: University of Cape Town.
   SALDRU. School of Economics. Carnegie Conference Paper
   #115. April, 1984. 46p.
Cock, Jacklyn and Emdon, E. and Klugman, B.
   "Research Report: Child Care and the Working Mother."
   South African Labour Bulletin. Volume 9 #7 1984. pp.
   58-59.
Cock, Jacklyn
   "The Missionary Articulation of Sexual Ideology and the
   Initial Incorporation of Black Women Into Wage Labour."
   Africa Perspective. Volume 13 1979. pp. 16-26.
Cock, Jacklyn
   "Black and White Women: A Socio-Historical Study of
   Domestic Workers and Their Employers in the Eastern
   Cape." Ph.D Dissertation: Rhodes University.
   Grahamstown, South Africa. 1979.
Cock, Jacklyn
   "The Plight of Domestic Servants." Sash. August, 1979.
Cock, Jacklyn
   "Settlers, Servants and Slaves on the Eastern Frontier."
   South African Outlook. Volume 111 #1301 November, 1979.
   pp. 172-178.
Cock, Jacklyn
   "Deference and Dependence: A Note on the Self-Imagery of

Domestic Workers." South African Labour Bulletin.
Volume 6 #1 July, 1980. pp. 9-21.

Cock, Jacklyn
"Domestic Servants in the Poitical Economy of South
Africa." Africa Perspective. Volume 15 1980. pp.
42-53.

Cock, Jacklyn
"Domestic Service: Apartheid's Deep South." South
African Outlook. Volume 111 #1301 November, 1979. pp.
165-168.

Du Toit, Bettie
Ukubamba Amadolo: Workers' Struggle in the South African
Textile Industry. London: Onyx Press. 1978. 145p.

Duncan, Sheena
"Aspects of Family Breakdown." Work in Progress. Volume
27. 1983. pp. 36-38.

Egan, Siobhan
"Black Women in South African Agriculture: An
Introductory Study of Life and Labour in the
Countryside." B.A. Honors Dissertation: University of
Natal. Durban, South Africa. 1983.

Faurie, K.M.
Die Loonstruktuur van Gegradueerde Blanke Vroue in 1981:
The Wage Structure of White Female Graduates in 1981.
Pretoria, South Africa: Human Sciences Research Council.
1981.

Favis, M.
Black Women in the South African Economy. Durban, South
Africa. 1983.

Flepp, Caroline
"Women Under Apartheid; A Triple Oppression." UNESCO
Courier. Volume 38 #4 April, 1985. pp. 14-15.

Freinkel, Joan C.
"Male and Female Managers: Where the Differences Lie."
B.A. Honors Dissertation: University of the
Witwatersrand. Johannesburg, South Africa. 1980.

Gaitskell, Deborah and Kimble, Judy
"Class, Race and Gender: Domestic Workers in South
Africa." Review of African Political Economy. #27/28
1983. pp. 86-108.

Gaitskell, Deborah
"Laundry, Liquor and 'Playing Ladish': African Women in
Johannesburg, 1903-1939." Paper Presented to the South
African Social History Workshop. London: University of
London. Centre for International and Area Studies.
1978.

Ginwala, Frene and Mashiane, Shirley
"Women and Apartheid: Black South African Women Stand on
the Lowest Rung of the Ladder of Oppression." UNESCO
Courier. Volume 33 #7 July, 1980. pp. 13-17.

Goldstein, Susan
"Women in Medicine." Critical Health. Volume 1 1980.
pp. 30-34.

Gon, Sylvia
   "The Effect of Legislation on Working Women." Paper
   Presented to the Conference on Women and the Economy.
   Johannesburg: Rand Afrikaans University. September 22,
   1980.
Goodwin, June
   Cry Amandla: South African Women and the Question of
   Power. New York: Holmes and Meier. 1984. 225p.
Gordon, S.
   Domestic Workers: A Guide for Employers. Johannesburg:
   South African Institute of Race Relations. 1978.
Graaff, Janet
   "Married to a Migrant." South African Outlook. Volume
   108 #1289 November, 1978. pp. 172-173.
Graaff, Janet
   "Will They be Together for Christmas?" South African
   Outlook. Volume 108 #1289. November, 1978. pp.
   163-165.
Guyer, Jane I.
   "Women in the Rural Economy: Contemporary Variations."
   (In) Hay, Margaret J. and Stichter, Sharon (eds.).
   African Women South of the Sahara. New York: Longman.
   1984. pp. 19-32.
Hamblin, E.
   "The Occupational Aspirations of Women in South Africa."
   D.Comm. Thesis: Rand Afrikaans University. Johannesburg,
   South Africa. 1980.
Hamilton, Carolyn A.
   "A Fragment of the Jigsaw: Authority and Labour Control
   Amongst the Early 19th Century Northern Nguni." B.A.
   Honors Dissertation: University of the Witwatersrand.
   Johannesburg, South Africa. 1980.
Harries, Jane
   "Women in Production in the Ciskei." B.A. Honors
   Dissertation: University of Cape Town. Cape Town, South
   Africa. 1979.
Hill, Alison M.
   "Materialist Feminism and South Africa: The Position of
   Black Working Class Women in Contemporary Cape Town."
   B.A. Honors Dissertation: University of Cape Town. Cape
   Town, South Africa. 1983.
Hirsch, A.
   "Ducking and Weaving: Problems of Worker Organization in
   the Textile Industry of Durban-Pinetown-
   Pietermaritzburg." B.A. Honors Dissertation: University
   of Cape Town. Cape Town, South Africa. 1978.
Kaplan, R.
   "Interview With Sarah Chitja, Deputy General Secretary of
   the National Union of Clothing Workers." South African
   Labour Bulletin. Volume 3 #4 1977. pp. 54-59.
Kiernan, J.P.
   "Spouses and Partners: Marriage and Career Among Urban

Zulu Zionists." Urban Anthropology. Volume 8 #1
Spring, 1979. pp. 95-110.
Klugman, Barbara
"Maternity Rights and Benefits and Protective Legislation
at Work." South African Labour Bulletin. Volume 9 #3
1983. pp. 25-51.
Knell, H.F.
"A Survey of the Attitudes and Experience of a Sample of
Women Working in Management Positions in South Africa."
M.Sc Thesis: University of Natal. Durban, South Africa.
1982.
Landis, Elizabeth
"African Women Under Apartheid." ISIS International
Bulletin. #9 Autumn, 1978. pp. 7-11.
Lapchick, Richard E. and Urdang, Stephanie
"The Effects of Apartheid on the Status of Women in
Employment in South Africa." Paper Presented at the
World Conference of the United Nations Decade for Women,
Copenhagen, Denmark, July 14-30, 1980. New York: United
Nations. 1980. 40p.
Lawton, L.
Working Women. Johannesburg: Raven Press. 1985.
Levitan, Ron
"Women in the 'Bachelor' Quarters." South African
Outlook. Volume 108 #1289 November, 1978. pp. 169-170.
Lewis, Jon
"Solly Sachs and the Garment Worker's Union." (In)
Webster, Eddie (ed.). Essays in Southern African Labour
History. Johannesburg: Raven Press. 1978. pp. 181-191.
Lotter, Johann M.
"The Effect of Urbanization and Education on the
Fertility of Blacks in South Africa." Humanitas. Volume
4 #1 1977. pp. 21-28.
Luckhardt, Ken and Wall, Brenda
"Women Play a Leading Role." (In) Luckhardt, Ken and
Wall, Brenda (eds.). Organise or Starve - The History of
the South African Congress of Trade Unions (SACTU). New
York: International Publishers. 1980. pp. 297-332.
Manona, C.W.
"Marriage, Family Life and Migrancy in a Ciskei Village."
(In) Mayer, Philip (ed.). Black Villagers in an
Industrial Society: Anthropological Perspectives on
Labour Migration in South Africa. New York: Oxford
University Press. 1980.
Manyosi, Maud
"Working Women in South Africa." Sechaba. January,
1980. pp. 23-24.
Mariotti, Amelia
"The Incorporation of African Women Into Wage Employment
in South Africa, 1920-1970." Ph.D Dissertation:
University of Connecticut, Storrs. Stoors, Connecticut.
1980. 338p.

Mariotti, Amelia
    "Capitalist Development and State Policy in South Africa:
    African Women, the Family and the Price of Labour Power."
    Paper Presented at the Conference on African Women in
    History. Santa Clara, California: University of Santa
    Clara. 1981.
Marks, Shula and Unterhalter, Elaine
    "Women and the Migrant Labour System in South Africa."
    Paper Presented at the Conference on Migrant Labour in
    Southern Africa. Lusaka, Zambia: United Nations Economic
    Commission For Africa (UNECA). 1978.
Martin, V.
    "The Role of Women in South African Manufacturing." B.A.
    Honors Dissertation: University of the Witwatersrand.
    Johannesburg, South Africa. 1982.
Mashaba, T.G.
    "The Composition of the Nursing Profession in South
    Africa in the Mid-Seventies and Its Implications for
    Provision of Health Care." Journal of Advanced Nursing.
    Volume 6 #5 September, 1981. pp. 339-347.
Matsepe, Ivy F.
    "African Women's Labor in the Political Economy of South
    Africa, 1880 -1970." Ph.D Dissertation: Rutgers
    University. New Brunswick, New Jersey. 1984. 327p.
Matsepe-Casaburri, Ivy F.
    Women and the Political Economy of Southern Africa.
    Harare, Zimbabwe. 1982. 100+p.
Matsepe-Casaburri, Ivy F.
    "Cheap Labour Policies and Their Implications for African
    Women in South Africa." Paper Presented at a Conference
    on Women's Development. Sussex, England: University of
    Sussex. 1978.
Matsetela, Ted
    "The Life Story of Nkgono MmaPooe: Aspects of
    Sharecropping and Proletatrianisation in the Northern
    Orange Free State, 1890-1930." (In) Marks, Shula and
    Rathbone, Richard (eds.). Industrialization and Social
    Change in South Africa: African Class Formation, Culture
    and Consciousness, 1870-1930. London: Longman. 1982.
Mawbey, John
    "Afrikaner Women of the Garment Union During the
    Thirities and Forties." (In) Webster, E. (ed.). Essays
    in South African Labour History. Johannesburg: Raven
    Press. 1978. pp. 192-206.
Meer, Fatima
    Women in the Apartheid Society. New York: United
    Nations. U.N. Centre Against Apartheid. April, 1985.
    31p.
Meer, Fatima
    Black Women in Industry, 1983: 988 Interviews, A
    Preliminary Report Conducted With African, Indian and

Coloured Women in the Greater Durban Metropolitan Area.
Durban, South Africa: Institute for Black Research.
Community and Labour Relations Research Group. 1983.
Meer, Fatima (ed.).
Black Women, Durban 1975: Case Studies of 85 Women at
Home and Work. Durban, South Africa: University of
Natal. Sociology Department. 1976.
Meer, Fatima (ed.).
Factory and Family: The Divided Lives of South Africa's
Women Workers. Durban, South Africa: Institute for Black
Research. 1984. 105p.
Mehta, Aasha
"Black Women in Wage Labour: A Factory Study Into Levels
of Class Consciousness." B.A. Honors Dissertation:
University of Natal. Durban, South Africa. 1983.
Millar, Shirley
"The Basic Conditions of Employment Act: The Position of
Women." South African Labour Bulletin. Volume 8 #6
June, 1983. pp. 1-4.
Mkalipe, Pauline C.M.
"A Sociological Study of Black Women in the Clothing
Industry." M.A. Thesis: University of South Africa.
Johannesburg, South Africa. 1981.
Mokgethi, S.S. and Matau, M.
"Adaptation to Industrialization: The Black Woman in
Industry." Pretoria, South Africa: Council for
Scientific and Industrial Research. 1978.
Mullins, Ann
"Working Women Speak." Work in Progress. Volume 27
1983. pp. 38-40.
Mullins, Elizabeth A.
"Working Women and the Dual Shift: A Case Study of a
Sample of Women in the Laundry, Drycleaning and Dyeing
Industry." B.A. Honors Dissertation: University of the
Witwatesrand. Johannesburg, South Africa. 1982.
Mvubelo, Lucy
"Women in Industry." South African Outlook. Volume 110
#1257 February, 1976. pp. 26.
Naidoo, Margaret
"Women at Work in the Community." South African Outlook.
Volume 110 #1257 February, 1976. pp. 27-28.
Nattrass, Nicoli
Street Trading in the Transkei: A Struggle Against
Poverty, Persecution, and Prosecution. Durban, South
Africa: University of Natal. Development Studies Unit.
Working Paper #7. 1984. 35p.
Nattrass, Nicoli
Street Trading in Transkei: A Struggle Against Poverty,
Persecution and Prosecution. Rondebosch, South Africa:
University of Cape Town. SALDRU. School of Economics.
Carnegie Conference Paper #237. 1984. 35p.
Nene, Daphne S.
"A Survey of African Women Petty Traders and

Self-Employed in Town and Country in South Africa." (In) International Labour Organization (ILO). Rural Development and Women in Africa. Geneva: ILO. 1984. pp. 147-154.

Nicol, Martin
"'Joh'burg Hotheads!' and 'Gullible Children of Cape Town': The Transvaal Garment Workers' Union Assault on Low Wages in the Cape Town Clothing Industry, 1930-1931." Paper Presented at the History Workshop, University of the Witwatersrand. Johannesburg, South Africa. 1984.

Nkabinde, C.
"The Legal Position of African Women in Employment." IPST Bulletin (University of Zululand). Volume 12 1978. pp. 27-32.

Norton, A.B.
"The Future of Women in South African Banks." South African Banker. Volume 74 #2 May, 1977. pp. 85-88.

Obery, Ingrid
"'Makobongwe Amakosikazi': The FSAW and Mass Struggle in the '50's." Africa Perspective. Volume 15 Autumn, 1980. pp. 36-41.

Oosthuizen, J.M.
"The Wage Perceptions of Hourly-Paid Coloured Female Workers: A Comparative Study in Seven Secondary Industry Companies." M.A. Thesis: University of Port Elizabeth. Port Elizabeth, South Africa. 1979.

Perold, Helene (ed.).
Working Women: A Portrait of South Africa's Black Women Workers. Braamfontein, South Africa: Raven Press. 1985. 144p.

Preston-Whyte, Eleanor
"Race Attitudes and Behavior: The Case of Domestic Employment in White South African Homes." (In) Orkin, F.M. and Welz, S.E. (eds.). Society in Southern Africa, 1975-1978: Proceedings of the Association for Sociology in Southern Africa. Johannesburg: ASSA. 1979.

Preston-Whyte, Eleanor M.
"Race Attitudes and Behavior: The Case of Domestic Employment in White South African Homes." African Studies. Volume 35 #2 1976. pp. 71-90.

Ricketts, D.J.
"Trends in the Employment of Women in the Banking Industry." Paper Presented to the Conference on Women and the Economy. Johannesburg: Rand Afrikaans University. September, 1980.

Saxe, Norma and Van Niekerk, J.P. de V.
"Women Doctors Wasted." South African Medical Journal. Volume 55 1979. pp. 760-762.

Schreiner, J.
"Divisions of Labour in the Manufacturing Industry in the Western Cape, 1950-1965, and the Implications for a Materialist Theory of Women's Subordination." African

Studies Honors Paper: University of Cape Town. Cape
Town, South Africa. 1981.
Schreiner, J.A.
"'Thina Singoomama Asinakubulawa': Forms of Organization
Adopted by the Federation of South African Women in the
Western Cape." B.A. Honors Thesis: University of Cape
Town. Cape Town, South Africa. 1982.
Sese, Lennox
"Cecilia Makiwane." South African Outlook. Volume 107
#1272 May, 1977. pp. 74-75.
Shindler, J.
The Reproductive Function and Ultra-Exploitability of
South African Domestic Workers. Johannesburg: University
of the Witwatersrand. Industrial Sociology Research
Project. 1978.
Shindler, J.
"The Effects of Influx Control and Labour-Saving
Appliances on Domestic Services." South African Labour
Bulletin. Volume 6 #1 July, 1980. pp. 22-34.
Showers, Kate
"A Note on Women, Conflict and Migrant Labour." South
African Labour Bulletin. Volume 6 #4 November, 1980.
Sibisi, Harriet N.
"How African Women Cope With Migrant Labor in South
Africa." Signs. Volume 3 #1 Autumn, 1977. pp.
167-177.
Sibisi, Harriet N.
"How African Women Cope With Migrant Labor in South
Africa." (In) Wellesley Editorial Committee. Women and
National Development: The Complexities of Change.
Chicago: University of Chicago Press. 1977. pp.
167-177.
Smit, G.J.
"Development of the Managerial Potential of South African
Women." M.B.L. Thesis: University of South Africa.
Pretoria, South Africa. 1978. 282p.
Smit, G.J.
"Capable Managers Needed: A Strategy for Developing
Women's Potential." South African Journal of Labour
Relations. Volume 2 #3 September, 1978. pp. 3-8.
South African Congress of Trade Unions
Conditions of Working Women in South Africa.
Dar-es-Salaam, Tanzania: South African Congress of Trade
Unions. June, 1979.
Spitz, Shirley
"Career Commitment of Professional Women: A Study Into
the Effects of an Encounter Group Experience on
Self-Esteem Self-Actualisation and Professional Image."
B.A. Honors Dissertation: University of the
Witwatersrand. Johannesburg, South Africa. 1983.
Spuy, Adelemarie V.
"Inequitable Legal and Economic Aspects of the
Discrimination Against Women, Especially Married Women in

South Africa Today." Plural Societies. Volume 9 #1
Spring, 1978. pp. 49-58.
Spuy, Adelmarie V.
"South African Women: The Other Discrimination." Munger
Africana Library Notes. July, 1978. pp. 1-15.
Stavrou, P.
"Social Psychological Manifestations of Worker
Alienation." B.Soc.Sci Honors Dissertation: University
of Natal. Durban, South Africa. 1983.
Tredoux, M.
"The Female Earth Scientist in Southern Africa II."
Geological Society of South Africa Quarterly News
Bulletin. Volume 24 #2 1981. pp. 34-36.
United Nations
The Plight of Black Women in Apartheid South Africa. New
York: United Nations. Department of Public Information.
1981. 35p.
United Nations
International Conference on Women and Apartheid Report.
New York: United Nations. 1982. 38p.
United Nations
The Effects of Apartheid on the Status of Women in
Southern Africa. New York: United Nations. July, 1980.
United Nations Centre Against Apartheid
"The Effects of Apartheid on the Status of Women in South
Africa." Black Scholar. Volume 10 #1 September, 1978.
pp. 11-21.
United Nations Centre Against Apartheid
African Women and Apartheid in Labour Matters. New York:
United Nations Centre Against Apartheid. Notes and
Documents Series #20/80. July, 1980. 13p.
United Nations Economic Commission for Africa (UNECA)
Apartheid and the Status of Women. Paper Presented at
the Regional Prepatory Meeting of the UNECA Second
Regional Conference for the Integration of Women in
Development, Lusaka, Zambia, December 3-7, 1979. Addis
Ababa, Ethiopia. 1979.
United Women's Organization (UWO) and Social Research Agency
(SRA)
The Federation of South African Women. Cape, Town, South
Africa: UWO and SRA. 1982.
Unterhalter, Beryl
"Women in Struggle--South Africa." Third World
Quarterly. Volume 5 #4 1983. pp. 886-893.
Unterhalter, Beryl
"Discrimination Against Women in the South African
Medical Profession." Social Science and Medicine.
Volume 20 #12 1985. pp. 1253-1258.
Urtel, Helga and Smit, Roberta
The Income Structure of Highly Qualified White Women on
July 1, 1976. Pretoria, South Africa: South African
Human Sciences Research Council. 1976. 28p.

Van Bart, Dawn
   "The Effects of the Mother's Work Experience on Her
   Preschool Child's Behavior." B.A. Honors Dissertation:
   University of the Witwatersrand. Johannesburg, South
   Africa. 1982.
Van Der Walt, Sunette
   An Investigation Into the Utilization of White Women
   Labour in the South African Industry (sic).
   Bloemfontein, South Africa: University of Orange Free
   State. Department of Industrial Psychology. Personnel
   Research Division. November, 1976. 45p.
Van Niekerk, K.
   "The Married Women in the Nursing Profession."
   Curationis. Volume 3 #2 September, 1980. pp. 32-35.
Van Onselen, Charles
   "The Witches of Suburbia: Domestic Service on the
   Witwatersrand, 1890-1914." (In) Van Onselen, Charles.
   Studies in the Social and Economic History of the
   Witwatersrand, 1886-1914. New Nineveh, South Africa:
   Raven Books. Volume 2. 1982. pp. 1-73.
Van Rensburg, L.R.
   "Part Time Specialization for Women Doctors." South
   African Medical Journal. Volume 55 #19 May 5, 1979.
   pp. 738-739.
Van Rooyen, Janice C.
   Women at Work: A Conceptualisation of Factors Affecting
   Female Career Commitment. Johannesburg: National
   Institute for Personnel Research. Council for Scientific
   and Industrial Research. Division of Management Studies.
   CSIR Special Report Pers 311. 1980. 54p.
Wessels, D.M.
   The Taxation of the Income of Married Women. Pretoria,
   South Africa: Institute of Manpower Research. 1977.
Wessels, D.M.
   "Where are Women in South Africa's Labour Force?" Paper
   Presented to the Conference on Women and the Economy.
   Johannesburg: Rand Afrikaans University. September 22,
   1980.
Wolmarans, Karen M.
   The Wage Structure of Graduate White Women in 1979.
   Pretoria, South Africa: Human Sciences Research Council.
   Research Finding M-R-67. 1979. 50p.
Wright, John
   "Control of Women's Labour in the Zulu Kingdom." (In)
   Peires, J.B. (ed.). Before and After Shaka: Papers in
   Nguni History. Grahamstown, South Africa: Rhodes
   University. Institute of Social and Economic Research.
   1983. pp. 82-99.
Yawitch, Joanne
   Black Women in South Africa: Capitalism, Employment and
   Reproduction. Johannesburg: Africa Perspective
   Dissertation #2. 1980.

Yawitch, Joanne
  Tightening the Noose: African Women and Influx Control in
  South Africa, 1950-1980. Rondebosch, South Africa:
  University of Cape Town. SALDRU. School of Economics.
  Carnegie Conference Paper #82. 1984. 36p.
Yawitch, Joanne
  "Tightening the Noose: African Women and Influx Control
  in South Africa, 1950-1980." Paper Presented to the
  Association for Sociology in Southern Africa.
  Johannesburg: University of the Witwatersrand. 1984.
Yawitch, Joanne
  "Sexism and the Sexual Division of Labour in South
  Africa." Africa Perspective. Volume 13 Spring, 1979.
Yawitch, Joanne
  "African Women and Labour Force Participation." Work in
  Progress. Volume 9 August, 1979. pp. 35-44.
Yawitch, Joanne
  "The Incorporation of African Women Into Wage Labour,
  1950-1980." South African Labour Bulletin. Volume 9 #3
  December, 1983. pp. 82-92.

EQUALITY AND LIBERATION

African National Congress (ANC)
  'Apartheid--You Shall Be Crushed': Women's Fight Against
  Apartheid. Lusaka, Zambia: ANC. 1981. 32p.
Anonymous
  The Effects of Apartheid on the Status of Women in South
  Africa. New York: United Nations. Centre Against
  Apartheid. Notices and Documents. 1978. 26p.
Anonymous
  "Effects of Apartheid on the Status of Women in South
  Africa." Objective Justice. Volume 10 #1 Spring, 1978.
Anonymous
  "Effects of Apartheid on the Status of Women in Southern
  Africa." Paper Presented at the World Conference of the
  United Nations Decade for Women, Copenhagen, Denmark,
  July 14-30, 1980. New York: United Nations. 1980.
Anonymous
  "'I Opened the Road for You': Dora Tamana and South
  Africa." ISIS International Bulletin. #21 1981.
Anonymous
  "Women and Changing Relations of Control." (In) South
  African Research Service (eds.). South Africa Review:
  Same Foundations New Facades. Johannesburg: Raven.
  1983. pp. 278-299.
Anonymous
  "The Women's Question in Azanian Revolution."
  Isandlwana. #8/9 July-December, 1981. pp. 18-44.
Baard, Francis
  "Banishment and Jail." (In) National Union of South
  African Students (NUSAS). NUSAS Conference on Women.
  Cape Town, South Africa: NUSAS Women's Directive. 1983.

Barrett, J. and Dawber, A. and Klugman, I. and Obery, I. and
Schindler, J. and Yawitch, Joanne
    Vukani Makhosikazi. South African Women Speak. London:
    Catholic Institute for International Relations. 1985.
Bozzoli, Belinda
    "Feminist Interpretations and South African Studies: Some
    Suggested Avenues for Exploration." Paper Presented at
    the University of Witwatersrand. Johannesburg:
    University of the Witwatersrand. African Studies
    Institute. October 19, 1981.
Bozzoli, Belinda
    "Marxism, Feminism and South African Studies." Journal
    of Southern African Studies. Volume 9 #2 April, 1983.
    pp. 137-171.
Brokensha, D.
    "Obituary: Monica Wilson, 1908-1982: An Appreciation."
    Africa. Volume 53 #3 1983. pp. 83-87.
Budlender, Debbie and Meintjes, Sheila and Schreiner, Jenny
    "Women and Resistance in South Africa: A Review Article."
    Journal of Southern African Studies. Volume 10 #1
    October, 1983. pp. 131+.
Cachalia, Amina
    "Indian Women in Resistance." Paper Presented at the
    National Union of South African Students (NUSAS)
    Conference on Women, July, 1982. Johannesburg:
    University of Witwatersrand. NUSAS Women's Directive.
    1983.
Church, Joan
    "Marriage and Human Rights: A Note on the Bophuthatswana
    Marriage Act." Codicillus. Volume 22 #2 1981. pp.
    220-266.
Federal Council of the National Party of South Africa
    Women, Our Silent Soldiers. Bloemfontein, South Africa:
    Federal Council of the National Party of South Africa.
    August, 1978.
Friedman, M.
    "Sexual Discrimination at a South African University With
    Special Reference to Sexual Harassment." Paper Presented
    at the Conference of the Association for Sociology in
    Southern Africa. Johannesburg: University of the
    Witwatersrand. 1984.
Goodwin, June
    Cry Amandla: South African Women and the Question of
    Power. New York: Holmes and Meier. 1984. 225p.
Griessel, Annette
    "CATAPAW (Cape Association to Abolish Passes for African
    Women) and the Anti-Pass Campaign in Cape Town in the
    Fifties." (In) Cooper, Linda and Kaplan, Dave (eds.).
    Selected Research Papers on Aspects of Organization in
    the Western Cape. Cape Town, South Africa: University of
    Cape Town. Department of Economic History. 1982.
Hermer, Carol
    The Diary of Maria Tholo. Johannesburg: Raven Press.
    1980.

Hill, Alison M.
    "Materialist Feminism and South Africa: The Position of
    Black Working Class Women in Contemporary Cape Town."
    B.A. Honors Dissertation: University of Cape Town. Cape
    Town, South Africa. 1983.
Intern. Defence and Aid Fund for Southern Africa (IDAF)
    You Have Struck a Rock: Women and Political Repression in
    Southern Africa. London: IDAF. 1980. 24p.
International Defense and Aid Fund (IDAF) and United Nations
Centre Against Apartheid
    To Honour Women's Day: Profiles of Leading Women in the
    South African and Namibian Liberation Struggles. London:
    IDAF/U.N. Centre Against Apartheid. 1981. 56p.
Kimble, Judy and Unterhalter, Elaine
    "We Opened the Road for You, You Must Go Forwards: ANC
    Women's Struggles, 1912-1982." Feminist Review. Volume
    12 1982. pp. 11-16.
Kimmons, Leona
    "Women in South Africa--Agony and Struggle." Wree-View.
    Fall, 1976. pp. 1-5.
Kros, Cynthia
    "Urban African Women's Organizations and Protest on the
    Rand, 1939-1956." B.A. Honors Dissertation: University
    of Witwatersrand. Johannesburg. 1978.
Kuzwayo, Ellen
    Call Me Woman. London: Women's Press. 1985. 266p.
Lapchick, Richard
    The Role of Women in the Struggle for Liberation in
    Zimbabwe, Namibia and South Africa. New York: United
    Nations. July, 1980. 37p.
Lapchick, Richard E.
    "The Role of Women in the Struggle Against Apartheid in
    South Africa." (In) Steady, Filomina C. (ed.). The
    Black Woman Cross-Culturally. Cambridge, Massachusetts:
    Schenkman Publishing. 1981. pp. 231-261.
Lapchick, Richard E. and Urdang, Stephanie
    Oppression and Resistance: The Struggle of Women in
    Southern Africa. Westport, Connecticut: Greenwood Press.
    Contributions in Women's Studies. #29. 1982. 234p.
Lipman, Beata
    We Make Freedom: Women in South Africa Speak. Boston:
    Pandora Press. 1984. 141p.
Lodge, Tom
    "Women Protest Movements in the 1950's." (In) Lodge,
    Tom. Black Politics in South Africa Since 1945. New
    York: Longman. 1983.
Mayne, Anne V. and Levett, Ann
    "Feminism in South Africa." off our backs. Volume 7
    April, 1977. pp. 4.
Ridd, Rosemary
    "Where Women Must Dominate: Response to Oppression in A
    South African Urban Community." (In) Ardener, Shirley

(ed.). Women and Space: Ground Rules and Social Maps.
New York: St. Martin's Press. 1981. pp. 187-204.
Robinson, Sally
"Women and Politics of Liberation in South Africa."
Ufahamu. Volume 6 #1 1976.
Schreiner, J.A.
"Organising Women in the Liberation Struggle." (In)
National Union of South African Students (NUSAS). NUSAS
Conference on Women, University of the Witwatersrand,
July, 1982. Cape Town, South Africa: NUSAS Women's
Directive. 1983.
Strangwaies-Booth, J.
A Cricket in the Thorn Tree: Helen Suzman and the
Progressive Party. London: Hutchinson. 1976. 320p.
Tsolo, Gladys
"Azania: My Experience in the National Liberation
Struggle." (In) Mies, Marie and Reddock, Rhoda (eds.).
National Liberation and Women's Liberation. Haque,
Netherlands: Institute for Social Studies. 1982. pp.
96-111.
United Nations Centre Against Apartheid
Mrs. Winnie Mandela: Profile in Courage and Defiance.
New York: United Nations Centre Against Apartheid.
February, 1978.
United Nations Secretary General
"The Role of Women in the Struggle for Liberation in
Zimbabwe, Namibia and South Africa: Report to the
Secretary General." Paper Presented at the World
Conference of the United Nations Decade for Women,
Copenhagen, Denmark, July 14-30. New York: United
Nations. 1980.
Unterhalter, Beryl
"Discrimination Against Women in the South African
Medical Profession." Social Science and Medicine.
Volume 20 #12 1985. pp. 1253-1258.
Unterholter, Elaine
"South Africa: Women in Struggle." Third World
Quarterly. Volume 5 #4 1983. pp. 886-893.
Urdang, Stephanie
"Ensuring a Revolution Within a Revolution." Southern
Africa. May, 1978. pp. 7-9.
Van Der Spuy, A.
"South African Women: The Other Discrimination." Munger
Africana Library Notes. #44. July, 1978. pp. 2-15.
Van Der Spuy, A.
"Inequitable Legal and Economic Aspects of the
Discrimination Against Women, Especially Married Women in
South Africa Today." Plural Societies. Volume 9 #1
Spring, 1978. pp. 49-58.
Van Vuuren, Nancy
Women Against Apartheid: The Fight for Freedom in South

Africa, 1920-1975. Palo Alto, California: R and E
Research Association. 1979. 133p.
Vaughan, Iris
    The Diary of Iris Vaughan. Cape Town, South Africa:
    Howard Timmins. 1982. 62p.
Walker, Cherryl
    Women's Suffrage Movement in South Africa. Capetown,
    South Africa: University of Capetown. Centre for African
    Studies. Communications #2. 1979. 121p.
Walker, Cherryl
    Women and Resistance in South Africa. London: Onyx
    Press. 1982. 309p.
Walker, Cherryl
    "Women in 20th Century South African Politics: The
    Federation of South African Women, Its Roots, Growth and
    Decline." M.A. Thesis: University of Capetown.
    Capetown, South Africa. 1978.
Walker, Cherryl
    "The Federation of South African Women, 1954-1962." (In)
    University of Witwatersrand. Conference on the History
    of Opposition in Southern Africa, January, 1978.
    Johannesburg: (Students') Development Studies Group of
    the University of the Witwatersrand. 1978. pp. 183-205.
Walker, Cherryl
    "Women and Politics: The Anti-Pass Campaign of the
    1950's." Paper Presented at the University of Cape Town
    Summer School. Cape Town, South Africa: University of
    Cape Town. 1979.
Walker, Cherryl
    "Women and Politics: The Women's Suffrage Movement Before
    1930." Paper Presented at the University of Cape Town
    Summer School. Cape Town, South Africa: University of
    Cape Town. 1979.
Wells, Julia C.
    "Women's Resistance to Passes in Bloemfontein During the
    Inter-War Period." Africa Perspective. Volume 15
    Autumn, 1980. pp. 16-35.
Wells, Julia C.
    "The History of Black Women's Struggle Against Pass Laws
    in South Africa, 1900-1960." Ph.D Dissertation: Columbia
    University. New York, New York. 1982. 414p.
Wells, Julia C.
    "Why Women Rebel: A Comparative Study of South African
    Women's Resistance in Bloemfontein (1913) and
    Johannesburg (1958)." Journal of Southern African
    Studies. Volume 10 #1 October, 1983. pp. 55-70.
Wells, Julia C.
    "Passes and Bypasses: Freedom of Movement for African
    Women Under the Urban Areas Act of South Africa." (In)
    Hays, Margaret J. and Wright, Marcia (eds.). African
    Women and the Law: Historical Perspectives. Boston:
    Boston University. African Studies Center. Boston

University Papers on Africa. Volume Seven. 1982. pp. 125-150.
Wells, Julia C.
    "'The Day the Town Stood Still': Women in Resistance in
    Potchefstroom, 1912-1930." (In) Bozzoli, Belinda (ed.).
    Town and Countryside in the Transvaal: Capitalist
    Penetration and Popular Response. Johannesburg: Raven
    Press. 1983.
Yawitch, Joanne
    "Natal 1959: The Women's Protests." Paper Presented at
    the Conference on the History of Opposition in Southern
    Africa. Johannesburg: (Student's) Development Studies
    Group of the University of the Witwatersrand. January,
    1978. pp. 206-223.
Yawittch, Joanne
    "Defining the Issues--Women: Towards a Methodology of
    Women." Work in Progress. Volume 9 August, 1979. pp.
    32-35.

FAMILY LIFE

Anonymous
    "Women: The Family Food Producers in South Africa."
    Apartheid Bulletin. #126 1978.
Beavon, K. and Rogerson, C.
    "The Changing Role of Women in the Informal Sector of
    South Africa." (In) Drakakissmith, D. (ed.).
    Urbanization in the Developing World. London: Croom
    Helm. 1980.
Bozzoli, Belinda
    "Migrant Women and South African Social Change:
    Biographical Approaches to Social Analysis." African
    Studies. Volume 44 #1 1985. pp. 87-96.
Brindley, Marianne
    "The Role of the Old Women in the Zulu Culture." Ph.D
    Dissertation: University of Zululand. Kwa-Dlangezwa,
    South Africa. 1982.
Brink, Elsabe
    "'Maar 'n Klomp Factory Meide': The Role of the Female
    Garment Workers in the Clothing Industry, Afrikaner
    Family and Community on the Witwatersrand During the
    1920's." Paper Presented at the History Workshop.
    Johannesburg: University of the Witwatersrand. 1984.
Bromberger, Norman and Gandor, Mark
    "Economic and Demographic Functioning of Rural Households
    in the Mahlabatini District Kwazulu." Social Dynamics.
    Volume 10 #2 June, 1984. pp. 20-37.
Chetty, Romila
    "The Changing Family: A Study of the Indian Family in
    South Africa." South African Journal of Sociology.
    Volume 11 #2 September, 1980. pp.26-39.

Chetty, Thiagaraj D.
    Job Satisfaction on Indian Married Women in the Clothing
    Manufacturing Industry in Durban and its Effects on the
    Interpersonal Family Relationships. Durban, South
    Africa: University of Durban-Westville. Institute for
    Social and Economic Research. 1983. 130p.
Duncan, Sheena
    "Aspects of Family Breakdown." Work in Progress. Volume
    27. 1983. pp. 36-38.
Fuchs, Jean R.
    "One Parent Families: Some Special Implications of
    Lone-Parenthood." M.A. Thesis: University of Cape Town.
    Cape Town, South Africa. 1980.
Graaff, Janet
    "Married to a Migrant." South African Outlook. Volume
    108 #1289 November, 1978. pp. 172-173.
Hermann, Anne
    "The Flight From Domesticity in Two South African
    Novels." Communications for Gender Research. #5
    Summer, 1985. pp. 1+
Krige, Eileen J.
    "A Comparative Analysis of Marriage and Social Structure
    Among the Southern Bantu." (In) Krige, Eileen J, and
    Comaroff, J.L. (eds.). Essays on African Marriage in
    Southern Africa. Cape Town, South Africa: Juta. 1981.
Krige, Eileen J.
    "Lovedu Marriage and Social Change." (In) Krige, Eileen
    J. and Comaroff, J.L. (eds.). Essays on African Marriage
    in Southern Africa. Cape Town, South Africa: Juta.
    1981.
Landau, J. and Griffiths, J.A.
    "Family Therapy in South Africa." Journal of Marital and
    Family Therapy. Volume 6 #1 1980. pp. 83-84.
Manona, C.W.
    "Marriage, Family Life and Migrancy in a Ciskei Village."
    (In) Mayer, Philip (ed.). Black Villagers in an
    Industrial Society: Anthropological Perspectives on
    Labour Migration in South Africa. New York: Oxford
    University Press. 1980.
Manyosi, Maud
    "Working Women in South Africa." Sechaba. January,
    1980. pp. 23-24.
Mariotti, Amelia
    "Capitalist Development and State Policy in South Africa:
    African Women, the Family and the Price of Labour Power."
    Paper Presented at the Conference on African Women in
    History. Santa Clara, California: University of Santa
    Clara. 1981.
Marks, Shula and Unterhalter, Elaine
    "Women and the Migrant Labour System in South Africa."
    Paper Presented at the Conference on Migrant Labour in

Southern Africa. Lusaka, Zambia: United Nations Economic Commission For Africa (UNECA). 1978.

Marwick, M.
"Household Composition and Marriage in a Witwatersrand African Township." (In) Argyle,J. and Preston-Whyte, E. (eds.). Social System and Tradition in Southern Africa. Cape Town, South Africa: Oxford University Press. 1978. pp. 36-54.

Matsepe-Casaburri, Ivy F.
"Changing Roles and Needs of Women in South Africa and Namibia." Paper Presented at the World Conference for the United Nations Decade for Women, Copenhagen, Denmark, July 14-30, 1980. New York: United Nations. 1980.

Meer, Fatima
Women in the Apartheid Society. New York: United Nations. U.N. Centre Against Apartheid. April, 1985. 31p.

Meer, Fatima (ed.).
Black Women, Durban 1975: Case Studies of 85 Women at Home and Work. Durban, South Africa: University of Natal. Sociology Department. 1976.

Meer, Fatima (ed.).
Factory and Family: The Divided Lives of South Africa's Women Workers. Durban, South Africa: Institute for Black Research. 1984. 105p.

Moeno, N.S.
"Illegitimacy in an African Urban Township in South Africa: An Ethnographic Note." African Studies. Volume 36 #1 1977. pp. 43-48.

Nash, Margaret
"Women and Children in Resettlement Areas." South African Outlook. Volume 111 #1324. October, 1981. pp. 154-157.

Nene, Daphne S.
"Role Enactment of Rural Women: A Sociological Exploratory Study of the Role Behavior and its Implications for Rural Development." M.A. Thesis: University of Zululand. Kwa-Dlangezwa, South Africa. 1983.

Ntantala, Phyllis
An African Tragedy: The Black Woman Under Apartheid. Detroit, Michigan: Agascha Productions. 1976. 137p.

Poinsette, Cheryl
"Black Women Under Apartheid: An Introduction." Harvard Women's Law Journal. Volume 8 Spring, 1985. pp. 93-119.

Preston-Whyte, E.
"Female Headed Households and Development: Lessons of Cross-Cultural Models for Research on Women in Southern Africa." Paper Presented to the Women's Studies Symposium. Umtata, South Africa: University of Transkei. March, 1984.

Preston-Whyte, Eleanor M.
    "Families Without Marriage: A Zulu Caste Study." (In)
    Argyle, W. and Preston-Whyte E. (eds.). Social Systems
    and Tradition in Southern Africa. Capetown, South
    Africa: Oxford University Press. 1978.
Roscani, Luisa
    "Qwa Qwa - Relocation and Survival: The Effects of
    Relocation on Women." B.Soc.Sci. Thesis: University of
    Natal. Durban, South Africa. 1983.
Russell, Kathryn
    "The Internal Relation Between Production and
    Reproduction: Reflections on the Manipulation of Family
    Life in South Africa." Journal of Social Philosophy.
    Volume 15 Summer, 1984. pp. 14-25.
Schweigart, M.A. and Mostert, W.P.
    "The Motivation of Women to Accept Family Planning."
    Tydskrif vir Rasse-Aangeleenthede. Volume 28 #1/2
    January-April, 1977. pp. 18-21.
Showers, Kate
    "A Note on Women, Conflict and Migrant Labour." South
    African Labour Bulletin. Volume 6 #4 November, 1980.
Sibisi, Harriet N.
    "How African Women Cope With Migrant Labor in South
    Africa." Signs. Volume 3 #1 Autumn, 1977. pp.
    167-177.
Sibisi, Harriet N.
    "How African Women Cope With Migrant Labor in South
    Africa." (In) Wellesley Editorial Committee. Women and
    National Development: The Complexities of Change.
    Chicago: University of Chicago Press. 1977. pp.
    167-177.
Smedley, L.N.
    "White Housewives: An Introductory Study." South African
    Journal of Sociology. Volume 17 April, 1978. pp.
    61-72.
Steyn, Anna F. and Uys, J.M.
    "The Changing Position of Black Women in South Africa."
    (In) Lupri, E. (ed.). The Changing Position of Women in
    Family and Society. Leiden, Netherlands: Brill. 1983.
    pp. 344-370.
United Nations Centre Against Apartheid
    "The Effects of Apartheid on the Status of Women in South
    Africa." Black Scholar. Volume 10 #1 September, 1978.
    pp. 11-21.
United Nations Economic Commission for Africa (UNECA)
    Apartheid and the Status of Women. Addis Ababa,
    Ethiopia: UNECA. Regional Prepatory Meeting of the UNECA
    Second Regional Conference for the Integration of Women
    in Development. Lusaka, Zambia. December 3-7, 1979.
Unterhalter, Beryl
    "Women in Struggle--South Africa." Third World
    Quarterly. Volume 5 #4 1983. pp. 886-893.

Van Bart, Dawn
    "The Effects of the Mother's Work Experience on Her
    Preschool Child's Behavior." B.A. Honors Dissertation:
    University of the Witwatersrand. Johannesburg, South
    Africa. 1982.
Whitelaw, D.A.
    "Socio-Economic Status and Use of Contraceptives Among
    Unmarried Primigravidas in Cape Town." South African
    Medical Journal. Volume 64 #18 October 22, 1983. pp.
    712-715.
Yawitch, Joanne
    Black Women in South Africa: Capitalism, Employment and
    Reproduction. Johannesburg: Africa Perspective
    Dissertation #2. 1980.
Yawitch, Joanne
    "Women and Squatting: A Winterveld Case Study." (In)
    University of Witwatersrand. Working Papers in Southern
    African Studies. Johannesburg: University of the
    Witwatersrand. May, 1979. pp. 199-227.
Yawitch, Joanne
    "Apartheid and Family Life." Work in Progress. Volume
    27 1983. pp. 40-42.

FAMILY PLANNING AND CONTRACEPTION

Barling, Julian and Lanham, W.
    "Beliefs Regarding the Consequences of Birth Control
    Among Black, Colored, Indian and White South Africans."
    Journal of Social Psychology. Volume 105 Part One June,
    1978. pp. 149-150.
Barling, Julian and Fincham, Frank
    "Locus of Control Beliefs in Male and Female Indian and
    White School Children in South Africa." Journal of
    Crosscultural Psychology. Volume 9 June, 1978. pp.
    227-236.
Barling, Julian
    "Multidimensional Locus of Control Beliefs Among English
    Speaking South African Mothers." Journal of Social
    Psychology. Volume 111 1st Quarter June, 1980. pp.
    139-140.
Bloch, B. and Davies, A.H.
    "Evaluation of a Combined Oestrogen-Progestogen
    Injectable Contraceptive." South African Medical
    Journal. Volume 53 #21 May 27, 1978. pp. 846-847.
Brown, Barbara B.
    The Political Economy of Population Policy in South
    Africa. Boston: Boston University. African Studies
    Center. African Studies Working Paper #71. 1983. 15p.
Castle, W.M. and Sapire, K.E. and Howard, K.A.
    "Efficacy and Acceptability of Injectable
    Medroxyprogesterone: A Comparison of Three Monthly and

Six Monthly Regimens." South African Medical Journal.
Volume 53 #21 May 27, 1978. pp. 842-845.

Erasmus, G.
"Decision-Making in Regard to the Use of Contraceptives
After Confinement: A Study Among Urban Black Women."
South African Journal of Sociology. Volume 15 #2 May,
1984. pp. 94-97.

Fernihough, T.J. and Munoz, W.P. and Mahadeyo, I.
"The Role of Brucella Abortus in Spontaneous Abortion
Among the Black Population." South African Medical
Journal. Volume 68 #6 September 14, 1985. pp. 379-380.

Groenewald, H.J.
Fertility and Family Planning in Atteridgeville: Data for
1969, 1974 and 1975. Pretoria, South Africa: South
African Human Sciences Research Council. Institute for
Sociological, Demographic and Criminological Research.
#S53 1978. 26p.

Groenewald, H.J.
Fertility and Family Planning in Chatsworth: Data for
1969, 1974, 1975, and 1977. Pretoria, South Africa:
South African Human Sciences Research Council. Institute
for Sociological, Demographic and Criminological
Research. #S57. 1978. 34p.

Groenewald, H.J.
"Multi-Purpose Survey Among Indians, 1977: Fertility and
Family Planning." Pretoria, South Africa: South African
Human Sciences Research Council. Institute for
Sociological, Demographic and Criminological Research.
#S117. 1978. 40p.

Hampson, M.E.
"Factors Involved in the Acceptance of Voluntary Female
Sterilization Among Indians in Natal." South African
Medical Journal. Volume 55 #18 April 28, 1979. pp.
719-721.

Hulka, J.F.
"Female Sterilization." South African Medical Journal.
Volume 55 #18 1979. pp. 118-124.

Letsema
"Family Planning in South Africa--A Kind of Genocide?"
African Communist. Volume 90 1982.

Lotter, Johann M.
"Some Aspects of Indian Fertility in South Africa."
Humanitas. Volume 3 #4 1976. pp. 419-426.

Lotter, Johann M.
"The Effect of Urbanization and Education on the
Fertility of Blacks in South Africa." Humanitas. Volume
4 #1 1977. pp. 21-28.

Lotter, Johann M.
Attitudes of Black South African Men Towards Fertility
and Family Planning. Pretoria, South Africa: South
African Human Sciences Research Council. Institute for
Sociological, Demographic and Criminological Research.
Research Finding #S-N-96. 1977. 16p.

Lotter, Johann M. and Van Tonder, J.L.
    Fertility and Family Planning Among Blacks in South
    Africa: 1974. Pretoria, South Africa: Human Sciences
    Research Council. Report No. S-39. 1976. 111p.
Lotter, Johann M. and Van Tonder, J.L.
    Certain Aspects of Human Fertility in Rural
    Bophuthatswana. Pretoria, South Africa: South African
    Human Sciences Research Council. Institute for
    Sociological, Demographic and Criminological Research.
    Report #S-54. 1978. 53p.
Mitchell, L.
    Tsonga Women: Changes in Production and Reproduction: A
    Working Paper. Minneapolis, Minnesota: University of
    Minnesota. African History Seminar. 1978.
Mostert, W.P. and Kok, P.C.
    The South African National Family Planning Programme:
    Contraceptive Projection and Service Efficiency During
    April, 1981. Pretoria, South Africa: Human Sciences
    Research Council. Institute for Sociological and
    Demographic Research. RGN.SRC Report #S-109. 1984.
    51p.
Nene, Daphne S.
    "Women Caught in Between: The Case of Rural Women in
    KwaZulu." Paper Presented to the Women's Studies
    Symposium, University of Transkei. Umtata, South Africa:
    University of Transkei. March, 1984.
Roux, A.
    "Family Planning Among A Group of Coloured Women." South
    African Medical Journal. Volume 65 #22 June 2, 1984.
    pp. 898-901.
Schweigart, M.A. and Mostert, W.P.
    "The Motivation of Women to Accept Family Planning."
    Tydskrif vir Rasse-Aangeleenthede. Volume 28 #1/2
    January-April, 1977. pp. 18-21.
Shindler, J.
    The Reproductive Function and Ultra-Exploitability of
    South African Domestic Workers. Johannesburg: University
    of the Witwatersrand. Industrial Sociology Research
    Project. 1978.
Snyman. I.
    "Social, Cultural and Psychological Barriers to Reduction
    of Fertility." Royal Society of South Africa.
    Transactions. Volume 43 Part One 1978. pp. 85-89.
Strauss, S.A.
    "We Need a Family Planning Act." Codicillus. Volume 19
    #1 May, 1978. pp. 4-6.
Van Regenmortel, P.J. and Van Harte, E.
    Family Planning in the Greater Cape Town Area: A
    Background Study. Bellville, South Africa: University of
    the Western Cape. Institute for Social Development.
    October, 1977. 107p.
Van Tonder, J.L.
    Fertility Survey 1981: Data Concerning the Coloured

Population of South Africa. Pretoria, South Africa:
Human Sciences Research Council. Institute for
Sociological and Demographic Research. Report #S-120.
1984. 204p.
Van Tonder, J.L.
Fertility Survey 1982: Data Concerning the Black
Population of South Africa. Pretoria, South Africa:
Human Sciences Research Council. Institute for
Sociological and Demographic Research. Report #S-129.
1985. 301p.
Verster, J.
Trend and Pattern of Fertility in Soweto: An Urban Bantu
Community: A Report on the Fertility Sample Survey of the
Bantu Population in Soweto. Braamfontein, South Africa:
University of the Witwatersrand Press. 1979.
Walker, Cherryl
Women and Resistance in South Africa. London: Onyx
Press. 1982. 309p.
Woodrow, E.P.
"Family Planning in South Africa: A Review." South
African Medical Journal. Volume 50 #53 December 11,
1976. pp. 2101-2103.
Yawitch, Joanne
Black Women in South Africa: Capitalism, Employment and
Reproduction. Johannesburg: Africa Perspective
Dissertation #2. 1980.

FERTILITY AND INFERTILITY

Brown, Barbara B.
The Political Economy of Population Policy in South
Africa. Boston: Boston University. African Studies
Center. African Studies Working Paper #71. 1983. 15p.
El-Attar, M. and Nouri, Mohamed O.
"Socioeconomic Characteristics and Fertility Level in the
Sudan." (In) American Statistical Association (ASA).
1983 Proceedings of the Social Statistics Section.
Washington, D.C.: ASA. 1983. pp. 407-411.
Groenewald, H.J.
Fertility and Family Planning in Atteridgeville: Data for
1969, 1974 and 1975. Pretoria, South Africa: South
African Human Sciences Research Council. Institute for
Sociological, Demographic and Criminological Research.
#S53 1978. 26p.
Groenewald, H.J.
Fertility and Family Planning in Chatsworth: Data for
1969, 1974, 1975, and 1977. Pretoria, South Africa:
South African Human Sciences Research Council. Institute
for Sociological, Demographic and Criminological
Research. #S57. 1978. 34p.
Groenewald, H.J.
Multi-Purpose Survey Among Indians, 1977: Fertility and
Family Planning. Pretoria, South Africa: South African

Human Sciences Research Council. Institute for
Sociological, Demographic and Criminological Research.
#S117. 1978. 40p.
Lotter, Johann M.
"Socio-Economic Status and Fertility: The Emergence of
New Trends Among White South Africans." Humanitas.
Volume 4 #3 1978. pp. 323-325.
Lotter, Johann M.
"Some Aspects of Indian Fertility in South Africa."
Humanitas. Volume 3 #4 1976. pp. 419-426.
Lotter, Johann M.
"The Effect of Urbanization and Education on the
Fertility of Blacks in South Africa." Humanitas. Volume
4 #1 1977. pp. 21-28.
Lotter, Johann M.
Attitudes of Black South African Men Towards Fertility
and Family Planning. Pretoria, South Africa: South
African Human Sciences Research Council. Institute for
Sociological, Demographic and Criminological Research.
Research Finding #S-N-96. 1977. 16p.
Lotter, Johann M. and Van Tonder, J.L.
Fertility and Family Planning Among Blacks in South
Africa: 1974. Pretoria, South Africa: Human Sciences
Research Council. Report No. S-39. 1976. 111p.
Lotter, Johann M. and Van Tonder, J.L.
Certain Aspects of Human Fertility in Rural
Bophuthatswana. Pretoria, South Africa: South African
Human Sciences Research Council. Institute for
Sociological, Demographic and Criminological Research.
Report #S-54. 1978. 53p.
Roberts, Mary and Rip, M.R.
"Black Fertility Patterns-Cape Town and Ciskei." South
African Medical Journal. Volume 66 #13 September 29,
1984. pp. 481-484.
Saghayroun, Atif A.R.
"Feasibility of Fertility Control in Rural Areas in the
Sudan." Economic and Social Research Council Bulletin.
#99 September, 1983.
Snyman. I.
"Social, Cultural and Psychological Barriers to Reduction
of Fertility." Royal Society of South Africa.
Transactions. Volume 43 Part One 1978. pp. 85-89.
Van Tonder, J.L.
Fertility Survey 1981: Data Concerning the Coloured
Population of South Africa. Pretoria, South Africa:
Human Sciences Research Council. Institute for
Sociological and Demographic Research. Report #S-120.
1984. 204p.
Van Tonder, J.L.
Fertility Survey 1982: Data Concerning the Black
Population of South Africa. Pretoria, South Africa:
Human Sciences Research Council. Institute for

Sociological and Demographic Research. Report #S-129. 1985. 301p.

Verster, J.
Trend and Pattern of Fertility in Soweto: An Urban Bantu Community: A Report on the Fertility Sample Survey of the Bantu Population in Soweto. Braamfontein, South Africa: University of the Witwatersrand Press. 1979.

HEALTH, NUTRITION AND MEDICINE

Anonymous
"Homeland Women." Critical Health. Volume 9 1983. pp. 36-39.

Anonymous
"Women and Mental Health: A Comment." Critical Health. Volume 9 1983. pp. 53-56.

Anonymous
"Women, Work and Health." Critical Health. Volume 9 1983. pp. 18-28.

Anonymous
"Women Health Workers." Critical Health. Volume 9 1983. pp. 5-10.

Anonymous
"Women Workers, Maternity Benefits and Trade Unions." Critical Health. Volume 9 1983. pp. 29-35.

Anonymous
"Rape." Critical Health. Volume 9 1983. pp. 52-62.

Anonymous
"A Chronology of Women's Struggles in Health." Critical Health. Volume 9 1983. pp. 11-15.

Arenson, Paul and Moizen, Inga
"Women Office Cleaners on Night Shift: A Report on the Study of the Effects on Night-Shift Work on the Health and Social Conditions of Women Office Cleaners in Some Johannesburg Office Blocks." South African Labour Bulletin. Volume 9 #3 December, 1983. pp. 74-81.

Armstrong, Henrietta E.
Camp Diary of Henrietta E.C. Armstrong: Experiences of a Boer Nurse in the Irene Concentration Camp, 6 April-11 October, 1901. Pretoria, South Africa: Human Sciences Research Council. Source Publication #8. 1980. 211p.

Baartman, D.
"Traditional and Modern Approaches to the Health Care of the Pregnant Woman in Xhosa Society." M.A. Thesis: University of South Africa. Pretoria, South Africa. 1983.

Barling, Julian and Lanham, W.
"Beliefs Regarding the Consequences of Birth Control Among Black, Colored, Indian and White South Africans." Journal of Social Psychology. Volume 105 Part One June, 1978. pp. 149-150.

Barlow, M.R.
"Woman Doctors of South Africa." South African Medical
Journal. Special Issue June 29, 1983. pp. 29-32.
Behr, D.
"Women and Work, in Psychological Perspective." Journal
of the University of Durban-Westville. Volume 2 #4 1976.
pp. 9-18.
Bloch, B. and Davies, A.H.
"Evaluation of a Combined Oestrogen-Progestogen
Injectable Contraceptive." South African Medical
Journal. Volume 53 #21 May 27, 1978. pp. 846-847.
Bloch, B.
"The Abortion and Sterilization Act of 1975: Experience
of the Johannesburg Hospital Pregnancy Advisory Service."
South African Medical Journal. Volume 53 #21 May 27,
1978. pp. 861-864.
Bolon, K. and Barling, J.I.
"Alcohol Consumption, Expectancy and Multi-Dimensional
Locus of Control in Female Social Drinkers." Journal of
Behavioral Science. Volume 2 #5 1978. pp. 331-337.
Booth, W.R.
"Paediatric Problems in a Rural Area of South Africa. A
Study in Southern Lebowa." South African Medical
Journal. Volume 61 #24 June 12, 1982. pp. 911-913.
Bradshaw, Evelyn
The Use of Tobacco and Alcoholic Beverages by Male and
Female Xhosa in Transkei in Relation to Cancer of the
Oesophagus. Grahamstown, South Africa: Rhodes
University. Institute of Social and Economic Research.
Occasional Paper #27. 1983. 46p.
Brindley, Marianne
"Old Women in Zulu Culture: The Old Woman and
Childbirth." South African Journal of Ethnology. Volume
8 #3 1985. pp. 98-108.
Budlender, Vivienne L
Unhooking the Gay Female From Drugs and Alcohol. Social
Work Dissertation: University of the Witwatersrand.
Johannesburg, South Africa. 1980.
Castle, W.M. and Sapire, K.E. and Howard, K.A.
"Efficacy and Acceptability of Injectable
Medroxyprogesterone: A Comparison of Three Monthly and
Six Monthly Regimens." South African Medical Journal.
Volume 53 #21 May 27, 1978. pp. 842-845.
Cheetham, R.W. and Rzadkowolski, A. and Rataemane, S.
"Psychiatric Disorders of the Puerperium in South African
Women of Nguni Origin--A Pilot Study." South African
Medical Journal. Volume 60 #13 September 26, 1981. pp
502-506.
Cock, Jacklyn
"Childcare and the Working Mother" Africa Perspective.
Volume 26 1985. pp. 29-60.
Cock, Jacklyn and Emdon, E.
"Child Care and the Working Mother." Paper Presented to

the Association for Sociology in Southern Africa.
Johannesburg: University of the Witwatersrand. 1984.
Cock, Jacklyn and Emdon, E. and Klugman, B.
Child Care and the Working Mother: A Sociological
Investigation of a Sample of Urban African Women.
Rondebosch, South Africa: University of Cape Town.
SALDRU. School of Economics. Carnegie Conference Paper
#115. April, 1984. 46p.
Cock, Jacklyn and Emdon, E. and Klugman, B.
"Research Report: Child Care and the Working Mother."
South African Labour Bulletin. Volume 9 #7 1984. pp.
58-59.
Cock, Jacklyn
"Women and Health." (In) National Union of South African
Students (NUSAS). NUSAS Conference on Women. Cape Town,
South Africa: NUSAS. Women's Directive. 1983.
Dommisse, J.
"The South African Gynaecologist's Attitude to the
Present Abortion Law." South African Medical Journal.
Volume 57 #25 June, 1980. pp. 1044-1045.
Drower, S.J. and Nash, E.S.
"Therapeutic Abortion on Psychiatric Ground. Part One: A
Local Study." South African Medical Journal. Volume 54
#15 October 7, 1978. pp. 604-608.
Drower, Sandra J.
"A Survey of Patients Referred for Therapeutic Abortion
on Psychiatric Grounds in a Cape Town Provincial
Hospital." Ph.D. Dissertation: University of Cape Town.
Cape Town, South Africa. 1977.
Duckitt, J.H.
"Psychological Factors Related to Subjective Health
Perception Among Elderly Women." Humanitas. Volume 9 #4
1983. pp. 441-449.
Emdon, S. and Gerard, U. and Jones, R.
"Knowledge About and Utilization of Facilities for
Cervical Smears Among Black Women in Johannesburg."
South African Medical Journal. Volume 65 #8 February
25, 1984. pp. 289-290.
Erasmus, G.
"Decision-Making in Regard to the Use of Contraceptives
After Confinement: A Study Among Urban Black Women."
South African Journal of Sociology. Volume 15 #2 May,
1984. pp. 94-97.
Farrand, Dorothy M. and Holdstock, T. Len
"Dreams of a Sangoma or Indigenous Healer." Journal of
African Studies. Volume 9 #2 Summer, 1982. pp. 68-75.
Fernihough, T.J. and Munoz, W.P. and Mahadeyo, I.
"The Role of Brucella Abortus in Spontaneous Abortion
Among the Black Population." South African Medical
Journal. Volume 68 #6 September 14, 1985. pp. 379-380.
Finch, Briony J.
"Male and Female Homosexuality: A Comparison of
Secretiveness, Promiscuity, Masculine/Feminine Role

Playing, Self-Concept and Self-Acceptance." B.A. Honors
Dissertation: University of the Witwatersrand.
Johannesburg, South Africa. 1980.
Flisher, A.J.
"The Development, Implementation and Evaluation of a
Training Program in Rape Crisis Intervention for Lay
Therapists: A Community Psychology Approach." M.Sc.
Thesis: University of Cape Town. Cape Town, South
Africa. 1981.
Furman, S.N.
"Attitudes of Middle-Class Mothers to Breast-Feeding."
South African Medical Journal. Volume 56 1979. pp.
722-723.
Gerdes, L.C.
"Personality Differences Between Men and Women in Marital
Roles." Social Welfare and Pensions. Volume 12 #1
June, 1977. pp. 6-12.
Goldstein, Susan
"Women in Medicine." Critical Health. Volume 1 1980.
pp. 30-34.
Grobler, I.
"Changes in the Body Image of Primiparous Women Before
and After Confinement." M.A. Thesis: University of
Pretoria. Pretoria, South Africa. 1980.
Gumede, M.V.
"Traditional Zulu Practitioners and Obstetric Medicine."
South African Medical Journal. Volume 53 #21 May 27,
1978. pp. 823-825.
Hampson, M.E.
"Factors Involved in the Acceptance of Voluntary Female
Sterilization Among Indians in Natal." South African
Medical Journal. Volume 55 #18 April 28, 1979. pp.
719-721.
Hoar, R.N.M.
"The Relevance of Mother's Speech in Communication With
the Pre-Verbal Child." M.A. Thesis: University of Natal.
Durban, South Africa. 1978.
Hulka, J.F.
"Female Sterilization." South African Medical Journal.
Volume 55 #18 1979. pp. 118-124.
Hyde, M.
"Personality Factors and Emotional Change in
Pre-Menopausal Women Undergoing Hysterectomy." M.Sc
Thesis: University of the Witwatersrand. Johannesburg,
South Africa. 1979.
Kaganas, F. and Murray, C.
"Rape in Marriage: Conjugal Right or Criminal Wrong?"
Acta Juridica. 1983. pp. 125-143.
Katz, I.B. and Brenner, B.N. and Sarzin, B.
"Pregnancy in the Unwed White South African." South
African Medical Journal. Volume 52 #2 July 9, 1977.
pp. 79-81.

Kilbourne, S.K.
"An Investigation of Ill Mothers and an Intervention
Programme Based on Their Observed Needs." M.A. Thesis:
University of the Witwatersrand. Johannesburg, South
Africa. 1979.
Kirsten, G.F. and Heese, H.D. and Watermeyer, S. and
Dempster, W.S. and Pocock, F. and Varkevisser, H.
"Zinc and Copper Levels in the Breastmilk of Cape Town
Mothers." South African Medical Journal. Volume 68 #6
September 14, 1985. pp. 402-405.
Klugman, Barbara
"Maternity Rights and Benefits and Protective Legislation
at Work." South African Labour Bulletin. Volume 9 #3
1983. pp. 25-51.
Klugman, Barbara
"The Political Economy of Population Control in South
Africa." B.A. Honors Dissertation: University of the
Witwatersrand. Johannesburg, South Africa. 1980.
Kopenhager, T. and Kort, H. and Bloch, B.
"An Analysis of the First 200 Legal Abortions of the
Johannesburg General Hospital." South African Medical
Journal. Volume 53 #21 May, 1978. pp. 858-860.
Labuschagne, G.P.
"Uterine Contraction Regularity During Labour in White
and Black Patients." South African Medical Journal.
Volume 63 #14 April 2, 1983.
Landau, J. and Griffiths, J.A.
"Family Therapy in South Africa." Journal of Marital and
Family Therapy. Volume 6 #1 1980. pp. 83-84.
Larsen, J.V. and Msane, C.L. and Monkhe, M.C.
"The Zulu Traditional Birth Attendant. An Evaluation of
Her Attitudes and Techniques and Their Implications for
Health Education." South African Medical Journal.
Volume 63 #14 April 2, 1983. pp. 540-542.
Larsen, J.V. and Msane, C.L. and Monkhe, M.C.
"The Fate of Women Who Deliver at Home in Rural Kwazulu:
Assessment of the Place of Traditional Birth Attendents
in the South African Health Services." South African
Medical Journal. Volume 63 #14 April 2, 1983. pp.
534-545.
Larsen, J.V. and Muller, E.J.
"Obstetric Care in a Rural Population." South African
Medical Journal. Volume 54 #27 December 30, 1978. pp.
1137-1140.
Letsema
"Family Planning in South Africa--A Kind of Genocide?"
African Communist. Volume 90 1982.
Levett, A.
"Considerations in the Provision of Adequate
Psychological Care for the Sexually Assaulted Woman."
M.Sc Thesis: University of Cape Town. Cape Town, South
Africa. 1981.

MacPhail, A.P. and Bothwell, T.H. and Torrance, J.D. and
Derman, D.P. and Bezwoda, W.R. and Charlton, R.W. and Mayet,
F.G.
    "Iron Nutrition in Indian Women at Different Ages."
    South African Medical Journal. Volume 59 #26 June 20,
    1981. pp. 932-942.
Mackenzie, D.J.
    "Influx Control, Health Regulation and African Women in
    Durban, c. 1917-1949." Paper Presented at the Workshop
    on Local History. Pietermaritzburg, South Africa. 1982.
Mark, G.
    "A Follow Up Study of Therapeutic Abortions: A Social
    Work Perspective." M.A. Thesis: University of South
    Africa. Pretoria, South Africa. 1981.
Mashaba, T.G.
    "The Composition of the Nursing Profession in South
    Africa in the Mid-Seventies and Its Implications for
    Provision of Health Care." Journal of Advanced Nursing.
    Volume 6 #5 September, 1981. pp. 339-347.
McCafferty, S.
    "An Analysis of Abortion on Mental Health Grounds Within
    the South African Context." Durban, South Africa:
    University of Natal. L.L.B. Research Project. 1980.
Melrose, E.B.
    "Maternal Deaths at King Edward VIII Hospital, Durban. A
    Review of 258 Consecutive Cases." South African Medical
    Journal. Volume 65 #5 February 4, 1984. pp. 161-165.
Mommsen, C.
    "A Psychodiagnostic Study of a Selected Group of Women
    Pregnant Out of Wedlock." M.A. Thesis: University of
    Orange Free State. Bloemfontein, South Africa. 1978.
Moodley, S.P. and Jialai, I. and Modley, J. and Naicker,
R.S. and Marivate, M.
    "Carbohydrate Metabolism in African Women With Twin
    Pregnancy." Diabetes Care. Volume 7 #1
    January-February, 1984. pp. 72-74.
Mostert, W.P. and Kok, P.C.
    The South African National Family Planning Programme:
    Contraceptive Projection and Service Efficiency During
    April, 1981. Pretoria, South Africa: Human Sciences
    Research Council. Institute for Sociological and
    Demographic Research. RGN.SRC Report #S-109. 1984.
    51p.
Mphahlele, M.
    "Dietary Restriction for the Prevention of Disproportion
    and Obstructed Labour Among the Pedis of Yester-Year."
    South African Medical Journal. Volume 61 #22 May 29,
    1982. pp. 842.
Nash, E.S. and Navias, M.
    "Therapeutic Abortion on Psychiatric Grounds. Part III:
    Implementing the Abortion and Sterilization Act
    (1975-1981)." South African Medical Journal. Volume 63
    #17 April 23, 1983. pp. 639-644.

Nash, E.S. and Navias, M.
    Termination of Pregnancy on Psychiatric Grounds, Part
    Three: Implementing the Abortion and Sterilization Act
    (1975-1981). Cape Town, South Africa: Hospital Services,
    Cape Provincial Administration. 1982.
Nel, C.J. and Roode, F. and De Wet, J.I.
    "The Attitude of South African Women to Mastectomy for
    Breast Cancer." South African Medical Journal. Volume
    67 #18 May 4, 1985. pp. 728-729.
O'Keefe, S.J.D. and Ndaba, N. and Woodward, A.
    "Relationship Between Nutritional Status, Dietary Intake
    Pattens and Plasma Lipoprotein Concentrations in Rural
    Black South Africans." Human Nutrition. Clinical
    Nutrition. Volume 39c #5 September, 1985. pp. 335-341.
Oldshue, R.
    "Maternal and Child Care Service in Rural KwaZulu."
    South African Medical Journal. Volume 55 #9 March 3,
    1979. pp. 344-346.
Pegoraro, R.J. and Nirmul, D. and Bryer, J.V. and Jordaan,
J.P. and Joubert, S.M.
    "Clinical Patterns of Presentation of Breast Cancer in
    Women of Different Racial Groups in South Africa." South
    African Medical Journal. Volume 68 #11 1985. pp.
    808-810.
Philpott, R.H.
    "What the Community Needs--Obstetric Care." South
    African Medical Journal. Volume 53 #21 May 27, 1978.
    pp. 831-833.
Richardson, B.D.
    "The Bearing of Diverse Patterns of Diet on Growth and
    Menarche in Four Ethnic Groups of South African Girls."
    Journal of Tropical Medicine and Hygiene. Volume 86 #1
    February, 1983. pp. 5-12.
Roberts, Mary and Rip, M.R.
    "Black Fertility Patterns-Cape Town and Ciskei." South
    African Medical Journal. Volume 66 #13 September 29,
    1984. pp. 481-484.
Ross, S.M. and MacPherson, T.A. and Naeye, R.L. and Khatree,
M.H.D. and Wallace, J.A.
    "Causes of Fetal and Neonatal Mortality in a South
    African Black Community." South African Medical Journal.
    Volume 61 #24 June 12, 1982. pp. 905-908.
Ross, S.M. and Van Middelkoop, A. and Khoza, N.C.
    "Breast Feeding Practices in a Black Community." South
    African Medical Journal. Volume 63 #1 January 1, 1983.
    pp. 23-25.
Roux, A.
    "Family Planning Among A Group of Coloured Women." South
    African Medical Journal. Volume 65 #22 June 2, 1984.
    pp. 898-901.
Saghayroun, Atif A.R.
    "Feasibility of Fertility Control in Rural Areas in the

Sudan." Economic and Social Research Council Bulletin.
#99 September, 1983.
Sandler, S.W.
"Spontaneous Abortion in Perspective: A Seven Year
Study." South African Medical Journal. Volume 52 #1
December 31, 1977. pp. 115, 118.
Saxe, Norma and Van Niekerk, J.P. de V.
"Women Doctors Wasted." South African Medical Journal.
Volume 55 1979. pp. 760-762.
Schafer, I.D.
"Human Artificial Insemination and the Law: Some Legal
Implications." Natal University Law Review. Volume 2 #2
1978. pp. 228-238.
Schuitevoerder, S.
"The Psychotherapeutic Intervention on the Stress Level
of Urban Africna Women During Childbirth." M.A. Thesis:
Rand Afrikaans University: Johannesburg, South Africa.
1983.
Schweigart, M.A. and Mostert, W.P.
"The Motivation of Women to Accept Family Planning."
Tydskrif vir Rasse-Aangeleenthede. Volume 28 #1/2
January-April, 1977. pp. 18-21.
Segal, I. and Walker, A.R.P. and Coupersmith, J.
"The Prevalence of Gallstones in Urban Black Women."
South African Medical Journal. Volume 68 #7 1985. pp.
530.
Shindler, J.
The Reproductive Function and Ultra-Exploitability of
South African Domestic Workers. Johannesburg: University
of the Witwatersrand. Industrial Sociology Research
Project. 1978.
Spitz, Shirley
"Career Commitment of Professional Women: A Study Into
the Effects of an Encounter Group Experience on
Self-Esteem Self-Actualisation and Professional Image."
B.A. Honors Dissertation: University of the
Witwatersrand. Johannesburg, South Africa. 1983.
Stavrou, P.
"Social Psychological Manifestations of Worker
Alienation." B.Soc.Sci Honors Dissertation: University
of Natal. Durban, South Africa. 1983.
Straker, G. and Altman, R.
"Psychological Factors Differentiating Unwed Mothers
Keeping Their Babies From Those Placing Them for
Adoption." South African Journal of Psychology. Volume
9 #1/2 1979. pp. 55-59.
Taitz, Jerold
"The Legal Consequences of a Sex Change: A Judicial
Dilemma." South African Law Review. Volume 97 1980.
pp. 65-76.
Thornton, L.
"Breastfeeding in South Africa: Social and Cultural

Aspects and Strategies for Promotion." Curationis.
Volume 7 #3 September, 1984. pp. 33-41.
Uken, J.M.
"Psychological Changes During Pregnancy With Special
Reference to Motherliness." Unisa Psychologia. Volume 5
1978. pp. 39-45.
Uken, J.M.
"The Psychological Changes During Pregnancy With Special
Reference to Motherliness." M.A. Thesis: University of
South Africa. Pretoria, South Africa. 1976.
Unterhalter, Beryl
"Discrimination Against Women in the South African
Medical Profession." Social Science and Medicine.
Volume 20 #12 1985. pp. 1253-1258.
Van Biljon, M.
"Women and Doctors." South African Medical Journal.
Volume 50 #24 June 5, 1976. pp. 911-912.
Van Coeverden de Groot, H.A.
"Trends in Maternal Mortality in Cape Town, 1953-1977."
Part One. South African Medical Journal. Volume 56 #14
September 29, 1979. pp. 547-552.
Van Coeverden de Groot, H.A.
"Trends in Maternal Mortality in Capetown, 1953-1977."
Part Two. South African Medical Journal. Volume 57 #7
February 16, 1980. pp. 224-225.
Van Coeverden de Groot, H.A. and Davey, D.A. and Howland,
R.C.
"The Peninsular Maternity and Neo-Natal Service: An Urban
Community Perinatal Programme." South African Medical
Journal. Volume 61 #2 January 9, 1982. pp. 35-36.
Van Coeverden de Groot, H.A.
"Deaths in Gynaecological Wards at Groote Schuur
Hospital, Cape Town, 1957-1977." South African Medical
Journal. Volume 56 #14 September 29, 1979. pp.
553-557.
Van Heyningen, Elizabeth B.
"The Social Evil of the Cape Colony, 1868-1902:
Prostitution and the Contagious Diseases Act." Journal
of Southern African Studies. Volume 10 #2 1984. pp.
170-197.
Van Heyningen, Elizabeth B.
"Prostitution and the Contagious Diseases Act: The Social
Evil in the Cape Colony, 1868-1902." (In) Saunders,
Christopher (ed.). Studies in the History of Cape Town.
Cape Town, South Africa: University of Cape Town. Centre
for African Studies and the History Department. Volume
Five. 1984. pp. 80-124.
Van Niekerk, Barend
"Class, Punishment and Rape in South Africa." Natal
University Law Review. Volume 1#5 1976. pp. 299-305.
Van Niekerk, G.
"Psychiatric Aspects of Therapeutic Abortion." South

African Medical Journal. Volume 55 #11 March, 1979.
"The Married Women in the Nursing Profession."
Curationis. Volume 3 #2 September, 1980. pp. 32-35.
Van Regenmortel, P.J. and Van Harte, E.
Family Planning in the Greater Cape Town Area: A
Background Study. Bellville, South Africa: University of
the Western Cape. Institute for Social Development.
"Part Time Specialization for Women Doctors." South
African Medical Journal. Volume 55 #19 May 5, 1979.
Vink, G. and Moodley, J.
"Gonorrhoea in Black Women Attending a Gynaecological
Outpatient Department." South African Medical Journal.
Volume 58 #22 November 29, 1980. pp. 901-902.
Walker, A.R.P. and Walker, B.F. and Tshabalala, E.N. and
Isaacson, C. and Segal, I.
"Low Survival of South African Urban Black Women With
Breast Cancer." British Journal of Cancer. Volume 49 #2
February, 1984. pp. 241-244.
Walker, A.R.P. and Walker, B.F. and Jones, J. and Verardi,
M. and Walker, Cherryl
"Nausea and Vomiting and Dietary Cravings and Aversions
During Pregnancy in South African Women." British
Journal of Obstetrics and Gynaecology. Volume 92 #5
May, 1985. pp. 484-489.
Walker, A.R.P. and Dison, E. and Walker, B.F.
"Dental Caries in South African Rural Black Women Who Had
Large Families and Long Lactations." Journal of Tropical
Medicine and Hygiene. Volume 86 #6 1983. pp. 201-205.
Walker, A.R.P. and Walker, B.F. and Jones, J. and Duvenhage,
A. and Mia, F.P.
"Knowledge of Nutrition Among Housewives in Three South
African Ethnic Groups." South African Medical Journal.
Volume 62 #17 October 16, 1982. pp. 605-610.
Walker, A.R.P. and Walker, B.F. and Ncongwane, J. and
"Age of Menopause in Black Women in South Africa."
British Journal of Obstetrics and Gynaecology. Volume 91
#8 August, 1984. pp. 797-801.
"Skin Deep: The Autobiography of a Woman Doctor."
Kommetjie, South Africa: Midgley. 1977. 171p.
Abortion in South Africa and Attitudes of Natal Medical
Practitioners Towards South African Abortion Legislation.
Durban, South Africa: University of Natal. Centre for
Applied Social Sciences and Abortion Reform Action Group.

Whitelaw, D.A.
    "Socio-Economic Status and Use of Contraceptives Among
    Unmarried Primigravidas in Cape Town." South African
    Medical Journal. Volume 64 #18 October 22, 1983. pp.
    712-715.
Woodrow, E.P.
    "Family Planning in South Africa: A Review." South
    African Medical Journal. Volume 50 #53 December 11,
    1976. pp. 2101-2103.
Woolfson, L.R.
    "Aetiological and Personality Factors Relating to
    Homosexual Behavior in Adult Females." M.A. Thesis:
    University of South Africa. Pretoria, South Africa.
    1977.
World Health Organization (WHO)
    Health Implications of Apartheid on Women. Geneva: WHO.
    1979.
Zlotnik, Zia
    "Achievement Motivation, Self-Concept, Feminine Role
    Perception and Feminity in White Female University
    Students." B.A. Honors Dissertation: University of the
    Witwatersrand. Johannesburg, South Africa. 1982.

HISTORY

Allen, Vivien
    Lady Trader: A Biography of Mrs. Sarah Heckford. London:
    Collins. 1979. 243p.
Anonymous
    Laundry, Liquor and 'Playing Ladish': African Women in
    Johannesburg, 1903-1939. London: University of London.
    Centre of International and Area Studies. South African
    Social History Workshop. Unpublished. June, 1978.
Armstrong, Henrietta E.
    Camp Diary of Henrietta E.C. Armstrong: Experiences of a
    Boer Nurse in the Irene Concentration Camp, 6 April-11
    October, 1901. Pretoria, South Africa: Human Sciences
    Research Council. Source Publication #8. 1980. 211p.
Beall, J.D.
    "Unwanted Guests: Indian Women in the Context of
    Indentured Immigation to the Natal." Paper Presented to
    the Conference Commemorating the 150th Anniversary of
    Indian Indentured Immigration and the Abolition of
    Slaves. Moka, Mauritius. October, 1984.
Beall, J.D.
    "Problems of Sociological Analysis in Historical
    Investigation: The Case of Women in Colonial Natal."
    Paper Presented at the History Workshop, University of
    Durban-Westville. Durban, South Africa: University of
    Durban-Westville. 1983.
Beall, J.D.
    "Changing Function and Status of Women in Zululand,

1818-1879." Paper Presented to the Development Studies
Research Group. Pietermarizburg, South Africa:
University of Natal. 1982.
Beall, J.D.
"The Changing Role and Status of African Women in the
Political Economy of Colonial Natal." Paper Presented at
the 13th Annual Congress of the Association of
Sociologists of Southern Africa. 1982.
Beall, J.D.
"Class, Race and Gender: The Political Economy of Women
in Colonial Natal." M.A. Thesis: University of Natal.
Durban, South Africa. 1982.
Beall, J.D.
"The Function and Status of African Women in the Social
and Economic Life of Natal and Zululand, 1818-1879."
B.A. Honors Dissertation: University of Natal. Durban,
South Africa. 1981.
Beckman, Joyce A.
Olive Schreiner: Feminism on the Frontier. St. Albans,
Vermont: Eden Press. 1979. 88p.
Beinart, William
"Amafelandawonye (the Diehards), Rural Popular Protest
and Women's Movements in Herschel District, South Africa
in the 1920's." Paper Presented at the History Workshop.
Johannesburg: University of the Witwatersrand. January,
1984.
Berger, Iris
Sources of Class Consciousness: The Experience of Women
Workers in South Africa, 1973-1980. Boston: Boston
University. African Studies Center. Working Paper #55.
1982. 27p.
Berger, Iris
"Sources of Class Consciousness: South African Women in
Recent Labor Struggles." International Journal of
African Historical Studies. Volume 16 #1 1983. pp.
49-66.
Berning, G.
"The Status and Position of Black Women in Natal Between
1845 and 1891." B.A.Honors Dissertation: University of
Natal. Pietermaritzburg, South Africa. 1980.
Blakeley, Brian L.
"Women and Imperialism: The Colonial Office and Female
Emigration to South Africa, 1901-1910." Albion. Volume
13 #2 1981. pp. 131-149.
Boddington, Erica
"Domestic Service: Changing Relations of Class
Domination, 1841-1948." M.A. Thesis: University of Cape
Town. Cape Town, South Africa. 1983.
Bozzoli, Belinda
"Feminist Interpretations and South African Studies: Some
Suggested Avenues for Exploration." Paper Presented at
the University of Witwatersrand. Johannesburg:
University of the Witwatersrand. African Studies

Institute. Johannesburg, South Africa. October 19, 1981.

Brink, Elsabe
"Plays, Poetry and Production: The Literature of the Garment Workers." South African Labour Bulletin. Volume 9 #8 1984. pp. 32-53.

Brink, Elsabe
"'Maar 'n Klomp Factory Meide': The Role of the Female Garment Workers in the Clothing Industry, Afrikaner Family and Community on the Witwatersrand During the 1920's." Paper Presented at the History Workshop. Johannesburg: University of the Witwatersrand. 1984.

Cock, Jacklyn
"The Missionary Articulation of Sexual Ideology and the Initial Incorporation of Black Women Into Wage Labour." Africa Perspective. Volume 13 1979. pp. 16-26.

Cock, Jacklyn
"Black and White Women: A Socio-Historical Study of Domestic Workers and Their Employers in the Eastern Cape." Ph.D Dissertation: Rhodes University. Grahamstown, South Africa. 1979.

Cock, Jacklyn
"Settlers, Servants and Slaves on the Eastern Frontier." South African Outlook. Volume 111 #1301 November, 1979. pp. 172-178.

De Villiers, Richard
"The Resistance to the Extension of Passes to Women, 1954-1960." Paper Presented to the African Studies Institute Post Graduate Seminar. Johannesburg: University of the Witwatersrand. September 24, 1979.

Fisher, F.
"Women in Pre-Capitalist Societies in South Africa." Paper Presented at the University of Cape Town Summer School. Cape Town, South Africa: University of Cape Town. January, 1979.

Gaitskell, Deborah
"Housewives, Maids or Mothers: Some Contradictions of Domesticity for Christian Women in Johannesburg, 1903-1939." Journal of African History. Volume 24 #2 1983. pp. 241-256.

Gaitskell, Deborah
"Female Mission Initiatives: Black and White Women in Three Witwatersrand Churches, 1903-1939." Ph.D Dissertation: University of London. London, England. 1981.

Gaitskell, Deborah
"'Christian Compounds for Girls': Church Hostels for African Women in Johannesburg, 1907-1970." Journal of Southern African Studies. Volume 6 #1 October, 1979. pp. 44-69.

Gaitskell, Deborah
"'Wailing for Purity': Prayer Unions, African Mothers and Adolescent Daughters, 1912-1940." (In) Marks, S. and

Rathbone, R. (eds.). Industrialization and Social Change
in South Africa... 1870-1930. New York: Longman. 1982.
357p.
Gaitskell, Deborah
"Laundry, Liquor and 'Playing Ladish': African Women in
Johannesburg, 1903-1939." Paper Presented to the South
African Social History Workshop. London: University of
London. Centre for International and Area Studies.
1978.
Hallett, Robin
"Policemen, Pimps and Prostitutes: Public Morality and
Police Corruption, Cape Town, 1902-1904." Paper
Presented at the History Workshop. Johannesburg:
University of the Witwatersrand. 1978.
Hamilton, Carolyn A.
"A Fragment of the Jigsaw: Authority and Labour Control
Amongst the Early 19th Century Northern Nguni." B.A.
Honors Dissertation: University of the Witwatersrand.
Johannesburg, South Africa. 1980.
Heberden, W.
"Diary of a Doctor's Wife During the Siege of Kimberley,
1899-1900." Military Historical Journal. Volume 3 1976.
pp. 166-174.
Hermer, Carol
The Diary of Maria Tholo. Johannesburg: Raven Press.
1980.
Hirshfield, Claire
"Liberal Women's Organizations and the War Against the
Boers, 1899-1902." Albion. Volume 14 #1 Spring, 1982.
pp. 27-49.
Kinsman, Margaret
"Beasts of Burden: The Subordination of Southern Tswana
Women, ca. 1800-1840." Journal of Southern African
Studies. Volume 10 #1 1983. pp. 39-54.
Kros, Cynthia
"Urban African Women's Organizations and Protest on the
Rand, 1939-1956." B.A. Honors Dissertation: University
of Witwatersrand. Johannesburg. 1978.
Kros, Cynthia
Urban African Women's Organizations and Protest on the
Rand From the Years 1939-1956. Johannesburg: Africa
Perspective Dissertation #3. 1980.
Lewis, Jon
"Solly Sachs and the Garment Worker's Union." (In)
Webster, Eddie (ed.). Essays in Southern African Labour
History. Johannesburg: Raven Press. 1978. pp. 181-191.
Lodge, Tom
"Women Protest Movements in the 1950's." (In) Lodge,
Tom. Black Politics in South Africa Since 1945. New
York: Longman. 1983.
Mackenzie, D.J.
"African Women and the Urbanization Process in Durban, c.
1920-1949." Paper Presented at the Workshop on African

Urban Life in Durban in the Twentieth Century. Durban,
South Africa: University of Natal. October, 1983.

Mackenzie, D.J.
"Influx Control, Health Regulation and African Women in
Durban, c. 1917-1949." Paper Presented at the Workshop
on Local History. Pietermaritzburg, South Africa. 1982.

Mackenzie, D.J.
"A Social History of African Women in Durban, 1920-1950."
M.Soc.Sci. Thesis: University of Natal. Durban, South
Africa. 1984.

Mariotti, Amelia
"The Incorporation of African Women Into Wage Employment
in South Africa, 1920-1970." Ph.D Dissertation:
University of Connecticut, Storrs. Stoors, Connecticut.
1980. 338p.

Matsepe, Ivy F.
"African Women's Labor in the Political Economy of South
Africa, 1880 -1970." Ph.D Dissertation: Rutgers
University. New Brunswick, New Jersey. 1984. 327p.

Matsetela, Ted
"The Life Story of Nkgono MmaPooe: Aspects of
Sharecropping and Proletatrianisation in the Northern
Orange Free State, 1890-1930." (In) Marks, Shula and
Rathbone, Richard (eds.). Industrialization and Social
Change in South Africa: African Class Formation, Culture
and Consciousness, 1870-1930. London: Longman. 1982.

Mawbey, John
"Afrikaner Women of the Garment Union During the
Thirities and Forties." (In) Webster, E. (ed.). Essays
in South African Labour History. Johannesburg: Raven
Press. 1978. pp. 192-206.

Merrett, Patricia L.
"Frances Ellen Colenso, 1848-1887: Her Life and Times in
Relation to the Victorian Sterotype of the Middle Class
Englishwoman." M.A. Thesis: University of Cape Town.
Cape Town, South Africa. 1980.

Nicol, Martin
"'Joh'burg Hotheads!' and 'Gullible Children of Cape
Town': The Transvaal Garment Workers' Union Assault on
Low Wages in the Cape Town Clothing Industry, 1930-1931."
Paper Presented at the History Workshop, University of
the Witwatersrand. Johannesburg, South Africa. 1984.

Parle, Julie
"Mrs. Florence MacDonald and University Education for
Non-Europeans in Natal c.1936-1952." B.A. Honors
Dissertation: University of Natal. Durban, South Africa.
1983.

Plaatje, S.T.
"The Mote and the Beam: An Epic on Sex-Relationship
'Twixt White and Black in British South Africa." English
in Africa. Volume 3 #2 September, 1976. pp. 85-92.

Riekert, Julian
"Race, Sex and the Law in Colonial Natal." Journal of
Natal and Zulu History. Volume 6 1983. pp. 82, 97.

Ross, R.
  "Sexuality and Slavery at the Cape in the Eighteenth
  Century." (In) University of London (eds.). The
  Societies of Southern Africa in the Nineteenth and
  Twentieth Centuries. London: University of London.
  Institute of Commonwealth Studies. Seminar Papers.
  Volume 8 #22. 1977.
Ross, Robert
  "The Age at Marriage of White South Africans, 1700-1951."
  (In) University of Edinburgh. African Historical
  Demography: Proceedings of a Seminar Held in the Centre
  of African Studies. Edinburgh, Scotland: University of
  Edinburgh. Volume Two. April 24-25, 1981. pp. 487-498.
Ross, Robert
  "Oppression, Sexuality and Slavery at the Cape of Good
  Hope." Historical Reflections. Volume 6 #2 1979. pp.
  421-433.
Schreiner, J.
  Divisions of Labour in the Manufacturing Industry in the
  Western Cape, 1950-1965, and the Implications for a
  Materialist Theory of Women's Subordination. African
  Studies Honors Paper: University of Cape Town. Cape
  Town, South Africa. 1981.
Schreiner, J.A.
  "Politics is the Search for Allies: The Women's Anti-Pass
  Campaigns and the Formation of CATAPAW in the Western
  Cape in the 1950's." Paper Presented to the Association
  for Sociology in Southern Africa. Johannesburg:
  University of Witwatersrand. 1984.
Schreiner, Olive
  "The Boer Woman and the Modern Woman's Question." (In)
  Schreiner, Olive. Thoughts on South Africa.
  Johannesburg: Africana Book Society. 1976. pp. 191-220.
Shingler, John P.
  Women of East London, 1900-1979. East London, South
  Africa: Griffith Standard Co. 1980.
Simkins, C.
  "The Distribution of the African Population of South
  Africa by Age, Sex and Region-Type, 1950-1980." (In)
  Simkins, C. (ed.). Four Essays on the Past, Present and
  Possible Future of the Distribution of the Black
  Population of South Africa. Rondebosch, South Africa:
  University of Cape Town. Southern African Labour and
  Development Research Unit. 1983.
Snyman, Rita
  "A Nurse Looks Back on the Seige of Ladysmith." Africana
  Notes and News. Volume 22 #5 March, 1977. pp. 180-194.
Spies, S.B.
  "Women and the War." (In) Warwick, Peter (ed.). The
  South African War: The Anglo-Boer War, 1899-1902.
  London: Longman. 1980. pp. 161-185.
Swaisland, C.F.
  "The Emigration of Women From the United Kingdom to South

Africa, 1820-1939." Paper Presented at the South African
Seminar. Johannesburg: Rhodes University. Institute for
Social and Economic Research. 1983.
Van Helten, Jean J. and Williams, Keith
"The Crying Need of South Africa: The Emigration of
Single British Women to the Transvaal, 1901-1910."
Journal of Southern African Studies. Volume 10 #1
October, 1983. pp. 17-38.
Van Heyningen, Elizabeth B.
"The Social Evil of the Cape Colony, 1868-1902:
Prostitution and the Contagious Diseases Act." Journal
of Southern African Studies. Volume 10 #2 1984. pp.
170-197.
Van Heyningen, Elizabeth B.
"Prostitution and the Contagious Diseases Act: The Social
Evil in the Cape Colony, 1868-1902." (In) Saunders,
Christopher (ed.). Studies in the History of Cape Town.
Cape Town, South Africa: University of Cape Town. Centre
for African Studies and the History Department. Volume
Five. 1984. pp. 80-124.
Van Onselen, Charles
"Prostitutes and Proletarians, 1886-1914." (In) Van
Onselen, C. Studies in the Social and Economic History
of the Witwatersrand, 1886-1914. New York: Longman.
Volume One: New Babylon. 1982. pp. 103-143.
Van Onselen, Charles
"The Witches of Suburbia: Domestic Service on the
Witwatersrand, 1890-1914." (In) Van Onselen, Charles.
Studies in the Social and Economic History of the
Witwatersrand, 1886-1914. New Nineveh, South Africa:
Raven Books. Volume 2. 1982. pp. 1-73.
Van Vuuren, Nancy
Women Against Apartheid: The Fight for Freedom in South
Africa, 1920-1975. Palo Alto, California: R and E
Research Association. 1979. 133p.
Walker, Cherryl
"Women and Politics: The Women's Suffrage Movement Before
1930." Paper Presented at the University of Cape Town
Summer School. Cape Town, South Africa: University of
Cape Town. 1979.
Wells, Julia C.
"Women's Resistance to Passes in Bloemfontein During the
Inter-War Period." Africa Perspective. Volume 15
Autumn, 1980. pp. 16-35.
Wells, Julia C.
"The History of Black Women's Struggle Against Pass Laws
in South Africa, 1900-1960." Ph.D Dissertation: Columbia
University. New York, New York. 1982. 414p.
Wells, Julia C.
"Why Women Rebel: A Comparative Study of South African
Women's Resistance in Bloemfontein (1913) and
Johannesburg (1958)." Journal of Southern African
Studies. Volume 10 #1 October, 1983. pp. 55-70.

Wells, Julia C.
"'The Day the Town Stood Still': Women in Resistance in
Potchefstroom, 1912-1930." (In) Bozzoli, Belinda (ed.).
Town and Countryside in the Transvaal: Capitalist
Penetration and Popular Response. Johannesburg: Raven
Press. 1983.

Wilson, Monica
"Xhosa Marriage in Historical Perspective." (In) Krige,
Eileen J. and Comarof, J.L. (eds.). Essays on African
Marriage in Southern Africa. Cape Town, South Africa:
Juta. 1981.

Wright, John
"Control of Women's Labour in the Zulu Kingdom." (In)
Peires, J.B. (ed.). Before and After Shaka: Papers in
Nguni History. Grahamstown, South Africa: Rhodes
University. Institute of Social and Economic Research.
1983. pp. 82-99.

Yawitch, Joanne
"Natal 1959: The Women's Protests." Paper Presented at
the Conference on the History of Opposition in Southern
Africa. Johannesburg: (Student's) Development Studies
Group of the University of the Witwatersrand. January,
1978. pp. 206-223.

Yawitch, Joanne
Tightening the Noose: African Women and Influx Control in
South Africa, 1950-1980. Rondebosch, South Africa:
University of Cape Town. SALDRU. School of Economics.
Carnegie Conference Paper #82. 1984. 36p.

Yawitch, Joanne
"Tightening the Noose: African Women and Influx Control
in South Africa, 1950-1980." Paper Presented to the
Association for Sociology in Southern Africa.
Johannesburg: University of the Witwatersrand. 1984.

LAW AND LEGAL ISSUES

Andre La Cock, J.
"Marriage by Way of Antenuptial Contract." De Rebus.
#194 February, 1984. pp. 76-77.

Anonymous
"Rape." Critical Health. Volume 9 1983. pp. 52-62.

Barnard, A.H.
"An Evaluation of the. Divorce Act 70 of 1979." Acta
Juridica. 1983. pp. 39-51.

Bekker, J.C.
Marriage, Money, Property and the Law: A Guide to the
Legal and Financial Consequences of a Marriage Between
Africans. Durban/Pretoria, South Africa: Butterworths.
1983. 53p.

Bekker, J.C.
"Grounds for Divorce in African Customary Marriages."

Comparative and International Law Journal of Southern
Africa. Volume 9 #3 November, 1976. pp. 346-355.
Bloch, B.
"The Abortion and Sterilization Act of 1975: Experience
of the Johannesburg Hospital Pregnancy Advisory Service."
South African Medical Journal. Volume 53 #21 May 27,
1978. pp. 861-864.
Burman, Sandra and Martine, Huvers
"Church Versus State: Divorce Legislation and Divided
South Africa." Journal of Southern African Studies.
Volume 12 #1 October, 1985. pp. 116-135.
Burman, Sandra
"Divorce and the Disadvantaged." (In) Hirschon, Renbee
(ed.). Women and Property, Women as Property. London:
Croom Helm. Oxford Women's Series. 1984.
Burman, Sandra B.
"Roman Dutch Family Law for Africans: The Black Divorce
Court in Action." Acta Juridica. 1983. pp. 171-190.
Cassim, N.A.
"Some Reflections on the Natal Code." Paper Presented at
the Conference on One Hundred Years of the Natal Code.
Kwa-Dlangezwa, South Africa: University of Zululand.
1980.
Cassim, N.A.
"Some Reflections on the Natal Code." Journal of African
Law. Volume 25 #2 Autumn, 1981. pp. 131-135.
Church, J.
"A New Dispensation for Black Women?: A Note on Act 6 of
1981 (KwaZulu)." Comparative and International Law
Journal of Southern Africa. Volume 16 #1 1983. pp.
100-102.
Church, Joan
"Marriage and Human Rights: A Note on the Bophuthatswana
Marriage Act." Codicillus. Volume 22 #2 1981. pp.
220-266.
Cooper, C. and Ensor, Linda
African Woman's Handbook on the Law. Johannesburg: South
African Institute of Race Relations. 1980. 41p.
Court, J.H.
"Pornography and Rape in White South Africa." De Jure.
Volume 12 #2 1979. pp. 236-241.
De Villiers, Richard
"The Resistance to the Extension of Passes to Women,
1954-1960." Paper Presented to the African Studies
Institute Post Graduate Seminar. Johannesburg:
University of the Witwatersrand. September 24, 1979.
Dlamini, C.R.
"The Transformation of a Customary Marriage in Zulu Law."
Comparative and International Law Journal of Southern
Africa. Volume 16 #3 November, 1983. pp. 383-392.
Dlamini, C.R.M.
"A Juridical Analysis and Critical Evaluation of Ilobolo
in a Changing Zulu Society." L.L.D Dissertation:

University of Zululand. Kwa-Dlangezwa, South Africa.
1983.

Duncan, Sheena
"Women Under Apartheid: African Women and the Pass Laws."
(In) National Union of South African Students Law
Directive and Law Students Council. Law in South Africa:
Lifting the Veil. Cape Town, South Africa: NAUSA. 1981.
pp. 54-63.

Fagan, J.J.
"New Rights for Married Women." Social Work. Volume 20
#4 1984. pp. 200-201.

Gon, Sylvia
"The Effect of Legislation on Working Women." Paper
Presented to the Conference on Women and the Economy.
Johannesburg: Rand Afrikaans University. September 22,
1980.

Gwazela, Sindiswa
"The Female Target: Behind Prison Bars in South Africa."
Resources for Feminist Research. Volume 14 December,
1985. pp. 23-25.

Handands, G.C.
"Prostitution in Cape Town." B. Soc.Sci. Honors
Dissertation: University of Cape Town. Cape Town, South
Africa. 1979.

Handands, G.C.
"Prostitution in Cape Town: An Exploratory Study." Paper
Presented to the Association for Sociology in Southern
Africa Conference. Cape Town, South Africa: University
of Cape Town. 1979.

Hlophe, J.M.
"The KwaZula Act on the Code of Zulu Law, 6 of 1981--A
Guide to Intending Spouses and Some Comments on the
Custom of Lobolo." Comparative and International Law
Journal of Southern Africa. Volume 17 #2 July, 1984.
pp. 163-171.

Kaganas, F. and Murray, C.
"Rape in Marriage: Conjugal Right or Criminal Wrong?"
Acta Juridica. 1983. pp. 125-143.

Kerr, A.J.
"Claims by South African Customary Union Widows and
Foreign Widows of Similar Unions in Respect of Loss of
Support on the Death of Their Husbands." Speculum Juris.
Volume 12 1983. pp. 37-44.

Kloppers, H.P. and Coertze, T.F.
Bantu Divorce Courts: Guide to Practice and Proceedure.
Cape Town, South Africa: Juta. Second Edition. 1976.
131p.

Klugman, Barbara
"Maternity Rights and Benefits and Protective Legislation
at Work." South African Labour Bulletin. Volume 9 #3
1983. pp. 25-51.

Kotze, J.J.
"Marital Privilege and the Competence and Compellability
of Customary Law: Spouses as Witnesses Against Each

Other." South African Journal of Criminal Law and Criminology. Volume 7 #2 1983. pp. 157-166.

Kunst, J. and Meiring, R.
"Abortion Law--A Need for Reform." De Rebus. # 198 June, 1984. pp.264-266.

McCafferty, S.
An Analysis of Abortion on Mental Health Grounds Within the South African Context. Durban, South Africa: University of Natal. L.L.B. Research Project. 1980.

Millar, Shirley
"The Basic Conditions of Employment Act: The Position of Women." South African Labour Bulletin. Volume 8 #6 June, 1983. pp. 1-4.

Nash, E.S. and Navias, M.
"Therapeutic Abortion on Psychiatric Grounds. Part III: Implementing the Abortion and Sterilization Act (1975-1981)." South African Medical Journal. Volume 63 #17 April 23, 1983. pp. 639-644.

Nathan, C.
"The Legal Status of Black Women in South African Society." (In) Saunders, A.J.G. (ed.). Southern Africa in Need of Law Reform. Durban, South Africa: Butterworth. 1981.

Nkabinde, C.
"The Legal Position of African Women in Employment." IPST Bulletin (University of Zululand). Volume 12 1978. pp. 27-32.

Ntantala, Phyllis
An African Tragedy: The Black Woman Under Apartheid. Detroit, Michigan: Agascha Productions. 1976. 137p.

Pascoe, Flavia
The Marriage and Divorce Book. Cape Town, South Africa: Tafelberg. 1978.

Peart, Nicola S.
"Civil or Christian Marriage and Customary Unions: The Legal Position of the Discarded Spouse and Children." Comparative and International Law Journal of South Africa. Volume 16 #1 1983. pp. 39-64.

Poinsette, Cheryl
"Black Women Under Apartheid: An Introduction." Harvard Women's Law Journal. Volume 8 Spring, 1985. pp. 93-119.

Riekert, Julian
"Race, Sex and the Law in Colonial Natal." Journal of Natal and Zulu History. Volume 6 1983. pp. 82, 97.

Satchwell, K.
"Women and the Law." (In) National Union of South African Students (NUSAS) and Law Students Council. Law in South Africa: Lifting the Veil. Cape Town, South Africa: NUSAS. 1981. pp. 42-53.

Schafer, I.D.
"Human Artificial Insemination and the Law: Some Legal

Implications." Natal University Law Review. Volume 2 #2
1978. pp. 228-238.
Schurink, W.J.
"Prostitution in Johannesburg: Preliminary Findings."
South African Journal of Criminal Law and Criminology.
Volume 6 #1 March, 1982. pp. 46-61.
Sinclair, June
"The Financial Consequences of Divorce in South Africa:
Judicial Determination or Private Ordering?"
International and Comparative Law Quarterly. Volume 32
#4 1983. pp. 785-811.
Sinclair, June
"Marriage: Is it Still a Commitment for Life Entailing a
Lifelong Duty of Support?" Acta Juridica. 1983. pp.
75-96.
Spuy, Adelemarie V.
"Inequitable Legal and Economic Aspects of the
Discrimination Against Women, Especially Married Women in
South Africa Today." Plural Societies. Volume 9 #1
Spring, 1978. pp. 49-58.
Staniland, H.
"Some Aspects of Co-Habitation and Home Ownership."
Natal University Law Review. Volume 2 #3 1979. pp.
285-297.
Strauss, S.A.
"We Need a Family Planning Act." Codicillus. Volume 19
#1 May, 1978. pp. 4-6.
Taitz, Jerold
"The Legal Consequences of a Sex Change: A Judicial
Dilemma." South African Law Review. Volume 97 1980.
pp. 65-76.
Thomson, R.C.
Some Discriminatory Laws and Their Effects on African
Women. Cape Town, South Africa: National Union of South
African Students (NUSAS). 1978.
Thomson, R.C.
"Some Discriminatory Laws and Their Effects on African
Women." Jure ac Legibus. Volume 3 1976. pp. 19-24.
Trengrove, J.J.
"Divorce Law Reform." De Rebus. #200 August, 1984.
pp. 353-358.
United Nations Centre Against Apartheid
African Women and Apartheid in Labour Matters. New York:
United Nations Centre Against Apartheid. Notes and
Documents Series #20/80. July, 1980. 13p.
University of Natal, Durban. Women's Movement.
"Women and the Law." (In) National Union of South
African Students (NUSAS). NUSAS Conference on Women.
Cape Town, South Africa: NUSAS. Women's Directive.
July, 1983.
Unterholter, Elaine
"South Africa: Women in Struggle." Third World
Quarterly. Volume 5 #4 1983. pp. 886-893.

Van Der Spuy, A.
"Inequitable Legal and Economic Aspects of the
Discrimination Against Women, Especially Married Women in
South Africa Today." Plural Societies. Volume 9 #1
Spring, 1978. pp. 49-58.

Van Heyningen, Elizabeth B.
"The Social Evil of the Cape Colony, 1868-1902:
Prostitution and the Contagious Diseases Act." Journal
of Southern African Studies. Volume 10 #2 1984. pp.
170-197.

Van Heyningen, Elizabeth B.
"Prostitution and the Contagious Diseases Act: The Social
Evil in the Cape Colony, 1868-1902." (In) Saunders,
Christopher (ed.). Studies in the History of Cape Town.
Cape Town, South Africa: University of Cape Town. Centre
for African Studies and the History Department. Volume
Five. 1984. pp. 80-124.

Van Niekerk, Barend
"Class, Punishment and Rape in South Africa." Natal
University Law Review. Volume 1#5 1976. pp. 299-305.

Van Wyk, A.H.
"Matrimonial Property Systems in Comparative
Perspective." Acta Juridica. 1983. pp. 53-74.

Vogelman, Lloyd
"The Client: A Study of Sexism and Prostitution." B.A.
Honors Dissertation: University of the Witwatersrand.
Johannesburg, South Africa. 1982.

Volpe, P.L.
"Enforceability of Marriage Brokage Contract." De Rebus.
#199 July, 1984. pp. 311-312.

Wells, Julia C.
"Women's Resistance to Passes in Bloemfontein During the
Inter-War Period." Africa Perspective. Volume 15
Autumn, 1980. pp. 16-35.

Wells, Julia C.
"The History of Black Women's Struggle Against Pass Laws
in South Africa, 1900-1960." Ph.D Dissertation: Columbia
University. New York, New York. 1982. 414p.

Wells, Julia C.
"Passes and Bypasses: Freedom of Movement for African
Women Under the Urban Areas Act of South Africa." (In)
Hays, Margaret J. and Wright, Marcia (eds.). African
Women and the Law: Historical Perspectives. Boston:
Boston University. African Studies Center. Boston
University Papers on Africa. Volume Seven. 1982. pp.
125-150.

Westmore, Jean
Abortion in South Africa and Attitudes of Natal Medical
Practitioners Towards South African Abortion Legislation.
Durban, South Africa: University of Natal. Centre for
Applied Social Sciences and Abortion Reform Action Group.
1977. 76p.

Women's Legal Status Committee
     Report of the 1976 National Convention to Advance Women's
     Legal Rights. Johannesburg: The Committee. 1976.
Yawitch, Joanne
     "Rural Natal 1959: The Women's Riots." Africa
     Perspective. Volume 5 1977. pp. 1-17.
Yawitch, Joanne
     Tightening the Noose: African Women and Influx Control in
     South Africa, 1950-1980. Rondebosch, South Africa:
     University of Cape Town. SALDRU. School of Economics.
     Carnegie Conference Paper #82. 1984. 36p.
Yawitch, Joanne
     "Tightening the Noose: African Women and Influx Control
     in South Africa, 1950-1980." Paper Presented to the
     Association for Sociology in Southern Africa.
     Johannesburg: University of the Witwatersrand. 1984.

LITERATURE

Abrahams, Cecil A.
     "The Tyranny of Place: The Context of Bessie Head's
     Fiction." World Literature Written in English (WLRE).
     April, 1978. pp. 22-29.
Anonymous
     "Interview With Hilda Bernstein." Women in South African
     History. #2 1983. pp. 3-15.
Anonymous
     "A Tribute to Ruth First." Review of African Political
     Economy. #25 September-December, 1982. pp. 3-64.
Beard, Linda S.
     "Doris Lessing, African Writer." (In) Parker, Carolyn A.
     and Arnold, Stephen H. (eds.). When the Drumbeat
     Changes. Washington, D.C.: Three Continents Press.
     1981. pp. 241-260.
Beckman, Joyce A.
     Olive Schreiner: Feminism on the Frontier. St. Albans,
     Vermont: Eden Press. 1979. 88p.
Brink, Elsabe
     "Plays, Poetry and Production: The Literature of the
     Garment Workers." South African Labour Bulletin. Volume
     9 #8 1984. pp. 32-53.
Brokensha, D.
     "Obituary: Monica Wilson, 1908-1982: An Appreciation."
     Africa. Volume 53 #3 1983. pp. 83-87.
Brown, Lloyd W.
     "Creating New Worlds in Southern Africa: Bessie Head and
     the Question of Power." Umoja. Volume 3 #1 Spring,
     1979. pp. 43-53.
Brown, Susan and Hofmeyer, Isabel and Rosenberg, Susan
(eds.)
     Lip From Southern African Women. Johannesburg: Raven
     Press. 1983. 232p.

Bruner, Charlotte H.
    "Bessie Head: Restless in a Distant Land." (In) Parker,
    Carolyn A. and Arnold, Stephen H. (eds). When the
    Drumbeat Changes. Washington D.C.: Three Continents
    Press. 1981. pp. 261-277.
Bruner, Charlotte H.
    "Bessie Head: Restless in a Distant Land." Paper
    Presented at the 1978 African Literature Association
    Convention. Baltimore, Maryland: University of Maryland.
    African-American Studies Department. 1978.
Bruner, Charlotte H.
    "Child Africa as Depicted by Bessie Head and Ama Ata
    Aidoo." Studies in the Humanities. Volume 7 #2 1979.
    pp. 5-11.
Cooke, John
    "Out of the Garden: The Fiction of Nadine Gordimer."
    Paper Presented at the 1979 African Literature
    Association Conference. Baltimore, Maryland: University
    of Maryland. African-American Studies Department. 1979.
Driver, D.
    "Pauline Smith--A Gentler Music of Her Own: South African
    Fiction of the 20's and 30's." Research in African
    Literature. Volume 15 #1 1984. pp. 45-71.
First, Ruth and Scott, Ann
    Olive Schreiner: A Biography. New York: Schocken Books.
    1980. 383p.
Gillard, Jillian
    "Perpetuation of a Capitalist Patriarchy: The Ideological
    Apparatus of the Women's Magazine in South Africa."
    B.Soc.Sci Honors Dissertation: University of Cape Town.
    Cape Town, South Africa. 1978.
Glen, I.
    "South African Women's Fiction: Fair Marais." Speak.
    Volume 1 #4 1978.
Gunner, Elizabeth
    "Women as Composers and Performers of Zulu Praise Poetry:
    Some Praise Poems." (In) University of York. Centre for
    Southern African Studies (ed.). Southern African
    Research in Progress. York, England: University of York.
    Collected Papers Volume 3. 1978. pp. 1-17.
Hermann, Anne
    "The Flight From Domesticity in Two South African
    Novels." Communications for Gender Research. #5
    Summer, 1985. pp. 1+
House, Amelia (ed.)
    Black Women Writers From South Africa: A Preliminary
    Checklist. Evanston, Illinois: Northwestern University.
    Northwestern University Program on Women. 1980.
Kunene, Mazisi
    Anthem of the Decades--A Zulu Epic Dedicated to the Women
    of Africa. London: Heinemann. African Writers Series
    #234. 1981. 312p.

Marquard, Jean
    "Bessie Head: Exile and Community in Southern Africa."
    London Magazine. December-January, 1978. pp. 49-61.
Marquard, Jean
    "The Farm: A Concept in the Writing of Olive Schreiner,
    Pauline Smith, Doris Lessing, Nadine Gordimer and Bessie
    Head." Paper Presented at the 1980 African Literature
    Association Convention. Baltimore, Maryland: University
    of Maryland. African-American Studies Department. 1980.
Moss, Rose
    "The Censor Repressions and Evasions in the Fiction of
    Some South African Women Writers." Paper Presented at
    the 1979 African Literature Association Convention.
    Baltimore, Maryland: University of Maryland.
    African-American Studies Department. 1979.
Murray, Colin
    ".....So Truth be in the Field...': A Short Appreciation
    of Monica Wilson." Journal of Southern African Studies.
    Volume 10 #1 1983. pp. 129-130.
Ode-Ade, Femi
    "Bessie Head's Alienated Heroine, Victim or Villain?"
    Paper Presented at the 1977 African Literature
    Association Convention. Baltimore, Maryland: University
    of Maryland. African-American Studies Department. 1977.
Ravenscroft, Arthur
    "The Novels of Bessie Head." (In) Heywood, Christopher
    (ed.). Aspects of South African Literature. London:
    Heinemann. 1976. pp. 174-186.
Schipper, Mineke
    "Inteview with Miriam Tlali." (In) Schipper, Mineke
    (ed.). Unheard Words: Women and Literature in Africa,
    the Arab World, Asia, the Caribbean and Latin America.
    New York: Allison and Busby. 1985. pp. 59-68.
Taiwo, Oladele
    "Bessie Head: When Rain Clouds Gather." (In) Taiwo,
    Oladele (ed.). Female Novelists of Modern Africa. New
    York: St. Martin's Press. 1984. pp. 186-190.
Topping-Bazin, Nancy
    "Feminist Perspectives in African Fiction: Bessie Head
    and Buchi Emecheta." Paper Presented at the Annual
    Meeting of the African Literature Association.
    Baltimore, Maryland: University of Maryland.
    African-American Studies Association. April, 1984.

MARITAL RELATIONS AND NUPTIALITY

Andre La Cock, J.
    "Marriage by Way of Antenuptial Contract." De Rebus.
    #194 February, 1984. pp. 76-77.
Barling, Julian and Lanham, W.
    "Beliefs Regarding the Consequences of Birth Control
    Among Black, Colored, Indian and White South Africans."

Journal of Social Psychology. Volume 105 Part One, June, 1978. pp. 149-150.

Barnard, A.H.
"An Evaluation of the Divorce Act 70 of 1979." Acta Juridica. 1983. pp. 39-51.

Bekker, J.C.
Marriage, Money, Property and the Law: A Guide to the Legal and Financial Consequences of a Marriage Between Africans. Durban/Pretoria, South Africa: Butterworths. 1983. 53p.

Bekker, J.C.
"Grounds for Divorce in African Customary Marriages." Comparative and International Law Journal of Southern Africa. Volume 9 #3 November, 1976. pp. 346-355.

Burman, Sandra and Martine, Huvers
"Church Versus State: Divorce Legislation and Divided South Africa." Journal of Southern African Studies. Volume 12 #1 October, 1985. pp. 116-135.

Burman, Sandra
"Divorce and the Disadvantaged." (In) Hirschon, Renbee (ed.). Women and Property, Women as Property. London: Croom Helm. Oxford Women's Series. 1984.

Burman, Sandra B. and Barry, J.
Divorce and Deprivation in South Africa. Rondebosch, South Africa: University of Cape Town. SALDRU, School of Economics. Carnegie Conference Paper #87. 1984. 54p.

Chetty, Romila
"The Changing Family: A Study of the Indian Family in South Africa." South African Journal of Sociology. Volume 11 #2 September, 1980. pp.26-39.

Chetty, Thiagaraj D.
Job Satisfaction on Indian Married Women in the Clothing Manufacturing Industry in Durban and its Effects on the Interpersonal Family Relationships. Durban, South Africa: University of Durban-Westville. Institute for Social and Economic Research. 1983. 130p.

Church, Joan
"Marriage and Human Rights: A Note on the Bophuthatswana Marriage Act." Codicillus. Volume 22 #2 1981. pp. 220-266.

De Haas, Mary
"Changing Patterns of Black Marriage and Divorce in Durban." M.Soc.Sci. Thesis: University of Natal. Durban, South Africa. 1984.

Dlamini, C.R.
"The Transformation of a Customary Marriage in Zulu Law." Comparative and International Law Journal of Southern Africa. Volume 16 #3 November, 1983. pp. 383-392.

Duncan, Sheena
"Aspects of Family Breakdown." Work in Progress. Volume 27. 1983. pp. 36-38.

El-Attar, M. and Nouri, Mohamed O.
"Socioeconomic Characteristics and Fertility Level in the

Sudan." (In) American Statistical Association (ASA).
1983 Proceedings of the Social Statistics Section.
Washington, D.C.: ASA. 1983. pp. 407-411.

Erasmus, G.
"Decision-Making in Regard to the Use of Contraceptives
After Confinement: A Study Among Urban Black Women."
South African Journal of Sociology. Volume 15 #2 May,
1984. pp. 94-97.

Fagan, J.J.
"New Rights for Married Women." Social Work. Volume 20
#4 1984. pp. 200-201.

Gaitskell, Deborah
"Housewives, Maids or Mothers: Some Contradictions of
Domesticity for Christian Women in Johannesburg,
1903-1939." Journal of African History. Volume 24 #2
1983. pp. 241-256.

Gerdes, L.C.
"Personality Differences Between Men and Women in Marital
Roles." Social Welfare and Pensions. Volume 12 #1
June, 1977. pp. 6-12.

Graaff, Janet
"Married to a Migrant." South African Outlook. Volume
108 #1289 November, 1978. pp. 172-173.

Graaff, Janet
"Will They be Together for Christmas?" South African
Outlook. Volume 108 #1289. November, 1978. pp.
163-165.

Hlophe, J.M.
"The KwaZula Act on the Code of Zulu Law, 6 of 1981--A
Guide to Intending Spouses and Some Comments on the
Custom of Lobolo." Comparative and International Law
Journal of Southern Africa. Volume 17 #2 July, 1984.
pp. 163-171.

Johnston, Thomas F.
"Levirate Practices of the Shangana-Tsonga, Seen Through
Widows Ritual Songs." Folklore. Volume 94 #1 1983. pp.
66-74.

Kaganas, F. and Murray, C.
"Rape in Marriage: Conjugal Right or Criminal Wrong?"
Acta Juridica. 1983. pp. 125-143.

Kerr, A.J.
"Claims by South African Customary Union Widows and
Foreign Widows of Similar Unions in Respect of Loss of
Support on the Death of Their Husbands." Speculum Juris.
Volume 12 1983. pp. 37-44.

Kiernan, J.P.
"Spouses and Partners: Marriage and Career Among Urban
Zulu Zionists." Urban Anthropology. Volume 8 #1
Spring, 1979. pp. 95-110.

Kloppers, H.P. and Coertze, T.F.
Bantu Divorce Courts: Guide to Practice and Proceedure.
Cape Town, South Africa: Juta. Second Edition. 1976.
131p.

Kotze, J.J.
    "Marital Privilege and the Competence and Compellability
    of Customary Law: Spouses as Witnesses Against Each
    Other." South African Journal of Criminal Law and
    Criminology. Volume 7 #2 1983. pp. 157-166.
Krige, Eileen J. and Comaroff, John L. (eds.).
    Essays on African Marriage in Southern Africa.   Cape
    Town, South Africa: Wetton. 1981. 205p.
Krige, Eileen J.
    "Women-Marriage, With Special Reference to the
    Lovedu--Its Significance for the Definition of Marriage."
    (In) Tiffany, Sharon W. (ed.). Women and Society: An
    Anthropological Reader. St. Albans, Vermont: Eden Press.
    1979. pp. 208-237.
Krige, Eileen J.
    "A Comparative Analysis of Marriage and Social Structure
    Among the Southern Bantu." (In) Krige, Eileen J, and
    Comaroff, J.L. (eds.). Essays on African Marriage in
    Southern Africa. Cape Town, South Africa: Juta. 1981.
Krige, Eileen J.
    "Lovedu Marriage and Social Change." (In) Krige, Eileen
    J. and Comaroff, J.L. (eds.). Essays on African Marriage
    in Southern Africa. Cape Town, South Africa: Juta.
    1981.
Kuper, Adam
    "Tied By Bridewealth: The Tsonga Case." (In) Krige, E.J.
    and Comaroff, J.L. (eds.). Essays on African Marriage in
    Southern Africa. Cape Town, South Africa: Juta. 1981.
Letsema
    "Family Planning in South Africa--A Kind of Genocide?"
    African Communist. Volume 90 1982.
Lotter, Johann M.
    "Some Aspects of Indian Fertility in South Africa."
    Humanitas. Volume 3 #4 1976. pp. 419-426.
Lotter, Johann M.
    "The Effect of Urbanization and Education on the
    Fertility of Blacks in South Africa." Humanitas. Volume
    4 #1 1977. pp. 21-28.
Lotter, Johann M.
    Attitudes of Black South African Men Towards Fertility
    and Family Planning. Pretoria, South Africa: South
    African Human Sciences Research Council. Institute for
    Sociological, Demographic and Criminological Research.
    Research Finding #S-N-96. 1977. 16p.
Lotter, Johann M. and Van Tonder, J.L.
    Fertility and Family Planning Among Blacks in South
    Africa: 1974. Pretoria, South Africa: Human Sciences
    Research Council. Report No. S-39. 1976. 111p.
Manona, C.W.
    "Marriage, Family Life and Migrancy in a Ciskei Village."
    (In) Mayer, Philip (ed.). Black Villagers in an
    Industrial Society: Anthropological Perspectives on

Labour Migration in South Africa. New York: Oxford
University Press. 1980.
Marks, Shula and Unterhalter, Elaine
"Women and the Migrant Labour System in South Africa."
Paper Presented at the Conference on Migrant Labour in
Southern Africa. Lusaka, Zambia: United Nations Economic
Commission For Africa (UNECA). 1978.
Marwick, M.
"Household Composition and Marriage in a Witwatersrand
African Township." (In) Argyle,J. and Preston-Whyte, E.
(eds.). Social System and Tradition in Southern Africa.
Cape Town, South Africa: Oxford University Press. 1978.
pp. 36-54.
Meer, Fatima (ed.).
Factory and Family: The Divided Lives of South Africa's
Women Workers. Durban, South Africa: Institute for Black
Research. 1984. 105p.
Nene, Daphne S.
"Role Enactment of Rural Women: A Sociological
Exploratory Study of the Role Behavior and its
Implications for Rural Development." M.A. Thesis:
University of Zululand. Kwa-Dlangezwa, South Africa.
1983.
Nene, Daphne S.
"Women Caught in Between: The Case of Rural Women in
KwaZulu." Paper Presented to the Women's Studies
Symposium, University of Transkei. Umtata, South Africa:
University of Transkei. March, 1984.
Ngubane, Harriet
"Marriage, Affinity and the Ancestral Realm: Zulu
Marriage in Female Perspective." (In) Krige, E.J. and
Comaroff, J.L. (eds.). Essays on African Marriage in
Southern Africa. Cape Town, South Africa: Juta. 1981.
Olmesdahl, M.J.C.
"Marriage and Cohabitation: Cross-Cultural Comparisons."
(In) Eekelaar, J.M. and Katz, S.N. (eds.). Marriage and
Cohabitation in Contemporary Societies: Areas of Legal,
Social and Ethical Change: An International and
Interdisciplinary Study. Toronto, Canada: Butterworth.
1980.
Pascoe, Flavia
The Marriage and Divorce Book. Cape Town, South Africa:
Tafelberg. 1978.
Peart, Nicola S.
"Civil or Christian Marriage and Customary Unions: The
Legal Position of the Discarded Spouse and Children."
Comparative and International Law Journal of South
Africa. Volume 16 #1 1983. pp. 39-64.
Radebe, M.D.
"A Study of Matrimonial Breakdown Among Urban Blacks."
M.A. Thesis: University of South Africa. Pretoria, South
Africa. 1978.

Ross, Robert
"The Age at Marriage of White South Africans, 1700-1951."
(In) University of Edinburgh. African Historical
Demography: Proceedings of a Seminar Held in the Centre
of African Studies. Edinburgh, Scotland: University of
Edinburgh. Volume Two. April 24-25, 1981. pp. 487-498.
Roux, A.
"Family Planning Among A Group of Coloured Women." South
African Medical Journal. Volume 65 #22 June 2, 1984.
pp. 898-901.
Russell, Kathryn
"The Internal Relation Between Production and
Reproduction: Reflections on the Manipulation of Family
Life in South Africa." Journal of Social Philosophy.
Volume 15 Summer, 1984. pp. 14-25.
Shindler, J.
The Reproductive Function and Ultra-Exploitability of
South African Domestic Workers. Johannesburg: University
of the Witwatersrand. Industrial Sociology Research
Project. 1978.
Showers, Kate
"A Note on Women, Conflict and Migrant Labour." South
African Labour Bulletin. Volume 6 #4 November, 1980.
Sibisi, Harriet N.
"How African Women Cope With Migrant Labor in South
Africa." Signs. Volume 3 #1 Autumn, 1977. pp.
167-177.
Sibisi, Harriet N.
"How African Women Cope With Migrant Labor in South
Africa." (In) Wellesley Editorial Committee. Women and
National Development: The Complexities of Change.
Chicago: University of Chicago Press. 1977. pp.
167-177.
Sinclair, June
"The Financial Consequences of Divorce in South Africa:
Judicial Determination or Private Ordering?"
International and Comparative Law Quarterly. Volume 32
#4 1983. pp. 785-811.
Sinclair, June
"Marriage: Is it Still a Commitment for Life Entailing a
Lifelong Duty of Support?" Acta Juridica. 1983. pp.
75-96.
Steyn, Anna F. and Uys, J.M.
"The Changing Position of Black Women in South Africa."
(In) Lupri, E. (ed.). The Changing Position of Women in
Family and Society. Leiden, Netherlands: Brill. 1983.
pp. 344-370.
Van Der Spuy, A.
"Inequitable Legal and Economic Aspects of the
Discrimination Against Women, Especially Married Women in
South Africa Today." Plural Societies. Volume 9 #1
Spring, 1978. pp. 49-58.

Van Der Vliet, Virginia N.
    "Black Marriage: Expectations and Aspirations in an Urban
    Environment." M.A. Thesis: University of the
    Witwatersrand. Johannesburg, South Africa. 1982.
Van Niekerk, K.
    "The Married Women in the Nursing Profession."
    Curationis. Volume 3 #2 September, 1980. pp. 32-35.
Van Regenmortel, P.J. and Van Harte, E.
    Family Planning in the Greater Cape Town Area: A
    Background Study. Bellville, South Africa: University of
    the Western Cape. Institute for Social Development.
    October, 1977. 107p.
Van Tonder, J.L.
    Fertility Survey 1982: Data Concerning the Black
    Population of South Africa. Pretoria, South Africa:
    Human Sciences Research Council. Institute for
    Sociological and Demographic Research. Report #S-129.
    1985. 301p.
Van Wyk, A.H.
    "Matrimonial Property Systems in Comparative
    Perspective." Acta Juridica. 1983. pp. 53-74.
Volpe, P.L.
    "Enforceability of Marriage Brokage Contract." De Rebus.
    #199 July, 1984. pp. 311-312.
Whitelaw, D.A.
    "Socio-Economic Status and Use of Contraceptives Among
    Unmarried Primigravidas in Cape Town." South African
    Medical Journal. Volume 646 #18 October 22, 1983. pp.
    712-715.
Wilson, Monica
    "Xhosa Marriage in Historical Perspective." (In) Krige,
    Eileen J. and Comarof, J.L. (eds.). Essays on African
    Marriage in Southern Africa. Cape Town, South Africa:
    Juta. 1981.
Yawitch, Joanne
    Black Women in South Africa: Capitalism, Employment and
    Reproduction. Johannesburg: Africa Perspective
    Dissertation #2. 1980.

MASS MEDIA

Bozzoli, Belinda
    "Women's Work: The Story of Mrs. S." (In) National Union
    of South African Students (NUSAS). NUSAS Conference on
    Women. Cape Town, South Africa: NUSAS Women's Directive.
    1983.
Frenkel, C.
    "Sensual ... But Not Too far From Innocent: A Critical
    Theory of Sexism in Advertising." Critical Arts. Volume
    1 #1 March, 1980.
Frenkel, C.
    "A Comparison of the Images of Black and White Women in

South African Magazine Advertisements." B.A. Honors
Dissertation: University of the Witwatersrand.
Johannesburg, South Africa. 1980.
Isaacs, Gayla C.
"The Media and the Ideal Woman." Africa Report. Volume
28 #2 March-April, 1983. pp. 48-51.
Zinn, Deborah
"Women's Role Portrayal in the South African Print
Media." B.A. Honors Dissertation: University of the
Witwatersrand. Johannesburg, South Africa. 1983.

MIGRATION

Bozzoli, Belinda
"Migrant Women and South African Social Change:
Biographical Approaches to Social Analysis." African
Studies. Volume 44 #1 1985. pp. 87-96.
Graaff, Janet
"Married to a Migrant." South African Outlook. Volume
108 #1289 November, 1978. pp. 172-173.
Graaff, Janet
"Will They be Together for Christmas?" South African
Outlook. Volume 108 #1289. November, 1978. pp.
163-165.
Manona, C.W.
"Marriage, Family Life and Migrancy in a Ciskei Village."
(In) Mayer, Philip (ed.). Black Villagers in an
Industrial Society: Anthropological Perspectives on
Labour Migration in South Africa. New York: Oxford
University Press. 1980.
Marks, Shula and Unterhalter, Elaine
"Women and the Migrant Labour System in South Africa."
Paper Presented at the Conference on Migrant Labour in
Southern Africa. Lusaka, Zambia: United Nations Economic
Commission For Africa (UNECA). 1978.
Showers, Kate
"A Note on Women, Conflict and Migrant Labour." South
African Labour Bulletin. Volume 6 #4 November, 1980.
Sibisi, Harriet N.
"How African Women Cope With Migrant Labor in South
Africa." Signs. Volume 3 #1 Autumn, 1977. pp.
167-177.
Sibisi, Harriet N.
"How African Women Cope With Migrant Labor in South
Africa." (In) Wellesley Editorial Committee. Women and
National Development: The Complexities of Change.
Chicago: University of Chicago Press. 1977. pp.
167-177.
Swaisland, C.F.
"The Emigration of Women From the United Kingdom to South
Africa, 1820-1939." Paper Presented at the South African
Seminar. Johannesburg: Rhodes University. Institute for
Social and Economic Research. 1983.

SOUTH AFRICA

MISCELLANEOUS

Anonymous
    "South Africa and Lesotho: Three Lesbian Conversations."
    Connexions. #3 Winter, 1982.
Bernstein, Hilda
    "Lilian Ngoyi: Isitwalandwe." Sechaba. August, 1982.
    pp. 16-19.
Court, J.H.
    "Pornography and Rape in White South Africa." De Jure.
    Volume 12 #2 1979. pp. 236-241.
Crause, H.L. and Botha, P.M.C.
    Prostitution: An Analysis of the Social System Centered
    in the Harbour Area of Port Elizabeth by Night. Port
    Elizabeth, South Africa: University of Port Elizabeth.
    Youth Research Project Publication #3. 1977.
Gillard, Jillian
    "Perpetuation of a Capitalist Patriarchy: The Ideological
    Apparatus of the Women's Magazine in South Africa."
    B.Soc.Sci Honors Dissertation: University of Cape Town.
    Cape Town, South Africa. 1978.
Grobler, I.
    "Changes in the Body Image of Primiparous Women Before
    and After Confinement." M.A. Thesis: University of
    Pretoria. Pretoria, South Africa. 1980.
Gwazela, Sindiswa
    "The Female Target: Behind Prison Bars in South Africa."
    Resources for Feminist Research. Volume 14 December,
    1985. pp. 23-25.
Hallett, Robin
    "Policemen, Pimps and Prostitutes: Public Morality and
    Police Corruption, Cape Town, 1902-1904." Paper
    Presented at the History Workshop. Johannesburg:
    University of the Witwatersrand. 1978.
Handands, G.C.
    "Prostitution in Cape Town." B. Soc.Sci. Honors
    Dissertation: University of Cape Town. Cape Town, South
    Africa. 1979.
Handands, G.C.
    "Prostitution in Cape Town: An Exploratory Study." Paper
    Presented to the Association for Sociology in Southern
    Africa Conference. Cape Town, South Africa: University
    of Cape Town. 1979.
Levitan, Ron
    "Women in the 'Bachelor' Quarters." South African
    Outlook. Volume 108 #1289 November, 1978. pp. 169-170.
Makunga, N.V.
    "Women and Achievement in a Changing Society." M.A.
    Thesis: University of Natal. Pietermaritzburg, South
    Africa. 1979.
Preston-Whyte, Eleanor and Nene, Sibongile
    Where the Formal Sector is not the Answer: Women and
    Poverty in Rural KwaZulu. Rondebosch, South Africa:

University of Cape Town. SALDRU, School of Economics.
Carnegie Conference Paper #235. 1984. 49p.
Schurink, W.J.
"Prostitution in Johannesburg: Preliminary Findings."
South African Journal of Criminal Law and Criminology.
Volume 6 #1 March, 1982. pp. 46-61.
Schurink, Willem J. and Levinthal, Terri
"Business Women Exchanging Sex for Money: A Descriptive
Survey." South African Journal of Sociology. Volume 14
#4 November, 1983. pp. 154-163.
Simkins, C.
"The Distribution of the African Population of South
Africa by Age, Sex and Region-Type, 1950-1980." (In)
Simkins, C. (ed.). Four Essays on the Past, Present and
Possible Future of the Distribution of the Black
Population of South Africa. Rondebosch, South Africa:
University of Cape Town. Southern African Labour and
Development Research Unit. 1983.
Van Heyningen, Elizabeth B.
"The Social Evil of the Cape Colony, 1868-1902:
Prostitution and the Contagious Diseases Act." Journal
of Southern African Studies. Volume 10 #2 1984. pp.
170-197.
Van Onselen, Charles
"Prostitutes and Proletarians, 1886-1914." (In) Van
Onselen, C. Studies in the Social and Economic History
of the Witwatersrand, 1886-1914. New York: Longman.
Volume One: New Babylon. 1982. pp. 103-143.
Vogelman, Lloyd
"The Client: A Study of Sexism and Prostitution." B.A.
Honors Dissertation: University of the Witwatersrand.
Johannesburg, South Africa. 1982.
Woolfson, L.R.
"Aetiological and Personality Factors Relating to
Homosexual Behavior in Adult Females." M.A. Thesis:
University of South Africa. Pretoria, South Africa.
1977.
Yawitch, Joanne
"Women and Squatting: A Winterveld Case Study." (In)
Bonner, P. (ed.). Working Papers in Southern African
Studies. Johannesburg: University of the Witwatersrand.
African Studies Institute. Raven Press. Volume 2.
1981.

NATIONALISM

African National Congress (ANC)
'Apartheid--You Shall Be Crushed': Women's Fight Against
Apartheid. Lusaka, Zambia: ANC. 1981. 32p.
Anonymous
"The Women's Question in Azanian Revolution."
Isandlwana. #8/9 July-December, 1981. pp. 18-44.

Barrett, J. and Dawber, A. and Klugman, I. and Obery, I. and
Schindler, J. and Yawitch, Joanne
     Vukani Makhosikazi. South African Women Speak. London:
     Catholic Institute for International Relations. 1985.
Bozzoli, Belinda
     "Feminist Interpretations and South African Studies: Some
     Suggested Avenues for Exploration." Paper Presented at
     the University of Witwatersrand. Johannesburg:
     University of the Witwatersrand. African Studies
     Institute. Johannesburg, South Africa. October 19,
     1981.
Bozzoli, Belinda
     "Marxism, Feminism and South African Studies." Journal
     of Southern African Studies. Volume 9 #2 April, 1983.
     pp. 137-171.
Budlender, Debbie and Meintjes, Sheila and Schreiner, Jenny
     "Women and Resistance in South Africa: A Review Article."
     Journal of Southern African Studies. Volume 10 #1
     October, 1983. pp. 131+.
De Villiers, Richard
     "The Resistance to the Extension of Passes to Women,
     1954-1960." Paper Presented to the African Studies
     Institute Post Graduate Seminar. Johannesburg:
     University of the Witwatersrand. September 24, 1979.
Duncan, Sheena
     "The Effect of Militarism on Women in South Africa."
     Paper Presented at the Workshop on War, Peace and
     Conscientious Objection in South Africa. Botha's Hill,
     South Africa. July 10-14, 1980.
Federal Council of the National Party of South Africa
     Women, Our Silent Soldiers. Bloemfontein, South Africa:
     Federal Council of the National Party of South Africa.
     August, 1978.
International Defense and Aid Fund (IDAF) and United Nations
Centre Against Apartheid
     To Honour Women's Day: Profiles of Leading Women in the
     South African and Namibian Liberation Struggles. London:
     IDAF/U.N. Centre Against Apartheid. 1981. 56p.
International Defense and Aid Fund for Southern Africa
     From You Have Struck a Rock: Women and Political
     Repression in Southern Africa. London: IDAFSA. 1980.
Kimble, Judy and Unterhalter, Elaine
     "We Opened the Road for You, You Must Go Forwards: ANC
     Women's Struggles, 1912-1982." Feminist Review. Volume
     12 1982. pp. 11-16.
Lapchick, Richard
     The Role of Women in the Struggle for Liberation in
     Zimbabwe, Namibia and South Africa. New York: United
     Nations. July, 1980. 37p.
Lapchick, Richard E.
     "The Role of Women in the Struggle Against Apartheid in
     South Africa." (In) Steady, Filomina C. (ed.). The

Black Woman Cross-Culturally. Cambridge, Massachusetts:
Schenkman Publishing. 1981. pp. 231-261.
Lapchick, Richard E. and Urdang, Stephanie
Oppression and Resistance: The Struggle of Women in
Southern Africa. Westport, Connecticut: Greenwood Press.
Contributions in Women's Studies. #29. 1982. 234p.
Lipman, Beata
We Make Freedom: Women in South Africa Speak. Boston:
Pandora Press. 1984. 141p.
Mayne, Anne V. and Levett, Ann
"Feminism in South Africa." off our backs. Volume 7
April, 1977. pp. 4.
Robinson, Sally
"Women and Politics of Liberation in South Africa."
Ufahamu. Volume 6 #1 1976.
Tsolo, Gladys
"Azania: My Experience in the National Liberation
Struggle." (In) Mies, Marie and Reddock, Rhoda (eds.).
National Liberation and Women's Liberation. Haque,
Netherlands: Institute for Social Studies. 1982. pp.
96-111
United Nations Secretary General
"The Role of Women in the Struggle for Liberation in
Zimbabwe, Namibia and South Africa: Report to the
Secretary General." Paper Presented at the World
Conference of the United Nations Decade for Women.
Copenhagen, Denamrk, July 14-30, 1980. New York: United
Nations. 1980.
Wells, Julia C.
"'The Day the Town Stood Still': Women in Resistance in
Potchefstroom, 1912-1930." (In) Bozzoli, Belinda (ed.).
Town and Countryside in the Transvaal: Capitalist
Penetration and Popular Response. Johannesburg: Raven
Press. 1983.
Yawitch, Joanne
"Natal 1959: The Women's Protests." Paper Presented at
the Conference on the History of Opposition in Southern
Africa. Johannesburg: (Student's) Development Studies
Group of the University of the Witwatersrand. January,
1978. pp. 206-223.

ORGANIZATIONS

Anonymous
"Maggie Oewies Talks About the Domestic Workers
Association." South African Labour Bulletin. Volume 6
#1 1980. pp. 35-36.
Anonymous
"Interview With Lucy Mvubelo." South African Labour
Bulletin. Volume 5 #3 October, 1979. pp. 97-100.
Anonymous
Garment Workers Unite: The Story of the Transvaal Garment

Workers Union. Salt River, South Africa: Labour History
Group. 1983. 51p.
Anonymous
"Women and Trade Unions: An Interview With Lydia
Ngwenya." South African Labour Bulletin. Volume 8 #6
June, 1983. pp. 63-68.
Anonymous
Women Workers. Durban, South Africa: Federation of South
African Trade Unions. 1984.
Anonymous
"Women Workers, Maternity Benefits and Trade Unions."
Critical Health. Volume 9 1983. pp. 29-35.
Anonymous
"Organising Women?" Work in Progress. Volume 21
February, 1982. pp. 14-22.
Anonymous
"Organising Women in Trade Unions: A Panel Discussion."
(In) National Union of South African Students (NUSAS).
NUSAS Conference on Women. Cape Town, South Africa:
NUSAS. Women's Directive. 1983.
Anonymous
"Interview With Mavis Nhlapo, Secretary of the Women's
Secretariat." Sechaba.   March, 1981. pp. 17-20.
Becker, Ruth
"The Sexual Division of Labour and its Implications for
Trade Union Organization: A Case Study." B.A. Honors
Dissertation: University of the Witwatersrand.
Johannesburg, South Africa. 1983.
Beinart, William
"Amafelandawonye (the Diehards), Rural Popular Protest
and Women's Movements in Herschel District, South Africa
in the 1920's." Paper Presented at the History Workshop.
Johannesburg: University of the Witwatersrand. January,
1984.
Berger, Iris
"Women in the South African Trade Union Movement." Ph.D
Dissertation: Boston University. Boston, Massachusetts.
1980.
Berger, Iris
"Garment Workers in the Transvaal: The Labour Process in
the Shaping of Ideology." Paper Presented at a
Conference on South Africa in the Comparative Study of
Class, Race and Nationalism. New York. 1982.
Bird, A.
"Organising Women in South Africa: Trade Unions." Paper
Presented to the Association for Sociology in Southern
Africa. Johannesburg: University of the Witwatersrand.
1984.
Carim, Shirene F.
The Role of Women in the South African Trade Union
Movement. New York: United Nations. Centre Against
Apartheid. Notices and Documents Series #7/80. April,
1980. 15p.

Dawber, Aneene
    "Transvaal Women Organise." Work in Progress. Volume 34
    1984. pp. 30-31.
Griessel, Annette
    "CATAPAW (Cape Association to Abolish Passes for African
    Women) and the Anti-Pass Campaign in Cape Town in the
    Fifties." (In) Cooper, Linda and Kaplan, Dave (eds.).
    Selected Research Papers on Aspects of Organization in
    the Western Cape. Cape Town, South Africa: University of
    Cape Town. Department of Economic History. 1982.
Hirsch, A.
    "Ducking and Weaving: Problems of Worker Organization in
    the Textile Industry of Durban-Pinetown-
    Pietermaritzburg." B.A. Honors Dissertation: University
    of Cape Town. Cape Town, South Africa. 1978.
Hirshfield, Claire
    "Liberal Women's Organizations and the War Against the
    Boers, 1899-1902." Albion. Volume 14 #1 Spring, 1982.
    pp. 27-49.
Kaplan, R.
    "Interview With Sarah Chitja, Deputy General Secretary of
    the National Union of Clothing Workers." South African
    Labour Bulletin. Volume 3 #4 1977. pp. 54-59.
Kimble, Judy and Unterhalter, Elaine
    "We Opened the Road for You, You Must Go Forwards: ANC
    Women's Struggles, 1912-1982." Feminist Review. Volume
    12 1982. pp. 11-16.
Kros, Cynthia
    "Urban African Women's Organizations and Protest on the
    Rand, 1939-1956." B.A. Honors Dissertation: University
    of Witwatersrand. Johannesburg. 1978.
Kros, Cynthia
    Urban African Women's Organizations and Protest on the
    Rand From the Years 1939-1956. Johannesburg: Africa
    Perspective Dissertation #3. 1980.
Lewis, Jon
    "Solly Sachs and the Garment Worker's Union." (In)
    Webster, Eddie (ed.). Essays in Southern African Labour
    History. Johannesburg: Raven Press. 1978. pp. 181-191.
Luckhardt, Ken and Wall, Brenda
    "Women Play a Leading Role." (In) Luckhardt, Ken and
    Wall, Brenda (eds.). Organise or Starve - The History of
    the South African Congress of Trade Unions (SACTU). New
    York: International Publishers. 1980. pp. 297-332.
Mawbey, John
    "Afrikaner Women of the Garment Union During the
    Thirities and Forties." (In) Webster, E. (ed.). Essays
    in South African Labour History. Johannesburg: Raven
    Press. 1978. pp. 192-206.
Nene, Daphne S.
    "The Role and Potential of Black Women's Voluntary
    Associations in Development: The Case of KwaZulu and
    Natal." Kwa Dlangezwa, South Africa: University of

Zululand. Publications of the University of Zululand.
Series B #19. 1982. 74p.
Nicol, Martin
"'Joh'burg Hotheads!' and 'Gullible Children of Cape
Town': The Transvaal Garment Workers' Union Assault on
Low Wages in the Cape Town Clothing Industry, 1930-1931."
Paper Presented at the History Workshop, University of
the Witwatersrand. Johannesburg, South Africa. 1984.
Obery, Ingrid
"'Makobongwe Amakosikazi': The FSAW and Mass Struggle in
the '50's." Africa Perspective. Volume 15 Autumn,
1980. pp. 36-41.
Schreiner, J.A.
"Politics is the Search for Allies: The Women's Anti-Pass
Campaigns and the Formation of CATAPAW in the Western
Cape in the 1950's." Paper Presented to the Association
for Sociology in Southern Africa. Johannesburg:
University of Witwatersrand. 1984.
Schreiner, J.A.
"Organising Women in the Liberation Struggle." (In)
National Union of South African Students (NUSAS). NUSAS
Conference on Women, University of the Witwatersrand,
July, 1982. Cape Town, South Africa: NUSAS Women's
Directive. 1983.
Schreiner, J.A.
"'Thina Singoomama Asinakubulawa': Forms of Organization
Adopted by the Federation of South African Women in the
Western Cape." B.A. Honors Thesis: University of Cape
Town. Cape Town, South Africa. 1982.
Shapiro, Janet
"Political and Economic Organization of Women in South
Africa: The Limitations of a Notion of 'Sisterhood' as a
Basis for Solidarity." Africa Perspective. Volume 15
Autumn, 1980. pp. 1-15.
South African Congress of Trade Unions
Conditions of Working Women in South Africa.
Dar-es-Salaam, Tanzania: South African Congress of Trade
Unions. June, 1979.
Strangwaies-Booth, J.
A Cricket in the Thorn Tree: Helen Suzman and the
Progressive Party. London: Hutchinson. 1976. 320p.
Thetele, Constance B.
"Women in South Africa: The WAAIC [Women's Association of
African Independent Churches]." (In) Appiah-Kubi, Kofi
and Torres, Sergio (eds.). African Theology in Route:
Papers From the Pan African Conference of Third World
Theologians, December 17-23, 1977, Accra, Ghana.
Maryknoll, New York: Orbis Books. 1979. pp. 150-154.
United Women's Organization (UWO) and Social Research Agency
(SRA)
The Federation of South African Women. Cape, Town, South
Africa: UWO and SRA. 1982.

Unterhalter, Beryl
  "Discrimination Against Women in the South African
  Medical Profession." Social Science and Medicine.
  Volume 20 #12 1985. pp. 1253-1258.
Walker, Cherryl
  "Women in 20th Century South African Politics: The
  Federation of South African Women, Its Roots, Growth and
  Decline." M.A. Thesis: University of Capetown.
  Capetown, South Africa. 1978.
Walker, Cherryl
  "The Federation of South African Women, 1954-1962." (In)
  University of Witwatersrand. Conference on the History
  of Opposition in Southern Africa, January, 1978.
  Johannesburg: (Students') Development Studies Group of
  the University of the Witwatersrand. 1978. pp. 183-205.
Women's Legal Status Committee
  Report of the 1976 National Convention to Advance Women's
  Legal Rights. Johannesburg: The Committee. 1976.

POLITICS AND GOVERNMENT

Africa Bureau
  The Status of Black Women in South Africa. London:
  Africa Bureau. Document Paper #21. 1979.
African National Congress (ANC)
  'Apartheid--You Shall Be Crushed': Women's Fight Against
  Apartheid. Lusaka, Zambia: ANC. 1981. 32p.
Anonymous
  The Effects of Apartheid on the Status of Women in South
  Africa. New York: United Nations. Centre Against
  Apartheid. Notices and Documents. 1978. 26p.
Anonymous
  "Effects of Apartheid on the Status of Women in South
  Africa." Objective Justice. Volume 10 #1 Spring, 1978.
Anonymous
  "Effects of Apartheid on the Status of Women in Southern
  Africa." Paper Presented at the World Conference of the
  United Nations Decade for Women, Copenhagen, Denmark,
  July 14-30, 1980. New York: United Nations. 1980.
Anonymous
  "'I Opened the Road for You': Dora Tamana and South
  Africa." ISIS International Bulletin. #21 1981.
Anonymous
  "South African Women." Sechaba. August, 1979. pp.
  19-21.
Anonymous
  "Women Under Apartheid." U.N. Chronicle. Volume 19
  July, 1982. pp. 40-41.
Anonymous
  Women Under Apartheid: In Photographs and Text. London:
  International Defense and Aid Fund for Southern Africa.
  1982. 120p.

SOUTH AFRICA

Anonymous
    "Women and Changing Relations of Control." (In) South
    African Research Service (eds.). South Africa Review:
    Same Foundations New Facades. Johannesburg: Raven.
    1983. pp. 278-299.
Anonymous
    "A Tribute to Ruth First." Review of African Political
    Economy. #25 September-December, 1982. pp. 3-64.
Anonymous
    "The Women's Question in Azanian Revolution."
    Isandlwana. #8/9 July-December, 1981. pp. 18-44.
Baard, Francis
    "Banishment and Jail." (In) National Union of South
    African Students (NUSAS). NUSAS Conference on Women.
    Cape Town, South Africa: NUSAS Women's Directive. 1983.
Beall, J.D.
    "The Changing Role and Status of African Women in the
    Political Economy of Colonial Natal." Paper Presented at
    the 13th Annual Congress of the Association of
    Sociologists of Southern Africa. 1982.
Beall, J.D.
    "Class, Race and Gender: The Political Economy of Women
    in Colonial Natal." M.A. Thesis: University of Natal.
    Durban, South Africa. 1982.
Bozzoli, Belinda
    "Feminist Interpretations and South African Studies: Some
    Suggested Avenues for Exploration." Paper Presented at
    the University of Witwatersrand. Johannesburg:
    University of the Witwatersrand. African Studies
    Institute. Johannesburg, South Africa. October 19,
    1981.
Bozzoli, Belinda
    "Marxism, Feminism and South African Studies." Journal
    of Southern African Studies. Volume 9 #2 April, 1983.
    pp. 137-171.
Brown, Barbara B.
    The Political Economy of Population Policy in South
    Africa. Boston: Boston University. African Studies
    Center. African Studies Working Paper #71. 1983. 15p.
Budlender, Debbie and Meintjes, Sheila and Schreiner, Jenny
    "Women and Resistance in South Africa: A Review Article."
    Journal of Southern African Studies. Volume 10 #1
    October, 1983. pp. 131+.
Burman, Sandra and Martine, Huvers
    "Church Versus State: Divorce Legislation and Divided
    South Africa." Journal of Southern African Studies.
    Volume 12 #1 October, 1985. pp. 116-135.
Cachalia, Amina
    "Indian Women in Resistance." Paper Presented at the
    National Union of South African Students (NUSAS)
    Conference on Women, July, 1982. Johannesburg:
    University of Witwatersrand. NUSAS Women's Directive.
    1983.

Church, Joan
    "Marriage and Human Rights: A Note on the Bophuthatswana
    Marriage Act." Codicillus. Volume 22 #2 1981. pp.
    220-266.
Cock, Jacklyn
    "Domestic Servants in the Poitical Economy of South
    Africa." Africa Perspective. Volume 15 1980. pp.
    42-53.
Cooper, C. and Ensor, Linda
    African Woman's Handbook on the Law. Johannesburg: South
    African Institute of Race Relations. 1980. 41p.
De Villiers, Richard
    "The Resistance to the Extension of Passes to Women,
    1954-1960." Paper Presented to the African Studies
    Institute Post Graduate Seminar. Johannesburg:
    University of the Witwatersrand. September 24, 1979.
Demissic, Fassil
    "Double Burden: African Women Under Apartheid." Ufahamu.
    Volume 14 #3 1985. pp. 52-77.
Duncan, Sheena
    "The Effect of Militarism on Women in South Africa."
    Paper Presented at the Workshop on War, Peace and
    Conscientious Objection in South Africa. Botha's Hill,
    South Africa. July 10-14, 1980.
Federal Council of the National Party of South Africa
    Women, Our Silent Soldiers. Bloemfontein, South Africa:
    Federal Council of the National Party of South Africa.
    August, 1978.
Gaitskell, Deborah and Kimble, Judy
    "Class, Race and Gender: Domestic Workers in South
    Africa." Review of African Political Economy. #27/28
    1983. pp. 86-108.
Ginwala, Frene and Mashiane, Shirley
    "Women and Apartheid: Black South African Women Stand on
    the Lowest Rung of the Ladder of Oppression." UNESCO
    Courier. Volume 33 #7 July, 1980. pp. 13-17.
Goodwin, June
    Cry Amandla: South African Women and the Question of
    Power. New York: Holmes and Meier. 1984. 225p.
Griessel, Annette
    "CATAPAW (Cape Association to Abolish Passes for African
    Women) and the Anti-Pass Campaign in Cape Town in the
    Fifties." (In) Cooper, Linda and Kaplan, Dave (eds.).
    Selected Research Papers on Aspects of Organization in
    the Western Cape. Cape Town, South Africa: University of
    Cape Town. Department of Economic History. 1982.
Gwazela, Sindiswa
    "The Female Target: Behind Prison Bars in South Africa."
    Resources for Feminist Research. Volume 14 December,
    1985. pp. 23-25.
Hallett, Robin
    "Policemen, Pimps and Prostitutes: Public Morality and
    Police Corruption, Cape Town, 1902-1904." Paper

Presented at the History Workshop. Johannesburg:
University of the Witwatersrand. 1978.
Hlophe, J.M.
"The KwaZula Act on the Code of Zulu Law, 6 of 1981--A
Guide to Intending Spouses and Some Comments on the
Custom of Lobolo." Comparative and International Law
Journal of Southern Africa. Volume 17 #2 July, 1984.
pp. 163-171.
Intern. Defence and Aid Fund for Southern Africa (IDAF)
You Have Struck a Rock: Women and Political Repression in
Southern Africa. London: IDAF. 1980. 24p.
International Defense and Aid Fund (IDAF) and United Nations
Centre Against Apartheid
To Honour Women's Day: Profiles of Leading Women in the
South African and Namibian Liberation Struggles. London:
IDAF/U.N. Centre Against Apartheid. 1981. 56p.
International Defense and Aid Fund for Southern Africa
"From You Have Struck a Rock: Women and Political
Repression in Southern Africa." London: IDAFSA. 1980.
Kimble, Judy and Unterhalter, Elaine
"We Opened the Road for You, You Must Go Forwards: ANC
Women's Struggles, 1912-1982." Feminist Review. Volume
12 1982. pp. 11-16.
Kimmons, Leona
"Women in South Africa--Agony and Struggle." Wree-View.
Fall, 1976. pp. 1-5.
Klugman, Barbara
"The Political Economy of Population Control in South
Africa." B.A. Honors Dissertation: University of the
Witwatersrand. Johannesburg, South Africa. 1980.
Kros, Cynthia
"Urban African Women's Organizations and Protest on the
Rand, 1939-1956." B.A. Honors Dissertation: University
of Witwatersrand. Johannesburg. 1978.
Kros, Cynthia
Urban African Women's Organizations and Protest on the
Rand From the Years 1939-1956. Johannesburg: Africa
Perspective Dissertation #3. 1980.
Lamula, Promise
"Women Under Apartheid." ISIS Women's World. #4
December, 1984.
Lapchick, Richard
The Role of Women in the Struggle for Liberation in
Zimbabwe, Namibia and South Africa. New York: United
Nations. July, 1980. 37p.
Lapchick, Richard E.
"The Role of Women in the Struggle Against Apartheid in
South Africa." (In) Steady, Filomina C. (ed.). The
Black Woman Cross-Culturally. Cambridge, Massachusetts:
Schenkman Publishing. 1981. pp. 231-261.
Lapchick, Richard E. and Urdang, Stephanie
Oppression and Resistance: The Struggle of Women in

Southern Africa. Westport, Connecticut: Greenwood Press.
Contributions in Women's Studies. #29. 1982. 234p.
Lodge, Tom
"Women Protest Movements in the 1950's." (In) Lodge,
Tom. Black Politics in South Africa Since 1945. New
York: Longman. 1983.
Mackenzie, D.J.
"Influx Control, Health Regulation and African Women in
Durban, c. 1917-1949." Paper Presented at the Workshop
on Local History. Pietermaritzburg, South Africa. 1982.
Mariotti, Amelia
"Capitalist Development and State Policy in South Africa:
African Women, the Family and the Price of Labour Power."
Paper Presented at the Conference on African Women in
History. Santa Clara, California: University of Santa
Clara. 1981.
Matsepe, Ivy F.
"African Women's Labor in the Political Economy of South
Africa, 1880 -1970." Ph.D Dissertation: Rutgers
University. New Brunswick, New Jersey. 1984. 327p.
Matsepe-Casaburri, Ivy F.
Women and the Political Economy of Southern Africa.
Harare, Zimbabwe. 1982. 100+p.
Matsepe-Casaburri, Ivy F.
"Cheap Labour Policies and Their Implications for African
Women in South Africa." Paper Presented at a Conference
on Women's Development. Sussex, England: University of
Sussex. 1978.
Meer, Fatima
Women in the Apartheid Society. New York: United
Nations. U.N. Centre Against Apartheid. April, 1985.
31p.
Nkabinde, C.
"The Legal Position of African Women in Employment."
IPST Bulletin (University of Zululand). Volume 12 1978.
pp. 27-32.
Ntantala, Phyllis
An African Tragedy: The Black Woman Under Apartheid.
Detroit, Michigan: Agascha Productions. 1976. 137p.
Poinsette, Cheryl
"Black Women Under Apartheid: An Introduction." Harvard
Women's Law Journal. Volume 8 Spring, 1985. pp.
93-119.
Riekert, Julian
"Race, Sex and the Law in Colonial Natal." Journal of
Natal and Zulu History. Volume 6 1983. pp. 82, 97.
Robinson, Sally
"Women and Politics of Liberation in South Africa."
Ufahamu. Volume 6 #1 1976.
Roscani, Luisa
"Qwa Qwa - Relocation and Survival: The Effects of
Relocation on Women." B.Soc.Sci. Thesis: University of
Natal. Durban, South Africa. 1983.

SOUTH AFRICA

Satchwell, K.
"Women and the Law." (In) National Union of South
African Students (NUSAS) and Law Students Council. Law
in South Africa: Lifting the Veil. Cape Town, South
Africa: NUSAS. 1981. pp. 42-53.
Schreiner, J.A.
"Politics is the Search for Allies: The Women's Anti-Pass
Campaigns and the Formation of CATAPAW in the Western
Cape in the 1950's." Paper Presented to the Association
for Sociology in Southern Africa. Johannesburg:
University of Witwatersrand. 1984.
Schreiner, J.A.
"Organising Women in the Liberation Struggle." (In)
National Union of South African Students (NUSAS). NUSAS
Conference on Women, University of the Witwatersrand,
July, 1982. Cape Town, South Africa: NUSAS Women's
Directive. 1983.
Shapiro, Janet
"Political and Economic Organization of Women in South
Africa: The Limitations of a Notion of 'Sisterhood' as a
Basis for Solidarity." Africa Perspective. Volume 15
Autumn, 1980. pp. 1-15.
Shindler, J.
"The Effects of Influx Control and Labour-Saving
Appliances on Domestic Services." South African Labour
Bulletin. Volume 6 #1 July, 1980. pp. 22-34.
Sikakane, Joyce
A Widow in Soweto. London: International Defense and Aid
Fund for Southern Africa. 1977. 80p.
Sikakane, Joyce
"Women Under Apartheid." Paper Presented at a Conference
Sponsored by the British Anti-Apartheid Movement.
London, England. April, 1976.
Strangwaies-Booth, J.
A Cricket in the Thorn Tree: Helen Suzman and the
Progressive Party. London: Hutchinson. 1976. 320p.
Thomson, R.C.
Some Discriminatory Laws and Their Effects on African
Women. Cape Town, South Africa: National Union of South
African Students (NUSAS). 1978.
Thomson, R.C.
"Some Discriminatory Laws and Their Effects on African
Women." Jure ac Legibus. Volume 3 1976. pp. 19-24.
Tsolo, Gladys
"Azania: My Experience in the National Liberation
Struggle." (In) Mies, Marie and Reddock, Rhoda (eds.).
National Liberation and Women's Liberation. Haque,
Netherlands: Institute for Social Studies. 1982. pp.
96-111
United Nations
The Plight of Black Women in Apartheid South Africa. New
York: United Nations. Department of Public Information.
1981. 35p.

United Nations
    International Conference on Women and Apartheid Report.
    New York: United Nations. 1982. 38p.
United Nations
    The Effects of Apartheid on the Status of Women in
    Southern Africa. New York: United Nations. July, 1980.
United Nations
    "The Effects of Apartheid on the Status of Women in South
    Africa and Namibia." Paper Presented at the United
    Nations World Conference of the United Nations Decade for
    Women: Equality, Development and Peace, Copenhagen. New
    York: United Nations. 1980. 37p.
United Nations
    The Effects of Apartheid on the Status of Women in South
    Africa, Namibia and Southern Rhodesia. New York: United
    Nations. 1978.
United Nations Centre Against Apartheid
    "The Effects of Apartheid on the Status of Women in South
    Africa." Black Scholar. Volume 10 #1 September, 1978.
    pp. 11-21.
United Nations Centre Against Apartheid
    African Women and Apartheid in Labour Matters. New York:
    United Nations Centre Against Apartheid. Notes and
    Documents Series #20/80. July, 1980. 13p.
United Nations Centre Against Apartheid
    Mrs. Winnie Mandela: Profile in Courage and Defiance.
    New York: United Nations Centre Against Apartheid.
    February, 1978.
United Nations Economic Commission for Africa (UNECA)
    "Apartheid and the Status of Women." Paper Presented at
    the Regional Prepatory Meeting of the UNECA Second
    Regional Conference for the Integration of Women in
    Development, Lusaka, Zambia, December 3-7, 1979. Addis
    Ababa, Ethiopia: UNECA.
United Nations Secretary General
    "The Role of Women in the Struggle for Liberation in
    Zimbabwe, Namibia and South Africa: Report to the
    Secretary General." Paper Presented at the World
    Conference of the United Nations Decade for Women,
    Copenhagen, Denmark, July 14-30, 1980. New York: United
    Nations. 1980.
Unterhalter, Beryl
    "Women in Struggle--South Africa." Third World
    Quarterly. Volume 5 #4 1983. pp. 886-893.
Unterholter, Elaine
    "South Africa: Women in Struggle." Third World
    Quarterly. Volume 5 #4 1983. pp. 886-893.
Urdang, Stephanie
    "Ensuring a Revolution Within a Revolution." Southern
    Africa. May, 1978. pp. 7-9.
Van Der Spuy, A.
    "South African Women: The Other Discrimination." Munger
    Africana Library Notes. #44. July, 1978. pp. 2-15.

Van Vuuren, Nancy
    Women Against Apartheid: The Fight for Freedom in South
    Africa, 1920-1975. Palo Alto, California: R and E
    Research Association. 1979. 133p.
Walker, Cherryl
    Women's Suffrage Movement in South Africa. Capetown,
    South Africa: University of Capetown. Centre for African
    Studies. Communications #2. 1979. 121p.
Walker, Cherryl
    Women and Resistance in South Africa. London: Onyx
    Press. 1982. 309p.
Walker, Cherryl
    "Women in 20th Century South African Politics: The
    Federation of South African Women, Its Roots, Growth and
    Decline." M.A. Thesis: University of Capetown.
    Capetown, South Africa. 1978.
Walker, Cherryl
    "The Federation of South African Women, 1954-1962." (In)
    University of Witwatersrand. Conference on the History
    of Opposition in Southern Africa, January, 1978.
    Johannesburg: (Students') Development Studies Group of
    the University of the Witwatersrand. 1978. pp. 183-205.
Walker, Cherryl
    "Women and Politics: The Anti-Pass Campaign of the
    1950's." Paper Presented at the University of Cape Town
    Summer School. Cape Town, South Africa: University of
    Cape Town. 1979.
Walker, Cherryl
    "Women and Politics: The Women's Suffrage Movement Before
    1930." Paper Presented at the University of Cape Town
    Summer School. Cape Town, South Africa: University of
    Cape Town. 1979.
Wells, J.
    "Interview With Josie Palmer." South African Institute
    of Race Relations Journal. October, 1977.
Wells, Julia C.
    "Women's Resistance to Passes in Bloemfontein During the
    Inter-War Period." Africa Perspective. Volume 15
    Autumn, 1980. pp. 16-35.
Wells, Julia C.
    "The History of Black Women's Struggle Against Pass Laws
    in South Africa, 1900-1960." Ph.D Dissertation: Columbia
    University. New York, New York. 1982. 414p.
Wells, Julia C.
    "Why Women Rebel: A Comparative Study of South African
    Women's Resistance in Bloemfontein (1913) and
    Johannesburg (1958)." Journal of Southern African
    Studies. Volume 10 #1 October, 1983. pp. 55-70.
Wells, Julia C.
    "Passes and Bypasses: Freedom of Movement for African
    Women Under the Urban Areas Act of South Africa." (In)
    Hays, Margaret J. and Wright, Marcia (eds.). African
    Women and the Law: Historical Perspectives. Boston:

Boston University. African Studies Center. Boston
University Papers on Africa. Volume Seven. 1982. pp.
125-150.

Wells, Julia C.
"'The Day the Town Stood Still': Women in Resistance in
Potchefstroom, 1912-1930." (In) Bozzoli, Belinda (ed.).
Town and Countryside in the Transvaal: Capitalist
Penetration and Popular Response. Johannesburg: Raven
Press. 1983.

Westmore, Jean
Abortion in South Africa and Attitudes of Natal Medical
Practitioners Towards South African Abortion Legislation.
Durban, South Africa: University of Natal. Centre for
Applied Social Sciences and Abortion Reform Action Group.
1977. 76p.

Women's Legal Status Committee
Report of the 1976 National Convention to Advance Women's
Legal Rights. Johannesburg: The Committee. 1976.

World Health Organization (WHO)
Health Implications of Apartheid on Women. Geneva: WHO.
1979.

Yawitch, Joanne
"Natal 1959: The Women's Protests." Paper Presented at
the Conference on the History of Opposition in Southern
Africa. Johannesburg: (Student's) Development Studies
Group of the University of the Witwatersrand. January,
1978. pp. 206-223.

Yawitch, Joanne
"Rural Natal 1959: The Women's Riots." Africa
Perspective. Volume 5 1977. pp. 1-17.

Yawitch, Joanne
Tightening the Noose: African Women and Influx Control in
South Africa, 1950-1980. Rondebosch, South Africa:
University of Cape Town. SALDRU. School of Economics.
Carnegie Conference Paper #82. 1984. 36p.

Yawitch, Joanne
"Tightening the Noose: African Women and Influx Control
in South Africa, 1950-1980." Paper Presented to the
Association for Sociology in Southern Africa.
Johannesburg: University of the Witwatersrand. 1984.

RELIGION AND WITCHCRAFT

Becken, Hans-Jurgen
"Give Me Water, Women of Samaria: The Pilgrimage of
Southern African Blacks in the 1980's." Journal of
Religion in Africa. Volume 14 #2 1983. pp. 115-129.

Burman, Sandra and Martine, Huvers
"Church Versus State: Divorce Legislation and Divided
South Africa." Journal of Southern African Studies.
Volume 12 #1 October, 1985. pp. 116-135.

Carstens, Peter
     "The Socio-Economic Context of Initiation Ceremonies
     Among Two Southern African Peoples." Canadian Journal of
     African Studies. Volume 16 #3 1982. pp. 502-522.
Chabaku, Motlalepula
     "'We Carry the Cross Close to Us': A South African Woman
     Talks About Her Land and Her Faith." Sojourners. Volume
     9 #7 July, 1980. pp. 16-18.
Cock, Jacklyn
     "The Missionary Articulation of Sexual Ideology and the
     Initial Incorporation of Black Women Into Wage Labour."
     Africa Perspective. Volume 13 1979. pp. 16-26.
Friedman, Annette
     "The Relationship Between Religiosity and Morality in a
     Group of Female College Students." B.A. Honors
     Dissertation: University of the Witwatersrand.
     Johannesburg, South Africa. 1978.
Gaitskell, Deborah
     "Housewives, Maids or Mothers: Some Contradictions of
     Domesticity for Christian Women in Johannesburg,
     1903-1939." Journal of African History. Volume 24 #2
     1983. pp. 241-256.
Gaitskell, Deborah
     "Female Mission Initiatives: Black and White Women in
     Three Witwatersrand Churches, 1903-1939." Ph.D
     Dissertation: University of London. London, England.
     1981.
Gaitskell, Deborah
     "'Christian Compounds for Girls': Church Hostels for
     African Women in Johannesburg, 1907-1970." Journal of
     Southern African Studies. Volume 6 #1 October, 1979.
     pp. 44-69.
Gaitskell, Deborah
     "'Wailing for Purity': Prayer Unions, African Mothers and
     Adolescent Daughters, 1912-1940." (In) Marks, S. and
     Rathbone, R. (eds.). Industrialization and Social Change
     in South Africa... 1870-1930. New York: Longman. 1982.
     357p.
Kiern, Susan M.
     "Convivial Sisterhood: Spirit Mediumship and Client-Core
     Network Among Black South African Women." (In)
     Hoch-Smith, J. and Spring, Anita (eds.). Women in Ritual
     and Symbolic Roles. New York: Plenum Press. 1978. pp.
     191-205.
Kiernan, J.P.
     "Spouses and Partners: Marriage and Career Among Urban
     Zulu Zionists." Urban Anthropology. Volume 8 #1
     Spring, 1979. pp. 95-110.
Krige, Eileen J. and Krige, J.D.
     The Realm of a Rain-Queen: A Study of the Pattern of
     Lovedu Society. New York: AMS Press. 1978. 335p.
Middleton-Keirn, Susan
     "Convivial Sisterhood: Spirit Mediumship and Client-Core
     Network Among Black South African Women." (In)

Hoch-Smith, Judith and Spring, Anita (eds.). Women in
Ritual and Symbolic Roles. New York: Plenum Press.
1978. pp. 191-205.
Mitchell, Mozella G.
"Howard Thurman and Olice Schreiner: Post-Modern Marriage
Post-Mortem." Journal of Religious Thought. Volume 38
Spring-Summer, 1981. pp. 62-72.
Peart, Nicola S.
"Civil or Christian Marriage and Customary Unions: The
Legal Position of the Discarded Spouse and Children."
Comparative and International Law Journal of South
Africa. Volume 16 #1 1983. pp. 39-64.
Thetele, Constance B.
"Women in South Africa: The WAAIC [Women's Association of
African Independent Churches]." (In) Appiah-Kubi, Kofi
and Torres, Sergio (eds.). African Theology in Route:
Papers From the Pan African Conference of Third World
Theologians, December 17-23, 1977, Accra, Ghana.
Maryknoll, New York: Orbis Books. 1979. pp. 150-154.

RESEARCH

Beall, J.D.
"Problems of Sociological Analysis in Historical
Investigation: The Case of Women in Colonial Natal."
Paper Presented at the History Workshop, University of
Durban-Westville. Durban, South Africa: University of
Durban-Westville. 1983.
Brokensha, D.
"Obituary: Monica Wilson, 1908-1982: An Appreciation."
Africa. Volume 53 #3 1983. pp. 83-87.
Cape Town. City Engineer. Technical Management Services
Mitchells Plain Survey of Coloured Females. Cape Town,
South Africa: City Engineers. March, 1979.
Driver, D.
"Pauline Smith--A Gentler Music of Her Own: South African
Fiction of the 20's and 30's." Research in African
Literature. Volume 15 #1 1984. pp. 45-71.
Preston-Whyte, E.
"Female Headed Households and Development: Lessons of
Cross-Cultural Models for Research on Women in Southern
Africa." Paper Presented to the Women's Studies
Symposium. Umtata, South Africa: University of Transkei.
March, 1984.
Yawittch, Joanne
"Defining the Issues--Women: Towards a Methodology of
Women." Work in Progress. Volume 9 August, 1979. pp.
32-35.

SEX ROLES

Anonymous
"General Questions on the Position of Black Women in South Africa: An Interview With Sheena Duncan, August, 1979." Africa Perspective. Volume 15 August, 1980. pp. 56-69.

Anonymous
Women Workers. Durban, South Africa: Federation of South African Trade Unions. 1984.

Anonymous
"Women: The Family Food Producers in South Africa." Apartheid Bulletin. #126 1978.

Anonymous
"South Africa: A Bulletin From Within." (In) Morgan, Robin (ed.). Sisterhood is Global. Garden City, New York: Anchor Books. 1984. pp. 618-620.

Baartman, D.
"Traditional and Modern Approaches to the Health Care of the Pregnant Woman in Xhosa Society." M.A. Thesis: University of South Africa. Pretoria, South Africa. 1983.

Barling, Julian
"Multidimensional Locus of Control Beliefs Among English Speaking South African Mothers." Journal of Social Psychology. Volume 111 1st Quarter June, 1980. pp. 139-140.

Barrett, Jane
"Knitmore: A Study in the Relationship Between Sex and Class." B.A. Honors Dissertation: University of the Witwatersrand. Johannesburg, South Africa. 1981.

Beall, J.
"Unwanted Guests: Indian Women in the Context of Indentured Immigation to the Natal." Paper Presented to the Conference Commemorating the 150th Anniversary of Indian Indentured Immigration and the Abolition of Slaves. Moka, Mauritius. October, 1984.

Beall, J.D.
"Changing Function and Status of Women in Zululand, 1818-1879." Paper Presented to the Development Studies Research Group. Pietermarizburg, South Africa: University of Natal. 1982.

Beall, J.D.
"The Changing Role and Status of African Women in the Political Economy of Colonial Natal." Paper Presented at the 13th Annual Congress of the Association of Sociologists of Southern Africa. 1982.

Beall, J.D.
"Class, Race and Gender: The Political Economy of Women in Colonial Natal." M.A. Thesis: University of Natal. Durban, South Africa. 1982.

Beall, J.D.
"The Function and Status of African Women in the Social

and Economic Life of Natal and Zululand, 1818-1879."
B.A. Honors Dissertation: University of Natal. Durban,
South Africa. 1981.

Beavon, K. and Rogerson, C.
"The Changing Role of Women in the Informal Sector of
South Africa." (In) Drakakissmith, D. (ed.).
Urbanization in the Developing World. London: Croom
Helm. 1980.

Becker, Ruth
"The Sexual Division of Labour and its Implications for
Trade Union Organization: A Case Study." B.A. Honors
Dissertation: University of the Witwatersrand.
Johannesburg, South Africa. 1983.

Behr, D.
"Women and Work, in Psychological Perspective." Journal
of the University of Durban-Westville. Volume 2 #4 1976.
pp. 9-18.

Boddington, Erica
"Domestic Service: Changing Relations of Class
Domination, 1841-1948." M.A. Thesis: University of Cape
Town. Cape Town, South Africa. 1983.

Bozzoli, Belinda
"Marxism, Feminism and South African Studies." Journal
of Southern African Studies. Volume 9 #2 April, 1983.
pp. 137-171.

Bozzoli, Belinda
"Migrant Women and South African Social Change:
Biographical Approaches to Social Analysis." African
Studies. Volume 44 #1 1985. pp. 87-96.

Bozzoli, Belinda
"Women's Work: The Story of Mrs. S." (In) National Union
of South African Students (NUSAS). NUSAS Conference on
Women. Cape Town, South Africa: NUSAS Women's Directive.
1983.

Brindley, Marianne
"Old Women in Zulu Culture: The Old Woman and
Childbirth." South African Journal of Ethnology. Volume
8 #3 1985. pp. 98-108.

Brindley, Marianne
"The Role of the Old Women in the Zulu Culture." Ph.D
Dissertation: University of Zululand. Kwa-Dlangezwa,
South Africa. 1982.

Brink, Elsabe
"'Maar 'n Klomp Factory Meide': The Role of the Female
Garment Workers in the Clothing Industry, Afrikaner
Family and Community on the Witwatersrand During the
1920's." Paper Presented at the History Workshop.
Johannesburg: University of the Witwatersrand. 1984.

Bromberger, Norman and Gandor, Mark
"Economic and Demographic Functioning of Rural Households
in the Mahlabatini District Kwazulu." Social Dynamics.
Volume 10 #2 June, 1984. pp. 20-37.

Bughwan, Devi
    "Discrimination Against and Exploitation of Women in the
    Work Place." Paper Presented to the Conference on Women
    and the Economy. Joahnnesburg: Rand Afrikaans
    University. September 22, 1980.
Burman, Sandra
    "Divorce and the Disadvantaged." (In) Hirschon, Renbee
    (ed.). Women and Property, Women as Property. London:
    Croom Helm. Oxford Women's Series. 1984.
Chabaku, Motlalepula
    "Southern Africa: Going Up the Mountain." (In) Morgan,
    Robin (ed.). Sisterhood is Global. Garden City, New
    York: Anchor Books. 1984. pp. 600-617.
Cock, Jacklyn
    Maids and Madams: A Study in the Politics of
    Exploitation. Johannesburg: Raven Press. 1980. 410p.
Cock, Jacklyn
    "Disposable Nannies: Domestic Servants in the Political
    Economy of South Africa." Review of African Political
    Economy. #21 May-September, 1981. pp. 63-83.
Dlamini, C.R.
    "The Transformation of a Customary Marriage in Zulu Law."
    Comparative and International Law Journal of Southern
    Africa. Volume 16 #3 November, 1983. pp. 383-392.
Duncan, Sheena
    "Aspects of Family Breakdown." Work in Progress. Volume
    27. 1983. pp. 36-38.
Egan, Siobhan
    "Black Women in South African Agriculture: An
    Introductory Study of Life and Labour in the
    Countryside." B.A. Honors Dissertation: University of
    Natal. Durban, South Africa. 1983.
Fagan, J.J.
    "New Rights for Married Women." Social Work. Volume 20
    #4 1984. pp. 200-201.
Favis, M.
    Black Women in the South African Economy. Durban, South
    Africa. 1983.
Finch, Briony J.
    "Male and Female Homosexuality: A Comparison of
    Secretiveness, Promiscuity, Masculine/Feminine Role
    Playing, Self-Concept and Self-Acceptance." B.A. Honors
    Dissertation: University of the Witwatersrand.
    Johannesburg, South Africa. 1980.
Fisher, F.
    "Women in Pre-Capitalist Societies in South Africa."
    Paper Presented at the University of Cape Town Summer
    School. Cape Town, South Africa: University of Cape
    Town. January, 1979.
Gaitskell, Deborah
    "Housewives, Maids or Mothers: Some Contradictions of
    Domesticity for Christian Women in Johannesburg,

1903-1939." Journal of African History. Volume 24 #2
1983. pp. 241-256.
Gaitskell, Deborah and Kimble, Judy
"Class, Race and Gender: Domestic Workers in South
Africa." Review of African Political Economy. #27/28
1983. pp. 86-108.
Gerdes, L.C.
"Personality Differences Between Men and Women in Marital
Roles." Social Welfare and Pensions. Volume 12 #1
June, 1977. pp. 6-12.
Harries, Jane
"Women in Production in the Ciskei." B.A. Honors
Dissertation: University of Cape Town. Cape Town, South
Africa. 1979.
Hermann, Anne
"The Flight From Domesticity in Two South African
Novels." Communications for Gender Research. #5
Summer, 1985. pp. 1+
Hill, Alison M.
"Materialist Feminism and South Africa: The Position of
Black Working Class Women in Contemporary Cape Town."
B.A. Honors Dissertation: University of Cape Town. Cape
Town, South Africa. 1983.
Isaacs, Gayla C.
"The Media and the Ideal Woman." Africa Report. Volume
28 #2 March-April, 1983. pp. 48-51.
Kiernan, J.P.
"Spouses and Partners: Marriage and Career Among Urban
Zulu Zionists." Urban Anthropology. Volume 8 #1
Spring, 1979. pp. 95-110.
Kinsman, Margaret
"Beasts of Burden: The Subordination of Southern Tswana
Women, ca. 1800-1840." Journal of Southern African
Studies. Volume 10 #1 1983. pp. 39-54.
Krige, Eileen J. and Comaroff, John L. (eds.).
Essays on African Marriage in Southern Africa. Cape
Town, South Africa: Wetton. 1981. 205p.
Krige, Eileen J.
"Women-Marriage, With Special Reference to the
Lovedu--Its Significance for the Definition of Marriage."
(In) Tiffany, Sharon W. (ed.). Women and Society: An
Anthropological Reader. St. Albans, Vermont: Eden Press.
1979. pp. 208-237.
Kubukeli, Pumla
"Women in Transkei." Paper Presented at the Women
Studies Symposium, University of Transkei. Umtata, South
Africa. March, 1984.
Lapchick, Richard E. and Urdang, Stephanie
Oppression and Resistance: The Struggle of Women in
Southern Africa. Westport, Connecticut: Greenwood Press.
Contributions in Women's Studies. #29. 1982. 234p.
Lawton, L.
Working Women. Johannesburg: Raven Press. 1985.

Mackenzie, D.J.
    "African Women and the Urbanization Process in Durban, c.
    1920-1949." Paper Presented at the Workshop on African
    Urban Life in Durban in the Twentieth Century. Durban,
    South Africa: University of Natal. October, 1983.
Marks, Shula and Unterhalter, Elaine
    "Women and the Migrant Labour System in South Africa."
    Paper Presented at the Conference on Migrant Labour in
    Southern Africa. Lusaka, Zambia: United Nations Economic
    Commission For Africa (UNECA). 1978.
Martin, V.
    "The Role of Women in South African Manufacturing." B.A.
    Honors Dissertation: University of the Witwatersrand.
    Johannesburg, South Africa. 1982.
Matsepe-Casaburri, Ivy F.
    "Changing Roles and Needs of Women in South Africa and
    Namibia." Paper Presented at the World Conference for
    the United Nations Decade for Women, Copenhagen,
    Denmark, July 14-30, 1980. New York: United Nations.
Meer, Fatima
    Black Women in Industry, 1983: 988 Interviews, A
    Preliminary Report Conducted With African, Indian and
    Coloured Women in the Greater Durban Metropolitan Area.
    Durban, South Africa: Institute for Black Research.
    Community and Labour Relations Research Group. 1983.
Meer, Fatima (ed.).
    Black Women, Durban 1975: Case Studies of 85 Women at
    Home and Work. Durban, South Africa: University of
    Natal. Sociology Department. 1976.
Meer, Fatima (ed.).
    Factory and Family: The Divided Lives of South Africa's
    Women Workers. Durban, South Africa: Institute for Black
    Research. 1984. 105p.
Mitchell, L.
    Tsonga Women: Changes in Production and Reproduction: A
    Working Paper. Minneapolis, Minnesota: University of
    Minnesota. African History Seminar. 1978.
Nene, Daphne S.
    "Role Enactment of Rural Women: A Sociological
    Exploratory Study of the Role Behavior and its
    Implications for Rural Development." M.A. Thesis:
    University of Zululand. Kwa-Dlangezwa, South Africa.
    1983.
Nene, Daphne S.
    "Women Caught in Between: The Case of Rural Women in
    KwaZulu." Paper Presented to the Women's Studies
    Symposium, University of Transkei. Umtata, South Africa:
    University of Transkei. March, 1984.
Ngubane, Harriet
    "Marriage, Affinity and the Ancestral Realm: Zulu
    Marriage in Female Perspective." (In) Krige, E.J. and
    Comaroff, J.L. (eds.). Essays on African Marriage in
    Southern Africa. Cape Town, South Africa: Juta. 1981.

Perold, Helene (ed.).
    Working Women: A Portrait of South Africa's Black Women
    Workers. Braamfontein, South Africa: Raven Press. 1985.
    144p.
Preston-Whyte, E.
    "Female Headed Households and Development: Lessons of
    Cross-Cultural Models for Research on Women in Southern
    Africa." Paper Presented to the Women's Studies
    Symposium. Umtata, South Africa: University of Transkei.
    March, 1984.
Preston-Whyte, Eleanor M.
    "Families Without Marriage: A Zulu Caste Study." (In)
    Argyle, W. and Preston-Whyte E. (eds.). Social Systems
    and Tradition in Southern Africa. Capetown, South
    Africa: Oxford University Press. 1978.
Ross, R.
    "Sexuality and Slavery at the Cape in the Eighteenth
    Century." (In) University of London (eds.). The
    Societies of Southern Africa in the Nineteenth and
    Twentieth Centuries. London: University of London.
    Institute of Commonwealth Studies. Seminar Papers.
    Volume 8 #22. 1977.
Schreiner, J.
    Divisions of Labour in the Manufacturing Industry in the
    Western Cape, 1950-1965, and the Implications for a
    Materialist Theory of Women's Subordination. African
    Studies Honors Paper: University of Cape Town. Cape
    Town, South Africa. 1981.
Schreiner, Olive
    "The Boer Woman and the Modern Woman's Question." (In)
    Schreiner, Olive. Thoughts on South Africa.
    Johannesburg: Africana Book Society. 1976. pp. 191-220.
Sibisi, Harriet N.
    "How African Women Cope With Migrant Labor in South
    Africa." Signs. Volume 3 #1 Autumn, 1977. pp.
    167-177.
Sibisi, Harriet N.
    "How African Women Cope With Migrant Labor in South
    Africa." (In) Wellesley Editorial Committee. Women and
    National Development: The Complexities of Change.
    Chicago: University of Chicago Press. 1977. pp.
    167-177.
Smedley, L.N.
    "White Housewives: An Introductory Study." South African
    Journal of Sociology. Volume 17 April, 1978. pp.
    61-72.
Spuy, Adelemarie V.
    "Inequitable Legal and Economic Aspects of the
    Discrimination Against Women, Especially Married Women in
    South Africa Today." Plural Societies. Volume 9 #1
    Spring, 1978. pp. 49-58.
Spuy, Adelmarie V.
    "South African Women: The Other Discrimination." Munger
    Africana Library Notes. July, 1978. pp. 1-15.

Steyn, Anna F. and Uys, J.M.
"The Changing Position of Black Women in South Africa."
(In) Lupri, E. (ed.). The Changing Position of Women in
Family and Society. Leiden, Netherlands: Brill. 1983.
pp. 344-370.
Stillman, Eric D. and Shapiro, Colin M.
"Scaling Sex Attitudes and Behavior in South Africa."
Archives of Sexual Behavior. Volume 8 January, 1979.
pp. 1-14.
Thomson, R.C.
Some Discriminatory Laws and Their Effects on African
Women. Cape Town, South Africa: National Union of South
African Students (NUSAS). 1978.
Thomson, R.C.
"Some Discriminatory Laws and Their Effects on African
Women." Jure ac Legibus. Volume 3 1976. pp. 19-24.
Van Der Spuy, A.
"Inequitable Legal and Economic Aspects of the
Discrimination Against Women, Especially Married Women in
South Africa Today." Plural Societies. Volume 9 #1
Spring, 1978. pp. 49-58.
Van Onselen, Charles
"The Witches of Suburbia: Domestic Service on the
Witwatersrand, 1890-1914." (In) Van Onselen, Charles.
Studies in the Social and Economic History of the
Witwatersrand, 1886-1914. New Nineveh, South Africa:
Raven Books. Volume 2. 1982. pp. 1-73.
Whitelaw, D.A.
"Socio-Economic Status and Use of Contraceptives Among
Unmarried Primigravidas in Cape Town." South African
Medical Journal. Volume 64 #18 October 22, 1983. pp.
712-715.
Wright, John
"Control of Women's Labour in the Zulu Kingdom." (In)
Peires, J.B. (ed.). Before and After Shaka: Papers in
Nguni History. Grahamstown, South Africa: Rhodes
University. Institute of Social and Economic Research.
1983. pp. 82-99.
Yawitch, Joanne
"Sexism and the Sexual Division of Labour in South
Africa." Africa Perspective. Volume 13 Spring, 1979.
Zinn, Deborah
"Women's Role Portrayal in the South African Print
Media." B.A. Honors Dissertation: University of the
Witwatersrand. Johannesburg, South Africa. 1983.
Zlotnik, Zia
"Achievement Motivation, Self-Concept, Feminine Role
Perception and Feminity in White Female University
Students." B.A. Honors Dissertation: University of the
Witwatersrand. Johannesburg, South Africa. 1982.

SLAVERY

Beall, J.
"Unwanted Guests: Indian Women in the Context of
Indentured Immigation to the Natal." Paper Presented to
the Conference Commemorating the 150th Anniversary of
Indian Indentured Immigration and the Abolition of
Slaves. Moka, Mauritius. October, 1984.
Cock, Jacklyn
"Settlers, Servants and Slaves on the Eastern Frontier."
South African Outlook. Volume 111 #1301 November, 1979.
pp. 172-178.
Ross, R.
"Sexuality and Slavery at the Cape in the Eighteenth
Century." (In) University of London (eds.). The
Societies of Southern Africa in the Nineteenth and
Twentieth Centuries. London: University of London.
Institute of Commonwealth Studies. Seminar Papers.
Volume 8 #22. 1977.
Ross, Robert
"Oppression, Sexuality and Slavery at the Cape of Good
Hope." Historical Reflections. Volume 6 #2 1979. pp.
421-433.

STATUS OF WOMEN

Africa Bureau
The Status of Black Women in South Africa. London:
Africa Bureau. Document Paper #21. 1979.
Anonymous
The Effects of Apartheid on the Status of Women in South
Africa. New York: United Nations. Centre Against
Apartheid. Notices and Documents. 1978. 26p.
Anonymous
"Effects of Apartheid on the Status of Women in South
Africa." Objective Justice. Volume 10 #1 Spring, 1978.
Anonymous
"Effects of Apartheid on the Status of Women in Southern
Africa." Paper Presented at the World Conference of the
United Nations Decade for Women, Copenhagen, Denmark,
July 14-30, 1980. New York: United Nations. 1980.
Anonymous
"Women and Apartheid." Objective Justice. Volume 12 #1
August, 1980. pp. 25-48.
Anonymous
"General Questions on the Position of Black Women in
South Africa: An Interview With Sheena Duncan, August,
1979." Africa Perspective. Volume 15 August, 1980.
pp. 56-69.
Anonymous
"South Africa: A Bulletin From Within." (In) Morgan,

Robin (ed.). Sisterhood is Global. Garden City, New
York: Anchor Books. 1984. pp. 618-620.
Barrett, J. and Dawber, A. and Klugman, I. and Obery, I. and
Schindler, J. and Yawitch, Joanne
Vukani Makhosikazi. South African Women Speak. London:
Catholic Institute for International Relations. 1985.
Barrett, Jane
"Knitmore: A Study in the Relationship Between Sex and
Class." B.A. Honors Dissertation: University of the
Witwatersrand. Johannesburg, South Africa. 1981.
Beall, J.D.
"Changing Function and Status of Women in Zululand,
1818-1879." Paper Presented to the Development Studies
Research Group. Pietermarizburg, South Africa:
University of Natal. 1982.
Beall, J.D.
"The Changing Role and Status of African Women in the
Political Economy of Colonial Natal." Paper Presented at
the 13th Annual Congress of the Association of
Sociologists of Southern Africa. 1982.
Beall, J.D.
"The Function and Status of African Women in the Social
and Economic Life of Natal and Zululand, 1818-1879."
B.A. Honors Dissertation: University of Natal. Durban,
South Africa. 1981.
Behardien, Gadaja and Lehulere, K. and Shaw, Anita
Domestic Workers in Poverty. Rondebosch, South Africa:
University of Cape Town. SALDRU. School of Economics.
Carnegie Conference Paper #114. 1984. 76p.
Berning, G.
"The Status and Position of Black Women in Natal Between
1845 and 1891." B.A.Honors Dissertation: University of
Natal. Pietermaritzburg, South Africa. 1980.
Boddington, Erica
"Economic Discrimination Against Women in South Africa:
Case Studies Involving White Middle Class Women." B.A.
Honors Dissertation: University of Cape Town. Cape Town,
South Africa. 1977.
Burman, Sandra
"Divorce and the Disadvantaged." (In) Hirschon, Renbee
(ed.). Women and Property, Women as Property. London:
Croom Helm. Oxford Women's Series. 1984.
Cassim, N.A.
"Some Reflections on the Natal Code." Paper Presented at
the Conference on One Hundred Years of the Natal Code.
Kwa-Dlangezwa, South Africa: University of Zululand.
1980.
Cassim, N.A.
"Some Reflections on the Natal Code." Journal of African
Law. Volume 25 #2 Autumn, 1981. pp. 131-135.
Flepp, Caroline
"Women Under Apartheid; A Triple Oppression." UNESCO
Courier. Volume 38 #4 April, 1985. pp. 14-15.

Ginwala, Frene and Mashiane, Shirley
    "Women and Apartheid: Black South African Women Stand on
    the Lowest Rung of the Ladder of Oppression." UNESCO
    Courier. Volume 33 #7 July, 1980. pp. 13-17.
Goodwin, June
    Cry Amandla: South African Women and the Question of
    Power. New York: Holmes and Meier. 1984. 225p.
Hermann, Anne
    "The Flight From Domesticity in Two South African
    Novels." Communications for Gender Research. #5
    Summer, 1985. pp. 1+
Hill, Alison M.
    "Materialist Feminism and South Africa: The Position of
    Black Working Class Women in Contemporary Cape Town."
    B.A. Honors Dissertation: University of Cape Town. Cape
    Town, South Africa. 1983.
Kimble, Judy and Unterhalter, Elaine
    "We Opened the Road for You, You Must Go Forwards: ANC
    Women's Struggles, 1912-1982." Feminist Review. Volume
    12 1982. pp. 11-16.
Kuzwayo, Ellen
    Call Me Woman. London: Women's Press. 1985. 266p.
Lapchick, Richard E. and Urdang, Stephanie
    "The Effects of Apartheid on the Status of Women in
    Employment in South Africa." Paper Presented at the
    World Conference of the United Nations Decade for Women,
    Copenhagen, Denmark, July 14-30, 1980. New York: United
    Nations. 1980. 40p.
Malveaux, J.
    "You Have Struck a Rock--A Note on the Status of Black
    Women in South Africa." Review of Black Political
    Economy. Volume 14 #2/3 1985. pp. 277-284.
Nathan, C.
    "The Legal Status of Black Women in South African
    Society." (In) Saunders, A.J.G. (ed.). Southern Africa
    in Need of Law Reform. Durban, South Africa:
    Butterworth. 1981.
Ntantala, Phyllis
    An African Tragedy: The Black Woman Under Apartheid.
    Detroit, Michigan: Agascha Productions. 1976. 137p.
Poinsette, Cheryl
    "Black Women Under Apartheid: An Introduction." Harvard
    Women's Law Journal. Volume 8 Spring, 1985. pp.
    93-119.
Rivkin, Elizabeth T.
    "The Black Woman in South Africa: An Azanian Profile."
    (In) Steady, Filomina C. (ed.). The Black Woman
    Cross-Culturally. Cambridge, Massachusetts: Schenkman
    Publishing. 1981. pp. 215-230.
Roscani, Luisa
    "Qwa Qwa - Relocation and Survival: The Effects of
    Relocation on Women." B.Soc.Sci. Thesis: University of
    Natal. Durban, South Africa. 1983.

Schmidt, Elizabeth S.
    "Women of South Africa Speak." Africa Today. Volume 31
    #2 1984. pp. 52-54.
Schreiner, Olive
    "The Boer Woman and the Modern Woman's Question." (In)
    Schreiner, Olive. Thoughts on South Africa.
    Johannesburg: Africana Book Society. 1976. pp. 191-220.
United Nations
    The Plight of Black Women in Apartheid South Africa. New
    York: United Nations. Department of Public Information.
    1981. 35p.
United Nations
    The Effects of Apartheid on the Status of Women in
    Southern Africa. New York: United Nations. July, 1980.
United Nations
    "The Effects of Apartheid on the Status of Women in South
    Africa and Namibia." Paper Presented at the United
    Nations World Conference of the United Nations Decade for
    Women: Equality, Development and Peace, Copenhagen,
    Denmark. New York: United Nations. 1980. 37p.
United Nations
    The Effects of Apartheid on the Status of Women in South
    Africa, Namibia and Southern Rhodesia. New York: United
    Nations. 1978.
United Nations Centre Against Apartheid
    "The Effects of Apartheid on the Status of Women in South
    Africa." Black Scholar. Volume 10 #1 September, 1978.
    pp. 11-21.
United Nations Economic Commission for Africa (UNECA)
    Apartheid and the Status of Women. Regional Prepatory
    Meeting of the UNECA Second Regional Conference for the
    Integration of Women in Development. Lusaka, Zambia.
    December 3-7, 1979. Addis Ababa, Ethiopia: UNECA. 1979.
Unterhalter, Beryl
    "Women in Struggle--South Africa." Third World
    Quarterly. Volume 5 #4 1983. pp. 886-893.
Urdang, Stephanie
    "Ensuring a Revolution Within a Revolution." Southern
    Africa. May, 1978. pp. 7-9.
Van Der Spuy, A.
    "South African Women: The Other Discrimination." Munger
    Africana Library Notes. #44. July, 1978. pp. 2-15.
Van Der Spuy, A.
    "Inequitable Legal and Economic Aspects of the
    Discrimination Against Women, Especially Married Women in
    South Africa Today." Plural Societies. Volume 9 #1
    Spring, 1978. pp. 49-58.
Yawittch, Joanne
    "Defining the Issues--Women: Towards a Methodology of
    Women." Work in Progress. Volume 9 August, 1979. pp.
    32-35.

URBANIZATION

Argyle, John
"Some African Meat-Sellers in Durban." Paper Presented
at the Workshop on African Urban Life in Durban in the
Twentieth Century. Johannesburg: University of the
Witwatersrand. October, 1983.
Hoosen, A.A. and Patel, M.
"The Incidence of Selected Vaginal Infections Among
Pregnant Urban Blacks." South African Medical Journal.
Volume 59 #23 May 30, 1981. pp. 827-829.
Kros, Cynthia
"Urban African Women's Organizations and Protest on the
Rand, 1939-1956." B.A. Honors Dissertation: University
of Witwatersrand. Johannesburg. 1978.
Kros, Cynthia
Urban African Women's Organizations and Protest on the
Rand From the Years 1939-1956. Johannesburg: Africa
Perspective Dissertation #3. 1980.
Lotter, Johann M.
"The Effect of Urbanization and Education on the
Fertility of Blacks in South Africa." Humanitas. Volume
4 #1 1977. pp. 21-28.
Mackenzie, D.J.
"African Women and the Urbanization Process in Durban, c.
1920-1949." Paper Presented at the Workshop on African
Urban Life in Durban in the Twentieth Century. Durban,
South Africa: University of Natal. October, 1983.
Radebe, M.D.
"A Study of Matrimonial Breakdown Among Urban Blacks."
M.A. Thesis: University of South Africa. Pretoria, South
Africa. 1978.
Ridd, Rosemary
"Where Women Must Dominate: Response to Oppression in A
South African Urban Community." (In) Ardener, Shirley
(ed.). Women and Space: Ground Rules and Social Maps.
New York: St. Martin's Press. 1981. pp. 187-204.
Segal, I. and Walker, A.R.P. and Coupersmith, J.
"The Prevalence of Gallstones in Urban Black Women."
South African Medical Journal. Volume 68 #7 1985. pp.
530.
Van Der Vliet, Virginia N.
"Black Marriage: Expectations and Aspirations in an Urban
Environment." M.A. Thesis: University of the
Witwatersrand. Johannesburg, South Africa. 1982.
Verster, J.
Trend and Pattern of Fertility in Soweto: An Urban Bantu
Community: A Report on the Fertility Sample Survey of the
Bantu Population in Soweto. Braamfontein, South Africa:
University of the Witwatersrand Press. 1979.
Wells, Julia C.
"Passes and Bypasses: Freedom of Movement for African
Women Under the Urban Areas Act of South Africa." (In)

Hays, Margaret J. and Wright, Marcia (eds.). African Women and the Law: Historical Perspectives. Boston: Boston University. African Studies Center. Boston University Papers on Africa. Volume Seven. 1982. pp. 125-150.

WOMEN AND THEIR CHILDREN

Bhana, Kastoor
"Indian Parents and Their Youth: Some Perceived and Actual Differences." South African Journal of Sociology. Volume 15 #3 August, 1984. pp. 124-128.

Cock, Jacklyn
"Childcare and the Working Mother" Africa Perspective. Volume 26 1985. pp. 29-60.

Hoar, R.N.M.
"The Relevance of Mother's Speech in Communication With the Pre-Verbal Child." M.A. Thesis: University of Natal. Durban, South Africa. 1978.

Nash, Margaret
"Women and Children in Resettlement Areas." South African Outlook. Volume 111 #1324. October, 1981. pp. 154-157.

Peart, Nicola S.
"Civil or Christian Marriage and Customary Unions: The Legal Position of the Discarded Spouse and Children." Comparative and International Law Journal of South Africa. Volume 16 #1 1983. pp. 39-64.

Saling, Michael M. and Cooke, Wendy-Lynne
"Cradling and Transport of Infants by South African Mothers: A Cross Cultural Study." Current Anthropology. Volume 25 #3 1984. pp. 333-335.

Straker, G. and Altman, R.
"Psychological Factors Differentiating Unwed Mothers Keeping Their Babies From Those Placing Them for Adoption." South African Journal of Psychology. Volume 9 #1/2 1979. pp. 55-59.

Van Bart, Dawn
"The Effects of the Mother's Work Experience on Her Preschool Child's Behavior." B.A. Honors Dissertation: University of the Witwatersrand. Johannesburg, South Africa. 1982.

Swaziland

Armstrong, Alice K. and Russell, Margo
    A Situation Analysis of Women in Swaziland. Kwaluseni,
    Swaziland: University of Swaziland. Social Science
    Research Unit. 1985. 105p.
Armstrong, Alice K. and Thandabantu, Nhlapo
    Law and the Other Sex: The Legal Position of Women in
    Swaziland. Kwaluseni, Swaziland: University of
    Swaziland. 1985. 150p.
Chaney, Elsa M.
    A Women in Development Project in Swaziland, Skills
    Training for Income Earning. New York: United Nations.
    Department of Technical Cooperation for Development.
    1982.
Derman, P.J.
    "Stock and Aristocracy: The Political Implications of
    Swazi Marriage." African Studies. Volume 36 #2 1977.
    pp. 119-129.
Ferraro, Gary
    Swazi Marital Patterns and Conjugal Roles: An Analysis
    and Policy Implications. Mbabane, Swaziland: University
    of Swaziland. Mimeograph. 1980.
Green, E.C.
    "Traditional Healers, Mothers and Childhood Diarreal
    Disease in Swaziland--The Interface of Anthropology and
    Health Education." Social Science and Medicine. Volume
    20 #3 1985. pp. 277-285.
Kuper, Adam
    "Rank and Preferential Marriage in Southern Africa: The
    Swazi." Man. Volume 13 #4 December, 1978. pp.
    567-579.
Lewis, Barbara C.
    "The Impact of Development Policies on Women." (In) Hay,
    Margaret J. and Stichter, Sharon (eds.). African Women
    South of the Sahara. New York: Longman. 1984. pp.
    170-187.

Low, Allan
  "From Farm-Homestead Theory to Rural Development Policy
  in Lesotho and Swaziland." (In) de Vletter, Fion (ed.).
  Labour Migration and Agricultural Development in Southern
  Africa. Rome: United Nations Food and Agriculture
  Organization. 1982.
Low, Allan
  Household Economics in Southern Africa. Mbabane,
  Swaziland: University of Swaziland. 1984.
Margo, R.
  The Production and Marketing of Women's Handicrafts in
  Swaziland. Kwaluseni, Swaziland: University of
  Swaziland. Social Science Research Unit. 1983.
Mbatha, Nikiwe D.
  The Ambiguities of Swazi Marriage. Kwaluseni, Swaziland:
  University of Swaziland. Social Science Research Unit.
  Research Paper #5. May, 1983. 10p.
McFadden, Patricia
  "Women in Wage-Labour in Swaziland: a Focus on
  Agriculture." South African Labour Bulletin. Volume 7
  #6 April, 1982. pp. 140-166.
McFadden, Patricia
  "Women in Wage Labour in Agriculture: Focus on
  Swaziland." Women in Southern African History. #2 May,
  1983. pp. 28-32.
Meheus, A. and Ballard, R. and Dlamini, M. and Van Dyck, E.
and Piot, P.
  "Epidemiology and Aetiology of Urethritis in Swaziland."
  International Journal of Epidemiology. Volume 9 1980.
  pp. 239.
Meheus, A.
  "Etiology of Genital Ulcerations in Swaziland." Sexually
  Transmitted Diseases. Volume 10 #1 January-March, 1983.
  pp. 33-35.
Meheus, A.
  "Genital Infections in Prenatal and Family Attendants in
  Swaziland." East African Medical Journal. Volume 57 #3
  March, 1980. pp. 212-217.
Nhlapho, R.T.
  Women and the Law: Report of Proceedings From Two
  Seminars Held in Swaziland. Kwaluseni, Swaziland:
  University of Swaziland. Department of Law. January,
  June, 1983. 93p.
O'Regan, F.
  "Women in Development Project, Swaziland." (In) O'Regan,
  F. and Hellinger, D. (eds.). The Pisces Studies:
  Assisting the Smallest Economic Activities of the Urban
  Poor: Part II Case Studies: Africa. Cambridge,
  Massachusetts: Accion International/AITEC. 1980.
Rosen-Prinz, B.
  Married Women and Taxation in Swaziland. Kwaluseni,
  Swaziland: University of Swaziland. Department of
  Sociology. 1981.

Swaziland. Ministry of Education
    The Survey of Roles, Tasks, Needs, Skills of Rural Women
    in Swaziland, 1978/1979. Mbabane, Swaziland: Ministry of
    Education. 1980.
Tabibian, N.
    Swazi Women's Income Generating Activities. Kwaluseni,
    Swaziland: University of Swaziland. DEMS. 1983.
Tabibian, Nasrin
    Directory of Women's Income-Generating Programmes in
    Swaziland. Amherst, Massachusetts: University of
    Massachusetts. Center for International Education.
    Kwaluseni, Swaziland: University of Swaziland. Division
    of Extra-Mural Services. April, 1983. 13p.
Tabibian, Nasrin
    "Women and Rural Development in Africa: A Case Study of
    Women's Income Generating Activities in Swaziland." Ph.D
    Dissertation: University of Masachusetts. Amherst,
    Massachusetts. 1985. 312p.
Te Riele, M.
    The Position of Rural Women in the Development Process:
    With Particular Reference to Swaziland. Reading England:
    University of Reading. Agricultural Extension and Rural
    Development Centre. 1982.
Wallender, Helena E.
    Demographic and Environmental Factors Affecting Fertility
    Decisions in Swaziland. Kwaluseni, Swaziland: University
    College of Swaziland. 1978. 178p.
Wallender, Helena E.
    "Demographic and Environmental Factors Affecting
    Fertility Decisions in Swaziland." Ph.D Dissertation:
    Michigan State University. Department of Family Ecology.
    East Lansing, Michigan. 1977. 153p.

Zambia

AGRICULTURE

Bardouille, Raj
  Women in the Informal Sector in Zambia: Towards a
  Framework of Analysis. Lusaka, Zambia: University of
  Zambia: Manpower Research Unit. Unpublished. 1981.
Chenoveth, F.A.
  Women in the Food System in Africa. Rome: United Nations
  Food and Agriculture Organization. Consultant Report,
  Zambia Field Document #1. 1984. 63p.
Cliffe, Lionel
  "Labour Migration and Peasant Differentiation: Zambian
  Experiences." Journal of Peasant Studies. Volume 5 #3
  1978. pp. 326-346.
Due, Jean M. and Mudenda, Timothy and Miller, Patricia
  How Do Rural Women Perceive Development? A Case Study in
  Zambia. East Lansing, Michigan: Michigan State
  University. Working Paper #63. August, 1984.
Due, Jean M. and Mudenda, Timothy and Miller, Patricia
  How Do Rural Women Perceive Development? A Case Study in
  Zambia. Urbana, Illinois: University of
  Illinois-Urbana-Champaign. Department of Agricultural
  Economics Staff Paper #83-E-265. 1983.
Due, Jean M.
  "Intra-Household Gender Issues in Farming Systems in
  Tanzania, Zambia and Malawi." (In) Poats, Susan V. and
  Schmink, Marianne and Spring, Anita (eds.). Gender
  Issues in Farming Systems Research and Extension.
  Boulder, Colorado: Westview Press. 1980. pp. 331-344.
Due, Jean M. and Mudenda, Timothy
  Women's Contributions to Farming Systems and Household
  Income in Zambia. East Lansing, Michigan: Michigan State
  University. Women in International Development. Working
  Paper #85. May, 1985. 29p.
Due, Jean M. and Mudenda, Timothy
  Women Made Visible Contributions: Of Farm and Market
  Women to Farming Systems and Household Incomes in
  Zambia. Champaign, Illinois: University of Illinois.

Agricultural Economics Staff Paper #84 E-285. 1984.
Gaobepe, M.G. and Mwenda, A.
    The Report on the Situation and Needs of Food Supplies:
    Women in Zambia. Lusaka, Zambia: United Nations Food and
    Agriculture Organization (FAO). 1980.
Geisler, Gisela G. and Keller, Bonnie B. and Chuzu, Pia M.
    The Needs of Rural Women in Northern Province: Analysis
    and Recommendations. Lusaka, Zambia: Government Printing
    Office. National Commission for Development Planning
    (NCDP). 1985. 138p.
Hansen, Karen T. and Spring, Anita
    "Women's Agricultural Work in Rural Zambia: From
    Valuation to Subordination." Paper Presented at the
    Annual Meeting of the African Studies Association. Paper
    #44. Los Angeles, California. 1979.
Hedlund, H. and Lundahl, M.
    "The Economic Role of Beer in Rural Zambia." Human
    Organization. Volume 43 Spring, 1984. pp. 61-65.
Jiggins, Janice
    "Female Headed Households Among Subsistence Cultivators
    in the Central and Northern Provinces of Zambia." Paper
    Presented at the Workshop on Women in Agricultural
    Production in Eastern and Southern Africa. Nairobi,
    Kenya. April 9-11, 1984.
Kamfwa, Franklin D.
    "Contributions of Women's Clubs to Rural Development in
    Ndola Rural East." Journal of Adult Education, Lusaka.
    Volume 1 #1 September, 1982. pp. 42-54.
Muntemba, M. Shimwaayi
    "Women as Food Producers and Suppliers in the 20th
    Century: The Case of Zambia." Development Dialogue.
    #1/2 1982. pp. 29-50.
Muntemba, M. Shimwaayi
    "Women and Agricultural Change in the Railway Region of
    Zambia: Dispossession and Counter Strategies, 1930-1970."
    (In) Bay, Edna (ed.). Women and Work in Africa.
    Boulder, Colorado: Westview Press. 1982. pp. 83-103.
Muntemba, M. Shimwaayi
    "The Changing Position of Women in Zambia as Food
    Producers and Suppliers: The 20th Century Experience."
    Paper Presented at the Conference on the History of the
    Family in Africa. London: Cambridge University. School
    of Oriental and African Studies. September, 1981.
Muntemba, Maude
    "The Underdevelopment of Peasant Agriculture in Zambia."
    Journal of Southern African Studies. Volume 5 #1 1978.
    pp. 58-85.
Safilios-Rothschild, C.
    The Policy Implications of the Roles of Women in
    Agriculture in Zambia. Lusaka, Zambia: Zambian Ministry
    of Agriculture and Water Development. National
    Commission for Development Planning. Planning Division
    Special Studies #20. November, 1985. 49p.
Spring, Anita and Hansen, Art
    "Women's Agricultural Work in Rural Zambia: From

Valuation to Subordination." Paper Presented at the
Annual Meeting of the African Studies Association. Paper
#44. Los Angeles, California. October 31, 1979. 25p.
Spring, Anita and Hansen, Art
"The Underside of Development: Agricultural Development
and Women in Zambia." Agriculture and Human Values.
Volume 2 #2 1985. pp. 60-67.
Wright, Marcia
"Technology, Marriage and Women's Work in the History of
Maize-Growers in Mazabuka, Zambia: A Reconnaissance."
Journal of Southern African Studies. Volume 10 #1
October, 1983. pp. 71-85.
Yates, Leslie M.
Integration of Women in Development in Zambia, Botswana
and Lesotho: AID's Efforts. Washington, D.C.: U.S.
Department of State. U.S. Agency for International
Development. Southern Africa Development Analysis.
1978. 92p.
Yates, Leslie M.
Integration of Women in Development in Southern Africa:
An Evaluation With Recommendations for U.S. AID Programs
in Botswana, Lesotho and Zambia. Sadex.
November-December, 1979. pp. 1-15.

ARTS

Dillon-Malone, Clive M.
The Korsten Basket Makers. Lusaka, Zambia: University of
Zambia. Institute for African Studies. 1978.

BIBLIOGRAPHIES

Bardouille, R.
An Annotated Bibliography of Research on Zambian Women.
Lusaka, Zambia: Zambia Association for Research and
Development. 1985. 159p.

CULTURAL ROLES

Ali, M.R.
A Study of Knowledge About Attitude Towards, and Practice
of Family Planning in Zambia. Lusaka, Zambia: University
of Zambia. Department of Psychology. Psychological
Studies: Reports of the Psychology Department. #7.
December, 1984. 51p.
Ault, James
"Making 'Modern' Marriage 'Traditional': State Power and
the Regulation of Marriage in Colonial Zambia." Theory
and Society. Volume 12 1983. pp. 181-210.
Ault, Jim
Traditionalizing 'Modern' Marriage: A Neglected Aspect of
Social Struggle on the Zambian Copperbelt. Mimeo. 1976.

Azefor, M.
"Family Household Statistics and Change in Zambia."
Paper Prepared for Feedback Seminar on Joint
ECA/Government of Zambia Survey on Interrelations Among
Infant and Childhood Mortality, Socio-Economic Factors
and Fertility. Kabwe, Zambia: United Nations Economic
Commission for Africa. April, 1982.

Bardouille, Raj
The Sexual Division of Labour in the Urban Informal
Sector: A Case Study of Lusaka, Zambia. Lusaka, Zambia:
University of Zambia. Manpower Research Unit.
Unpublished. 1981.

Bardouille, Raj
"The Sexual Division of Labour in the Urban Informal
Sector: The Case of Some Townships in Lusaka." African
Social Research. #32 1981. pp. 29-54.

Bardouille, Raj
"The Sexual Division of Labour in the Urban Informal
Sector: A Case Study of Lusaka." (In) Woldring, Klaus
and Chibaye, Chibwe (eds.). Beyond Political
Independence: Zambia's Development Predicament in the
1980's. Berlin, Germany: Moutan. 1984. pp. 161-182.

Bardouille, Raj
Women in the Informal Sector in Zambia: Towards a
Framework of Analysis. Lusaka, Zambia: University of
Zambia: Manpower Research Unit. Unpublished. 1981.

Canter, Richard S.
"Family Dispute: Settlement and the Zambian Judiciary:
Local Level Legal Adaptation." (In) Roberts, Simon
(ed.). Law and the Family in Africa. Hague,
Netherlands: Mouton. 1977. pp. 69-91.

Chanock, Martin
"Making Customary Law: Men, Women and Courts in Colonial
Northern Rhodesia." (In) Hay, M.J. and Wright, M.
(eds.). African Women and the Law: Historical
Perspectives. Boston: Boston University. Papers on
Africa. Volume 7 1982. pp. 53-67.

Chauncey, George
"The Locus of Reproduction: Women's Labour in the Zambian
Copperbelt, 1927-1953." Journal of Southern African
Studies. Volume 7 #2 April, 1981. pp. 135-164.

Chenoveth, F.A.
Women in the Food System in Africa. Rome: United Nations
Food and Agriculture Organization. Consultant Report,
Zambia Field Document #1. 1984. 63p.

Clarke, Sarah H.
The Position of Women in Education and Employment in
Zambia: Some Problems Worthy of Further Research.
Lusaka, Zambia: Unpublished Manuscript. 1976.

Cliffe, Lionel
"Labour Migration and Peasant Differentiation: Zambian
Experiences." Journal of Peasant Studies. Volume 5 #3
1978. pp. 326-346.

Crehan, Kate
"Women and Development in Northwest Zambia: From Producer

to Housewife." Review of African Political Economy. #27/28 1984. pp. 51-66.

Cutshall, Charles R.
The Role of Women in Disputing Among the Ila of Zambia: Political Adaptation in Legal Change. Boston: Boston University. African Studies Center. Working Paper #46. 1981. 50p.

Cutshall, Charles R. and McCold, Paul E.
"Patterns of Stock Theft Victimization and Formal Response Strategies Among the Ila of Zambia." Victimology. Volume 9 #1 1984. pp. 181+.

Dillon-Malone, Clive M.
The Korsten Basket Makers. Lusaka, Zambia: University of Zambia. Institute for African Studies. 1978.

Due, Jean M. and Mudenda, Timothy (eds.).
Women's Contributions Made Visible: Of Farm and Market Women to Farming Systems and Household Incomes in Zambia, 1982. Urbana, Illinois: University of Illinois. Department of Agriculture Economics. Staff Paper #285. 1984. 45p.

Due, Jean M.
"Intra-Household Gender Issues in Farming Systems in Tanzania, Zambia and Malawi." (In) Poats, Susan V. and Schmink, Marianne and Spring, Anita (eds.). Gender Issues in Farming Systems Research and Extension. Boulder, Colorado: Westview Press. 1980. pp. 331-344.

Due, Jean M. and Mudenda, Timothy
Women's Contributions to Farming Systems and Household Income in Zambia. East Lansing, Michigan: Michigan State University. Women in International Development. Working Paper #85. May, 1985. 29p.

Due, Jean M. and Mudenda, Timothy
Women Made Visible Contributions: Of Farm and Market Women to Farming Systems and Household Incomes in Zambia. Champaign, Illinois: University of Illinois. Agricultural Economics Staff Paper #84 E-285. 1984.

Epstein, Arnold L.
Urbanization and Kinship: The Domestic Domain on the Copperbelt of Zambia, 1950-1956. New York: Academic Press. 1981. 364p.

Freund, Paul J. and Kalumba, Katele
"Maternal Health and Child Survival Rates in Zambia: A Comparative Community Study." Medical Journal of Zambia. Volume 18 #2 June, 1984.

Gaobepe, M.G. and Mwenda, A.
The Report on the Situation and Needs of Food Supplies: Women in Zambia. Lusaka, Zambia: United Nations Food and Agriculture Organization (FAO). 1980.

Geisler, Gisela G. and Keller, Bonnie B. and Chuzu, Pia M.
The Needs of Rural Women in Northern Province: Analysis and Recommendations. Lusaka, Zambia: Government Printing Office. National Commission for Development Planning (NCDP). 1985. 138p.

Hansen, Karen T.
"When Sex Becomes a Critical Variable: Married Women and

Extra-Domestic Work in Lusaka, Zambia." African Social Research. #30 December, 1980. pp. 831-850.

Hansen, Karen T.
"Planning Productive Work for Married Women in a Low-Income Settlement in Lusaka: The Case for a Small Scale Handicrafts Industry." African Social Research. #33 1982. pp. 211-223.

Hansen, Karen T.
"Prospects for Wage Labor Among Married Women in Lusaka, Zambia." Paper Presented at the Annual Meeting of the African Studies Association. Paper #31. Houston, Texas. 1977. 24p.

Hansen, Karen T.
"The Work History: Disaggregating the Changing Terms of Poor Women's Entry into Lusaka's Labour Force." Paper Presented at the Annual Meeting of the African Studies Association. Paper #38. Washington, D.C. November 4-7, 1982.

Hansen, Karen T.
"When Sex Becomes a Critical Variable: Married Women and Extradomestic Work in Lusaka, Zambia." Paper Presented at the Annual Meeting of the African Studies Association. Paper #45. Los Angeles, California. 1979. 22p.

Hansen, Karen T. and Spring, Anita
"Women's Agricultural Work in Rural Zambia: From Valuation to Subordination." Paper Presented at the Annual Meeting of the African Studies Association. Paper #44. Los Angeles, California. 1979.

Hansen, Karen T.
"Negotiating Sex and Gender in Urban Zambia." Journal of Southern African Studies. Volume 10 #2 April, 1984. pp. 219-238.

Hansen, Karen T.
Zambian Women and Access to Urban Labor. Seattle, Washington: University of Washington. 1978.

Hansen, Karen T.
"The Urban Informal Sector as a Development Issue: Poor Women and Work in Lusaka, Zambia." Urban Anthropology. Volume 9 #2 Summer, 1980. pp. 199-226.

Hansen, Karen T.
Gender Ideology and Work Prospects: The Beer and Sex Link in Urban Zambia. Mimeo. 1983.

Hedlund, H. and Lundahl, M.
"The Economic Role of Beer in Rural Zambia." Human Organization. Volume 43 Spring, 1984. pp. 61-65.

Himonga, C.N.
"Some Aspects of the Zambian Marriage Act." Zambia Law Journal. Volume 11 1979. pp. 23-44.

Hussain, S.J.
"Breakdown of Marriage in Zambia: Judicial Response and Challenge." Zambia Law Journal. Volume 13 1981.

Jiggins, Janice
"Female Headed Households Among Subsistence Cultivators in the Central and Northern Provinces of Zambia." Paper Presented at the Workshop on Women in Agricultural

Production in Eastern and Southern Africa. Nairobi,
Kenya. April 9-11, 1984.
Jules-Rosette, Bennetta
Women's Work in the Informal Sector: A Zambian Case
Study. San Diego, California: University of California,
San Diego. 1981. 24p.
Jules-Rosette, Bennetta
Women's Work in the Informal Sector: A Zambian Case
Study. East Lansing, Michigan: Michigan State
University. Office of Women in International
Development. WID Working Papers #3. 1982. 24p.
Konie, Gwendoline
"Zambia: Feminist Progress-More Difficult than
Decolonization." (In) Morgan, Robin (ed.). Sisterhood
is Global. Garden City, New York: Anchor Books. 1984.
pp. 739-745.
Kwofie, Kwamie and Brew-Graves, Ekow and Adika, G.H.
"Malnutrition and Pregnancy Wastage in Zambia." Social
Science and Medicine. Volume 17 #9 1983. pp. 539-543.
Lancaster, Chet S.
The Goba of the Zambezi: Sex Roles, Economics and Change.
Norman, Oklahoma: University of Oklahoma Press. 1981.
350p.
Mbikusita-Lewanika, Inonge
"Kinship Terms and Family Relationships: The Case of
Bulozi-Zambia." Paper Presented at the Seminar on the
Changing Family in the African Context, Maseru,
Lesotho, 1983. Paris: United Nations Educational,
Scientific and Cultural Organization. 1984. 16p.
Mburugu, Edward K.
"Structural Moderization and Differential Fertility in
Zambia." Ph.D Dissertation: University of
Wisconsin-Madison. Madison, Wisconsin. 1978. 190p.
Merry, Sally E.
"The Articulation of Legal Spheres." (In) Hays, Margaret
J. and Wright, Marcia (eds.). African Women and the Law:
Historical Perspectives. Boston, Masachusetts: Boston
University. 1982. pp. 68-89.
Munachonga, Monica
The Conjugal Power Relationship: An Urban Case Study in
Zambia. Sussex, England: Sussex University. 1984.
Muntemba, M. Shimwaayi·
"Women as Food Producers and Suppliers in the 20th
Century: The Case of Zambia." Development Dialogue.
#1/2 1982. pp. 29-50.
Muntemba, M. Shimwaayi
"The Changing Position of Women in Zambia as Food
Producers and Suppliers: The 20th Century Experience."
Paper Presented at the Conference on the History of the
Family in Africa. London: Cambridge University. School
of Oriental and African Studies. September, 1981.
Muntemba, M. Shimwaayi
"Dispossession and Counter Strategies in Zambia,
1930-1970." Development: Seeds of Change. #4 1984. pp.
15-17.

ZAMBIA

Muntemba, Maude
"The Underdevelopment of Peasant Agriculture in Zambia."
Journal of Southern African Studies. Volume 5 #1 1978.
pp. 58-85.
Nag, Prithvish
"The Role of Women in Internal Migration in Zambia."
Population Geography. Volume 5 #1-2 June-December,
1983. pp. 60-69.
Ngulube, Clare
"Marriage in Zambia." Africa Woman. #12
November-December, 1977. pp. 62-63.
Ngwisha, Kaluba J.
"Urbanization and Family Structure: A Study of the Family
on the Copperbelt of Zambia." Ph.D Dissertation:
Brandeis University. Florence Heller Graduate School for
Advanced Studies in Social Welfare. Waltham,
Massachusetts. 1978. 463p.
Parpart, Jane L.
Working Class Wives and Collective Labor Action on the
Northern Rhodesian Copperbelt, 1926-1964. Boston: Boston
University. African Studies Center. Working Paper #98.
1985.
Parpart, Jane L.
Class and Gender on the Copperbelt: Women in Northern
Rhodesian Copper Mining Areas, 1926-1964. Boston: Boston
University. African Studies Center. Working Paper #77.
1983. 29p.
Perrings, Charles
"Consciousness, Conflict and Proletarianization: An
Assessment of the 1935 Mineworkers' Strike on the
Northern Rhodesian Copperbelt." Journal of Southern
African Studies. Volume 4 #1 October, 1977. pp. 31-51.
Poewe, Karla O.
"Matriliny in the Throes of Change: Kinship, Descent and
Marriage in Luapula, Zambia." Part One. Africa. Volume
48 #3 1978. pp. 205-367.
Poewe, Karla O.
"Matriliny in the Throes of Change: Kinship, Descent and
Marriage in Luapula, Zambia." Part Two. Africa. Volume
48 #4 1978. pp. 353-367.
Poewe, Karla O.
"Marriage, Descent and Kinship: On the Differential
Primacy of Institutions in Luapula and Longana." Africa.
Volume 50 #1 1980. pp. 73-95.
Poewe, Karla O.
Matrilineal Ideology: Male-Female Dynamics in Luapula,
Zambia. New York: Academic Press. For the International
African Institute. 1981. 140p.
Poewe, Karla O.
"Religion, Matriliny and Change: Jehovah's Witnesses and
Seventh-Day Adventists in Luapula, Zambia." American
Ethnologist. Volume 5 #2 1978.
Rennie, J.K.
"Cattle, Conflict and Court-Cases: The Praise Poetry of
Ila Leadership." Research in African Literatures.

461

Volume 15 #4 1984. pp. 530-567.
Richards, Audrey I.
   Chisungu: a Girls' Initiation Ceremony Among the Bemba of
   Zambia. New York: Tavistock. 1982. 224p.
Schuster, Ilsa M.
   Cycles of Dependence and Independence: Westernization and
   the African Heritage of Lusaka's Young Women. East
   Lansing, Michigan: Michigan State University. Office of
   Women in International Development. Working Paper #7.
   June, 1982. 30p.
Schuster, Ilsa M.
   New Women of Lusaka. Palo Alto, California: Mayfield
   Publishing. Explorations in World Ethnology. 1979.
   209p.
Schuster, Ilsa M.
   "Constraints and Opportunities in Political
   Participation: The Case of Zambian Women."
   Geneve-Afrique. Volume 21 #2 1983. pp. 7-37.
Schuster, Ilsa M.
   "Marginal Lives: Conflict and Contradiction in the
   Position of Female Traders in Lusaka, Zambia." (In) Bay,
   Edna G. (ed.). Women and Work in Africa. Boulder,
   Colorado: Westview Press. Westview Special Studies in
   Africa. 1982. pp. 105-126.
Schuster, Ilsa M.
   "Marginal Lives: Conflict and Contradiction in the
   Position of Female Traders in Lusaka, Zambia." Paper
   Presented at the Symposium, Women and Work in Africa.
   Urbana, Illinois: University of Illinois-Urbana. April
   29-May 1, 1979.
Schuster, Ilsa M.
   "Constraints and Opportunities in Political
   Participation: The Case of Zambian Women." Paper
   Presented at the Workshop on Women in the African
   Political Process. London: University of London. School
   of Oriental and African Studies. 1981. September 22,
   1982.
Spring, Anita
   "Women's Rituals and Natality Among the Luvale of
   Zambia." Ph.D Dissertation: Cornell University. Ithaca,
   New York. 1976. 258p.
Spring, Anita
   "An Indigenous Therapeutic Style and Its Consequences for
   Natality: The Luvale of Zambia." (In) Marshall, John F.
   and Polgar, Steven (eds.). Culture, Natality and Family
   Planning. Chapel Hill, North Carolina: University of
   North Carolina. Carolina Population Center. 1976. pp.
   99-125.
Spring, Anita
   "Epidemiology of Spirit Possession Among the Luvale of
   Zambia." (In) Hoch-Smith, Judith and Spring, Anita
   (eds.). Women in Ritual and Symbolic Roles. New York:
   Plenum Press. 1978. pp. 165-190.
Spring, Anita and Hansen, Art
   "Women's Agricultural Work in Rural Zambia: From

Valuation to Subordination." Paper Presented at the
Annual Meeting of the African Studies Association. Paper
#44. Los Angeles, California. October 31, 1979. 25p.
Tembo, Lyson P.
"The Changing Family in the African Context: The Zambian
Case." Paper Presented at the Seminar on the Changing
Family in the African Context, Maseru, Lesotho, 1983.
Paris: United Nations Educational, Scientific and
Cultural Organization. 1984. 21p.
Van Binsbergen, Wim M.
"Law in Context of Nkoya Society." (In) Roberts, Simon
(ed.). Law and the Family in Africa. Hague,
Netherlands: Mouton. 1977. pp. 39-68.
Van Rouveroy van Nieuwall, Emile and Van Rouveroy van
Nieuwall, Els
"To Claim or Not to Claim: Changing Views About the
Restitution of Marriage Prestations Among the Anufom in
Northern Tonga." (In) Roberts, Simon (ed.). Law and the
Family in Africa. Hague, Netherlands: Mouton. 1977.
pp. 93-115.
Wenlock, R.W.
"Birth Spacing and Prolonged Lactation in Rural Zambia."
Journal of Biosocial Science. Volume 9 #4 October,
1977. pp. 481-485.
Wright, Marcia
"Justice, Women and the Social Order in Abercorn,
Northeastern Rhodesia, 1898-1903." (In) Hay, M.J. and
Wright, M. (eds.). African Women and the Law: Historical
Perspectives. Boston: Boston University. African
Studies Center. Boston University Papers on Africa.
Volume Seven. 1982. pp. 33-50.
Wright, Marcia
"Technology, Marriage and Women's Work in the History of
Maize-Growers in Mazabuka, Zambia: A Reconnaissance."
Journal of Southern African Studies. Volume 10 #1
October, 1983. pp. 71-85.

DEVELOPMENT AND TECHNOLOGY

Akerele, Olubanke
Women Workers in Ghana, Kenya, Zambia: A Comparative
Analysis of Women's Employment in the Modern Wage
Sector. Addis Ababa, Ethiopia: United Nations Economic
Commission for Africa. African Training and Research
Center for Women. 1979. 109p.
Bardouille, Raj
The Sexual Division of Labour in the Urban Informal
Sector: A Case Study of Lusaka, Zambia. Lusaka, Zambia:
University of Zambia. Manpower Research Unit.
Unpublished. 1981.
Bardouille, Raj
"The Sexual Division of Labour in the Urban Informal
Sector: The Case of Some Townships in Lusaka." African
Social Research. #32 1981. pp. 29-54.

Bardouille, Raj
"The Sexual Division of Labour in the Urban Informal
Sector: A Case Study of Lusaka." (In) Woldring, Klaus
and Chibaye, Chibwe (eds.). Beyond Political
Independence: Zambia's Development Predicament in the
1980's. Berlin, Germany: Moutan. 1984. pp. 161-182.

Bardouille, Raj
Women in the Informal Sector in Zambia: Towards a
Framework of Analysis. Lusaka, Zambia: University of
Zambia: Manpower Research Unit. Unpublished. 1981.

Chenoveth, F.A.
Women in the Food System in Africa. Rome: United Nations
Food and Agriculture Organization. Consultant Report,
Zambia Field Document #1. 1984. 63p.

Crehan, Kate
"Women and Development in Northwest Zambia: From Producer
to Housewife." Review of African Political Economy.
#27/28 1984. pp. 51-66.

Due, Jean M. and Mudenda, Timothy and Miller, Patricia
How Do Rural Women Perceive Development? A Case Study in
Zambia. East Lansing, Michigan: Michigan State
University. Working Paper #63. August, 1984.

Due, Jean M. and Mudenda, Timothy and Miller, Patricia
How Do Rural Women Perceive Development? A Case Study in
Zambia. Urbana, Illinois: University of
Illinois-Urbana-Champaign. Department of Agricultural
Economics Staff Paper #83-E-265. 1983.

Due, Jean M. and White, M.
Differences in Earnings, Labor Input, Decision Making,
and Perceptions of Development Between Farm and Market
Women: A Case Study of Zambia. Urbana, Illinois:
University of Illinois-Urbana-Champaign. Department of
Agricultural Economics. Agricultural Economics Staff
Paper #83-E-319. 1983.

Due, Jean M. and Mudenda, Timothy
Women's Contributions to Farming Systems and Household
Income in Zambia. East Lansing, Michigan: Michigan State
University. Women in International Development. Working
Paper #85. May, 1985. 29p.

Due, Jean M. and Mudenda, Timothy
Women Made Visible Contributions: Of Farm and Market
Women to Farming Systems and Household Incomes in
Zambia. Champaign, Illinois: University of Illinois.
Agricultural Economics Staff Paper #84 E-285. 1984.

Geisler, Gisela G. and Keller, Bonnie B. and Chuzu, Pia M.
The Needs of Rural Women in Northern Province: Analysis
and Recommendations. Lusaka, Zambia: Government Printing
Office. National Commission for Development Planning
(NCDP). 1985. 138p.

Hansen, Karen T.
"The Urban Informal Sector as a Development Issue: Poor
Women and Work in Lusaka, Zambia." Urban Anthropology.
Volume 9 #2 Summer, 1980. pp. 199-226.

Jiggins, Janice
"Female Headed Households Among Subsistence Cultivators

in the Central and Northern Provinces of Zambia." Paper
Presented at the Workshop on Women in Agricultural
Production in Eastern and Southern Africa. Nairobi,
Kenya. April 9-11, 1984.

Jules-Rosette, Bennetta
Women's Work in the Informal Sector: A Zambian Case
Study. San Diego, California: University of California,
San Diego. 1981. 24p.

Jules-Rosette, Bennetta
Women's Work in the Informal Sector: A Zambian Case
Study. East Lansing, Michigan: Michigan State
University. Office of Women in International
Development. WID Working Papers #3. 1982. 24p.

Kamfwa, Franklin D.
"Contributions of Women's Clubs to Rural Development in
Ndola Rural East." Journal of Adult Education, Lusaka.
Volume 1 #1 September, 1982. pp. 42-54.

Keller, Bonnie B.
Report on Current Efforts to Integrate Zambian Women in
Development. Lusaka, Zambia: University of Zambia.
Department of African Development Studies. 1984.

Keller, Bonnie B.
The Integration of Zambian Women in Development. Lusaka,
Zambia: NORAD. November, 1984. 71p.

Muntemba, M. Shimwaayi
"Women as Food Producers and Suppliers in the 20th
Century: The Case of Zambia." Development Dialogue.
#1/2 1982. pp. 29-50.

Muntemba, M. Shimwaayi
"Women and Agricultural Change in the Railway Region of
Zambia: Dispossession and Counter Strategies, 1930-1970."
(In) Bay, Edna (ed.). Women and Work in Africa.
Boulder, Colorado: Westview Press. 1982. pp. 83-103.

Muntemba, M. Shimwaayi
"The Changing Position of Women in Zambia as Food
Producers and Suppliers: The 20th Century Experience."
Paper Presented at the Conference on the History of the
Family in Africa. London: Cambridge University. School
of Oriental and African Studies. September, 1981.

Muntemba, M. Shimwaayi
"Dispossession and Counter Strategies in Zambia,
1930-1970." Development: Seeds of Change. #4 1984. pp.
15-17.

Muntemba, Maude
"The Underdevelopment of Peasant Agriculture in Zambia."
Journal of Southern African Studies. Volume 5 #1 1978.
pp. 58-85.

Mwanamwabwa, Catherine
Suggested Income Generating Activities for Women:
Proposal for a Pilot Program. Lusaka, Zambia. August,
1977.

Safilios-Rothschild, C.
The Policy Implications of the Roles of Women in
Agriculture in Zambia. Lusaka, Zambia: Zambian Ministry
of Agriculture and Water Development. National

Commission for Development Planning. Planning Division
Special Studies #20. November, 1985. 49p.

Schuster, Ilsa M.
Cycles of Dependence and Independence: Westernization and
the African Heritage of Lusaka's Young Women. East
Lansing, Michigan: Michigan State University. Office of
Women in International Development. Working Paper #7.
June, 1982. 30p.

Schuster, Ilsa M.
Female White Collar Workers: A Case Study of Successful
Development in Lusaka, Zambia. East Lansing, Michigan:
Michigan State University. Office of Women in
International Development. Working Paper #29. August,
1983. 31p.

Schuster, Ilsa M.
"Perspectives in Development: The Problem of Nurses and
Nursing in Zambia." Journal of Development Studies.
Volume 17 #3 April, 1981. pp. 77-99.

Schuster, Ilsa M.
New Women of Lusaka. Palo Alto, California: Mayfield
Publishing. Explorations in World Ethnology. 1979.
209p.

Spring, Anita and Hansen, Art
"The Underside of Development: Agricultural Development
and Women in Zambia." Agriculture and Human Values.
Volume 2 #2 1985. pp. 60-67.

Tembo, Lyson P.
"The Changing Family in the African Context: The Zambian
Case." Paper Presented at the Seminar on the Changing
Family in the African Context, Maseru, Lesotho, 1983.
Paris: United Nations Educational, Scientific and
Cultural Organization. 1984. 21p.

United Nations Economic Commission for Africa (UNECA)
African Women's Employment in the Modern Wage Sector.
Background Document. Regional Prepatory Meeting of the
U.N. Economic Commission for Africa Second Regional
Conference for the Integration of Women in Development.
Lusaka, Zambia. Addis Ababa, Ethiopia: UNECA. December
3-7, 1979.

Wright, Marcia
"Technology, Marriage and Women's Work in the History of
Maize-Growers in Mazabuka, Zambia: A Reconnaissance."
Journal of Southern African Studies. Volume 10 #1
October, 1983. pp. 71-85.

Yates, Leslie M.
Integration of Women in Development in Zambia, Botswana
and Lesotho: AID's Efforts. Washington, D.C.: U.S.
Department of State. U.S. Agency for International
Development. Southern Africa Development Analysis.
1978. 92p.

Yates, Leslie M.
Integration of Women in Development in Southern Africa:
An Evaluation With Recommendations for U.S. AID Programs
in Botswana, Lesotho and Zambia. Sadex.
November-December, 1979. pp. 1-15.

ECONOMICS

Akerele, Olubanke
   Women Workers in Ghana, Kenya, Zambia: A Comparative
   Analysis of Women's Employment in the Modern Wage
   Sector. Addis Ababa, Ethiopia: United Nations Economic
   Commission for Africa. African Training and Research
   Center for Women. 1979. 109p.
Bardouille, Raj
   The Sexual Division of Labour in the Urban Informal
   Sector: A Case Study of Lusaka, Zambia. Lusaka, Zambia:
   University of Zambia. Manpower Research Unit.
   Unpublished. 1981.
Bardouille, Raj
   "The Sexual Division of Labour in the Urban Informal
   Sector: The Case of Some Townships in Lusaka." African
   Social Research. #32 1981. pp. 29-54.
Bardouille, Raj
   "The Sexual Division of Labour in the Urban Informal
   Sector: A Case Study of Lusaka." (In) Woldring, Klaus
   and Chibaye, Chibwe (eds.). Beyond Political
   Independence: Zambia's Development Predicament in the
   1980's. Berlin, Germany: Moutan. 1984. pp. 161-182.
Chenoveth, F.A.
   Women in the Food System in Africa. Rome: United Nations
   Food and Agriculture Organization. Consultant Report,
   Zambia Field Document #1. 1984. 63p.
Clarke, Sarah H.
   The Position of Women in Education and Employment in
   Zambia: Some Problems Worthy of Further Research.
   Lusaka, Zambia: Unpublished Manuscript. 1976.
Cliffe, Lionel
   "Labour Migration and Peasant Differentiation: Zambian
   Experiences." Journal of Peasant Studies. Volume 5 #3
   1978. pp. 326-346.
Crehan, Kate
   "Women and Development in Northwest Zambia: From Producer
   to Housewife." Review of African Political Economy.
   #27/28 1984. pp. 51-66.
Dillon-Malone, Clive M.
   The Korsten Basket Makers. Lusaka, Zambia: University of
   Zambia. Institute for African Studies. 1978.
Due, Jean M. and Mudenda, Timothy (eds.).
   Women's Contributions Made Visible: Of Farm and Market
   Women to Farming Systems and Household Incomes in Zambia,
   1982. Urbana, Illinois: University of Illinois.
   Department of Agriculture Economics. Staff Paper #285.
   1984. 45p.
Due, Jean M. and White, M.
   Differences in Earnings, Labor Input, Decision Making,
   and Perceptions of Development Between Farm and Market
   Women: A Case Study of Zambia. Urbana, Illinois:
   University of Illinois-Urbana-Champaign. Department of

Agricultural Economics. Agricultural Economics Staff
Paper #83-E-319. 1983.
Due, Jean M.
"Intra-Household Gender Issues in Farming Systems in
Tanzania, Zambia and Malawi." (In) Poats, Susan V. and
Schmink, Marianne and Spring, Anita (eds.). Gender
Issues in Farming Systems Research and Extension.
Boulder, Colorado: Westview Press. 1980. pp. 331-344.
Due, Jean M. and Mudenda, Timothy
Women's Contributions to Farming Systems and Household
Income in Zambia. East Lansing, Michigan: Michigan State
University. Women in International Development. Working
Paper #85. May, 1985. 29p.
Due, Jean M. and Mudenda, Timothy
Women Made Visible Contributions: Of Farm and Market
Women to Farming Systems and Household Incomes in
Zambia. Champaign, Illinois: University of Illinois.
Agricultural Economics Staff Paper #84 E-285. 1984.
Hansen, Karen T.
"When Sex Becomes a Critical Variable: Married Women and
Extra-Domestic Work in Lusaka, Zambia." African Social
Research. #30 December, 1980. pp. 831-850.
Hansen, Karen T.
"Planning Productive Work for Married Women in a
Low-Income Settlement in Lusaka: The Case for a Small
Scale Handicrafts Industry." African Social Research.
#33 1982. pp. 211-223.
Hansen, Karen T.
"Prospects for Wage Labor Among Married Women in Lusaka,
Zambia." Paper Presented at the Annual Meeting of the
African Studies Association. Paper #31. Houston, Texas.
1977. 24p.
Hansen, Karen T.
"The Work History: Disaggregating the Changing Terms of
Poor Women's Entry into Lusaka's Labour Force." Paper
Presented at the Annual Meeting of the African Studies
Association. Paper #38. Washington, D.C. November 4-7,
1982.
Hansen, Karen T.
"When Sex Becomes a Critical Variable: Married Women and
Extradomestic Work in Lusaka, Zambia." Paper Presented
at the Annual Meeting of the African Studies Association.
Paper #45. Los Angeles, California. 1979. 22p.
Hansen, Karen T.
Zambian Women and Access to Urban Labor. Seattle,
Washington: University of Washington. 1978.
Hansen, Karen T.
"The Urban Informal Sector as a Development Issue: Poor
Women and Work in Lusaka, Zambia." Urban Anthropology.
Volume 9 #2 Summer, 1980. pp. 199-226.
Hedlund, H. and Lundahl, M.
"The Economic Role of Beer in Rural Zambia." Human
Organization. Volume 43 Spring, 1984. pp. 61-65.
Jules-Rosette, Bennetta
Women's Work in the Informal Sector: A Zambian Case

Study. San Diego, California: University of California,
San Diego. 1981. 24p.

Jules-Rosette, Bennetta
Women's Work in the Informal Sector: A Zambian Case
Study. East Lansing, Michigan: Michigan State
University. Office of Women in International
Development. WID Working Papers #3. 1982. 24p.

Kamfwa, Franklin D.
"Contributions of Women's Clubs to Rural Development in
Ndola Rural East." Journal of Adult Education, Lusaka.
Volume 1 #1 September, 1982. pp. 42-54.

Keller, Bonnie B.
Report on Current Efforts to Integrate Zambian Women in
Development. Lusaka, Zambia: University of Zambia.
Department of African Development Studies. 1984.

Keller, Bonnie B.
The Integration of Zambian Women in Development. Lusaka,
Zambia: NORAD. November, 1984. 71p.

Muntemba, M. Shimwaayi
"Women as Food Producers and Suppliers in the 20th
Century: The Case of Zambia." Development Dialogue.
#1/2 1982. pp. 29-50.

Muntemba, M. Shimwaayi
"Women and Agricultural Change in the Railway Region of
Zambia: Dispossession and Counter Strategies, 1930-1970."
(In) Bay, Edna (ed.). Women and Work in Africa.
Boulder, Colorado: Westview Press. 1982. pp. 83-103.

Muntemba, M. Shimwaayi
"The Changing Position of Women in Zambia as Food
Producers and Suppliers: The 20th Century Experience."
Paper Presented at the Conference on the History of the
Family in Africa. London: Cambridge University. School
of Oriental and African Studies. September, 1981.

Muntemba, M. Shimwaayi
"Dispossession and Counter Strategies in Zambia,
1930-1970." Development: Seeds of Change. #4 1984. pp.
15-17.

Muntemba, Maude
"The Underdevelopment of Peasant Agriculture in Zambia."
Journal of Southern African Studies. Volume 5 #1 1978.
pp. 58-85.

Mwanamwabwa, Catherine
Suggested Income Generating Activities for Women:
Proposal for a Pilot Program. Lusaka, Zambia. August,
1977.

Perrings, Charles
"Consciousness, Conflict and Proletarianization: An
Assessment of the 1935 Mineworkers' Strike on the
Northern Rhodesian Copperbelt." Journal of Southern
African Studies. Volume 4 #1 October, 1977. pp. 31-51.

Schuster, Ilsa M.
Cycles of Dependence and Independence: Westernization and
the African Heritage of Lusaka's Young Women. East
Lansing, Michigan: Michigan State University. Office of
Women in International Development. Working Paper #7.

June, 1982. 30p.

Schuster, Ilsa M.
Female White Collar Workers: A Case Study of Successful
Development in Lusaka, Zambia. East Lansing, Michigan:
Michigan State University. Office of Women in
International Development. Working Paper #29. August,
1983. 31p.

Schuster, Ilsa M.
New Women of Lusaka. Palo Alto, California: Mayfield
Publishing. Explorations in World Ethnology. 1979.
209p.

Schuster, Ilsa M.
"Marginal Lives: Conflict and Contradiction in the
Position of Female Traders in Lusaka, Zambia." (In) Bay,
Edna G. (ed.). Women and Work in Africa. Boulder,
Colorado: Westview Press. Westview Special Studies in
Africa. 1982. pp. 105-126.

Schuster, Ilsa M.
"Marginal Lives: Conflict and Contradiction in the
Position of Female Traders in Lusaka, Zambia." Paper
Presented at the Symposium, Women and Work in Africa.
Urbana, Illinois: University of Illinois-Urbana. April
29-May 1, 1979.

Spring, Anita and Hansen, Art
"Women's Agricultural Work in Rural Zambia: From
Valuation to Subordination." Paper Presented at the
Annual Meeting of the African Studies Association. Paper
#44. Los Angeles, California. October 31, 1979. 25p.

Tadesse, Zenebeworke
An Oveview on the Role of Women's Organizations in
Africa: Case Study of Ethiopia, Zambia, Mozambique and
Tanzania. Lusaka, Zambia: P/O Box RW 514. 1978.

Tembo, Lyson P.
"The Changing Family in the African Context: The Zambian
Case." Paper Presented at the Seminar on the Changing
Family in the African Context, Maseru, Lesotho, 1983.
Paris: United Nations Educational, Scientific and
Cultural Organization. 1984. 21p.

United Nations Economic Commission for Africa (UNECA)
African Women's Employment in the Modern Wage Sector.
Background Document. Regional Prepatory Meeting of the
U.N. Economic Commission for Africa Second Regional
Conference for the Integration of Women in Development.
Lusaka, Zambia. Addis Ababa, Ethiopia: UNECA. December
3-7, 1979.

United Nations Economic Commission for Africa (UNECA)
Women Workers in Ghana-Kenya-Zambia: A Comparative
Analysis of Women's Employment in the Modern Wage
Sector. Addis Ababa, Ethiopia: UNECA. 1979.

Yates, Leslie M.
Integration of Women in Development in Zambia, Botswana
and Lesotho: AID's Efforts. Washington, D.C.: U.S.
Department of State. U.S. Agency for International
Development. Southern Africa Development Analysis.
1978. 92p.

Yates, Leslie M.
   Integration of Women in Development in Southern Africa:
   An Evaluation With Recommendations for U.S. AID Programs
   in Botswana, Lesotho and Zambia. Sadex.
   November-December, 1979. pp. 1-15.

EDUCATION AND TRAINING

Clarke, Sarah H.
   The Position of Women in Education and Employment in
   Zambia: Some Problems Worthy of Further Research.
   Lusaka, Zambia: Unpublished Manuscript. 1976.
Himonga, H.B.
   "An Approach to the Detection of Malnutrition in Rural
   Children Using Socio-Economic Indices and Level of
   Education of Mother as Proxy." Medical Journal of
   Zambia. Volume 16 #2 February-April, 1982. pp. 17-21.
Kamfwa, Franklin D.
   "Contributions of Women's Clubs to Rural Development in
   Ndola Rural East." Journal of Adult Education, Lusaka.
   Volume 1 #1 September, 1982. pp. 42-54.
Tadesse, Zenebeworke
   An Oveview on the Role of Women's Organizations in
   Africa: Case Study of Ethiopia, Zambia, Mozambique and
   Tanzania. Lusaka, Zambia: P/O Box RW 514. 1978.

EMPLOYMENT AND LABOR

Akerele, Olubanke
   Women Workers in Ghana, Kenya, Zambia: A Comparative
   Analysis of Women's Employment in the Modern Wage
   Sector. Addis Ababa, Ethiopia: United Nations Economic
   Commission for Africa. African Training and Research
   Center for Women. 1979. 109p.
Bardouille, Raj
   The Sexual Division of Labour in the Urban Informal
   Sector: A Case Study of Lusaka, Zambia. Lusaka, Zambia:
   University of Zambia. Manpower Research Unit.
   Unpublished. 1981.
Bardouille, Raj
   "The Sexual Division of Labour in the Urban Informal
   Sector: The Case of Some Townships in Lusaka." African
   Social Research. #32 1981. pp. 29-54.
Bardouille, Raj
   "The Sexual Division of Labour in the Urban Informal
   Sector: A Case Study of Lusaka." (In) Woldring, Klaus
   and Chibaye, Chibwe (eds.). Beyond Political
   Independence: Zambia's Development Predicament in the
   1980's. Berlin, Germany: Moutan. 1984. pp. 161-182.
Bardouille, Raj
   Women in the Informal Sector in Zambia: Towards a
   Framework of Analysis. Lusaka, Zambia: University of
   Zambia: Manpower Research Unit. Unpublished. 1981.

Chauncey, George
   "The Locus of Reproduction: Women's Labour in the Zambian
   Copperbelt, 1927-1953." Journal of Southern African
   Studies. Volume 7 #2 April, 1981. pp. 135-164.
Clarke, Sarah H.
   The Position of Women in Education and Employment in
   Zambia: Some Problems Worthy of Further Research.
   Lusaka, Zambia: Unpublished Manuscript. 1976.
Cliffe, Lionel
   "Labour Migration and Peasant Differentiation: Zambian
   Experiences." Journal of Peasant Studies. Volume 5 #3
   1978. pp. 326-346.
Dillon-Malone, Clive M.
   The Korsten Basket Makers. Lusaka, Zambia: University of
   Zambia. Institute for African Studies. 1978.
Due, Jean M. and Mudenda, Timothy (eds.).
   Women's Contributions Made Visible: Of Farm and Market
   Women to Farming Systems and Household Incomes in Zambia,
   1982. Urbana, Illinois: University of Illinois.
   Department of Agriculture Economics. Staff Paper #285.
   1984. 45p.
Due, Jean M. and White, M.
   Differences in Earnings, Labor Input, Decision Making,
   and Perceptions of Development Between Farm and Market
   Women: A Case Study of Zambia. Urbana, Illinois:
   University of Illinois-Urbana-Champaign. Department of
   Agricultural Economics. Agricultural Economics Staff
   Paper #83-E-319. 1983.
Due, Jean M.
   "Intra-Household Gender Issues in Farming Systems in
   Tanzania, Zambia and Malawi." (In) Poats, Susan V. and
   Schmink, Marianne and Spring, Anita (eds.). Gender
   Issues in Farming Systems Research and Extension.
   Boulder, Colorado: Westview Press. 1980. pp. 331-344.
Due, Jean M. and Mudenda, Timothy
   Women's Contributions to Farming Systems and Household
   Income in Zambia. East Lansing, Michigan: Michigan State
   University. Women in International Development. Working
   Paper #85. May, 1985. 29p.
Due, Jean M. and Mudenda, Timothy
   Women Made Visible Contributions: Of Farm and Market
   Women to Farming Systems and Household Incomes in
   Zambia. Champaign, Illinois: University of Illinois.
   Agricultural Economics Staff Paper #84 E-285. 1984.
Hansen, Karen T.
   "When Sex Becomes a Critical Variable: Married Women and
   Extra-Domestic Work in Lusaka, Zambia." African Social
   Research. #30 December, 1980. pp. 831-850.
Hansen, Karen T.
   "Planning Productive Work for Married Women in a
   Low-Income Settlement in Lusaka: The Case for a Small
   Scale Handicrafts Industry." African Social Research.
   #33 1982. pp. 211-223.
Hansen, Karen T.
   "Prospects for Wage Labor Among Married Women in Lusaka,

Zambia." Paper Presented at the Annual Meeting of the
African Studies Association. Paper #31. Houston, Texas.
1977. 24p.

Hansen, Karen T.
"The Work History: Disaggregating the Changing Terms of
Poor Women's Entry into Lusaka's Labour Force." Paper
Presented at the Annual Meeting of the African Studies
Association. Paper #38. Washington, D.C. November 4-7,
1982.

Hansen, Karen T.
"When Sex Becomes a Critical Variable: Married Women and
Extradomestic Work in Lusaka, Zambia." Paper Presented
at the Annual Meeting of the African Studies Association.
Paper #45. Los Angeles, California. 1979. 22p.

Hansen, Karen T. and Spring, Anita
"Women's Agricultural Work in Rural Zambia: From
Valuation to Subordination." Paper Presented at the
Annual Meeting of the African Studies Association. Paper
#44. Los Angeles, California. 1979.

Hansen, Karen T.
"Negotiating Sex and Gender in Urban Zambia." Journal of
Southern African Studies. Volume 10 #2 April, 1984.
pp. 219-238.

Hansen, Karen T.
Zambian Women and Access to Urban Labor. Seattle,
Washington: University of Washington. 1978.

Hansen, Karen T.
"The Urban Informal Sector as a Development Issue: Poor
Women and Work in Lusaka, Zambia." Urban Anthropology.
Volume 9 #2 Summer, 1980. pp. 199-226.

Hansen, Karen T.
Gender Ideology and Work Prospects: The Beer and Sex Link
in Urban Zambia. Mimeo. 1983.

Jules-Rosette, Bennetta
Women's Work in the Informal Sector: A Zambian Case
Study. San Diego, California: University of California,
San Diego. 1981. 24p.

Jules-Rosette, Bennetta
Women's Work in the Informal Sector: A Zambian Case
Study. East Lansing, Michigan: Michigan State
University. Office of Women in International
Development. WID Working Papers #3. 1982. 24p.

Keller, Bonnie B.
Report on Current Efforts to Integrate Zambian Women in
Development. Lusaka, Zambia: University of Zambia.
Department of African Development Studies. 1984.

Keller, Bonnie B.
The Integration of Zambian Women in Development. Lusaka,
Zambia: NORAD. November, 1984. 71p.

Mubanga, Foster
"Freedom and Labour: Women and Nationalist Movement."
(In) Allen, C. and Willians, G. (eds.). Subsaharan
Africa. London: MacMillan. Sociology of Developing
Societies Series. 1982. pp. 58-62.

Muntemba, M. Shimwaayi
"Women as Food Producers and Suppliers in the 20th
Century: The Case of Zambia." Development Dialogue.
#1/2 1982. pp. 29-50.
Muntemba, M. Shimwaayi
"Women and Agricultural Change in the Railway Region of
Zambia: Dispossession and Counter Strategies, 1930-1970."
(In) Bay, Edna (ed.). Women and Work in Africa.
Boulder, Colorado: Westview Press. 1982. pp. 83-103.
Muntemba, M. Shimwaayi
"The Changing Position of Women in Zambia as Food
Producers and Suppliers: The 20th Century Experience."
Paper Presented at the Conference on the History of the
Family in Africa. London: Cambridge University. School
of Oriental and African Studies. September, 1981.
Mwanamwabwa, Catherine
Suggested Income Generating Activities for Women:
Proposal for a Pilot Program. Lusaka, Zambia. August,
1977.
Parpart, Jane L.
Working Class Wives and Collective Labor Action on the
Northern Rhodesian Copperbelt, 1926-1964. Boston: Boston
University. African Studies Center. Working Paper #98.
1985.
Parpart, Jane L.
Class and Gender on the Copperbelt: Women in Northern
Rhodesian Copper Mining Areas, 1926-1964. Boston: Boston
University. African Studies Center. Working Paper #77.
1983. 29p.
Perrings, Charles
"Consciousness, Conflict and Proletarianization: An
Assessment of the 1935 Mineworkers' Strike on the
Northern Rhodesian Copperbelt." Journal of Southern
African Studies. Volume 4 #1 October, 1977. pp. 31-51.
Safilios-Rothschild, C.
The Policy Implications of the Roles of Women in
Agriculture in Zambia. Lusaka, Zambia: Zambian Ministry
of Agriculture and Water Development. National
Commission for Development Planning. Planning Division
Special Studies #20. November, 1985. 49p.
Schuster, Ilsa M.
Female White Collar Workers: A Case Study of Successful
Development in Lusaka, Zambia. East Lansing, Michigan:
Michigan State University. Office of Women in
International Development. Working Paper #29. August,
1983. 31p.
Schuster, Ilsa M.
"Perspectives in Development: The Problem of Nurses and
Nursing in Zambia." Journal of Development Studies.
Volume 17 #3 April, 1981. pp. 77-99.
Schuster, Ilsa M.
New Women of Lusaka. Palo Alto, California: Mayfield
Publishing. Explorations in World Ethnology. 1979.
209p.

Schuster, Ilsa M.
    "Marginal Lives: Conflict and Contradiction in the
    Position of Female Traders in Lusaka, Zambia." (In) Bay,
    Edna G. (ed.). Women and Work in Africa. Boulder,
    Colorado: Westview Press. Westview Special Studies in
    Africa. 1982. pp. 105-126.
Schuster, Ilsa M.
    "Marginal Lives: Conflict and Contradiction in the
    Position of Female Traders in Lusaka, Zambia." Paper
    Presented at the Symposium, Women and Work in Africa.
    Urbana, Illinois: University of Illinois-Urbana. April
    29-May 1, 1979.
Spring, Anita and Hansen, Art
    "Women's Agricultural Work in Rural Zambia: From
    Valuation to Subordination." Paper Presented at the
    Annual Meeting of the African Studies Association. Paper
    #44. Los Angeles, California. October 31, 1979. 25p.
Spring, Anita and Hansen, Art
    "The Underside of Development: Agricultural Development
    and Women in Zambia." Agriculture and Human Values.
    Volume 2 #2 1985. pp. 60-67.
United Nations Economic Commission for Africa (UNECA)
    African Women's Employment in the Modern Wage Sector.
    Background Document. Regional Prepatory Meeting of the
    U.N. Economic Commission for Africa Second Regional
    Conference for the Integration of Women in Development.
    Lusaka, Zambia. Addis Ababa, Ethiopia: UNECA. December
    3-7, 1979.
United Nations Economic Commission for Africa (UNECA)
    Women Workers in Ghana-Kenya-Zambia: A Comparative
    Analysis of Women's Employment in the Modern Wage
    Sector. Addis Ababa, Ethiopia: UNECA. 1979.

EQUALITY AND LIBERATION

Kankassa, B.C.
    Report on the Development of the Status of Zambian
    Women. Lusaka, Zambia: Zambian Information Services and
    Freedom House. 1976.
Konie, Gwendoline
    "Zambia: Feminist Progress-More Difficult than
    Decolonization." (In) Morgan, Robin (ed.). Sisterhood
    is Global. Garden City, New York: Anchor Books. 1984.
    pp. 739-745.
Longwe, Sara H. and Shakakata, Regina C. (eds.).
    Women's Rights in Zambia: Proceedings of the Second
    National Women's Rights Conference, March 22-24, 1985.
    Lusaka, Zambia: Zambia Association for Research and
    Development. 1985. 191p.
Mubanga, Foster
    "Freedom and Labour: Women and Nationalist Movement."
    (In) Allen, C. and Willians, G. (eds.). Subsaharan
    Africa. London: MacMillan. Sociology of Developing
    Societies Series. 1982. pp. 58-62.

FAMILY LIFE

Azefor, M.
"Family Household Statistics and Change in Zambia."
Paper Prepared for Feedback Seminar on Joint
ECA/Government of Zambia Survey on Interrelations Among
Infant and Childhood Mortality, Socio-Economic Factors
and Fertility. Kabwe, Zambia: United Nations Economic
Commission for Africa. April, 1982.
Canter, Richard S.
"Family Dispute: Settlement and the Zambian Judiciary:
Local Level Legal Adaptation." (In) Roberts, Simon
(ed.). Law and the Family in Africa. Hague,
Netherlands: Mouton. 1977. pp. 69-91.
Crehan, Kate
"Women and Development in Northwest Zambia: From Producer
to Housewife." Review of African Political Economy.
#27/28 1984. pp. 51-66.
Due, Jean M. and Mudenda, Timothy (eds.).
Women's Contributions Made Visible: Of Farm and Market
Women to Farming Systems and Household Incomes in Zambia,
1982. Urbana, Illinois: University of Illinois.
Department of Agriculture Economics. Staff Paper #285.
1984. 45p.
Due, Jean M.
"Intra-Household Gender Issues in Farming Systems in
Tanzania, Zambia and Malawi." (In) Poats, Susan V. and
Schmink, Marianne and Spring, Anita (eds.). Gender
Issues in Farming Systems Research and Extension.
Boulder, Colorado: Westview Press. 1980. pp. 331-344.
Epstein, Arnold L.
Urbanization and Kinship: The Domestic Domain on the
Copperbelt of Zambia, 1950-1956. New York: Academic
Press. 1981. 364p.
Lancaster, Chet S.
The Goba of the Zambezi: Sex Roles, Economics and
Change. Norman, Oklahoma: University of Oklahoma Press.
1981. 350p.
Mbikusita-Lewanika, Inonge
"Kinship Terms and Family Relationships: The Case of
Bulozi-Zambia." Paper Presented at the Seminar on the
Changing Family in the African Context, Maseru, Lesotho,
1983. Paris: United Nations Educational, Scientific and
Cultural Organization. 1984. 16p.
Ngwisha, Kaluba J.
"Urbanization and Family Structure: A Study of the Family
on the Copperbelt of Zambia." Ph.D Dissertation:
Brandeis University. Florence Heller Graduate School for
Advanced Studies in Social Welfare. Waltham,
Massachusetts. 1978. 463p.
Parpart, Jane L.
Working Class Wives and Collective Labor Action on the
Northern Rhodesian Copperbelt, 1926-1964. Boston: Boston

University. African Studies Center. Working Paper #98.
1985.
Parpart, Jane L.
Class and Gender on the Copperbelt: Women in Northern
Rhodesian Copper Mining Areas, 1926-1964. Boston: Boston
University. African Studies Center. Working Paper #77.
1983. 29p.
Poewe, Karla O.
Matrilineal Ideology: Male-Female Dynamics in Luapula,
Zambia. New York: Academic Press. For the International
African Institute. 1981. 140p.
Poewe, Karla O.
"Religion, Matriliny and Change: Jehovah's Witnesses and
Seventh-Day Adventists in Luapula, Zambia." American
Ethnologist. Volume 5 #2 1978.
Tembo, Lyson P.
"The Changing Family in the African Context: The Zambian
Case." Paper Presented at the Seminar on the Changing
Family in the African Context. Paris: United Nations
Educational, Scientific and Cultural Organization. 1983.
Maseru, Lesotho. 1984. 21p.
Van Binsbergen, Wim M.
"Law in Context of Nkoya Society." (In) Roberts, Simon
(ed.). Law and the Family in Africa. Hague,
Netherlands: Mouton. 1977. pp. 39-68.

FAMILY PLANNING AND CONTRACEPTION

Ali, M.R.
A Study of Knowledge About Attitude Towards, and Practice
of Family Planning in Zambia. Lusaka, Zambia: University
of Zambia. Department of Psychology. Psychological
Studies: Reports of the Psychology Department. #7.
December, 1984. 51p.
Azefor, M.
"Family Household Statistics and Change in Zambia."
Paper Prepared for Feedback Seminar on Joint
ECA/Government of Zambia Survey on Interrelations Among
Infant and Childhood Mortality, Socio-Economic Factors
and Fertility. Kabwe, Zambia: United Nations Economic
Commission for Africa. April, 1982.
Chauncey, George
"The Locus of Reproduction: Women's Labour in the Zambian
Copperbelt, 1927-1953." Journal of Southern African
Studies. Volume 7 #2 April, 1981. pp. 135-164.
Mburugu, Edward K.
"Structural Moderization and Differential Fertility in
Zambia." Ph.D Dissertation: University of
Wisconsin-Madison. Madison, Wisconsin. 1978. 190p.
Spring, Anita
"Women's Rituals and Natality Among the Luvale of
Zambia." Ph.D Dissertation: Cornell University. Ithaca,
New York. 1976. 258p.

Spring, Anita
"An Indigenous Therapeutic Style and Its Consequences for
Natality: The Luvale of Zambia." (In) Marshall, John F.
and Polgar, Steven (eds.). Culture, Natality and Family
Planning. Chapel Hill, North Carolina: University of
North Carolina. Carolina Population Center. 1976. pp.
99-125.
Wenlock, R.W.
"Birth Spacing and Prolonged Lactation in Rural Zambia."
Journal of Biosocial Science. Volume 9 #4 October,
1977. pp. 481-485.

FERTILITY AND INFERTILITY

Azefor, M.
"Family Household Statistics and Change in Zambia."
Paper Prepared for Feedback Seminar on Joint
ECA/Government of Zambia Survey on Interrelations Among
Infant and Childhood Mortality, Socio-Economic Factors
and Fertility. Kabwe, Zambia: United Nations Economic
Commission for Africa. April, 1982.
Chauncey, George
"The Locus of Reproduction: Women's Labour in the Zambian
Copperbelt, 1927-1953." Journal of Southern African
Studies. Volume 7 #2 April, 1981. pp. 135-164.
Mburugu, Edward K.
"Structural Moderization and Differential Fertility in
Zambia." Ph.D Dissertation: University of
Wisconsin-Madison. Madison, Wisconsin. 1978. 190p.
Zambia. Central Statistics Office (CSO)
1980 Population and Housing Census of Zambia Analytical
Report (Volume Four): Fertility and Mortality Levels and
Trends. Lusaka, Zambia: CSO. 1985. 116p.

HEALTH, NUTRITION AND MEDICINE

Azefor, M.
"Family Household Statistics and Change in Zambia."
Paper Prepared for Feedback Seminar on Joint
ECA/Government of Zambia Survey on Interrelations Among
Infant and Childhood Mortality, Socio-Economic Factors
and Fertility. Kabwe, Zambia: United Nations Economic
Commission for Africa. April, 1982.
Freund, Paul J. and Kalumba, Katele
"Maternal Health and Child Survival Rates in Zambia: A
Comparative Community Study." Medical Journal of Zambia.
Volume 18 #2 June, 1984.
Grech, E.S.
"Obstetric Deaths in Lusaka." Medical Journal of Zambia.
Volume 12 #2 April-May, 1978. pp. 45-53.
Himonga, H.B.
"An Approach to the Detection of Malnutrition in Rural
Children Using Socio-Economic Indices and Level of

Education of Mother as Proxy." Medical Journal of
Zambia. Volume 16 #2 February-April, 1982. pp. 17-21.
Kwofie, Kwamie and Brew-Graves, Ekow and Adika, G.H.
"Malnutrition and Pregnancy Wastage in Zambia." Social
Science and Medicine. Volume 17 #9 1983. pp. 539-543.
Schuster, Ilsa M.
"Perspectives in Development: The Problem of Nurses and
Nursing in Zambia." Journal of Development Studies.
Volume 17 #3 April, 1981. pp. 77-99.
Spring, Anita
"An Indigenous Therapeutic Style and Its Consequences for
Natality: The Luvale of Zambia." (In) Marshall, John F.
and Polgar, Steven (eds.). Culture, Natality and Family
Planning. Chapel Hill, North Carolina: University of
North Carolina. Carolina Population Center. 1976. pp.
99-125.
Wadhawan, S.
"Obstetrical Performance in Elderly Zambian Parturients."
Medical Journal of Zambia. Volume 15 #2 February-March,
1981. pp. 37-40.
Watts, T.
"A Case-Control Study of Still Births at a Teaching
Hospital in Zambia, 1979-1980: Antenatal Factors."
Bulletin of the World Health Organization. Volume 60 #6
1982. pp. 971-979.
Wenlock, R.W.
"Birth Spacing and Prolonged Lactation in Rural Zambia."
Journal of Biosocial Science. Volume 9 #4 October,
1977. pp. 481-485.
Zambia. Central Statistics Office (CSO)
1980 Population and Housing Census of Zambia Analytical
Report (Volume Four): Fertility and Mortality Levels and
Trends. Lusaka, Zambia: CSO. 1985. 116p.

HISTORY

Ault, James
"Making 'Modern' Marriage 'Traditional': State Power and
the Regulation of Marriage in Colonial Zambia." Theory
and Society. Volume 12 1983. pp. 181-210.
Chanock, Martin
"Making Customary Law: Men, Women and Courts in Colonial
Northern Rhodesia." (In) Hay, M.J. and Wright, M.
(eds.). African Women and the Law: Historical
Perspectives. Boston: Boston University. Papers on
Africa. Volume 7 1982. pp. 53-67.
Chauncey, George
"The Locus of Reproduction: Women's Labour in the Zambian
Copperbelt, 1927-1953." Journal of Southern African
Studies. Volume 7 #2 April, 1981. pp. 135-164.
Merry, Sally E.
"The Articulation of Legal Spheres." (In) Hays, Margaret
J. and Wright, Marcia (eds.). African Women and the Law:
Historical Perspectives. Boston, Masachusetts: Boston

University. 1982. pp. 68-89.
Muntemba, M. Shimwaayi
    "Women and Agricultural Change in the Railway Region of
    Zambia: Dispossession and Counter Strategies, 1930-1970."
    (In) Bay, Edna (ed.). Women and Work in Africa.
    Boulder, Colorado: Westview Press. 1982. pp. 83-103.
Muntemba, M. Shimwaayi
    "Dispossession and Counter Strategies in Zambia,
    1930-1970." Development: Seeds of Change. #4 1984. pp.
    15-17.
Perrings, Charles
    "Consciousness, Conflict and Proletarianization: An
    Assessment of the 1935 Mineworkers' Strike on the
    Northern Rhodesian Copperbelt." Journal of Southern
    African Studies. Volume 4 #1 October, 1977. pp. 31-51.
Schuster, Ilsa M.
    "Constraints and Opportunities in Political
    Participation: The Case of Zambian Women."
    Geneve-Afrique. Volume 21 #2 1983. pp. 7-37.
Schuster, Ilsa M.
    "Constraints and Opportunities in Political
    Participation: The Case of Zambian Women." Paper
    Presented at the Workshop on Women in the African
    Political Process. London: University of London. School
    of Oriental and African Studies. 1981. September 22,
    1982.
Wright, Marcia
    "Justice, Women and the Social Order in Abercorn,
    Northeastern Rhodesia, 1898-1903." (In) Hay, M.J. and
    Wright, M. (eds.). African Women and the Law: Historical
    Perspectives. Boston: Boston University. African
    Studies Center. Boston University Papers on Africa.
    Volume Seven. 1982. pp. 33-50.

LAW AND LEGAL ISSUES

Canter, Richard S.
    "Family Dispute: Settlement and the Zambian Judiciary:
    Local Level Legal Adaptation." (In) Roberts, Simon
    (ed.). Law and the Family in Africa. Hague,
    Netherlands: Mouton. 1977. pp. 69-91.
Chanock, Martin
    "Making Customary Law: Men, Women and Courts in Colonial
    Northern Rhodesia." (In) Hay, M.J. and Wright, M.
    (eds.). African Women and the Law: Historical
    Perspectives. Boston: Boston University. Papers on
    Africa. Volume 7. 1982. pp. 53-67.
Cutshall, Charles R.
    The Role of Women in Disputing Among the Ila of Zambia:
    Political Adaptation in Legal Change. Boston: Boston
    University. African Studies Center. Working Paper #46.
    1981. 50p.
Cutshall, Charles R. and McCold, Paul E.
    "Patterns of Stock Theft Victimization and Formal

Response Strategies Among the Ila of Zambia."
Victimology. Volume 9 #1 1984. pp. 181+.

Hansen, Karen T.
"Negotiating Sex and Gender in Urban Zambia." Journal of
Southern African Studies. Volume 10 #2 April, 1984.
pp. 219-238.

Himonga, C.N.
"Some Aspects of the Zambian Marriage Act." Zambia Law
Journal. Volume 11 1979. pp. 23-44.

Hussain, S.J.
"Breakdown of Marriage in Zambia: Judicial Response and
Challenge." Zambia Law Journal. Volume 13 1981.

Longwe, Sara H. and Shakakata, Regina C. (eds.).
Women's Rights in Zambia: Proceedings of the Second
National Women's Rights Conference, March 22-24, 1985.
Lusaka, Zambia: Zambia Association for Research and
Development. 1985. 191p.

Merry, Sally E.
"The Articulation of Legal Spheres." (In) Hays, Margaret
J. and Wright, Marcia (eds.). African Women and the Law:
Historical Perspectives. Boston, Masachusetts: Boston
University. 1982. pp. 68-89.

Van Binsbergen, Wim M.
"Law in Context of Nkoya Society." (In) Roberts, Simon
(ed.). Law and the Family in Africa. Hague,
Netherlands: Mouton. 1977. pp. 39-68.

Wright, Marcia
"Justice, Women and the Social Order in Abercorn,
Northeastern Rhodesia, 1898-1903." (In) Hay, M.J. and
Wright, M. (eds.). African Women and the Law: Historical
Perspectives. Boston: Boston University. African
Studies Center. Boston University Papers on Africa.
Volume Seven. 1982. pp. 33-50.

LITERATURE

Rennie, J.K.
"Cattle, Conflict and Court-Cases: The Praise Poetry of
Ila Leadership." Research in African Literatures.
Volume 15 #4 1984. pp. 530-567.

MARITAL RELATIONS AND NUPTIALITY

Ali, M.R.
A Study of Knowledge About Attitude Towards, and Practice
of Family Planning in Zambia. Lusaka, Zambia: University
of Zambia. Department of Psychology. Psychological
Studies: Reports of the Psychology Department. #7.
December, 1984. 51p.

Ault, James
"Making 'Modern' Marriage 'Traditional': State Power and
the Regulation of Marriage in Colonial Zambia." Theory
and Society. Volume 12 1983. pp. 181-210.

Ault, Jim
    Traditionalizing 'Modern' Marriage: A Neglected Aspect of
    Social Struggle on the Zambian Copperbelt. Mimeo. 1976.
Azefor, M.
    "Family Household Statistics and Change in Zambia."
    Paper Prepared for Feedback Seminar on Joint
    ECA/Government of Zambia Survey on Interrelations Among
    Infant and Childhood Mortality, Socio-Economic Factors
    and Fertility. Kabwe, Zambia: United Nations Economic
    Commission for Africa. April, 1982.
Canter, Richard S.
    "Family Dispute: Settlement and the Zambian Judiciary:
    Local Level Legal Adaptation." (In) Roberts, Simon
    (ed.). Law and the Family in Africa. Hague,
    Netherlands: Mouton. 1977. pp. 69-91.
Chauncey, George
    "The Locus of Reproduction: Women's Labour in the Zambian
    Copperbelt, 1927-1953." Journal of Southern African
    Studies. Volume 7 #2 April, 1981. pp. 135-164.
Due, Jean M. and Mudenda, Timothy (eds.).
    Women's Contributions Made Visible: Of Farm and Market
    Women to Farming Systems and Household Incomes in Zambia,
    1982. Urbana, Illinois: University of Illinois.
    Department of Agriculture Economics. Staff Paper #285.
    1984. 45p.
Epstein, Arnold L.
    Urbanization and Kinship: The Domestic Domain on the
    Copperbelt of Zambia, 1950-1956. New York: Academic
    Press. 1981. 364p.
Hansen, Karen T.
    "When Sex Becomes a Critical Variable: Married Women and
    Extra-Domestic Work in Lusaka, Zambia." African Social
    Research. #30 December, 1980. pp. 831-850.
Hansen, Karen T.
    "Prospects for Wage Labor Among Married Women in Lusaka,
    Zambia." Paper Presented at the Annual Meeting of the
    African Studies Association. Paper #31. Houston, Texas.
    1977. 24p.
Hansen, Karen T.
    "When Sex Becomes a Critical Variable: Married Women and
    Extradomestic Work in Lusaka, Zambia." Paper Presented
    at the Annual Meeting of the African Studies Association.
    Paper #45. Los Angeles, California. 1979. 22p.
Hansen, Karen T.
    "Negotiating Sex and Gender in Urban Zambia." Journal of
    Southern African Studies. Volume 10 #2 April, 1984.
    pp. 219-238.
Himonga, C.N.
    "Some Aspects of the Zambian Marriage Act." Zambia Law
    Journal. Volume 11 1979. pp. 23-44.
Hussain, S.J.
    "Breakdown of Marriage in Zambia: Judicial Response and
    Challenge." Zambia Law Journal. Volume 13 1981.
Lancaster, Chet S.
    The Goba of the Zambezi: Sex Roles, Economics and Change.

Norman, Oklahoma: University of Oklahoma Press. 1981.
350p.
Mburugu, Edward K.
"Structural Moderization and Differential Fertility in
Zambia." Ph.D Dissertation: University of
Wisconsin-Madison. Madison, Wisconsin. 1978. 190p.
Munachonga, Monica
The Conjugal Power Relationship: An Urban Case Study in
Zambia. Sussex, England: Sussex University. 1984.
Nag, Prithvish
"The Role of Women in Internal Migration in Zambia."
Population Geography. Volume 5 #1-2 June-December,
1983. pp. 60-69.
Ngulube, Clare
"Marriage in Zambia." Africa Woman. #12
November-December, 1977. pp. 62-63.
Ngwisha, Kaluba J.
"Urbanization and Family Structure: A Study of the Family
on the Copperbelt of Zambia." Ph.D Dissertation:
Brandeis University. Florence Heller Graduate School for
Advanced Studies in Social Welfare. Waltham,
Massachusetts. 1978. 463p.
Parpart, Jane L.
Working Class Wives and Collective Labor Action on the
Northern Rhodesian Copperbelt, 1926-1964. Boston: Boston
University. African Studies Center. Working Paper #98.
1985.
Parpart, Jane L.
Class and Gender on the Copperbelt: Women in Northern
Rhodesian Copper Mining Areas, 1926-1964. Boston: Boston
University. African Studies Center. Working Paper #77.
1983. 29p.
Poewe, Karla O.
"Matriliny in the Throes of Change: Kinship, Descent and
Marriage in Luapula, Zambia." Part One. Africa. Volume
48 #3 1978. pp. 205-367.
Poewe, Karla O.
"Matriliny in the Throes of Change: Kinship, Descent and
Marriage in Luapula, Zambia. Part Two. Africa. Volume
48 #4 1978. pp. 353-367.
Poewe, Karla O.
"Marriage, Descent and Kinship: On the Differential
Primacy of Institutions in Luapula and Longana." Africa.
Volume 50 #1 1980. pp. 73-95.
Poewe, Karla O.
Matrilineal Ideology: Male-Female Dynamics in Luapula,
Zambia. New York: Academic Press. For the International
African Institute. 1981. 140p.
Poewe, Karla O.
"Religion, Matriliny and Change: Jehovah's Witnesses and
Seventh-Day Adventists in Luapula, Zambia." American
Ethnologist. Volume 5 #2 1978.
Tembo, Lyson P.
"The Changing Family in the African Context: The Zambian
Case." Paper Presented at the Seminar on the Changing

ZAMBIA

Family in the African Context, Maseru, Lesotho, 1983.
Paris: United Nations Educational, Scientific and
Cultural Organization. 1984. 21p.
Van Rouveroy van Nieuwall, Emile and Van Rouveroy van
Nieuwall, Els
    "To Claim or Not to Claim: Changing Views About the
    Restitution of Marriage Prestations Among the Anufom in
    Northern Tonga." (In) Roberts, Simon (ed.). Law and the
    Family in Africa. Hague, Netherlands: Mouton. 1977.
    pp. 93-115.
Wenlock, R.W.
    "Birth Spacing and Prolonged Lactation in Rural Zambia."
    Journal of Biosocial Science. Volume 9 #4 October,
    1977. pp. 481-485.
Wright, Marcia
    "Technology, Marriage and Women's Work in the History of
    Maize-Growers in Mazabuka, Zambia: A Reconnaissance."
    Journal of Southern African Studies. Volume 10 #1
    October, 1983. pp. 71-85.

MIGRATION

Chauncey, George
    "The Locus of Reproduction: Women's Labour in the Zambian
    Copperbelt, 1927-1953." Journal of Southern African
    Studies. Volume 7 #2 April, 1981. pp. 135-164.
Cliffe, Lionel
    "Labour Migration and Peasant Differentiation: Zambian
    Experiences." Journal of Peasant Studies. Volume 5 #3
    1978. pp. 326-346.
Nag, Prithvish
    "The Role of Women in Internal Migration in Zambia."
    Population Geography. Volume 5 #1-2 June-December,
    1983. pp. 60-69.

NATIONALISM

Mubanga, Foster
    "Freedom and Labour: Women and Nationalist Movement."
    (In) Allen, C. and Willians, G. (eds.). Subsaharan
    Africa. London: MacMillan. Sociology of Developing
    Societies Series. 1982. pp. 58-62.

ORGANIZATIONS

Kamfwa, Franklin D.
    "Contributions of Women's Clubs to Rural Development in
    Ndola Rural East." Journal of Adult Education, Lusaka.
    Volume 1 #1 September, 1982. pp. 42-54.
Longwe, Sara H. and Shakakata, Regina C. (eds.).
    Women's Rights in Zambia: Proceedings of the Second
    National Women's Rights Conference, March 22-24, 1985.

Lusaka, Zambia: Zambia Association for Research and
Development. 1985. 191p.
Tadesse, Zenebeworke
An Overview on the Role of Women's Organizations in
Africa: Case Study of Ethiopia, Zambia, Mozambique and
Tanzania. Lusaka, Zambia: P/O Box RW 514. 1978.

POLITICS AND GOVERNMENT

Ault, James
"Making 'Modern' Marriage 'Traditional': State Power and
the Regulation of Marriage in Colonial Zambia." Theory
and Society. Volume 12 1983. pp. 181-210.
Cutshall, Charles R.
The Role of Women in Disputing Among the Ila of Zambia:
Political Adaptation in Legal Change. Boston: Boston
University. African Studies Center. Working Paper #46.
1981. 50p.
Mubanga, Foster
"Freedom and Labour: Women and Nationalist Movement."
(In) Allen, C. and Willians, G. (eds.). Subsaharan
Africa. London: MacMillan. Sociology of Developing
Societies Series. 1982. pp. 58-62.
Muntemba, M. Shimwaayi
"Dispossession and Counter Strategies in Zambia,
1930-1970." Development: Seeds of Change. #4 1984. pp.
15-17.
Schuster, Ilsa M.
"Constraints and Opportunities in Political
Participation: The Case of Zambian Women."
Geneve-Afrique. Volume 21 #2 1983. pp. 7-37.
Schuster, Ilsa M.
"Constraints and Opportunities in Political
Participation: The Case of Zambian Women." Paper
Presented at the Workshop on Women in the African
Political Process. London: University of London. School
of Oriental and African Studies. 1981. September 22,
1982.
Yates, Leslie M.
Integration of Women in Development in Zambia, Botswana
and Lesotho: AID's Efforts. Washington, D.C.: U.S.
Department of State. U.S. Agency for International
Development. Southern Africa Development Analysis.
1978. 92p.
Yates, Leslie M.
Integration of Women in Development in Southern Africa:
An Evaluation With Recommendations for U.S. AID Programs
in Botswana, Lesotho and Zambia. Sadex.
November-December, 1979. pp. 1-15.

RELIGION AND WITCHCRAFT

Poewe, Karla O.
"Religion, Matriliny and Change: Jehovah's Witnesses and
Seventh-Day Adventists in Luapula, Zambia." American
Ethnologist. Volume 5 #2 1978.
Richards, Audrey I.
Chisungu: a Girls' Initiation Ceremony Among the Bemba of
Zambia. New York: Tavistock. 1982. 224p.
Spring, Anita
"Epidemiology of Spirit Possession Among the Luvale of
Zambia." (In) Hoch-Smith, Judith and Spring, Anita
(eds.). Women in Ritual and Symbolic Roles. New York:
Plenum Press. 1978. pp. 165-190.

RESEARCH

Due, Jean M.
"Intra-Household Gender Issues in Farming Systems in
Tanzania, Zambia and Malawi." (In) Poats, Susan V. and
Schmink, Marianne and Spring, Anita (eds.). Gender
Issues in Farming Systems Research and Extension.
Boulder, Colorado: Westview Press. 1980. pp. 331-344.

SEX ROLES

Ault, Jim
Traditionalizing 'Modern' Marriage: A Neglected Aspect of
Social Struggle on the Zambian Copperbelt. Mimeo. 1976.
Bardouille, Raj
The Sexual Division of Labour in the Urban Informal
Sector: A Case Study of Lusaka, Zambia. Lusaka, Zambia:
University of Zambia. Manpower Research Unit.
Unpublished. 1981.
Bardouille, Raj
"The Sexual Division of Labour in the Urban Informal
Sector: The Case of Some Townships in Lusaka." African
Social Research. #32 1981. pp. 29-54.
Bardouille, Raj
"The Sexual Division of Labour in the Urban Informal
Sector: A Case Study of Lusaka." (In) Woldring, Klaus
and Chibaye, Chibwe (eds.). Beyond Political
Independence: Zambia's Development Predicament in the
1980's. Berlin, Germany: Moutan. 1984. pp. 161-182.
Chauncey, George
"The Locus of Reproduction: Women's Labour in the Zambian
Copperbelt, 1927-1953." Journal of Southern African
Studies. Volume 7 #2 April, 1981. pp. 135-164.
Cliffe, Lionel
"Labour Migration and Peasant Differentiation: Zambian
Experiences." Journal of Peasant Studies. Volume 5 #3
1978. pp. 326-346.

Crehan, Kate
     "Women and Development in Northwest Zambia: From Producer
     to Housewife." Review of African Political Economy.
     #27/28 1984. pp. 51-66.
Cutshall, Charles R.
     The Role of Women in Disputing Among the Ila of Zambia:
     Political Adaptation in Legal Change. Boston: Boston
     University. African Studies Center. Working Paper #46.
     1981. 50p.
Due, Jean M. and Mudenda, Timothy (eds.).
     Women's Contributions Made Visible: Of Farm and Market
     Women to Farming Systems and Household Incomes in Zambia,
     1982. Urbana, Illinois: University of Illinois.
     Department of Agriculture Economics. Staff Paper #285.
     1984. 45p.
Due, Jean M.
     "Intra-Household Gender Issues in Farming Systems in
     Tanzania, Zambia and Malawi." (In) Poats, Susan V. and
     Schmink, Marianne and Spring, Anita (eds.). Gender
     Issues in Farming Systems Research and Extension.
     Boulder, Colorado: Westview Press. 1980. pp. 331-344.
Due, Jean M. and Mudenda, Timothy
     Women Made Visible Contributions: Of Farm and Market
     Women to Farming Systems and Household Incomes in
     Zambia. Champaign, Illinois: University of Illinois.
     Agricultural Economics Staff Paper #84 E-285. 1984.
Hansen, Karen T. and Spring, Anita
     "Women's Agricultural Work in Rural Zambia: From
     Valuation to Subordination." Paper Presented at the
     Annual Meeting of the African Studies Association. Paper
     #44. Los Angeles, California. 1979.
Hansen, Karen T.
     "Negotiating Sex and Gender in Urban Zambia." Journal of
     Southern African Studies. Volume 10 #2 April, 1984.
     pp. 219-238.
Hansen, Karen T.
     Gender Ideology and Work Prospects: The Beer and Sex Link
     in Urban Zambia. Mimeo. 1983.
Himonga, C.N.
     "Some Aspects of the Zambian Marriage Act." Zambia Law
     Journal. Volume 11 1979. pp. 23-44.
Jiggins, Janice
     "Female Headed Households Among Subsistence Cultivators
     in the Central and Northern Provinces of Zambia." Paper
     Presented at the Workshop on Women in Agricultural
     Production in Eastern and Southern Africa. Nairobi,
     Kenya. April 9-11, 1984.
Jules-Rosette, Bennetta
     Women's Work in the Informal Sector: A Zambian Case
     Study. San Diego, California: University of California,
     San Diego. 1981. 24p.
Jules-Rosette, Bennetta
     Women's Work in the Informal Sector: A Zambian Case
     Study. East Lansing, Michigan: Michigan State

University.   Office of Women in International
Development.   WID Working Papers #3.   1982.   24p.
Lancaster, Chet S.
The Goba of the Zambezi: Sex Roles, Economics and
Change.   Norman, Oklahoma: University of Oklahoma Press.
1981.   350p.
Mbikusita-Lewanika, Inonge
"Kinship Terms and Family Relationships: The Case of
Bulozi-Zambia."   Paper Presented at the Seminar on the
Changing Family in the African Context, Maseru,
Lesotho, 1983.   Paris: United Nations Educational,
Scientific and Cultural Organization.   1984.   16p.
Mubanga, Foster
"Freedom and Labour: Women and Nationalist Movement."
(In) Allen, C. and Willians, G. (eds.).   Subsaharan
Africa.   London: MacMillan.   Sociology of Developing
Societies Series.   1982.   pp. 58-62.
Munachonga, Monica
The Conjugal Power Relationship: An Urban Case Study in
Zambia.   Sussex, England: Sussex University.   1984.
Muntemba, M. Shimwaayi
"Women as Food Producers and Suppliers in the 20th
Century: The Case of Zambia."   Development Dialogue.
#1/2 1982.   pp. 29-50.
Muntemba, M. Shimwaayi
"Women and Agricultural Change in the Railway Region of
Zambia: Dispossession and Counter Strategies, 1930-1970."
(In) Bay, Edna (ed.).   Women and Work in Africa.
Boulder, Colorado: Westview Press.   1982.   pp. 83-103.
Muntemba, M. Shimwaayi
"The Changing Position of Women in Zambia as Food
Producers and Suppliers: The 20th Century Experience."
Paper Presented at the Conference on the History of the
Family in Africa.   London: Cambridge University.   School
of Oriental and African Studies.   September, 1981.
Muntemba, Maude
"The Underdevelopment of Peasant Agriculture in Zambia."
Journal of Southern African Studies.   Volume 5 #1 1978.
pp. 58-85.
Nag, Prithvish
"The Role of Women in Internal Migration in Zambia."
Population Geography.   Volume 5 #1-2 June-December,
1983.   pp. 60-69.
Ngwisha, Kaluba J.
"Urbanization and Family Structure: A Study of the Family
on the Copperbelt of Zambia."   Ph.D Dissertation:
Brandeis University.   Florence Heller Graduate School for
Advanced Studies in Social Welfare.   Waltham,
Massachusetts.   1978.   463p.
Parpart, Jane L.
Working Class Wives and Collective Labor Action on the
Northern Rhodesian Copperbelt, 1926-1964.   Boston: Boston
University.   African Studies Center.   Working Paper #98.
1985.

Parpart, Jane L.
    Class and Gender on the Copperbelt: Women in Northern
    Rhodesian Copper Mining Areas, 1926-1964. Boston: Boston
    University. African Studies Center. Working Paper #77.
    1983. 29p.
Poewe, Karla O.
    "Matriliny in the Throes of Change: Kinship, Descent and
    Marriage in Luapula, Zambia." Part One. Africa. Volume
    48 #3 1978. pp. 205-367.
Poewe, Karla O.
    "Matriliny in the Throes of Change: Kinship, Descent and
    Marriage in Luapula, Zambia. Part Two. Africa. Volume
    48 #4 1978. pp. 353-367.
Poewe, Karla O.
    "Marriage, Descent and Kinship: On the Differential
    Primacy of Institutions in Luapula and Longana." Africa.
    Volume 50 #1 1980. pp. 73-95.
Poewe, Karla O.
    Matrilineal Ideology: Male-Female Dynamics in Luapula,
    Zambia. New York: Academic Press. For the International
    African Institute. 1981. 140p.
Safilios-Rothschild, C.
    The Policy Implications of the Roles of Women in
    Agriculture in Zambia. Lusaka, Zambia: Zambian Ministry
    of Agriculture and Water Development. National
    Commission for Development Planning. Planning Division
    Special Studies #20. November, 1985. 49p.
Spring, Anita
    "Women's Rituals and Natality Among the Luvale of
    Zambia." Ph.D Dissertation: Cornell University. Ithaca,
    New York. 1976. 258p.
Spring, Anita
    "An Indigenous Therapeutic Style and Its Consequences for
    Natality: The Luvale of Zambia." (In) Marshall, John F.
    and Polgar, Steven (eds.). Culture, Natality and Family
    Planning. Chapel Hill, North Carolina: University of
    North Carolina. Carolina Population Center. 1976. pp.
    99-125.
Spring, Anita
    "Epidemiology of Spirit Possession Among the Luvale of
    Zambia." (In) Hoch-Smith, Judith and Spring, Anita
    (eds.). Women in Ritual and Symbolic Roles. New York:
    Plenum Press. 1978. pp. 165-190.
Spring, Anita and Hansen, Art
    "Women's Agricultural Work in Rural Zambia: From
    Valuation to Subordination." Paper Presented at the
    Annual Meeting of the African Studies Association. Paper
    #44. Los Angeles, California. October 31, 1979. 25p.
Tembo, Lyson P.
    "The Changing Family in the African Context: The Zambian
    Case." Paper Presented at the Seminar on the Changing
    Family in the African Context, Maseru, Lesotho, 1983.
    Paris: United Nations Educational, Scientific and
    Cultural Organization. 1984. 21p.

Van Binsbergen, Wim M.
   "Law in Context of Nkoya Society." (In) Roberts, Simon
   (ed.). Law and the Family in Africa. Hague,
   Netherlands: Mouton. 1977. pp. 39-68.
Van Rouveroy van Nieuwall, Emile and Van Rouveroy van
Nieuwall, Els
   "To Claim or Not to Claim: Changing Views About the
   Restitution of Marriage Prestations Among the Anufom in
   Northern Tonga." (In) Roberts, Simon (ed.). Law and the
   Family in Africa. Hague, Netherlands: Mouton. 1977.
   pp. 93-115.
Wright, Marcia
   "Technology, Marriage and Women's Work in the History of
   Maize-Growers in Mazabuka, Zambia: A Reconnaissance."
   Journal of Southern African Studies. Volume 10 #1
   October, 1983. pp. 71-85.

STATUS OF WOMEN

Bardouille, Raj
   Women in the Informal Sector in Zambia: Towards a
   Framework of Analysis. Lusaka, Zambia: University of
   Zambia: Manpower Research Unit. Unpublished. 1981.
Kankassa, B.C.
   Report on the Development of the Status of Zambian Women.
   Lusaka, Zambia: Zambian Information Services and Freedom
   House. 1976.
Konie, Gwendoline
   "Zambia: Feminist Progress-More Difficult than
   Decolonization." (In) Morgan, Robin (ed.). Sisterhood
   is Global. Garden City, New York: Anchor Books. 1984.
   pp. 739-745.
Longwe, Sara H. and Shakakata, Regina C. (eds.).
   Women's Rights in Zambia: Proceedings of the Second
   National Women's Rights Conference, March 22-24, 1985.
   Lusaka, Zambia: Zambia Association for Research and
   Development. 1985. 191p.

URBANIZATION

Bardouille, Raj
   The Sexual Division of Labour in the Urban Informal
   Sector: A Case Study of Lusaka, Zambia. Lusaka, Zambia:
   University of Zambia. Manpower Research Unit.
   Unpublished. 1981.
Bardouille, Raj
   The Sexual Division of Labour in the Urban Informal
   Sector: The Case of Some Townships in Lusaka. African
   Social Research. #32 1981. pp. 29-54.
Bardouille, Raj
   "The Sexual Division of Labour in the Urban Informal
   Sector: A Case Study of Lusaka." (In) Woldring, Klaus
   and Chibaye, Chibwe (eds.). Beyond Political

Independence: Zambia's Development Predicament in the
1980's. Berlin, Germany: Moutan. 1984. pp. 161-182.
Epstein, Arnold L.
Urbanization and Kinship: The Domestic Domain on the
Copperbelt of Zambia, 1950-1956. New York: Academic
Press. 1981. 364p.
Hansen, Karen T.
"Negotiating Sex and Gender in Urban Zambia." Journal of
Southern African Studies. Volume 10 #2 April, 1984.
pp. 219-238.
Hansen, Karen T.
Zambian Women and Access to Urban Labor. Seattle,
Washington: University of Washington. 1978.
Hansen, Karen T.
"The Urban Informal Sector as a Development Issue: Poor
Women and Work in Lusaka, Zambia." Urban Anthropology.
Volume 9 #2 Summer, 1980. pp. 199-226.
Hansen, Karen T.
Gender Ideology and Work Prospects: The Beer and Sex Link
in Urban Zambia. Mimeo. 1983.
Munachonga, Monica
The Conjugal Power Relationship: An Urban Case Study in
Zambia. Sussex, England: Sussex University. 1984.
Ngwisha, Kaluba J.
"Urbanization and Family Structure: A Study of the Family
on the Copperbelt of Zambia." Ph.D Dissertation:
Brandeis University. Florence Heller Graduate School for
Advanced Studies in Social Welfare. Waltham,
Massachusetts. 1978. 463p.

WOMEN AND THEIR CHILDREN

Freund, Paul J. and Kalumba, Katele
"Maternal Health and Child Survival Rates in Zambia: A
Comparative Community Study." Medical Journal of Zambia.
Volume 18 #2 June, 1984.
Himonga, H.B.
"An Approach to the Detection of Malnutrition in Rural
Children Using Socio-Economic Indices and Level of
Education of Mother as Proxy." Medical Journal of
Zambia. Volume 16 #2 February-April, 1982. pp. 17-21.

Zimbabwe

AGRICULTURE

Bond-Stewart, K.
    Women's Problems. Harare, Zimbabwe: Zimbabwe Publishing
    House. 1984. 44p.
Cheater, Angela P.
    "Women and Their Participation in Commercial Agricultural
    Production: The Case of Medium-Scale Freehold in
    Zimbabwe." Development and Change. Volume 12 #3 July,
    1981. pp. 349-378.
Cheater, Angela P.
    "Cattle and Class? Rights to Grazing Land, Family
    Organization and Class Formation in Msengezi." Africa.
    Volume 53 #4 1983. pp. 59-74.
Jacobs, Susie
    "Women and Land Resettlement in Zimbabwe." Review of
    African Political Economy. #27/28 1984. pp. 33-50.
McCalman, Kate
    "Zimbabwe: Rural Women Speak Out." Ideas and Action
    Bulletin. #158 1984.
McCalman, Kate
    We Carry a Heavy Load: Rural Women in Zimbabwe Speak Out:
    Report of a Survey Carried Out by the Zimbabwe Women's
    Bureau. Harare, Zimbabwe: Zimbabwe Women's Bureau.
    December, 1981. 51p.
Muchena, Olivia N.
    "The Changing Position of African Women in
    Zimbabwe-Rhodesia." Zimbabwe Journal of Economics.
    Volume 1 #1 March, 1979. pp. 44-61.
Muchena, Olivia N.
    "Women, Subsistence Farming and Extension Services in the
    Tribal Trust Lands of Rhodesia." Ms Thesis: Cornell
    University. Ithaca, New York. 1977. 294p.
Muchena, Olivia N.
    A Socio-Economic Overview: Zimbabwe Women. Addis Ababa,
    Ethiopia: United Nations Economic Commission for Africa.

African Training and Research Centre for Women. 1982.
48p.

Mundondo, Mabel
"The Decimation of Zimbabwe's Women." Africa Women. #6
1976.

Mungate, D.
"Women, the Silent Farm Managers in the Small Scale
Commercial Areas of Zimabawe." Zimbabwe Agriculture
Journal. Volume 2 #80 1983. pp. 245-249.

Ndebele, S.
"Problems Faced by the YWCA of Rhodesia in Involving
Women and Girls in Rural Development." (In) University
College of Botswana. Proceedings of the Afro Workshop on
Rural Environment and Development Planning in Southern
Africa. Gaborone, Botswana: University College of
Botswana. 1978. pp. 52-67.

Ranger, T.O.
Some Issues in Land Resettlement in Zimbabwe: Experiences
of Shona Women in Resettlement Schemes. London:
University of London. Institute of Commonwealth Studies.
Center for African Studies. Discussion Paper. December
3, 1985.

Tendengu, L.
"An Investigation Into Factors Contributing to the Low
Ratio of Women to Men Studying Formal Vocational and
Professional Agriculture in Zimbabwe." M.Ed.
Dissertation: University of Zimbabwe. Harare, Zimbabwe.
1985.

Truscott, Kate
Female Focused Extension--A Contribution to the National
Extension Framework Study. Harare, Zimbabwe: Ministry of
Lands, Agriculture and Rural Resettlement. Monitoring
and Evaluation Section. AGRITEX. 1985.

United Nations Economic Commission for Africa (UNECA)
A Socio-Economic Overview: Zimbabwe Women. Addis Ababa,
Ethiopia: UNECA. Research Series. 1982.

BIBLIOGRAPHIES

Muchena, Olivia N.
Women and Development in Zimbabwe: An Annotated
Bibliography. Addis Ababa, Ethiopia: United Nations
Economic Commission for Africa. Bibliography Series #9.
1984. 50p.

CULTURAL ROLES

Anonymous
"Zimbabwe's Women: Throwing Off the Past." Southern
Africa. November-December, 1979. pp. 7-8+.

Anonymous
    What the Women are Saying About the Unmarried Girl, Her
    Child. Salisbury, Rhodesia: Division of African
    Education. 1977. 18p.
Bond-Stewart, K.
    Women's Problems. Harare, Zimbabwe: Zimbabwe Publishing
    House. 1984. 44p.
Bonnerjea, Lucy
    "Invisible Women." Zambezia. Volume 9 #2 1981.
Brown, Judith K.
    "Economic Organization and the Position of Women Among
    the Iroquois (and Bemba)." (In) Tiffany, Sharon W.
    (ed.). Women and Society: An Anthropological Reader.
    St. Albans, Vermont: Eden Press. Women's Publications.
    1979. pp. 48-74.
Castle, W.M.
    "The Extent of the Practice of Family Planning Among
    Africans in Mashonaland." Central African Journal of
    Medicine. Volume 22 #8 August, 1976. pp. 147-151.
Castle, W.M. and Hakutangwi, K.
    "Patterns of Fertility Among Africans in Glen Norah
    Township, Salisbury." Central African Journal of
    Medicine. Volume 25 #6 June, 1979. pp. 126-130.
Chavunduka, G.L.
    "Witchcraft and the Law in Zimbabwe." Zambezia. Volume
    8 #2 1980. pp. 129-147.
Cheater, Angela P.
    "Women and Their Participation in Commercial Agricultural
    Production: The Case of Medium-Scale Freehold in
    Zimbabwe." Development and Change. Volume 12 #3 July,
    1981. pp. 349-378.
Cheater, Angela P.
    "Cattle and Class? Rights to Grazing Land, Family
    Organization and Class Formation in Msengezi." Africa.
    Volume 53 #4 1983. pp. 59-74.
Chizengeni, Siphikelelo
    Customary Law and Family Predicaments : A Report on the
    Application of Customary Law in a Changing Society and
    its Effects on the Family With Special Reference to Women
    and Children in Zimbabwe. Harare, Zimbabwe: University
    of Zimbabwe. Center for Applied Social Sciences. 1979.
    78p.
Cook, G.
    "Teurai Ropa Mhongo: Zimbabwe Minister of Community
    Development and Women's Affairs (Interview)." Africa
    Report. Volume 26 #2 April, 1981. pp. 49-50.
Drakakis-Smith, D.W.
    "The Changing Economic Role of Women in the Urbanization
    Process: A Preliminary Report From Zimbabwe."
    International Migration Review. Volume 18 #4 Winter,
    1984. pp. 1278-1292.
Gelfand, M.
    Midwifery in Tropical Africa: The Growth of Maternity

Services in Rhodesia. Salisbury, Rhodesia: University of
Rhodesia. 1978. 88p.
Heald, Madeline
Down Memory Lane With Some Early Rhodesian Women,
1897-1923. Bulawayo, Rhodesia: Books of Rhodesia. 1979.
323p.
Jacobs, Susie
"Women and Land Resettlement in Zimbabwe." Review of
African Political Economy. #27/28 1984. pp. 33-50.
Jules-Rosette, Bennetta
"Family and Ceremonial Authority: The Sources of
Leadership in an Indigenous African Church." (In)
Oppong, C. and Adaba, G. and Bekombo-Priso, M. and Mogey,
J. (eds.). Marriage, Fertility and Parenthood in West
Africa. Canberra, Australia: Australian National
University. Department of Demography. Volume One.
1978. pp. 123+.
MacPherson, T.A.
"A Retrospective Study of Maternal Deaths in the
Zimbabwean Black." Central African Journal of Medicine.
Volume 27 #4 April, 1981. pp. 57-60.
Makamure, Nyaradzo
"Women and Revolution: The Women's Movement of Zimbabwe."
Journal of African Marxists. #6 October, 1984.
pp. 74-86.
May, Joan
"Social Aspects of the Legal Position of Women in
Zimbabwe-Rhodesia." M.Phil Thesis: University of
Zimbabwe-Rhodesia. Harare, Zimbabwe. 1980. 38p.
May, Joan
Zimbabwean Women in Colonial and Customary Law.
Edinburgh, Scotland: Holmes McDougall. Zambeziana #14.
1983. 128p.
May, Joan
African Women in Urban Development. Gwelo, Zimbabwe:
Mambo Press. 1979.
May, Joan
African Women in Urban Employment: Factors Influencing
Their Employment in Zimbabwe. Gwelo, Zimbabwe: Mambo
Press. Mambo Occasional Papers. Socio-Economic Series
#12. 1979. 83p.
May, Joan
Zimbabwean Women in Customary and Colonial Law. Gweru,
Zimbabwe: Mambo Press. Zambeziana #14. 1985. 128p.
May, Joan
Women's Guide to Law Through Life. Harare, Zimbabwe:
University of Zimbabwe. Center for Inter-Racial Studies.
Women and Development Research Unit. April, 1979.
McCalman, Kate
"Zimbabwe: Rural Women Speak Out." Ideas and Action
Bulletin. #158 1984.
McCalman, Kate
We Carry a Heavy Load: Rural Women in Zimbabwe Speak Out:

Report of a Survey Carried Out by the Zimbabwe Women's Bureau. Harare, Zimbabwe: Zimbabwe Women's Bureau. December, 1981. 51p.

Muchena Olivia N.
"Zimbabwe: It Can be Only Handled by Women." (In) Morgan, Robin (ed.). Sisterhood is Global. Garden City, New York: Anchor Books. 1984. pp. 746-755.

Muchena, Olivia N.
"Education and Rural Development as Mission: Some Experiences From Zimbabwe." International Review of Missions. Volume 73 July, 1984. pp. 296-302.

Muchena, Olivia N.
"Women and Participation." Ecumenical Review. Volume 36 #1 January, 1984. pp. 22-24.

Muchena, Olivia N.
"The Changing Position of African Women in Zimbabwe-Rhodesia." Zimbabwe Journal of Economics. Volume 1 #1 March, 1979. pp. 44-61.

Muchena, Olivia N.
Women in Town: A Socioeconomic Survey of African Women in Highfield Township, Salisbury. Harare, Zimbabwe: University of Zimbabwe. Women in Development. Research Unit. Centre for Applied Social Sciences. 1980. 97p.

Muchena, Olivia N.
A Socio-Economic Overview: Zimbabwe Women. Addis Ababa, Ethiopia: United Nations Economic Commission for Africa. African Training and Research Centre for Women. 1982. 48p.

Mundondo, Mabel
"The Decimation of Zimbabwe's Women." Africa Women. #6 1976.

Mungate, D.
Delineation of Areas of Decision Making by Farm Women in Chitomborwizi and Vuti Small Scale Commercial Areas of Mashonaland West Province of Zimbabwe. Harare, Zimbabwe: Ministry of Agriculture. 1985.

Mungate, D.
"Delineation of Area of Decision Making by Farm Women in Chitomborwizi and Vuti Small Scale Commercial Areas of Mashonaland West Province of Zimbabwe." Zimbabwe Agricultural Journal. Volume 2 #82 1985. pp. 47-51.

Mungate, D.
"Women, the Silent Farm Managers in the Small Scale Commercial Areas of Zimabawe." Zimbabwe Agriculture Journal. Volume 2 #80 1983. pp. 245-249.

Mutasa, Joyce and Muzanenhamo, Regina
"Women in Liberation Struggles--Zimbabwe." ISIS International Bulletin. April, 1977. pp. 14+.

Mutunhu, Tendai
"Nehanda of Zimbabwe: A Story of a Woman Liberation Fighter." Ufahamu. Volume 7 #1 1976.

Ngweny,J.
"Women and Liberation in Zimbabwe." (In) Davies, M.

(ed.). Third World Women-Second Sex: Women's Struggles and National Liberation. Third World Women Speak Out. London: Zed Press. 1983. pp. 78-83.

Nhariwa, Margaret
"Women and the Health System in Zimbabwe." ISIS International Bulletin. #20 1981. pp. 25-27.

Nkomo, Jester
"Women's Role in the Struggle." Zimbabwe Review. Volume 7 #1 1978. pp. 10-11.

Nyasha, Rose
"Four Years of Armed Struggle in Zimbabwe." (In) Davies, M. (ed.). Third World-Second Sex: Women's Struggles and National Liberation. Third World Women Speak Out. London: Zed Press. 1983. pp. 99-107.

Penny, O.M.
"The First Midwifery Unit at Harare Hospital." Central African Journal of Medicine. Volume 23 #7 July, 1977. pp. 162-163.

Ranger, T.O.
Some Issues in Land Resettlement in Zimbabwe: Experiences of Shona Women in Resettlement Schemes. London: University of London. Institute of Commonwealth Studies. Center for African Studies. Discussion Paper. December 3, 1985.

Ranger, T.O.
Women in the Politics of Makoni District Zimbabwe, 1890-1980. Manchester, England: University of Manchester. Department of History. 1982.

Ropa, T.
"Women Have Total Involvement in the Struggle." Zimbabwe News. Volume 10 #3 1978. pp. 29-30.

Seidman, Gay W.
"Women in Zimbabwe: Post Independence Struggles." Feminist Studies. Volume 10 #3 Fall, 1984. pp. 419-440.

Shaw, S.
"Bottom of the Pile--Yet Again." New Statesman. Volume 109 May 31, 1985. pp. 20.

Slapgard, Sigrun
"Zimbabwe--Tradition Against the Law." UNICEF News. #122 1985. pp. 26-27.

Tendengu, L.
"An Investigation Into Factors Contributing to the Low Ratio of Women to Men Studying Formal Vocational and Professional Agriculture in Zimbabwe." M.Ed. Dissertation: University of Zimbabwe. Harare, Zimbabwe. 1985.

Thompson, Carol B. (ed.)
"Women in the National Liberation Struggle in Zimbabwe, an Interview of Naomi Nhiwatiwa." Women's Studies International Forum. #2/3 Summer/Fall, 1982. pp. 247-252.

Tsele, Lindiwe M.
   Women in Chimurenga: A Personal Synoptic Account of the
   Experiences of Some of the Women of Zimbabwe During the
   Liberation War for the Freedom of Zimbabwe. London:
   Black Women's Centre. 1981. 64p.
Weinrich, A.K.H.
   "Changes in the Political and Economic Roles of Women in
   Zimbabwe Since Independence." Cultures. Volume 8 #4
   1982. pp. 43-62.
Weinrich, A.K.H.
   Women and Racial Discrimination in Rhodesia. Paris:
   United Nations Educational, Scientific and Cultural
   Organization. 1979. 143p.
Weinrich, A.K.H.
   African Marriage in Zimbabwe and the Impact of
   Christianity. Edinburgh, Scotland: Holmes McDougall.
   1982. 212p.
Weiss, Ruth
   Women of Zimbabwe. Harare, Zimbabwe: Nehanda Publishers.
   Nairobi, Kenya: Savannah Publishers. 1985. 190p.
Women's Action Group.
   Women of Zimbabwe Speak Out: Report of the Women's Action
   Group Workshop, Harare, May, 1984. Harare, Zimbabwe:
   Women's Action Group. 1984. 41p.
Zimbabwe African National Union (ZANU)
   Women's Liberation in the Zimbabwean Struggle. Maputo,
   Zimbabwe: ZANU. A Document Prepared by the ZANU Women's
   Seminar. May, 1979.
Zimbabwe African Patriotic Union (ZAPU)
   "Role of Zimbabwean Women in the Liberation Struggle."
   Paper Presented at the Afro-Asian People's Solidarity
   Organization Conference. Lusaka, Zambia. April, 1979.
Zimbabwe National Family Planning Council (ZNFPC)
   Zimbabwe Reproductive Health Survey, 1984. Harare,
   Zimbabwe: ZNFPC. 1985. 209p.
Zimbabwe. Ministry of Comm. Develop. and Women's Studies
   Report on the Situation of Women in Zimbabwe. Harare,
   Zimbabwe: The Ministry. 1982. 159p.
Zvobgo, Eddison
   "Women in Zimbabwe: Removing Laws That Oppress Women."
   Africa Report. Volume 28 #2 March-April, 1983. pp.
   45-47.
Zvobgo, Eddison
   "Women in Zimbabwe: Transforming the Law." Africa
   Report. Volume 30 #2 March-April, 1985. pp. 64-65.

DEVELOPMENT AND TECHNOLOGY

Cheater, Angela P.
   "Women and Their Participation in Commercial Agricultural
   Production: The Case of Medium-Scale Freehold in

Zimbabwe." Development and Change. Volume 12 #3 July, 1981. pp. 349-378.

Cook, G.
"Teurai Ropa Mhongo: Zimbabwe Minister of Community Development and Women's Affairs (Interview)." Africa Report. Volume 26 #2 April, 1981. pp. 49-50.

Drakakis-Smith, D.W.
"The Changing Economic Role of Women in the Urbanization Process: A Preliminary Report From Zimbabwe." International Migration Review. Volume 18 #4 Winter, 1984. pp. 1278-1292.

Jacobs, Susie
"Women and Land Resettlement in Zimbabwe." Review of African Political Economy. #27/28 1984. pp. 33-50.

Jorgensen, Kirsten (ed.)
Women's Programmes in Zimbabwe. Copenhagen, Denmark: K.U.L.U. Women and Development. 1982. 107p.

Made, P. and Lagerstrom, B.
Zimbabwean Women in Industry. Harare, Zimbabwe: Zimbabwe Publishing House. 1985. 61p.

May, Joan
African Women in Urban Development. Gwelo, Zimbabwe: Mambo Press. 1979.

May, Joan
African Women in Urban Employment: Factors Influencing Their Employment in Zimbabwe. Gwelo, Zimbabwe: Mambo Press. Mambo Occasional Papers. Socio-Economic Series #12. 1979. 83p.

McCalman, Kate
"Zimbabwe: Rural Women Speak Out." Ideas and Action Bulletin. #158 1984.

McCalman, Kate
We Carry a Heavy Load: Rural Women in Zimbabwe Speak Out: Report of a Survey Carried Out by the Zimbabwe Women's Bureau. Harare, Zimbabwe: Zimbabwe Women's Bureau. December, 1981. 51p.

Muchena, Olivia N.
"Education and Rural Development as Mission: Some Experiences From Zimbabwe." International Review of Missions. Volume 73 July, 1984. pp. 296-302.

Muchena, Olivia N.
"The Changing Position of African Women in Zimbabwe-Rhodesia." Zimbabwe Journal of Economics. Volume 1 #1 March, 1979. pp. 44-61.

Muchena, Olivia N.
Women in Town: A Socioeconomic Survey of African Women in Highfield Township, Salisbury. Harare, Zimbabwe: University of Zimbabwe. Women in Development. Research Unit. Centre for Applied Social Sciences. 1980. 97p.

Muchena, Olivia N.
"Women, Subsistence Farming and Extension Services in the Tribal Trust Lands of Rhodesia." Ms Thesis: Cornell University. Ithaca, New York. 1977. 294p.

Muchena, Olivia N.
    Women's Organizations in Zimbabwe: An Assessment of Their
    Needs, Achievement and Potential. Harare, Zimbabwe:
    University of Zimbabwe. Centre for Applied Social
    Science. July, 1980. 32p.
Muchena, Olivia N.
    A Socio-Economic Overview: Zimbabwe Women. Addis Ababa,
    Ethiopia: United Nations Economic Commission for Africa.
    African Training and Research Centre for Women. 1982.
    48p.
Muchena, Olivia N.
    Women and Development in Zimbabwe: An Annotated
    Bibliography. Addis Ababa, Ethiopia: United Nations
    Economic Commission for Africa. Bibliography Series #9.
    1984. 50p.
Mundondo, Mabel
    "The Decimation of Zimbabwe's Women." Africa Women. #6
    1976.
Mungate, D.
    Delineation of Areas of Decision Making by Farm Women in
    Chitomborwizi and Vuti Small Scale Commercial Areas of
    Mashonaland West Province of Zimbabwe. Harare, Zimbabwe:
    Ministry of Agriculture. 1985.
Mungate, D.
    "Delineation of Area of Decision Making by Farm Women in
    Chitomborwizi and Vuti Small Scale Commercial Areas of
    Mashonaland West Province of Zimbabwe." Zimbabwe
    Agricultural Journal. Volume 2 #82 1985. pp. 47-51.
Ndebele, S.
    "Problems Faced by the YWCA of Rhodesia in Involving
    Women and Girls in Rural Development." (In) University
    College of Botswana. Proceedings of the Afro Workshop on
    Rural Environment and Development Planning in Southern
    Africa. Gaborone, Botswana: University College of
    Botswana. 1978. pp. 52-67.
Shaw, S.
    "Bottom of the Pile--Yet Again." New Statesman. Volume
    109 May 31, 1985. pp. 20.
Shifferraw, Maigenet
    "Educational Policy and Practice Affecting Females in
    Zambian Secondary Schools." Ph.D Dissertation:
    University of Wisconsin-Milwaukee. Milwaukee, Wisconsin.
    1982. 176p.
Tendengu, L.
    "An Investigation Into Factors Contributing to the Low
    Ratio of Women to Men Studying Formal Vocational and
    Professional Agriculture in Zimbabwe." M.Ed.
    Dissertation: University of Zimbabwe. Harare, Zimbabwe.
    1985.
Truscott, Kate
    Female Focused Extension--A Contribution to the National
    Extension Framework Study. Harare, Zimbabwe: Ministry of

Lands, Agriculture and Rural Resettlement. Monitoring
and Evaluation Section. AGRITEX. 1985.
United Nations Economic Commission for Africa (UNECA)
   A Socio-Economic Overview: Zimbabwe Women. Addis Ababa,
   Ethiopia: UNECA. Research Series. 1982.
Women's Action Group.
   Women of Zimbabwe Speak Out: Report of the Women's Action
   Group Workshop, Harare, May, 1984. Harare, Zimbabwe:
   Women's Action Group. 1984. 41p.

ECONOMICS

Bond-Stewart, K.
   Women's Problems. Harare, Zimbabwe: Zimbabwe Publishing
   House. 1984. 44p.
Cheater, Angela P.
   "Women and Their Participation in Commercial Agricultural
   Production: The Case of Medium-Scale Freehold in
   Zimbabwe." Development and Change. Volume 12 #3 July,
   1981. pp. 349-378.
Cook, G.
   "Teurai Ropa Mhongo: Zimbabwe Minister of Community
   Development and Women's Affairs (Interview)." Africa
   Report. Volume 26 #2 April, 1981. pp. 49-50.
Drakakis-Smith, D.W.
   "The Changing Economic Role of Women in the Urbanization
   Process: A Preliminary Report From Zimbabwe."
   International Migration Review. Volume 18 #4 Winter,
   1984. pp. 1278-1292.
England, K.
   "A Political Economy of Black Female Labor in Zimbabwe,
   1900-1980." B.A. Thesis: University of Manchester.
   Honors School of History. Manchester, England. 1982.
Jacobs, Susie
   "Women and Land Resettlement in Zimbabwe." Review of
   African Political Economy. #27/28 1984. pp. 33-50.
Jorgensen, Kirsten (ed.)
   Women's Programmes in Zimbabwe. Copenhagen, Denmark:
   K.U.L.U. Women and Development. 1982. 107p.
May, Joan
   African Women in Urban Development. Gwelo, Zimbabwe:
   Mambo Press. 1979.
May, Joan
   African Women in Urban Employment: Factors Influencing
   Their Employment in Zimbabwe. Gwelo, Zimbabwe: Mambo
   Press. Mambo Occasional Papers. Socio-Economic Series
   #12. 1979. 83p.
McCalman, Kate
   "Zimbabwe: Rural Women Speak Out." Ideas and Action
   Bulletin. #158 1984.
McCalman, Kate
   We Carry a Heavy Load: Rural Women in Zimbabwe Speak Out:

Report of a Survey Carried Out by the Zimbabwe Women's
Bureau. Harare, Zimbabwe: Zimbabwe Women's Bureau.
December, 1981. 51p.

Muchena, Olivia N.
"The Changing Position of African Women in
Zimbabwe-Rhodesia." Zimbabwe Journal of Economics.
Volume 1 #1 March, 1979. pp. 44-61.

Muchena, Olivia N.
"Women in Town: A Socioeconomic Survey of African Women
in Highfield Township, Salisbury. Harare, Zimbabwe:
University of Zimbabwe. Women in Development. Research
Unit. Centre for Applied Social Sciences. 1980. 97p.

Muchena, Olivia N.
"Women, Subsistence Farming and Extension Services in the
Tribal Trust Lands of Rhodesia." Ms Thesis: Cornell
University. Ithaca, New York. 1977. 294p.

Muchena, Olivia N.
A Socio-Economic Overview: Zimbabwe Women. Addis Ababa,
Ethiopia: United Nations Economic Commission for Africa.
African Training and Research Centre for Women. 1982.
48p.

Mundondo, Mabel
"The Decimation of Zimbabwe's Women." Africa Women. #6
1976.

Mungate, D.
"Women, the Silent Farm Managers in the Small Scale
Commercial Areas of Zimabawe." Zimbabwe Agriculture
Journal. Volume 2 #80 1983. pp. 245-249.

Shaw, S.
"Bottom of the Pile--Yet Again." New Statesman. Volume
109 May 31, 1985. pp. 20.

Tendengu, L.
"An Investigation Into Factors Contributing to the Low
Ratio of Women to Men Studying Formal Vocational and
Professional Agriculture in Zimbabwe." M.Ed.
Dissertation: University of Zimbabwe. Harare, Zimbabwe.
1985.

Tshuma, Jester and Holmes, Anni
"Publishing for Women in Zimbabwe." ISIS Women's
International Journal. #2 1984.

United Nations Economic Commission for Africa (UNECA)
A Socio-Economic Overview: Zimbabwe Women. Addis Ababa,
Ethiopia: UNECA. Research Series. 1982.

Weinrich, A.K.H.
"Changes in the Political and Economic Roles of Women in
Zimbabwe Since Independence." Cultures. Volume 8 #4
1982. pp. 43-62.

Weinrich, A.K.H.
Women and Racial Discrimination in Rhodesia. Paris:
United Nations Educational, Scientific and Cultural
Organization. 1979. 143p.

EDUCATION AND TRAINING

Anonymous
What the Women are Saying About the Unmarried Girl, Her Child. Salisbury, Rhodesia: Division of African Education. 1977. 18p.

Bond-Stewart, K.
Women's Problems. Harare, Zimbabwe: Zimbabwe Publishing House. 1984. 44p.

Jorgensen, Kirsten (ed.)
Women's Programmes in Zimbabwe. Copenhagen, Denmark: K.U.L.U. Women and Development. 1982. 107p.

Muchena, Olivia N.
"Education and Rural Development as Mission: Some Experiences From Zimbabwe." International Review of Missions. Volume 73 July, 1984. pp. 296-302.

Muchena, Olivia N.
"The Changing Position of African Women in Zimbabwe-Rhodesia." Zimbabwe Journal of Economics. Volume 1 #1 March, 1979. pp. 44-61.

Muchena, Olivia N.
"Women, Subsistence Farming and Extension Services in the Tribal Trust Lands of Rhodesia." Ms Thesis: Cornell University. Ithaca, New York. 1977. 294p.

Muchena, Olivia N.
Women's Organizations in Zimbabwe: An Assessment of Their Needs, Achievement and Potential. Harare, Zimbabwe: University of Zimbabwe. Centre for Applied Social Science. July, 1980. 32p.

Ndebele, S.
"Problems Faced by the YWCA of Rhodesia in Involving Women and Girls in Rural Development." (In) University College of Botswana. Proceedings of the Afro Workshop on Rural Environment and Development Planning in Southern Africa. Gaborone, Botswana: University College of Botswana. 1978. pp. 52-67.

Shifferraw, Maigenet
"Educational Policy and Practice Affecting Females in Zambian Secondary Schools." Ph.D Dissertation: University of Wisconsin-Milwaukee. Milwaukee, Wisconsin. 1982. 176p.

Tendengu, L.
"An Investigation Into Factors Contributing to the Low Ratio of Women to Men Studying Formal Vocational and Professional Agriculture in Zimbabwe." M.Ed. Dissertation: University of Zimbabwe. Harare, Zimbabwe. 1985.

Truscott, Kate
Female Focused Extension--A Contribution to the National Extension Framework Study. Harare, Zimbabwe: Ministry of Lands, Agriculture and Rural Resettlement. Monitoring and Evaluation Section. AGRITEX. 1985.

Weinrich, A.K.H.
"Changes in the Political and Economic Roles of Women in
Zimbabwe Since Independence." Cultures. Volume 8 #4
1982. pp. 43-62.
Weinrich, A.K.H.
Women and Racial Discrimination in Rhodesia. Paris:
United Nations Educational, Scientific and Cultural
Organization. 1979. 143p.
Women's Action Group.
Women of Zimbabwe Speak Out: Report of the Women's Action
Group Workshop, Harare, May, 1984. Harare, Zimbabwe:
Women's Action Group. 1984. 41p.

EMPLOYMENT AND LABOR

Cheater, Angela P.
"Women and Their Participation in Commercial Agricultural
Production: The Case of Medium-Scale Freehold in
Zimbabwe." Development and Change. Volume 12 #3 July,
1981. pp. 349-378.
Drakakis-Smith, D.W.
"The Changing Economic Role of Women in the Urbanization
Process: A Preliminary Report From Zimbabwe."
International Migration Review. Volume 18 #4 Winter,
1984. pp. 1278-1292.
England, K.
"A Political Economy of Black Female Labor in Zimbabwe,
1900-1980." B.A. Thesis: University of Manchester.
Honors School of History. Manchester, England. 1982.
Made, P. and Lagerstrom, B.
Zimbabwean Women in Industry. Harare, Zimbabwe: Zimbabwe
Publishing House. 1985. 61p.
May, Joan
African Women in Urban Development. Gwelo, Zimbabwe:
Mambo Press. 1979.
May, Joan
African Women in Urban Employment: Factors Influencing
Their Employment in Zimbabwe. Gwelo, Zimbabwe: Mambo
Press. Mambo Occasional Papers. Socio-Economic Series
#12. 1979. 83p.
McCalman, Kate
"Zimbabwe: Rural Women Speak Out." Ideas and Action
Bulletin. #158 1984.
McCalman, Kate
We Carry a Heavy Load: Rural Women in Zimbabwe Speak Out:
Report of a Survey Carried Out by the Zimbabwe Women's
Bureau. Harare, Zimbabwe: Zimbabwe Women's Bureau.
December, 1981. 51p.
Muchena, Olivia N.
Women in Town: A Socioeconomic Survey of African Women in
Highfield Township, Salisbury. Harare, Zimbabwe:

University of Zimbabwe. Women in Development. Research Unit. Centre for Applied Social Sciences. 1980. 97p.

Muchena, Olivia N.
"Women, Subsistence Farming and Extension Services in the Tribal Trust Lands of Rhodesia." Ms Thesis: Cornell University. Ithaca, New York. 1977. 294p.

Muchena, Olivia N.
A Socio-Economic Overview: Zimbabwe Women. Addis Ababa, Ethiopia: United Nations Economic Commission for Africa. African Training and Research Centre for Women. 1982. 48p.

Mungate, D.
Delineation of Areas of Decision Making by Farm Women in Chitomborwizi and Vuti Small Scale Commercial Areas of Mashonaland West Province of Zimbabwe. Harare, Zimbabwe: Ministry of Agriculture. 1985.

Mungate, D.
"Delineation of Area of Decision Making by Farm Women in Chitomborwizi and Vuti Small Scale Commercial Areas of Mashonaland West Province of Zimbabwe." Zimbabwe Agricultural Journal. Volume 2 #82 1985. pp. 47-51.

Ndebele, S.
"Problems Faced by the YWCA of Rhodesia in Involving Women and Girls in Rural Development." (In) University College of Botswana. Proceedings of the Afro Workshop on Rural Environment and Development Planning in Southern Africa. Gaborone, Botswana: University College of Botswana. 1978. pp. 52-67.

Seidman, Gay W.
"Women in Zimbabwe: Post Independence Struggles." Feminist Studies. Volume 10 #3 Fall, 1984. pp. 419-440.

Shaw, S.
"Bottom of the Pile--Yet Again." New Statesman. Volume 109 May 31, 1985. pp. 20.

Tshuma, Jester and Holmes, Anni
"Publishing for Women in Zimbabwe." ISIS Women's International Journal. #2 1984.

United Nations Economic Commission for Africa (UNECA)
A Socio-Economic Overview: Zimbabwe Women. Addis Ababa, Ethiopia: UNECA. Research Series. 1982.

Weinrich, A.K.H.
"Changes in the Political and Economic Roles of Women in Zimbabwe Since Independence." Cultures. Volume 8 #4 1982. pp. 43-62.

Women's Action Group.
Women of Zimbabwe Speak Out: Report of the Women's Action Group Workshop, Harare, May, 1984. Harare, Zimbabwe: Women's Action Group. 1984. 41p.

EQUALITY AND LIBERATION

Anonymous
    "Zimbabwe's Women: Throwing Off the Past." Southern
    Africa. November-December, 1979. pp. 7-8+.
Bare, Tendai
    Report on the Situation of Women in Zimbabwe. Harare,
    Zimbabwe: Ministry of Community Development and Women's
    Affairs. February, 1982.
Bond-Stewart, Kathy and Leocardia, C. Murdimu
    Young Women in the Liberation Struggle. Harare,
    Zimbabwe: Zimbabwe Publishing House. 1984.
Makamure, Nyaradzo
    "Women and Revolution: The Women's Movement of Zimbabwe."
    Journal of African Marxists. #6 October, 1984.
    pp. 74-86.
Mgabi, Sally and Munyati, Tsitse and Chengetayi, Confidence
    "Zimbabwe: My Experience in the National Liberation
    Struggle." (In) Mies, Maria and Reddock, Rhoda (eds.).
    National Liberation and Women's Liberation. Hague,
    Netherlands: Institute of Social Studies. 1982. pp.
    73-94.
Mutasa, Joyce and Muzanenhamo, Regina
    "Women in Liberation Struggles--Zimbabwe." ISIS
    International Bulletin. April, 1977. pp. 14+.
Mutunhu, Tendai
    "Nehanda of Zimbabwe: A Story of a Woman Liberation
    Fighter." Ufahamu. Volume 7 #1 1976.
Ngweny,J.
    "Women and Liberation in Zimbabwe." (In) Davies, M.
    (ed.). Third World Women-Second Sex: Women's Struggles
    and National Liberation. Third World Women Speak Out.
    London: Zed Press. 1983. pp. 78-83.
Nkomo, Jester
    "Women's Role in the Struggle." Zimbabwe Review. Volume
    7 #1 1978. pp. 10-11.
Nyasha, Rose
    "Four Years of Armed Struggle in Zimbabwe." (In) Davies,
    M. (ed.). Third World-Second Sex: Women's Struggles and
    National Liberation. Third World Women Speak Out.
    London: Zed Press. 1983. pp. 99-107.
Ropa, T.
    "Women Have Total Involvement in the Struggle." Zimbabwe
    News. Volume 10 #3 1978. pp. 29-30.
Seidman, Gay W.
    "Women in Zimbabwe: Post Independence Struggles."
    Feminist Studies. Volume 10 #3 Fall, 1984. pp.
    419-440.
Thompson, Carol B. (ed.)
    "Women in the National Liberation Struggle in Zimbabwe,
    an Interview of Naomi Nhiwatiwa." Women's Studies
    International Forum. #2/3 Summer/Fall, 1982. pp.
    247-252.

Tshuma, Jester and Holmes, Anni
    "Publishing for Women in Zimbabwe." ISIS Women's
    International Journal. #2 1984.
Zimbabwe African National Union (ZANU)
    Women's Liberation in the Zimbabwean Struggle. Maputo,
    Zimbabwe: ZANU. A Document Prepared by the ZANU Women's
    Seminar. May, 1979.
Zimbabwe African Patriotic Union (ZAPU)
    "Role of Zimbabwean Women in the Liberation Struggle."
    Paper Presented at the Afro-Asian People's Solidarity
    Organization Conference. Lusaka, Zambia. April, 1979.

FAMILY LIFE

Cheater, Angela P.
    "Cattle and Class? Rights to Grazing Land, Family
    Organization and Class Formation in Msengezi." Africa.
    Volume 53 #4 1983. pp. 59-74.
Chizengeni, Siphikelelo
    Customary Law and Family Predicaments : A Report on the
    Application of Customary Law in a Changing Society and
    its Effects on the Family With Special Reference to Women
    and Children in Zimbabwe. Harare, Zimbabwe: University
    of Zimbabwe. Center for Applied Social Sciences. 1979.
    78p.
Cook, G.
    "Teurai Ropa Mhongo: Zimbabwe Minister of Community
    Development and Women's Affairs (Interview)." Africa
    Report. Volume 26 #2 April, 1981. pp. 49-50.
Drakakis-Smith, D.W.
    "The Changing Economic Role of Women in the Urbanization
    Process: A Preliminary Report From Zimbabwe."
    International Migration Review. Volume 18 #4 Winter,
    1984. pp. 1278-1292.
Jules-Rosette, Bennetta
    "Family and Ceremonial Authority: The Sources of
    Leadership in an Indigenous African Church." (In)
    Oppong, C. and Adaba, G. and Bekombo-Priso, M. and Mogey,
    J. (eds.). Marriage, Fertility and Parenthood in West
    Africa. Canberra, Australia: Australian National
    University. Department of Demography. Volume One.
    1978. pp. 123+.
May, Joan
    African Women in Urban Employment: Factors Influencing
    Their Employment in Zimbabwe. Gwelo, Zimbabwe: Mambo
    Press. Mambo Occasional Papers. Socio-Economic Series
    #12. 1979. 83p.
Muchena, Olivia N.
    Women in Town: A Socioeconomic Survey of African Women in
    Highfield Township, Salisbury. Harare, Zimbabwe:
    University of Zimbabwe. Women in Development. Research
    Unit. Centre for Applied Social Sciences. 1980. 97p.

Seidman, Gay W.
"Women in Zimbabwe: Post Independence Struggles."
Feminist Studies. Volume 10 #3 Fall, 1984. pp.
419-440.
Weinrich, A.K.H.
"Changes in the Political and Economic Roles of Women in
Zimbabwe Since Independence." Cultures. Volume 8 #4
1982. pp. 43-62.
Weinrich, A.K.H.
Women and Racial Discrimination in Rhodesia. Paris:
United Nations Educational, Scientific and Cultural
Organization. 1979. 143p.
Weinrich, A.K.H.
African Marriage in Zimbabwe and the Impact of
Christianity. Edinburgh, Scotland: Holmes McDougall.
1982. 212p.

FAMILY PLANNING AND CONTRACEPTION

Bond-Stewart, K.
Women's Problems. Harare, Zimbabwe: Zimbabwe Publishing
House. 1984. 44p.
Castle, W.M.
"The Extent of the Practice of Family Planning Among
Africans in Mashonaland." Central African Journal of
Medicine. Volume 22 #8 August, 1976. pp. 147-151.
Zimbabwe National Family Planning Council (ZNFPC)
Zimbabwe Reproductive Health Survey, 1984. Harare,
Zimbabwe: ZNFPC. 1985. 209p.

FERTILITY AND INFERTILITY

Castle, W.M. and Hakutangwi, K.
"Patterns of Fertility Among Africans in Glen Norah
Township, Salisbury." Central African Journal of
Medicine. Volume 25 #6 June, 1979. pp. 126-130.
Zimbabwe National Family Planning Council (ZNFPC)
Zimbabwe Reproductive Health Survey, 1984. Harare,
Zimbabwe: ZNFPC. 1985. 209p.

HEALTH, NUTRITION AND MEDICINE

Bond-Stewart, K.
Women's Problems. Harare, Zimbabwe: Zimbabwe Publishing
House. 1984. 44p.
Castle, W.M.
"The Extent of the Practice of Family Planning Among
Africans in Mashonaland." Central African Journal of
Medicine. Volume 22 #8 August, 1976. pp. 147-151.
Castle, W.M. and Hakutangwi, K.
"Patterns of Fertility Among Africans in Glen Norah

Township, Salisbury." Central African Journal of
Medicine. Volume 25 #6 June, 1979. pp. 126-130.
Gelfand, M.
Midwifery in Tropical Africa: The Growth of Maternity
Services in Rhodesia. Salisbury, Rhodesia: University of
Rhodesia. 1978. 88p.
Gelfand, Michael
A Service to the Sick: A History of the Health Services
for Africans in Southern Rhodesia, 1890-1953. Harare,
Zimbabwe: Mambo Press. 1976. 187p.
MacPherson, T.A.
"A Retrospective Study of Maternal Deaths in the
Zimbabwean Black." Central African Journal of Medicine.
Volume 27 #4 April, 1981. pp. 57-60.
Nhariwa, Margaret
"Women and the Health System in Zimbabwe." ISIS
International Bulletin. #20 1981. pp. 25-27.
Nhariwa, Margaret
"Women and the Health System in Zimbabwe." ISIS:
International Women's Journal. #20. 1981.
Penny, O.M.
"The First Midwifery Unit at Harare Hospital." Central
African Journal of Medicine. Volume 23 #7 July, 1977.
pp. 162-163.
Zimbabwe National Family Planning Council (ZNFPC)
Zimbabwe Reproductive Health Survey, 1984. Harare,
Zimbabwe: ZNFPC. 1985. 209p.

HISTORY

England, K.
"A Political Economy of Black Female Labor in Zimbabwe,
1900-1980." B.A. Thesis: University of Manchester.
Honors School of History. Manchester, England. 1982.
Gelfand, Michael
A Service to the Sick: A History of the Health Services
for Africans in Southern Rhodesia, 1890-1953. Harare,
Zimbabwe: Mambo Press. 1976. 187p.
Heald, Madeline
Down Memory Lane With Some Early Rhodesian Women,
1897-1923. Bulawayo, Rhodesia: Books of Rhodesia. 1979.
323p.
May, Joan
Zimbabwean Women in Colonial and Customary Law.
Edinburgh, Scotland: Holmes McDougall. Zambeziana #14.
1983. 128p.
May, Joan
Zimbabwean Women in Customary and Colonial Law. Gweru,
Zimbabwe: Mambo Press. Zambeziana #14. 1985. 128p.
Mutunhu, Tendai
"Nehanda of Zimbabwe: A Story of a Woman Liberation
Fighter." Ufahamu. Volume 7 #1 1976.

Ranger, T.O.
  Women in the Politics of Makoni District Zimbabwe,
  1890-1980. Manchester, England: University of
  Manchester. Department of History. 1982.
Seidman, Gay W.
  "Women in Zimbabwe: Post Independence Struggles."
  Feminist Studies. Volume 10 #3 Fall, 1984. pp.
  419-440.

LAW AND LEGAL ISSUES

Chavunduka, G.L.
  "Witchcraft and the Law in Zimbabwe." Zambezia. Volume
  8 #2 1980. pp. 129-147.
Chizengeni, Siphikelelo
  Customary Law and Family Predicaments : A Report on the
  Application of Customary Law in a Changing Society and
  its Effects on the Family With Special Reference to Women
  and Children in Zimbabwe. Harare, Zimbabwe: University
  of Zimbabwe. Center for Applied Social Sciences. 1979.
  78p.
May, Joan
  "Social Aspects of the Legal Position of Women in
  Zimbabwe-Rhodesia." M.Phil Thesis: University of
  Zimbabwe-Rhodesia. Harare, Zimbabwe. 1980. 38p.
May, Joan
  Zimbabwean Women in Colonial and Customary Law.
  Edinburgh, Scotland: Holmes McDougall. Zambeziana #14.
  1983. 128p.
May, Joan
  Zimbabwean Women in Customary and Colonial Law. Gweru,
  Zimbabwe: Mambo Press. Zambeziana #14. 1985. 128p.
May, Joan
  Women's Guide to Law Through Life. Harare, Zimbabwe:
  University of Zimbabwe. Center for Inter-Racial Studies.
  Women and Development Research Unit. April, 1979.
Slapgard, Sigrun
  "Zimbabwe--Tradition Against the Law." UNICEF News.
  #122 1985. pp. 26-27.
Zvobgo, Eddison
  "Women in Zimbabwe: Removing Laws That Oppress Women."
  Africa Report. Volume 28 #2 March-April, 1983. pp.
  45-47.
Zvobgo, Eddison
  "Women in Zimbabwe: Transforming the Law." Africa
  Report. Volume 30 #2 March-April, 1985. pp. 64-65.

LITERATURE

Gardzanwa, Rodo B.
  Images of Women in Zimbabwean Literature. Harare,
  Zimbabwe: University of Zimbabwe Press. 1985.

MARITAL RELATIONS AND NUPTIALITY

Castle, W.M.
"The Extent of the Practice of Family Planning Among
Africans in Mashonaland." Central African Journal of
Medicine. Volume 22 #8 August, 1976. pp. 147-151.
May, Joan
"Social Aspects of the Legal Position of Women in
Zimbabwe-Rhodesia." M.Phil Thesis: University of
Zimbabwe-Rhodesia. Harare, Zimbabwe. 1980. 38p.
May, Joan
African Women in Urban Employment: Factors Influencing
Their Employment in Zimbabwe. Gwelo, Zimbabwe: Mambo
Press. Mambo Occasional Papers. Socio-Economic Series
#12. 1979. 83p.
Weinrich, A.K.H.
African Marriage in Zimbabwe and the Impact of
Christianity. Edinburgh, Scotland: Holmes McDougall.
1982. 212p.

MIGRATION

Bond-Stewart, Kathy and Leocardia, C. Murdimu
Young Women in the Liberation Struggle. Harare,
Zimbabwe: Zimbabwe Publishing House. 1984.
Drakakis-Smith, D.W.
"The Changing Economic Role of Women in the Urbanization
Process: A Preliminary Report From Zimbabwe."
International Migration Review. Volume 18 #4 Winter,
1984. pp. 1278-1292.

NATIONALISM

Anonymous
"Zimbabwe's Women: Throwing Off the Past." Southern
Africa. November-December, 1979. pp. 7-8+.
Makamure, Nyaradzo
"Women and Revolution: The Women's Movement of Zimbabwe."
Journal of African Marxists. #6 October, 1984.
pp. 74-86.
Mgabi, Sally and Munyati, Tsitse and Chengetayi, Confidence
"Zimbabwe: My Experience in the National Liberation
Struggle." (In) Mies, Maria and Reddock, Rhoda (eds.).
National Liberation and Women's Liberation. Hague,
Netherlands: Institute of Social Studies. 1982. pp.
73-94.
Mutasa, Joyce and Muzanenhamo, Regina
"Women in Liberation Struggles--Zimbabwe." ISIS
International Bulletin. April, 1977. pp. 14+.

Mutunhu, Tendai
   "Nehanda of Zimbabwe: A Story of a Woman Liberation
   Fighter." Ufahamu. Volume 7 #1 1976.
Ngweny,J.
   "Women and Liberation in Zimbabwe." (In) Davies, M.
   (ed.). Third World Women-Second Sex: Women's Struggles
   and National Liberation. Third World Women Speak Out.
   London: Zed Press. 1983. pp. 78-83.
Nkomo, Jester
   "Women's Role in the Struggle." Zimbabwe Review. Volume
   7 #1 1978. pp. 10-11.
Nyasha, Rose
   "Four Years of Armed Struggle in Zimbabwe." (In) Davies,
   M. (ed.). Third World-Second Sex: Women's Struggles and
   National Liberation. Third World Women Speak Out.
   London: Zed Press. 1983. pp. 99-107.
Ropa, T.
   "Women Have Total Involvement in the Struggle." Zimbabwe
   News. Volume 10 #3 1978. pp. 29-30.
Seidman, Gay W.
   "Women in Zimbabwe: Post Independence Struggles."
   Feminist Studies. Volume 10 #3 Fall, 1984. pp.
   419-440.
Thompson, Carol B. (ed.)
   "Women in the National Liberation Struggle in Zimbabwe,
   an Interview of Naomi Nhiwatiwa." Women's Studies
   International Forum. #2/3 Summer/Fall, 1982. pp.
   247-252.
Zimbabwe African National Union (ZANU)
   Women's Liberation in the Zimbabwean Struggle. Maputo,
   Zimbabwe: ZANU. A Document Prepared by the ZANU Women's
   Seminar. May, 1979.
Zimbabwe African Patriotic Union (ZAPU)
   "Role of Zimbabwean Women in the Liberation Struggle."
   Paper Presented at the Afro-Asian People's Solidarity
   Organization Conference. Lusaka, Zambia. April, 1979.

ORGANIZATIONS

Jorgensen, Kirsten (ed.)
   Women's Programmes in Zimbabwe. Copenhagen, Denmark:
   K.U.L.U. Women and Development. 1982. 107p.
Muchena, Olivia N.
   Women's Organizations in Zimbabwe: An Assessment of Their
   Needs, Achievement and Potential. Harare, Zimbabwe:
   University of Zimbabwe. Centre for Applied Social
   Science. July, 1980. 32p.
Ndebele, S.
   "Problems Faced by the YWCA of Rhodesia in Involving
   Women and Girls in Rural Development." (In) University
   College of Botswana. Proceedings of the Afro Workshop on
   Rural Environment and Development Planning in Southern

Africa. Gaborone, Botswana: University College of
Botswana. 1978. pp. 52-67.
Women's Action Group.
Women of Zimbabwe Speak Out: Report of the Women's Action
Group Workshop, Harare, May, 1984. Harare, Zimbabwe:
Women's Action Group. 1984. 41p.

POLITICS AND GOVERNMENT

Anonymous
"Zimbabwe's Women: Throwing Off the Past." Southern
Africa. November-December, 1979. pp. 7-8+.
Cook, G.
"Teurai Ropa Mhongo: Zimbabwe Minister of Community
Development and Women's Affairs (Interview)." Africa
Report. Volume 26 #2 April, 1981. pp. 49-50.
Jacobs, Susie
"Women and Land Resettlement in Zimbabwe." Review of
African Political Economy. #27/28 1984. pp. 33-50.
Makamure, Nyaradzo
"Women and Revolution: The Women's Movement of Zimbabwe."
Journal of African Marxists. #6 October, 1984.
pp. 74-86.
May, Joan
Zimbabwean Women in Customary and Colonial Law. Gweru,
Zimbabwe: Mambo Press. Zambeziana #14. 1985. 128p.
Mgabi, Sally and Munyati, Tsitse and Chengetayi, Confidence
"Zimbabwe: My Experience in the National Liberation
Struggle." (In) Mies, Maria and Reddock, Rhoda (eds.).
National Liberation and Women's Liberation. Hague,
Netherlands: Institute of Social Studies. 1982. pp.
73-94.
Mundondo, Mabel
"The Decimation of Zimbabwe's Women." Africa Women. #6
1976.
Mutasa, Joyce and Muzanenhamo, Regina
"Women in Liberation Struggles--Zimbabwe." ISIS
International Bulletin. April, 1977. pp. 14+.
Ngweny,J.
"Women and Liberation in Zimbabwe." (In) Davies, M.
(ed.). Third World Women-Second Sex: Women's Struggles
and National Liberation. Third World Women Speak Out.
London: Zed Press. 1983. pp. 78-83.
Nkomo, Jester
"Women's Role in the Struggle." Zimbabwe Review. Volume
7 #1 1978. pp. 10-11.
Nyasha, Rose
"Four Years of Armed Struggle in Zimbabwe." (In) Davies,
M. (ed.). Third World-Second Sex: Women's Struggles and
National Liberation. Third World Women Speak Out.
London: Zed Press. 1983. pp. 99-107.

Ranger, T.O.
   Some Issues in Land Resettlement in Zimbabwe: Experiences
   of Shona Women in Resettlement Schemes. London:
   University of London. Institute of Commonwealth Studies.
   Center for African Studies. Discussion Paper. December
   3, 1985.
Ranger, T.O.
   Women in the Politics of Makoni District Zimbabwe,
   1890-1980. Manchester, England: University of
   Manchester. Department of History. 1982.
Ropa, T.
   "Women Have Total Involvement in the Struggle." Zimbabwe
   News. Volume 10 #3 1978. pp. 29-30.
Seidman, Gay W.
   "Women in Zimbabwe: Post Independence Struggles."
   Feminist Studies. Volume 10 #3 Fall, 1984. pp.
   419-440.
Thompson, Carol B. (ed.)
   "Women in the National Liberation Struggle in Zimbabwe,
   an Interview of Naomi Nhiwatiwa." Women's Studies
   International Forum. #2/3 Summer/Fall, 1982. pp.
   247-252.
Truscott, Kate
   Female Focused Extension--A Contribution to the National
   Extension Framework Study. Harare, Zimbabwe: Ministry of
   Lands, Agriculture and Rural Resettlement. Monitoring
   and Evaluation Section. AGRITEX. 1985.
Weiss, Ruth
   Women of Zimbabwe. Harare, Zimbabwe: Nehanda Publishers.
   Nairobi, Kenya: Savannah Publishers. 1985. 190p.
Women's Action Group.
   Women of Zimbabwe Speak Out: Report of the Women's Action
   Group Workshop, Harare, May, 1984. Harare, Zimbabwe:
   Women's Action Group. 1984. 41p.
Zimbabwe African Patriotic Union (ZAPU)
   "Role of Zimbabwean Women in the Liberation Struggle."
   Paper Presented at the Afro-Asian People's Solidarity
   Organization Conference. Lusaka, Zambia. April, 1979.
Zvobgo, Eddison
   "Women in Zimbabwe: Removing Laws That Oppress Women."
   Africa Report. Volume 28 #2 March-April, 1983. pp.
   45-47.
Zvobgo, Eddison
   "Women in Zimbabwe: Transforming the Law." Africa
   Report. Volume 30 #2 March-April, 1985. pp. 64-65.

RELIGION AND WITCHCRAFT

Chavunduka, G.L.
   "Witchcraft and the Law in Zimbabwe." Zambezia. Volume
   8 #2 1980. pp. 129-147.

Jules-Rosette, Bennetta
    "Family and Ceremonial Authority: The Sources of
    Leadership in an Indigenous African Church." (In)
    Oppong, C. and Adaba, G. and Bekombo-Priso, M. and Mogey,
    J. (eds.). Marriage, Fertility and Parenthood in West
    Africa. Canberra, Australia: Australian National
    University. Department of Demography. Volume One.
    1978. pp. 123+.
Muchena, Olivia N.
    "Education and Rural Development as Mission: Some
    Experiences From Zimbabwe." International Review of
    Missions. Volume 73 July, 1984. pp. 296-302.
Muchena, Olivia N.
    "Women and Participation." Ecumenical Review. Volume 36
    #1 January, 1984. pp. 22-24.
Weinrich, A.K.H.
    African Marriage in Zimbabwe and the Impact of
    Christianity. Edinburgh, Scotland: Holmes McDougall.
    1982. 212p.

SEX ROLES

Bond-Stewart, K.
    Women's Problems. Harare, Zimbabwe: Zimbabwe Publishing
    House. 1984. 44p.
Bonnerjea, Lucy
    "Invisible Women." Zambezia. Volume 9 #2 1981.
Brown, Judith K.
    "Economic Organization and the Position of Women Among
    the Iroquois (and Bemba)." (In) Tiffany, Sharon W.
    (ed.). Women and Society: An Anthropological Reader.
    St. Albans, Vermont: Eden Press. Women's Publications.
    1979. pp. 48-74.
Cheater, Angela P.
    "Cattle and Class? Rights to Grazing Land, Family
    Organization and Class Formation in Msengezi." Africa.
    Volume 53 #4 1983. pp. 59-74.
Drakakis-Smith, D.W.
    "The Changing Economic Role of Women in the Urbanization
    Process: A Preliminary Report From Zimbabwe."
    International Migration Review. Volume 18 #4 Winter,
    1984. pp. 1278-1292.
England, K.
    "A Political Economy of Black Female Labor in Zimbabwe,
    1900-1980." B.A. Thesis: University of Manchester.
    Honors School of History. Manchester, England. 1982.
May, Joan
    "Social Aspects of the Legal Position of Women in
    Zimbabwe-Rhodesia." M.Phil Thesis: University of
    Zimbabwe-Rhodesia. Harare, Zimbabwe. 1980. 38p.
May, Joan
    Zimbabwean Women in Customary and Colonial Law. Gweru,
    Zimbabwe: Mambo Press. Zambeziana #14. 1985. 128p.

Muchena, Olivia N.
  "The Changing Position of African Women in
  Zimbabwe-Rhodesia." Zimbabwe Journal of Economics.
  Volume 1 #1 March, 1979. pp. 44-61.
Muchena, Olivia N.
  "Women, Subsistence Farming and Extension Services in the
  Tribal Trust Lands of Rhodesia." Ms Thesis: Cornell
  University. Ithaca, New York. 1977. 294p.
Mungate, D.
  Delineation of Areas of Decision Making by Farm Women in
  Chitomborwizi and Vuti Small Scale Commercial Areas of
  Mashonaland West Province of Zimbabwe. Harare, Zimbabwe:
  Ministry of Agriculture. 1985.
Mungate, D.
  "Delineation of Area of Decision Making by Farm Women in
  Chitomborwizi and Vuti Small Scale Commercial Areas of
  Mashonaland West Province of Zimbabwe." Zimbabwe
  Agricultural Journal. Volume 2 #82 1985. pp. 47-51.
Mungate, D.
  "Women, the Silent Farm Managers in the Small Scale
  Commercial Areas of Zimabawe." Zimbabwe Agriculture
  Journal. Volume 2 #80 1983. pp. 245-249.
Nkomo, Jester
  "Women's Role in the Struggle." Zimbabwe Review. Volume
  7 #1 1978. pp. 10-11.
Ranger, T.O.
  Some Issues in Land Resettlement in Zimbabwe: Experiences
  of Shona Women in Resettlement Schemes. London:
  University of London. Institute of Commonwealth Studies.
  Center for African Studies. Discussion Paper. December
  3, 1985.
Shaw, S.
  "Bottom of the Pile--Yet Again." New Statesman. Volume
  109 May 31, 1985. pp. 20.
Tendengu, L.
  "An Investigation Into Factors Contributing to the Low
  Ratio of Women to Men Studying Formal Vocational and
  Professional Agriculture in Zimbabwe." M.Ed.
  Dissertation: University of Zimbabwe. Harare, Zimbabwe.
  1985.
Tsele, Lindiwe M.
  Women in Chimurenga: A Personal Synoptic Account of the
  Experiences of Some of the Women of Zimbabwe During the
  Liberation War for the Freedom of Zimbabwe. London:
  Black Women's Centre. 1981. 64p.
Weinrich, A.K.H.
  "Changes in the Political and Economic Roles of Women in
  Zimbabwe Since Independence." Cultures. Volume 8 #4
  1982. pp. 43-62.
Weiss, Ruth
  Women of Zimbabwe. Harare, Zimbabwe: Nehanda Publishers.
  Nairobi, Kenya: Savannah Publishers. 1985. 190p.

STATUS OF WOMEN

Bare, Tendai
    Report on the Situation of Women in Zimbabwe. Harare,
    Zimbabwe: Ministry of Community Development and Women's
    Affairs. February, 1982.
Bond-Stewart, Kathy and Leocardia, C. Murdimu
    Young Women in the Liberation Struggle. Harare,
    Zimbabwe: Zimbabwe Publishing House. 1984.
Makamure, Nyaradzo
    "Women and Revolution: The Women's Movement of Zimbabwe."
    Journal of African Marxists. #6 October, 1984.
    PP.74-86.
Muchena Olivia N.
    "Zimbabwe: It Can be Only Handled by Women." (In)
    Morgan, Robin (ed.). Sisterhood is Global. Garden City,
    New York: Anchor Books. 1984. pp. 746-755.
Mutasa, Joyce and Muzanenhamo, Regina
    "Women in Liberation Struggles--Zimbabwe." ISIS
    International Bulletin.   April, 1977. pp. 14+.
Ngweny,J.
    "Women and Liberation in Zimbabwe." (In) Davies, M.
    (ed.). Third World Women-Second Sex: Women's Struggles
    and National Liberation. Third World Women Speak Out.
    London: Zed Press. 1983. pp. 78-83.
Nkomo, Jester
    "Women's Role in the Struggle." Zimbabwe Review. Volume
    7 #1 1978. pp. 10-11.
Ropa, T.
    "Women Have Total Involvement in the Struggle." Zimbabwe
    News. Volume 10 #3 1978. pp. 29-30.
Slapgard, Sigrun
    "Zimbabwe--Tradition Against the Law." UNICEF News.
    #122 1985. pp. 26-27.
Thompson, Carol B. (ed.)
    "Women in the National Liberation Struggle in Zimbabwe,
    an Interview of Naomi Nhiwatiwa." Women's Studies
    International Forum. #2/3 Summer/Fall, 1982. pp.
    247-252.
Weinrich, A.K.H.
    "Changes in the Political and Economic Roles of Women in
    Zimbabwe Since Independence." Cultures. Volume 8 #4
    1982. pp. 43-62.
Weinrich, A.K.H.
    Women and Racial Discrimination in Rhodesia. Paris:
    United Nations Educational, Scientific and Cultural
    Organization. 1979. 143p.
Women's Action Group.
    Women of Zimbabwe Speak Out: Report of the Women's Action
    Group Workshop, Harare, May, 1984. Harare, Zimbabwe:
    Women's Action Group. 1984. 41p.
Zimbabwe African National Union (ZANU)
    Women's Liberation in the Zimbabwean Struggle. Maputo,

Zimbabwe: ZANU. A Document Prepared by the ZANU Women's
Seminar. May, 1979.
Zimbabwe African Patriotic Union (ZAPU)
"Role of Zimbabwean Women in the Liberation Struggle."
Paper Presented at the Afro-Asian People's Solidarity
Organization Conference. Lusaka, Zambia. April, 1979.
Zimbabwe. Ministry of Community Development and Women's
Studies
Report on the Situation of Women in Zimbabwe. Harare,
Zimbabwe: The Ministry. 1982. 159p.

URBANIZATION

Drakakis-Smith, D.W.
"The Changing Economic Role of Women in the Urbanization
Process: A Preliminary Report From Zimbabwe."
International Migration Review. Volume 18 #4 Winter,
1984. pp. 1278-1292.

WOMEN AND THEIR CHILDREN

Anonymous
What the Women are Saying About the Unmarried Girl, Her
Child. Salisbury, Rhodesia: Division of African
Education. 1977. 18p.
Bond-Stewart, K.
Women's Problems. Harare, Zimbabwe: Zimbabwe Publishing
House. 1984. 44p.
Chizengeni, Siphikelelo
Customary Law and Family Predicaments : A Report on the
Application of Customary Law in a Changing Society and
its Effects on the Family With Special Reference to Women
and Children in Zimbabwe. Harare, Zimbabwe: University
of Zimbabwe. Center for Applied Social Sciences. 1979.
78p.

Author Index

Abbas, Ibrahim 123,146,149,151
Abbott, Susan 5,12
Abdalla, Raqiya 2,10,15,123,171,168
Abdelraman, Mohammed A. 271,275
Abegaz, Berhanu 28,29,36,53
Abrahams, Cecil A. 410
Abrahams, R. 235
Abrahams, R.G. 181,219,225
Abu-Bakr, Salah 123,147,151,159
Adagala, Kavetsa 43,58,63,72
Adam, Abbas Y. 123(2),146(2),149(2)
Adan, Amina H. 116
Adika, G.H. 460
Adlakha, Arjun 83,88,93
Adnan, Amal M. 123,147,151,159
Adu-Bobie, Gemma 42,106
Africa Bureau 320,352,427,445
African National Congress (ANC) 320,373,421,427
Agbasi, Gabriel O. 84
Aggarwal, V.P. 37(2),80,89(2)
Ahlberg, B.M. 37,42,58,63
Aitchison, Roberta 19
Akello, Grace 235
Akerele, Olubanke 58,63,72,463,467,471
Ali, M.R. 456,477,481
Ali, Mohamed A. 123,136,140,149
Ali, Nur 123,142,145,163
Allen, Vivien 352,397
Almagor, Uri 21,27,34
Alopaeus-Stahl, Dorrit 176,181,190,197,204,222
Alpers, E.A. 181,190,217(2),224(2),225,312
Alpers, Edward 2,12
Altman, R. 394,450
Alverson, Hoyt 256,277,328

Amobi, Nnambi K.   84
Anandajayasekeram   178,183,227
Anderson, Mary B.   37(2),42(2),41(2),63,69,72,107
Andre La Cock, J.   404,412
Anker, Richard   38,42,63(2),69,72(2),84(4),101
Anonymous   13,20,21(2),42,58(2),63,172,182,210,223,226,
    232,239(2),245,248(2),249,250,253,285(2),288,289,290(2),
    292,301,302(2),312(2),319,320(6),321(2),328(12),329(2),
    351,352(2),360(10),361(4),373(6),378,387(7),397,404,
    410(2),420,421,423(3),424(6),427(7),428(3),438(4),
    445(6),493,494,503,506,511,513,518
Arenson, Paul   329,361,387
Argyle, John   352,361,449
Arkutu, A.A.   215,216
Armon, P.J.   216
Armstrong, Alice K.   451(2)
Armstrong, Amanda   348,361
Armstrong, Henrietta E.   387,397
Aromasodu, M.C.   123,151,174,256,271
Arungu-Olende, Rose   42,107
Arya, O.P.   235
Asayehgn, Desta   182,197,202,204,226
Assaad, Fawzia   124,151,169
Attallah, N.L.   151
Ault, James (Jim)   456(2),479,481,482,485,486
Austoker, Joyce   359,361
Ayiemba, Elias H.   42,81,85
Azefor, M.   457,476,477,478(2),482
Aziz, F.   124,151,169

Baard, Francis   321,373,428
Baartman, D.   329,387,438
Baasher, Taha A.   124(3),151,152(2),169(3)
Babiker, Abdel B.   119,124,142,164
Bader, Zinnat   176,182,190,210,226
Badran, Margot   120,152
Badri, Amina E.   124,136,139,141(2),161(3),165
Badri, Amira   123,141,145,164
Badri, Gasim Y.   124(2),125,141,145,152(3),165,169(2),174
Badri, Malik   125(2),152,153,169,170
Bakr, Salah A.   125(2),153(2),170(2)
Bakri, Z.B.   125,139,141,162,173   See also: El-Bakri, Z.B.
Balisidya, M.L.   182,202,219
Ballard, R.   452
Bardouille, Raj   454,456,457(4),463,464(2),467(3),471(4),
    486(3),490(4)
Bare, Tendai   506,517
Barling, J.I.   388
Barling, Julian   329(3),382(3),387,412,438
Barlow, M.R.   388
Barnabas, G.   21,29
Barnard, A.H.   351,404,413
Barnard, Alan   256,278
Barnes, Carolyn   38,42,107
Barnes, Virginia L.   162,235

Barnes-Dean, Virginia L. 125,153,170
Barrett, J. 374,422,446
Barrett, Jane 329,438,446
Barry, J. 332,351,413
Bauer, Dan F. 21,28,34
Baxter, Diana 120(3),125,126(2),134(3),139(2),142(2),143,
  145,165(2),173(2)
Bayoumi, Ahmed 126,153,165
Beall, J. 321,329(3),330,438,445
Beall, J.D. 321,352(3),397(3),398(3),428(2),437,438(4),
  446(3)
Beaman, Anne C. 60,107
Beard, Linda S. 410
Beavon, K. 330,348,352,361,378,439
Becken, Hans-Jurgen 330,435
Becker, Ruth 330,361,424,439
Becker, Stan 49,51,70,71,83(3),87(2),88,99(2),100
Beckman, Joyce A. 398,410
Beddada, Belletech 22(4),29(4),35(2)
Bedri, Balghis Y. 120,134,139,141
Behardien, Gadaja 330,352,361,446
Behr, D. 330,361,388,439,
Beidelman, T.O. 312
Beinart, William 321,398,424
Bekele, Abebech 121,128,137,139,143,165,173
Bekker, J.C. 330(2),351,352,404(2),413(2)
Bella, H. 126,153
Benedict, Burton 115
Benedict, Marion 115
Benson, Susan 126,139,143,146
Bentley, G.R. 256,271
Berger, Iris 2(2),14(2),330(2),353(3),362(4),398(2),
  424(2)
Berio, Ann 120,136,139,143
Bernal, V. 120,126,143,165
Bernard, Roger P. 119(2),135(2),148(2),158(2),160(2)
Berning, G. 330,398,446
Bernstein, Hilda 420
Besha, R.M. 7,13
Bettles, F.M. 254,261,265
Bezwoḍa, W.R. 392
Bhana, Kastoor 330,450
Bifani, Patricia 42,43,58(2),63,72,106,241,242,249
Bijleveld, Catrien 132,156,172
Binford, Martha B. 312
Bird, A. 353,362,424
Bjeran, Gunilla 22,28,32,34
Blakeley, Brian L. 331,398
Bliese, Loren F. 22,35
Bloch, B. 318(2),331,382,388(2),391,405
Bloch, Maurice 305(2)
Blok, P.G. 56,92,93,114
Boddington, Erica 321(2),353,362(2),398,439,446
Boddy, J. 126,153,162,170
Boerma, J.T. 89

Bolon, K. 388
Bond, C.A. 254,261,265
Bond-Stewart, K. 492,494,501,503,506,508(2),511,515,517,
  518
Bongaarts, John 91
Bonnerjea, Lucy 494,515
Booth, W.R. 388
Botha, P.M.C. 333,420
Bothwell, T.H. 392
Botswana. Ministry of Agriculture 254,261,265,278
Bourgoyne, Clarissa 20,22,25,31,35
Bozzoli, Belinda 331(2),353(2),362,374(2),378,398,418,
  419,422(2),428(2),439(3)
Bradshaw, Evelyn 331,388
Brain, James L. 177,182(3),190,191,197,205,219,224,226
Brainard, J.M. 43,89,114
Brantley, Cynthia 43,105
Brass, W. 310
Brenner, B.N. 336,390
Brew-Graves, Ekow 460
Brindley, Marianne 331(2),378,388,439(2)
Brink, Elsabe 353,362(2),378,399(2),410,439
Broche-Due, Vigdis 38,43,58
Brokensha, D. 374,410,437
Bromberger, Norman 331,353,378,439
Brown, Barbara B. 256(3),263(3),266(4),268(3),273,274(2),
  275,278(2),281,321,331,353,382,385,428
Brown, Judith K. 494,515
Brown, Lloyd W. 410
Bruner, Charlotte H. 411(3)
Bryant, Coralie 256,263,266,268,275,281
Bryceson, Deborah F. 177(4),182(3),191(5),197(3),198(2),
  202(2),205(3),210,217,221,226(3),232
Bryer, J.V. 393
Budlender, Debbie 374,422,428
Budlender, Vivienne L. 331,388
Bughwan, Devi 353,362,440
Bujra, Janet M. 43(2),63,64,72,73,93(2),113
Bullough, C.H. 306
Burkhart, Marianne 57,93
Burman, Sandra B. 331(2),332,351(4),404(3),413(3),428,
  435,440,446
Burton, John F. 126,146,159
Burton, John W. 126(4),159,162(2),165,173
Butler, Lorna M. 284,289,290,306
Butterfield, Cynthia 64,73
Buzzard, Shirley 64,73,112

Cachalia, Amina 321,332,374,428
Campbell, C.A. 41,43
Canter, Richard S. 457,476,480,482
Cape Town. City Engineer. Technical Management Services
  321,437
Caplan, A.P. 224,231
Caplan, Patricia 2,6,12(2),15,17,174,177,182,183(2),

191(2),198(3),205(2),216,224,226
Carim, Shirene F. 353,363,424
Caron, James W. 43,107,114
Carstens, Peter 332,436
Casale, Dorothy M. 235
Cassiers, Anne 22,28
Cassim, N.A. 405(2),446(2)
Castle, W.M. 382,388,494(2),508(4),511
Catchpole, David R. 239,249
Chabaku, Motlalepula 332(2),436,440
Chale, Freda U. 177(2),191(2),198(2),202,205,210,226,234
Chandler, Dale 42,106
Chaney, Elsa M. 451
Chanock, Martin 457,479,480
Charlton, R.W. 392
Chauncey, George 457,472,477,478,479,482,484,486
Chavunduka, G.L. 494,510,514
Cheater, Angela P. 492(2),494(2),498,501,504,507,515
Cheetham, R.W. 332,388
Chengelela, Rustica 192,203,210,226
Chengetayi, Confidence 511,513
Chenoveth, F.A. 454,457,464,467
Chernichovsky, Dov 256(2),266(2),268(2),270(2),271(2),
  273(2)
Chetty, Romila 332,378,413
Chetty, Thiagaraj D. 332,363,379,413
Chi, I-Cheng 119,134,148,158
Chiffelle, Suzanne 20,22,27,28,35
Chijumba, Beat J. 183,198,205,219,227
Chimwaza, B.M. 306
Chipande, G. 306
Chiume, Kanyama 192,198,205
Chizengeni, Siphikelelo 494,507,510,518
Chung. Ah-Fong 310
Church, J. 332,405
Church, Joan 332,374,405,413,429
Chuzu, Pia M. 455,458,464
Ciancanelli, Penelope 43,98,107,112
Clark, Carolyn M. 38,43,94,107
Clark, Isobel 126,153,170
Clark, Mari H. 43,64,107
Clark, Noreen 38,42,69
Clarke, Sarah H. 457,467,471,472
Cliffe, Lionel 454,457,467,472,484,486
Cloudsley, Anne 126,127,153,162,170(2)
Cobbe, Louise B. 290,292(2)
Cochrane, Judith 43,44,97
Cock, Jacklyn 321,322,332(2),333(3),354(3),363(11),
  364(2),388(2),389(3),399(3),429,436,440(2),445,450
Coertze, T.F. 351,406,414
Collier, J.F. 256,276,278
Collins, Carole 315(2),
Comaroff, John L. 256,257(2),273(3),274,278,337,415,441
Comhaire, Jean 20,22,25,31
Constantinides, Pamela 127,153,162,165

Cook, G.   494,499,501,507,513
Cook, Robert   127,153,162,170
Cook, Sheila   270,271
Cooke, John   411
Cooke, Wendy-Lynne   343,450
Cooper, C.   322,333,405,429
Cooper, Carole   239,246
Cooper, David   257(2),263(2),266(2),268(2),275(2),278(2),
  281(2)
Cooper, Frederick   38,73,94,111,177,205,217,232
Coupersmith, J.   394,449
Court, J.H.   405,420
Cox, J.L.   235
Crause, H.L.   333,420
Crehan, Kate   457,464,467,476,487
Croll, E.J.   177,183,192,198,205,227
Cronje, Gillian   315
Cronje, Suzanne   315
Crummey, Donald   20(3),23(5),31(3),32(2)
Curtin, Patricia R.   44,98
Cutshall, Charles R.   458(2),480(2),485,487

Daka, Kebebew   23,28,32,35
Date-Bah, Eugenia   254,257,261,267,278
Davey, D.A.   395
Davies, A.H.   331,382,388
Davison, J.   44,59
Davison, Jean   38,44,70,103
Dawber, A.   422,446
Dawber, Aneene   322,374,425
De Haas, Mary   333,351,413
De Heusch, Luc   312
De Jager, Thea   262,268
De Villiers, F.   257,269,270
De Villiers, Richard   322,399,405,422,429
De Wet, J.I.   393
Deheusch, L.   238,239,247,250
Delmet, C.   127,146,159,163
Demissic, Fassil   322,429
Dempster, W.S.   391
Derman, D.P.   392
Derman, P.J.   451
Dey, Jennie M.   120,134,143,165
Diaz, Christina   126,153,170
Diepenhorst, M.J.   81,85
Dillon-Malone, Clive M.   456,458,467,472
Dirasse, Laketch   23,25,33
Dison, E.   347,396
Dissevelt, A.G.   89
Dlamini, C.R.M.   333(2),405(2),413,440
Dlamini, M.   452
Dodoo, Nii M.S.   127,147,149
Dommisse, J.   318,389
Donley, L.   44,94,98
Donne, L.   85,149,296

Doodoh, A. 119,134,148,158
Dow, Thomas E. 44(4),81(5),85(2),98(4)
Drakakis-Smith, D.W. 494,499,501,504,507,511,515,518
Driver, D. 411,437
Drower, Sandra J. 318(2),333,389(2)
Du Pradal, Pia 257,269,270,274
Du Toit, Bettie 354,364
Dualeh, Raqiya H. 116(2)
Duckitt, J.H. 333,389
Due, Jean M. 178(2),183(2),198,206,210,222,227(2),306,
  454(5),458(4),464(5),467(2),468(3),472(5),476(2),482,
  487(3)
Duffield, Mark 126,139,143,146
Duncan, M.E. 29
Duncan, Sheena 322,333,364,379,406,413,422,429,440
Durban Women's Bibliography Group 239,327
Duvenhage, A. 347,396
Duza, M. Badrud 235

Eastman, C.M. 41,43,44,77,98,107
Edwards, Felicity 239,249,250
Eelens, Frank 49,73,85(2),87,89,149,286,296(2),297
Egan, Siobhan 319,333,364,440
El Awad alal el Din, Mohamed 127,159,175
El Awad Galal El Din, Mohamed 127,147,149,163,174
El Bagir, Ibrahim 120,136,143,165
El Dareer, A.A. 154(2),170(2) See also: El-Dareer, A.A.
El Din Abdu, Anwar S. 119,124,142,164
El Meheina, Rabab H. 120,136,141,173
El Sadaawi, Nawal 127,157,163,171
El Sayed, M. 127,128,154(2),163(2),171(2)
El Sayed, Mahasin K. 120,121(2),128,141,143,165
El-Attar, M. 333,385,413
El-Bakri, Z.B. 128,139,143,163 See also: Bakri, Z.B.
El-Bushra, Judy 121,128,137,139,143,165,173
El-Dareer, Asma A. 128(6),154(4),155(2),171(6)
  See also: El Dareer, A.A.
El-Kashef, Samy 129,146,159,166
El-Nagar, S. 129,163
El-Sayyid, Mahasin K. 129(2),137(2),143(2),166(2)
El-Tom, Abdul R. 129,147,155
El-Wassela, Negeya 137,144
Elias, Misrak 5(2),6,7,241(2),243(2)
Elmalik, Khitma H. 129,166
Emdon, E. 363(3),388,389(2)
Emdon, S. 389
Emereuwaonu, Ernest U. 44,70,81(2),85(2),98(2)
England, K. 501,504,515
Ensminger, J. 38,44,101,107
Ensor, Linda 239,246,322,333,405,429
Epstein, Arnold L. 458,476,482,491
Eraj, Yusuf A. 81,89
Erasmus, G. 334,383,389,414
Erasto, Muga 2,13,239,248
Evans, J. 306(2),307

Evans, Jennifer 45,97
Evans-Pritchard, E.E. 129,163
Evens, T.M. 129,163
Ewbank, Douglas C. 183(2),212(2),214(2),216(2),219,220
Eyben, Rosalind 141,144,173

Fagan, J.J. 334,406,414,440
Fam, Murman L. 310
Farah, Abdul-Aziz 119(3),147(2),149,155(3)
Farid, Samir 147,149,160
Farrand, Dorothy M. 334,389
Faruqee, Rashid 85
Faurie, K.M. 354,364
Favis, M. 354,364,440
Federal Council of the National Party of South Africa
   322,334,374,422,429
Feldman, Rayah 38(2),45,59(2),73,102
Fenn, Thomas 129,147,155
Ferguson, J.G. 119,135,148,158,160
Fernihough, T.J. 334,383,389
Ferraro, Gary 451
Ferry, Benoit 45,81,85
Finch, Briony J. 389,440
Finch, Charles S. 24,31
Fincham, Frank 329,382
Findley, Sally E. 183(3),212(3),214(3),233(3)
Finlayson, Rosalie 334
First, Ruth 411
Fisher, F. 334,399,440
Fjellman, Stephen M. 45,107
Flanagan, William G. 184,206,211,220,233
Flepp, Caroline 322,334,364,446
Fleuret, A. 192,199,206
Flisher, A.J. 359,390
Fluehr-Lobban, Carolyn 121,129,130(2),137,159,162,163,
   166(2)
Fomulu, J.N. 87,91
Forni, Elisabetta 116
Forsey, T. 29
Fortmann, Louise P. 178(4),184(2),192(4),199(4),206(4),
   227(2),254(3),257(2),261(3),263,264(2),278(2)
Foucher, Emile 23,34
Founou-Tchuigoua, B. 121,130,137,144
Fowkes, F.G. 30
Franks, James A. 296,297
Freinkel, Joan C. 364
Frenkel, C. 418(2)
Freund, Paul J. 458,478,491
Friedman, Annette 334,359,374,436
Frost, O. 30
Fruzzetti, L. 121,130,155,166
Fuchs, Jean R. 334,379
Furman, S.N. 334,390

Gabba, Anna 223

Gachuhi, J. Mugo 82
Gachukia, Eddah W. 38(3),45,59(3),103(2)
Gaitskell, Deborah 322,334(2),335(3),354,364(2),399(4),
  400,414,429,436(4),440,441
Gakuo, Mumbi 45,59,64,112
Gandor, Mark 331,353,378,439
Gaobepe, M.G. 455,458
Gardzanwa, Robo B. 510
Gatara, Timothy H. 45,70,77,85,99,105
Gay, Judith S. 285(2),290(3),292,298,302
Gay, Judy S. 284(2),285(2),289,290(3),291,293(3),294(3),
  300(3),302
Gebre-Medhim, Mehari 30(2),36
Gebre-Selassie, Alasebu 2,5,17,21,24,30,34,36
Geiger, Susan 178,192,199,203
Geisler, Gisela G. 455,458,464
Gelfand, M. 494,509
Generose, Ngonyani 177,191,198,205,210,234
Gerais, Abdel S. 130,147,155
Gerard, U. 389
Gerdes, L.C. 335,390,414,441
Germain, Adrienne 1,2,5,15,238,239,241,249
Getechah, W. 39,42
Gilfoun, Nadia 130,146,160,166
Gill, H.S. 216
Gillard, Jillian 354,411,420
Ginwala, Frene 322,335,354,364,429,447
Gizuli, Shahwa 130,141,155
Gjerstad, O. 312
Glazier, Jack 45
Glen, I. 411
Gold, Alice 39,45,94,107
Goldstein, Susan 364,390
Gomm, Roger 45,105
Gon, Sylvia 365,406
Goodwin, June 322,335,365,374,429,447
Gordon, Elizabeth 285,286(3),291(2),293(3),294(2),295(2),
  298(2),299(2),300(3),303(2)
Gordon, S. 365
Gore, Paul W. 130(3),137,150(2),155(2),160
Gorfain, Phyllis 45
Graaff, Janet 365(2),379,414(2),419(2)
Grainger, C.R. 115,
Grassivaro, Gallo P. 116
Grech, E.S. 478
Greeley, Edward H. 45,86,89
Green, E.C. 451
Greene, P.A. 39,59,64,70
Griessel, Annette 322,374,425,429
Griffiths, Anne 257,273,276,282
Griffiths, J.A. 379,391
Grobler, I. 390,420
Groenewald, H.J. 383(3),385(3)
Gruenbaum, Ellen 121,130(2),137,144,155,166,172,173
Guenther, Mathias G. 238,239,244

Gumede, M.V. 335,390
Gunner, Elizabeth 327(2),335(2),411
Gupta, Anirudha 45,59,64,112
Gutto, S.B.O. 49,78,96,100,111
Gutto, Shadrack B. 46(2),59(2),96,107,108,112(2)
Guyer, Jane I. 255,258,261,264,267,279,319,348,354,365
Gwazela, Sindiswa 322,406,420,429
Gyepi-Garbrah, Benjamin 86

Hafkin, Nancy J. 21,24,34
Haile, Daniel 23,30,32,36
Hakem, Ahmed M. 131,158
Hakutangwi, K. 494
Hall, Marjorie J. 131(2),159,172,173
Hallett, Robin 400,420,429
Hamblin, E. 354,365
Hamdani, Salha 178,192,199,206,227
Hamilton, Carolyn A. 323,335,365,400
Hammour, Fatima A. 131,137,141,144,166
Hammour, Fawzia 121,128,137,139,143,165,173
Hampson, M.E. 335,383,390
Handands, G.C. 406(2),420(2)
Hanoomanjee, Esther 310
Hansen, Art 455,456,462,466,470,475(2),489
Hansen, H. 312
Hansen, Karen T. 455,458,459(9),464,468(7),472(3),473(7),
    481,482(4),487(3),491(4)
Hansen, R. 312
Harries, Jane 319,365,441
Harris, Joan 46,77,104,112
Hart, R.H. 216
Hassan, Kamil I. 121,131,140,144,167
Hassan, Majda M. 124,136,139,141,165
Hathi, Jee T. 176,183,216
Hay, Margaret J. 46(2),60,64,94(2),96
Hazzard, Virginia 1,4,7,15
Heald, Madeline 495,509
Heberden, W. 400
Hecht, Elisabeth-Dorothea 23,33,35
Hedlund, H. 455,459,468
Heese, H.D. 391
Hein, Catherine R. 245,246,247,310(2)
Henderson, Francene I. 255,258,262,277
Henin, Roushdi A. 2,9,10,86(2)
Henn, Jeanne K. 178,192,199,206,227
Hermann, Anne 379,411,441,447
Hermer, Carol 323,374,400
Hernell, Olle 30
Heyneman, Stephen P. 235
Hill, Alison M. 365,375,441,447
Hill, G.B. 297
Hill, Sylvia 312
Himonga, C.N. 459,481,482,487
Himonga, H.B. 471,478,491
Hirsch, A. 365,425

Hirschmann, David 307(5)
Hirshfield, Claire 400,425
Hishongwa, Ndentala 315
Hlophe, J.M. 336,406,414,430
Hoar, R.N.M. 390,450
Hofmeyer, Isabel 410
Holdstock, T. Len 334,389
Hollander, Roberta B. 46,95,104,108,184,217,223,227
Holmes, Anni 502,505
Hoosen, A.A. 449
Horn, Nancy 255,258,262,264,267,277,279
Hosken, Fran P. 2(2),3(10),4(2),8,9(2),10(10),11(4),15,
  16(10),17(3)
House, Amelia 411
Howard, K.A. 388
Howland, R.C. 395
Hrbek, Ivan 131,158
Huelsman, Ben R. 4,11,17
Hughes, C.A. 237
Hulka, J.F. 383,390
Hull, Valerie 46,82,90,114
Hussain, S.J. 459,481,482
Hutchinson, Sharon 131,167
Huth, Mary J. 193,199,206,232,233
Hyde, M. 390

Ibrahim, Fouad N. 121(2),131(2),144,167
Ibrahim, Suad A. 122,131,167
Igbinovia, Patrick E. 4,7,13,15,240,244,248,250
Internation Co-Operative Alliance 193,203
International Defence and Aid Fund for Southern Africa
  (IDAF) 315(2),323,336,375(2),422(2),430(3)
International Labour Organization (ILO) 39,60,64
International Statistical Institute (ISI) 86,150(2),156,
  296
Isaacman, Allen 313(2)
Isaacman, Barbara 313(2)
Isaacs, Gayla C. 247,336,419,441
Isaacson, C. 396
Ismail, Bakhita A. 131,172,173
Ismail, Edna A. 116,117(3)
Ismail, Ellen T. 131,146,160,167
Izzard, Wendy 258(4),264(4),267(4),269(4),274,275(4),
  279(3),282(3)

Jackson, Kennell A. 46,77,90,95
Jacobs, Susie 492,495,499,501,513
Jahn, Samia A. 122,132,137,167
Jalal el-Deen, Mohamed A. 132,147
Janelid, Ingrid 284,286,289,302,303
Jansen, A.A. 48,90(2),91(2),113
Jelley, D. 313
Jialai, I. 340,392
Jiggins, Janice 455,459,464,487
Johnson, Willene 193,199,207,233

Johnston, Bruce F.   5(2),9(2),11(2),14(2)
Johnston, Thomas F.   327,336,414
Jones, J.   347,396(2)
Jones, R.   389
Jordaan, J.P.   393
Jorgensen, Kirsten   499,501,503,512
Joseph, Rosemary   327,336
Joubert, S.M.   393
Jules-Rosette, Bennetta   240,249,253,460(2),465(2),468,
  469,473(2),487(2),495,515
Junge, B.J.   23,26,36

Kabwegyere, Tarsis   46,64,77,82(2),86(2)
Kaganas, F.   390,406,414
Kaha, Ulla   262,264,276
Kalule-Sabiti, I.   86,123,146,149,151,287,297,299,303
Kalumba, Katele   458,478,491
Kamau, G.K.   46,85,96,106
Kameir, E.M.   125,128,139(2),141,143,162(2),173
Kamfwa, Franklin D.   455,465,469,484
Kamuzora, C. Lwechungura   174,193,217,214,227
Kangi, M.W.   46,82,86,90,113
Kankassa, B.C.   475,490
Kanyiri, Elisha M.   47,65,73,82
Kaplan, R.   365,425
Kariuki, Patricia W.   43,58,63,72
Karrar, Gaafar   132,147
Kartunnen, Maryatta   141,144,173
Kashif-Badri, Hagga   138(2),142(2),144(2),164(2),173(2)
Kasulamemba, Sylvia   184,207,210,220,234
Katumba, Rebecca   236(2)
Katz, I.B.   336,390
Kayongo-Male, Diana   5,7(2),14,60,65,73,106,108
Kayuni, F.   308(3)
Keller, Bonnie B.   455,458,464,465(2),469(2),473(2)
Kelley, Allen C.   47,65,77
Kenya. Central Bureau of Statistics   86,90
Kenya. Ministry of Finance and Economic Planning   47(5),
  60(2),65(2),70,82(4),86,87(3),98(3),108,112
Kerr, A.J.   336,406,414
Kershaw, Greet   47(2),65(2),78,108(2)
Kertzer, David I.   132,156,167
Kerven, Carol   255,258,262,264(2),269,275,279,282
Ketema, Teserach   24,28(2),30,32
Kettel, Bonnie   47,108
Khalifa, Mona A.   132(6),147(2),148(4),150(3),156,160,163,
  174
Khatree, M.H.D.   393
Khider, M.   122,132,144,167
Khoza, N.C.   343,393
Khulumani, P.   259,272
Kibet, M.   49,70,71,83(2),87(2),99(2)
Kibuka, E.P.   236
Kidane-Mariam, Widad   30
Kiern, Susan M.   336,436

Kiernan, J.P.   336,365,414,436,441
Kigozi, Dorcus   236
Kikopa, Jane R.   184(2),210,218,223,228,232,234
Kilbourne, S.K.   391
Kilbride, Janet E.   236
Kilbride, Philip L.   236
Kimane, I.   286,289,293,303
Kimaryo, Scholastica   185,193,199,217,228,234
Kimble, Judy   322,334,336,354,364,375,422,425,429,430,
  441,447
Kimenya, P.   39,60,70,74
Kimmons, Leona   323,336,375,430
Kinsman, Margaret   253,258,272,279,336,351,400,441
Kipury, N.   47,99
Kirsten, G.F.   391
Kisekka, Mere N.   236
Klein, H.   4,12,17
Klima, George   185,218,220,228
Kloppers, H.P.   351,406,414
Klugman, B.   363(2),389(2),391(2)
Klugman, Barbara   336,354,366,406,430
Klugman, I.   374,422,446
Kneerim, Jill   65,73,103
Knell, H.F.   366
Knotts, Mary A.   65,73,78,102,113
Knowles, James C.   38,42,63(2),69,72(2),83(3),101
Kocher, James E.   179(4),185(6),193(5),200(2),213(5),
  214(3),215(3),216(2),222,228(5)
Koda, Bertha   185,194,201,207,210,222,228
Kok, P.C.   384,392
Kokuhirwa, Hilda N.   185,194,201(2),211,220
Komma, Toru   48(2),65,70,73,90,103(2)
Kongstad, P.   48,93,78
Konie, Gwendoline   240,248,250,460,475,490
Konner, M.J.   258(2),270,272(2),279,282,315
Kopenhager, T.   318,391
Kort, H.   318,391
Korten, Ailsa   86
Kosgei, Sally J.   48,65,95
Kossoudji, Sherrie   255,259,265,269,279
Kotze, J.J.   337,406,414
Kramer, Joyce M.   48,97,90
Krause, Richard A.   327,337
Kreysler, J.   259,272
Krige, Eileen J.   337(5),379(2),415(4),436,441(2)
Krige, J.D.   337,436
Kromstedt, Katherine   25,27
Kros, Cynthia   375,400(2),425(2),430(2),449(2)
Kruks, Sonia   313(2)
Krystall, Abigail   40,41,62,63,68,70,75,77
Kubukeli, Pumla   337,441
Kune, J.B.   48,65,78,90,109,114
Kunene, Mazisi   337,411
Kunst, J.   318,407
Kuper, Adam   240,245,247,250,337,415,451

Kuria, Gibson K. 48,78,96,99,108
Kusin, Jane A. 90(3),91,114
Kuzwayo, Ellen 323,337,375,447
Kwast, B.E. 30
Kwofie, Kwamie 460
Kyaruzi, Agnes 222

Labuschagne, G.P. 391
Lacko, W. 91,113
Ladipo, O.A. 9,11
Ladner, Joyce A. 179,194,200,223
Lagerstrom, B. 499,504
Lagerwerf, Levy 259
Lakhani, S.A. 48,90(2),91(3),113
Lamba, Isaac C. 307
Lambek, Michael 283
Lamula, Promise 323,337,430
Lancaster, Chet S. 476,482,488
Landau, J. 379,391
Landis, Elizabeth 323,337,349,354,366
Langley, Myrtle S. 48,106,117
Lanham, W. 329,382,387,412
Lapchick, Richard E. 315,316,323((2),338(3),355(2),366,
    375(3),422(2),423,430(3),441,447
Larsen, J.V. 338(2),391(3)
Larsen, Lorne E. 186,224
Larsen, Ulla 87,91,150,156
Larson, M.K. 259,272
Larson, Thomas J. 259(2),277(2)
Laukaran, Virginia 91
Lauro, Donald 129,147,155
Lawton, L. 338,355,366,441
Lee, Lily W. 91
Lee, Richard B. 253,259(2),267,276,279,316
Lehulere, K. 330,352,361,446
Leland, Stephanie 245,249
Leocardia, C. Murdimu 506,511,517
Leonard, D.K. 39(2),40,60(2),70(2),71,74,75,92,104
Lesotho. Central Bureau of Statistics 296
Lesthaeghe, Ron J. 49(2),70,71,83(3),87(3),99(2),286,297
Letsema 383,391,415
Levett, A. 391
Levett, Ann 339,375,423
LeVine, Robert A. 48,49,70,78,99(2),108
LeVine, Sarah 48,49(2),99(2),108(2)
Levinthal, Terri 343,357,421
Levitan, Ron 366,420
Levy, Wendy 132,156,172
Lewis, Barbara C. 39,60,66,74,451
Lewis, Jon 366,400,425
Liao, Kharia F. 130,147,155
Lightfoot-Klein, H. 132,156,172
Lihamba, Amandina 181,186
Likimani, Muthoni G. 49,60,66,104,112
Lindsay, Beverly 49,60,66(4),71(3),74(2),104,112,113

AUTHOR INDEX

Lipman, Beata 323,338,249,355,375,423
Lisasi, D. 217,222
Llewelyn-Davies, Melissa 32(2),95,109(2)
Locke, M. 323,338,349,359
Lodge, Tom 375,400,431
Lonnerdal, Bo 30
Longwe, Sara H. 475,481,484,490
Lotter, Johann M. 323,338(4),339,355,359,366,383(3),
  384(2),386(6),415(4),449
Low, Allan 296,291,293,299,301,303,452(2)
Lowe, Linda T. 194,200,207,233
Lowenfels, A. 4,11,13,17,117
Lowenstein, L.F. 133,156,172
Luckhardt, Ken 366,425
Luhanga, Emily 186,194,218,232
Lundahl, M. 455,459,468
Lura, Russell P. 49,52,71,83,87,88,100

MacGaffey, Wyatt 4,8,12(2),15,240,245,246,247,250
Machel, S.M. 313
Mackay, B. 21,25,29,34
Mackenzie, D.J. 339(2),392,400,401(2),431,442,449
MacPhail, A.P. 392
MacPherson, T.A. 393,495,509
Made, P. 499,504
Madison, Oker B.B. 132,156,167
Madland, M. 284,286,289,303
Madsen, Birgit 179,186,194,200,207
Magnarella, P.J. 133,162,164
Mahadeyo, I. 334,383,389
Maina, Rose 49,78,96,100,111
Maitum, Mary I.D. 236
Majma, Sachak 191,197,202,210,232
Makamure, Nyaradzo 495,506,511,513,517
Makenete, S.T. 295,296,297,299
Makokha, A.E. 91
Makunga, N.V. 420
Malahleha, Gwen M. 286,303
Malawi Ministry of Agriculture (MOA) 307
Malveaux, J. 339,447
Mamashela, M. 286,289,298,299,303
Mandala, Elias 307(2)
Mandeville, Elizabeth 236
Manona, C.W. 339,366,379,415,419
Manyeneng, W.G. 259,272
Manyosi, Maud 339,355,366,379
Maqutu, W.C.M. 286,298,299,303
Marasha, M. 51,83
Margo, R. 452
Mariotti, Amelia 349(2),355(2),366,367,379,401,431
Marivate, M. 340,392
Mark, G. 318,392
Marks, Shula 6,7,13,318,339,367,379,416,419,442
Marquard, Jean 412(2)
Martin, P.M. 297

Martin, V. 367,442
Martine, Huvers 351,405,413,428,435
Marwick, M. 339,380,416
Mascarenhas, Ophelia 181(2),194,225(2)
Mashaba, T.G. 367,392
Mashiane, Shirley 322,335,354,364,429,447
Matau, M. 356,368
Mathews, T. 87,91
Mati, J.K.G. 11,14,37(3),51,80,83,87,89(3),91,94(2)
Matsepe, Ivy F. 238,241,242,245(2),248(3),250,349,355,
   367,401,431
Matsepe-Casaburri, Ivy F. 238,240(2),241(2),242,246,249,
   251,316,323,339(2),349(3),355(3),359,367(2),380,431(2),
   442
Matsetela, Ted 320,356,367,401
Matteru, May 186,203,219
Mauritius. Ministry of Health 310
Mawbey, John 367,401,425
May, Nicky 40,53,61,110
May, Joan 495(6),499(2),501(2),504(2),507,509(2),510(4),
   511(2),513,515(2)
Mayes, Janis 97
Mayet, F.G. 392
Mayne, Anne V. 339,375,423
Mbatha, Nikiwe D. 452
Mbevi, Grace 49,91,100
Mbikusita-Lewanika, Inonge 460,476,488
Mbilinyi, Marjorie J. 7,15,177,179(4),181(2),182(2),
   186(5),187(2),191,194(4),195,197,200(3),203(2),205,
   207(3),210,211(2),213,215,218(4),223,225(2),226(2),
   228,229(5),232
Mbughuni, Patricia 50(2),97(2)
Mbula, J. 33,77,78,82,86,109
Mburu, F.M. 92,114
Mburugu, Edward K. 460,477,478,483
McAdoo, Harriette P. 50,78,109,113
McCafferty, S. 319,392,407
McCalman, Kate 492(2),495(2),499(2),501(2),504(2)
McCold, Paul E. 458,480
McDowell, James 1,4,5,7,15
McFadden, Patricia 240,243,244,452(2)
Mcharo, N.E. 187,195,203
McHenry, Dean E. 180,187,195,200,208,229
Meer, Fatima 324,339,340(2),356,367(2),368(2),380(3),416,
   431,442(3)
Meghji, Zakia 195,200,208,229
Meheus, A. 452(3)
Mehta, Aasha 356,368
Mehta, S.R. 311
Meintjes, Sheila 331,422,428
Meiring, R. 318,407
Melrose, E.B. 392
Merrett, Patricia L. 401
Merry, Sally E. 460,479
Merryman, Nancy H. 39,33,78

Meyer, Anthony J.   5(2),9,11(2),14(2)
Mgabi, Sally   511,513
Mgaya, Mary   187,195,200,208
Mgone, C.S.   4,11,17
Mhloyi, Marvellous M.   50,83,88,91,287,296,297(2)
Mia, F.P.   347,396
Mickelwait, Donald R.   39,60,66,73,284,289,291,293
Middleton-Keirn, Susan   340,436
Mies, M.   1,6,8,238,243,244
Millar, Shirley   368,407
Miller, Patricia   454(2),464(2)
Minnis, Robert L.   296,297
Mitchell, L.   340,384,442
Mitchell, Mozella G.   340,437
Mkalipe, Pauline C.M.   368
Mkangi, George C.   50,66,71,88
Mlama, Penina   181,197,204,219,231
Modawi, Osman   133(2),156(2),167(2)
Modawi, Suleiman   133(2),156,157,172(2)
Modley, J.   340,392
Moeno, N.S.   340,380
Mohammed, Nadia   123,142,145,164
Mohan, P.C.   39,61,66,73
Moharib, Samir R.   133,142,145,150,160
Moizen, Inga   329,361,387
Mokgethi, S.S.   356,368
Molise, Ngoakoane M.   287,299
Molokomme, Athaliah   259,274,281
Mommsen, C.   340,392
Monkhe, M.C.   338(2),391(2)
Monstead, Mette   39(2),33(3),74(2),79(2),100(2),109(2)
Monsted, Mette   40(2),48,61,66,73,74,77,79,100,103,109
Moock, P.R.   40,61,66,73
Moodley, J.   396
Moodley, S.P.   340,392
Moody, Elizabeth J.   239,241,242,243,244,249,340,349,356
Mosley, W. Henry   51(2),83(2),88(2),100(2)
Moss, Rose   412
Mostert, W.P.   343,381,384(2),392,394
Motsete, Ruth K.   262,265,276
Motshologane, S.R.   259,269,274,279,281,282
Mott, Frank L.   51,67,73,79,109
Mott, S.H.   51,91
Mott, Susan H.   34,61,71,83,88,92,114
Mphahlele, M.   392
Mpiti, A.M.   287,297,299,303
Msane, C.L.   338(2),391(2)
Mtimavalye, L.A.   216,217,222
Mubanga, Foster   473,475,484,485,488
Muchai, V.W.   49,78,96,100,111
Muchena, Olivia N.   240,242,243,492(3),493,496(6),499(4),
   500(3),502(4),503(4),504,505(2),507,512,515(2),516(2),
   517
Mudenda, Timothy   454(4),458(3)464(4),467,468(2),472(3),
   476,482,487(2)

AUTHOR INDEX

Mueller, Eva 255,259(2),265,269(2),279,280
Mueller, Martha B. 287(3),289(2),299,303(2),304
Muganzi, Zibeon S. 92,114
Mukurasi, Laeticia 208,222,223,229
Muller, A.S. 56(2),89,92,93(3),102,114
Muller, E.J. 391
Mullins, Ann 368
Mullins, Elizabeth A. 356,368
Muludiang, Venansio T. 133,140,145,161,174
Munachonga, Monica 460,483,488
Mundondo, Mabel 313,493,496,500,502,513
Munene, Fibi 61,67,71
Mungate, D. 493,496(3),500(2),502,505(2),516(3)
Munoz, W.P. 334,383,389
Munroe, Robert L. 51,109
Munroe, Ruth H. 51,109
Muntemba, M. Shimwaayi 455(3),460(3),465(4),469(4),
  474(3),480(2),485,488(3)
Muntemba, Maude 455,460,465,469,488
Munyati, Tsitse 511,513
Murdock, Muneera S. 122,133,138,168
Muriuki, Margaret N. 7,8,14,243,244,248
Muro, Asseny 180(2),187(3),195(3),201(2),204(3),208(3),
  229,230
Muro, M. 218,220,230
Murphy, D. 313
Murray, C. 390,406,414
Murray, Colin G. 238,240,243,244,246,247(2),287(7),
  291(4),293(3),294(2),295(5),299,300(2),301(6),304(4),
  412
Murray, Joselyn 51,92,95,106,111
Murray-Hudson, A. 316
Murugu, N.M. 37,94
Mushanga, Tibamanya M. 4,13,14
Musialele, E. 316
Mustafa, Asha 122,134,168
Mustafa, M.Y. 134,146,150,160,161,174
Musyoki, Rachel N. 71,83
Mutasa, Joyce 245,249,496,506,511,513,517
Mutiso, G.C. 12,79
Mutiso, Roberta M. 40,74,102
Mutungi, O.K. 51,97,106
Mutunhu, Tendai 496,506,509,512
Muzaale, P. 39,60,70,74
Muzale, P. 40,71,75,92,100
Muzanenhamo, Regina 496,506,511,513,517
Muze, Siphiwe 187,211,220
Mvubelo, Lucy 356,368
Mwanamwabwa, Catherine 465,469,474
Mwaniki, M.K. 51,83
Mwaniki, N. 51,83
Mwaria, Cheryl B. 51,67,75,79,102,109,111
Mwenda, A. 455,458
Mwenda, Deborah 222
Mwobobia, I. 86

N'ska, Leci 8,14
Naeye, R.L. 393
Nag, Prithvish 461,483,484,488
Nagashima, Nobuhiro 51,52,100(2)
Naicker, R.S. 340,392
Naidoo, Margaret 368
Naisho, Joyce 134,157
Naishom, Joyce 134,157,168
Namfua, Pelad P. 188,215,220,230
Nash, E.S. 318,319(2),333,389,392,393,407
Nash, Margaret 380,450
Nathan, C. 407,447
National Association of Negro Business and Professional
  Women's Clubs 307
National Union of Eritrean Women 33,34,36
Nattrass, Nicoli 340,356(2),368(2)
Navias, M. 319(2),392,393,407
Ncongwane, J. 396
Ndaba, N. 393
Ndebele, S. 493,500,503,505,512
Nel, C.J. 393
Nelson, Nici 52(5),61,67,75,79(3),101(2),104,109,110(2)
Nene, Daphne S. 320(2),340(2),341,349(2),356,359,368,380,
  384,416(2),425,442(2)
Nene, Sibongile 324,342,420
Newman, James L. 52,83,88
Ngalula, Theresia K. 180,188(2),196,201,208,211,220,
  213(2)
Ngcobo, Lauretta 246
Ngubane, Harriet 341(2),416,442
Ngugi, D. 39,60,70,74
Ngulube, Clare 461,483
Ngweny, J. 496,506,512,513,517
Ngwisha, Kaluba J. 461,476,483,488,491
Nhariwa, Margaret 497
Nhlapho, R.T. 452
Nicol, Martin 356,369,401,426
Nirmul, D. 393
Njau, Rebeka 52
Njoki, Margaret 52(2),53,92(3),111
Njuki, Caroline W. 53,71
Nkabinde, C. 324,341,368,407,431
Nkambule-Kanyima, Brenda 255,258,262,264,267,277,279
Nkomo, Jester 497,506,512,513,516,517
Norton, A.B. 350,357,369
Nouri, Mohamed O. 134,148,150,333,385,413
Nsanze, H. 235
Ntantala, Phyllis 324,341,380,407,431,447
Ntozi, James P. 236
Ntsoaki 316
Ntuyabaliwe, W.K. 217,222
Nujumi, Elhan E. 124,136,139,141,165
Nur, Osman el-H. M. 134,148(2),150,157(2)
Nwankwo, Chimalum M. 97(2)

Nyasha, Rose 497,506,512,513
Nyonyntono, Rebecca M. 53,61,67(2),75,79

O'Brien, Denise 240,247,250
O'Brien, M. 180,188,195,208,230
O'Keefe, S.J.D. 393
O'Regan, F. 452
Obbo, Christine S. 236
Obeid, Marwa A. 124,136,139,141,165
Obery, I. 369,374,422,446
Obery, Ingrid 426
Oboler, Regina S. 53(4),67,101,110(3)
Ocholla-Ayayo, A.B. 134,160,168
Ode-Ade, Femi 412
Ogutu, M.A. 67,75,95
Ohadike, Patrick O. 188,211,213,215,220
Ojiambo, Julia 57,61,67,75
Ojwang, J.B. 63,95,96,106
Okeyo, Achola P. 40,53,95   See also: Pala, Achola O.
Okonkwo, J.I. 117
Oldshue, R. 393
Olekambaine, Priscilla 195,204
Olivecrona, Thomas 30
Olmesdahl, M.J.C. 341,416
Olusanya, P.O. 36,84,92,288,296,297,311
Ombina, O. 40,53,61,110
Omer, E.E. 140
Omiat, John 235
Omondi, Odhiambo 56(2),89,93(2),102
Omran, S. 130,147,155
Onyango, Philista P.M. 4,6,8(2),17
Oomen-Myin, Marie A. 180,196,201,208,230
Oosthuizen, J.M. 357,369
Opolot, J.A. 236
Opondo, Diana 61,67,104
Organization of Angolan Women 253
Orr, Ann C. 183(2),212(2),214(2),233(2)
Osman, Ali K. 134(3),157(3)
Otaala, Barnabas 260,267,269,272,280,281
Otoo, S.N.A. 117
Ottenheimer, M. 283
Oucho, John O. 4,8,9(2),13
Ouma, J.H. 92,114
Oyugi, W. 39,60,70,74

Page, Hilary J. 62,81,85
Pala, Achola O. 40(3),41(2),54(4),61(2),62(2),67,68(5),
  71,72,75,104,105,109(2),113   See also: Okeyo, Achola P.
Palmer, Ingrid 25,26,27,34,62,68,75,105,238,240,243,245,
  247(2)
Pankhurst, Richard K. 24(2),31,36
Parker, C. 54,97
Parkin, David 54,101
Parle, Julie 359,401
Parpart, Jane L. 461(2),474(2),476,477,483(2),488,489

Pascoe, Flavia 351,407,416
Pasquet, Marie-Ange 138,140,161
Patel, M. 449
Peart, Nicola S. 341,351,407,416,437,450
Pegoraro, R.J. 393
Penny, O.M. 497,509
Perold, Helene 341,369,443
Perrings, Charles 461,469,474
Peters, Pauline E. 255,260(4),262(3),267,270(3),272,
  277(2),280(3),281
Pettit, John J. 26,28,33
Pfeifer, G. 49,99,108
Philpott, R.H. 393
Phiri, Kings M. 307
Pieters, Guy 4,11,13,17,117
Piot, P. 452
Plaatje, S.T. 324,341,401
Plummer, F.A. 92
Pocock, F. 391
Poewe, Karla O. 461(5),477(2),483(5),486,489(4)
Poinsette, Cheryl 324,341,380,407,431,447
Porter, Abioseh 97
Potash, Betty 54,101
Poulter, Sebastian 288(3),290,295(3),298(4),300
Presley, Cora A. 54(2),75,95(2),102
Preston-Whyte, Eleanor M. 324(3),341,342(3),350,369(2),
  380,381,420,437,443(2)
Princess Elizabeth of Toro 236

Radebe, M.D. 342,416,449
Radel, David 84,88
Ramsay, V.P. 93
Ranger, T.O. 493,497(2),510,514(2),516
Rataemane, S. 332,388
Ravenscroft, Arthur 412
Reese, M.C. 217
Reining, Priscilla 54,80,88,110,113
Rennie, J.K. 461
Richards, Audrey I. 462,486
Richardson, B.D. 393
Richter, Kerry 84,88,93
Ricketts, D.J. 357,369
Ridd, Rosemary 324,342,375,449
Riegelman, Mary Ann 39,60,66,74,284,289,291,293
Riekert, Julian 324,342,401,407,431
Rip, M.R. 342,386,393
Riria Ouko, J.V.N. 54,62(2),72,77,104
Rivkin, Elizabeth T. 342,447
Roberts, Mary 342,386,393
Roberts, S. 257,273(2),278
Roberts, Simon 260,273,274,280
Robertson, A.F. 237
Robertson, Claire 243
Robins, Catherine 237
Robinson, Sally 342,376,423,431

Rodriguez, A. 313
Rogers, Susan G. 180,188(2),196(2),201(2),208,218,222,
  230(2),232
Rogerson, C. 330,348,352,361,378,439
Roode, F. 393
Ropa, T. 497,506,512,514,517
Rosaldo, M.Z. 256,276,278
Roscani, Luisa 324,342,381,431,447
Rosen-Prinz, B. 452
Rosenberg, Susan 410
Rosenfeld, Chris P. 31(2)
Ross, R. 324,402,443,445
Ross, Robert 342(2),402(2),417,445
Ross, S.M. 343,393(2)
Roux, A. 343,384,393,417
Rubens, Bernice 288,294,295,301,304
Rushwan, Hamid E. 119(3),134,135,148(2),158(3),160
Rushwan, James G. 119,135,148,158,160
Russell, Annemarie 122,135,138,168
Russell, Joan 54
Russell, Kathryn 325,343,381,417
Russell, Margo 451
Rycroft, David K. 343
Rzadkowolski, A. 332,388

Sackak, Najma 196,201,209,223
Sadaty, Fahima Z. 138,140,145,174
Saed, Ebrahim M. 30
Safilios-Rothschild, Constantina 284(2),288(2),289(2),
  291(2),304(2),455,474,489
Saghayroun, Atif A.R. 135,146,151,168,174,343,386,393
Saling, Michael M. 343,450
Sanders, A.J.G.M. 260,263,273,274
Sanderson, Lilian P. 135,158,172
Sandler, S.W. 319,343,394
Santilli, Kathy 55,103,105
Sapire, K.E. 382,388
Sarazin, C. 312
Sarzin, B. 336,390
Satchwell, K. 407,432
Sawyerr, Akilagpa 188,212,219,221
Saxe, Norma 369,394
Schafer, I.D. 394,407
Schapera, I. 260,273
Schierling, Marla J. 240
Schindler, J. 374,446
Schipper, Mineke 412
Schmidt, Elizabeth S. 319,343,448
Schreiner, Jenny 331,422,428,443
Schreiner, J.A. 325,343,369,370,376,402(2),426(3),432(2)
Schreiner, Olive 402,443,448
Schuitevoerder, S. 394
Schulpen, T.W. 55,63,76
Schurink, Willem J. 343,357,408,421(2)
Schuster, Ilsa M. 462(6),466(4),469,470(4),474(3),475(2),

479,480(2),485(2)
Schweigart, M.A.   343,381,384,394
Scott, Ann   411
Sebatane, E. Molapi   288,292,294,295,300,301
Seeley, Janet   55,89,96
Segal, I.   394,396,449
Seidman, Gay W.   497,505,506,508,510,512,514
Sekatawa, Emmanuel K.   188(2),213(2),215(2),221(2),230(2)
Selolwane, Onalenna   260,268,270,280
Sembajwe, I.S.L.   189,212,213,221,231,233
Sembajwe, Israel S.   237
Senkoro, F.E.M.K.   98,219
Sequeira, E.   91,113
Sese, Lennox   370
Shabo, Mariam K.   124,136,139,141,165
Shakakata, Regina C.   475,481,484,490
Shamebo, D.   29,30
Shapiro, Colin M.   345
Shapiro, D.   51,67,74,79,109
Shapiro, Janet   357,426,432
Shaw, Anita   330,352,361,446
Shaw, S.   497,500,502,505,516
Shepherd, Gilliam M.   55,84,93,283,
Shields, Nwanganga G.   196,201,209,233
Shifferraw, Maigenet   500,503
Shimmin, Harold S.   51,209
Shindler, J.   370(2),384,394,417,422,432
Shingler, John P.   343,402
Shostak, Marjorie   260(2),280(2)
Showers, Kate   343,370,381,417,419
Shuenyane, Esline N.   344,359
Sibisi, Harriet N.   344(3),350,357,359,370(2),381(2),
   417(2),419(2),443(2)
Sidahmed, Awatif   161,162
Sijaona, S.T.   196,201,209,233
Sikakane, Joyce   325(2),344(2),432(2)
Silkin, Trish   24,33,34,36
Simkins, C.   402,421
Simpson, Mayling   46,82,90,114
Sinclair, June   344(2),351,408(2),417(2)
Sindiga, Isaac   88,93
Singleton, Michael   189,224
Slapgard, Sigrun   497,510,517
Slottved, Astrid   117
Smedley, L.N.   344,381,443
Smit, G.J.   350(2),357,360(3),370(2)
Smit, Roberta   358,371
Smith, C.   308(3)
Smith, Susan E.   84,88
Smock, Audrey C.   41,55(2),62,68,72,75,84,110(2)
Snyder, M.   138,140,145(2),168
Snyman, Rita   344,402
Snyman, I.   344,384,386
Somali Women's Democratic Organization   117
Somalia. Ministry of Health   117

South African Congress of Trade Unions   344,357,370,426
South West Africa People's Organization (SWAPO)   313,
   316(2)
South West Africa People's Organization Women's Council
   316
Spens, M.T.   308
Spies, S.B.   345,402
Spitz, Shirley   370,394
Spring, Anita   308(9),455(2),456,459,462(4),466,470,473,
   475(2),477,478,479,487,489(4)
Spuy, Adelemarie V.   345(2),357(2),370,371,408,443(2)
   See also: Van Der Spuy, A.
Staniland, H.   345,408
Staudt, Kathleen A.   41(2),55(5),62(2),68(2),77,95,105(5),
   111
Stavrou, P.   371,394
Stephen, June   313
Stephens, Betsy   280,271,272,274
Stevens, Yvette   257,261,267,278
Steyn, Anna F.   345,381,417,444
Stichter, Sharon B.   55(2),56,68(2),75(3),80(2),95,101,
   111,114
Stillman, Eric D.   345,444
Straker, G.   394,450
Strangwaies-Booth, J.   376,426,432
Strauss, S.A.   384,408
Strobel, Margaret A.   56(2),62,68,76,96(2),104,106,112
Sudan. Department of Statistics   151,158
Sudan. Ministry of Health   151,158
Sundkler, Bengt   224
Svanberg, Ulf   30
Swaisland, C.F.   402,419
Swantz, Marja-Liisa   180(2),189(3),196(3),202(2),209(3),
   224(2),225,231(2)
Swartz, Audrey R.   56,101,111
Swartz, Caroline   47,65,77
Swartz, Marc J.   56(2),101(2),111(2)
Swaziland. Ministry of Education   453
Sweet, Charles F.   39,60,66,74,284,289,291,293
Sweetman, David   298,302
Szklut, Jay   5,13

Taber, S.R.   235
Tabibian, Nasrin   453(3)
Tadesse, Zenebeworke   21(2),24,25(3),26(6),27,33(2),36,
   202(2),204(2),223(2),313(2),470,471,485
Taitz, Jerold   394,408
Taiwo, Oladele   412
Te Riele, M.   453
Tegegne, D.   23,26,36
Tembo, Lyson P.   463,466,470,477,483,489
Tendengu, L.   493,497,500,502,503,516
Thadani, Veena N.   56(3),62,69(2),76(2),80,102,111,114
Thairu, R.W.   42,106
Thandabantu, Nhlapo   451

Thein, M. 30
Thelejane, T.S. 241,244,246,251
Thetele, Constance B. 345,426,437
Thiong'o, Ngugi W. 41,56
Thiuri, B. 90
Thomas, Rosalind 246
Thompson, Carol B. 497,506,512,514,517
Thompson, Richard W. 237
Thomson, R.C. 345(2),408(2),432(2),444(2)
Thornton, L. 345,394
Thrupp, Lori-Ann 41,62,76
Tiffany, Sharon W. 237,261,268,270,280,282
Tmannetje, W. 90(2)
Tobisson, Eva 180,189,209,217,231
Topping-Bazin, Nancy 412
Torrance, J.D. 392
Toubia, Nahid F. 135,158,172
Tredoux, M. 350,371
Trengrove, J.J. 352,408
Truscott, Kate 493,500,503,514
Tsehai, Berhane S. 24
Tsele, Lindiwe M. 498,516
Tshabalala, E.N. 396(2)
Tshumu, Jester 502,505
Tsolo, Gladys 376,423,432
Turshen, Meredith 189,217,224
Turton, David 24,32

U.S. Department of Commerce. Bureau of the Census 62,
   106,196,225
Uba, Sam 241,242,246,248
Uken, J.M. 395(2)
United Nations 242,244,245,316(2),325(5),345(3),346,357,
   371(3),432,433(4),448(4)
United Nations Centre Against Apartheid 315,325(3),
   346(2),357,371(2),376,381,408,422,430,433(3),448
United Nations Economic Commission for Africa (UNECA)
   26,27(4),56,69,76,88,101,122,138(2),140(2),161,162,189,
   162,189,196,209,212,217,231,232,234,288,300,309,311,326,
   346,358,371,381,433,448,466,470(2),475,493,501,502,505
United Nations Educational, Scientific and Cultural
   Organization 135,164,237
United Nations Secretary-General 242,244,316,376,423,433
United Women's Organization (UWO) 371,426
University of North Carolina 117
University of Natal, Durban. Women's Movement 408
Unterhalter, Beryl 326,346,371(2),376,381,395,427,433,
   448
Unterhalter, Elaine 6,7,13,326,336,346,367,375,376,379,
   408,416,419,422,425,430,433,442,447
Urdang, Stephanie 253,314(4),316,323,338(2),355,366,375,
   376,423,430,433,441,447,448
Urtel, Helga 358,371
Uys, J.M. 345,381,417

Vail, L.   314
Van Bart, Dawn   372,382,450
Van Biljon, M.   395
Van Binsbergen, Wim M.   463,477,481,490
Van Coeverden de Groot, H.A.   327,346(2),395(4)
Van De Wall-Bake, Titia   262,268
Van der Horst, Sheila T.   242,243,245
Van der Merwe, Sandra   347,350,358
Van Der Spuy, A.   346,358,376(2),409,417,433,444,448(2)
  See also: Spuy, Adelemarie V.
Van Der Vliet, Virginia N.   346,418,449
Van Der Walt, Sunette   372
Van Dyck, E.   452
Van Ginneken, J.K.   56(2),89,93(3),102
Van Harte, E.   347,384,396,418
Van Helten, Jean J.   403
Van Heyningen, Elizabeth B.   346(2),395(2),403(2),409(2),
  421
Van Middelkoop, A.   343
Van Niekerk, G.   319,395
Van Niekerk, K.   372,396,418
Van Niekerk, Barend   395,409
Van Niekerk, J.P. de V.   369,394
Van Onselen, Charles   347,372,403(2),421,444
Van Regenmortel, P.J.   347,384,396,418
Van Rensburg, L.R.   372,396
Van Rooyen, Janice C.   372
Van Rouveroy van Nieuwall, Els   463,484,490
Van Rouveroy van Nieuwall, Emile   463,484,490
Van Sertima, Ivan 31
Van Steenbergen, W.M.   93
Van Tonder, J.L.   323,338,339,347,384(3),385,386(4),415,
  418
Van Vuuren, Nancy   326,347,376,403,434
Van Wyk, A.H.   347,409,418
Vanderhoeft, C.   32,70,71,83(2),87(2),99(2)
Varkevisser, H.   391
Vaughan, Iris   326,377
Vaughan, Megan   307,309
Ventura, Dias   41,62,69,76
Verardi, M.   396
Vercoutter, Jean   131,158
Verster, J.   347,385,387,449
Villaume, Mary L.   122,135,138,168
Vink, G.   396
Virji, Parin   197,209
Vogelman, Lloyd   409,421
Volkman, Toby A.   261,280
Volpe, P.L.   409,418
Voorhoeve, A.M.   56,57(2),79(2),89,93(3),102
Vourela, Ulla   191,221,231

Wachtel, Andy   62,69,104
Wachtel, Eleanor   62,69(2),76,104
Wada, Shonei   189

Wadhawan, S.   479
Wadsworth, Gail M.   1,5,15,239,242,250
Wagner, Albert   120,136,143,165
Wahlstrom, Per-Ake   224
Waife, Ronald S.   57,94
Walker, A.R.P.   347(2),394,396(5),449
Walker, B.F.   347(2),396(5)
Walker, Cherryl   326,377(6),385,403,427(2),434(6)
Walker, Jean S.   396
Wall, Brenda   366,425
Wallace, J.A.   393
Wallace, Wendy   135,149,158,160
Wallender, Helena E.   453(2)
Waller, R.D.   57,96
Waltons, S.M.   89,94
Wanjala, Esther   58,63,69,76,79,93
Wanjala, S.   37
Warsame, M.   118(2)
Wasow, Bernard   63,69,76,102
Watermeyer, S.   391
Watson, D.S.   241,249
Watts, T.   479
Way, Ann A.   259,272
Webster, D.   314
Weinrich, A.K.H.   498(3),502(2),504(2),505,508(3),511,515,
  516,517(2)
Weisner, Thomas S.   5,12
Weiss, Ruth   498,514,516
Welch, Gita H.   314
Wells, J.   326,433
Wells, Julia C.   326(4),347,377(4),378,403(3),404,409(3),
  423,434(4),435,449
Wenlock, R. June   28,30
Wenlock, R.W.   28,30,463,478,479,484
Werner, Linda H.   44(4),51(2),81(5),83(2),85(2),86,88(2),
  98(4),100(2)
Wessels, D.M.   358(2),372(2)
Westmore, Jean   319,396,409,435
White, L.   314
White, Luise S.   57(3),76(3),96(2),102(2),103,105
White, M.   467,472
White, Susan   314
Whitelaw, D.A.   347,382,397,418,444
Whiting, Beatrice B.   57(2),72,80
Whiting, Martha   58,57,63,77
Wienpahl, Jan   41,57,111
Wikan, G.   255,262,265
Wiley, Liz   180,181,190,197,202
Wilkinson, R.C.   288,292,294,296,301,304
Willard, Fran   245,249
Williams, Keith   403
Williams, Larry   24,31
Willis, Roy G.   190,202,233
Wilmsen, Edwin N.   261(2),271(2),272(2)
Wilson, G.M.   58,77,103

Wilson, Monica H.   190,221,231,309,348,404,418
Winikoff, Beverly   91
Winston C.   130,147,155
Wisner, B.   313
Wolmarans, Karen M.   358,372
Women's Action Group   498,501,504,505,513,514,517
Women's Legal Status Committee   410,427,435
Women's Studies Documentation Unit   122,164
Woodrow, E.P.   385,397
Woodward, A.   393
Woolfson, L.R.   397,421
World Health Organization (WHO)   326,347,397,435
Worthman, C.   258,270,272
Wright, John   347,372,404,444
Wright, K.   24,33,35
Wright, Marcia   1,6(2),7,190,212,225,456,463(2),466,480,
    481,484,490
Wykstra, Ronald A.   285,292,294
Wylie, Liz   190,197,209

Xenos, Christos   311

Yates, Leslie M.   255(2),262,263,265(2),276(2),277,285(2),
    290(2),292(2),302(3),456(2),466(2),470,471,485(2)
Yawitch, Joanne   320,326,327(3),347(3),350(3),358(4),372,
    373(5),374,378(2),382(3),385,404(3),410(3),418,421,422,
    423,435(4),437,444,446,448
Young, Sherilynn   314
Young, William C.   135,140,145,146,168
Youssef, Humam A.   129,146,159,166

Zambia.   Central Statistics Office (CSO)   478,479
Zimbabwe.   Ministry of Community Development and Women's
    Studies   498,518
Zimbabwe African National Union (ZANU)   498,507,512,517
Zimbabwe African Patriotic Union (ZAPU)   498,507,512,514,
    518
Zimbabwe National Family Planning Council (ZNFPC)   498,
    508(2),509
Zinn, Deborah   419,444
Zlotnik, Zia   347,397,444
Zvobgo, Eddison   498(2),510(2),514(2)

About the Compiler

Native Californian Davis A. Bullwinkle was raised in the San Francisco Bay area. Early interest in Black history and African Studies led to undergraduate degrees in History and Anthropology from California State University-Chico. Under the guidance of professors in History and Anthropology, Mr. Bullwinkle specialized in African Studies. He received a Masters of Library Science degree from Emporia State University in Kansas.

Mr. Bullwinkle has published bibliographic articles on Drought and Desertification in Africa, Nomadism and Pastoralism in Africa, and Women in Africa during the 1970's. All were published in the former Washington, D.C., African Bibliographic Center's "Current Bibliography on African Affairs." He is presently employed by the Arkansas State Library in Little Rock, Arkansas, where he is the Senior Reference Librarian. He recently married and has three stepchildren.